Accounting

Nick Gunther

2L, Harvard Law School

33 Concord Ave, Cambridge

864-6921

University Casebook Series

December, 1982

ACCOUNTING AND THE LAW, Fourth Edition (1978), with Problems Pamphlet (Successor to Dohr, Phillips, Thompson & Warren)

George C. Thompson, Professor, Columbia University Graduate School of Business.
Robert Whitman, Professor of Law, University of Connecticut.
Ellis L. Phillips, Jr., Member of the New York Bar.
William C. Warren, Professor of Law Emeritus, Columbia University.

ACCOUNTING FOR LAWYERS, MATERIALS ON (1980)

David R. Herwitz, Professor of Law, Harvard University.

ADMINISTRATIVE LAW, Seventh Edition (1979), with 1983 Problems Supplement (Supplement edited in association with Paul R. Verkuil, Dean and Professor of Law, Tulane University)

Walter Gellhorn, University Professor Emeritus, Columbia University.
Clark Byse, Professor of Law, Harvard University.
Peter L. Strauss, Professor of Law, Columbia University.

ADMIRALTY, Second Edition (1978), with Statute and Rule Supplement

Jo Desha Lucas, Professor of Law, University of Chicago.

ADVOCACY, see also Lawyering Process

AGENCY, see also Enterprise Organization

AGENCY—PARTNERSHIPS, Third Edition (1982)

Abridgement from Conard, Knauss & Siegel's Enterprise Organization, Third Edition.

ANTITRUST AND REGULATORY ALTERNATIVES (1977), Fifth Edition

Louis B. Schwartz, Professor of Law, University of Pennsylvania.
John J. Flynn, Professor of Law, University of Utah.

ANTITRUST SUPPLEMENT—SELECTED STATUTES AND RELATED MATERIALS (1977)

John J. Flynn, Professor of Law, University of Utah.

BUSINESS ORGANIZATION, see also Enterprise Organization

BUSINESS PLANNING (1966), with 1982 Supplement

David R. Herwitz, Professor of Law, Harvard University.

BUSINESS TORTS (1972)

Milton Handler, Professor of Law Emeritus, Columbia University.

CHILDREN IN THE LEGAL SYSTEM (1983)

Walter Wadlington, Professor of Law, University of Virginia.
Charles H. Whitebread, Professor of Law, University of Southern California.
Samuel Davis, Professor of Law, University of Georgia.

i

CIVIL PROCEDURE, see Procedure

CLINIC, see also Lawyering Process

COMMERCIAL AND CONSUMER TRANSACTIONS, Second Edition (1978)

William D. Warren, Dean of the School of Law, University of California, Los Angeles.
William E. Hogan, Professor of Law, Cornell University.
Robert L. Jordan, Professor of Law, University of California, Los Angeles.

COMMERCIAL LAW, CASES & MATERIALS ON, Third Edition (1976), with 1982 Supplement

E. Allan Farnsworth, Professor of Law, Columbia University.
John Honnold, Professor of Law, University of Pennsylvania.

COMMERCIAL PAPER, Second Edition (1976)

E. Allan Farnsworth, Professor of Law, Columbia University.

COMMERCIAL PAPER AND BANK DEPOSITS AND COLLECTIONS (1967), with Statutory Supplement

William D. Hawkland, Professor of Law, University of Illinois.

COMMERCIAL TRANSACTIONS—Principles and Policies (1982)

Alan Schwartz, Professor of Law, University of Southern California.
Robert E. Scott, Professor of Law, University of Virginia.

COMPARATIVE LAW, Fourth Edition (1980)

Rudolf B. Schlesinger, Professor of Law, Hastings College of the Law.

COMPETITIVE PROCESS, LEGAL REGULATION OF THE, Second Edition (1979), with Statutory Supplement and 1982 Case Supplement

Edmund W. Kitch, Professor of Law, University of Chicago.
Harvey S. Perlman, Professor of Law, University of Virginia.

CONFLICT OF LAWS, Seventh Edition (1978), with 1982 Supplement

Willis L. M. Reese, Professor of Law, Columbia University,
Maurice Rosenberg, Professor of Law, Columbia University.

CONSTITUTIONAL LAW, Sixth Edition (1981), with 1982 Supplement

Edward L. Barrett, Jr., Professor of Law, University of California, Davis.
William Cohen, Professor of Law, Stanford University.

CONSTITUTIONAL LAW: THE STRUCTURE OF GOVERNMENT (Reprinted from CONSTITUTIONAL LAW, Sixth Edition), with 1982 Supplement

Edward L. Barrett, Jr., Professor of Law, University of California, Davis.
William Cohen, Professor of Law, Stanford University.

CONSTITUTIONAL LAW, CIVIL LIBERTY AND INDIVIDUAL RIGHTS, Second Edition (1982)

William Cohen, Professor of Law, Stanford Law School.
John Kaplan, Professor of Law, Stanford Law School.

CONSTITUTIONAL LAW, Tenth Edition (1980), with 1982 Supplement

Gerald Gunther, Professor of Law, Stanford University.

CONSTITUTIONAL LAW, INDIVIDUAL RIGHTS IN, Third Edition (1981), with 1982 Supplement (Reprinted from CONSTITUTIONAL LAW, Tenth Edition)

Gerald Gunther, Professor of Law, Stanford University.

UNIVERSITY CASEBOOK SERIES—Continued

CONTRACT LAW AND ITS APPLICATION, Second Edition (1977)

The late Addison Mueller, Professor of Law, University of California, Los Angeles.
Arthur I. Rosett, Professor of Law, University of California, Los Angeles.

CONTRACT LAW, STUDIES IN, Second Edition (1977)

Edward J. Murphy, Professor of Law, University of Notre Dame.
Richard E. Speidel, Professor of Law, University of Virginia.

CONTRACTS, Fourth Edition (1982)

John P. Dawson, Professor of Law Emeritus, Harvard University.
William Burnett Harvey, Professor of Law and Political Science, Boston University.
Stanley D. Henderson, Professor of Law, University of Virginia.

CONTRACTS, Third Edition (1980), with Statutory Supplement

E. Allan Farnsworth, Professor of Law, Columbia University.
William F. Young, Professor of Law, Columbia University.

CONTRACTS, Second Edition (1978), with Statutory and Administrative Law Supplement (1978)

Ian R. Macneil, Professor of Law, Cornell University.

COPYRIGHT, PATENTS AND TRADEMARKS, see also Competitive Process

COPYRIGHT, PATENT, TRADEMARK AND RELATED STATE DOCTRINES, Second Edition (1981), with Problem Supplement and Statutory Supplement

Paul Goldstein, Professor of Law, Stanford University.

COPYRIGHT, Unfair Competition, and Other Topics Bearing on the Protection of Literary, Musical, and Artistic Works, Third Edition (1978)

Benjamin Kaplan, Professor of Law Emeritus, Harvard University,
Ralph S. Brown, Jr., Professor of Law, Yale University.

CORPORATE FINANCE, Second Edition (1979), with 1982 New Developments Supplement

Victor Brudney, Professor of Law, Harvard University.
Marvin A. Chirelstein, Professor of Law, Yale University.

CORPORATE READJUSTMENTS AND REORGANIZATIONS (1976)

Walter J. Blum, Professor of Law, University of Chicago.
Stanley A. Kaplan, Professor of Law, University of Chicago.

CORPORATION LAW, BASIC, Second Edition (1979), with Documentary Supplement

Detlev F. Vagts, Professor of Law, Harvard University.

CORPORATIONS, see also Enterprise Organization

CORPORATIONS, Fifth Edition—Unabridged (1980)

William L. Cary, Professor of Law, Columbia University.
Melvin Aron Eisenberg, Professor of Law, University of California, Berkeley.

CORPORATIONS, Fifth Edition—Abridged (1980)

William L. Cary, Professor of Law, Columbia University.
Melvin Aron Eisenberg, Professor of Law, University of California, Berkeley.

CORPORATIONS, Second Edition (1982)

Alfred F. Conard, Professor of Law, University of Michigan.
Robert N. Knauss, Dean of the Law School, University of Houston.
Stanley Siegel, Professor of Law, University of California, Los Angeles.

CORPORATIONS, THE LAW OF: WHAT CORPORATE LAWYERS DO (1976)

Jan G. Deutsch, Professor of Law, Yale University.
Joseph J. Bianco, Professor of Law, Yeshiva University.

CORPORATIONS COURSE GAME PLAN (1975)

David R. Herwitz, Professor of Law, Harvard University.

CORRECTIONS, SEE SENTENCING

CREDIT TRANSACTIONS AND CONSUMER PROTECTION (1976)

John Honnold, Professor of Law, University of Pennsylvania.

CREDITORS' RIGHTS, see also Debtor-Creditor Law

CRIMINAL JUSTICE, THE ADMINISTRATION OF, Second Edition (1969)

Francis C. Sullivan, Professor of Law, Louisiana State University.
Paul Hardin III, Professor of Law, Duke University.
John Huston, Professor of Law, University of Washington.
Frank R. Lacy, Professor of Law, University of Oregon.
Daniel E. Murray, Professor of Law, University of Miami.
George W. Pugh, Professor of Law, Louisiana State University.

CRIMINAL JUSTICE ADMINISTRATION, Second Edition (1982)

Frank W. Miller, Professor of Law, Washington University.
Robert O. Dawson, Professor of Law, University of Texas.
George E. Dix, Professor of Law, University of Texas.
Raymond I. Parnas, Professor of Law, University of California, Davis.

CRIMINAL LAW, Second Edition (1979)

Fred E. Inbau, Professor of Law Emeritus, Northwestern University.
James R. Thompson, Professor of Law Emeritus, Northwestern University.
Andre A. Moenssens, Professor of Law, University of Richmond.

CRIMINAL LAW (1982)

Peter W. Low, Professor of Law, University of Virginia.
John C. Jeffries, Jr., Professor of Law, University of Virginia.
Richard C. Bonnie, Professor of Law, University of Virginia.

CRIMINAL LAW, Third Edition (1980)

Lloyd L. Weinreb, Professor of Law, Harvard University.

CRIMINAL LAW AND PROCEDURE, Fifth Edition (1977)

Rollin M. Perkins, Professor of Law Emeritus, University of California, Hastings
   College of the Law.
Ronald N. Boyce, Professor of Law, University of Utah.

CRIMINAL PROCEDURE, Second Edition (1980), with 1982 Supplement

Fred E. Inbau, Professor of Law Emeritus, Northwestern University.
James R. Thompson, Professor of Law Emeritus, Northwestern University.
James B. Haddad, Professor of Law, Northwestern University.
James B. Zagel, Chief, Criminal Justice Division, Office of Attorney General of
   Illinois.
Gary L. Starkman, Assistant U. S. Attorney, Northern District of Illinois.

CRIMINAL PROCEDURE, CONSTITUTIONAL (1977), with 1980 Supplement

James E. Scarboro, Professor of Law, University of Colorado.
James B. White, Professor of Law, University of Chicago.

CRIMINAL PROCESS, Third Edition (1978), with 1982 Supplement

Lloyd L. Weinreb, Professor of Law, Harvard University.

DAMAGES, Second Edition (1952)

Charles T. McCormick, late Professor of Law, University of Texas.
William F. Fritz, late Professor of Law, University of Texas.

DEBTOR–CREDITOR LAW, Second Edition (1981), with Statutory Supplement

William D. Warren, Dean of the School of Law, University of California, Los Angeles.
William E. Hogan, Professor of Law, New York University.

DECEDENTS' ESTATES (1971)

Max Rheinstein, late Professor of Law Emeritus, University of Chicago.
Mary Ann Glendon, Professor of Law, Boston College.

DECEDENTS' ESTATES AND TRUSTS, Sixth Edition (1982)

John Ritchie, Emeritus Dean and Wigmore Professor of Law, Northwestern University.
Neill H. Alford, Jr., Professor of Law, University of Virginia.
Richard W. Effland, Professor of Law, Arizona State University.

DECEDENTS' ESTATES AND TRUSTS (1968)

Howard R. Williams, Professor of Law, Stanford University.

DOMESTIC RELATIONS, see also Family Law

DOMESTIC RELATIONS, Third Edition (1978), with 1980 Supplement

Walter Wadlington, Professor of Law, University of Virginia.
Monrad G. Paulsen, Dean of the Law School, Yeshiva University.

ELECTRONIC MASS MEDIA, Second Edition (1979)

William K. Jones, Professor of Law, Columbia University.

EMPLOYMENT DISCRIMINATION (1983)

Joel W. Friedman, Professor of Law, Tulane University.
George M. Strickler, Professor of Law, Tulane University.

ENERGY LAW (1983)

Donald N. Zillman, Professor of Law, University of Utah.
Laurence Lattman, Dean of Mines and Engineering, University of Utah.

ENTERPRISE ORGANIZATION, Third Edition (1982), with 1982 Corporation and Partnership Statutes, Rules and Forms Supplement

Alfred F. Conard, Professor of Law, University of Michigan.
Robert L. Knauss, Dean of the Law School, University of Houston.
Stanley Siegel, Professor of Law, University of California, Los Angeles.

ENVIRONMENTAL POLICY LAW (1982)

Thomas J. Schoenbaum, Professor of Law, Tulane University.

EQUITY, see also Remedies

EQUITY, RESTITUTION AND DAMAGES, Second Edition (1974)

Robert Childres, late Professor of Law, Northwestern University.
William F. Johnson, Jr., Professor of Law, New York University.

ESTATE PLANNING, Second Edition (1982), with Documentary Supplement

David Westfall, Professor of Law, Harvard University.

ETHICS, see Legal Profession, and Professional Responsibility

ETHICS AND PROFESSIONAL RESPONSIBILITY (1981) (Reprinted from THE LAWYERING PROCESS)

Gary Bellow, Professor of Law, Harvard University.
Bea Moulton, Legal Services Corporation.

EVIDENCE, Fourth Edition (1981)

David W. Louisell, late Professor of Law, University of California, Berkeley.
John Kaplan, Professor of Law, Stanford University.
Jon R. Waltz, Professor of Law, Northwestern University.

EVIDENCE (1968)

Francis C. Sullivan, Professor of Law, Louisiana State University.
Paul Hardin, III, Professor of Law, Duke University.

EVIDENCE, Seventh Edition (1983) with Rules and Statute Supplement (1981)

Jack B. Weinstein, Chief Judge, United States District Court.
John H. Mansfield, Professor of Law, Harvard University.
Norman Abrams, Professor of Law, University of California, Los Angeles.
Margaret Berger, Professor of Law, Brooklyn Law School.

FAMILY LAW, see also Domestic Relations

FAMILY LAW (1978), with 1983 Supplement

Judith C. Areen, Professor of Law, Georgetown University.

FAMILY LAW AND CHILDREN IN THE LEGAL SYSTEM, STATUTORY MATERIALS (1981)

Walter Wadlington, Professor of Law, University of Virginia.

FEDERAL COURTS, Seventh Edition (1982)

Charles T. McCormick, late Professor of Law, University of Texas.
James H. Chadbourn, Professor of Law, Harvard University.
Charles Alan Wright, Professor of Law, University of Texas.

FEDERAL COURTS AND THE FEDERAL SYSTEM, Hart and Wechsler's Second Edition (1973), with 1981 Supplement

Paul M. Bator, Professor of Law, Harvard University.
Paul J. Mishkin, Professor of Law, University of California, Berkeley.
David L. Shapiro, Professor of Law, Harvard University.
Herbert Wechsler, Professor of Law, Columbia University.

FEDERAL PUBLIC LAND AND RESOURCES LAW (1981)

George C. Coggins, Professor of Law, University of Kansas.
Charles F. Wilkinson, Professor of Law, University of Oregon.

FEDERAL RULES OF CIVIL PROCEDURE, 1982 Edition

FEDERAL TAXATION, see Taxation

FOOD AND DRUG LAW (1980), with Statutory Supplement

Richard A. Merrill, Dean of the School of Law, University of Virginia.
Peter Barton Hutt, Esq.

FUTURE INTERESTS (1958)

Philip Mechem, late Professor of Law Emeritus, University of Pennsylvania.

FUTURE INTERESTS (1970)

Howard R. Williams, Professor of Law, Stanford University.

FUTURE INTERESTS AND ESTATE PLANNING (1961), with 1962 Supplement

W. Barton Leach, late Professor of Law, Harvard University.
James K. Logan, formerly Dean of the Law School, University of Kansas.

GOVERNMENT CONTRACTS, FEDERAL (1975), with 1980 Supplement

John W. Whelan, Professor of Law, Hastings College of the Law.
Robert S. Pasley, Professor of Law Emeritus, Cornell University.

INJUNCTIONS (1972)

Owen M. Fiss, Professor of Law, Yale University.

INSTITUTIONAL INVESTORS, 1978

David L. Ratner, Professor of Law, Cornell University.

INSURANCE (1971)

William F. Young, Professor of Law, Columbia University.

INTERNATIONAL LAW, see also Transnational Legal Problems and United Nations Law

INTERNATIONAL LAW IN CONTEMPORARY PERSPECTIVE (1981), with Essay Supplement

Myres S. McDougal, Professor of Law, Yale University.
W. Michael Reisman, Professor of Law, Yale University.

INTERNATIONAL LEGAL SYSTEM, Second Edition (1981), with Documentary Supplement

Joseph Modeste Sweeney, Professor of Law, Tulane University.
Covey T. Oliver, Professor of Law, University of Pennsylvania.
Noyes E. Leech, Professor of Law, University of Pennsylvania.

INTERNATIONAL TRADE AND INVESTMENT, REGULATION OF (1970)

Carl H. Fulda, late Professor of Law, University of Texas.
Warren F. Schwartz, Professor of Law, University of Virginia.

INTRODUCTION TO LAW, see also Legal Method, On Law in Courts, and Dynamics of American Law

INTRODUCTION TO THE STUDY OF LAW (1970)

E. Wayne Thode, late Professor of Law, University of Utah.
Leon Lebowitz, Professor of Law, University of Texas.
Lester J. Mazor, Professor of Law, University of Utah.

JUDICIAL CODE and Rules of Procedure in the Federal Courts with Excerpts from the Criminal Code, 1981 Edition

Henry M. Hart, Jr., late Professor of Law, Harvard University.
Herbert Wechsler, Professor of Law, Columbia University.

JURISPRUDENCE (Temporary Edition Hardbound) (1949)

Lon L. Fuller, Professor of Law Emeritus, Harvard University.

JUVENILE, see also Children

JUVENILE JUSTICE PROCESS, Second Edition (1976), with 1980 Supplement

Frank W. Miller, Professor of Law, Washington University.
Robert O. Dawson, Professor of Law, University of Texas.
George E. Dix, Professor of Law, University of Texas.
Raymond I. Parnas, Professor of Law, University of California, Davis.

LABOR LAW, Ninth Edition (1981), with Statutory Supplement

Archibald Cox, Professor of Law, Harvard University.
Derek C. Bok, President, Harvard University.
Robert A. Gorman, Professor of Law, University of Pennsylvania.

LABOR LAW, Second Edition (1982), with Statutory Supplement

Clyde W. Summers, Professor of Law, University of Pennsylvania.
Harry H. Wellington, Dean of the Law School, Yale University.
Alan Hyde, Professor of Law, Rutgers University.

LAND FINANCING, Second Edition (1977)

Norman Penney, Professor of Law, Cornell University.
Richard F. Broude, Member of the California Bar.

LAW AND MEDICINE (1980)

Walter Wadlington, Professor of Law and Professor of Legal Medicine, University
of Virginia.
Jon R. Waltz, Professor of Law, Northwestern University.
Roger B. Dworkin, Professor of Law, Indiana University, and Professor of Bio-
medical History, University of Washington.

LAW, LANGUAGE AND ETHICS (1972)

William R. Bishin, Professor of Law, University of Southern California.
Christopher D. Stone, Professor of Law, University of Southern California.

**LAWYERING PROCESS (1978), with Civil Problem Supplement and Criminal
Problem Supplement**

Gary Bellow, Professor of Law, Harvard University.
Bea Moulton, Professor of Law, Arizona State University.

LEGAL METHOD (1980)

Harry W. Jones, Professor of Law Emeritus, Columbia University.
John M. Kernochan, Professor of Law, Columbia University.
Arthur W. Murphy, Professor of Law, Columbia University.

LEGAL METHODS (1969)

Robert N. Covington, Professor of Law, Vanderbilt University.
E. Blythe Stason, late Professor of Law, Vanderbilt University.
John W. Wade, Professor of Law, Vanderbilt University.
Elliott E. Cheatham, late Professor of Law, Vanderbilt University.
Theodore A. Smedley, Professor of Law, Vanderbilt University.

LEGAL PROFESSION (1970)

Samuel D. Thurman, Dean of the College of Law, University of Utah.
Ellis L. Phillips, Jr., Professor of Law, Columbia University.
Elliott E. Cheatham, late Professor of Law, Vanderbilt University.

UNIVERSITY CASEBOOK SERIES—Continued

LEGISLATION, Fourth Edition (1982) (by Fordham)

Horace E. Read, late Vice President, Dalhousie University.
John W. MacDonald, Professor of Law Emeritus, Cornell Law School.
Jefferson B. Fordham, Professor of Law, University of Utah.
William J. Pierce, Professor of Law, University of Michigan.

LEGISLATIVE AND ADMINISTRATIVE PROCESSES, Second Edition (1981)

Hans A. Linde, Judge, Supreme Court of Oregon.
George Bunn, Professor of Law, University of Wisconsin.
Fredericka Paff, Professor of Law, University of Wisconsin.
W. Lawrence Church, Professor of Law, University of Wisconsin.

LOCAL GOVERNMENT LAW, Revised Edition (1975)

Jefferson B. Fordham, Professor of Law, University of Utah.

MASS MEDIA LAW, Second Edition (1982)

Marc A. Franklin, Professor of Law, Stanford University.

MENTAL HEALTH PROCESS, Second Edition (1976), with 1981 Supplement

Frank W. Miller, Professor of Law, Washington University.
Robert O. Dawson, Professor of Law, University of Texas.
George E. Dix, Professor of Law, University of Texas.
Raymond I. Parnas, Professor of Law, University of California, Davis.

MUNICIPAL CORPORATIONS, see Local Government Law

NEGOTIABLE INSTRUMENTS, see Commercial Paper

NEGOTIATION (1981) (Reprinted from THE LAWYERING PROCESS)

Gary Bellow, Professor of Law, Harvard Law School.
Bea Moulton, Legal Services Corporation.

NEW YORK PRACTICE, Fourth Edition (1978)

Herbert Peterfreund, Professor of Law, New York University.
Joseph M. McLaughlin, Dean of the Law School, Fordham University.

OIL AND GAS, Fourth Edition (1979)

Howard R. Williams, Professor of Law, Stanford University.
Richard C. Maxwell, Professor of Law, University of California, Los Angeles.
Charles J. Meyers, Dean of the Law School, Stanford University.

ON LAW IN COURTS (1965)

Paul J. Mishkin, Professor of Law, University of California, Berkeley.
Clarence Morris, Professor of Law Emeritus, University of Pennsylvania.

PERSPECTIVES ON THE LAWYER AS PLANNER (Reprint of Chapters One through Five of Planning by Lawyers) (1978)

Louis M. Brown, Professor of Law, University of Southern California.
Edward A. Dauer, Professor of Law, Yale University.

PLANNING BY LAWYERS, MATERIALS ON A NONADVERSARIAL LEGAL PROCESS (1978)

Louis M. Brown, Professor of Law, University of Southern California.
Edward A. Dauer, Professor of Law, Yale University.

PLEADING AND PROCEDURE, see Procedure, Civil

PROPERTY—PERSONAL, Third Edition (1954)

Everett Fraser, late Dean of the Law School Emeritus, University of Minnesota. Third Edition by Charles W. Taintor, late Professor of Law, University of Pittsburgh.

PROPERTY—INTRODUCTION, TO REAL PROPERTY, Third Edition (1954)

Everett Fraser, late Dean of the Law School Emeritus, University of Minnesota.

PROPERTY—REAL AND PERSONAL, Combined Edition (1954)

Everett Fraser, late Dean of the Law School Emeritus, University of Minnesota. Third Edition of Personal Property by Charles W. Taintor, late Professor of Law, University of Pittsburgh.

PROPERTY—REAL PROPERTY AND CONVEYANCING (1954)

Edward E. Bade, late Professor of Law, University of Minnesota.

PROPERTY—FUNDAMENTALS OF MODERN REAL PROPERTY, Second Edition (1982)

Edward H. Rabin, Professor of Law, University of California, Davis.

PROPERTY—PROBLEMS IN REAL PROPERTY (Pamphlet) (1969)

Edward H. Rabin, Professor of Law, University of California, Davis.

PROSECUTION AND ADJUDICATION, Second Edition (1982)

Reprint of Chapters 11–26 of Miller, Dawson, Dix and Parnas' Criminal Justice Administration, Second Edition.

PUBLIC REGULATION OF DANGEROUS PRODUCTS (paperback) (1980)

Marshall S. Shapo, Professor of Law, Northwestern University.

PUBLIC UTILITY LAW, see Free Enterprise, also Regulated Industries

REAL ESTATE PLANNING (1980), with 1980 Problems, Statutes and New Materials Supplement

Norton L. Steuben, Professor of Law, University of Colorado.

REAL ESTATE TRANSACTIONS (1980), with Statute, Form and Problem Supplement

Paul Goldstein, Professor of Law, Stanford University.

RECEIVERSHIP AND CORPORATE REORGANIZATION, see Creditors' Rights

REGULATED INDUSTRIES, Second Edition, 1976

William K. Jones, Professor of Law, Columbia University.

REMEDIES (1982)

Edward D. Re, Chief Judge, U. S. Court of International Trade.

RESTITUTION, Second Edition (1966)

John W. Wade, Professor of Law, Vanderbilt University.

SALES (1980)

Marion W. Benfield, Jr., Professor of Law, University of Illinois.
William D. Hawkland, Chancellor, Louisiana State University Law Center.

SALES AND SALES FINANCING, Fourth Edition (1976), with 1982 Supplement

John Honnold, Professor of Law, University of Pennsylvania.

UNIVERSITY CASEBOOK SERIES—Continued

SALES LAW AND THE CONTRACTING PROCESS (1982)

Reprint of Chapters 1–10 of Schwartz and Scott's Commercial Transactions.

SECURITIES REGULATION, Fifth Edition (1982), with 1982 Selected Statutes, Rules and Forms Supplement

Richard W. Jennings, Professor of Law, University of California, Berkeley.
Harold Marsh, Jr., Member of the California Bar.

SECURITIES REGULATION (1982), with 1983 Supplement

Larry D. Soderquist, Professor of Law, Vanderbilt University.

SENTENCING AND THE CORRECTIONAL PROCESS, Second Edition (1976)

Frank W. Miller, Professor of Law, Washington University.
Robert O. Dawson, Professor of Law, University of Texas.
George E. Dix, Professor of Law, University of Texas.
Raymond I. Parnas, Professor of Law, University of California, Davis.

SOCIAL WELFARE AND THE INDIVIDUAL (1971)

Robert J. Levy, Professor of Law, University of Minnesota.
Thomas P. Lewis, Dean of the College of Law, University of Kentucky.
Peter W. Martin, Professor of Law, Cornell University.

TAX, POLICY ANALYSIS OF THE FEDERAL INCOME (1976)

William A. Klein, Professor of Law, University of California, Los Angeles.

TAXATION, FEDERAL INCOME (1976), with 1982 Supplement

Erwin N. Griswold, Dean Emeritus, Harvard Law School.
Michael J. Graetz, Professor of Law, University of Virginia.

TAXATION, FEDERAL INCOME, Fourth Edition (1982)

James J. Freeland, Professor of Law, University of Florida.
Stephen A. Lind, Professor of Law, University of Florida.
Richard B. Stephens, Professor of Law Emeritus, University of Florida.

TAXATION, FEDERAL INCOME, Volume I, Personal Income Taxation (1972), with 1982 Supplement; Volume II, Taxation of Partnerships and Corporations, Second Edition (1980)

Stanley S. Surrey, Professor of Law, Harvard University.
William C. Warren, Professor of Law Emeritus, Columbia University.
Paul R. McDaniel, Professor of Law, Boston College Law School.
Hugh J. Ault, Professor of Law, Boston College Law School.

TAXATION, FEDERAL WEALTH TRANSFER, Second Edition (1982)

Stanley S. Surrey, Professor of Law, Harvard University.
William C. Warren, Professor of Law Emeritus, Columbia University.
Paul R. McDaniel, Professor of Law, Boston College Law School.
Harry L. Gutman, Instructor, Harvard Law School and Boston College Law School.

TAXATION OF INDIVIDUALS, PARTNERSHIPS AND CORPORATIONS, PROBLEMS in the (1978)

Norton L. Steuben, Professor of Law, University of Colorado.
William J. Turnier, Professor of Law, University of North Carolina.

TAXES AND FINANCE—STATE AND LOCAL (1974)

Oliver Oldman, Professor of Law, Harvard University.
Ferdinand P. Schoettle, Professor of Law, University of Minnesota.

TORT LAW AND ALTERNATIVES: INJURIES AND REMEDIES, Second Edition (1979)

Marc A. Franklin, Professor of Law, Stanford University.

TORTS, Seventh Edition (1982)

William L. Prosser, late Professor of Law, University of California, Hastings College.

John W. Wade, Professor of Law, Vanderbilt University.

Victor E. Schwartz, Professor of Law, American University.

TORTS, Third Edition (1976)

Harry Shulman, late Dean of the Law School, Yale University.

Fleming James, Jr., Professor of Law Emeritus, Yale University.

Oscar S. Gray, Professor of Law, University of Maryland.

TRADE REGULATION (1975), with 1979 Supplement

Milton Handler, Professor of Law Emeritus, Columbia University.

Harlan M. Blake, Professor of Law, Columbia University.

Robert Pitofsky, Professor of Law, Georgetown University.

Harvey J. Goldschmid, Professor of Law, Columbia University.

TRADE REGULATION, see Antitrust

TRANSNATIONAL LEGAL PROBLEMS, Second Edition (1976) with 1982 Case and Documentary Supplement

Henry J. Steiner, Professor of Law, Harvard University.

Detlev F. Vagts, Professor of Law, Harvard University.

TRIAL, see also Evidence, Making the Record, Lawyering Process and Preparing and Presenting the Case

TRIAL ADVOCACY (1968)

A. Leo Levin, Professor of Law, University of Pennsylvania.

Harold Cramer, of the Pennsylvania Bar.

Maurice Rosenberg, Professor of Law, Columbia University, Consultant.

TRUSTS, Fifth Edition (1978)

George G. Bogert, late Professor of Law Emeritus, University of Chicago.

Dallin H. Oaks, President, Brigham Young University.

TRUSTS AND SUCCESSION (Palmer's), Third Edition (1978)

Richard V. Wellman, Professor of Law, University of Georgia.

Lawrence W. Waggoner, Professor of Law, University of Michigan.

Olin L. Browder, Jr., Professor of Law, University of Michigan.

UNFAIR COMPETITION, see Competitive Process and Business Torts

UNITED NATIONS IN ACTION (1968)

Louis B. Sohn, Professor of Law, Harvard University.

UNITED NATIONS LAW, Second Edition (1967), with Documentary Supplement (1968)

Louis B. Sohn, Professor of Law, Harvard University.

WATER RESOURCE MANAGEMENT, Second Edition (1980), with 1983 Supplement

Charles J. Meyers, Dean of the Law School, Stanford University.

A. Dan Tarlock, Professor of Law, Indiana Unversity.

WILLS AND ADMINISTRATION, Fifth Edition (1961)

Philip Mechem, late Professor of Law, University of Pennsylvania.

Thomas E. Atkinson, late Professor of Law, New York University.

WORLD LAW, see United Nations Law

University Casebook Series

EDITORIAL BOARD

MATERIALS ON

ACCOUNTING FOR LAWYERS

By

DAVID R. HERWITZ

Professor of Law, Harvard University

Mineola, New York

THE FOUNDATION PRESS, INC.

1980

Printed in the United States of America

Library of Congress Cataloging in Publication Data

Herwitz, David R
  Materials on accounting for lawyers.

  (University casebook series)
  Includes index.
  1. Lawyers—United States—Accounting. I. Title.
II. Series.
KF320.A2H47   1980   657'.834   80–18163

ISBN0–88277–014–4

Herwitz–Acc't. For Lawyers UCB
1st Reprint—1983

PREFACE

This book is a successor to Materials on Accounting (Amory & Hardee, 3rd edition by Herwitz and Trautman, 1959). Although my colleague on that earlier work, Professor Donald T. Trautman, has not participated in this effort, these materials certainly continue to benefit from our earlier association. And of course this book is still reaping where my predecessors, former Professors Robert Amory, Jr. and Covington Hardee, so well sowed, starting with Bob Amory's pioneering first casebook on accounting for law students in 1948, and including the splendid second edition on which he was joined by Cuz Hardee in 1953.

The primary goal of the materials is to make accounting as teachable as possible to law students, most of whom approach the subject with considerable trepidation (and often a good deal of disinterest as well). Fortunately, even in these days of elective curricula many students are still willing at least to give the subject a whirl (perhaps encouraged by the current interest in litigation, and a recognition that a high proportion of today's lawsuits arise under the securities laws and are bottomed on financial statements). The aim of this book is to instill confidence in the students that they can indeed master the principals of accounting and develop command of the basic tools needed to serve the lawyer's function in this field.

To accomplish this objective, the materials are built around explanatory text designed to lead the students through the technical aspects of the subject. Wherever possible, the bookkeeping alternatives are laid out, with detailed illustrations of the various entries, so that the students' efforts can be directed less to accounting mechanics and more to analyzing the comparative merits of the various possible alternatives. To serve as vehicles for such analysis, one or more problems are included in each section, and both the materials and the problems seek to highlight the lawyer's role in dealing with accounting issues.

As in the predecessor version, the book starts with the Introduction to Bookkeeping which has proved successful in introducing students to the mechanics of the accounting process. This chapter is divided into five sections: debit and credit, income and expense accounts, deferral, accrual, and inventory accounting; each of these topics is accompanied by a problem designed to be covered in one class period. Chapter 2 deals with the development of accounting principles (including the roles played by both the profession and the SEC); the auditing function; and the current litigation setting under the federal securities laws (including disciplinary proceedings by the SEC against accountants for failure to comply with professional standards). Chapter 3 focuses on accounting for corporate proprietorship, with an introduction to dividend law; a closer look at the balance sheet, particularly classification of assets between current and non-current, and the various balance sheet ratios used in financial analysis; the treatment of extraordinary items; and valuation of assets, both for accounting purposes and under dividend law, plus an introduction to consolidated accounting. Chapter 4 covers deferral of expenses in a variety of contexts, including goodwill, research and development, and interest during construction, plus deferral of income. Chapter 5 deals with accrual: first, expenses, with special emphasis on contingencies and the importance of the lawyer's role in disclosing contingent liabilities; then, accrual of income, both in typical sales transactions and in more complicated kinds of long-term installment transactions like retail sales of land lots, with the concomitant requirement of an allowance for uncollectible accounts.

Chapter 6 covers inventory, and contains a new section dealing with accounting for the work-in-process and finished goods of a manufacturing enterprise, to provide some exposure to the issues of cost accounting. Chapter 7 addresses depreciation, with particular attention to the impact of inflation. Chapter 8 represents a comprehensive treatment of the problems involved in allocation of taxes, especially in connection with accelerated depreciation. Chapter 9 offers a wholly new set of materials relating to long-term indebtedness.

While the amount of time devoted to particular topics will, of course, vary with the inclination of the instructor (and the diligence of the students), I do not find it possible to cover all the material in the approximately 26 60-minute sessions we normally have for our two-credit, one-term course. The introduction to bookkeeping takes some five hours, and another four to five hours seem needed to cover Chapters 2 and 3 (even without spending any time on balance sheet ratios or consolidated accounting). Chapter 4 requires about four hours, and so does Chapter 5 (without doing anything on the subject of leases). This means that we are usually somewhere in Chapter 5 at the end of 16 hours, at which point, under the system we have been using here for some years, students are allowed to terminate the course (and get only one credit) by taking a pass-fail examination. In the remaining nine to ten hours of class I usually do no better than complete the chapter on depreciation, after covering inventory (but omitting the material on cost accounting), so we usually do not reach tax allocation (to say nothing of long-term indebtedness). That is a glaring omission, given the importance and complexity of tax allocation, but a hard one to cure since this topic does not lend itself to a once-over-lightly treatment squeezed in at the end of the term.

In addition to the source acknowledgements which appear at appropriate points throughout the following materials, special mention should be made of the permission granted by the Financial Accounting Standards Board to reprint substantial excerpts from its Statements and other documents. The FASB wishes to have particular attention called to the fact that the appendices to its various documents, although largely omitted in the following materials, constitute integral parts of the respective documents. Complete copies of each FASB document are available from the Board, at High Ridge Park, Stamford, Conn. 06905.

DAVID R. HERWITZ

July, 1980

*

SUMMARY OF CONTENTS

*

TABLE OF CONTENTS

TABLE OF CONTENTS

*

TABLE OF OFFICIAL ACCOUNTING PROMULGATIONS

Page

TABLE OF OFFICIAL ACCOUNTING PROMULGATIONS

TABLE OF CASES

The principal cases are in italic type. Cases excerpted or discussed are in roman.
References are to Pages.

*

MATERIALS ON ACCOUNTING FOR LAWYERS

Chapter 1

INTRODUCTION TO BOOKKEEPING

Preliminary Remarks: Accounting problems of concern to a lawyer ordinarily demand much the same kind of analysis and judgment as is required for solution of legal problems. The lawyer's job is to unscramble other people's troubles or, if he is fortunate enough, to help avoid trouble before it develops. Before he can take on the job where accounting issues are involved, however, the lawyer faces a special difficulty. Accountants, and more generally people in business and finance, have their own way of expressing the data with which they are concerned. At first, it may seem akin to an unfamiliar language. But the basic principles on which this language is built are simple enough. This chapter is designed to show you that if you— rather than, as historians tell us, a Renaissance monk named Paciolo —had set out to devise a system for recording financial data, you might well have come out about the same way.

However, it is not to be assumed that every aspect of the system, as it has been worked out, was inevitable. Certainly the application of the system in particular situations is open to doubt and to analysis, and in later chapters of this book, which deal with the function of accounting statements in business life, we will often question the appropriateness of the "language" as applied in particular contexts.

That is not our concern here. For the moment, we are only interested in understanding the language itself, "bookkeeping".

1. THE BALANCE SHEET

The object of bookkeeping is to make it as easy as possible for anyone who understands the language to get a clear and accurate summary of how well a business is doing. Suppose we want a financial picture of E. Tutt, who recently graduated from law school. Certainly one important facet is how much he owns. Since we really are concerned with his business and not his personal affairs, we forget his car, his clothes, and other personal property, and we look to see what he has in his office:

(a) Office furniture

(b) Office equipment

(c) Stationery and supplies

(d) Library

(e) Cash in the bank

All of these would be understood by laymen to be what the accountant calls them: *assets*.

We would also want some measurement of these assets; i. e., we would want to put a dollar figure on them. And since the price at which the property was bought is ordinarily much easier to ascertain and less subjective than the "present value" of the property, it would make sense to record E. Tutt's assets at *cost*.

If E. Tutt bought all his property out of his own funds and has not yet earned anything, we could simply add up the assets to find out how E. Tutt stands in his business. But if he has borrowed money from a bank to buy some of his assets or, perhaps more likely, has bought some on credit, E. Tutt's personal "stake" in the business would not be as large as if he had bought everything from his own funds. In order to give a true picture of his financial position, we would want to know where the money came from to buy the assets. Suppose we find that he acquired the assets as follows:

(a) Office furniture: bought on credit from Frank Co. for $400;

(b) Office equipment: bought on credit from Elmer Co. for $300;

(c) Stationery and supplies: bought from Stanley for $100 on a promissory note;

(d) Library: purchased for $200 cash, out of Tutt's original "stake" of $1,000;

(e) $800 cash: balance of Tutt's original "stake" remaining.

We could then list, in parallel columns, the assets and their sources:

Assets		**Sources**	
(a) Office furniture	$ 400	Frank Co.	$ 400 (a)
(b) Office equipment	300	Elmer Co.	300 (b)
(c) Stationery and supplies	100	Stanley	100 (c)
(d) Library	200		
(e) Cash (balance remaining)	800	E. Tutt	1,000 (d, e)
	$1,800		$1,800

This parallel listing of assets and their sources is what the accountant calls a *balance sheet*. It shows, at any point in time, what assets the business now has and where the money came from to acquire them. Since that is all it is, no matter how complicated the business or how long its history the totals of the two columns are always equal.

To give a somewhat clearer picture of how well off E. Tutt himself is, we can separate the sources of assets into two groups: "outside" sources, or here, money owed by the business to outsiders; and "inside" sources, here, what Tutt himself has put into the business. The outside sources, which are usually called *"Liabilities"*, may be money owed on open account, usually called an "account payable;" another "outside" source is money advanced on a note, a "note payable". The "inside" source here is E. Tutt's contribution (his "stake" or equity in the business) which is often called *"Proprietorship"*. We might also rearrange the assets, listing them in the order in which they are likely to be used up. The result would be a somewhat more refined balance sheet that might look like this:

Assets		Liabilities & Proprietorship	
		Liabilities:	
(e) Cash	$ 800	Accounts Payable	
(c) Supplies	100	Frank Co.	$ 400 (a)
(a) Furniture	400	Elmer Co.	300 (b)
(b) Equipment	300	Notes Payable	
		Stanley	100 (c)
(d) Library	200	Proprietorship	1,000 (d, e)
	$1,800		$1,800

Note that no change has been made except a change in presentation. The essential meaning is the same. But because clear disclosure is one of the accountant's main concerns, matters of presentation are important.

2. DOUBLE–ENTRY BOOKKEEPING

As Tutt engages in practice, many events will occur to affect his financial position, and the balance sheet figures will change. If, for example, in transaction (f), he pays off the note to Stanley, his cash would decrease by $100, so that the cash balance remaining would be $700, and the liability to Stanley of $100 would disappear. If, in transaction (g), Tutt paid Elmer Co. $200 of the amount owed for equipment, cash would be further decreased, to $500, and the liability of $300 to Elmer Co. would be decreased to $100. After these two transactions Tutt's balance sheet would read as follows:

	Assets		**Liabilities & Proprietorship**	
(e, f, g)	Cash	$ 500	A/P Frank Co.	$ 400 (a)
(c)	Supplies	100	A/P Elmer Co.	100 (b, g)
(a)	Furniture	400		
(b)	Equipment	300		
(d)	Library	200	Proprietorship	1,000 (d, e)
		$1,500		$1,500

Note that each of these two transactions affected two items on the balance sheet and did so in equal amounts. This is not a coincidence; the fact is that every transaction has two separate aspects of equal importance. If, (h), Tutt bought more books for $100 in cash, it would tell only half the story to record just the decrease in cash of $100; his "holdings" of books—represented by the asset, "Library"—have increased by $100. If, (i), Tutt took a chair costing $50 from his office for use thereafter at home, reducing "Office Furniture" by $50 would not tell the whole story because his "stake" in the enterprise, Proprietorship, has also been reduced by $50.

Tutt's balance sheet after these two transactions:

	Assets		**Liabilities & Proprietorship**	
(e, f, g, h)	Cash	$ 400	A/P Frank Co.	$ 400 (a)
(c)	Supplies	100	A/P Elmer Co.	100 (b, g)
(a, i)	Furniture	350		
(b)	Equipment	300		
(d, h)	Library	300	Proprietorship	950 (d, e, i)
		$1,450		$1,450

You will note that recognition of the two aspects of each transaction, which are always equal in amount, may change the totals of the balance sheet columns but does not upset their equality. That should not be surprising: we have already seen that the two columns of the balance sheet represent simply the assets and their sources at any given time, and the inherent equality of what are in effect opposite sides of the same coin cannot be affected by changes in the mix of assets and sources. To illustrate, an increase in an asset may come about in one of two ways: either another asset has been exchanged for it, or an additional source of funds has been supplied to acquire it (as, for example, if Tutt bought an asset on credit from a new supplier). On the balance sheet, the increase in the asset column would either be offset by a decrease in the asset column or be balanced by an increase in the sources column. Likewise, a decrease in an asset may come about in one of two ways. If assets have been exchanged, we have the transaction already discussed, but stated in reverse order, and the decrease in assets will be accompanied by an increase in assets reflecting the acquisition of the new asset; the other possibility is a decrease in the sources column, reflecting use of an asset to pay off a claim, as with the use of cash to discharge the note payable to Stanley. Finally, there can be an exchange of sources, which would be reflected by equal increases and decreases in the sources column, as, for example, if Tutt should give a note to a creditor to whom he owed money on open account.

In order eventually to simplify the number of possible combinations involved, we might first set out all the possibilities:

One Effect of Transaction	Accompanying Effect
(1) Increase in Asset	(a) Increase in Source (b) Decrease in Asset
(2) Decrease in Asset	(a) Decrease in Source (b) Increase in Asset
(3) Increase in Source	(a) Increase in Asset (b) Decrease in Source
(4) Decrease in Source	(a) Increase in Source (b) Decrease in Asset

Obviously, a number of these possibilities simply restate others, but in reverse order: e. g., (1)(a) and (3)(a). Indeed, the four types of balance sheet effects involved could be grouped as follows:

Increase in Asset	Increase in Source
Decrease in Source	Decrease in Asset

for all transactions are some combination of an item on one side of this table with one of the two items on the other side of the table.

The balance sheet itself is simply the summary to date of all the individual transactions, and the inherent equality of its columns is confirmed by the fact that each individual transaction has two equal effects on the balance sheet.

A single transaction can have more than two effects. If (j), Tutt bought another piece of office equipment from Elmer Co. for $100, paying $50 down, office equipment would increase $100, cash would decrease $50, and the liability to Elmer Co. would increase $50. This transaction shows that sometimes two combinations may be involved at the same time; the transaction here involves an increase in an asset balanced half by a decrease in an asset and half by an increase in a source.

Tutt's balance sheet, after the above transaction:

	Assets			**Liabilities and Proprietorship**		
(e, f, g, h, j)	Cash	$ 350		A/P Frank Co.	$ 400	(a)
(c)	Supplies	100		A/P Elmer Co.	150	(b, g, j)
(a, i)	Furniture	350				
(b, j)	Equipment	400				
(d, h)	Library	300		Proprietorship	950	(d, e, f)
		$1,500			$1,500	

Even with these few transactions, the balance sheet has been changed several times. While we could rewrite the balance sheet every time something happened, it is more efficient for the bookkeeper to keep a separate record of the ups and downs of each item on the balance sheet, so that he can determine at any time the net effect on that item of all transactions since he drew up the last balance sheet. Look at cash. Tutt's first balance sheet, shown earlier, showed a cash balance of $800. The bookkeeper would take a separate card, or page in a book, entitle it "Cash", and enter the $800 from the balance sheet as the opening balance. Since we ultimately want the net result of all the ups and downs in the cash, it would be convenient to divide the page into two columns, one for recording the increases in cash, the other for reflecting the decreases; and it would be sensible to use the same column for increases as the one which has the opening balance. This record is called the cash "Account." Here, transactions (e), (f), (g), (h) and (j) would produce an "entry" in the cash account. When the time for drawing up a new balance sheet arrived, it would be simple to add the total of the increases in cash to the opening balance and subtract the total of the decreases to find the cash now on hand. The process is about the same as entering balance forward, deposits and withdrawals in the stubs of a checkbook. The cash account for Tutt, beginning at the date of the balance sheet on page 2, would look like this:

Order in which entries were made			Cash	
			(+)	(−)
(e)	Opening balance (from last balance sheet)		(e) $800	
(f)	To pay off Stanley			$100 (f)
(g)	To pay off Elmer Co.			200 (g)
(h)	To purchase books			100 (h)
(j)	To purchase equipment			50 (j)
	Current balance		$350	

Because this record is shaped like a "T," it is often called a "T-account". The total of the plus column of the T-account, showing the opening cash balance plus any increases, less the total of the minus column, showing decreases, gives the current balance of $350, which would appear on the new balance sheet.

The T-accounts for the other assets, with the opening balance in each case coming from the previous balance sheet, would be as follows:

		Office Furniture	
		(+)	(–)
(a)	Opening balance	(a) $400	
(i)	On removal of chair from business		$50 (i)
	Current balance	$350	

		Office Equipment	
		(+)	(–)
(b)	Opening balance	(b) $300	
(j)	On new purchase from Elmer Co.	(j) 100	
	Current balance	$400	

	Office Supplies	
	(+)	(–)
(c) Opening balance	(c) $100	

(No further entries, as nothing has happened to affect the Office Supplies account.)

		Library	
		(+)	(–)
(d)	Opening balance	(d) $200	
(h)	On purchase of new books	(h) 100	
	Current balance	$300	

In the T-accounts for assets, it is customary to enter the opening balance in the left-hand column. This corresponds to the fact that assets are recorded on the left-hand side of the balance sheet. As noted, the increases are entered in the same column as the opening balance, just as bank deposits are added to the previous balance in a checkbook.

T-accounts similar to those illustrated for the asset accounts are also set up for the liability and the proprietorship accounts. By a convention to be analyzed in the next paragraph, the opening balance in these accounts (which, as with assets, comes from the last previous balance sheet) is entered on the right-hand side of the T-account. To keep this important switch in mind, remember that these accounts are the ones on the right-hand side of the balance sheet. As with assets, increases in these accounts are entered on the same side as the opening balance; but for these accounts that means the right-hand side, with decreases on the left. Tutt's liability and proprietor-ship T-accounts are as follows:

A/P Frank Co.

(−)	(+)
	$400 (a)

(a)   Opening balance

A/P Elmer Co.

(−)	(+)
	$300 (b)
(g) $200	
	50 (j)
Current balance	$150

(b)   Opening balance
(g)   To show partial payment of the account
(j)   On new purchase of equipment

Current balance

N/P Stanley

(−)	(+)
	$100 (c)
(f) $100	
Current balance	$ 0

(c)   Opening balance
(f)   To show payment of note

Current balance

Proprietorship

(−)	(+)
	$1,000 (d,e)
(i) $50	
Current balance	$ 950

(d, e)   Opening balance
(i)   On removal of chair from business

Current balance

At first, this switch of the plus and minus columns may seem clumsy. But it has one very practical advantage which makes the bookkeeper's job easier: it results in having every transaction, no matter what accounts are affected, give rise to equal left-hand and right-hand entries in the T-accounts. To see that this is so, you should first recognize that a transaction affecting accounts on only one side of the balance sheet must produce an equal increase and decrease, and never two increases alone, or two decreases alone. Therefore, if a transaction affects only one side of the balance sheet, e. g., Assets only or Sources only, one entry will be a left-hand entry and the other a right-hand entry. In these cases there is no necessity for any convention calling for a switch between Asset accounts and Source accounts as to the side of the T-account on which an increase or decrease is entered.

It is when a transaction affects both sides of the balance sheet that the advantage of this convention appears. Remember that a transaction affecting accounts on both sides produces either an equal increase on both sides or an equal decrease on both sides, but never an increase on one and a decrease on the other. Whether the change on both sides of the balance sheet is an increase or a decrease, by virtue of this convention the change on one side will be a left-hand entry and the change on the other a right-hand entry. For example, an increase in assets is a left-hand entry, whereas the corresponding equal increase in the liabilities or proprietorship is a right-hand entry. Again, a decrease in the assets column will be a right-hand entry, and the corresponding decrease in liabilities and proprietorship will be a left-hand entry. The table given earlier, then, actually constitutes a summary of the possible combinations of left-hand and right-hand entries:

Left-hand entries	Right-hand entries
Increase in Asset	Increase in Source
Decrease in Source	Decrease in Asset

This convention as to the side of the T-accounts on which increases and decreases are entered, operating in conjunction with the fact that every transaction has two equal aspects which must be recorded, forms the basis of the system often called "double-entry bookkeeping".

To see how double-entry bookkeeping is used, take another look at the transaction already considered. When Tutt paid off Stanley's note, there was a decrease in a liability, the note payable to Stanley, a left-hand entry, and a decrease in an asset, cash, a right-hand entry. And when Tutt bought more office equipment from Elmer Co. for $100, paying $50 down, the left-hand entry showed a $100 increase in an asset, office equipment; the right-hand entry included a $50 decrease in an asset, cash, and a $50 increase in a liability, the account payable to Elmer Co. The left-hand and right-hand entries for each transaction are equal, no matter how many accounts are affected.

The terms "left-hand entry" and "right-hand entry" are cumbersome. Bookkeepers instead use shorthand terms. Left-hand entries are "debits", or "charges", and right-hand entries are "credits". When Tutt buys more books, the bookkeeper speaks of a "debit" (or "charge") to Library, or "debiting" (or "charging") Library, and a "credit" to Cash, or "crediting" Cash. Whatever meaning these terms have in other contexts, here debit (or charge) and credit mean nothing more than left-hand and right-hand entries in the T-accounts.

For convenience, the bookkeeper first records transactions chronologically in a separate book, usually referred to as the "Journal". The account to be debited as a result of the transaction and the amount of the debit is written first, and then on the following line, but indented, is written the account to be credited and the amount. Indentation separates the "credits" from the "debits". These items are generally followed by a brief description of the transaction which makes it possible to check later to see whether the transaction was recorded properly. Representative "journal entries" for some of Tutt's transactions would be:

(f)	Note payable: Stanley	$100	
	Cash		$100
	(To record payment of the note to Stanley)		
(h)	Library	$100	
	Cash		$100
	(To record the purchase of additional books)		
(j)	Office equipment	$100	
	Cash		$ 50
	Account payable: Elmer Co.		50
	(To record purchase of additional business equipment from Elmer Co.)		

These entries are then recorded in the appropriate T-accounts, a process know as "posting" from the Journal to the T-accounts.

PROBLEM

You have now met the basic foundations of bookkeeping. What is called for at this point is some practice in applying these techniques yourself. Immediately following is the balance sheet for E. Tutt on January 1 of his second year of practice, followed by a list of some of Tutt's transactions during the month of January, on the dates indicated. Set up on a separate sheet of paper T-accounts for each of the items on the balance sheet, with the opening balance on the appropriate side. Then on another piece of paper write the journal entry for each of the transactions listed, and then "post" them to the appropriate T-accounts, adding new T-accounts as necessary.

E. TUTT, ESQUIRE

Balance sheet, January 1

Assets		Liabilities & Proprietorship	
Cash	$ 450	Accounts Payable:	
Supplies	50	Brown	$ 200
Furniture	550	Frank Co.	250
Equipment	420		
Library	630	Proprietorship	1,650
	$2,100		$2,100

Transactions in January:

Jan. 1.   Bought a new chair for the office for $75 cash.

    4.   Paid Brown $100 on account.

    6.   Purchased a new office machine from Jones Co. for $220 on credit.

7.   Purchased a new copy of the Ames Code Annotated from the East Publishing Co. for $120, paying $60 down, with the other $60 due in February.

9.   Received a birthday gift from his parents of $300 cash to help him stay in business—he deposited the money in his business bank account.

11. Paid Frank Co. the $250 he owed it.

12. Gave some law books he no longer needed, which cost him $100, to his law school's library.

3. THE INCOME STATEMENT

The balance sheet shows the present status of the assets and the "sources of assets" resulting from all transactions since the business was formed.   It is drawn up at regular intervals which will vary with the needs of the business.   There is another, and increasingly more important, basic financial statement: the *income statement*.   The income statement is a statement for a period of time, giving a summary of earnings between balance sheet dates.   A fundamental distinction between the two is that the balance sheet speaks as of a particular date, while the income statement covers a period of time between successive balance sheet dates.   In later chapters of this book we will have occasion to consider the relative importance of these two statements;   here the question is simply their relation.   You will need a little time to understand the relation and to get used to the way in which double-entry bookkeeping performs a neat "bridging function" between the two.   But there is nothing mysterious about the income statements as such.

It may be easiest to start by drawing up an income statement for E. Tutt, say for the month of June.   Suppose that during the month he receives legal fees of $600 and $400.

(1) Professional Income	$600
(2) Professional Income	$400

To find his net income, we have to subtract his expenses for the month.   Suppose that the operating expenses were as follows:

(3) Rent	$200
(4) Secretary	$230
(5) Telephone	$ 15
(6) Heat & Light	$ 5
(7) Miscellaneous	$ 5

In addition, during the month Tutt suffered a loss when a thief broke into his office and stole $20 cash. This loss is treated as just another expense:

(8) Theft loss $ 20

There is no particular form required for an income statement, so long as it is a clear and fair statement of the information. An acceptable one might look like this:

INCOME STATEMENT—E. TUTT, JUNE

(1 & 2)	Professional Income		$1,000
	Less: Expenses		
(3)	Rent	$200	
(4)	Secretary	230	
(5)	Telephone	15	
(6)	Heat & Light	5	
(7)	Miscellaneous	5	
(8)	Theft Loss	20	
	Total Expenses		475
	NET INCOME		$525

To get started on seeing how the income statement fits into the balance sheet we might ask where "net income" shows up on a balance sheet. In lay terms, it is an increase in the owner's stake in the business, which we call "Proprietorship". Hence, if no other change in Proprietorship occurs, the balance sheet figure for Proprietorship on June 30 should be $525 larger than on June 1.

How does this work out in the accounts? Upon receipt of the $600 fee received for legal work done in June, Tutt will debit Cash, since cash has increased $600:

```
        Cash                              $600
          ?                                        $600
```

Since the corresponding entry must be a credit of $600, the alternatives are a decrease in assets, an increase in liabilities, or an increase in proprietorship (or some combination thereof). But no asset has decreased, nor has any liability increased. Therefore, the credit must be an increase in proprietorship of $600.

This result makes sense. The assets of Tutt's law practice have increased, and since he is the residual owner of this enterprise the increase redounds to his benefit; in other words, his stake in the enterprise has gone up. But common sense tells us that Tutt's "stake" has not been augmented by a full $600. Light, heat, rent, supplies, secretarial services and miscellaneous items have all gone to produce this

$600 fee (and while the theft loss of $20 has not actually helped to produce any fees, it too is a cost of doing business). These items, then, should appear as decreases in Proprietorship; in the same way that income increases the stake of the proprietor, expenses decrease his stake. For example, when rent is paid, the entry could be:

| Proprietorship | $200 | |
| Cash | | $200 |

If all income and expenses were entered in the Proprietorship account, at the end of the period that account would reflect the net increase or decrease in proprietorship for the period. The T-accounts for Cash and Proprietorship for Tutt would be:

Cash

(Opening bal.)	$350	
(1)	600	$200 (3)
(2)	400	230 (4)
		15 (5)
		5 (6)
		5 (7)
		20 (8)
(Current bal.)	$875	

Proprietorship

		$950 (Opening bal.)
(3)	$200	
(4)	230	
(5)	15	
(6)	5	
(7)	5	600 (1)
(8)	20	400 (2)
		$1,475 (Current bal.)

Just as it is inconvenient to draw up a new balance sheet every time something happens, so it would be inconvenient, and indeed uninformative, to enter all the many "operating" items directly in Proprietorship. Instead, the Proprietorship account is broken up into separate T-accounts. The left-hand side of the Proprietorship account, the side on which decreases in proprietorship are recorded, is subdivided into separate T-accounts, called "expense" accounts (e. g., Rent Expense, Utility Expense), or sometimes "loss" accounts (e. g., Theft Loss), and the decreases in proprietorship resulting from operations are entered in those accounts rather than directly in the Proprietorship account. Similarly, the right-hand side of the Proprietorship account, on which increases are recorded, is subdivided into separate T-accounts called "income" accounts (e. g., Professional Income, Dividend Income), and increases arising from operations are recorded in those accounts. The relationship between the expense and income T-accounts and the Proprietorship T-account might be symbolized in the following manner:

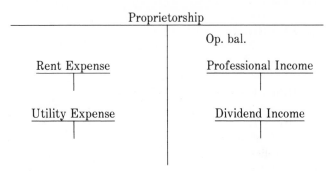

Since an expense constitutes a decrease in proprietorship, which is a debit entry, an expense is of course reflected by a debit or left-hand entry in the appropriate expense T-account. Indeed, since the expense T-accounts are subdivisions of just the left-hand side of the Proprietorship account, you may wonder why the expense accounts themselves have two sides. The answer is simply a practical one: sometimes a portion of an expense previously paid is refunded, perhaps as a rebate, or because it was inadvertently overpaid, and it seems more sensible to record this as a reduction in the expense, by a right-hand entry in the expense T-account, than as an increase in Proprietorship, either by a credit directly to that account or to some income account.

In the same vein, since income constitutes an increase in proprietorship, which is a credit, an income item is reflected by a credit or right-hand entry in the appropriate income T-account; and the presence of a left-hand side in the income T-accounts is simply to make it convenient to reflect any refund of an income item (e. g., a return by E. Tutt of an overpayment of a fee) as a reduction in the income, by a debit to the income T-account.

The number of different expense and income T-accounts set up depends upon the extent to which we want to identify separately in the books the various items of income and expense. For example, Tutt here may want to show rent and secretarial expense as separate items, because they are individually important, but may be satisfied to lump together telephone, heat and light in a single "Utility Expense" account.

Tutt's journal entries for the income and expense transactions during the month would be as follows:

(1) Cash	$600	
Prof. Income		$600
(2) Cash	400	
Prof. Income		400
(3) Rent Expense	200	
Cash		200
(4) Secretarial Expense	230	
Cash		230
(5) Utility Expense	15	
Cash		15
(6) Utility Expense	5	
Cash		5
(7) Miscellaneous Expense	5	
Cash		5
(8) Theft Loss	20	
Cash		20

As these entries show, cash received for professional income has as its corresponding right-hand entry a credit to Professional Income, which is in effect an increase in Proprietorship; and when cash is paid out for expenses for the period, there are corresponding left-hand entries in the various expense accounts that are in effect decreases in Proprietorship. When these entries have been posted to the T-accounts, the T-accounts would appear as follows:

Cash	
bal. $350	
(1) 600	$200 (3)
(2) 400	230 (4)
	15 (5)
	5(6)
	5(7)
	20 (8)
bal. $875	

Proprietorship
$950 bal.

[Expense Items]

Rent Expense

(3) $200	

[Income Items]

Professional Income

	$600 (1)
	400 (2)

Secretarial Expense

(4) $230	

Utility Expense

(5) $15	
(6) 5	

Miscellaneous Expense

(7) $5	

Theft Loss

(8) $20	

Income and expense accounts differ from other accounts in one important respect: as subsidiary accounts of proprietorship, they never appear on the balance sheet. Instead, after the accounts have performed their function of collecting in one place all items of the same kind of income or expense for the period, the net balances in these accounts are brought together in a single account. The net figure in that account, net income, shows the effect of the operations of the period on Proprietorship. In other words, whereas at the beginning of the period we broke the Proprietorship account down into several sub-accounts for income and expense items, at the end of the period we bring these sub-accounts back together, and the net figure is the increase (or decrease) in Proprietorship due to operations.

Of course, the income and expense accounts could be brought back together in the Proprietorship account itself, by simply debiting the Proprietorship account with the various expense items, and crediting Proprietorship with the income items. That is ordinarily not done, however, since it is desirable to isolate in a single special account all the items *relating to operations* for the particular period. If the income and expense items were brought back together in the Proprietorship account, that isolation would not be achieved, since the Proprietorship account also reflects other transactions having nothing to do with the operations of the business—for example, a withdrawal from the business during the period, such as Tutt's removal of the chair from the office. A separate account is needed to show just the results of operations; that account called *Profit and Loss*, serves as the consolidating account for all the income and expense items. Accordingly, the income and expense items are transferred, or, in accounting jargon, "closed" to the Profit and Loss account.

The bookkeeper uses journal entries to transfer the balances in these individual accounts to Profit and Loss. Since the separate income and expense accounts are to disappear, the bookkeeper makes an entry in each of these accounts equal to and on the opposite side from the net balance found in the account. This entry, by making the two sides of the account equal, "closes" the account, and the bookkeeper draws a double line across the bottom of the account to show that it is closed. The corresponding "opposite-hand" entry is then made to Profit and Loss, thus putting the balance in each account on the same side of Profit and Loss as it was in the account from which it came, i. e., expenses on the left-hand side, income on the right. Tutt's "closing entries":

(a) Professional Income	$1,000	
Profit and Loss		$1,000
(b) Profit and Loss	$ 200	
Rent Expense		$ 200
(c) Profit and Loss	$ 230	
Secretarial Expense		$ 230
(d) Profit and Loss	$ 20	
Utility Expense		$ 20
(e) Profit and Loss	$ 5	
Miscellaneous Expense		$ 5
(f) Profit and Loss	$ 20	
Theft Loss		$ 20

The T-accounts then become:

Cash		Proprietorship	
bal. $350			$950 bal.
(1) 600	$200 (3)		
(2) 400	250 (4)		
	15 (5)		
	5 (6)	**[Expense Items]**	**[Income Items]**
	5 (7)		
	20 (8)	Rent Expense	Professional Income
bal. $875			

Rent Expense

(3) $200	
	$200 (b)

Professional Income

	$600 (1)
(a) $1,000	400 (2)

Secretarial Expense

(4) $230	
	$230 (c)

Utility Expense

(5) $ 15	
(6) 5	$ 20 (d)

Miscellaneous Expense

(7) $ 5	
	$ 5 (e)

Theft Loss

(8) $ 20	
	$ 20 (f)

Profit and Loss

(b) $200	$1,000 (a)
(c) 230	
(d) 20	
(e) 5	
(f) 20	
	$ 525

What has been achieved? Compare the Profit and Loss account with the income statement which we made up at the beginning of this section. They are of course essentially the same, for the income statement is nothing more than a somewhat more verbal presentation of Profit and Loss. But the creation of separate income and expense accounts in effect sets up slots for recording the transactions as they occur; it permits the immediate classification of the various categories of income and expense and provides a single place for the orderly accumulation and preservation of all items of the same category. And the utility of a separate Profit and Loss account, reflecting solely the operations of the business, will become increasingly apparent.

The final step is to "close" Profit and Loss into Proprietorship: since at present the net figure in Profit and Loss is a credit of $525, we need a debit to Profit and Loss of $525 to close the account, and a credit to Proprietorship in the same amount:

(g) Profit and Loss	$525	
Proprietorship		$525

Nothing more is happening, of course, than to transfer the credit of $525 to Proprietorship, where it would have been in the first place if we had not created the separate income and expense accounts. The final T-accounts then:

Cash		Proprietorship	
(closing bal.) $875			$950 (op. bal.) 525 (g)
		bal.	$1,475

	Profit and Loss	
(b) $200		$1,000 (a)
(c) 230		
(d) 20		
(e) 5		
(f) 20		
		525
(g) 525		

The circle is now complete; the resulting balances of $875 in cash and $1,475 in Proprietorship are exactly the same as we saw earlier in this section, before we went through the bookkeeping processes for expense and income items. If no change in other assets or liabilities has occurred, so that the balances in those accounts remain as they were on page 6, the ending balance sheet would be:

Assets		**Liabilities & Proprietorship**	
Cash	$ 875	Accounts payable	
Furniture	350	Frank Co.	$ 400
Equipment	400	Elmer Co.	150
Supplies	100		
Library	300	Proprietorship	1,475
	$2,025		$2,025

PROBLEM

Here are the rest of E. Tutt's transactions for the month of January. Prepare the journal entries for these transactions, and post them to the appropriate T-accounts, setting up any additional T-accounts that may be needed (including of course the necessary expense and income accounts). Then close the expense and income accounts to the Profit and Loss account, and close Profit and Loss to Proprietorship. Prepare an income statement for the month of January and a balance sheet as of the end of January, using the forms set out after the list of transactions. (To aid you in checking your work, the correct Net Income figure is $375, and the balance sheet columns should each total $2605.)

Additional Transactions in January:

Jan. 13.   Gave Smith some legal advice and received $150.

15.   Got a reminder from his landlord that he had not paid the rent of $150 for his office for January, and sent a check immediately.

16.   Paid his secretary her salary of $200 for the first half of January.

20.   Received $375 for his work during January on Bolton's Estate.

23.   Paid an electrician $20 to repair a lighting fixture.

25.   Purchased some supplies for $75 cash from Stanley Co.

27.   Did some work for Sam's Book Store, and in exchange received a new East's Digest which sells for $220.

29.   Prepared a deed for Ingersoll and received a fee of $250.

30.   Paid his secretary $200 for the second half of January.

31.   Went to Telephone Co. and paid his bill of $50 for the month of January.

Income Statement—January

Professional Income $ _995_

       Less: Expenses
           Rent $_150_
           Secretary   _400_
           Telephone _50_
           Miscellaneous _20_   _620_
Net Income   _375_

Balance Sheet, January 31

Assets		Liabilities & Proprietorship	
Cash	$ _345_	Accounts Payable:	
Supplies	_125_	Brown	$ _100_
Furniture	_625_	Jones Co.	_60_
Equipment	_640_	East Publish. Co.	_220_
Library	_870_	Proprietorship	_2225_
Total	_2605_	Total	_2605_

4. DEFERRAL OF EXPENSE AND INCOME

The fact that both assets and expenses are increased by a debit and decreased by a credit is not fortuitous. There is a significant relationship between assets and expenses. Suppose when Tutt first hangs out his shingle, he pays $12,000 to purchase a small building to use as his office; he would debit the asset "Building" $12,000, and credit Cash in the same amount, and no income or expense account would be affected. If instead he pays a week's rent for an office, a debit to Rent Expense would be appropriate. But what if he pays advance rent for six months? Ten years? Ninety-nine years? Clearly at some point it can no longer be said that Tutt is "out" or "poorer" by the amount of the advance payment, or that his stake in the enterprise has been reduced in that amount. Rather he has exchanged cash for an asset, just as he did when he purchased a building; here the asset would be the right to occupy the office for the period covered by the payment.

Actually any expense paid in advance creates an asset, although that asset may be short-lived; even the payment of rent in advance for a week gives rise to an asset, the right to occupy for one week. By the end of the week, however, the asset has been used up, and the payment has become an expense. By the same token, almost all assets are simply prepaid expenses, since ultimately they will be used up and disappear. For the key to deciding how much of an advance payment is an expense and how much is an asset, remember that the income and expense accounts collect the items affecting proprietorship *in a particular period.* The amount of an advance payment which is used up during the period is an expense for that period; any portion of the payment not used up in the current period is something the business still owns, and hence is an asset as of the end of the period. Thus if Tutt pays $12,000 advance rental for ten years, at the end of the first year $1,200 is an expense, and $10,800 remains as an asset. If, as we have been assuming, Tutt prepares statements each month, then for the first month $100 (1/120 x $12,000) is an expense, and the remaining $11,900 is an asset at the end of the first month.

If for simplicity we assume that the useful life of a building can be estimated with precision and we ignore scrap or other salvage value, the purchase of a building with a useful life of 10 years for $12,000 may be thought of in exactly the same way as an advance rental for ten years. Like the advance rental, the cost of the building will be completely used up at the end of the tenth year; therefore that cost should be apportioned among the periods in which the building helps to produce income.

To see how the bookkeeper uses entries to handle this, suppose that on January 1 of his first year Tutt pays $3,000 for rent for three years in advance. At the end of the first year, no matter how the entries are made during the year, he should end up with an expense of $1,000 and an asset of $2,000. Since a payment for rent seems like an expense at first blush, Tutt's bookkeeper might make this entry on January 1:

Rent Expense	$3,000	
Cash		$3,000

Assuming for the moment that we are only concerned with Tutt's annual statements, the various income and expense accounts will be closed into the profit and loss account at the end of the year. But only $1,000 of the $3,000 now in the rent expense T-account "belongs" to the first year; thus if the whole $3,000 is closed to profit and loss, rent expense for that year will be overstated and net income will be understated. At the same time Tutt's balance sheet for December 31 will not include all of his assets since the asset representing the right to occupy the premises for two more years will be missing. What is needed, then, is a reduction of the expense to the amount actually used up, and the creation of an asset to show what Tutt actually still owns. To show the existence of the asset, that is, the "Right-to-Occupy", a debit of $2,000 should be made to that account. To decrease the expense from $3,000 to $1,000, a credit to the Rent Expense of $2,000 is needed. A single entry would accomplish both objectives. The entry could be journalized as follows:

Right-to-Occupy (asset)	$2,000	
Rent Expense		$2,000

This process of reducing an expense to the amount actually used up during the period with the corresponding creation of an asset to show something the business still has on hand is called "deferral". The name appropriately connotes the fact that part of the expense is held back from the current period because it has not yet been used. Accordingly, the asset created is often called a "Deferred Expense"— here the asset would be called "Deferred Rent Expense" instead of the more cumbersome "Right-to-Occupy". It is also common to refer to such an asset as a "Prepaid Expense", in this case, "Prepaid Rent Expense", which, of course, connotes the fact that a future expense has been paid in advance. And the fact that a single entry, often referred to as an *"adjusting"* entry, accomplishes both the reduction in the expense and the creation of the asset in the proper amount is just one example of the neat "bridging function" which double-entry bookkeeping performs between the balance sheet and the income statement.

Look now at the case in which, at the beginning of his first year, Tutt purchases a building with a useful life of ten years to use as his office. This is clearly a purchase of an asset, and the entry would be:

Building	$12,000	
Cash		$12,000

Unless some entry is made at the end of the first year, however, the balance sheet drawn up then will show the asset "Building" at $12,000. That would be an overstatement of Tutt's assets, since the building would have a remaining useful life of only nine years. In addition, Tutt's net income for the first year would be overstated, since there would be no deduction for the expense of using an office, although one-tenth of the total life of the building has been "used up" during the year. What is called for, then, is the creation of an expense of $1,200, usually called "Depreciation Expense", and a reduction of the asset "Building" to $10,800. Again a single entry will do the job:

Depreciation Expense	$1,200	
Building [1]		$1,200

This adjusting entry properly puts an expense of $1,200 into the current year and reduces the asset figure to $10,800 to show what is really left for future years.

It might be noted, incidentally, that the advance payment for rent could have been handled in exactly the same way, rather than as we did it above. Upon payment of the $3,000 on January 1 of the first year, the entire payment could have been recorded as a Deferred Rent Expense asset:

Deferred Rent Expense	$3,000	
Cash		$3,000

---

1. As we shall see later, this credit ordinarily would not be made directly to the Building account, but to a separate account called Accumulated Depreciation, which would appear on the balance sheet as an offset to the Building account.

In that event, on December 31 an adjusting entry creating an expense of $1,000 and decreasing the asset by the same amount would have been necessary to show that one-third of the asset had been used up:

Rent Expense	$1,000	
Deferred Rent Expense		$1,000

The product of these two entries is exactly the same as the one we obtained by first recording the entire advance payment as an expense and then deferring the portion not used up during the period.

Which of these methods the bookkeeper uses depends entirely upon whether he initially records an expenditure as an asset or an expense; the end result is the same. Therefore, if you find it easier, handle any advance payment which may not be used up in the current period just as you would an obvious asset like a building—that is, first record the payment as an asset, and then at the end of the period reduce the asset and create an expense to the extent that the asset was used up during the period. In practice, however, the initial entry for an expenditure often depends upon whether it "looks" more like an expense or an asset in the lay sense; hence a payment of rent to a landlord will normally be debited to an expense account initially, even though it may cover far more than the current period. That is because the bookkeeper's functions are fairly mechanical and do not include determining the length of time over which an advance payment will be used up. The often difficult question of how much of a particular expenditure belongs to the current period, which will receive considerable attention in later chapters of this book, is then resolved by the accountant who supervises the closing of the books at the end of the period, and makes whatever adjusting entries are necessary.

A relation similar to that between expenses and assets exists between income items and liabilities, both of which are decreased by a debit and increased by a credit. Consider the bookkeeping for Ohner, the lessor of the building in which E. Tutt rents office space for three years by paying $3,000 in advance. When Ohner receives the $3,000, he might make the following entry in his books:

Cash	$3,000	
Rental Income		$3,000

Without some further entry, this $3,000 item will be closed into the profit and loss account along with the other income and expense items at the end of the year. Again it must be remembered, however, that the income accounts, like the expense accounts, are supposed to collect items affecting proprietorship *in the current period.* The entire $3,000 of rent income does not "belong" to the first year; $2,000 of that amount was received for the second and third years. Thus if the whole $3,000 is closed to Profit and Loss for the first year, rent income for that year will be overstated, which will result in an overstatement of net income for the year. And net income for each of the next two years would be understated, since there would be no rent income for those years, although there would still be such expenses as insurance, janitor service, property taxes and the like.

At the same time, there would be an item missing from Ohner's balance sheet for the end of the first year. If for some reason Ohner defaulted in his agreement to furnish Tutt with office space for the next two years, presumably Ohner would at least be required to refund to Tutt the $2,000 paid for those two years. To put it another way, as of the end of the first year Ohner has an obligation to provide office space to Tutt for the next two years, and the most convenient measure of this obligation is the $2,000 Tutt paid for those two years. This obligation should appear on Ohner's balance sheet as a liability at the end of the first year.

What is needed, then, is a reduction of rent income to the amount actually applicable to the current period, here $1,000, and the creation of a liability in the amount of $2,000 to show Ohner's future obligation. To reduce rent income to $1,000, a debit of $2,000 should be made to that account. To create the liability account, which is usually called "Deferred Income" (or here perhaps, for greater precision, "Deferred Rent Income") because it results from deferring income from the current period, a credit of $2,000 should be made to that account. The entry would be journalized as follows:

Rent Income	$2,000	
Deferred Rent Income		$2,000

Once again a single adjusting entry has accomplished both objectives —and we see here another example of the "bridging" function of double-entry bookkeeping.

Just as it is permissible to record an advance payment which may not be used up during the current period initially as an asset rather than as an expense, so an advance receipt can properly be recorded first by a credit to the appropriate "Deferred Income" liability account. Such an entry for Ohner in this situation would be:

Cash	$3,000	
Deferred Rent Income		$3,000

In that event, at the close of the period it would be necessary to make an adjusting entry crediting Rent Income in the amount of $1,000 and decreasing the liability by the same amount. Again a single entry will do the job:

Deferred Rent Income	$1,000	
Rent Income		$1,000

This entry properly puts income of $1,000 into the current year, and reduces the liability to $2,000 to show a more meaningful measure of Ohner's obligation for future years. The product of these two entries is exactly the same as the one we obtained by first recording the entire advance receipt as income and then deferring the amount not applicable to the current period.

Determination of the period or periods in which to reflect, or as the accountants say, *"recognize"*, the income represented by a payment received in advance is not always as easy as in the foregoing illustration. Actually, the advance rent example, in which the total income involved is allocated pro rata among the periods affected, is somewhat atypical; in many situations, all of the income from a single transaction is recognized in just one period, and not allocated among several periods. That is because of an important general rule governing the recognition of income, which will be developed in more detail later but should at least be introduced here: income is recognized only in the period in which it is *"earned"*, and normally none of the income from a particular transaction is considered to have been earned until the recipient has substantially completed performance of everything he is required to do on his side of the bargain. Under this test, a lawyer who receives a fee from a client for a professional undertaking which is not completed until a later period would normally not recognize any income from the transaction until the period in which he in fact completes the assignment, even if he does some of the work in a prior period; and any portion of the fee received earlier would be treated as deferred income until that later period when the performance is completed. Similarly, a seller of goods who receives payment in advance ordinarily would not recognize any of the income from the transaction until the period in which a transfer of the goods to the customer (or some counterpart indication of substantial completion of performance) occurs, at which time all of the income from the transaction would be reflected; even if some of the work is done in the period in which the advance receipt was received, or in an intervening period, none of the income would be allocated to such period(s), and all of the advance payment would be deferred until the period in which performance is substantially completed. (As you might expect, some close questions arise as to what constitutes a single transaction, whether in the practice of law, the sale of goods, or whatever the activity; we will examine issues of this kind later in these materials.)

Development of the rule governing recognition of income was significantly influenced by an historic accounting doctrine known as "conservatism"; in a nutshell, the thrust of the doctrine is that accounting principles should lean toward the pessimistic side, to offset the natural optimism (if not to say exuberance) of business owners or managers in reporting the results of their operations. The theme of the doctrine of conservatism is summed up in the adage, "Recognize all losses, anticipate no gains", which simply means that in order to avoid later unpleasant surprises an effort should be made to reflect all losses or expenses as soon as they appear likely, while delaying the recognition of income or gain until it is virtually assured. Although this doctrine still has considerable impact, today there is growing awareness that undue pessimism in reporting financial results can be just as harmful as over-optimism, for example, to an investor who is led by unduly discouraging financial statements to sell his investment for a lower price.

Returning to our example involving Ohner's receipt of an advance payment of rent for three years, it might seem that Ohner would not have completed his agreed-upon performance until the end of the third year, and therefore would not have "earned" any of the income involved in the transaction until that time. However, transactions in which the performance by the recipient of income consists primarily of permitting another to enjoy the use of property or money for a period of time, as in the case of rent or interest, are usually treated differently from the standard types of business activity like practice of law or the sale of goods. These transactions involving leasing property, or lending money at interest, which produce income by virtue of the passage of time, are viewed as though they consisted of a series of separable agreements covering the consecutive accounting periods over which the entire transaction runs, and the income proportionate to the passage of time during each accounting period is regarded as having been earned in that period. Hence, one-third of the income from Ohner's advance receipt of three years' rent would be treated as earned at the end of the first of the three years. Similarly, for anyone interested in monthly periods, one-twelfth of the one-third earned in the first year would be regarded as earned during each of the twelve months of that first year. (Some justification for this difference in treatment may be found in the fact that even under the most conservative view of things it is unlikely that the lender of money or the lessor of property will (or even could) fail to perform his agreement in full, since no further effort on his part is called for.)

PROBLEM

Below is the balance sheet for E. Tutt on March 1, followed by some of Tutt's transactions during March. Make the journal entries for these transactions and post them to the appropriate T-accounts. (Ignore depreciation.)

Balance Sheet, March 1

Assets		Liabilities & Proprietorship	
Cash	$ 345	Accounts Payable	
Accounts Rec.		Stanley	$ 100
Potter Corp.	225	Jones Co.	220
Smith Estate	500	Tel. Exp. Pay.	40
Furn. & Equip.	1250		
Library	870	Deferred Income	300
Supplies	110		
Def. Secretar. Exp.	200	Proprietorship	2840
Total	$3500	Total	$3500

Transactions in March:

March   1.   Purchased a three-section Super Fireproof Safe for $480 from Jarald Co. on credit.

         2.   Paid the landlord $150 rent for his office for March.

         5.   Paid $120 for a one-year liability insurance policy ordered the week before and running through next Feb. 28.

         7.   Paid $60 for a one-year subscription to the local weekly legal journal, to start on April 1.

         9.   Purchased a $100 treatise on bankruptcy from East Publishing Company on credit.

      11.   Received $350 from Homer Co. for legal advice given during the week.

      13.   A new client, Fashion Corp., sent him $250 as a retainer for an argument on a motion scheduled for April 10.

      14.   Completed the work for which Anderson paid him $300 in advance last month.

5. ACCRUAL OF EXPENSE AND INCOME

Thus far we have been considering the proper treatment of expense and income items when cash has been paid or received. We have seen that cash receipts or payments do not necessarily determine the amount of income or expense for the current period. As a matter of fact, the time when cash changes hands in a business transaction is often governed by factors which have little to do with the question of when the income or expense represented by the cash should be reflected. That holds true whether the cash moves beforehand, as in the deferral cases we have been considering, or moves afterward: the absence of cash receipts or payment does not negative current income or expense. Let us look at a situation where no cash has moved. Suppose Tutt took a three-year lease of office space calling for rent of $1,000 per year, payable at the end of each year. Obviously, if Tutt paid the $1,000 due for rent at the end of the first year, an entry debiting Rent Expense in the amount of $1,000 and crediting cash in the same amount would be routine. But suppose instead that due to inadvertence or otherwise Tutt failed to pay the rent due at the end of the first year. If the movement of cash were controlling, then there would not be any entry reflecting rent expense during the first year; hence when Tutt closed his books at the end of that first year, net income for the year would be overstated since there would be no deduction for the expense of using an office during the year. Moreover, when Tutt pays the $1,000 for the first year's rent shortly into the second year, presumably it would be debited to the current Rent Expense account at that time; but if Tutt also pays the rent for the second year by the end of that year, as he is supposed to, that too would be charged to current rent expense, with the result that Profit and Loss for the second year would be burdened with $2,000 of rent expense, and net income for the year would be seriously understated.

What is needed, then, is the creation of an expense in the first year in the amount properly allocable to that year. That is, the first year should bear its fair share of the total cost of utilizing office space, even though none of that cost was actually paid during the first year. A bookkeeping entry can be used to accomplish this purpose. The debit part is simple enough, for that is dictated by the "judgment decision" that rent expense in the amount of $1,000 "belongs" in the current (first) year; there is only one way to reflect an expense in a particular year, and that is to debit the appropriate expense account in that year, so that it will be closed to the Profit and Loss account at the end of the year, to be netted with all of the other expense and income items for the period.

Rent Expense $1,000
        ?
                                                        $1,000

As to the credit, of course if cash had been paid that would be easy. But since Tutt has not paid, as he was supposed to, is it not clear that he owes the $1,000 at the close of the year, just as clearly if he had bought more office equipment for $1,000 on account? The credit, therefore, should be to a liability account, to reflect his obligation to pay. This process of pulling an expense into the current period even though it has not yet been paid, with the corollary creation of a liability account reflecting the obligation to pay, is known as "Accrual". Taken together with deferral, accrual makes it possible to free the reporting of expense items from the movement of cash: when cash has moved in an amount greater than the expense that belongs in the current period, deferral makes it possible to charge only the proper amount to expense for the current period; when an expense belongs in the current period even though the cash has not moved as yet, accrual makes it possible to reflect the expense in the current period.

Incidentally, with regard to the name given the liability account which is created when an expense is accrued, it would probably not be called an "Account Payable", since that term is usually reserved for credit purchases of goods and supplies; moreover, it is often helpful to identify other liabilities as to their source. Hence, the liability would more likely be called "Accrued Rent Expense", which serves as a reminder that the liability results from the accrual of an expense into the current period. Another common term for such a liability, which we will often use in these materials, is "Expense Payable", here "Rent Expense Payable", or perhaps just "Rent Payable", which similarly connotes the fact that the liability is the product of reflecting an expense currently although it has not yet been paid. So the entry here might be:

Rent Expense	$1,000	
Rent Expense Payable		$1,000

This entry puts $1,000 of rent expense into the current year, and creates a liability account to show that Tutt owes this amount for rent at the end of the first year.

Now suppose that Tutt's lease of office space for three years had not called for payments at the end of either of the first two years, but instead provided that the total of $3,000 should all be paid at the end of the third year. Once again, unless some entry is made when Tutt closes his books at the end of the first year, net income for the first year will be overstated since there will be no deduction for the expense of using an office during the year. Moreover, presumably the entire $3,000 payment in the third year would have to be treated as an expense of that year, with the result that net income for the third year would be greatly understated. Here, too, we need to accrue in the first year the amount of rent expense properly applicable to that year, even though no amount has been paid during that year. Since it seems clear that the one-third of the total rent of $3,000 is properly applicable to the first year, an entry exactly the same as before is called for, with a debit of $1,000 to Rent Expense, and a credit of $1,000 to Rent Expense Payable or Accrued Rent Expense.

To be sure, since in this case Tutt has agreed to pay only at the end of the third year, strictly speaking he is under no legal obligation to pay anything at the end of the first year. Nevertheless, in an accounting sense Tutt does "owe" $1,000 at the end of the first year, since he must pay it ultimately, and, what is more significant, $1,000 of the total commitment has been used up in the current period. Hence it is entirely appropriate to credit a Rent Expense Payable (or Accrued Rent Expense) liability account, although on the balance sheet it may be desirable to segregate liabilities of this sort, which do not have to be paid for quite some time, from those which must be paid rather shortly, in the ordinary course of business. The important point is that an expense which belongs in the period may be accrued, that is, reflected in a current expense account, even though it not only has not been paid but there is not yet even a current obligation to pay it.

Notice that in this case of a three-year lease with none of the rent due until the end of the third year, when the rent expense is accrued for the first year the Rent Expense Payable (or Accrued Rent Expense) liability account reflects only an amount equal to the expense charged to that year, not the entire rent obligation for the three-year period. That is because the very purpose of accrual is to reflect an expense currently, with the creation of the liability being simply a corollary, to provide a companion credit to go along with the debit to an expense account, and obviously that credit must be in the same amount as the debit. Indeed, unlike the case of an advance payment, when of course some entry must be made to reflect the reduction in cash even though not all of the payment is chargeable to current expense (which is where deferral comes in), in the case of an expected future payment usually no entry at all need be made in the current period unless, and then only to the extent that, a charge to current expense is called for. So if Tutt signed a three-year lease for office space during the year before the beginning of the lease, no entry at all relating to the lease commitment would be called for in that year. (However, it might be desirable to disclose, in the financial statements for that year, the existence of the lease commitment scheduled to start the following year; similarly, it might be well to disclose in the financial statements at the end of the first year that the $1,000 shown in the Rent Payable liability account does not represent the entire rent commitment. As we shall see, the use of footnotes or other adjuncts to the financial statements may provide suitable mechanisms for such disclosure.[2])

2. There may be some occasions, perhaps in cases where an obligation to make future payments is relatively very large, or is all currently due as a matter of contract, when the full amount of the obligation should be recorded on the balance sheet (rather than just disclosed, say, in a footnote), even though some, or even all, of the obligation is not yet properly chargeable to current expense because some (or even all) of the benefit remains to be enjoyed in future periods. In that event, the entire amount of the obligation would have to be credited to the Expense Payable liability account (which might then need a different name). As to the accompanying debit in such a case, the only sensible one, except for any amount charged

When the rent is ultimately paid, the debit will be to Rent Payable, just as any debtor who pays money owed on open account debits the account payable:

Rent Expense Payable	$1,000	
Cash		$1,000

The important fact is that no account on the income statement is affected by the actual payment, which is as it should be since the expense has already been reflected at an earlier time.

Similar accrual techniques are available where income should be recognized in a period prior to the receipt of cash. Look at the bookkeeping for Ohner when he leases an office to Tutt for three years, for a total rent of $3,000. Ohner's recognition of income from this transaction should not depend upon when he receives the cash; the amount of income reflected in the first year (or any subsequent year, for that matter) should be the same, whether Ohner (1) received cash during the year or (2) was entitled to receive cash but Tutt inadvertently failed to pay, or (3) was not entitled to receive any cash until the end of the three years. As to the amount of income to be reflected in the first year, recall that under the rules for recognizing income noted earlier, the income represented by rent (and interest) is regarded as earned uniformly with the passage of time. Accordingly, at the end of the first year Ohner has earned $1,000 of the rent, and therefore he should recognize $1,000 in current income, even if no cash has been received, or is even due as yet.

Once a judgment has been made that $1,000 of rent income belongs in the first year, it follows that a credit in that amount must be made to the Rent Income account for that year. (As with the counterpart reflection of an expense, the only way that any income item can ever be put into a particular year is to credit a current income account during that year.) This is another example of accrual; the rent income is accrued, i. e., pulled into the current period, although the cash has not yet been received. As to the accompanying debit (which would of course have been to cash if the $1,000 had been received), a receivable should be created, to reflect the fact that although the cash has not been received Ohner has a right to receive it in the future. This receivable might be called "Accrued Rent Income", or "Rent Income Receivable" (or perhaps just "Rent Receivable"), terms which connote the fact that the receivable reflects

to current expense, would be a debit to a Deferred Expense Account (with the recording of the liability serving as a kind of substitute for the payment of cash which is the usual basis for creating a deferred expense asset).

the right to receive an amount which has been recognized as income prior to the receipt of cash. So the entry might be:

Rent Income Receivable	$1,000	
Rent Income		$1,000

Notice that if the lease provided that none of the rent was due until the end of the third year, then technically Ohner would not have any legal right to $1,000 at the end of the first year. Nevertheless, in the same sense that Tutt "owed" $1,000 at the end of the first year even though he was not obligated to pay anything until the end of the third year, so Ohner would have a "right" to $1,000 at the end of the first year since he is entitled to receive it ultimately, and it has been "earned" during the first year. Therefore, it is entirely appropriate to debit a "Rent Income Receivable" (or Accrued Rent Income) account, although again on the balance sheet it may be desirable to segregate receivables like this, on which the cash will not be received for some time, from those on which the cash will be received shortly, in the ordinary course of business. Note that, paralleling the accrual of expenses, the primary purpose of accrual of income is to reflect an item in current income even though cash has not yet been received, and the creation of an Income Receivable (or Accrued Income) account is merely an adjunct needed to show that there is a right to receive the cash in the future. Hence, as with the counterpart payables discussed earlier, these receivables will normally show only that portion of a future receipt which has been earned, rather than the full amount of the expected future payment.

When Ohner ultimately receives the money, the credit will be to the Rent Income Receivable account, just as a creditor who receives money owed to him on open account credits the account receivable:

Cash	$1,000	
Rent Income Receivable		$1,000

The important fact is that no account on the income statement is affected by the actual receipt, which is as it should be since the income has already been recognized at an earlier time.

As we noted in connection with advance receipts, transactions involving the rental of property, as here, or lending money at interest, are atypical so far as recognition of income is concerned, because in such cases the income is viewed as earned by the passage of time. For standard types of income-producing activity, like practice of law or sale of goods, the general rule applies, to the effect that all of the income from a transaction is to be recognized in the period in which substantial completion of performance occurs. (Sometimes, recognition of income from performance of services is delayed until a bill has been sent, in order to avoid the need for estimation, and perhaps also provide greater assurance that performance has indeed been completed.) The important point is that it does not matter whether the cash has been received as yet, so long as the income has been earned; and accrual provides the mechanics for recognizing the income in the period in which it is earned, even though no cash has been received.

Notice that, unlike the case of an advance receipt where some entry must be made to reflect the receipt of cash even though the related income has not been earned in the current period, in the case of an expected future receipt no entry is called for in the current period if the income has not yet been earned. An entry will be made only in the period when the income is finally earned, unless, of course, the cash moves sooner, in which event the case becomes simply one of an advance receipt.

One special aspect of the treatment of an expected receipt deserves brief mention here. It arises because accounting, mirroring business in this regard, still attributes considerable importance to the ultimate receipt of cash, even though it does not make such receipt a pre-condition for the recognition of income. (Obviously, no question about the ultimate receipt of cash can arise in cases involving advance receipts, because by hypothesis the cash has already been received.) In the case of an expected future receipt, if there is substantial doubt as to the ultimate collectibility of cash, because of the insolvency of the debtor or otherwise, no income is recognized from the transaction even though it has been earned in the current period. It should be emphasized that this qualification applies only when there is some special reason for concern about collectability, not just the general risk of non-payment that is inherent in any business done on credit; for the latter, other tools exist, which will be introduced when this subject is discussed in more detail later.

PROBLEM

Here are the rest of E. Tutt's transactions for March. Prepare the journal entries and post them to the appropriate T-accounts; then make up the income statement for the month of March and the balance sheet as of March 31. (Blank forms for these financial statements, showing the correct net income figure and balance sheet totals, are set out after the list of transactions.)

Additional Transactions in March:

March 15.   Borrowed $480 from First State Bank on a one-year note, with interest at 10%, payable at maturity, and immediately paid his debt to Jarald Co.

March 16. Paid $50 to Manpower, Inc. for temporary typing assistance last week.

17. Received bill from landlord for additional rent of $15 due for March under the fuel adjustment clause in his lease.

20. Sent $40 to the telephone company to pay his outstanding bill.

21. Gave tax advice to Olson and received $200 for it.

22. Prepared and filed incorporation papers for Nelson, Inc. and sent a bill for $250.

24. Received $300 of the $500 due from Smith's Estate.

26. Rented a section of his new safe to Bilder, a lawyer in the adjacent office, for 90 days, at a rental of $90 payable at the end of the term.

30. Paid his secretary $100 of the $200 owed to her for the second half of March.

31. Checked with telephone company and learned that his bill for March would be $45.

Income Statement, March

Professional Income	_____	
Rent Income	_____	_____
Less Expenses:		
Rent	_____	
Insurance	_____	
Secretarial	_____	
Telephone	_____	
Interest	_____	_____
Net Income		$433

Balance Sheet, March 31

Assets		Liabilities & Proprietorship	
Cash	_____	Accounts Payable	_____
Accounts Rec.	_____	Note Payable	_____
Income Rec.	_____	Expenses Payable	_____
Furn. & Equip.	_____		
Library	_____	Deferred Income	_____
Supplies	_____		
Deferred Exp.	_____	Proprietorship	_____
TOTAL	$4,585	TOTAL	$4,585

6. PRACTICE PROBLEM

Deferral and accrual are the most important tools of bookkeeping, and it is therefore essential that you master the mechanics of these two techniques. They are easy enough to summarize: deferral problems arise only after cash has moved, and the objective is to allocate an expenditure or a receipt between the current period and future periods; accrual problems arise only when cash has not yet moved, and the objective is to bring into the current period an item of income or expense which properly belongs there. However, here, as in so many areas, there is no substitute for practice. To gain the necessary confidence in handling these mechanics you must satisfy yourself that you can make them work as they should. Then we will be ready to turn to the matters that make the field of Accounting worth your time and attention as a prospective lawyer, that is, the questions of judgment and discretion involved in determining the period in which particular items of income and expense should be recognized.

The following problem is designed to afford some additional practice in bookkeeping. Set out after the list of transactions are the appropriate journal entries, with explanatory comments, the completed T-accounts, and the final balance sheet and income statement. However, you would do best to work out the problem on your own, before looking at the recommended solution and the comments.

Assume that E. Tutt's balance sheet on June 30 was as follows:

E. TUTT, ESQ.

Assets		Liabilities & Proprietorship		
Cash	$1,150	Robertson Law Book Co.	$	40
Accounts Rec.				
Southacre Corp.	300			
Georgina Hats, Inc.	100			
Jack Self Clothes	125			
Library	650			
Office Equipment	575	Proprietorship		2,860
	$2,900			$2,900

The following transactions occurred during the month of July (depreciation will be ignored):

July 1. Purchased a piece of land for a contemplated new office building for $1,800. He paid $600 down, and gave a one-year 5% note for the balance, interest payable at maturity.

     2. Paid $75 cash to landlord for rent for July.

July   3.   Paid $100 cash to Douds for painting interior of office.

        5.   Bought adding machine for $200 from P. M. Ryan on account.

        9.   Received $150 cash for legal services rendered on July 7 and 8 to Jones.

      11.   Mailed bill for $225 to Potter for legal services rendered in July.

      13.   Paid Ryan $100 cash on account.

      15.   Received check from Southacre for $200 on account.

      16.   Paid temporary secretarial replacement $180 cash for salary for first three weeks in July.

      18.   Jack Self settled account with $25 cash and a suit of clothes for Mr. Tutt.

      20.   Paid Robertson Law Book Company $40 cash.

      21.   Uncle Zeke Tutt's executor delivered law books worth $100 which had been bequeathed to E. Tutt.

      25.   Paid $15 filing fee to Clerk of County for client Coogan in Coogan v. Sargeant.

      26.   Tutt carelessly dropped a cigarette, starting a fire which destroyed books costing $120, for which he had no insurance.

      28.   Received $200 advance retainer from Annan.

      29.   Received telephone bill of $25 for July.

      30.   Probate Court allowed $1,000 fee for services to executor of Estate of Smith.

      31.   Paid temporary secretary $180 salary for last week in July and first two weeks in August.

July
1   Land $1,800
         Cash $ 600
         Note Payable   1,200

Comment: This entry records Tutt's purchase of land, partly for cash, and partly on credit by giving a note. The Note Payable account is basically the same kind of account as an Account Payable, except that the term "Note Payable" (or, in the case of bonds, "Bonds Payable") is used when a written instrument is given. A separate account is particularly desirable when the written instruments are negotiable. Notice that nothing is done at this time to record the obligation for interest, since no interest is yet due.

2   Rent Expense $75
         Cash $75

Comment: Tutt debits "Rent Expense" because he wants a separate record of his rent payments. If he had no interest in identification of rent payments, the debit might be simply to "Miscellaneous Expense". Since this payment is all for July, it is all an expense for July, and no asset will appear on the balance sheet on July 31.

3	Miscellaneous Expense	$100	
	Cash		$100

Comment: Here a separate account for "Maintenance Expense" might have been used, in which case the debit would have been to that account. Note also that there is a deferral problem: since the paint job will doubtless have utility beyond the month of July, should all this expense be considered a cost of doing business in the month of July? Factors affecting the accounting judgment of whether some of the $100 should be allocated to later periods will be considered in a later chapter; here, for simplicity, Tutt treats this item as an expense of the current period.

5	Office Equipment	$200	
	Account Payable: Ryan		$200

Comment: If Tutt distinguished among the various kinds of office equipment that he had, e. g., "Typewriters", "Mimeographing Machines" and "Bookkeeping Machines", the debit would then be to the appropriate one of these accounts, which would be in effect "sub-accounts" of Office Equipment. (Note that in fact Tutt has moved in the opposite direction, and now includes both Furniture and Equipment in the Office Equipment account.)

9	Cash	$150	
	Professional Income		$150

Comment: Since Tutt has performed all the services called for by the agreement, the income arising from this receipt has been earned and is therefore income for the current period.

11	Account Receivable: Potter	$225	
	Professional Income		$225

Comment: Although no cash has yet been received, Tutt has earned the income in July. Therefore, unless Potter is insolvent or for some other reason collection is not reasonably assured, the income should be recognized in the current period. The debit might just as appropriately be to "Fee Receivable: Potter"; there is no uniform practice where income from personal services is involved.

If Tutt had not yet sent a bill, he might postpone the recognition of this income: the recognition of income from services is often postponed until the sending of a bill, even though the services have been completed and collection of the income is reasonably assured, because of uncertainty as to the amount to be charged.

13	Account Payable: Ryan	$100	
	Cash		$100

Comment: This is exactly like payment of the amount due Elmer Co., described earlier in this chapter; note that the transaction affects both sides of the balance sheet, resulting in a decrease on both sides of $100.

15	Cash	$200	
	Account Receivable: Southacre		$200

Comment: Note that the income account is not affected. An entry like that of July 11 had already been made in a prior period, and Tutt is now simply converting into cash the asset he then recorded.

16	Secretarial Expense	$180	
	Cash		$180

Comment: Since this payment will be completely used up in July, it is recorded immediately as an expense for the current period, and no deferral problem will arise.

18	Cash	$ 25	
	Proprietorship	100	
	Account Receivable: Jack Self		$125

Comment: The troublesome element, the debit of $100 to Proprietorship, is exactly the same in theory as the entry upon Tutt's removal of a chair from the office for use at home.

20	Account Payable: Robertson	$40	
	Cash		$40

21	Library	$100	
	Proprietorship		$100

Comment: Here, in effect, Tutt has contributed $100 more assets to the business, and there is an increase in Proprietorship.

25	Account Receivable: Coogan	$15	
	Cash		$15

Comment: The $15 is chargeable to Coogan, and is not an expense of Tutt's.

26	Fire Loss	$120	
	Library		$120

Comment: Here Tutt lost one of his assets other than cash. Nevertheless, this loss, like the theft loss described earlier in the text, is one of the costs of doing business, and is therefore treated like an expense. "Fire Loss" may be regarded as simply shorthand for "Fire Loss Expense". The credit to "Library" reduces that account by the amount of the books lost.

	28	Cash		$200	
			Deferred Income		$200

Comment: Since Tutt has not yet performed the services for which this fee was received, the income arising from this advance receipt has not been earned. Therefore the income should not be recognized in the current period and the credit is to "Deferred Income". If by the end of the current period Tutt were to complete performance of all the services called for by the agreement, the income would be recognized currently, by a debit to "Deferred Income" and a credit to "Professional Income"; since he does not, "Deferred Income" will appear as a liability account on the balance sheet at the end of July.

	29	Telephone Expense		$25	
		Telephone Expense Payable			$25

Comment: This is an example of accrual of expense. Since this expense is clearly applicable to the current period it should be reflected in this period. Even if no bill had been received, Tutt would still reflect this expense in the current period. Recognition of an expense applicable to the current period is usually not postponed until the receipt of a bill, even though there is uncertainty as to the amount of the charge; instead a reasonable estimate of the charge is made. This differs somewhat from the treatment often adopted in connection with accrual of income. See the Comment to the entry on July 11.

	30	Account Receivable: Smith Estate	$1,000	
		Professional Income		$1,000

Comment: The accrual problem here is exactly like that in the transaction of July 11.

	31	Deferred Salary Expense	$180	
		Cash		$180

Comment: Here the payment will not be completely used up by the end of the period. If, as here, Tutt initially records the payment as an asset, he must make an adjusting entry at the end of the period, to create an expense and reduce the asset in the amount used up during the period. The entry:

(a) Salary Expense $60
         Deferred Salary Expense $60

It would be equally proper first to record the payment as an expense; in that event, upon closing his books at the end of the period, Tutt's adjusting entry would defer the amount not used up during the period.

One other adjusting entry is necessary:

(b) Interest Expense $5
         Interest Expense Payable $5

Comment: Recall that no entry reflecting interest expense was made at the time of the borrowing transaction on July 1, since the note had then just been given. However, the interest which Tutt will ultimately have to pay should not all be charged, i. e. debited, as an expense in the month when he makes the payment. This is just like the situation in the text above in which we saw that Tutt should not charge the entire payment for rent for three years to the third year simply because it was all paid in that year. Instead, Tutt should charge a *pro rata* share of the total interest expense to each month during the time that he has the use of the money, just as he charged a *pro rata* share of the rent expense to each of the years in which he had the use of the office premises. Since the interest charge per year is 5% of $1,200, or $60, one-twelfth of $60, or $5, should be charged as an expense in each month. Hence the debit is to an expense account, here Interest Expense, to reflect this expense in the current period; the credit is to an expense payable account, here Interest Expense Payable, to reflect the eventual liability for this current expense.

Note that no entry is called for to reflect the fact that the due date of the principal amount of the note is one month closer. Just as the borrowing of the funds did not affect Tutt's income statement, neither will the repayment. Therefore, no further entry need be made in connection with the ultimate liability to pay the principal until the note is actually discharged, at which time the entry will be simply:

        Note Payable $1,200
            Cash $1,200

Cash			
(op.)	$1,150		
(9)	150	$600	(1)
(15)	200	75	(2)
(18)	25	100	(3)
(28)	200	100	(13)
		180	(16)
		40	(20)
		15	(25)
		180	(31)
	$ 435		

A/R: Southacre			
(op.)	$300		
		$200	(15)
	$100		

A/R: Georgina		
(op.)	$100	

A/R: Jack Self			
(op.)	$125		
		$125	(18)
	0		

Library			
(op.)	$650		
(21)	100	$120	(26)
	$630		

Office Equipment		
(op.)	$575	
(5)	200	
	$775	

A/R: Potter		
(11)	$225	

A/R: Coogan		
(25)	$15	

A/R: Smith Estate		
(30)	$1,000	

A/P: Robertson			
		$40	(op.)
(20)	$40		

Proprietorship			
		$2,860	(op.)
(18)	$100	100	(21)
		810	(j)
		$3,670	

Note Payable		
		$1,200	(1)

Interest Payable		
		$5	(b)

A/P: Ryan			
		$200	(5)
(13)	$100		
		$100	

Telephone Exp. Pay.		
		$25	(29)

Deferred Income		
		$200	(28)

Rent Expense			
(2)	$75		
		$75	(c)

Miscellaneous Expense			
(3)	$100		
		$100	(d)

Salary Expense			
(16)	$180		
(a)	60		
		$240	(e)

Telephone Expense			
(29)	$25		
		$25	(f)

Deferred Salary Expense

(31)	$180		
		$60	(a)
	$120		

Land

(1)	$1,800	

Fire Loss Exp.

(26)	$120		
		$120	(g)

Interest Expense

(b)	$5		
		$5	(h)

Professional Income

		$ 150	(9)
		225	(11)
		1,000	(30)
		$1,375	
(i)	$1,375		

Profit and Loss

(c)	$ 75	$1,375	(i)
(d)	100		
(e)	240		
(f)	25		
(g)	120		
(h)	5		
		$810	
(j)	$810		

Income Statement, July

Professional Income		$1,375
Expenses:		
Rent	$ 75	
Secretarial	240	
Telephone	25	
Miscellaneous	100	
Fire Loss	120	
Interest	5	565
NET INCOME		$ 810

Balance Sheet, July 31

Assets			Liabilities & Proprietorship	
Cash		$435	Account Payable Ryan	$100
Accounts Receivable:				
Southacre	$ 100		Note Payable	1,200
Georgina	100			
Potter	225		Expenses Payable	30
Coogan	15			
Smith Estate	1,000	1,400		
Deferred Secr. Exp.		120	Deferred Income	200
Library		630		
Equipment		775		
Land		1,800	Proprietorship	3,670
		$5,200		$5,200

7. INVENTORY ACCOUNTING

Many businesses earn profits from the sale of goods rather than, like Tutt, from providing services. In such a business, one of the basic assets is "Inventory", representing the goods held for sale. Inventory is a somewhat different kind of asset from those which Tutt has, because the goods it represents are constantly turning over; sales take goods out of inventory, and purchases are made to replace them. (For an enterprise engaged in manufacturing, the process is a bit more complex: the manufactured, or, as they are often termed, "completed", goods are sold, to be replaced by purchases of raw materials which will be turned into completed goods through the manufacturing operations.) This section is designed to introduce you to the special techniques which are used to deal with the problems which this constant turnover creates.

To take a simple example, suppose Jones is a retailer of shoes, and during the month of January he sells 1,000 pairs of shoes for $10 a pair. Jones must include in his expenses not only the ones that Tutt had, like rent, utilities, salaries, etc., but also the cost of the shoes sold. In bookkeeping language, Jones has Sales Income of $10,000, from which he must deduct the cost of the goods sold, as well as his other expenses, in order to determine his net income. If the shoes cost Jones $7 a pair, and his other expenses for the month came to $1,000, his net income would be $2,000, and a simplied version of his income statement might look something like this:

Income Statement—January

Sales Income	$10,000	
Cost of Goods Sold	7,000	
Gross Profit on Sales		$3,000
Expenses		1,000
Net Income		$2,000

The chief differences between this statement and Tutt's, in addition to the introduction of the Cost of Goods Sold account, are the different name given to the Income account and the introduction of a new caption, Gross Profit on Sales. Sales Income is simply another type of income (i. e., increase in proprietorship resulting from operations), and it reflects the total amount of sales completed during the period. As to Gross Profit on Sales, that figure is often of considerable significance in a business which sells goods, since it is frequently a better guide to market conditions and the efficiency of the selling operations than the Net Income figure.

There are various ways to determine the figure for the cost of goods sold at the end of a period. For example, Jones might keep a record of the cost of each pair of shoes as they are sold; then at the end of the period the total shown by this record would give him the cost of all the shoes sold during the period. Ordinarily, however, it might be difficult, and it would certainly be time-consuming, to identify the cost of each pair of shoes. Usually it would be simpler for Jones merely to keep a record of the cost of the shoes on hand at the beginning of the period and the cost of the shoes acquired during the period. Then at the end of the period Jones can "take inventory", that is, count up the number of shoes he has left and determine their total cost. By subtracting the cost of what he has left from the sum of what he had at the beginning of the period and what he acquired during the period, he can compute the cost of what he sold.

Suppose, for example, that Jones had an inventory at the beginning of January of 300 pairs of shoes which cost $7 per pair, and that during the month he purchased another 1200 pairs of shoes at $7 per pair. Since Jones sold 1000 pairs of shoes during January, upon taking inventory at the end of the month, he would find 500 pairs of shoes which cost a total of $3,500. The difference between that figure and the sum of what Jones had on hand and what he acquired, $10,500, gives the cost of goods sold figure of $7,000 which we had previously assumed. A somewhat more detailed version of his income statement might then look like this:

Income Statement—January

Sales		$10,000
Cost of Goods Sold:		
Opening Inventory	$ 2,100	
Purchases	8,400	
	10,500	
Less:		
Closing Inventory	3,500	7,000
Gross Profit on Sales		3,000
Expenses		1,000
Net Income		$ 2,000

Let us now see how the bookkeeper uses T-accounts and entries to make these computations. On his balance sheet at the beginning of the period, Jones has an asset, "Inventory", in the amount of $2,-100. This account, which was derived by "taking inventory" at the close of the period just ended, becomes "Opening Inventory" for the new period. During the period Jones opens a T-account called "Purchases", to which the amount of purchases made during the period is debited; the corresponding credit is to cash or an account payable, depending upon whether the purchase is made for cash or on credit. (Actually, the purchases during the period could as well be debited directly to the Inventory T-account, thus eliminating the need for opening a new Purchases T-account; but in practice it appears that a separate T-account for purchases is commonly used.) Thus if Jones purchased the entire $8,400 worth of goods acquired in January in a single transaction, and for cash, the entry would be:

(a) Purchases	$8,400	
Cash		$8,400

And of course whether or not Jones purchased all the goods at the same time, or purchased them all for cash, the T-account for Purchases would show a total debit of $8,400 at the end of the month of January.

At the end of the period the bookkeeper sets up a new T-account called "Cost of Goods Sold". As we have already seen, Cost of Goods Sold is an expense and therefore this account should be increased by a debit and decreased by a credit. The bookkeeper then closes Opening Inventory and Purchases to the Cost of Goods Sold account in much the same way that expense and income accounts are closed to the Profit and Loss account. Here the entries would consist of debits to the Cost of Goods Sold account, and credits to the Opening Inventory and Purchases accounts respectively to close them out:

(b) Cost of Goods Sold	$2,100	
Opening Inventory		$2,100
(c) Cost of Goods Sold	8,400	
Purchases		8,400

The bookkeeper then learns from the person who "took inventory" at the end of the month how much inventory is left—here $3,500. This information has two aspects of equal significance to the bookkeeper. It tells him that there remains at the end of the period an asset of $3,500 of closing inventory which should appear on the balance sheet at the end of the period. It also tells him that the cost of goods sold is $3,500 less than would be indicated simply by adding together the opening inventory and the purchases. He can reflect both these facts by a single journal entry:

(d) Closing Inventory $3,500
     Cost of Goods Sold $3,500

The amount debited to closing inventory is balanced by a credit to the Cost of Goods Sold account, and that account performs the subtraction of what Jones has left from the sum of what he had at the beginning of the period plus what he bought during the period; the net debit in the Cost of Goods Sold account is the cost of what was sold during the period.

A little thought will show that this entry debiting the amount of the goods still on hand at the close of the period to Closing Inventory, and crediting the same figure to the Cost of Goods Sold account, is just another example of deferral. The sum of what Jones originally had on hand and what he bought during the period constitutes an overstatement of the expense applicable to the current period; the cost of merchandise remaining at the end of the period should not be included as an expense of the current period, but rather should be deferred to later periods. Thus "Closing Inventory" is just another, but more descriptive, name for "Deferred Cost of Goods Sold Expense". The closing inventory will appear as an asset, usually called simply "Inventory", on the balance sheet at the end of the period, like any other deferred item; the Inventory account on the balance sheet will then become "Opening Inventory" for the new period, and the cycle will start all over again.

It is not necessary to use separate T-accounts for opening inventory and closing inventory. Instead, the bookkeeper usually uses a single T-account called simply "Inventory". At the close of each period this account is temporarily closed out with a credit, when the amount of the opening inventory is closed to the left-hand side of the Cost of Goods Sold account, and is then reopened with a debit in the amount of the closing inventory.

Once the net figure in the Cost of Goods Sold account is arrived at, here $7,000, that cost, like any other expense, is closed to Profit and Loss:

(e) Profit and Loss $7,000
     Cost of Goods Sold $7,000

Here is a summary of the journal entries described above, along with the related T-accounts.

(a) Purchases	$8,400	
Cash		$8,400
(b) Cost of Goods Sold	2,100	
Opening Inventory		2,100
(c) Cost of Goods Sold	8,400	
Purchases		8,400
(d) Closing Inventory	3,500	
Cost of Goods Sold		3,500
(e) Profit and Loss	7,000	
Cost of Goods Sold		7,000

Inventory		Cost of Goods Sold	
Bal. $2,100	$2,100 (b)	(b) $2,100	
		(c) 8,400	
(d) $3,500			$3,500 (d)
		$7,000	
			$7,000 (e)

Purchases	
(a) $8,400	$8,400 (c)

The Profit and Loss account would then look like this (after Cost of Goods Sold, together with Sales Income of $10,000 and other expenses of $1,000 have been closed to it) :

Profit and Loss	
(e) $7,000	$10,000
1,000	
	2,000

and this balance of $2,000 would be closed to Proprietorship.

The foregoing illustrates the mechanics of handling inventory under what is known as the periodic inventory system, which relies upon a physical count of closing inventory at the end of a period to determine the amount of inventory sold during the period. As you might expect, some difficult problems can arise in particular situations—for example, determining the "cost" of the closing inventory when the price has been fluctuating during the period. It is not necessary to do more than allude to such problems here, however; they are considered in detail in a later chapter.

8.　NIFTY–NOVELTY PROBLEM

The following problem is designed to provide some experience in handling the mechanics of accounting for inventory, as well as some additional practice in bookkeeping generally.

The Nifty-Novelty Company was organized as a partnership on February 1, to operate a wholesale knick-knack business at rented premises formerly occupied by Mr. Nifty. The following transactions during February are to be recorded on the company's books. Make the appropriate journal entries and post them to the T-accounts. Draw up a simplified income statement and a balance sheet as of February 28. (Depreciation and taxes should again be ignored.)

Feb.　1.　Samuel Nifty contributed store fixtures valued at $10,000; Hiram Novelty contributed merchandise valued at $2,000 and $8,000 in cash.

　　　1.　Paid February rent for store of $200.

　　　2.　Paid painter $72 for lettering on store front which will not have to be redone for a year.

　　　3.　Purchased costume jewelry on account from Acme, Inc., for $1,000.

　　　4.　Purchased counter and trays for displaying merchandise from Blake & Co. for $1,500 on account.

　　　6.　Sold merchandise for $550 cash.

　　　8.　Received $400 from Ritter for goods to be delivered in March.

　　　9.　Sold party decorations and favors to Lincoln Hotel on account for $310.

　　11.　Paid February wages of $260 to salesperson.

　　12.　Paid $500 on account to Acme, Inc.

　　15.　Sold merchandise for $2,150 cash.

　　17.　Purchased merchandise from Klips Corp. giving note for $1,300 due in six months.

　　20.　A display tray which cost $19 was accidentally destroyed.

　　22.　Received $100 on account from Lincoln Hotel.

　　24.　Paid Blake & Co. $1,000 on account.

　　26.　Sold merchandise for $700 cash.

　　28.　Determined that telephone bill for February will amount to $20.

　　28.　$100 was distributed to each of the partners.

Assume further that:

(i) Rent of $105 will be due Smith Corp. on April 30 for storage space leased to Nifty Novelty on Feb. 1 for 3 months.

(ii) A physical inventory on February 28 discloses $1,700 worth of merchandise on hand.

As a check on your work on this problem, the income statement should show net income of $570 for the month of February and the balance sheet columns should each total $23,125 on February 28.

NIFTY NOVELTY COMPANY

Income Statement, February

Sales		$ 3710
Cost of Goods Sold		
Opening Inventory	$ 2000	
Purchases	2300	
Total	$ 4300	
Less: Closing Inventory	1700	2600
Gross Profit on Sales		1110
Less: Expenses		540
Net Income		$ 570

Balance Sheet, February 28

Cash	$ 9668	Accounts Payable	$ 1000	
Accounts Receivable	210	Note Payable	1300	
Inventory	1700	Expenses Payable	55	
Store Fixtures	11481	Deferred Income	400	
Deferred Expenses	66	Partners' Capital	20,370	
Total	$ 23,125	Total	$ 23,125	

QUESTIONS

1. Suppose the Nifty-Novelty bookkeeper was not aware of the lease of storage space from Smith Corp. referred to in (i) on the previous page, and made no entry reflecting this transaction. What would the effect of this omission be on Nifty-Novelty's financial statements?

  a. Could any of the transactions listed on page 49 have been overlooked by the bookkeeper, and hence not recorded, without changing either the balance sheet totals or the net income figure given on page 50?

2. Read pages 83–92 and 108–111. If you were called upon to audit the financial statements of Nifty-Novelty as of the close of February, what steps would you take? What questions would you ask and to whom would you address them?

3. Suppose that the Nifty-Novelty "management" had decided not to defer the sales income involved in the transaction of February 8, on the ground that "these things even up over time". As the outside auditor, what would your response be? Consider pages 92–101, especially bottom of 96–98 (including footnote 189).

9. ILLUSTRATIVE FINANCIAL STATEMENTS

Here is a modern example of the financial statements of a large industrial corporation. Though these statements are far more complicated than those of E. Tutt, they were prepared by applying the same principles discussed in this chapter. The important difference lies in the many difficult questions of judgment which had to be resolved in the preparation of these statements. They are inserted here merely for the purpose of illustration and later reference.

COLT INDUSTRIES, INC. AND SUBSIDIARIES

CONSOLIDATED BALANCE SHEET

December 31.

Assets		(In thousands)	
		1978	1977
Current Assets	Cash, including certificates of deposit of $31,270 and $34,506	$ 32,438	$ 47,782
	Marketable securities, at cost (approximates market)	133,630	57,147
	Accounts and notes receivable—		
	Trade	241,212	211,500
	Other	10,087	9,170
		251,299	220,670
	Less reserves	6,425	5,106
		244,874	215,564
	Inventories (Notes 1 and 12)—		
	Finished goods	94,408	92,425
	Work in process and finished parts	235,068	205,611
	Raw materials and supplies	101,390	94,462
		430,866	392,498
	Less reserves	32,896	27,550
		397,970	364,948
	Deferred income taxes (Note 2)	17,761	16,515
	Other current assets	9,280	6,973
	Total current assets	835,953	708,929
Property, Plant, and Equipment, at Cost (Notes 1, 3, and 12)	Land and improvements	23,616	23,389
	Buildings and equipment	144,340	127,479
	Machinery and equipment	627,057	575,151
	Leasehold improvements	7,206	7,119
	Construction in progress	26,646	29,050
		828,865	762,188
	Less accumulated depreciation and amortization	456,485	411,724
		372,380	350,464
	Funds held by custodian for pollution equipment	161	1,667
		372,541	352,131
Other Assets	Notes receivable from officers and employees	4,955	3,406
	Other assets (Note 1)	50,364	47,771
		$1,263,813	$1,112,237

		(In thousands, of dollars, except par values)	
Liabilities and Shareholders' Equity		1978	1977
Current Liabilities	Notes payable to banks (Note 3)	$ 25,275	$ 18,218
	Current maturities of long-term debt (Note 3)	19,998	18,908
	Accounts payable	127,629	84,467
	Accrued expenses—		
	Salaries, wages, and employee benefits	59,943	53,839
	Taxes	62,095	34,728
	Interest	4,877	3,936
	Other	32,695	21,715
		159,610	114,218
	Total current liabilities	332,512	235,811
Noncurrent Liabilities	Long-term debt (Note 3)	294,296	301,326
	Reserves—		
	Employee benefits	17,517	12,287
	Losses on long-term leases	2,623	2,736
	Other	1,707	2,223
		21,847	17,246
	Deferred income taxes (Note 2)	48,391	51,286
	Minority interest in subsidiaries	3,226	2,971
	Commitments and contingencies (Note 11)		
Shareholders' Equity (Notes 3, 4, and 6)	Preferred stock— $1 par value, 2,438,901 and 2,860,476 shares authorized, 783,406 and 1,204,981 shares outstanding (involuntary liquidation value at December 31, 1978—$62,209)	783	1,205
	Common stock— $1 par value, 30,000,000 and 15,000,000 shares authorized, 13,040,902 and 8,106,164 shares issued	13,041	8,106
	Capital in excess of par value	169,220	167,605
	Retained earnings	387,041	333,225
		570,085	510,141
	Less cost of 174,525 and 116,350 shares of common stock in treasury	6,544	6,544
		563,541	503,597
		$1,263,813	$1,112,237

COLT INDUSTRIES, INC. AND SUBSIDIARIES

CONSOLIDATED STATEMENT OF EARNINGS

For the five years ended December 31, 1978.

		(In thousands, except per share data)				
		1978	1977	1976	1975	1974
Revenue	Net sales	$1,807,882	$1,525,484	$1,345,764	$1,103,681	$1,210,909
Costs and Expenses	Cost of sales	1,446,844	1,222,948	1,074,428	905,664	968,821
	Selling and administrative	181,785	153,407	137,004	89,120	91,901
	Interest expense	29,804	25,328	22,996	20,363	22,285
	Interest income	(13,191)	(5,419)	(5,115)	(8,772)	(10,534)
	Total costs and expenses	1,645,242	1,396,264	1,229,313	1,006,375	1,072,473
Earnings	Earnings before income taxes	162,640	129,220	116,451	97,306	138,436
	Provision for income taxes (Note 2)	75,620	59,760	49,606	39,870	60,133
	Net earnings	87,020	69,460	66,845	57,436	78,303
	Dividends on preferred stock	3,282	4,246	4,372	4,400	4,403
	Net earnings applicable to common stock	$ 83,738	$ 65,214	$ 62,473	$ 53,036	$ 73,900
Earnings Per Share Data	Earnings per common share including common equivalent share (Notes 1 and 4)	$6.66	$5.40	$5.24	$4.54	$6.40
	Earnings per common share assuming full dilution (Notes 1 and 4)	$6.07	$4.87	$4.71	$4.11	$5.67
	Average number of shares (Notes 1 and 4)— Common and common equivalent basis	12,565	12,073	11,912	11,690	11,549
	Fully diluted basis	14,304	14,230	14,146	13,919	13,784
	Cash dividends per common share	$2.03⅓	$1.70⅚	$1.50	$1.33⅓	$ .83⅓

COLT INDUSTRIES, INC. AND SUBSIDIARIES

**CONSOLIDATED STATEMENT OF CHANGES IN
FINANCIAL POSITION**

For the five years ended December 31, 1978.

		(In thousands)				
		1978	1977	1976	1975	1974
Source of Funds	Net earnings	$ 87,020	$ 69,460	$ 66,845	$ 57,436	$ 78,303
	Items not requiring use of working capital—					
	Depreciation and amortization	44,192	37,051	35,309	29,065	27,817
	Deferred income taxes	(4,141)	7,925	2,430	2,837	(928)
	Working capital provided from operations	127,071	114,436	104,584	89,338	105,192
	Long-term debt	24,847	50,401	84,975	2,611	25,568
		151,918	164,837	189,559	91,949	130,760
Application of Funds	Acquisition of Garlock Inc (excluding working capital of $48,656)	—	—	—	38,744	—
	Additions to properties	55,981	46,131	44,547	38,683	60,657
	Decrease in long-term debt	41,359	23,760	77,324	18,646	18,792
	Dividends paid	28,774	24,204	20,418	17,521	12,547
	Other—net	(4,519)	(9,803)	(1,691)	(2,765)	(1,653)
		121,595	84,292	140,598	110,829	90,343
Working Capital	Increase (decrease) in working capital	30,323	80,545	48,961	(18,880)	40,417
	At beginning of year	473,118	392,573	343,612	362,492	322,075
	At end of year	$503,441	$473,118	$392,573	$343,612	$362,492

		Increase (decrease) in working capital				
		1978	1977	1976	1975	1974
Changes in Components of Working Capital	Cash, including certificates of deposit	$(15,344)	$ 24,060	$ 869	$ (2,021)	$ (606)
	Marketable securities	76,483	10,550	33,683	(28,054)	(6,402)
	Accounts and notes receivable	29,310	40,121	11,888	(2,019)	27,897
	Inventories	33,022	19,095	15,287	26,872	48,543
	Deferred income taxes	1,246	3,985	2,247	633	3,650
	Other current assets	2,307	(2,963)	(1,886)	5,194	902
	Notes payable to banks	(7,057)	(3,407)	(1,499)	(8,450)	(2,441)
	Current maturities of long-term debt	(1,090)	(4,694)	(3,238)	(1,548)	(1,361)
	Accounts payable	(43,162)	(6,763)	2,610	5,708	(20,622)
	Accrued expenses	(45,392)	561	(11,000)	(15,195)	(9,143)
		$ 30,323	$ 80,545	$ 48,961	$(18,880)	$ 40,417

COLT INDUSTRIES, INC. AND SUBSIDIARIES
NOTES TO FINANCIAL STATEMENTS

December 31, 1978.

1. Summary of Accounting Policies

Principles of Consolidation—Investments in which the company's ownership of common voting stock is over 50 percent are consolidated in the financial statements. Corporations in which the company has stock ownership of at least 20 percent but not over 50 percent are accounted for on the equity basis. Intercompany transactions are eliminated.

* * *

Inventories—Inventories are valued at the lower of cost or market less reserves for potential losses from obsolete or slow moving inventories. Cost elements included in inventory are material, labor, and factory overhead. Cost on approximately 47 percent of the domestic inventory is determined on the last-in, first-out basis and on the remainder of the inventory is generally determined on the first-in, first-out basis. The excess of current cost over last-in, first-out cost at December 31, 1978 and 1977 was approximately $85,000,000 and $70,000,000, respectively.

Beginning and ending inventories used in the determination of cost of goods sold were as follows (in thousands):

December 31, 1978	$397,970
December 31, 1977	364,948
December 31, 1976	345,853
December 31, 1975	330,566
December 31, 1974	303,694
December 31, 1973	255,151

Property and Depreciation—Depreciation and amortization of plant and equipment are provided for by the company and its subsidiaries, generally using the straight-line method, based on estimated useful lives of the assets, which in some instances may be less than the lives allowed for tax purposes. For federal income tax purposes, most assets are depreciated using allowable accelerated methods and the Class Life Asset Depreciation Range System (ADR).

The ranges of estimated useful lives used in computing depreciation and amortization for financial reporting were as follows:

	Years
Land improvements	10–50
Buildings and equipment	10–50
Machinery and equipment	3–25
Leasehold improvements	Generally life of lease

Renewals and betterments are capitalized by additions to the related asset accounts, while repair and maintenance costs are charged against earnings. The company and its subsidiaries generally record retirements by removing the cost and accumulated depreciation from the asset and reserve accounts, reflecting any resulting gain or loss in earnings.

At December 31, 1978 and 1977, the company and certain of its subsidiaries had the following assets recorded under capital leases (in thousands):

	1978	1977
Land and improvements	$ 360	$ 351
Buildings and equipment	16,286	4,962
Machinery and equipment	26,317	19,481
Construction in progress	—	832
	42,963	25,626
Less—Accumulated depreciation and amortization	21,290	9,823
	$21,673	$15,803

Certain leases, entered into prior to January 1, 1977 and meeting the criteria for classification as capital leases, were accounted for as operating leases at December 31, 1977. Such leases were capitalized as of January 1, 1978, increasing assets and liabilities by $9,600,000. The impact on earnings in 1977 and in prior years had such leases been capitalized would not have been significant in amount.

Start-up Costs—Start-up costs related to new operations and major facilities are expensed as incurred.

Revenue Recognition—Revenue on the majority of the company's products and services is recorded at the time deliveries or acceptances are made and the company has the contractual right to bill.

Excess of Cost over Net Tangible Assets—In compliance with Opinion No. 17 of the Accounting Principles Board, the excess of cost ($14,252,000) arising from acquisitions subsequent to October 31, 1970 is being amortized on a straight-line basis, over 40 years, and the excess of cost arising from acquisitions prior to October 31, 1970 ($10,466,000) is not being amortized since there is no indication of any impairment in the value of these intangibles.

Earnings Per Share—Earnings per common share, including common equivalent share, are computed by dividing net earnings less dividends on preferred stock by the weighted average number of shares of common stock and common stock equivalents outstanding during each period. Common stock equivalents are shares issuable on the exercise of stock options when dilutive, net of shares assumed to have been purchased with the proceeds.

Earnings per share, assuming full dilution, are computed as above with additional assumptions that all the dilutive convertible securities were converted and related dividends were eliminated.

2. Income Taxes

The provision for income taxes is as follows:

| | (In thousands) | | | | |
	1978	1977	1976	1975	1974
Current	$79,761	$51,835	$47,176	$37,033	$61,061
Deferred	(4,141)	7,925	2,430	2,837	(928)
Total	$75,620	$59,760	$49,606	$39,870	$60,133

Current includes foreign income taxes of $3,523,000, $3,094,000, $5,-430,000, $2,918,000, and $1,957,000; and deferred includes foreign income taxes of $1,283,000, $1,971,000, $148,000, $185,000, and $207,-000 for 1978, 1977, 1976, 1975, and 1974, respectively.

Deferred income taxes result principally from timing differences in the recognition of revenue and expense for tax and financial reporting. Significant items were as follows:

| | (In thousands) | | | | |
	1978	1977	1976	1975	1974
Depreciation	$ 1,897	$ 5,976	$ 3,707	$2,486	$ 2,330
Employee benefits	1,426	3,544	182	605	(739)
Other (not individually significant)	(7,464)	(1,595)	(1,459)	(254)	(2,519)
Total	$(4,141)	$ 7,925	$ 2,430	$2,837	$ (928)

The tax provisions were determined as follows:

| | (In thousands) | | | | |
	1978	1977	1976	1975	1974
Tax at statutory U.S. federal income tax rate	$78,067	$62,025	$55,896	$46,707	$66,449
Increases (decreases):					
Investment tax credit	(4,500)	(3,800)	(2,986)	(2,635)	(2,556)
Foreign losses with no tax benefit, DISC, capital gains, etc.	2,053	1,535	(3,304)	(4,202)	(3,760)
	$75,620	$59,760	$49,606	$39,870	$60,133
Effective tax rate	46.5%	46.25%	42.6%	41.0%	43.4%

3. Long-Term Debt

	(In thousands)	
	1978	1977
Colt Industries Inc (a)—		
9¾% senior promissory notes due 1982–1996	$115,000	$115,000
8½% senior promissory notes due 1979–1992	46,666	50,000
6% notes due 1979–1980	5,000	8,000
Pollution control bonds 6%–7% due 1998–2008	11,975	11,500
Capital lease obligations 4.2%–9.2% due 1979–2008 (c)	18,485	19,902
	197,126	204,402
Subsidiaries—(* indicates average interest rates for 1978)		
First mortgage sinking fund bonds 5.3%–6⅞% due serially 1979–1992 (b)	49,230	54,764
8⅞% notes payable to insurance company in installments to 1990	23,000	24,500
Notes due 1979–1989—9.0% *	20,797	20,718
Capital lease obligations 3.9%–11.9% due 1979–2070 (c)	9,246	354
Other long-term debt due 1979–1992—7.9% *	14,895	15,496
	314,294	320,234
Less—Amounts due within one year	19,998	18,908
	$294,296	$301,326

(a) The company's loan agreements provide that, for the company and all restricted subsidiaries, current assets shall not be less than 175 percent of current liabilities and that working capital shall not be less than 100 percent of funded debt. In addition, dividends declared subsequent to December 31, 1975 are limited to the sum of $50,000,000, plus net earnings since December 31, 1975. At December 31, 1978, $157,000,000 of consolidated retained earnings was available for dividends. The loan agreements also provide that the company cannot incur any additional funded debt unless at the time such funded debt is incurred and after giving effect thereto, net tangible assets would then exceed 200 percent of funded debt and 250 percent of senior funded debt.

(b) The mortgage bond indentures, secured by approximately $195,000,000 of assets, principally property, plant, and equipment, provide for restrictions on the disposition of property and the creation of additional indebtedness.

(c) The amounts payable under capital lease obligations are as follows (in thousands):

1979	$ 5,139
1980	4,898
1981	3,406
1982	2,487
1983	2,407
Remainder	40,623
Total minimum lease payments	58,960
Less—Amount representing interest	31,229
Present value of net minimum lease payments, included in long-term debt	$27,731

(d) Minimum payments on long-term debt, including capital lease obligations, due within five years from December 31, 1978 are as follows (in thousands):

1979	$19,998
1980	17,916
1981	15,709
1982	21,590
1983	21,362

(e) At December 31, 1978, the company had unused lines of credit aggregating $50,000,000 for short-term bank borrowings. The company has understandings with the banks regarding compensating balances for these credit arrangements but the aggregate amount of such compensating balances was not material at December 31, 1978. During 1978, the average short-term borrowing outstanding was $21,-856,000, with $25,275,000 being the maximum amount outstanding at any month-end. The weighted average interest rate on short-term borrowing, principally related to foreign borrowing, was 10.6 percent during the year and 11.2 percent at year-end. The average interest rate during the year was calculated by weighting the short-term borrowing outstanding for each month.

(f) During January, 1979, the company entered into two Revolving Credit Agreements for a total of $150,000,000. A commitment fee of 1/2 of 1 percent per annum is payable on the unused portions.

4. Capital Stock

On May 4, 1978, the Board of Directors authorized a three-for-two stock split in the form of a 50 percent stock dividend. In connection with the stock split, 4,198,955 shares (including 58,175 treasury shares) were issued with the par value of these additional shares

($4,198,955) being transferred from retained earnings to common stock. Cash was paid in lieu of issuing fractional shares.

All share and per share amounts have been adjusted to give effect of the stock split.

* * *

5. Pension and Retirement Plans

The company and certain of its subsidiaries have in effect, for substantially all employees, pension and retirement plans under which funds are deposited with trustees. As of December 31, 1978, the actuarially computed vested benefits, using a 6 percent interest factor, were $348,789,000, exceeding the market values of fund assets by $132,223,000.

Pension expense of $41,389,000, $38,272,000, $36,103,000, $28,-892,000, and $23,129,000 was charged to earnings in 1978, 1977, 1976, 1975, and 1974, respectively, and is the maximum annual provision permitted by Opinion No. 8 of the Accounting Principles Board, including amortization of prior service cost at 10 percent per year.

6. Stock Option Plans

* * *

8. Segment Information

The company's operations are conducted through divisions within five industry segments consisting of:

Industrial and Power Equipment—fabricated metal products, weighing systems, industrial diesel engines and accessories, compressors, machine tools and measuring equipment, transformers, and firearms;

Fluid Control Systems—automotive carburetors, pumps and aerospace fuel systems and controls;

Materials—specialty carbon and low-alloy steels, stainless and other special purpose steels;

Industrial Seals and Components—gaskets, packings, valves, and other devices to prevent leakage and seal out contaminants;

Shock Mitigation Systems—aircraft landing gear assemblies and other shock mitigation and flight control systems.

Information on the company's industry segments for the two years ended December 31, 1978 is as follows (in millions):

Industry Segments	Operating Income	Sales	Total Assets	Depreciation and Amortization	Additions to Properties
1978					
Industrial and Power Equipment	$ 55.2	$ 516	$ 318	$ 8.5	$16.3
Fluid Control Systems	48.4	320	116	6.4	6.1
Materials	44.3	664	395	20.3	20.0
Industrial Seals and Components	31.9	250	190	6.6	8.8
Shock Mitigation Systems	14.2	92	74	2.1	4.7
Intersegment elimination	—	(34)	—	—	—
Total segments	194.0	1,808	1,093	43.9	55.9
Interest expense	(29.8)	—	—	—	—
Interest income	13.1	—	—	—	—
Corporate unallocated	(14.7)	—	171	.3	.1
Consolidated	$162.6	$1,808	$1,264	$44.2	$56.0
1977					
Industrial and Power Equipment	$ 48.2	$ 453	$ 296	$ 8.0	$14.6
Fluid Control Systems	35.4	238	101	5.9	3.8
Materials	42.8	582	375	15.9	18.7
Industrial Seals and Components	25.3	206	177	5.6	6.9
Shock Mitigation Systems	11.0	77	65	1.5	2.0
Intersegment elimination	—	(31)	—	—	—
Total segments	162.7	1,525	1,014	36.9	46.0
Interest expense	(25.3)	—	—	—	—
Interest income	5.4	—	—	—	—
Corporate unallocated	(13.6)	—	98	.2	.1
Consolidated	$129.2	$1,525	$1,112	$37.1	$46.1

Information on the company's operations by geographic segments for the two years ended December 31, 1978 is as follows (in millions):

Geographic Segments	Earnings Before Income Taxes	Sales	Total Assets
1978			
Domestic Operations	$160.9	$1,664	$1,189
Foreign Operations	1.7	164	139
Intersegment elimination	—	(20)	(64)
Consolidated	$162.6	$1,808	$1,264
1977			
Domestic Operations	$123.2	$1,404	$1,044
Foreign Operations	6.0	138	132
Intersegment elimination	—	(17)	(64)
Consolidated	$129.2	$1,525	$1,112

9. Quarterly Sales and Earnings (Unaudited)

For the two years ended December 31, 1978 (in thousands of dollars, except per share data):

1978	1st	2nd	3rd	4th
		Quarter		
Net sales	$421,484	$458,566	$447,550	$480,282
Gross profit	75,829	92,784	90,892	101,533
Net earnings	16,020	22,722	22,006	26,272
Earnings per common share—				
Including common equivalent share	1.23	1.77	1.67	1.98
Assuming full dilution	1.12	1.59	1.53	1.83

1977	1st	2nd	3rd	4th
Net sales	$357,756	$395,154	$368,115	$404,459
Gross profit	62,786	79,410	75,103	85,237
Net earnings	11,104	19,301	17,234	21,821
Earnings per common share—				
Including common equivalent share	.84	1.51	1.34	1.71
Assuming full dilution	.78	1.35	1.21	1.53

The above per share amounts have been adjusted to give effect to the stock split (see Note 4).

10. Supplementary Earnings Information

	1978	1977	1976	1975	1974
			(In thousands)		
Maintenance	$89,158	$73,935	$63,570	$51,860	$51,691
Depreciation and amortization	44,192	37,051	35,309	29,065	27,817
Taxes, other than federal income taxes—					
Payroll	36,005	29,796	25,804	20,610	21,571
Property	7,449	7,445	6,916	6,089	5,729
State and local	14,610	10,323	10,649	9,071	13,506
Other	3,986	3,674	3,508	3,197	3,093
	62,050	51,238	46,877	38,967	43,899
Rent	17,869	17,390	16,427	14,339	13,809
Rental income	(4,159)	(3,743)	(3,797)	(3,591)	(3,439)
	13,710	13,647	12,630	10,748	10,370
Research and development costs	18,835	17,665	15,475	13,558	13,925

11. Commitments and Contingencies

The company and certain of its subsidiaries are contingently liable as guarantors of certain leases and are defendants in various lawsuits. In the opinion of management, these contingent liabilities are not significant in relation to the financial position of the company and its subsidiaries.

The company and certain of its subsidiaries are obligated under operating lease commitments, expiring on various dates after December 31, 1979 to pay rentals totaling $59,277,000, as follows:

$7,461,000 in 1979, $6,310,000 in 1980, $5,258,000 in 1981, $3,977,000 in 1982, $3,286,000 in 1983, and $32,985,000 in later years. These rent payments are before reduction for related sublease rentals of $20,901,000.

12.   Replacement Cost Data (Unaudited)

In compliance with rules of the Securities and Exchange Commission, management has estimated the replacement cost of certain inventories and productive capacity of the company and its consolidated subsidiaries as of December 31, 1978 and 1977, together with cost of sales and depreciation on the basis of replacement cost for the two years then ended.

The replacement cost information presented below does not reflect all of the effects of inflation and other economic factors on the company's current costs of operating the business. The SEC rule does not require consideration of these effects on assets and liabilities other than inventories and productive capacity. Further, the replacement cost information standing alone does not recognize the customary relationships between cost changes and changes in selling prices. The company has attempted over the years to adjust selling prices to maintain profit margins. Competitive conditions permitting, the company expects to modify its selling prices to recognize future cost changes. Accordingly, it is management's view that the limited replacement cost data presented herein cannot be used alone to compute the total effect of inflation on net earnings as reported.

Management also cautions that this information should not be interpreted to indicate that the company actually has present plans to replace such assets and that actual replacement would take place in the form and manner assumed in developing these estimates. The replacement cost information is based on the hypothetical assumption that the company would replace its entire inventory and productive capacity at the end of its fiscal year, whether or not such instant replacement were physically possible. In the normal course of business, the company will replace its productive capacity over an extended period of time. Decisions concerning replacement will be made in the light of economic, regulatory, and competitive conditions existing on the dates such determinations are made and could differ substantially from the assumptions on which the data included herein are based. If the company's productive capacity were to be replaced in the manner assumed in the calculation of replacement cost of existing productive capacity many costs in addition to depreciation (e. g., direct labor costs, repairs and maintenance, utility, and other indirect costs) would be altered. Although these expected cost changes cannot be quantified with any precision, the current level of operating costs other than depreciation would be reduced as a result of the technological improvements assumed in the hypothetical replacement.

It must be recognized that these required replacement cost data are, by their nature, limited in scope, imprecise, and predicated upon certain assumptions and subjective judgments which may vary over time and from company to company.

Set forth below is an analysis of management's estimates of the replacement cost of certain of the inventories and productive capacity of the company and its subsidiaries at December 31, 1978 and 1977, together with an estimate of the replacement cost of sales and depreciation for the two years then ended. Comparable related historical amounts with respect to these same assets, as stated in the accompanying consolidated balance sheet and statement of earnings, are also included for informational purposes.

| | (In thousands) | | | |
| | 1978 | | 1977 | |
	Replacement Cost (Unaudited)	Historical Cost (a)	Replacement Cost (Unaudited)	Historical Cost (a)
Inventories—				
Finished goods	$ 116,024	$ 94,408	$ 112,466	$ 92,425
Work in process and finished parts	288,989	235,068	252,729	205,611
Raw materials and supplies	115,268	101,390	104,225	94,462
	520,281	430,866	469,420	392,498
Less reserves	32,896	32,896	27,550	27,550
	$ 487,385	$ 397,970	$ 441,870	$ 364,948
Property, Plant, and Equipment—				
Land improvements	$ 26,501	$ 12,305	$ 24,408	$ 11,949
Buildings and equipment	387,008	144,340	343,640	127,479
Machinery and equipment	1,201,184	627,218	1,088,227	584,330
Leasehold improvements	12,740	7,206	11,756	7,119
	1,627,433	791,069	1,468,031	730,877
Less accumulated depreciation and amortization	1,138,837	456,485	997,416	411,724
	$ 488,596	$ 334,584	$ 470,615	$ 319,153
Cost of Sales	$1,459,654	$1,446,844	$1,235,782	$1,222,948
Depreciation—				
Included in cost of sales	$ 53,664	$ 40,702	$ 46,275	$ 33,793
Included in other operating costs	4,603	3,490	4,649	3,258
	$ 58,267	$ 44,192	$ 50,924	$ 37,051

(a) For purposes of comparison with replacement cost, the historical cost data excludes land, ($11,311,000 and $11,440,000), and construction in progress, ($26,646,000 and $21,538,000) at December 31, 1978 and 1977, respectively. Machinery and equipment, at historical cost, includes capital expenditures for pollution equipment of $161,000 and $9,179,000 at December 31, 1978 and 1977, respectively. This pollution equipment, at December 31, 1978 is reported as funds held by custodian and at December 31, 1977 as construction in progress ($7,512,000) and funds held by custodian ($1,667,000).

With respect to inventories, replacement cost has been estimated based on quantities on hand at the end of the year. The excess of replacement cost over historical cost, stated at LIFO included above, at December 31, 1978 and 1977 was approximately $85,000,000 and $70,000,000 respectively. There is no significant effect on the components of inventory such as depreciation, direct labor costs, repairs and maintenance, utility, or other indirect costs as a result of the assumed replacement cost of productive capacity.

Replacement cost of sales was estimated through adjustment of historical cost of sales for the approximate time lag between incurring inventory costs and their subsequent conversion into sales revenue. The replacement cost of sales amount does not include any cost savings in direct labor, repairs and maintenance, utility, and other indirect costs which may result from the replacement of existing assets with assets of improved technology.

The estimated replacement cost of productive capacity was determined by adjusting historical cost by indices of reproduction cost relevant to the plant and equipment of the company. The result was modified by vendor quotations and engineering studies to reflect major technological improvements which management intends to incorporate into the productive capacity through normal capital expenditure programs and to reflect anticipated environmental expenditures.

Accumulated depreciation and depreciation expense, on a replacement cost basis, are based on the expired economic lives used for historical cost purposes and are calculated using the straight-line method. Accumulated depreciation and depreciation expense on a replacement cost basis were computed by adjusting historical cost depreciation by the same reproduction cost indices used to develop the estimated replacement cost of productive capacity. The result was modified by the effect on depreciation of changes to productive capacity resulting from technological replacements and anticipated environmental expenditures. In certain instances, historical depreciation is calculated on an accelerated basis with the corresponding replacement depreciation calculated on a straight-line basis.

Auditors' Report

To the Board of Directors and Shareholders Colt Industries Inc:

We have examined the consolidated balance sheet of Colt Industries Inc. (a Pennsylvania corporation) and subsidiaries as of December 31, 1978 and 1977, and the consolidated statements of earnings, retained earnings, capital in excess of par value and changes in financial position for each of the five years in the period ended December 31, 1978. Our examination was made in accordance with generally accepted auditing standards, and accordingly included such tests of the accounting records and such other auditing procedures as we considered necessary in the circumstances.

In our opinion, the accompanying financial statements present fairly the financial position of Colt Industries Inc. and subsidiaries as of December 31, 1978 and 1977, and the results of their operations and changes in their financial position for each of the five years in the period ended December 31, 1978 in conformity with generally accepted accounting principles consistently applied during the periods.

ARTHUR ANDERSEN & CO.

New York, N.Y.,
January 26, 1979.

FINANCIAL REVIEW

Sales and Earnings

In 1978, the company established record sales, net earnings, earnings per share, new orders and, as of year end, record backlogs. Sales in 1978 were $1,808 million, up 19 percent from $1,525 million in 1977. Net earnings for the year 1978 increased 25 percent to $87.0 million as compared with the $69.5 million recorded in 1977. Sales and operating income of each of the company's industry segments improved over 1977, contributing to a higher overall corporate margin. Strong gains were recorded by the Fluid Control Systems, Industrial Seals and Components, and Shock Mitigation Systems segments, where sales and operating income increased substantially.

The results for the year reflect the improved demand from broad industrial markets served by the company's diverse businesses. Order input remained strong throughout the year and backlogs increased steadily. The broad base of the company's balanced earnings power is evident from the earnings contribution of 29 percent, 25 percent and 23 percent of total operating income by the Industrial and Power Equipment, Fluid Control Systems, and Materials industry segments, respectively.

Sales and earnings increases in 1977 over 1976 were attributed to increased demand for Crucible specialty steels plus strong performances throughout the year by almost all of the company's industrial products businesses.

Cost of Sales

Cost of sales in 1978 increased 18 percent over 1977. The increases in cost of sales are directly related to the increased volume of business and to the inflationary cost increases of energy, materials, supplies, maintenance, wages, payroll taxes, and fringe benefits. Depreciation and amortization expense increases in 1978 over 1977 were attributable principally to additions to property, plant, and equipment. The increase in cost of sales in 1977 over 1976 was due directly to the volume of business and also to the prolonged cold weather in January and February, 1977 and a ten-week strike at two West Hartford, Connecticut divisions.

Selling and Administrative Expense

The increases in selling and administrative expense result from the increased volume of business and higher costs. State and local income and franchise taxes increased $4.0 million due to higher earnings in 1978 compared with 1977. In 1978 and 1977, the company incurred foreign exchange losses, including the effect of translating inventories as sold at the new exchange rates, of $1.3 million and $4.4 million after taxes, respectively. The 1978 loss was principally due to the decline of the U. S. dollar in relation to other currencies while the 1977 loss was principally due to the devaluation of the Mexican peso.

Interest Expense and Interest Income

The $4.5 million increase in interest expense for 1978 compared with 1977 was due mainly to the issuance of $40 million of 9¾ percent senior promissory notes in December 1977. Interest income in 1978 increased $7.7 million compared with 1977 due to higher average cash balances and higher yields.

Taxes

The effective income tax rates for the years 1978, 1977, and 1976 were 46.5 percent, 46.25 percent, and 42.6 percent, respectively. The rate in 1977 was higher than in 1976 principally because of the reduction of DISC benefits pursuant to the Tax Reform Act of 1976, nondeductible foreign exchange losses, and acquisition costs.

Financial Information by Industry Segment

*   *   *

Order Backlog

The order backlog of $791.7 million at December 31, 1978 set a new high for the company and was up 29 percent over the December 31, 1977 order backlog of $613.3 million. Every industry segment ended the year with backlogs up compared with 1977, and most divisions within each segment participated in this increase. The rate of order input during 1978 and high backlog at year-end reflect both current and ongoing strength in demand for the company's products.

Financial Position

The company's financial position at December 31, 1978 was stronger than at anytime in its history. Capital expenditures of $56.0 million and record dividends of $28.8 million were more than adequately covered by internally generated cash. Cash and marketable securities were $166.1 million at December 31, 1978, an increase of $61.1 million over the prior year-end.

The continued improvement in the company's liquidity is demonstrated by its increase in working capital, reduction in long-term debt to shareholders' equity ratio, improved inventory turnover, and lower receivable days outstanding.

Working capital increased during the year by $30.3 million to a record $503.4 million at December 31, 1978. The ratio of long-term debt to total shareholders' equity improved from 59.8 percent at the end of 1977 to 52.2 percent as of December 31, 1978. This improvement was achieved despite the addition to long-term debt at December 31, 1978 to $7.2 million of capital lease obligations in accordance with a new accounting rule effective January 1, 1978. Inventory turned over 3.29 times for 1978 compared with 2.97 times in 1977. Receivable days outstanding at December 31, 1978 were 51 days compared with 52 days at the end of 1977.

In January 1979, the company arranged $150 million revolving credit agreements with six banks under which the company has available at its option $100 million for a three-year revolving period, with conversion to a five-year term loan; as well as $50 million for a one-year revolving period. Interest for the revolving periods will be at the prime rate.

Capital Expenditures

Plant and equipment expenditures during 1978 totaled $56.0 million. Environmental control projects continued at the Midland Pennsylvania specialty steels mill. In order to meet increasing market demand, production capacity is being expanded by the Central Moloney Transformer Division and the Holley Carburetor Division and at certain Industrial Seals and Components facilities. Machining capabilities were increased at the Menasco California and Texas plants. Modernization of the company's specialty steels mill in Syracruse, New York was continued in 1978 to improve operating efficiencies and eliminate production bottlenecks. The company maintains its policy of selective expansion, cost reductions, modernization, and pollution control improvements to assure continued future production capacity to satisfy the increasing demand for its products. Capital expenditures for 1979 are expected to be in excess of the total amount spent in 1978 and are expected to be more than adequately financed by depreciation and internally generated cash.

Dividends

Record dividends of $28.8 million were paid to the company's shareholders in 1978 and consisted of $25.5 million to common shareholders, up 31 percent compared with 1977; and $3.3 million to preferred shareholders, compared with $4.2 million in 1977.

Quarterly cash dividends on the common stock were paid at the rate of 45⅝¢ per share for the first quarter of 1978; and in May, the Board of Directors increased the quarterly dividend to 52½¢ and voted a three-for-two stock split in the form of a 50 percent stock dividend. The per share data reflects the additional shares distributed on June 30, 1978.

Quarterly dividends on the company's preferred stocks were paid during 1978 and 1977 at the respective annual amounts stated in the titles of such preferred stocks. The lower total amount paid in 1978 reflects the result of voluntary conversions to common stock by preferred holders.

The following tabulation sets forth, for each series of convertible preferred stock, the number of shares outstanding at December 31, 1978; the annual dividend rate per share; and the aggregate dividends per share receivable if converted into common stock based on the current annual dividend rate of $2.10 per share of common stock:

Series	Shares Outstanding December 31, 1978	Annual Dividend Rate Per Share	Aggregate Dividends Per Share Receivable If Converted Into Common Stock
A	222,797	$1.60	$ 1.68
B	10,815	4.50	15.97
C	12,785	4.25	4.76
D	475,567	4.25	4.55

NOTE ON STATEMENT OF CHANGES IN FINANCIAL POSITION

Under accrual accounting, as we have seen, determination of expenses and income for a period is not controlled by the movement of cash. That does not mean, however, that the movement of cash into and out of the enterprise, often referred to as "cash flow", is unimportant. In order to remain in business a company must either have on hand, or have access to, the cash needed to meet its regular recurring expenses, like payroll and rent, to pay its accounts payable to suppliers, and to discharge its outstanding debt obligations as they fall due from time to time. In addition, any distributions to the owners of the enterprise normally come from cash. Accordingly, judging the future prospects of a company calls for some consideration (and comparison) of its cash-generating potential and its cash needs, over both the short term and the long pull.

Obviously, a company's revenues from operations are its primary source of cash, while its expenses are the principal cash drain; hence, estimated future earnings do provide some index to expected cash resources. But this is only a starting point, since cash may be significantly increased or decreased by transactions not reflected in the income statement, such as borrowing, or purchasing capital assets for cash. It must also be kept in mind that, as a corollary of accrual accounting, there will be some expenses which do not involve any current or prospective cash outflow. One example is the periodic charge-off (or amortization) of a deferred expense asset, like E. Tutt's deferred insurance expense (and a much more important illustration, as a practical matter, is depreciation on tangible fixed assets): in those cases the actual expenditure of cash has occurred in an earlier period. On the other side of the coin, while normally any recognition of income under the accrual method reflects an expected receipt of cash, there may sometimes be a substantial time lag between income recognition and cash receipt, and this can be a significant element in the company's total financial picture.

Some useful information relating to cash flow may be gleaned from the current balance sheet, plus a comparison with the balance sheet for the prior year. For example, the relative amounts of cash and accounts receivable, and the change in those figures from the prior year, would be of some significance. However, there are a number of important kinds of transactions, like borrowing, issuing new stock, or buying capital assets, which may greatly affect cash but are not reflected in the income statement for the period and are simply recorded on the balance sheet at the end of the period as accomplished facts (although it is possible to tell what happened by making a comparison with the prior balance sheet).

In any event there is clearly room for another financial statement, primarily directed to detailing the effect on cash of both the company's regular operations during the year and those other types of significant transactions like issuance of stock and acquisition of assets (which of course do not always affect cash, as, for example, when new stock is issued in exchange for capital assets). That is the role of the Statement of Changes in Financial Position, an example of which appears in the illustrative financial statements above, at page 55. Immediately below is the latest authoritative pronouncement governing the Statement of Changes in Financial Position, together with excerpts from a recent comment on such Statements:

APB OPINION NO. 19 *

Reporting Changes in Financial Position

March, 1971.

INTRODUCTION

1. In 1963 the Accounting Principles Board issued Opinion No. 3, *The Statement of Source and Application of Funds.* Support of

---

* Copyright ©️ by the American Institute of Certified Public Accountants, Inc.   Portions of the text and all footnotes omitted.

that Opinion by the principal stock exchanges and its acceptance by the business community have resulted in a significant increase in the number of companies that present a statement of sources and uses of funds (funds statement) in annual financial reports to shareholders. . . .

2.   APB Opinion No. 3 encouraged but did not require presentation of a funds statement.   In view of the present widespread recognition of the usefulness of information on sources and uses of funds, the Board has considered whether presentation of such a statement should be required to complement the income statement and the balance sheet. . . .

* * *

DISCUSSION

4.   The objectives of a funds statement are (1) to summarize the financing and investing activities of the entity, including the extent to which the enterprise has generated funds from operations during the period, and (2) to complete the disclosure of changes in financial position during the period.   The information shown in a funds statement is useful to a variety of users of financial statements in making economic decisions regarding the enterprise.

5.   The funds statement is related to both the income statement and the balance sheet and provides information that can be obtained only partially, or at most in piecemeal form, by interpreting them.   An income statement together with a statement of retained earnings reports results of operations but does not show other changes in financial position.   Comparative balance sheets can significantly augment that information, but the objectives of the funds statement require that all such information be selected, classified, and summarized in meaningful form.   The funds statement cannot supplant either the income statement or the balance sheet but is intended to provide information that the other statements either do not provide or provide only indirectly about the flow of funds and changes in financial position during the period.

6.   The concept of *funds* in funds statements has varied somewhat in practice, with resulting variations in the nature of the statements.   For example, *funds* is sometimes interpreted to mean *cash* or its equivalent, and the resulting funds statement is a summary of cash provided and used.   Another interpretation of *funds* is that of *working capital*, i. e., current assets less current liabilities, and the resulting funds statement is a summary of working capital provided and used.   However, a funds statement based on either the cash or the working capital concept of funds sometimes excludes certain financing and investing activities because they do not directly affect cash or working capital during the period.   For example, issuing equity securities to acquire a building is both a financing and investing transaction but does not affect either cash or working capital.   To meet all of its objectives, a funds statement should disclose separately the financing and investing aspects of all significant transactions that affect financial position during a period.   These transactions include acquisition or disposal of property in exchange for debt or equity securities and conversion of long-term debt or preferred stock to common stock.

OPINION

Applicability

7. The Board concludes that information concerning the financing and investing activities of a business enterprise and the changes in its financial position for a period is essential for financial statement users, particularly owners and creditors, in making economic decisions. When financial statements purporting to present both financial position (balance sheet) and results of operations (statement of income and retained earnings) are issued, a statement summarizing changes in financial position should also be presented as a basic financial statement for each period for which an income statement is presented. . . .

Concept

8. The Board also concludes that the statement summarizing changes in financial position should be based on a broad concept embracing all changes in financial position and that the title of the statement should reflect this broad concept. The Board therefore recommends that the title be Statement of Changes in Financial Position (referred to below as "the Statement"). The Statement of each reporting entity should disclose all important aspects of its financing and investing activities regardless of whether cash or other elements of working capital are directly affected. For example, acquisitions of property by issuance of securities or in exchange for other property, and conversions of long-term debt or preferred stock to common stock, should be appropriately reflected in the Statement.

Format

9. The Board recognizes the need for flexibility in form, content, and terminology of the Statement to meet its objectives in differing circumstances. For example, a working capital format is not relevant to an entity that does not distinguish between current and noncurrent assets and liabilities. Each entity should adopt the presentation that is most informative in its circumstances. The Board believes, however, that the guides set forth in the paragraphs that follow should be applied in preparing and presenting the Statement.

10. The ability of an enterprise to provide working capital or cash from operations is an important factor in considering its financing and investing activities. Accordingly, the Statement should prominently disclose working capital or cash provided from or used in operations for the period, and the Board believes that the disclosure is most informative if the effects of extraordinary items . . . are reported separately from the effects of normal items. The Statement for the period should begin with income or loss before extraordinary items, if any, and add back (or deduct) items recognized in determining that income or loss which did not use (or provide) working capital or cash during the period. Items added and deducted in accordance with this procedure are not sources or uses of working capital or cash, and the related captions should make this clear, e. g., "Add—Expenses not requiring outlay of working capital in the current period." An acceptable alternative procedure, which gives the same result, is to begin with total revenue that provided working cap-

ital or cash during the period and deduct operating costs and expenses that required the outlay of working capital or cash during the period. In either case the resulting amount of working capital or cash should be appropriately described, e. g., "Working capital provided from [used in] operations for the period, exclusive of extraordinary items." This total should be immediately followed by working capital or cash provided or used by income or loss from extraordinary items, if any; extraordinary income or loss should be similarly adjusted for items recognized that did not provide or use working capital or cash during the period.

11.   Provided that these guides are met, the Statement may take whatever form gives the most useful portrayal of the financing and investing activities and the changes in financial position of the reporting entity.   The Statement may be in balanced form or in a form expressing the changes in financial position in terms of cash, of cash and temporary investments combined, of all quick assets, or of working capital.   The Statement should disclose all important changes in financial position for the period covered;   accordingly, types of transactions reported may vary substantially in relative importance from one period to another.

Content

12.   Whether or not working capital flow is presented in the Statement, net changes in each element of working capital (as customarily defined) should be appropriately disclosed for at least the current period, either in the Statement or in a related tabulation.

   a.   If the format shows the flow of cash, changes in other elements of working capital (e. g., in receivables, inventories, and payables) constitute sources and uses of cash and should accordingly be disclosed in appropriate detail in the body of the Statement.

   b.   If the format shows the flow of working capital and two-year comparative balance sheets are presented, the changes in each element of working capital for the current period (but not for earlier periods) can be computed by the user of the statements.   Nevertheless, the Board believes that the objectives of the Statement usually require that the net change in working capital be analyzed in appropriate detail in a tabulation accompanying the Statement, and accordingly this detail should be furnished.

13.   The effects of other financing and investing activities should be individually disclosed.   For example, both outlays for acquisitions and proceeds from retirements of property should be reported; both long-term borrowings and repayments of long-term debt should be reported; and outlays for purchases of consolidated subsidiaries should be summarized in the consolidated Statement by major categories of assets obtained and obligations assumed.   Related items should be shown in proximity when the result contributes to the clarity of the Statement.   Individual immaterial items may be combined.

14.   In addition to working capital or cash provided from operations (see paragraph 10) and changes in elements of working capital (see paragraph 13), the Statement should clearly disclose:

a. Outlays for purchase of long-term assets (identifying separately such items as investments, property, and intangibles).

b. Proceeds from sale (or working capital or cash provided by sale) of long-term assets (identifying separately such items as investments, property, and intangibles) not in the normal course of business, less related expenses involving the current use of working capital or cash.

c. Conversion of long-term debt or preferred stock to common stock.

d. Issuance, assumption, redemption, and repayment of long-term debt.

e. Issuance, redemption, or purchase of capital stock for cash or for assets other than cash.

f. Dividends in cash or in kind or other distributions to shareholders (except stock dividends and stock split-ups . . .).

Terminology

15. The amount of working capital or cash provided from operations is not a substitute for or an improvement upon properly determined net income as a measure of results of operations and the consequent effect on financial position. Terms referring to "cash" should not be used to describe amounts provided from operations unless all non-cash items have been appropriately adjusted. The adjusted amount should be described accurately, in conformity with the nature of the adjustments, e. g., "Cash provided from operations for the period" or "Working capital provided from operations for the period" as appropriate. The Board strongly recommends that isolated statistics of working capital or cash provided from operations, especially per-share amounts, not be presented in annual reports to shareholders. If any per-share data relating to flow of working capital or cash are presented, they should as a minimum include amounts for inflow from operations, inflow from other sources, and total outflow, and each per-share amount should be clearly identified with the corresponding total amount shown in the Statement.

HEATH, LET'S SCRAP THE "FUNDS" STATEMENT

146 J. Accountancy (Oct. 1978) 94.

Funds statements found in practice today are a hodgepodge of miscellaneous information presented in a confusing and misleading way.

Many accountants see the problem as one of defining "funds." They attribute the confusion over the funds statement to confusion over what is meant by the term "funds." . . .

In my opinion, the fundamental problem is not a definitional one. Confusion over what is meant by the term funds is merely a symptom of a more basic problem: confusion over the objectives of the funds statement. The solution does not lie in redefining funds; it lies in scrapping the funds statement, identifying the objectives it tries but fails to meet and designing statements that achieve those objectives.

Specious Objectives

The stated objectives of funds statements in Accounting Principles Board Opinion no. 19, *Reporting Changes in Financial Position,* are specious. Superficially they appear to be reasonable but when analyzed and applied in practice they are unclear, misleading and unattainable. According to the opinion, the objectives are "(1) to summarize the financing and investing activities of the entity, including the extent to which the enterprise has generated funds from operations during the period, and (2) to complete the disclosure of changes in financial position during the period."

The meaning of the first objective is unclear. It begs the question of what effects of financing and investing activities should be summarized. Financing and investing activities, like all business activities, have many different effects. A single transaction may affect cash, working capital, total assets, capital structure, net assets and so forth. Obviously not all of those effects can be portrayed in a single statement, but the opinion is silent as to which one or ones are the object or objects of attention in the statement. Paragraph 8 says only that the statement "should be based on a broad concept embracing all changes in financial position" without even saying a broad concept of what! The problem reflects more than just poor draftsmanship; it reflects the absence of an underlying concept.

The second objective is unattainable. As noted, business activities have many effects. No statement can possibly "complete the disclosure of changes in financial position" (par. 4) or "disclose all important changes in financial position for the period covered" (par. 11). A meaningful statement must focus on a specific aspect or dimension of financial position such as cash, working capital, net assets, monetary assets and so forth. The possibilities are almost limitless. No statement can portray in an understandable way all effects of all activities on all possible measures of financial position. . . .

Implicit Objectives

Although the APB's stated objectives in Opinion no. 19 are unclear, a careful reading of the opinion suggests that the board was concerned with reporting the effects of *all* business activities (not just financing and investing activities) on at least two and perhaps three different measures of financial position.

The first was to report changes in some measure of the cash or near-cash resources of a company, that is, changes in some measure of its debt-paying ability. A number of specific provisions of the opinion support that view. Paragraph 10 requires that "the Statement should prominently disclose working capital or cash provided from or used in operations for the period." Paragraph 11 states, "The Statement may be in balanced form or in a form expressing the changes in financial position in terms of cash, or cash and temporary investments combined, of all quick assets, or of working capital." Paragraph 14 further specifically requires that "outlays for purchase of long-term assets . . . proceeds from sale (or working capital or cash provided by sale) of long-term assets" and "dividends in cash" all be disclosed.

The second type of change that the board appears to have been concerned with having reported was capital structure changes. Capital structure refers to the claims on the resources used to operate a business enterprise, including both debt and equity claims. Changes in the size of a company's capital structure result from activities such as the borrowing and repayment of debt, sale and repurchase of capital stock, profit-directed activities and cash or property dividends. Changes in the composition of a company's capital structure result from activities such as the conversion of convertible securities into common stock and refinancing operations including the "swapping" of one type of financial instrument for another in a financial reorganization.

Many changes in the size and composition of a company's capital structure also affect its cash, its working capital and other measures of debt-paying ability, but some of them do not. Evidence that the board was concerned with having changes in the size and composition of a company's capital structure as well as changes in its debt-paying ability reported is found in . . . [both paragraphs 6 and 14].

The third type of change that the board seems to have been concerned with having reported is changes in a company's long-term assets such as plant and equipment and long-term investments. Many of the increases in those assets would, of course, be revealed by a statement that shows only changes in cash or working capital. Some, however, such as those resulting from the issuance of debt or equity securities, would be excluded from that type of statement.

*   *   *

In summary, the APB may have intended to require the disclosure of all increases in long-term assets, but its intentions are not clear. It certainly gave no indication of any desire to show decreases in long-term assets; only the "proceeds from sale (or working capital or cash provided by sale) of long-term assets," not the book value of assets sold, is required to be disclosed.

Relevant Objectives

Changes in all three of the measures of financial position discussed in the last section are clearly of interest to investors, creditors and other external users of financial statements. Changes in debt-paying ability are of such obvious interest to creditors and investors that the matter hardly requires comment; the only real issue is which measure of debt-paying ability is likely to be most useful. Changes in the size and composition of a company's capital structure are also clearly of interest. One of the most widely used financial ratios in credit analysis is the ratio of debt to equity. That ratio would obviously be affected by changes in the composition of a company's capital structure such as the conversion of debentures into common stock and various kinds of refinancing operations. The nature of those activities and a report of how they affect a company's capital structure would, therefore, also be of interest. Changes in the amount or composition of long-term assets are likely to signal changes in a company's future profits and future cash needs so that they, too, are likely to be of interest to investors and creditors.

Conflicting Objectives

The basic problem with Opinion no. 19 is not, therefore, that it requires disclosure of unimportant or irrelevant information but that it requires too many different types of information to be disclosed on the same statement. The result is a confusing statement.

Financial statements are maps of economic territory; they portray the financial characteristic of business enterprises. Different maps are needed for different purposes because only a limited amount of information can be portrayed on a single map. A single geographic map designed to portray changes in annual rainfall, changes in educational level of the population, changes in agricultural crops and changes in unemployment is not likely to portray any of that information clearly. Similarly, a single financial statement designed to portray many different types of changes in the financial position of a business enterprise is not likely to portray any of that information clearly. That, however, is exactly what Opinion no. 19 requires of the funds statement. To achieve the multiple and disparate objectives of that statement, the term funds was defined so broadly that it has become meaningless, and a funds statement based on a meaningless concept of funds does not communicate information effectively. That is the heart of the problem of the confusing funds statements found in practice today.

Recommendation

Once the basis of the confusion over the funds statement is diagnosed, the general nature of a solution becomes obvious; several different statements are needed to communicate clearly the information now crammed into a single statement. Specifically, three statements are needed to replace the funds statement and achieve its objectives: a statement of cash receipts and payments, a statement of financing activities and a statement of investing activities.

Statement of Cash Receipts and Payments

One of the relevant objectives of funds statements is to report changes in some measure of debt-paying ability. Both historically and currently the measure of debt-paying ability used most frequently in funds statements has been working capital. That measure is rejected here in favor of cash.

The principal reason for recommending a change from working capital as a measure of debt-paying ability to cash is that the approach to evaluation of a company's solvency, or "credit analysis" as it is often called, has changed and the information needs of financial statement users have therefore also changed. During the 1920s when funds statements based on working capital changes were developed, the adequacy of a company's working capital position, particularly as measured by its current ratio, was considered the "alpha and omega" of credit analysis. It was argued that current liabilities are paid with current assets and current assets must therefore exceed current liabilities by an "adequate margin."

During the 1950s there was a searching reappraisal of working capital as a measure of debt-paying ability. Arthur Stone Dewing wrote in 1953 that "bankers learned by tragic experience that there was no mystical significance in the two-to-one ratio. They observed that in many types of business, under the stress of general disaster, inventories could not be sold, and if such an attempt should be made, not a two-to-one or even a three- or four-to-one ratio would bring them the immediate payment of their debts. If the business failed, the relative amounts of current capital in the days before failure had little significance in the final liquidation of the bankrupt business."

*   *   *

Those views are widely accepted by financial analysts today. The emphasis in credit analysis has shifted from analysis of current working capital position to dynamic analysis of future cash receipts and payments in much the same way that the emphasis in security analysis shifted from static analysis of balance sheet values to dynamic analysis of net income some thirty or forty years earlier.

The central question in credit analysis today is not whether a company's working capital is "adequate" but whether the cash expected to be received within a given time period will equal or exceed required cash payments within that same period. Analysis of working capital position does not provide that information. A company's principal sources of cash are from sale of its products or services to its customers, from borrowing and from issuance of stock to investors. Its principal uses are payments to employees, suppliers and governments, repayment of debt and purchase of plant and equipment. Most of the cash a company will receive within the following year is not represented by assets classified as current, and most of the obligations it will have to pay are not represented by liabilities classified as current.

The only concept of current assets as the source from which current liabilities will be paid is meaningless under this framework of analysis. Current liabilities are not paid with current assets; they are paid with cash. Whether a company's current or its noncurrent assets were the source of its cash is an unanswerable question. One can no more determine whether current or noncurrent assets provided the cash generated by a company's operations than he can determine which blade of the scissors cut the cloth, because both were clearly necessary.

The rationale for recommending a statement of cash receipts and payments as one of the statements to replace the funds statement is implicit in the above discussion. If a financial statement user's primary object of attention is the future cash receipts and payments of a company, then it follows that a statement of past cash receipts and payments would be useful for the same reason that historical income statements are useful in predicting the future income of a company: both provide a basis for predicting future performance.

Reporting cash receipts and payments is widely advocated today by many financial statement users, particularly bankers. For example, Walter B. Wriston, chairman of the board of Citibank, N. A., stated in a recent speech before Peat, Marwick, Mitchell & Co. personnel, "When I came into the banking business, we were asset-conscious and we loaned money on that basis. Well, assets give you a warm feeling, but they don't generate cash. The first question I would ask any borrower these days is, 'What is your break-even cash flow?' That's the one thing we can't find out from your audit reports and it's the single most important question we ask. It's important that you figure out a way to present the difference between real cash flow and accrual cash flow."

An example of the form of cash receipts and payments statement recommended, together with a recommended supporting schedule showing details of cash provided by operations, is presented for Example, Inc., in exhibit 1, page 82.

Only business activities that affected cash are shown on the statement of cash receipts and payments. If financing and investing activities that did not affect cash are shown on statements of cash receipts and payments as if they did, users will become confused over the purpose of the statement and what it shows. Financing transactions that did not affect cash are shown on the recommended statement of financing activities; investing transactions that did not affect cash are shown on the recommended statement of investing activities.

For the purpose of clarity of presentation, details of cash provided by profit-directed activities or what are called operations (to simplify terminology on the statement) are shown on a separate schedule rather than on the face of the statement of cash receipts and payments. Both the absolute magnitude of many of the cash receipts and payments from operations (such as the amount of cash collected from customers and the amount paid for merchandise) as well as the many types of cash payments would tend to overshadow some of the other items on the statement of cash receipts and payments (such as cash borrowed and fixed assets purchased), which may be of greater significance to the financial statement user in estimating future cash receipts and payments.

The schedule of the cash provided by operations illustrates the direct (as opposed to the indirect) method of calculating that amount. When the direct method is used, the schedule shows the actual sources and uses of cash. If the indirect method was used, the schedule would start with net income and adjust that figure for all revenues and expenses that did not affect cash. Those are the two alternative methods of presenting funds provided by operations in statements of changes in financial position that the APB described as acceptable in Opinion no. 19.

The indirect method is basically a set of worksheet adjustments rather than an explanation of how operating activities affected cash. It is analogous to calculating income by subtracting stockholders' equity at the beginning of the year from stockholders' equity at the end of the year and then adjusting the difference for nonincome items, such as dividends and purchases and sales of capital stock. This method, of course, will always "work" if the proper adjustments are made, but if accountants were to prepare income statements in this way, many financial statement users would be confused. They would begin to describe dividends, for example, as a "source" of income in the same way they now describe depreciation as a "source" of funds because they are both "add-backs" when the indirect method of calculation is used. The indirect method of calculating cash provided by operations is pernicious because it is almost certain to continue to confuse financial statement users by reinforcing the incredible belief that profits and depreciation are sources of cash. The direct method, on the other hand, is likely to be useful in dispelling some of the confusion that now exists over the relationship between business activities and cash receipts and payments because it shows clearly that profits are neither cash nor a source of cash, that cash comes from customers, that it is paid for merchandise, administrative and selling expenses, taxes and so forth and that depreciation is neither a source nor a use of cash.

* * *

EXHIBIT 1

EXAMPLE, INC.
CASH RECEIPTS AND PAYMENTS STATEMENT
Year ending December 31, 1977.

Cash balance December 31, 1976		$15,666
Sources of cash:		
Cash provided by operations (schedule 1)	$27,537	
Sale of marketable securities	3,062	
Sale of land, buildings and equipment	12,793	
Net amount borrowed	31,092	
Received from sale of common stock	7,495	81,979
Cash available		97,645
Uses of cash:		
Land, buildings and equipment purchased	62,119	
Dividends paid	13,558	75,677
Cash balance December 31, 1977		$21,968

Schedule 1

Calculation of cash provided by operations

Cash collected from customers		$783,545
Interest and dividends received		1,417
Total cash receipts from operations		784,962
Cash payments:		
For merchandise inventories	$457,681	
For administrative and selling expenses	264,577	
For interest	6,941	
For other expenses	14,953	
For taxes	13,273	757,425
Cash provided by operations		$ 27,537

Chapter 2

THE DEVELOPMENT OF ACCOUNTING PRINCIPLES

1. INTRODUCTION

Take a look at the following data relating to a hypothetical Z Corporation, which was organized in 1974 to manufacture wire-tapping equipment for the quasi-governmental market. In 1978 the owners of the company decided that the future of their business was somewhat doubtful, and decided to liquidate it rather than convert to the production of burglar alarm systems. The following summary tabulation of receipts and expenditures from organization to liquidation is available:

Receipts		Expenditures	
Original investment	$ 250,000	Organization expenses	$ 12,000
		Land	18,000
Borrowings	300,000	Construction of factory	300,000
		Purchase of machinery	400,000
Payments from customers	4,200,000	Raw materials	1,400,000
		Freight charges	75,000
Insurance received for		Salaries and wages	1,500,000
fire loss	75,000	Property taxes	45,000
		Income taxes	400,000
Interest received on		Utility charges	80,000
bank deposits	15,000	Insurance premiums	30,000
		Interest paid	55,000
Proceeds of sale of plant		Miscellaneous expenses	45,000
and machinery	220,000	Dividends	200,000
		Repayments of loans	300,000
		Amount left for stockhold-	
		ers upon liquidation	200,000
	$5,060,000		$5,060,000

Since the business venture involved is over, and everything has been reduced to cash, it is very simple to construct a picture of how well the enterprise did during its existence and how much the owners received on their investment. Clearly, if this simple exercise in arithmetic plus orderly collection of data were all there is to accounting, it would hardly deserve to be considered a profession, and learning about it would not be worth your time and attention. But of course normally financial statements are being prepared for an on-going enterprise—indeed, the statements for a business which is terminating its existence are usually of little importance. The various parties concerned with the welfare and prospects of a going enterprise—particularly existing and prospective investors and creditors—need a

83

picture of the financial position and the results of operations of the business on an interim basis, typically, at least annually. It is here that problems abound, and nice judgments are needed; for business enterprises have a way of not coming to a stop just to facilitate drawing an accounting picture. Thus at the end of any period, whether it be a year in length, a quarter of a year, or a month, a business is likely to be in various stages of many different transactions, and the matter of how to reflect, or "account for", these partially-completed transactions in the most meaningful fashion poses a host of difficult questions.

Obviously, there is a need for ground rules and guidelines as to the manner of presenting various types of financial data in the financial statements. Some are virtually self-evident: for example, it is clearly desirable that similar transactions be similarly treated, in order to provide comparability, both among different companies, and among successive periods for the same company. But with regard to the question on the merits as to what form of presentation is most meaningful for any particular type of transaction or item, there is much room for difference of opinion; and if there are two or more acceptable modes, how is the choice to be made? Ground rules and conventions covering these kinds of matters constitute accounting principles, and one may properly inquire as to where these principles come from. However, before pursuing that we must consider the question of who bears the ultimate responsibility for a company's financial statements, and what the role of the accounting profession is.

Historically, there has been little doubt that corporate financial statements are the representations of the management of the company. The managers of the company are, after all, intimately acquainted with its affairs, and they are well-positioned to prepare the financial statements. However, one of the important functions of the financial statements is to report on how the managers have employed the resources entrusted to them, and how successful they have been— their "stewardship", as it is often termed. But of course the managers are not the most objective reporters of their own performance; accordingly, from the beginning the owners of an enterprise who did not manage it often engaged independent accountants to review the records of the managers and verify the financial statements prepared by these "stewards". As the ownership of incorporated enterprises passed into the hands of large disparate groups of public stockholders, it became all the more important to have independent accountants "audit" the managers' reports, to be sure that they were not manipulated to give an unduly rosy hue to the picture, or, even worse, to conceal improprieties.

Hence, the practice developed of having an independent public accountant—the auditor—report on, that is, express an opinion on (or "certify", as it used to be called before accountants grew wary of that term because it was thought to connote an unattainable degree of certainty) whether the management's financial statements were consistent with fact and presented in accordance with accounting principles which are generally accepted as sound and appropriate in the circumstances. Notice the two-fold responsibility involved in the auditing process: (1) some check on the underlying facts represented in the financial statements (e. g., confirming that the company actually has the inventory it shows, and owes no more than the liabilities indicated); and (2) a review of the principles applied in portraying the information (e. g., whether a particular expenditure should be recorded as an expense of the current year). If the auditor finds that the financial statements are deficient in any respect, he will not give an unqualified report, or "clean certificate" as it is sometimes termed, but instead will qualify his opinion or perhaps even give an adverse opinion, depending upon the particular circumstances; and of course anything other than an unqualified opinion is a most unwelcome development from management's point of view.*

* For an illustration of an unqualified opinion, see footnote 26 on page 111, infra. Compare the following example of a qualified opinion, from the Annual Report of Cannon Mills Company for the calendar year 1963:

We have examined the balance sheet of Cannon Mills Company as of December 31, 1963 and the related statement of income and earned surplus for the year then ended. Our examination was made in accordance with generally accepted auditing standards, and accordingly included such tests of the accounting records and such other auditing procedures as we considered necessary in the circumstances.

As explained in the [note below], in 1963 the Company made payments on cotton exported in 1963 and expensed such amounts, thereby reducing net income [after taxes] approximately $1,975,000. The accounting treatment given this disbursement, in our opinion, is at variance with generally accepted accounting principles.

In our opinion, except as stated in the preceding paragraph, the accompanying financial statements present fairly the financial position of the Company at December 31, 1963 and the results of its operations for the year then ended, in conformity with generally accepted accounting principles applied on a basis consistent with that of the preceding year.—Accountants' Opinion, March 12, 1964.

The footnote to the Company's financial statements referred to in the Accountants' Opinion read as follows:

During the year ended December 31, 1963, Cannon Mills Company paid its cotton suppliers $0.925 a pound on approximately 45,500,000 pounds of cotton which the suppliers exported or caused to be exported in 1963. In consideration for these payments, the suppliers agreed to deliver to the Company an equal quantity of cotton during the first seven months of 1964 at prices substantially below the price of "unrestricted" cotton on the domestic market. Since the cotton was exported in 1963 and payment was made in 1963, in the opinion of management such payments represent cost applicable to the year ended December 31, 1963.

In order to instill greater public confidence in the role of independent accountants, the various states developed standards of education and experience as minimum qualifications for accountants authorized to perform this function. In addition, guidelines were developed for assuring that the reporting accountant would be independent of the subject company and its management (although of course there remains the inherent conflict resulting from the fact that the management is at least instrumental in, and may completely control, selection—and dismissal—of the auditor).

2. THE ROLE OF THE SEC

This audit responsibility of accountants received a tremendous boost with the enactment of the federal securities laws in 1933–34. These statutes were a response to the financial collapse of 1929, and they were designed to provide greater assurance that financial statements, particularly those of companies whose stocks were traded in the nation's securities markets, would not be misleading. The Securities and Exchange Commission (SEC) was given the responsibility of overseeing the requirements of companies subject to the jurisdiction of the SEC. The securities laws require filing of financial statements with the SEC by any company proposing to offer new securities to the public; in addition, most of the country's largest corporations, whose shares are listed on a national securities exchange like the New York Stock Exchange, or which meet certain tests relating to total assets and number of shareholders, must file financial reports periodically with the SEC.

It seems clear that under these federal statutes the SEC could have prescribed the accounting rules to be followed by companies subject to its jurisdiction, at least as to financial statements filed with the Commission (and maybe as to all financial statements for such companies, including the annual report to stockholders). Section 19 (a) of the Securities Act of 1933 provides as follows:

> ". . . the Commission shall have authority, for the purposes of this title, to prescribe the form or forms in which required information shall be set forth, the items or details to be shown in the balance sheet and earning statement, and the methods to be followed in the preparation of accounts, in the appraisal or valuation of assets and liabilities, . . . in the differentiation of recurring and nonrecurring income . . .."

However, the SEC has never chosen to implement the full reach of its power over accounting principles, preferring instead to leave the development of accounting principles to the profession. As the Chairman of the SEC in 1964 put it, "from its inception, the Commission has preferred cooperation with the profession to governmental action, and has actively encouraged accountants to take the initiative in regulating their practices and in setting standards of conduct". But the SEC strongly endorsed the role of the profession as the auditor of management's statements, by requiring that financial statements filed with the Commission be accompanied by the report of an independent accountant who has performed the two-fold auditing function. Specifically, the accountant's report (required under SEC Regulation S–X, referred to below must (1) state whether the audit was made in accordance with generally accepted auditing standards (and make specific reference to any appropriate auditing procedures which may have been omitted); and (2) state clearly the opinion of the accountant in respect of the financial statements covered by the report and the accounting principles and practices reflected therein (including comment on the company's consistency in applying such principles). The SEC also sought to strengthen the independence requirement, by expressly precluding from the auditing function any accountant who has a direct or material indirect financial interest in the subject company, or is "connected" with the company as a director, officer, employee, etc.

Thus, the SEC has embraced the traditional view of the respective roles of management and the auditor in connection with the preparation of financial statements. This was expressly confirmed in one of the SEC's early opinions, Interstate Hosiery Mills, Inc., 4 SEC 721 (1939):

> "The fundamental and primary responsibility for the accuracy of information filed with the Commission and disseminated among investors rests upon management. Management does not discharge its obligations in this respect by the employment of independent public accountants, however reputable. Accountants' certificates are required not as a substitute for management's accounting of its stewardship, but as a check upon that accounting."

Although the SEC has chosen the path of leaving the development of accounting principles largely to the profession rather than attempting to mandate them administratively, the Commission has by no means been entirely passive in this area. The SEC's Regulation S–X is a lengthy and detailed statement prescribing the specific items which must be disclosed or dealt with in financial statements filed with the Commission. In addition, the SEC has published a number of Accounting Series Releases (ASR's) on accounting principles when it felt that the profession had failed to deal with a particular type of item or problem area, and these pronouncements have had considerable influence on accounting developments.

A new, more informal dimension was added to the SEC accounting scene with the announcement, in ASR No. 180 (Nov. 4, 1975), of the institution of a new series of SEC Staff Accounting Bulletins. These Bulletins are "intended to achieve a wider dissemination of the administrative interpretations and practices utilized by the Commission's staff in reviewing financial statements. The statements in the Bulletin are not rules or interpretations of the Commission, nor are they published as bearing the Commission's official approval; they represent interpretations and practices followed by the Division [of Corporation Finance] and the Chief Accountant in administering the disclosure requirements of the federal securities laws." The first of these Bulletins, Staff Accounting Bulletin No. 1, was promulgated simultaneously with ASR No. 180, and one section of it is particularly relevant at this point:

G.   Requirements for Audited or Certified Financial Statements

Facts: Amendments adopted in Accounting Series Release No. 155 changed the requirement in various forms from "certified" to "audited" financial statements.

Question: Does the word "audited" have the same meaning as the word "certified"?

Interpretive Response: No difference in meaning or change in requirements was intended or effected by ASR No. 155 which was a continuation of a program to conform the terminology used in the forms to that currently applied by the accounting profession (see ASR No. 125).

Facts: The accountants' report is qualified as to scope of audit, or the accounting principles used.

Question: Does the staff consider the requirements for audited or certified financial statements met when the auditors' opinion is so qualified?

Interpretive Reponse: The staff does not accept as consistent with the requirements of Rule 2–02(b) of Regulation S–X financial statements on which the auditors' opinions are qualified because of a limitation on the scope of the audit, since in these situations the auditor was unable to perform all the procedures required by professional standards to support the expression of an opinion. This position was discussed in ASR No. 90 in connection with representations concerning the verification of prior years' inventories in first audits.

Financial statements for which the auditors' opinions contain qualifications relating to the acceptability of accounting principles used or the completeness of disclosures made are also unacceptable.

For a more detailed description of auditing standards and procedures, see pages 108–111, infra in these materials. Other excerpts from Staff Accounting Bulletin No. 1 and subsequent Bulletins will appear at various points later herein.

Some years ago the SEC also moved in the direction of exerting greater influence over the financial statements which are not filed with the Commission, notably the annual financial report customarily sent to stockholders. The SEC's proxy regulations require that financial statements be sent to stockholders whenever proxies are solicited from stockholders (which is almost always the case), in connection with an annual meeting of stockholders at which directors are to be elected. While compliance with all of the SEC's promulgations is not required for these statements, SEC Rule 14a–3, adopted in 1967, does require the company to note and explain any material discrepancies between the statements presented to stockholders and those filed with the SEC, resulting from differences in accounting principles or practices. Since most companies would prefer not to have to pinpoint any such differences, let alone undertake to explain and reconcile them, the SEC's accounting promulgations embodied in Regulation S–X and the various ASR's are becoming well-nigh determinative for all the published financial statements for any corporation subject to the jurisdiction of the SEC.

In 1974 Rule 14a–3 was amended to require that the financial statements sent to stockholders in conjunction with a solicitation of proxies (1) be certified (as would normally have been the case anyway, but at least in theory was within the discretion of the management); (2) contain a textual summary of operations by the management which discusses and analyzes material changes from period to period in various categories of revenues and expenses, and changes in accounting principles or practices which have a material effect on reported income; and, as further amended in 1977, (3) contain a breakdown of accounting data among the company's various industry segments, plus information relating to classes of similar products or services, foreign and domestic operations, and export sales.

3. DEVELOPMENT OF ACCOUNTING PRINCIPLES BY THE PROFESSION

How has leaving the development of accounting principles to the profession worked out? The first formal efforts came in 1939, when the principal national association of accountants, the American Institute of Certified Public Accountants (AICPA) created a Committee on Accounting Procedure, charged with responsibility for determining the proper accounting approach (or approaches) in particular areas of current concern, and a Committee on Accounting Terminology, whose function was to make recommendations as to the definition of certain accounting terms and their subsequent use in financial statements. The two committees published their views in the form of Accounting Research Bulletins (ARB's) which were widely circulated; but their pronouncements were not binding upon the profession, much less on anyone else: each ARB bore the concluding comment that "the authority of the bulletins rests upon the general acceptability of opinions so reached". In 1953 the substantive determinations of the Committee on Accounting Procedure contained in the first forty-two ARB's were consolidated (and reconfirmed, with very few changes of substance) in ARB No. 43, which is divided into chapters covering most of the subjects dealt with in the earlier bulletins; the terminology pronouncements were amplified and replaced by Accounting Terminology Bulletin No. 1. Although many of these early statements have been modified by the promulgations of subsequent principle-setting groups, those which have not been remain in force, and reference to some of these appears from time to time later in these materials.

Although the ARB's represented a useful start, they did not carry great weight in the profession. One patent deficiency was the fact that the ARB's were not supported by any significant amount of research by the AICPA, and instead simply represented a consensus of committee members based primarily upon their experience and viewpoints. Hence the ARB's frequently sponsored alternative practices or were otherwise equivocal, often reflecting the compromises on conclusions and wording needed to obtain the necessary two-thirds vote of the committee members.

In an effort to give more effective leadership in the determination of accounting principles, in 1959 the AICPA established the Accounting Principles Board (APB); the Board consisted of Institute members, mostly in public practice, with a representative from each of the largest accounting firms (the "Big Eight") as well as a number of smaller firms and some academics, and was supported by a greatly expanded research capacity. The APB was first to consider and reach some conclusions on basic concepts and principles of accounting (aided by detailed research studies undertaken by staff members) and then to try to resolve the more important current problem areas involving accounting practices and financial reporting. The overall objective was "to narrow the areas of difference and inconsistency in practice" in as expeditious a manner as practicable, but on the basis of adequate research and consideration. By the time of its dissolution in June, 1973, the APB had issued thirty-one "Opinions" and four "Statements", which defined and narrowed the acceptable perimeters of accounting methodology. (Hereinafter APB opinions are referred to as "APB Op. No. ——", or sometimes just "APB No. ——".)

Despite the added research dimension, the APB suffered from some of the same deficiencies which marked its predecessor. The compromises needed to secure the necessary two-thirds vote of the members often led to results that failed to satisfy anyone (and sometimes produced long delays before any conclusion at all could be reached). There was also a continuing disquiet about whether the practicing members could sufficiently divorce themselves from the desires of their major clients on various issues. More and more observers reached the conclusion that the existing system was unworkable, and that a total overhaul was called for.

As a result, in 1971 the Board of Directors of the AICPA appointed a Committee on the Establishment of Accounting Principles, under the chairmanship of Francis M. Wheat, a distinguished securities lawyer (and former SEC commissioner). Pursuant to the recommendations of that Committee, in 1972 a new body, called the Financial Accounting Standards Board (FASB), was created to replace the APB as the organ responsible for determining and promulgating accounting principles. The FASB consists of seven full-time members, appointed for staggered five-year terms. To assure independence, members of the FASB must terminate all other employment ties and are paid a very generous salary, upwards of $100,000 per year.

The members of the Board are appointed by the Trustees of the Financial Accounting Foundation, a newly-created, independent charitable corporation. Of the nine Trustees, one is the president of the AICPA, and the other eight are appointed by the Board of Directors of the AICPA, four of them with the assistance and advice of organizations respectively representing business executives, corporate financial officers, financial analysts and accounting educators. The Trustees also nominate the twenty members of the Financial Accounting Advisory Council, drawn from various disciplines, who function as advisers to the FASB. Under the guidelines governing the FASB's activities, provision is made for extensive research, issuance of detailed discussion memoranda focusing issues under consideration by the Board, publication of exposure drafts of contemplated Statements, conduct of public hearings, and promulgation of formal Statements of Financial Accounting Standards. (Hereinafter such FASB Statements are referred to as "FASB Statement No. ——", or sometimes just "FASB No. ——".) In addition, the FASB issues interpretations of its Statements, and also of presently outstanding APB opinions and ARB's, which the FASB's rules indicate are to be viewed as continuing in force until amended or replaced by an FASB Statement. The AICPA's involvement in the establishment of accounting principles is now limited to making its views known to the FASB by means of position papers and other communications from the Institute's Accounting Standards Executive Committee.

The FASB is assured of a more authoritative role in setting accounting standards than its predecessors enjoyed, by virtue of the

AICPA's adoption in 1972 of Rule 203 of the restated Code of Professional Ethics; that rule forbids members to express an opinion that financial statements are in conformity with generally accepted accounting principles if the statements contain any departure from an accounting principle sanctioned by the FASB (which includes prior APB opinions and ARB's not supplanted by the FASB) and such departure has a material effect on the statements taken as a whole. The only exception allowed is where the auditor believes that the statements would otherwise be misleading, in which event the departure and its effects must be disclosed. See footnote 189 and accompanying text, pages 98–99, infra. The prior rule had only required disclosure of any departure from a principle approved by the APB.

One of the most thoughtful and constructive critics of the current scene is Professor Melvin Eisenberg, who described the situation this way in his excellent article, Legal Models of Management Structure in the Modern Corporation: Officers, Directors, and Accountants, 63 Cal.L.Rev. 375, 417–429 (1975) : *

A. THE FAILURE OF THE ACCOUNTANTS

1. Responsibility for Selecting Accounting Principles

Since a major purpose of financial statements is to measure management's performance, and since the financial data reported by a corporation depend in significant part on discretionary choices among competing accounting principles, it is reasonable to expect that the principles employed in the preparation of a corporation's financial statements will be selected by the corporation's outside accountant, and not by its managers. The outside accountant, after all, is a professional, skilled in accounting principles and practice, and presumably objective in the exercise of his discretion. In contrast, the manager typically has no advanced training in accounting and is invariably highly self-interested in selecting those principles that show off his performance in the best possible light.

Yet the official position of the American Institute of Certified Public Accountants is that "the accounts of a company are primarily the responsibility of *management*. The [only] responsibility of the auditor is to express his opinion concerning the financial statements and to state clearly such explanations, amplifications, disagreement, or disapproval as he deems appropriate". To put this differently, the accountants' position is that their role is not to determine which accounting principles most appropriately present the financial results, but only to certify that the principles selected by management are not completely inappropriate. As an academic accountant has stated: "An analogy might be having the baseball batter calling the balls and the strikes".

2. Discretion in Selecting Among Competing Accounting Principles; the Test for Certification

Placing responsibility for selecting accounting principles with management rather than with the accountants might perhaps be tolerable if management's discretion in selecting among competing accounting principles were relatively circumscribed. But here too reasonable expectations have been confounded. Since the accountant's major control over the financials is his power to withhold or qualify his certification, the test for determining whether a clean certificate will be granted is critical to the integrity of the process. The test the accountants have formulated is whether the financial statements "present fairly the financial position of [the company] and the results of its operations . . . in conformity with generally accepted accounting principles . . . ." As elaborated and applied this test has been fundamentally defective, because an accounting principle may be "generally accepted" without being fair, and because certification has been deemed permissible even though the corporation's financial statements do not fairly present its financial position and the results of its operations.

a. *"Generally accepted accounting principles"*. It might seem reasonable to expect that the essential standard for certifying the acceptabilty of an accounting principle would be that the principle presents fairly the transaction it describes. The accountants, however, do not so interpret the matter. In their view, a principle can be certified as "generally accepted" merely on the basis of past use in other financial statements or support in the literature. Since accounting principles are selected by management, however, the test of past use need only mean that a few accountants have agreed not to object to a management decision, while the test of support in the literature need only mean that a single accountant has published his reasons for not objecting to such a decision. Furthermore, when the significance of past use is combined with the power of management to determine what principles are used—subject only to the test of past use by other managements—it follows that an accountant may certify a statement even though he believes that the principles employed in its preparation do not account for the underlying transactions as fairly as competing principles that management has rejected. This in turn provides further support for the principle, and since managers of competing companies are evaluated by comparing the financial results of their corporations with those of their competitors, there is great pressure for inferior principles to spread throughout an industry. The net result is a frequent tendency toward general deterioration of both accounting principles and financial statements. As one accountant has put it: "[T]his chain reaction . . . leads to a reverse of keeping up with the Joneses; it is keeping *down* with the Joneses. As Leonard Spacek has observed, the tendency noted by Gresham's Law, that bad money drives out the good, seems to apply to accounting: The bad alternatives drive out the good alternatives".

The rule that "general acceptance" can rest on past use or support in the literature, which is the foundation of this tendency in accounting, was far from inevitable. Even if individual accountants did not want to render a judgment on the fairness of individual accounting principles—notwithstanding the language of their certification—the

AICPA's Accounting Principles Board (APB) was empowered to issue authoritative opinions on accounting principles generally.   If the principles approved in those opinions had been deemed to preempt competing principles, the criterion of past use might gradually have given way to a criterion of analytical soundness.   Unfortunately, the AICPA took just the opposite position:

    1.   "Generally accepted accounting principles" are those principles which have substantial authoritative support.

    2.   Opinions of the Accounting Principles Board constitute "substantial authoritative support".

    3.   "Substantial authoritative support" can exist for accounting principles that differ from Opinions of the Accounting Principles Board.[165]

Of course, in some cases an APB opinion would either cast grave doubt on some or all competing principles or explicitly render competing principles unacceptable.   But since the APB was practitioner-dominated and notoriously weak, in many areas it did not speak at all, in many others it did not speak decisively, and even where it spoke decisively its opinions often failed to drive out unsound accounting practices.

The accountants' rejection of a standard of fairness in the all-too-frequent absence of an authoritative opinion by an organ of the AICPA, and their readiness to rely on past use as the standard in certifying general acceptability, is well-illustrated by the leading case of Escott v. BarChris Construction Corp.[169] and the critical comment it engendered.   In that case, BarChris was engaged in the construction of bowling alleys and had entered into a transaction under which an alley it built for a wholly-owned subsidiary was "sold" to a factor, which then leased the alley back to a second subsidiary whose obligations to the factor were guaranteed by BarChris.   Thus the transaction was in substance (and to a large extent in form) a loan by the factor to BarChris on the security of the alley and BarChris's guarantee.   In its financial statements, however, BarChris treated the amount it had received from the factor as sales income and did not show the amount owing to the factor as a direct liability.   BarChris's accountants—Peat, Marwick, Mitchell & Co.—certified that the financials were prepared in accordance with generally accepted accounting principles.   Obviously, no sound accounting principle would have permitted this transaction to be accounted for as a sale.   The cash that changed hands was not the result of an arm's-length price paid by a willing buyer, but simply a loan by a factor engaged in the business of lending, and when all the shooting was over BarChris retained both the use of the property (through its wholly-owned subsidiary) and the economic risks of ownership (through its guarantee).   In a private action against Peat, Marwick and others, brought under section 11 of the

---

165.   AICPA, Disclosure of Departures from Opinions of the Accounting Principles Board (Special Bull. 1964) . . . . [Ed. note: However, as its name indicates, this Special Bulletin did require disclosure when any accounting principle that differed materially from one approved in an APB Opinion was utilized.   In addition, the Special Bulletin provided that the prior ARB's were to be accorded the same status as APB Opinions, unless and until revoked or amended by the APB.]

169.   283 F.Supp. 643 (S.D.N.Y.1968).

Securities Exchange Act by purchasers of BarChris convertible debentures, the certification was accordingly found wanting and liability was imposed on the accountants.

Subsequently, an article published in the Journal of Accountancy criticized this result. The authors did not specifically assert that the accounting treatment of the transaction was *fair*. Instead they argued, in substance, that in determining whether an accounting principle selected by management is certifiable, fairness is irrelevant:

> In BarChris the Court ruled that profits on a sale-leaseback should have been eliminated; however, the AICPA statements on accounting principles at the time of the transaction were silent as to the need for eliminating such profits . . . .

> Let us re-examine the BarChris sale-leaseback transaction in the light of then existing accounting principles to answer the claims of some commentators that the relevant principles were sufficiently defined before the case was brought to trial. One might advance several reasons to explain why BarChris should [not have reported profit from the sale-leaseback transaction] . . . . . [T]he overriding doctrine of fairness might be invoked; one might argue profit [from the transaction] should be eliminated so that financial statements would fairly present the financial position and results of operations for BarChris.

> But the doctrine of fairness is necessarily egocentric. He who espouses it presumes to know the one and only correct interpretation of a given transaction. Unfortunately, fairness like beauty exists in the eye of the beholder. What appears fair to one often appears unfair to another. No one denies the propriety of fairness, but accountants need more explicit guidelines . . . . [R]easonable doubt existed as to what was required in accordance with the generally accepted accounting principles circa 1960. . . .

Thus the authors' position—which seems to reflect the prevalent attitude of the accounting profession and indeed the official position of the AICPA—appears to be that an accounting principle can be considered generally accepted if it is in use and has not been specifically disapproved by an authoritative institution, whether or not it fairly accounts for the transaction it describes. That position, however, rests on a fallacious premise—that "[h]e who espouses [a test of fairness] presumes to know the one and only correct interpretation of a given transaction". One need not know the "one and only correct interpretation" of a transaction to know when an interpretation is obviously incorrect. This is perfectly illustrated by the *BarChris* case itself, because the possibility that there was more than one fair way to describe the transaction clearly does not mean it could be accounted for in any way management chose. No one would claim, for example, that the transaction could have been accounted for as a gift, and it was equally inappropriate to account for it as a sale yielding sales income. An argument that accounting for the transaction as a sale was permissible because others were doing it and the APB had not forbidden it simply demonstrates the moral and intellectual poverty of the term "generally accepted accounting principles" as interpreted by the accountants.

b. *"Presented fairly"*. Vesting in management the power to select the principles applied to audit its own performance might perhaps have been made tolerable by narrowly confining management's discretion in selecting among competing principles; this the accountants failed to do. Alternatively, vesting in management wide discretion to select among competing principles might perhaps have been made tolerable by forbidding a clean certificate even though each principle selected by management was generally accepted, if the financial statements *taken as a whole* failed to present fairly the corporation's financial picture. This interpretation of the accountant's role seems called for by the legitimate expectations of the statement-using public and by the very language of the certificate itself—that the company's financial statements *"present fairly* . . . in accordance with generally accepted accounting principles"* its financial position and operating results. To read this language as satisfied simply because each principle employed in the preparation of the financial statements is generally accepted would be to read the term "fairly" right out of the certification: If a statement prepared in accordance with generally accepted accounting principles is presented fairly by virtue of that fact alone, there would be no difference between "present . . . in accordance with" and "present *fairly* . . . in accordance with".

Once more, however, the accountants have managed to subvert legitimate expectations by interpreting their role in a minimalist way. While the AICPA has failed to give a definitive interpretation of the language in question, many or most accountants take the position that as long as the financials are prepared in accordance with generally accepted accounting principles, certification is proper even if the auditor believes that the statements are not fairly presented.[174]

* * *

3. The Selection and Dismissal of Acccountants

Virtually the only substantive limit placed on management's discretion by the accountants is that the principles management selects in preparing its financial statements must be "generally accepted".[176] Virtually the accountant's only mechanism for enforcing this limit is his power to withhold a clean certificate from the corporation's finan-

---

174. . . . [Ed. note: For the latest word on the concept of "present fairly in accordance with generally accepted accounting principles", see Statement on Auditing Standards No. 5, set out at pages 101–103, infra.]

176. A further limit is the requirement that the financial statements "present fairly [the position of the company] . . . in conformity with [GAAP] applied on a basis *consistent with that of the previous year."* AUDITING STANDARDS, supra note 158, § 511.04 at 81 (emphasis added). In practice, however, at least until recently, management has been able to switch principles with virtually no constraint. For example, in 1968–69 more than 60 corporations, including many of the largest steel companies, switched from accelerated to straight-line depreciation for no apparent reason other than to increase reported earnings. Inland Steel raised its reported 1968 income $17.3 million by the switch, and U.S. Steel raised its 1968 reported income $94 million by this and other switches. Similarly, in 1970–71 a number of corporations changed their inventory accounting method from LIFO to FIFO to raise reported profits, despite the fact that such a switch results in a very substantial increase in taxes. Allegheny Ludlum, for example, increased its taxes for 1970 by $6 million through this switch . . . . .

cial statements. Yet by law, and largely by practice, the selection, tenure, and dismissal of an accountant is entirely in the hands of the management. Moreover, management is not hesitant to use this power. During the 18-month period of November 1971 to April 1973 there were approximately 400 accountant changes among the corporations which must file Form 8–K's with the SEC, and during the 18-month period of January 1973 to June 1974, there were approximately 700 such changes. At least 10 percent of these changes, and almost certainly more, were made against a background of disputes over accounting principles.[177]

The accountant's dependence on management for his tenure, when combined with management's discretion in selecting among competing accounting principles and the low standards set by the accountants for determining whether a given principle is "generally accepted", result in an almost irresistible pressure on the accountant to go along with marginal principles. The accountant " 'can swallow his convictions or he can qualify his opinion, or he can resign. Usually the latter two courses are one and the same' ".

The pressure on the accountants to go along in marginal (and even less-than-marginal) cases is considerably augmented by the fact that if an incumbent accountant does balk, a more flexible auditor can almost always be found. The result is that an accountant who uses or threatens to use his only real control over management's selection of accounting principles is likely to lose his own position without materially benefiting those who use the corporation's financial statements. Many accountants appear to regard the withholding of a clean opinion under such circumstances as a quixotic gesture.

B.   STRUCTURAL REFORM OF THE ACCOUNTANT'S CORPORATE ROLE

The accountant plays a critical role in the modern corporation: objective auditing of management's performance is and must be a central concern of the corporate system, and only through the accountant can such auditing be achieved. But the structure of the ac-

177. . . . Until 1971, it was almost impossible to gather meaningful information on the real reasons for auditor changes . . . .. In 1971, however, the SEC amended its Form 8–K (which requires registered corporations to report specified types of events within ten days after the close of the month in which they occur) to include a new Item 12, calling for (i) a report when a new accountant is engaged, and (ii) a letter

stating whether in the eighteen months preceding such engagement there were any disagreements with the former principal accountant on any matter of accounting principles or practices, financial statement disclosure, or auditing procedure, which disagreements if not resolved to the satisfaction of the former accountant would have caused him to make reference in connection with his opinion to the subject matter of the disagreement.

The registrant was also required to request the former accountant to furnish a comparable letter. Even these provisions did not produce entirely reliable information, and recently the 8–K was further amended to broaden the scope of the disclosure and require that the information called for in the separate letter be supplied in the 8–K itself. Related amendments were made in Regulation S–X and the Proxy Rules. SEC Securities Act of 1933 Release No. 5550 (Dec. 20, 1974); . . . ..

countant's role is seriously—even fundamentally—flawed. It is impossible to expect objective reporting from an institutional structure which combines (1) power of selection of accounting principles by the very managers whose activities are being accounted for, (2) wide discretion in making that selection, and (3) auditing of that selection by persons hired and fired by the very managers who make the selection. As long as management rather than the accountant is empowered to make discretionary choices among competing accounting principles, such choices will often lack soundness and will invariably lack objectivity. As long as management hires and fires those who audit management, there can be no true auditing. To achieve an objective flow of information on the results achieved by management, one of two conditions must prevail. Either accounting principles must be made so narrow and mutually exclusive that selection among them becomes a mechanical rather than a discretionary act, or the power to select applicable accounting principles must be vested in accountants who are truly independent of management.[183] Since the former condition is not practicably attainable, corporate law must aim at establishing the latter.

1. Responsibility for Selecting Accounting Principles

Although at first glance a shift of responsibility for selecting accounting principles from management to the accountants might appear so radical as to be unrealistic, in many respects it would simply carry to their logical conclusion a series of recent developments in the courts, the SEC, and the accounting profession itself. In the accounting profession, for example, in 1964 the AICPA Council issued a Special Bulletin recommending that financial statements disclose any departure from principles recognized by the APB, even where the principle utilized in the statement has substantial authoritative support. In 1971 the APB issued Opinion No. 20, which states a presumption that an accounting principle once adopted by a firm should not be changed in accounting for later events and transactions of a similar type—a presumption that can be overcome only by the justification that a new principle is preferable to the old one. In 1972 the AICPA replaced the part-time, practitioner-dominated APB with a Financial Accounting Standards Board (FASB), which is expected to narrow the choice of generally accepted accounting principles. In contrast to the APB, three of the FASB's seven members need not be CPA's, and all are to serve full-time five-year terms and must sever their former employment or partnership ties. Finally, in 1973 the AICPA adopted a new rule which makes it unethical for a member to "express an opinion that financial statements are presented in conformity with generally accepted accounting principles if such statements contain any departure from an accounting principle promulgated by [the APB or FASB] which has a material effect on the statements taken as a whole, unless the member can demonstrate that due to unusual circumstances the financial statements would otherwise have been misleading".[189]

183. Responsibility for the data underlying the financial statements would of course remain with management, while responsibility for auditing that data would remain with the accountants.

189. See AICPA, Restatement of the Code of Professional Ethics Rule 203 (1972). Where a departure is justified under this test, the accountant's report "must describe the departure,

A second line of developments leading to increased responsibility for accountants is taking place in the courts and the SEC. To begin, with, those accountants who do not meet even the minimum standards of their own profession are being exposed to severe sanctions. Partners in Lybrand, Ross Bros. & Montgomery and Peat, Marwick, Mitchell & Co. have been found guilty of criminal violations. Arthur Andersen & Co. has been censured by the SEC. Private actions against Haskins & Sells, Arthur Andersen, Lybrand, Arthur Young, and Peat, Marwick have been settled for amounts ranging from $300,000 to just under $5 million. As of 1973, claims against accountants involving more than 500 companies were either in process or in litigation, and in 1974 Arthur Andersen alone had lawsuits pending against it involving 34 companies. The heavy pressure exerted by this criminal and civil litigation is causing accountants to be both more careful and more scrupulous in observing their own minimal standards.

Of perhaps greater import, the courts are beginning to upgrade the standards of the profession in the first instance. This upgrading is most dramatically exemplified by *Escott v. BarChris Construction Corp.* and *United States v. Simon.*[199] The *BarChris* case, discussed earlier, focused on liability for certifying a principle that does not fairly account for the transaction being described; *Simon* focused on liability for certifying a financial statement that is unfair taken as a whole.

The problem in *Simon* grew out of the use by Harold Roth of two corporations under his control, Continental and Valley, to finance personal stock-market transactions, by causing Continental to loan money to Valley, which in turn lent the money to him. The purpose of making the loans through Valley, rather than directly from Continental to Roth, was to dress up Continental's balance sheet: the loans were shown on Continental's books as an account receivable from Valley rather than from Roth. At the end of fiscal 1962, Continental's account receivable from Valley arising out of loans destined for Roth exceeded $3.5 million. Before Continental's financial statements for that year were certified, its accountants learned that the Valley receivable was uncollectible (and therefore could not be shown on Continental's books as an asset) because Roth was unable to repay Valley

the approximate effects thereof, if practicable, and the reasons why compliance with the [APB or FASB] principle would result in a misleading statement". Predecessor rules had merely required disclosure of a departure . . . [see footnote 165, supra].

The AICPA's trial board is empowered to admonish or expel a member for violations of professional ethics, but has no power to impose fines or to bar a person from the practice of accounting. It has been charged that the AICPA's enforcement of its ethics code has been less than rigorous . . . . .

Although rule 203 does not explictly require disregard of authoritative principles whose application would result in unfair presentation, an interpretation issued by the AICPA's Division of Professional Ethics states that "upon occasion there may be unusual circumstances where the literal application of pronouncements on accounting principles would have the effect of rendering financial statements misleading. In such cases, the proper accounting treatment is that which will render the financial statements not misleading". AICPA, Restatement of the Code of Professional Ethics 35 (1972).

199. 425 F.2d 796 (2d Cir. 1969), certiorari denied 397 U.S. 1006, 90 S.Ct. 1235, 25 L.Ed.2d 420 (1970).

the amount it had lent him, an amount far exceeding Valley's net worth. To remedy this, Roth collateralized the Valley receivable, but the collateral consisted principally of stock and convertible debentures in Continental itself. The accountants, aware of all the relevant facts, nevertheless certified the $3.5 million Valley receivable with only the following qualification, which appeared in a footnote:

> The amount receivable from Valley Commercial Corp. (an affiliated company of which Mr. Harold Roth is an officer, director and stockholder) bears interest at 12% a year. Such amount, less the balance of the notes payable to that company, is secured by the assignment to the Company of *Valley's equity in certain marketable securities.* As of February 15, 1963, the amount of such equity at current market quotations exceeded the net amount receivable.

Subsequently the accountants were indicted under the Securities Exchange Act for certifying a false or misleading financial statement.[201] At the trial they called as witnesses eight expert accountants, constituting, in the words of the Second Circuit, "an impressive array of leaders of the profession", who testified that the failure to disclose in the footnote the purpose of the loans to Valley and the nature of the collateral was in no way inconsistent with generally acceptable accounting principles. The defendants asked for instructions which, in substance, would have told the jury that "a defendant could be found guilty only if, *according to generally accepted accounting principles,* the financial statements as a whole did not fairly present the financial condition of Continental at September 30, 1962, and then only if his departure from accepted standards was due to willful disregard of those standards with knowledge of the falsity of the statements and an intent to deceive". The trial court declined to give this instruction—which would have given the defendants a complete defense in light of the expert testimony—but instead instructed that the critical issue was whether the financial statements *as a whole* fairly presented Continental's financial position and accurately reported its operations. If they did not, the basic issue was whether defendants had acted in good faith. Proof of compliance with generally accepted accounting principles would be "evidence which may be very persuasive but not necessarily conclusive" on that issue.

A jury verdict against the accountants was sustained by the Second Circuit in an opinion by Judge Friendly. Thereafter, in a speech to the AICPA, the Chairman of the SEC described the result of the case as follows:

> [T]he court established that it is not enough to merely adhere to rules, even if they are generally accepted principles or stand-

---

201. The indictment was based on (1) the failure of the note to disclose the purpose of the loans to Valley and the nature of the collateral, and (2) the fact that in determining the value of the collateral and the extent to which the Valley receivable was collateralized, the accountants improperly netted Continental's account payable to Valley against its Valley receivable, failed to discover that there was a lien of $1 million against the pledged securities, and failed to disclose that the amount of the receivable had risen by $400,000 between the end of the fiscal year and the date of certification, while the value of the collateral had declined by more than $270,000 between the date of certification and the date the financial statements were mailed. Id. at 801, 805–08.

ards.   Rather a critical test is whether the financial statement, as a whole, fairly presents the position of the company and accurately reports its operation for the period it purports to cover. To meet this test and establish good faith, an accounting report has to reflect pertinent information which those who prepare it have, or in due diligence, should obtain, whether or not the disclosure of that information is required by specific generally accepted principles or standards.

To put the matter differently, just as *BarChris* held, in effect, that an accountant cannot rely on general acceptance to support his certification of a principle that does not fairly account for the transaction being described, *Simon* held that an accountant cannot rely on the general acceptance of each principle employed in the preparation of a financial statement to support his certification of a statement that is not fair as a whole.   To comply with these decisions the accountants will need to increase significantly their control over the financial statements they certify.   Taken together with the cases holding accountants to their own existing standards, as well as the trends within the accounting profession itself, *BarChris* and *Simon* indicate that a shift of power over the selection of accounting principles utilized in the preparation of financial statements from the managers to the accountants is not only appropriate on policy grounds, but also carries forward an institutional momentum that seems to be building to just such a climax.

* * *

STATEMENT ON AUDITING STANDARDS NO. 5 *

Auditing Standards Executive Committee, 1975.

THE MEANING OF "PRESENT FAIRLY IN CONFORMITY WITH GENERALLY ACCEPTED ACCOUNTING PRINCIPLES" IN THE INDEPENDENT AUDITOR'S REPORT

1.   An independent auditor's unqualified opinion usually reads as follows:

> "In our opinion, the financial statements referred to above present fairly the financial position of X Company as of (at) December 31, 19XX, and the results of its operations and the changes in its financial position for the year then ended, in conformity with generally accepted accounting principles applied on a basis consistent with that of the preceding year."

The purpose of this Statement is to explain the meaning of the phrase "present fairly . . . in conformity with generally accepted accounting principles" in the independent auditor's report.

2. The first standard of reporting requires an auditor who has examined financial statements in accordance with generally accepted auditing standards to state in his report whether the statements are presented in accordance with generally accepted accounting principles. The phrase "generally accepted accounting principles" is a technical accounting term which encompasses the conventions, rules, and procedures necessary to define accepted accounting practice at a particular time. It includes not only broad guidelines of general application, but also detailed practices and procedures . . . . Those conventions, rules, and procedures provide a standard by which to measure financial presentations.

3. The independent auditor's judgment concerning the "fairness" of the overall presentation of financial statements should be applied within the framework of generally accepted accounting principles. Without that framework the auditor would have no uniform standard for judging the presentation of financial position, results of operations, and changes in financial position in financial statements.

4. The auditor's opinion that financial statements present fairly an entity's financial position, results of operations, and changes in financial position in conformity with generally accepted accounting principles should be based on his judgment as to whether (a) the accounting principles selected and applied have general acceptance (see paragraphs 5 and 6); (b) the accounting principles are appropriate in the circumstances (see paragraphs 7–9); (c) the financial statements, including the related notes, are informative of matters that may affect their use, understanding, and interpretation . . . ; (d) the information presented in the financial statements is classified and summarized in a reasonable manner, that is, neither too detailed nor too condensed . . . ; and (e) the financial statements reflect the underlying events and transactions in a manner that presents the financial position, results of operations, and changes in financial position stated within a range of acceptable limits, that is, limits that are reasonable and practicable to attain in financial statements.

5. Generally accepted accounting principles are relatively objective; that is, they are sufficiently established so that independent auditors usually agree on their existence. Nevertheless, the identification of an accounting principle as generally accepted in particular circumstances requires judgment. No single source of reference exists for all established accounting principles. Rule 203 of the AICPA Code of Professional Ethics requires compliance with accounting principles promulgated by the body designated by Council to establish such principles, unless due to unusual circumstances the financial statements would otherwise be misleading . . . . The pronouncements comprehended by Rule 203 are statements and interpretations issued by the Financial Accounting Standards Board, APB opinions, and AICPA accounting research bulletins.

6. In the absence of pronouncements comprehended by Rule 203, the auditor should consider other possible sources of established accounting principles, such as AICPA accounting interpretations, AICPA industry audit guides and accounting guides, and industry accounting practices. Depending on their relevance in the circumstances, the auditor may also wish to refer to APB statements, AICPA statements of position, pronouncements of other professional associa-

tions and regulatory agencies, such as the Securities and Exchange Commission, and accounting textbooks and articles . . . . . Independent auditors should be alert to pronouncements that change accounting principles. They should also be alert to changes that become acceptable as a result of common usage in business, rather than as a result of pronouncements.

7. Generally accepted accounting principles recognize the importance of recording transactions in accordance with their substance. The auditor should consider whether the substance of transactions differs materially from their form.

8. The auditor should be familiar with alternative accounting principles that may be applicable to the transaction or facts under consideration and realize that an accounting principle may have only limited usage but still have general acceptance. On occasion, established accounting principles may not exist for recording and presenting a specific event or transaction because of developments such as new legislation or the evolution of a new type of business transaction. In certain instances, it may be possible to account for the event or transaction on the basis of its substance by selecting an accounting principle that appears appropriate when applied in a manner similar to the application of an established principle to an analogous event or transaction.

9. Specifying the circumstances in which one accounting principle should be selected from among alternative principles is the function of bodies having authority to establish accounting principles. When criteria for selection among alternative accounting principles have not been established to relate accounting methods to circumstances, the auditor may conclude that more than one accounting principle is appropriate in the circumstances. The auditor should recognize, however, that there may be unusual circumstances in which the selection and application of specific accounting principles from among alternative principles may make the financial statements taken as a whole misleading.

The Statement entitled "The Meaning of 'Present Fairly in Conformity with Generally Accepted Accounting Principles' in the Independent Auditor's Report" was adopted by the assenting votes of twenty members of the committee, of whom three, Messrs. Konkel, Nelson, and Solomon, assented with qualifications. Mr. Brasseaux dissented.

Note: Statements on Auditing Standards are issued by the Auditing Standards Executive Committee, the senior technical committee of the Institute designated to issue pronouncements on auditing matters. Rule 202 of the Institute's Code of Professional Ethics requires adherence to the applicable generally accepted auditing standards promulgated by the Institute. It recognizes Statements on Auditing Standards as interpretations of generally accepted auditing standards, and requires that members be prepared to justify departures from such Statements.

NOTE ON THE FINANCIAL ACCOUNTING STANDARD BOARD'S PROJECT TO ESTABLISH FUNDAMENTAL ACCOUNTING CONCEPTS

In addition to its pronouncements on particular accounting principles, i.e., the Statements of Financial Accounting Standards and a variety of "Interpretations", the Board has been engaged in a comprehensive project seeking to distill the fundamentals on which financial accounting and reporting standards should be based. The Board's conclusions will be incorporated in a series of "Statements of Financial Accounting Concepts", which the Board describes as "intended to establish the objectives and concepts that the FASB will use in developing standards of financial accounting and reporting". The ultimate aim is to create a basic, comprehensive framework within which to resolve particular issues of accounting principle.

The first such Statement of Financial Accounting Concepts, captioned "Objectives of Financial Reporting by Business Enterprises", was issued in 1978. It constitutes a broad compilation of the basic purposes of financial statements, in the light of the potential users of such statements and the kind of information that should be included. A second Statement of Financial Accounting Concepts was promulgated in 1979, in the form of a so-called "Exposure Draft" (a tentative statement circulated for public comment), in which the objectives of FASB Concepts Statement No. 1 are summarized as follows *:

> Financial reporting should provide information that is useful to present and potential investors and creditors and other users in making rational investment, credit, and similar decisions. The information should be comprehensible to those who have a reasonable understanding of business and economic activities and are willing to study the information with reasonable diligence.

> Financial reporting should provide information to help present and potential investors and creditors and other users in assessing the amounts, timing, and uncertainty of prospective cash receipts from dividends or interest and the proceeds from the sale, redemption, or maturity of securities or loans. The prospects for those cash receipts are affected by an enterprise's ability to generate enough cash to meet its obligations when due and its other cash operating needs, to reinvest in operations, and to pay cash dividends and may also be affected by perceptions of investors and creditors generally about that ability, which affect market prices of the enterprise's securities. Thus, financial reporting should provide information to help investors, creditors, and others assess the amounts, timing, and uncertainty of prospective net cash inflows to the related enterprise.

Financial reporting should provide information about the economic resources of an enterprise, the claims to those resources (obligations of the enterprise to transfer resources to other entities and owners' equity), and the effects of transactions, events, and circumstances that change resources and claims to those resources.

Financial reporting should provide information about an enterprise's financial performance during a period. Investors and creditors often use information about the past to help in assessing the prospects of an enterprise. Thus, although investment and credit decisions reflect investors' and creditors' expectations about future enterprise performance, those expectations are commonly based at least partly on evaluations of past enterprise performance.

The primary focus of financial reporting is information about an enterprise's performance provided by measures of earnings and its components.

Financial reporting should provide information about how an enterprise obtains and spends cash, about its borrowing and repayment of borrowing, about its capital transactions, including cash dividends and other distributions of enterprise resources to owners, and about other factors that may affect an enterprise's liquidity or solvency.

Financial reporting should provide information about how management of an enterprise has discharged its stewardship responsibility to owners (stockholders) for the use of enterprise resources entrusted to it.

Financial reporting should provide information that is useful to managers and directors in making decisions in the interests of owners.

The 1979 Exposure Draft referred to above is entitled "Qualitative Characteristics: Criteria for Selecting and Evaluating Financial Accounting and Reporting Policies". The highlights of that opinion are set out at the outset, in the following form:

HIGHLIGHTS

This Statement is concerned with the criteria for selecting and evaluating financial accounting and reporting policies. Policy issues arise whenever alternative accounting and reporting methods or disclosures are possible. Examples of alternatives include choosing the attributes of assets and liabilities to be measured, selecting methods of cost allocation, and deciding on levels of disaggregation and formats for disclosure. Those who prepare, audit, and use financial reports, as well as the Financial Accounting Standards Board, must often select or evaluate accounting alternatives. The qualitative criteria are intended to guide those who choose between accounting and reporting alternatives to produce the "best" or most useful information to investors, creditors, and other users.

Decision making is the central concern, whether financial reporting is oriented to stewardship or to the sale, purchase, or redemption of investors' or creditors' securities or loans. A hierarchy of informational qualities described in this Statement places *decision usefulness* at its head.

Relevance and *reliability* are the two primary qualities that make accounting information useful for decision making. Subject to constraints imposed by cost and materiality, increased relevance and increased reliability are the characteristics that make information a more desirable commodity—that is, one useful to decision makers.

The qualities of useful information and the criteria for choice that they imply are the same whether the judgment about an accounting alternative is being made by the Board or a preparer. The criteria, however, cannot always be expected to produce agreement on a preferred choice. The Board must try to balance the needs of all members of its constituency, yet the preferences of different individuals and groups will not always coincide. Individual or private interests will, therefore, at times have to be sacrificed in selecting that accounting or reporting policy most useful to all.

Relevance is defined as the capability of information to make a difference to the decision maker by affecting the assessment of the probability of occurrence of some event relating to the attainment of a goal. Information is also relevant if it changes a decision maker's expectations about the results or consequences of actions or events, or if it confirms expectations. A reduction in the degree of uncertainty about the occurrence of a future action or event will be regarded as useful information by most decision makers. There are degrees of relevance—information can make a big difference or a small difference. In addition, what is relevant depends on the needs of the user, the information already available, and the ability to digest new information.

Timeliness and *understandability* are secondary aspects of relevance. Anything that improves these qualities increases the relevance of information.

Reliability is defined as the quality of information that allows users to depend on it to represent the conditions or events that it purports to represent. To be useful, information must be reliable as well as relevant. Reliability rests upon the extent to which the accounting description or measurement is *verifiable* and *representationally faithful*. Reliability also implies *completeness* of information, at least within the bounds of what is material and feasible, considering the cost.

Verifiability is a quality that may be demonstrated by securing a high degree of consensus among independent measurers using the same measurement methods. *Representational faithfulness*, on the other hand, refers to the correspondence between the accounting numbers and the resources or events that those numbers purport to represent. A high degree of correspondence, however, does not guarantee that an accounting measurement will be relevant to the user's needs if the resources or events represented by the measurement are inappropriate to the purpose at hand.

Relevance and reliability interact with each other. Though, ideally, the choice of an accounting alternative should produce information that is both more reliable and more relevant, it may be necessary to sacrifice some of one quality for a gain in the other. Moreover, measurements that are more representationally faithful may be less verifiable, making it difficult to say that the net result is a higher quality of information.

Materiality. Those who make accounting decisions about financial presentations constantly face the need to make judgments about materiality. The meaning of materiality has evolved mostly within the judicial process and under the Securities Acts. Materiality is a pervasive concept that is difficult to appreciate except as it relates to the other qualitative criteria, especially relevance and reliability. Generally, the omission or misstatement of an item in a financial report is material if it is probable that the judgment of a reasonable person relying upon the report would have been changed or influenced by the inclusion or correct statement of the item.

Quantitative materiality criteria may be given by the Board in specific standards in the future, as in the past, where appropriate. Nonetheless, it does not seem desirable for the Board to issue a set of general quantitative materiality guidelines for broad application.

Neutrality. A choice between accounting alternatives that is neutral is one that is free from bias towards a predetermined result. If information is relevant, reliable, and complete, it will be neutral. The Board's due process emphasizes the importance of choosing methods that produce neutral or "evenhanded" information. The Board will consider the economic effects of financial accounting standards—both before and after they are issued—as well as their costs and benefits.

Comparability. Information about a particular enterprise that is comparable with information about other enterprises is more useful than noncomparable information to those who must evaluate relative economic opportunities or performance. Likewise, *consistency* in the application of methods over time increases the informational value of many period-to-period comparisons of individual enterprise data.

Comparability and consistency do not require the use of an accounting or reporting alternative when better methods are at hand. Uniform reporting requirements or the continued use of an outmoded method imposed without regard for differences in the circumstances and informational needs of the individual enterprise can result in information that is not genuinely comparable and may also involve a loss of relevance or reliability.

Costs and *Benefits.* Whether the choice of an alternative is to be made at the level of the standard setter or the individual enterprise, consideration of the *costs* and *benefits* of supplying that information is essential. The costs and benefits of information are widely diffused and fall unevenly throughout the economy. Hence the task of assessment is extremely complex and subjective, but thinking about such issues imposes a discipline on the standard-setting process which cannot fail to be salutary.

4. THE DEVELOPMENT OF AUDITING STANDARDS

FIFLIS, CURRENT PROBLEMS OF ACCOUNTANTS' RESPONSIBILITIES TO THIRD PARTIES *

28 Vand.L.Rev. 31, 35–42 (1975).

* * *

B. THE AUDIT FUNCTION—A THUMBNAIL SKETCH

In essence, like most communication tasks, an audit consists of:

(a) Investigation and collection of data;

(b) Drawing of inferences from the findings; and

(c) Presentation of conclusions.

Many variations of an "audit" are possible, ranging from a complete, transaction by transaction reconstruction and investigation of everything done by the client's recordkeepers and other employees, to the opposite extreme of merely reading a statement of accounts receivable. Of necessity, practical limitations and the purpose of the examination will dictate the scope of the audit . . . .

(i) The Preliminary Survey of Facts

The first stage undertaken is planning the audit in conformity with the scope of the engagement. When an accountant is employed for a full audit of a client for the first time, usually the partner in charge will make a preliminary survey of the business, gleaning information about the nature of the business, sales trends, manufacturing, and marketing techniques, sources of raw materials, conditions in the industry, major customers, products, personnel, budgeting and accounting systems, characteristics of management, affiliations and the like. . . . Also, the basic accounting policies being followed by the client will be ascertained. These policies may be contained in company manuals and minutes or no consistent policies may be followed. . . .

(ii) Planning the "Audit Program"

After this preliminary survey, the next step in the planning stage is development of the "audit program," the guide to the audit describing the "audit procedures"; the what, how and when to do certain things in checking the client's accounting. . . .

"Auditing procedures" are designed to establish the reliability and integrity of the client's system of "internal controls" over its activities. "Internal control" means the client's record-keeping system and its system of checking the operations of the business, for example, the subsystem of matching reports of the receiving department for goods received with vendors' invoices. Audit procedures further include independent checking, such as confirmation of accounts receivable with customers ** or of bank balances with banks. . . . Although [the

---

** Ed note: The need for such confirmation had been dramatically illustrated in the late 1930's by the McKesson & Robbins, Inc. scandal. As Professor Fiflis described it, at pages 54–55 of his article, the AICPA's prior ambivalence on whether to require external confirmation of accounts re-

auditor] is not an insurer against fraud on the client, he must always give consideration to "the possibility [that] fraud may exist." Moreover, an even higher awareness must be had of the possibility of deliberate misrepresentation by management to investors. . . .

Based on the results of his review and testing of the client's internal control system as well as the results of the study of the preliminary survey, he will prepare a revised audit program, which will consist of specific procedures to test the reliability of the financial statements including, for example, such matters as testing and sampling the books of account for accuracy, reading corporate minutes, contracts and leases (internal evidence), and confirming bank accounts with the bank and receivables with the client's debtors (external evidence). . . .

(iii) Implementation and Adjustment of the Audit Program

The planning stage is completed at this point and the audit program is ready for implementation. In this stage of the process, the auditor must continue his healthy skepticism, for example, scrutinizing documents closely for suspicious deletions or interlineations, backdating, lack of dating, forgeries and the like. In every case, materiality and the probabilities of the situation will call for more or less attention. . . . Financial insecurity of the business also has a significant influence on how far the auditor's procedures must go.

When the auditor begins the audit program he will record in "working papers" his work and findings. . . . [S]tandard work-

ceivable, or independent verification of inventories, "enabled one Philip Musica, a twice-convicted confidence man, who rose to the presidency of McKesson & Robbins, Inc., to falsify the statements of that company to the tune of about 20 million dollars, about half being overstated accounts receivable and the rest fictitious inventories. Musica and his henchmen pretended to order goods from vendors who supposedly retained the goods in storage in their own warehouses for shipment to customers of McKesson & Robbins. Musica then caused checks to be issued in the names of the vendors, intercepted them and used the proceeds to make partial payments to McKesson & Robbins on resales pretended to have been made for the company. About 2.8 million dollars remained glued to the Musica gang's fingers. The result was that inventories as well as receivables were fictitious. The accountants failed to confirm the receivables or take any physical views of the inventories and hence failed to detect the wrongs."

This blatant fraud spurred the AICPA to try to put its auditing house in order. A new Committee on Auditing

Procedures was created, and the Committee's first Statement on Auditing Procedures specifically required that thereafter inventories should be actually observed by the auditor and the amount of receivables confirmed with the company's debtors. Noting this development with approval, the SEC refrained from undertaking to establish auditing procedures on its own, and instead followed the same path adopted with regard to accounting principles of leaving the development of standards largely to the profession. In 1974 the more than fifty statements promulgated by the AICPA Committee, subsequently renamed the Auditing Standards Executive Committee, were combined and republished as Statement on Auditing Standards No. 1. By 1980 the Committee had published 24 more Statements on Auditing Standards (which are customarily referred to by the abbreviation "SAS"). Under Rule 202 of the AICPA Code of Professional Ethics, these Statements on Auditing Standards are "considered to be interpretations of the generally accepted auditing standards, and departures from such statements must be justified by those who do not follow them".

ing papers are data from the corporate charter, by-laws, and minutes and analyses of accounts, prescribed by the audit program. One of the last working papers will be the management's "letter of representation" executed by the top officers. stating that no relevant post-balance-sheet-date events or other matters make the financial statements misleading, that disclosure of all known shortages has been made, that complete and correct corporate minutes have been supplied, and other matters of like import. . . .

(iv) The Auditor's Report

After completion of the field work and discussions with management of questions raised as to the form of the financial statements, the auditor will "report" on whether he conducted his examination in accordance with generally accepted auditing standards (GAAS) and whether the statements are presented in accordance with generally accepted accounting principles (GAAP) consistently observed in relation to the prior period. The distinction between accounting principles on the one hand and auditing standards and procedures on the other must be kept in mind for much misunderstanding has occurred in judicial opinions and other lawyers' work because of a lack of discrimination between them, even among sophisticated corporate lawyers. This may be because in some cases the two overlap. Nevertheless, by and large they are separate domains.

"Auditing standards" address the objectives to be attained by the audit and fix the standard of quality of performance of the audit procedures. GAAS, as established by the AICPA, require the auditor to exercise skill, independence and care, compel adequate planning and supervision of the audit including evaluation of the client's internal controls and independent confirmations, and require the report of compliance with GAAP.[24]

---

24. The "generally accepted auditing standards" as established by the AICPA have been briefly stated:

General Standards

1. The examination is to be performed by a person or persons having adequate technical training and proficiency as an auditor.
2. In all matters relating to the assignment, an independence in mental attitude is to be maintained by the auditor or auditors.
3. Due professional care is to be exercised in the performance of the examination and the preparation of the report.

Standards of Field Work

1. The work is to be adequately planned and assistants, if any, are to be properly supervised.
2. There is to be a proper study and evaluation of the existing internal control as a basis for reliance thereon and for the determination of the resultant extent of the tests to which auditing procedures are to be restricted.
3. Sufficient competent evidential matter is to be obtained through inspection, observation, inquiries, and confirmations to afford a reasonable basis for an opinion regarding the financial statements under examination.

Standards of Reporting

1. The report shall state whether the financial statements are presented in accordance with generally accepted accounting principles.
2. The report shall state whether such principles have been consistently observed in the current period in relation to the preceding period.

* * *

The auditor's report may be:

(a) "Unqualified"—indicating that the statements are presented fairly, that his opinion was formed on the basis of an examination made in accordance with GAAS, and that the statements conform with GAAP consistently applied, and include all disclosures necessary to make the statements not misleading. This is the standard accountant's report found affixed to most audited financial statements.[26]

(b) "Qualified"—same as above with certain qualifications and clearly explained reasons and descriptions of the effect on the statements.

(c) "Adverse"—stating that the statements are not fairly presented in conformity with GAAP, or

(d) A "Disclaimer of Opinion"—stating that the auditor is unable to express an opinion because of a serious limitation on the scope of the examination.

This completes the audit.

* * *

Currently, one of the matters of most concern to auditors is the extent of their responsibility to detect fraud or other improprieties:

3. Informative disclosures in the financial statements are to be regarded as reasonably adequate unless otherwise stated in the report.

4. The report shall either contain an expression of opinion regarding the financial statements, taken as a whole, or an assertion to the effect that an opinion cannot be expressed. When an overall opinion cannot be expressed, the reasons therefor should be stated. In all cases where an auditor's name is associated with financial statements, the report should contain a clear-cut indication of the character of the auditor's examination, if any, and the degree of responsibility he is taking.

SAS No. 1, ...

26. Typically, it reads:
Auditors' Report
To the Shareholders of X Corporation:
We have examined the consolidated balance sheet of X Corporation (a Delaware corporation) and subsidiaries as of December 31, 19—, and the related statements of consolidated earnings retained for requirements of the business and consolidated application of funds for the year then ended. Our examination was made in accordance with generally accepted auditing standards, and accordingly included such tests of the accounting records and such other auditing procedures as we considered necessary in the circumstances.

In our opinion, the financial statements described above present fairly the financial position of X Corporation and subsidiaries as of December 31, 19—, and the results of their operations and application of funds for the year then ended, in conformity with generally accepted accounting principles applied on a basis consistent with that of the preceding year.

Chicago, Illinois, March 19, 19—
/s/Readem & Weep

STATEMENT ON AUDITING STANDARDS NO. 16 *

Auditing Standards Executive Committee, 1977.

THE INDEPENDENT AUDITOR'S RESPONSIBILITY
FOR THE DETECTION OF ERRORS
OR IRREGULARITIES

1.   This Statement provides guidance on the independent auditor's responsibility for detecting errors or irregularities when making an examination of financial statements in accordance with generally accepted auditing standards. It also discusses procedures that the auditor should perform when his examination indicates that material errors or irregularities may exist.

2.   The term *errors* refers to unintentional mistakes in financial statements and includes mathematical or clerical mistakes in the underlying records and accounting data from which the financial statements were prepared, mistakes in the application of accounting principles, and oversight or misinterpretation of facts that existed at the time the financial statements were prepared.

3.   The term *irregularities* refers to intentional distortions of financial statements, such as deliberate misrepresentations by management, sometimes referred to as management fraud, or misappropriations of assets, sometimes referred to as defalcations.[1] Irregularities in financial statements may result from the misrepresentation or omission of the effects of events or transactions; manipulation, falsification, or alteration of records or documents; omission of significant information from records or documents; recording of transactions without substance; intentional misapplication of accounting principles; or misappropriation of assets for the benefit of management, employees, or third parties. Such acts may be accompanied by the use of false or misleading records or documents and may involve one or more individuals among management, employees, or third parties.

Relationship of Independent Audits to Other Business Controls

4.   Generally, entities operate with certain controls. Examples of controls for business entities include legal requirements, the monitoring of management activities by boards of directors and their audit committees, the internal audit function, and internal accounting control procedures. Those who rely on financial statements look to entities' controls together with independent audits to provide reasonable assurance that financial statements are not materially misstated as a result of errors or irregularities.

The Auditor's Responsibility

5.   The independent auditor's objective in making an examination of financial statements in accordance with generally accepted

---

1.   For guidance on other actions that an independent auditor should consider with respect to the possible illegality of such acts, see SAS No. 17, "Illegal Acts by Clients." [Footnotes are by the Committee.]

auditing standards is to form an opinion on whether the financial statements present fairly financial position, results of operations, and changes in financial position in conformity with generally accepted accounting principles consistently applied. Consequently, under generally accepted auditing standards the independent auditor has the responsibility, within the inherent limitations of the auditing process (see paragraphs 11–13), to plan his examination (see paragraphs 6–10) to search for errors or irregularities that would have a material effect on the financial statements, and to exercise due skill and care in the conduct of that examination. The auditor's search for material errors or irregularities ordinarily is accomplished by the performance of those auditing procedures that in his judgment are appropriate in the circumstances to form an opinion on the financial statements; extended auditing procedures are required if the auditor's examination indicates that material errors or irregularities may exist (see paragraph 14). An independent auditor's standard report implicitly indicates his belief that the financial statements taken as a whole are not materially misstated as a result of errors or irregularities.

The Possibility of Errors or Irregularities

6. The independent auditor's plan for an examination in accordance with generally accepted auditing standards is influenced by the possibility of material errors or irregularities. The auditor should plan and perform his examination with an attitude of professional skepticism, recognizing that the application of his auditing procedures may produce evidential matter indicating the possibility of errors or irregularities. The scope of the auditor's examination would be affected by his consideration of internal accounting control, by the results of his substantive tests, and by circumstances that raise questions concerning the integrity of management.

Internal Accounting Control and Substantive Tests

7. Management is responsible for establishing and maintaining internal accounting control procedures including appropriate supervisory review procedures necessary for adherence to adopted policies and prescribed procedures and for identification of errors and irregularities. On the other hand, the auditor evaluates internal accounting control to establish a basis for any reliance thereon in determining the nature, timing, and extent of audit tests to be applied in his examination of the financial statements. SAS No. 1, section 320.65–.66, suggests the following approach to the auditor's evaluation of internal accounting control:

A conceptually logical approach to the auditor's evaluation of accounting control, which focuses directly on the purpose of preventing or detecting material errors and irregularities in financial statements, is to apply the following steps in considering each significant class of transactions and related assets involved in the audit:

a Consider the types of errors and irregularities that could occur.

b Determine the accounting control procedures that should prevent or detect such errors and irregularities.

c Determine whether the necessary procedures are prescribed and are being followed satisfactorily.

d Evaluate any weaknesses—i. e., types of potential errors and irregularities not covered by existing control procedures—to determine their effect on (1) the nature, timing, or extent of auditing procedures to be applied and (2) suggestions to be made to the client.

In the practical application of the foregoing approach, the first two steps are performed primarily through the development of questionnaires, checklists, instructions, or similar generalized material used by the auditor. However, professional judgment is required in interpreting, adapting, or expanding such generalized material as appropriate in particular situations. The third step is accomplished through the review of the system and tests of compliance and the final step through the exercise of professional judgment in evaluating the information obtained in the preceding steps.

In evaluating internal accounting control, the auditor uses accumulated experience and understanding of the points of risk for possible errors and irregularities.

8. Effective internal accounting control reduces the probability that errors or irregularities will occur, but does not eliminate the possibility that they may occur. There are inherent limitations that should be recognized in considering the potential effectiveness of internal accounting control procedures. Further, whether the objectives of internal accounting control will be achieved depends in substantial part on the competence and integrity of company personnel. Consequently, the auditor does not place complete reliance on internal accounting control. . . .

Thus, the auditor's examination includes substantive tests that are designed to obtain evidential matter concerning the validity and propriety of the accounting treatment of transactions and balances or, conversely, evidential matter indicating the possibility of material errors or irregularities therein even in the absence of material weaknesses [2] in internal accounting control. Examples of circumstances that may lead the auditor to question whether material errors or possible irregularities exist include the following: (a) discrepancies within the accounting records, such as a difference between a control account and its supporting subsidiary records; (b) differences disclosed by confirmations; (c) significantly fewer responses to confirmation requests than expected; (d) transactions not supported by proper documentation; (e) transactions not recorded in accordance with management's general or specific authorization; and (f) the completion of unusual transactions at or near year end. However, the existence of any of those circumstances does not necessarily mean that material errors or irregularities do exist.

2. SAS No. 1, section 320.68, defines a material weakness as follows:
" . . . a condition in which the auditor believes the prescribed procedures or the degree of compliance with them does not provide reasonable assurance that errors or irregularities in amounts that would be material in the financial statements being audited would be prevented or detected within a timely period by employees in the normal course of performing their assigned functions."

Integrity of Management

9.   The auditor should recognize that management can direct subordinates to record or conceal transactions in a manner that could result in a material misstatement of the financial statements. Thus, management can perpetrate irregularities by overriding controls that would prevent similar irregularities by other employees. Consequently, the auditor should be aware of the importance of management's integrity to the effective operation of internal accounting control procedures and should consider whether there are circumstances that might predispose management to misstate financial statements. Such circumstances might include those of a company that is in an industry experiencing a large number of business failures, or that lacks sufficient working capital or credit to continue operations.

10.   The auditor should consider the possibility that management may have made material misrepresentations or may have overridden control procedures. The auditor's consideration should include factors such as the nature of the entity being audited, the susceptibility to irregularities of the item or transaction being examined, the degree of authority vested at various management levels, and prior experience with the entity. For example, the following circumstances, although not necessarily indicative of the presence of irregularities, may cause the auditor to be concerned about the possibility that management may have made material misrepresentations or overridden internal control procedures: (a) the company does not correct material weaknesses in internal accounting control that are practicable to correct; (b) key financial positions, such as controller, have a high turnover rate; or (c) the accounting and financial functions appear to be understaffed, resulting in a constant crisis condition and related loss of controls. However, unless the auditor's examination reveals evidential matter to the contrary, it is reasonable for him to assume that management has not made material misrepresentations or has not overridden control procedures.

Inherent Limitations of an Audit

11.   An examination made in accordance with generally accepted auditing standards is subject to the inherent limitations of the auditing process. As with certain business controls, the costs of audits should bear a reasonable relationship to the benefits expected to be derived. As a result, the concept of selective testing of the data being examined, which involves judgment both as to the number of transactions to be examined and as to the areas to be tested, has been generally accepted as a valid and sufficient basis for an auditor to express an opinion on financial statements. Thus, the auditor's examination, based on the concept of selective testing of the data being examined, is subject to the inherent risk that material errors or irregularities, if they exist, will not be detected.

12.   The risk that material errors or irregularities will not be detected is increased by the possibility of management's override of internal controls, collusion, forgery, or unrecorded transactions. Certain acts, such as collusion between client personnel and third parties or among management or employees of the client, may result in misrepresentations being made to the auditor or in the presentation to the auditor of falsified records or documents that appear truthful and

genuine. Unless the auditor's examination reveals evidential matter to the contrary, his reliance on the truthfulness of certain representations and on the genuineness of records and documents obtained during his examination is reasonable. Examples of representations that are normally accepted by the auditor are (a) those of management concerning its intent or knowledge and the completeness of the entity's records and (b) those of third parties, such as confirmations of accounts receivable by debtors and accounts payable by creditors, and confirmations and other documents received from banks or other depositaries. Further, the auditor cannot be expected to extend his auditing procedures to seek to detect unrecorded transactions unless evidential matter obtained during his examination indicates that they may exist. For example, an auditor ordinarily would not extend his auditing procedures to seek failures to record the receipt of cash from unexpected sources.

13. In view of those and other limitations on the effectiveness of auditing procedures, the subsequent discovery that errors or irregularities existed during the period covered by the independent auditor's examination does not, in itself, indicate inadequate performance on his part. The auditor is not an insurer or guarantor; if his examination was made in accordance with generally accepted auditing standards, he has fulfilled his professional responsibility.

Procedures When the Examination Indicates That Errors or Irregularities May Exist

14. If the independent auditor's examination causes him to believe that material errors or irregularities may exist, he should consider their implications and discuss the matter and the extent of any further investigation with an appropriate level of management that is at least one level above those involved. If after such discussions the auditor continues to believe that material errors or irregularities may exist, he should determine that the board of directors or its audit committee is aware of the circumstances. Also, he should attempt to obtain sufficient evidential matter to determine whether in fact material errors or irregularities exist and, if so, their effect. In this regard, the auditor may wish to consult with the client's legal counsel on matters concerning questions of law. If practicable, the auditor should extend his auditing procedures in an effort to obtain such evidential matter. In some circumstances, however, it may be impracticable or impossible to obtain sufficient evidential matter to determine the existence, or related effect, of material errors or possible irregularities, or management may impose a limitation on the scope of the auditor's search for the evidential matter needed to reach a conclusion.[3] When the auditor's examination indicates the presence of errors or possible irregularities, and the auditor remains uncertain about whether these errors or possible irregularities may materially affect the financial statements, he should qualify his opinion or disclaim an opinion on the financial statements and, depending on the circumstances, consider withdrawing from the engagement, indicating his reasons and findings in

---

3. For a discussion of the effect of a restriction on the scope of an auditor's examination whether imposed by the client or by circumstances, see SAS No. 2, "Reports on Audited Financial Statements," paragraphs 10 through 13.

writing to the board of directors. In such circumstances, the auditor may wish to consult with his legal counsel.

15. The independent auditor's examination may reveal errors or possible irregularities that he concludes could not be so significant as to materially affect the financial statements he is examining. For example, irregularities involving peculations from a small imprest fund would normally be of little significance because both the manner of operating the fund and its size would tend to establish a limitation on the amount of a loss. The auditor should refer such matters to an appropriate level of management that is at least one level above those involved, with the recommendation that the matter be pursued to a conclusion. Also, the auditor should consider the effect of any immaterial irregularity as it may relate to other aspects of his examination, such as the role of the personnel involved in the system of internal accounting control.

The Statement entitled "The Independent Auditor's Responsibility for the Detection of Errors or Irregularities" was adopted by the assenting votes of nineteen members of the Committee, of whom four, Messrs. Lamb, Ross, Solomon, and Tiano, assented with qualifications. Messrs. Groveman and Nelson dissented.

Mr. Solomon qualifies his assent to the issuance of this Statement because he objects to paragraph 5 since it does not provide with sufficient clarity that an examination in accordance with generally accepted auditing standards is not required to include specific procedures designed to detect errors and irregularities. He believes that paragraph 5 should clearly state his belief of what was intended, that such an examination requires only that the auditor plan his examination with an awareness of the possibility of errors or irregularities that would have a material effect on the financial statements.

Mr. Tiano approves the issuance of this Statement, but qualifies his assent because he believes that paragraph 5 may be misinterpreted to convey conclusions regarding the auditor's responsibility to detect irregularities that go beyond the responsibility he understands was intended to be established by the Statement. This is in part caused by the referenced paragraphs 11 through 13 not clearly stating that, because of the inherent limitations of the auditing process, even an extension of customary auditing procedures to most or all recorded transactions or records of an entity would not necessarily assure that financial statements are not materially misstated as a result of errors or irregularities. The possible misinterpretation is also due to not discussing separately the different levels of risk and probability of detection that exist with respect to errors as distinguished from irregularities. He believes that an examination made in accordance with generally accepted auditing standards does provide a reasonable basis for a professional judgment by the independent auditor that the financial statements are not materially misstated as a result of errors; however, the magnitude of the inherent limitations of the auditing process and the reliance which the auditor, in the absence of indications to the contrary, places on evidential matter which appears truthful and genuine (as described in paragraph 12), do not provide a basis for the auditor to indicate implicitly or otherwise a positive belief that the financial statements are not materially misstated as a result of irregularities, as appears to be suggested in paragraph 5. Instead, the auditor, in expressing his opinion on the financial statements, is only indicating that as a result of his auditing procedures, he has no reason to believe that the financial statements are materially misstated as a result of irregularities (as defined in paragraph 3).

Mr. Tiano also believes that misinterpretation of the penultimate sentence of paragraph 5 is possible because it does not clearly convey what he understands was intended; that is, that the Statement does not contemplate auditing procedures beyond those customarily performed under existing generally accepted auditing standards and that additional procedures are required only when the auditor suspects that irregularities do exist rather than when there is merely a possibility that irregularities may exist. . . .

NOTE ON INTERNAL ACCOUNTING CONTROL

Both Professor Fiflis' article and SAS No. 16 indicate how important a company's internal accounting control is to the audit process in particular and the overall accounting picture in general. As noted earlier, it is management's responsibility to prepare financial statements for the enterprise, and appropriate procedures for recording and collecting the relevant financial data are essential for this purpose. (In addition, management has the responsibility of safe-guarding the resources under its stewardship, which requires a comprehensive system of accountability.) To be sure, management's data will be subjected to careful review by the auditors, including a variety of tests to confirm the validity of the figures; but it is obviously not feasible to check every item and transaction for the period, and hence the management figures must be relied upon to a considerable extent. This makes the auditors' examination of the company's internal accounting control all the more important; the stronger the internal control system, the more the auditor may justifiably rely upon the company's data, though of course some independent confirmation is essential in any event.

The role of internal accounting control was increased by an order of magnitude as a result of enactment of the federal Foreign Corrupt Practices Act of 1977. That Act amended § 13(b) of the Securities Exchange Act by adding a new Section 2, which provides that companies subject to the jurisdiction of the SEC are required to—

(A) make and keep books, records, and accounts, which, in reasonable detail, accurately and fairly reflect the transactions and dispositions of the assets of the issuer; and

(B) devise and maintain a system of internal accounting controls sufficient to provide reasonable assurances that—

(i) transactions are executed in accordance with management's general or specific authorization;

(ii) transactions are recorded as necessary (I) to permit preparation of financial statements in conformity with generally accepted accounting principles or any other criteria applicable to such statements, and (II) to maintain accountability for assets;

(iii) access to assets is permitted only in accordance with management's general or specific authorization; and

(iv) the recorded accountability for assets is compared with the existing assets at reasonable intervals and appropriate action is taken with respect to any differences.

Notice that although the revelations about improper overseas payments during the 1970's undoubtedly served as the catalyst for enactment of the FCPA, and a number of its provisions do indeed deal expressly with extra-territorial bribery, the above-quoted sections are not at all limited to cases involving foreign corruption. Rather they apply generally to all subject companies, and these provisions certainly represent the most substantial legislative foray into the accounting arena in recent memory. Just how far they go is obvious from a glance at paragraph A, which in effect mandates proper bookkeeping (and maybe more, depending upon the scope of the "accurately" requirement). Equally significant is the fact that the clauses of paragraph B come almost verbatim from the statement of the objectives of internal accounting control contained in the AICPA's SAS No. 1 (see page 109, supra). However, remember that the objectives stated in SAS No. 1 are aimed at providing guidance to auditors with respect to the evaluation of internal accounting control in the context of reviewing the financial statements. The FCPA provisions, on the other hand, are applicable directly to the companies, and hence management has a statutory obligation to comply with the requirements. The FCPA does not contain any scienter requirement, unlike § 10(b) of the Exchange Act, page 125, infra, or any express reference to materiality either, although it may be that the sprinkling of the qualifying adjective "reasonable" throughout the statute will provide protection against liability for inadvertent or insignificant errors.

Because the FCPA became a part of the Securities Exchange Act, the SEC has general authority to promulgate rules and regulations thereunder. In 1979 the Commission published for comment a set of proposed rules, in Release No. 34–15772, which would require a statement by management on the state of the company's internal accounting control, plus a report on that statement by the independent auditor. The proposed rules have provoked substantial opposition, on the ground, inter alia, that they go beyond the statute. See, e. g., the report of a special ABA committee, under the heading "Statement of Management on Internal Accounting Control", 35 Bus.Law. 311 (1979). This is probably only the opening salvo in what seems destined to be a lengthy period of controversy, as management, the accounting profession, and the courts adjust to the new accounting environment created by this unprecedented statutory sally into the domain of internal accounting control.

—————

5. THE CURRENT RELATIONSHIP BETWEEN THE SEC AND THE PROFESSION IN THE ESTABLISHMENT OF ACCOUNTING PRINCIPLES

As the following materials indicate, the SEC has expressly agreed to treat promulgations of the FASB as determinative of whether particular accounting principles have substantial authoritative support, but not everyone in the profession was pleased by this development:

ACCOUNTING SERIES RELEASE NO. 150

Securities and Exchange Commission, 1973.

Various Acts of Congress administered by the Securities and Exchange Commission clearly state the authority of the Commission to prescribe the methods to be followed in the preparation of accounts and the form and content of financial statements to be filed under the Acts and the responsibility to assure that investors are furnished with information necessary for informed investment decisions. In meeting this statutory responsibility effectively, in recognition of the expertise, energy and resources of the accounting profession, and without abdicating its responsibilities, the Commission has historically looked to the standard-setting bodies designated by the profession to provide leadership in establishing and improving accounting principles. The determinations by these bodies have been regarded by the Commission, with minor exceptions, as being responsive to the needs of investors.

The body presently designated by the Council of the American Institute of Certified Public Accountants (AICPA) to establish accounting principles is the Financial Accounting Standards Board (FASB). This designation by the AICPA followed the issuance of a report in March 1972 recommending the formation of the FASB, after a study of the matter by a broadly based study group. The recommendations contained in that report were widely endorsed by industry, financial analysts, accounting educators, and practicing accountants. The Commission endorsed the establishment of the FASB in the belief that the Board would provide an institutional framework which will permit prompt and responsible actions flowing from research and consideration of varying viewpoints. The collective experience and expertise of the members of the FASB and the individuals and professional organizations supporting it are substantial. Equally important, the commitment of resources to the FASB is impressive evidence of the willingness and intention of the private sector to support the FASB in accomplishing its task. In view of these considerations, the Commission intends to continue its policy of looking to the private sector for leadership in establishing and improving accounting principles and standards through the FASB with the expectation that the body's conclusions will promote the interests of investors.

In Accounting Series Release No. 4 (1938) the Commission stated its policy that financial statements prepared in accordance with accounting practices for which there was no substantial authoritative support were presumed to be misleading and that footnote or other disclosure would not avoid this presumption. It also stated that, where there was a difference of opinion between the Commission and a registrant as to the proper accounting to be followed in a particular case, disclosure would be accepted in lieu of correction of the financial statements themselves only if substantial authoritative support existed for the accounting practices followed by the registrant and the position of the Commission had not been expressed in rules, regulations or other official releases. For purposes of this policy, principles, standards and practices promulgated by the FASB in its Statements and Interpretations [1] will be considered by the Commission as having substantial authoritative support, and those contrary to such FASB promulgations will be considered [2] to have no such support.

In the exercise of its statutory authority with respect to the form and content of filings under the Acts, the Commission has the responsibility to assure that investors are provided with adequate information. A significant portion of the necessary information is provided by a set of basic financial statements (including the notes thereto) which conform to generally accepted accounting principles. Information in addition to that included in financial statements conforming to generally accepted accounting principles is also necessary. Such additional disclosures are required to be made in various fashions, such as in financial statements and schedules reported on by independent public accountants or as textual statements required by items in the applicable forms and reports filed with the Commission. The Commission will continue to identify areas where investor information needs exist and will determine the appropriate methods of disclosure to meet these needs.

It must be recognized that in its administration of the Federal Securities Acts and in its review of filings under such Acts, the Commission staff will continue as it has in the past to take such action on a day-to-day basis as may be appropriate to resolve specific problems of accounting and reporting under the particular factual circumstances involved in filings and reports of individual registrants.

The Commission believes that the foregoing statement of policy provides a sound basis for the Commission and the FASB to make sig-

1. Accounting Research Bulletins of the Committee on Accounting Procedure of the American Institute of Certified Public Accountants and effective opinions of the Accounting Principles Board of the Institute should be considered as continuing in force with the same degree of authority except to the extent altered, amended, supplemented, revoked or superseded by one or more Statements of Financial Accounting Standards issued by the FASB.

2. It should be noted that Rule 203 of the Rules of Conduct of the Code of Ethics of the AICPA provides that it is necessary to depart from accounting principles promulgated by the body designated by the Council of the AICPA if, due to unusual circumstances, failure to do so would result in misleading financial statements. In such a case, the use of other principles may be accepted or required by the Commission.

nificant contributions to meeting the needs of registrants and investors.

By the Commission.

George A. Fitzsimmons
[*Secretary*]

ARTHUR ANDERSEN & CO. v. SEC

United States District Court, Northern District Illinois, 1976.
CCH Fed.Sec.L.Rep., 1976–7 Transl.Bind., ¶ 95,720.

TRANSCRIPT OF PROCEEDINGS

THE COURT: . . . I had hoped I would have something written for you this morning, but . . . I will give it to you orally. If any of the parties desire review of the decision, the reporter will transcribe it for you, and I will sign it as written findings and conclusions.

* * *

Defendant's alleged wrong is said to consist of violations of the rule-making provisions of the Administrative Procedure Act, . . . the SEC's own rule-making regulations . . . and generally of the laws and Constitution of the United States.

The plaintiff, Arthur Andersen & Company, is a general partnership organized and existing under the laws of the State of Illinois with its principal office located in Chicago. It is a firm of independent public accountants. The firm's activities include the examination of and reporting on the financial statements of business enterprises and public bodies. Many of the firm's clients are subject to the jurisdiction of the SEC and are required to include financial statements together with Arthur Andersen's audit reports thereon and filings under the various Acts which are administered and enforced by the SEC. These filings include, but are not limited to registration statements filed pursuant to the Securities Act of 1933 and annual and periodic reports and proxy statements filed pursuant to the Securities Exchange Act of 1934.

In all of these filings, the plaintiff is required to observe the rules and regulations promulgated by the SEC which govern the form and content of financial statements; in particular, the plaintiff is required to observe the SEC's Regulation SX governing accounting presentations and filings with the SEC, Rule 202(c) of [which] . . . requires plaintiff to express an opinion relating to the financial statements filed by its clients with the SEC and the accounting principles and practices reflected therein.

The rule does not by itself define or impose any limitations or prerequisites concerning the accounting principles and practices used in preparing the statements; however, the defendant has issued a series of statements known as Accounting Series Releases which are incorporated into . . . Regulation SX . . . . .

* * *

The plaintiff seeks a preliminary injunction enjoining and restraining the defendant from enforcing or applying two issuances known as ASR–150 and ASR–177 *, the content and details of which will be touched upon momentarily.

The standards for the issuance of a preliminary injunction are well-known, and the parties and their counsel have addressed them.

The first, in view of the immediacy of the relief which is given, is that the plaintiff demonstrate a likelihood of success on the merits. The second is that the plaintiff demonstrate that it will suffer irreparable harm if the preliminary relief is not granted. The third is that there be a showing that the defendant will not suffer irreparable harm as a consequence of any preliminary relief. And the fourth is that the issuance of the preliminary relief will not be adverse to the public interest.

The first item in controversy is defendant's ASR–150, which was issued on December the 20th, 1973. The defendant concedes that the rule-making provisions of the Administrative Procedure Act and the Commission were not followed prior to the issuance of ASR–150 because as defendant asserts, it is not a rule; rather it is concerned with defendant's recognition of certain accounting principles enjoying widespread recognition in the accounting profession.

Some history, brief history, is warranted in appraising the significance, purpose and impact of ASR–150.

On April 25, 1938, prior to the enactment of the Administrative Procedure Act, the defendant issued its ASR–4 [described in ASR No. 150, above].

* * *

The meaning of the expression "substantial authoritative support" contained in ASR–4 was left, as I perceive the record and briefs, to a case-by-case determination. While the Committee on Accounting Procedures of the American Institute of Certified Public Accountants issued research bulletins in respect to accounting principles from time to time, and later the Accounting Principles Board of the Institute issued opinions in regard to those principles, there was, as we see it, no single source of authoritative standards. Although the defendant Commission has and has had the power to promulgate its own accounting standards, it has elected historically in deference to and in cooperation with the accounting profession not to do so.

In 1973, conditions within the accounting profession changed. The American Institute of Certified Public Accountants designated the Financial Accounting Standards Board of the Financial Accounting Foundation as the body to establish authoritative accounting principles pursuant to Rule 203 of the American Institute of Certified Public Accountants, which rule was in turn made obligatory upon the members of the AICPA.

It was thereafter that ASR–150 was issued by the SEC. After summarizing the content and import of ASR–4, ASR–150 provides in that respect, as I perceive it, deemed offensive by the plaintiff, as follows: "For the purposes of this policy"—that being the policy previously articulated in ASR–4—"For the purposes of this policy, principles, standards and practices promulgated by the FASB in its state-

---

* Portions of the opinion dealing with
ASR No. 177 omitted.

ments and interpretations will be considered by the Commission as having substantial authoritative support, and those contrary to such FASB promulgations will be considered to have no such support."

By ASR–150, the defendant SEC has said no more than that it will henceforth, in making its long-standing inquiry into whether a financial statement has been prepared in accord with accepted accounting principles, apply and look to the substantial authoritative support provided by the FASB, will be considered as having substantial authoritative support, while those contrary to the principles approved by the FASB will not be.

In taking this position, in my judgment, the SEC has done no more than state the obvious. Now that an authoritative profession-accepted collection of accounting principles exists, it will look to them first in making its own judgment on the question of authoritative support.

On the other hand, a principle contrary to the FASB standards will be considered without support. No mention is made for a principle which is neither embraced by nor rejected by the FASB.

ASR–150 emerges, then, as a method by which the SEC will evaluate accounting principles. It does not ordain the result of that evaluation. It does not prescribe per se approval to or rejection of any accounting principle. It merely acknowledges a fact, the existence of an authoritative body of principles, and says that it will credit those principles.

It is not a conditional imperative, which is the characteristic of a substantive rule.

Nor is ASR–150 rendered invalid by the hyperbole that the SEC has delegated impermissibly its rule-making authority to FASB. True, ASR–150 will encompass not only past, but future accounting principles approved by the FASB, but those prospective principles will have no greater force than the present ones do. The SEC will consider them authoritative, which they clearly are and will be, but ASR–150 does not even suggest that the SEC will abdicate its ultimate responsibility to judge the propriety of the accounting principles employed by a registrant.

Accordingly, as to ASR–150, we have concluded preliminarily that the plaintiff has failed to show the requisite likelihood of success on the merits, so as to entitle it to preliminary relief.

* * *

There is in the case another question which is traditionally a threshold inquiry: plaintiff's standing to complain. We have doubts on that score, but because the resolution of that issue adverse to the plaintiff would result in the termination of the action, we decline in this hurried setting to resolve it. That can await more mature deliberations even while this order is reviewed by a reviewing court, should that be the course the plaintiff takes.*

---

* In a later opinion it was held that the plaintiff lacked standing to sue. CCH Fed.Sec.L.Rep. ¶ 96,374 (D.C.N.D.Ill. 1978). The court found that the plaintiff had not shown sufficient likelihood of injury to itself, its clients, or the public interest from compliance with these SEC pronouncements to confer standing.

We turn briefly, however, to the questions of irreparable harm. Insofar as plaintiff is concerned, we see no harm flowing to it from the SEC's application of the evaluative standards articulated in ASR–150. Plaintiff has pointed out none which are offensive to it. We must assume on this record that plaintiff abides the teachings of the FASB in its day-by-day practice.

On the other hand, a preliminary injunction could work irreparable harm to the SEC in the discharge of its duties. What would be the consequence of such an injunction? Would the SEC be precluded from giving any credence to the FASB standards? And what credence should the balance of the accounting profession give those standards?

* * *

For the foregoing reasons, the plaintiff's motion for a preliminary injunction will be denied.

---

6. THE CURRENT LITIGATION SETTING UNDER THE FEDERAL SECURITIES LAWS

The tremendous proliferation of law suits against accountants referred to by Professor Eisenberg above is merely one aspect of the explosion in securities law actions brought by all sorts of plaintiffs against defendants of every stripe: the issuing corporation; individual officers, directors and stockholders; underwriters and brokers; and various outside professionals, such as accountants and lawyers. These actions are normally predicated upon one or more of the many provisions in the federal securities laws imposing liability, either expressly or by implication, upon practically anyone involved in a securities transaction who is guilty of, or abets, a failure to make full, fair and accurate disclosure about the securities. Obviously, the very heart of this required disclosure is the financial information contained in the accounting statements of the company whose securities are involved; hence accountants, with their special responsibility for reviewing the financial statements, have found themselves right in the eye of this litigation storm churned up by disappointed investors, along side the company itself (which has often become defunct) and its management.

From the range of provisions in the securities laws upon which such liability may be based, it is sufficient here merely to note the two most important categories: sections 11 and 12 of the Securities Act of 1933, which prohibit false statements in connection with offerings of new securities, and impose what in effect amounts to a reasonable care standard; and SEC Rule 10b–5 (set out in footnote 5 on page 131, infra), which was promulgated under § 10(b) of the Securities Exchange Act of 1934 and prohibits misrepresentation in connection with any purchase or sale or securities, subject to a standard which after considerable uncertainty has been definitively determined by the Supreme Court to require *scienter*, that is, some intention or at least knowledge, something more than negligence, at least in private damage actions. Ernst & Ernst v. Hochfelder, 425 U.S. 185, 96 S.Ct. 1375, 47 L.Ed.2d 668 (1976).

The following case should be read "once over lightly" at this point, just to get a feel for the role of financial statements in the current litigation context under the federal securities laws:

HERZFELD v. LAVENTHOL, KREKSTEIN, HORWATH & HORWATH *

United States Court of Appeals, Second Circuit, 1976.
540 F.2d 27.

MOORE, CIRCUIT JUDGE: Laventhol, Krekstein, Horwath & Horwath, a firm of certified public accountants ("Laventhol") appeals from an amended judgment for the amount of $153,000, entered against it and in favor of plaintiff, Gerald L. Herzfeld ("Herzfeld") after a trial to the Court. . . .

Originally, Herzfeld had sued Laventhol and eleven other defendants primarily to recover $510,000 which he claimed that he had paid for certain securities of Firestone Group, Ltd. ("FGL"), namely, two FGL units, each unit consisting of a $250,000 FGL note and 5000 shares of FGL stock at $1 a share, a total of $255,000 per unit. The substance of Herzfeld's charges was that the representations made to him by the defendants in connection with the purchase were materially misleading and that there were omissions of material facts, all of which were inducing factors, and on which he relied, in making his purchase and in not exercising his right of rescission. Herzfeld predicated his suit upon alleged violations of the securities laws of the United States, Section 352–c of the New York General Business Law and common law fraud.

That suit was settled by all defendants except Laventhol for $357,000. Thereafter, by an amended complaint, Herzfeld sought, to recoup the balance ($153,000) of the $510,000 from Laventhol. . . .

FGL was a California company engaged principally in the business of purchasing real estate and thereafter syndicating or reselling it. In November 1969, FGL planned to raise $7,500,000 by the private placement through Allen and Company, Incorporated, of the aforementioned units. Lee Meyer, a defendant, was an Allen vice-president and also a FGL director.

Through friends, Herzfeld became interested in the venture. A purchase agreement, entitled "Note and Stock Purchase Agreement", dated November 10, 1969, was delivered to Herzfeld by FGL with an accompanying letter which advised him that the closing date for the sale of the notes would be December 16, 1969, "to permit the preparation of audited financial statements, as at and for the eleven months ended November 30, 1969, copies of which will be delivered to you."

---

* Portions of the opinion dealing with the defendant's claims for contribution from others, and many of the footnotes, omitted.

The letter added that these "audited statements will serve as the basis for confirming the unaudited Projected Financial Statements annexed to the Note and Stock Purchase Agreement as Exhibit B."

Exhibit B was a balance sheet and income statement. It portrayed FGL as a strikingly profitable corporation with over $20 million in assets, a net worth of close to a million dollars, sales of over $17 million, deferred income of $2.7 million and an after-tax of $315,-000. FGL warranted that it fairly presented its financial condition as at November 30, 1969.

Herzfeld read the entire income statement and the balance sheet and noted that it represented FGL as being very profitable, with earnings of approximately $2 a share for the period ending November 30, 1969. He then signed the agreement to purchase two units thereunder.

To prepare the promised audit (to be as of November 30, 1969), FGL retained Laventhol as the accountants for the task. The Herzfeld-Laventhol lawsuit and this appeal therefrom involve only the deeds and alleged misdeeds of Laventhol in making its audit which was submitted to FGL and thereafter to the security purchasers, including Herzfeld. . . .

The spotlight of Herzfeld's claim of a materially misleading audit, knowingly made with admitted awareness of the facts, focuses upon Laventhol's accounting treatment of two real estate transactions in which FGL allegedly engaged in late November 1969, referred to herein as the FGL-Monterey purchase and the FGL-Continental sale. Purporting to reflect these transactions are two agreements. Each agreement is on an identical printed form entitled "Agreement for Sale of Real Estate" and certain typewritten provisions have been inserted therein. The first is dated November 22, 1969 and is between Monterey Nursing Inns, Inc. ("Monterey") as seller and FGL as buyer. The transaction was subject to two conditions: (1) the buyer's approval of a preliminary title report and CC&R's of Record on each property (there is no evidence that any such documents were ever prepared, delivered or approved); and (2) execution of a NNN lease per terms of "Exhibit D attached hereto" (no such exhibit appears to have been attached). Twenty-three (23) nursing homes were the subject of the sale "as per Exhibit 'A' attached hereto" (no such exhibit appears to have been attached). The purchase price is stated as $13,362,-500, $5,000 of which was payable before November 30, 1969 (i. e., upon the signing of the contract).

On an identical printed form with almost identical typewritten inserts is an agreement by FGL as seller to sell to Continental Recreation Company, Ltd. ("Continental") as buyer. Again, there is no Exhibit A listing the properties. The purchase price is stated as $15,-393,000 with $25,000 as a down payment, other payments to be made in 1970 and thereafter.

This purchase and sale of nursing homes, if ever consummated, would have been the largest single transaction in the history of FGL. Placing these two purported agreements side by side, if the obligations therein were ever fulfilled in the future, FGL would have bought Monterey for $13,362,500 and sold it for $15,393,000, thus producing a profit, when, as and if the transactions were consummated, of $2,030,-500, no part of which was even contemplated as having been received prior to November 30, 1969, and only payments of $5,000 by FGL to Monterey and $25,000 from Continental to FGL may have been made.

A comparison of the financial condition of FGL with and without these transactions demonstrates the importance of them to FGL:

	Monterey Included	Monterey Excluded
Sales	$22,132,607	$6,739,607
Total Current Assets	6,290,987	1,300,737
Net Income	66,000	[169,000]
Deferred Profit	1,795,000	–0–
Earnings/Share	$0.10	[0.25]

Thus, the accounting treatment of these transactions determined the health of FGL's financial picture. Laventhol knew this was so. By this treatment, namely, immediate recognition of a so-called profit, Laventhol notes, dated November 30, 1969, reveal the conversion of estimated $772,108 losses into a $1,257,892 gain by the addition of the $2,030,500 "profit". These work papers contain the following entries:

"Estimated loss 4 months ended 4/30/69	200,000
Estimated loss 7 months ended 11/30/69	572,108
Loss before sale to Continental Recreation	772,108
Profit on sale to Continental Recreation	2,030,000 [sic]
Profit before income taxes	1,257,892" [sic]

Little wonder that when at the outset a Laventhol partner was discussing the situation from an accounting standpoint, he referred to it as a "fictitious or proposed or artificial transaction." Appendix ("App.") p. 887. But Laventhol undertook the task, albeit it had to engage in considerable soul-searching during it. Laventhol also learned that Monterey transactions were nowhere recorded in the FGL books and that there were no corporate minutes or resolutions approving or even adverting to the transactions. The absence was remedied by Laventhol, who prepared adjusting entries and ordered the FGL controller to enter them in the FGL books. Illustrative is the letter from Laventhol's audit manager to FGL's controller enclosing "the journal entries which we *generated* for the financial statements at November 30" (emphasis added). These very entries were prepared by Laventhol as if the transaction had been consummated: yet the agreements on their face showed that no profits could result therefrom until long after November 30.

Under date of November 30, 1969, appears as a general journal entry (Journal No. 9) an item "Profit on sale $2,030,500" and also a credit of $3,995,000 "to record purchase and sale of various hospitals from Monterey . . .". A further Laventhol paper, dated December 6, 1969, reverses a tax liability entry on the Continental sale which reads that Laventhol "will not record as sale since not enough deposit was given to Firestone".

The November 22 and 26 contracts came to Laventhol's attention on or about December 1st through its partners, Chazen and Lipkin, and Schwabb, the audit manager. Schwabb sought Lipkin's advice about the proper way to report the transactions in the audit. Lipkin sought to gather the pertinent information by meeting with Scott, a FGL vice-president, and Firestone. Scott told him that FGL was busy acquiring the necessary documentation. Firestone said that the agreements were legitimate and described Continental's principal, Max Ruderian, as an experienced real estate operator and a wealthy individual. Laventhol learned that Continental had a net worth of $100,-000 and that its assets consisted of "miniature golf courses plus other assets". Ruderian's business practice was to "buy and resell prior to final payment on his sales contracts".

Lipkin also examined the sales contracts. He was an attorney but had only practiced one year. He concluded that the contracts were legally enforcible. He consulted another Laventhol partner who assured him that there need be no concern about Ruderian. Ruderian's references concurred in the appraisal.

Lipkin also consulted over the telephone with a Los Angeles attorney. The attorney did not see the contracts, nor were the contracts in their entirety read to him, despite the fact that his offices were only one-half hour away by cab. Nevertheless, the attorney gave a telephone opinion that they were valid and enforcible.

The first tangible results of Laventhol's accounting efforts appear in its audit enclosed in its letter to FGL, dated December 6, 1969. In the consolidated balance sheet as of November 30, 1969, the amount of $1,795,500 was recorded "as unrealized gross profit". The same characterization was given to this assumed profit in the income statement with a reference to an explanatory Note 4. This Note only explained the $1,795,500 by stating that "because of the circumstances and nature of the transactions, $1,795,500 of the gross profit thereon will be considered realized when the January 30, 1970 payment is received." The $1,795,500 was apparently arrived at by first adding the $25,000 paid upon execution of the Continental agreement, the $25,000 not yet due (until January 2, 1970) and $185,000—a liquidated damage figure for non-performance. These amounts totalled $235,-000. They were apparently considered as received and were deducted from the then fictitious profit of $2,030,500, resulting in the figure of $1,795,500. This first December 6, 1969 report is marked "Withdrawn & Superseded".

The reason for the withdrawal is found in the testimony that FGL wanted the audit to reflect the entire amount of $2,030,500 as pre-November 30, 1969, income resulting from a sale by FGL to Continental. On December 4, 1969, Chazen and Lipkin met with FGL officers. Firestone objected to the tentative accounting treatment of the Monterey transactions, and FGL threatened to withdraw its account and sue Laventhol if the private financing did not go through.

A second report (also dated December 6, 1969) was then submitted by Laventhol. In the income statement "unrealized gross profits (Note 4)" was changed to "Deferred gross profit (Note 4)" and Note 4, itself to read:

> "Of the total gross profit of $2,030,500, $235,000 is included in the Consolidated Income Statement and the balance $1,795,500 will be considered realized when the January 30, 1970 payment

is received. The latter amount is included in deferred income in the consolidated balance sheet."

It was this second report which was distributed to the investors, including Herzfeld.

Unlike the initial report, the opinion letter accompanying this second and final report was qualified. It stated:

"In our opinion, subject to collectibility of the balance receivable on the contract of sale (see Note 4 of Notes to Financial Statements) the accompanying consolidated balance sheet and related consolidated statements of income and retained earnings present fairly the financial position of [FGL] . . . ."

Recognizing the difference between the financial statements (Exhibit B to the purchase agreement of November 10, 1969) and the Laventhol audit (December 6, 1969) submitted to Herzfeld and others, on December 16, 1969, FGL attempted to explain by a letter of that date the shift of $1,795,500 from a current to a deferred basis. The financial statements and the qualified opinion letter accompanied the FGL letter which purported to "explain" the distinctions between unaudited projections originally contained in the Agreement and Laventhol's report. No claim is made that Laventhol in any way participated in, or was responsible for, this FGL letter.

The FGL letter reads:

"One transaction which is reflected in the November 30 audited financial statements has been treated as producing deferred gross profit rather than current gross profit. While the combination of current and deferred income is actually higher than projected ($1,411,557 as compared with $1,360,000 projected) the shift of $1,795,500 of gross profit on this transaction from a current basis to deferred basis by the auditors has reduced current net income below that originally projected. . . .

"Deferred income shown on the audited balance sheet has been increased to $2,834,133 as against $1,421,000 projected. A breakdown of the components of the deferred income account is shown in the audited financial statements. . . .

"If for any reason you find that the changes reflected in the audited financial statements are of a nature which would have resulted in a change in your investment decision, we will arrange to promptly refund to you your subscription payment. . . ."

Herzfeld read this letter outlining the differences, the "Consolidated Statement of Income and Retained Earnings" and noted the deferred gross profit item of $1,795,500. He did not read the Laventhol opinion letter or Note 4. Apparently, relying on what he had seen, he was satisfied with his investment and did not take advantage of the rescission offer.

Neither the Monterey nor the Continental transactions were consummated and somewhat over a year later FGL filed a petition under Chapter XI of the Bankruptcy Act. A 10% dividend was eventually paid . . ., leaving a balance of $153,000 unpaid on Herzfeld's original investment, for which, by this suit, he claims that Laventhol, because of its materially misleading audit, is responsible.

The Trial Court first considered Herzfeld's claim under § 10(b) of the Securities Exchange Act of 1934, and Rule 10b–5 thereunder. . . .[5] The Court found that "Laventhol knew that its audited report was required for the FGL private placement and that investors would be relying on the financial statements"; that Laventhol had access to information concerning FGL which was not available to investors. As to Laventhol's legal duty, the Court held that it was the policy of the securities laws that investors be provided "with all the facts needed to make intelligent investment decisions [which] can only be accomplished if financial statements fully and fairly portray the actual financial condition of the company." 378 F.Supp. at 122.

After analyzing the facts, the Court concluded that "the Laventhol report was materially misleading." Id. at p. 124. The Court found that Note 4, claimed by Laventhol to be fully explanatory, was misleading: (1) in not disclosing that Continental, obligated to pay almost $5,000,000, had assets of only some $100,000; (2) in affirmatively stating that FGL had "acquired" the nursing homes (when it had not); (3) in reporting that $1,795,500 was deferred income; and (4) in stating that there was a lease back (when apparently no such lease existed). The Court's conclusion was that "the inclusion of the Monterey transaction in sales and income was misleading without a full disclosure by Laventhol of all the material facts about the transactions." Id. at p. 125.

Examining the report as a whole, the Court also found ten materially misleading omissions in Laventhol's failure to disclose (1) Continental's net worth; (2) the printed form language which suggested that they were mere options; (3) the absence of Ruderian's personal liability; (4) Ruderian's practice of reselling property before he paid for it; (5) the absence of any records of the Monterey transactions in FGL books; (6) the relative importance of the contracts; (7) the loss FGL would suffer if the sales fell through; (8) the absence of any title search; (9) that FGL had not acquired title; and (10) that the attorney ventured his opinion about the enforcibility of the contract without having examined the printed forms.

The Court held that Laventhol had the necessary *scienter* (merely the Latin adverb for "knowingly"), namely, "knowledge of the fact that the figures created a false picture . . .", and in addition, that Laventhol "had actual knowledge of the omitted facts which render[ed] its report misleading." Id. at p. 127. In light of Laventhol's concession that it was actually aware of the facts which the Trial Court correctly determined made Laventhol's affirmations misleading,

5. "§ 240.10b–5 Employment of manipulative and deceptive devices.

It shall be unlawful for any person, directly or indirectly, by the use of any means or instrumentality of interstate commerce, or of the mails or of any facility of any national securities exchange,

(a) To employ any device, scheme, or artifice to defraud,

(b) To make any untrue statement of a material fact or to omit to state a material fact necessary in order to make the statements made, in the light of the circumstances under which they were made, not misleading, or

(c) To engage in any act, practice, or course of business which operates or would operate as a fraud or deceit upon any person, in connection with the purchase or sale of any security."

we need not dwell upon the particular evidentiary items which the Court invoked to supplement its rationale.

The Laventhol report, if not the original inducing factor for the purchase, was read by Herzfeld. The Court therefore concluded that "The report's false picture of FGL's financial condition was, thus, a substantial, even crucial, factor in convincing Herzfeld that his investment decision to purchase the securities was right," Id. at p. 129, and that Herzfeld had shown sufficient reliance thereon. Characterizing the case as one of affirmative misrepresentations, the Court held that the correct test was whether the misrepresentations were a substantial factor in Herzfeld's decision to go through with his purchase of the FGL securities and determined that the Laventhol material was such a factor.

Laventhol contends that the Court erred and would have us attribute Herzfeld's purchase of the securities to his own enthusiasm, his acquaintance's touting, the FGL letter which accompanied the Laventhol report—in short, to everything but the Laventhol material. As to the Laventhol material, Laventhol argues that Herzfeld ignored it and emphasizes that Herzfeld read neither the opinion letter nor footnote 4 to which both the opinion letter and the income statement referred. This, to Laventhol, is fatal because it contends, *inter alia*, that the only statement made by an auditor upon which an investor is entitled to rely is the auditor's opinion letter. We agree with none of these arguments.

The Trial Court invoked the appropriate reliance test. Generally speaking, a plaintiff in a Rule 10b–5 damage action must prove that the misrepresentation was a "substantial factor" in his securities activities.

The Trial Court correctly applied the "substantial factor" test. Even assuming that persons other than Laventhol first aroused Herzfeld's interest in FGL, or that the FGL cover letter which accompanied the Laventhol material may have influenced Herzfeld somewhat, these considerations do not defeat Herzfeld's claim. Herzfeld was not required to prove that the Laventhol material was the sole and exclusive cause of his action, he must only show that it was "substantial", i. e., a significant contributing cause.

The Laventhol material was clearly a substantial factor. Looking at the transaction as a whole, it becomes clear that the investment decision was predicated upon confirmation of the Agreement's financial presentation by the Laventhol audit. The FGL letter explicitly informed the tentative investors of this fact and the Agreement itself conditioned its financial data on the auditor's confirmation. Herzfeld examined the Agreement and its income statement which suggested that FGL was a "very profitable company". When the Laventhol material was distributed he checked its income statement which provided the crucial corroboration of the Agreement's picture of corporate health. As the Trial Court observed "He paid particular attention to the earnings indicated and was very impressed by the deferred gross profit of $1,795,000. [sic] The latter figure, he understood, meant 'that this is a profit that the company had made and was going to pick up in a subsequent accounting period.'" In reliance upon this corroborative Laventhol financial statement, Herzfeld completed his investment in FGL securities.

In view of our imposition of liability on the ground that the Laventhol audit was materially and knowingly misleading and that Herzfeld relied thereon, we need not pass upon the questions whether there was a violation of New York State statutory or common law.

The issue here is not one of negligence, but of the "materially misleading" treatment of facts known to Laventhol in its submitted audit.

The function of an accountant is not merely to verify the correctness of the addition and subtraction of the company's bookkeepers. Nor does it take a fiscal wizard to appreciate the elemental and universal accounting principle that revenue should not be recognized until the "earning process is complete or virtually complete", and "an exchange has taken place." [6] Insofar as FGL's interest in the Monterey transactions is concerned, the earning process had hardly commenced, let alone neared completion. As of November 30, 1969, FGL had paid only $5,000 cash out of $13.2 million dollar purchase price and accepted a $25,000 "deposit" under a $15.3 million contract. Conditions for closing were unsatisfied. There remained the consummation of its purchase from Monterey, the furnishing to Continental of current title reports, and the delivery of the CC&R's and a copy of a lease. By the close of November 30, 1969, title had not passed. Nor was this the exceptional instance of a conditional sale or a long-term lease with purchase option, where the retention of title does not vitiate the economic reality of a consummated exchange.

Reference to the SEC's Accounting Series Release No. 95, 28 F.R. 276, 5 CCH Fed.Securities Rep. ¶ 72,117, p. 62,272 ("ASR #95") points toward the same conclusion. That release lists several factors whose presence, according to the SEC, singly or in combination, raises a question of the propriety of current recognition of profit in real estate transactions. Not less than three of these factors inhere in the Monterey transaction including (1) evidence of financial weakness of the purchaser (Continental's insignificant net worth relative to the resale property price); (2) substantial uncertainty as to amount of proceeds to be realized because of form of consideration—e. g., nonrecourse notes; (3) small or no down payment. Because the FGL offer was a private placement, ASR #95 was not directly applicable to Laventhol's audit. But since ASR #95 merely codifies basic principles of accrual accounting theory, we do not reject its corroboration of our own independent conclusions.

If the hoped-for profit of $2,030,500 were ever to be realized, it could only come after the transactions had been consummated—and consummation was never even contemplated before the audit date, November 30, 1969. FGL's profit till for this transaction as of that date was as bare of profits as Mother Hubbard's cupboard, bare of bones.

An accountant should not represent on an audited statement that income and profit exist unless underlying facts justify that conclusion. Here, the underlying facts known to Laventhol dictated precisely the contrary course, namely, that income should not have been recognized for the accounting period ending November 30, 1969. And were it not for Laventhol's disregard of Statements on Accounting Proce-

---

6. American Institute of Certified Public Accountants, Accounting Principles Board, Statement No. 4 § 150; 2 CCH Accounting Principles p. 9086.

dure No. 33, Ch. 2, p. 16 (1963) ("SAP 33") it would have confronted additional evidence pointing in the same direction. SAP 33 states:

> "Sufficient competent evidential matter is to be obtained through inspection, observation, inquiries and confirmations to affirm a reasonable basis for an opinion regarding the financial statements under examination".

Laventhol knew that the issuance of FGL securities depended upon a correct ascertainment of that condition. It is undisputed that, without the Monterey-Continental transactions, for the eleven months preceding November 30, FGL had sustained a loss of $772,108. Query: by what accounting legerdemain was this figure converted into a substantial profit? The Monterey purchase added nothing to the FGL till. To the contrary, it reduced it by $5,000 (if the check was honored). The Continental sale produced a down payment of $25,000 (if made) but no profit. In fact, if the hoped-for profit of $2,030,500 were ever to be realized, it could only come after the transactions had been consummated—and consummation was never even contemplated before the audit date, November 30, 1969.

Laventhol points to the Trial Court's finding that the Monterey-Continental transactions were not "phony". This finding, however, only implies that there were signed agreements between the parties. By no stretch of the imagination does it imply that profits of $2,030,-500 were realized therefrom before November 30, 1969, or would be at any time until consummation. In fact, both agreements showed on their face that the principal payments were to be made in 1970.

In such circumstances, the recognition of Monterey transactions was a materially misleading statement which, once included at the top of the income statement as a sale, resulted in, or necessitated, compensating adjustments which distorted all the financial figures which followed. A reasonable man in Herzfeld's position might well have acted otherwise than to purchase the FGL securities, had the truth been told and the Monterey transactions not been misleadingly represented as a consummated purchase and sale. .   .   .

This misleading impression was aggravated by Laventhol's labelling of the $1,795,500 as "deferred" as opposed to "unrealized" gross profit. Such nomenclature conveyed the erroneous impression that all that profit was so much cash in hand and would be recognized periodically *in futuro* just as if it were prepaid interest or management fees. But as Laventhol well knew, net cash had increased only $20,000, and the transaction was still in doubt.

Having engendered its own quandary, it ill behooves Laventhol to seek the solace of SAP 33, which concerns the rendition of a qualified auditing opinion. But even assuming the propriety of allowing Laventhol to extricate itself by the simple expedient of disclaiming or qualifying its opinion of the very financial statements which it concocted, Laventhol did not follow the route proscribed by SAP 33. At Chapter 10, page 58, SAP 33 provides, *inter alia*:

> "When a qualification is so material as to negative an expression of opinion as to the fairness of the financial statement as a whole, either a disclaimer of opinion or an adverse opinion is required."

*   *   *

"When a qualified opinion is intended by the independent auditor, the opinion paragraph of the standard short-form report should be modified in a way that makes clear the nature of the qualification. It should refer specifically to the subject of the qualification and should give a *clear explanation of the reasons for the qualification* and of the effect on financial position and results of operations, if reasonably determinable." (emphasis added)

But Laventhol did not provide a *clear explanation of the reasons for the qualification*. A simple note would have sufficed saying in substance:

"Agreements for the purchase of Monterey Nursing Inns, Inc. for $13,362,500 and the sale thereof to Continental Recreation, Inc. for $15,393,000, have been executed. When, as and if these transactions are consummated, FGL expects to realize a profit of $2,030,500."

Instead, Laventhol chose to delete from its first so-called explanatory Note 4, the sentence "Because of the circumstances and nature of the transaction, $1,795,500 of the gross profit therein will be considered realized when the January 30, 1970 payment is received" and substituted therefor the sentence "Of the total gross profit of $2,030,500, $235,000 is included in the Consolidated Income Statement and the balance, $1,795,500 will be considered realized when the January 30, 1969 payment is received." The substituted note also changed "unrealized gross profit" to "deferred income". Even in the first Note, there is no explanation of what were the circumstances and nature of the transaction or, in the second Note, how or why $235,000 could qualify as gross profit or income as of November 30, 1969.

From the very outset of the audit, the danger signals were flashing.

(1) Even if Laventhol accepted the agreements as not "phony", on the face of the Monterey agreement were two conditions to be performed, i. e., approval by FGL of a title search and a lease back. There was no proof that they were performed or that Laventhol made any effort to verify these facts.

(2) Normally on transactions of such magnitude and vital importance, corporate minutes, resolutions and other corporate papers authenticating the transaction would be examined. No proof of such examination was presented.

(3) Laventhol demonstrated an awareness that the legality of the agreement with Continental might be important. However, a telephone call to an attorney who did not even see or read the agreement and who only heard such excerpts as Laventhol's partner chose to read to him, scarcely qualifies as a legal opinion as to enforcibility.

(4) As for Continental, Laventhol knew that it had contractually committed itself to pay $15,300,000 to FGL and that Continental had assets of only some $100,000, consisting mostly of miniature golf courses. Laventhol was aware that Max Ruderian was a well-known, successful, and wealthy real estate operator and had signed the Continental agreement but there is no document which evidences that Ruderian's wealth was in any way committed to the Continental purchase.

(5) The absence of entries of the transactions on FGL's books and the necessity for Laventhol to create journal entries thereof.

(6) Laventhol, whose duty it was to reveal the truth rather than be subservient to the dictates of its clients, FGL, should have taken warning from FGL's pressurizing tactics to change "unrealized profits" to "deferred".

In sum, we affirm the result reached by the Trial Court in holding that the Laventhol report contained materially misleading omissions and misrepresentations. The term "result" is used advisedly. Although we agree with the facts as found by the Trial Court, we do not accept its opinion that all of the ten items specified therein were required to be included in Laventhol's report. The vice of the report was its representation that the Monterey transactions were consummated and the concomitant statement that current and deferred profit had been realized. This would have been remedied by simply not recognizing the sales as completed transactions for the accounting period ending November 30, 1969. A specific listing of the facts which dictated that treatment would have been unnecessary. . . .

NOTE ON DISCIPLINING ACCOUNTANTS FOR UNPROFESSIONAL CONDUCT

While the AICPA has the power to admonish or expel a member for violation of the rules of professional ethics, including the rules requiring conformity to the established guidelines for accounting principles and auditing standards, the Institute has no power to bar a person from practicing accounting. The right to practice accounting is governed by state statutory law, and every jurisdiction has legislation dealing with both admission to practice and procedures for revocation of the license to practice. Typically, the statutory powers are lodged in some type of Board, whose members are drawn largely from the profession. However, policing of the professional competence of accountants through this channel has turned out to be quite limited. There is, of course, the historic reluctance of the professions to "go after" their own. In addition, there may be a special basis for hesitance where, as is so often the case today, the alleged impropriety is one constituting a violation of the federal securities laws: in such cases the accountant whose conduct is under question is likely to be a defendant in one or more suits under the securities laws, and the Board may be fearful that a parallel disciplinary proceeding could prejudice the accountant's defense in those suits. In these days of seemingly endless delay in litigation, by the time the civil action(s) have been resolved the matter may have become too "old and cold" to justify commencement of a new professional inquiry.

The SEC has stepped into this perceived gap and sought to discipline accountants under Rule 2(e) of its Rules of Practice, which provides that professionals may be disqualified from practice before the Commission if they are found to have engaged in improper professional conduct or to have violated the federal securities laws. Since the SEC defines "practice" before it to include preparing any opinion to be filed with the Commission, including the opinion of an auditor on a company's financial statements, disqualification would prevent an accounting firm from auditing the statements of any of the thousands of companies required to file with the SEC. Although the SEC statutes do not expressly confer the power to disqualify from practice before the Commission which Rule 2(e) assumes, it was recently upheld by the Court of Appeals for Second Circuit. Touche Ross & Co. v. SEC, 609 F.2d 570 (2d Cir. 1979).

Commission opinions in Rule 2(e) proceedings are promulgated as Accounting Series Releases, in part because they usually express some views on acceptable accounting principles or proper auditing practices. Here is one example:

ACCOUNTING SERIES RELEASE NO. 248

Securities and Exchange Commission, 1978.

[This was a proceeding before the SEC to discipline a major accounting firm (E & E) and two of its partners, Isensee and Maurer, for alleged shortcomings in auditing the financial statements of Westec, a Houston-based conglomerate, for the years 1964 and 1965. Westec was the product of a merger in September, 1964 of two companies, one principally engaged in mining and the other a manufacturer of geophysical equipment. Westec's stock rose from $3\frac{1}{2}$ on the American Stock Exchange in September 1964 to more than 67 in the spring of 1967; as it turned out, this was largely the result of a conspiracy on the part of the top officers of the company, Hall and Williams, to raise the price of the stock by manipulating the earnings to show substantial annual increases. The conspiracy began to unravel in August, 1966 and within weeks Westec was in bankruptcy; Hall and Williams subsequently went to prison.

The Commission affirmed the findings of an administrative law judge that Westec's financial statements for 1964 and 1965 were inconsistent with generally accepted accounting principles and were materially misleading, and that the respondents had failed to comply with generally accepted auditing standards. Among the many items reviewed by the Commission were the following:]

B. *Sale of Carved-Out Production Payments*

Of Westec's reported 1965 earnings of almost $4.9 million, about $1.3 million represented net income on Camerina's [a subsidiary] sale of "carved-out production payments." A carved-out production payment is created when the owner of a mineral working interest, usually in consideration for an immediate cash payment, carves out by assignment an amount payable out of future production from that interest.

On December 22, 1965, Camerina sold two production payments for cash totalling almost $3 million. These payments were sold with no liability on the part of Camerina in the event production should not be sufficient to equal the amount of the payments, but Camerina was required to pay all "lifting costs" associated with production. The properties involved in these sales were seasoned oil properties. Based on normal operations, it would have taken about four years' production to liquidate one payment and about seven years' production to liquidate the other.

The net income of $1.3 million from the sale of the two payments was arrived at by deducting from the gross proceeds the costs applicable to the sale, including depletion, depreciation, amortization and estimated lifting costs based on an independent engineering study. With respondents' approval, the net income was taken *in toto* into Westec's 1965 income under the so-called current income method of accounting. A note to the financial statements stated that "under an alternative generally accepted method of accounting for sales of carved-out production payments, proceeds from such sales are accounted for as deferred income to be included in sales as the oil or gas . . . required to liquidate such payments is produced." The note further indicated that had this deferred income method been followed, no or very little income on the sales would have been recognized in 1965.

The Chief Accountant alleged, and the administrative law judge found, that by 1965 the current income method was no longer acceptable and that its use rendered the 1965 financial statements materially false and misleading. Respondents urge that this method was still regarded at that time as a generally accepted alternative accounting principle.

The record shows that from 1963 on our Chief Accountant took the position that the deferred income method was the only acceptable method except in very unusual circumstances. That position was based in part on a survey of financial statements of oil and gas producing companies which indicated substantial uniformity of treatment. As of the time Westec's 1965 financial statements were issued, however, this Commission had published no rules, regulations or other official releases or opinions of the Chief Accountant on this accounting question, nor had the AICPA issued any pronouncements.

There is no doubt that respondents were familiar with our staff's position. In fact, in 1963 another E&E client had changed from the current to the deferred method after our staff had objected to use of the former. The record shows that Henry J. Hogan, an E&E partner, advised Westec's management that use of the current method might be challenged by our staff and recommended use of the deferred method. Management, however, stated that it intended to use the current method, if that were an acceptable alternative method of accounting. Hogan, Halvorson [another E&E partner] and Isensee concluded that it was. They insisted, however, on inclusion of the footnote quoted above.

The administrative law judge noted that respondents could have discussed the matter with our staff if they had an honest difference of opinion with its position. No doubt that would have been preferable. But the critical issue is whether in 1965 the current income method was still a generally accepted accounting principle, i. e., a principle which had "substantial authoritative support." Early in its existence the Commission stated its policy that financial statements prepared in accordance with accounting practices for which there was no substantial authoritative support were presumed to be misleading and that disclosure would not avoid this presumption. It also stated that where there was a difference of opinion between the Commission and a registrant as to the proper accounting to be followed in a particular case, disclosure would be accepted in lieu of correction of the financial statements themselves only if substantial authoritative support existed for the accounting practices followed by the registrant and the position of the Commission had not been expressed in rules, regulations or other official releases.

The question of whether in 1965 there was still substantial authoritative support for the current income method is a close one. But we are not persuaded that the Chief Accountant has met its burden of proving the absence of such support.

It is absolutely clear, as the Chief Accountant's brief points out, that as of the time in question the current income method had been rejected by the Commission's accounting staff and that it had fallen into increasing disfavor even for use in financial statements not subject to Commission review. On the other hand, the method was still recognized as an alternative method in contemporary accounting literature.

Moreover, respondents' expert witnesses who testified on the question, including one who was chief accountant of our Division of Corporation Finance until March 1965, expressed the unanimous view that while the deferred method had become dominant, the current method was still a generally accepted accounting principle.

We also note certain circumstances, pertaining to the filing which precipitated the Chief Accountant's 1963 directive to the accounting staff. The company involved had been using the current income method. The staff recommended that the Commission require the company to follow the deferred method. The Commission did not act on that recommendation. Instead it approved a compromise under which current income accounting would be continued for past sales, but deferred income accounting would be used for future sales. As part of the compromise, the company included in its 1963 financial statements a note stating that under "an alternative generally accepted method of accounting (now more commonly used) for sales of carved-out production payments, proceeds from such sales are accounted for as deferred income." The note went on to state that if "this alternative" method had been followed in the past, net income would have been reduced by specified amounts, and that such method would be followed with respect to future sales. While we recognize that the solution arrived at was a compromise, it reflects some recognition of the continuing legitimacy of the current income method.

C. *Weco Oil Property Sales*

The largest single profit item reported by Westec for 1965 was a net gain of $2,042,840 on the purported sale by its subsidiary, Weco, of interests in oil and gas properties to Irving Petroleum Investment, Inc. on December 29, 1965. According to the income statement, the sale price was $2,250,000; the net gain represented the difference between that figure and the cost of $207,160. The sale was in fact a sham transaction engineered by Hall and Williams to inflate Westec's income. Irving was a corporation created by Hall's brother at Hall's instance for the purpose of effecting the transaction. Respondents did not know that the transaction was not *bona fide*. But the administrative law judge found, as charged by the Chief Accountant, that their lack of knowledge resulted from a failure to comply with generally accepted auditing standards in their examination of the transaction. We agree.

Weco was incorporated in January 1965. Its accounting records were maintained at Westec's offices under Belcher's [Westec's controller and a former employee of E&E] supervision. From the time of its organization through December 1965, Weco participated through investment in the drilling of about 90 wells, of which 16 became producers, and incurred expenses of more than $500,000 in connection with its drilling activities. The "sale" to Irving covered substantially all of Weco's oil and gas properties, including its entire interest in the producing wells.

Of the total purchase price, half was paid in cash on or before December 31, 1965. Irving gave Weco a note for the balance, which was paid in full on January 10, 1966. There is no evidence that respondents ever saw the note or that it remained in Westec's files following payment. The funds with which payment was made were obtained in part from the sale of Westec shares which had been held in McGregor's [apparently a sometime associate of Hall and Williams] name and were transferred to Irving, and the balance from loans obtained by Irving from companies owned or controlled by Hall's brothers.

In September 1965, Maurer was informed by Belcher that Weco had sold some oil properties during the year. Before Maurer began his field work in January 1966, he received copies of the conveyance documents relating to the December 29 sale. He subsequently inquired of Belcher concerning the prior sales which Belcher had mentioned and was told those sales had fallen through, but that Weco had been able to dispose of the properties involved and other properties in the sale to Irving. Maurer testified that he was satisfied from his examination that the Irving sale had been consummated and he accepted Belcher's word as to the earlier sales.

While two earlier sales transactions were recorded in Weco's books, those transactions in fact never took place. Sometime after June 30, 1965, Belcher prepared a document as of that date providing for Weco's sale of carved-out production payments to McGregor for $500,000. Belcher gave the document to Hall for the purpose of obtaining the signatures of Weco's president and McGregor, but it was never signed. Nevertheless, Weco recorded a gain of about $490,000 on the transaction, which Belcher included in Westec's unaudited consolidated statement of earnings for the six months ended June 30, 1965. That statement was included in an interim report issued by Westec for the second quarter of 1965 and in Westec's Form 9–K report for the first half of 1965 filed with the Commission.

In September 1965, Hall told Belcher that Weco had made another sale of oil properties for $650,000. No conveyance document was prepared. The purported gain of $626,000 was included in the three-month and nine-month unaudited consolidated earnings statements which were included in Westec's third quarter interim report.

In reviewing E&E's working papers for Weco in early April 1966, Isensee noted the absence of a schedule analyzing the accounting for the year-end transaction, and he requested the audit staff to prepare such a schedule. Garland R. Shelton, an accountant working under Maurer, prepared a schedule based on Weco's accounting records. That schedule reflected the two earlier purported sales, noting that the first of these was to McGregor. The underlying "journal voucher" for that transaction referred to a June 30 sale and was prepared on October 23, 1965 as of August 31, 1965. The voucher for the second purported sale for $650,000 was prepared on December 30, 1965 and carried an October 30, 1965 "as of" date. The schedule also reflected a journal voucher as of December 31, 1965 recording the sale of property for notes receivable of $1.1 million, "reclassifying" the two earlier sales and reflecting aggregate sales of $2.25 million. As Shelton explained, the procedure used on Weco's records was to "book the net difference" rather than to reverse the earlier transactions and book the full $2.25 million. The schedule noted that "essentially," the total sales transaction "was recorded at three times during the year."

Shelton asked Belcher to explain the relationship between the apparent earlier sales and the year-end sale. According to Shelton's testimony, Belcher told him that Weco had sold some properties and recorded the sales, but those sales had fallen through and substantially all of Weco's producing properties had been sold at the year's end. Belcher testified that he advised Shelton that Hall had informed him that the prior sales were to McGregor and that he (Belcher) did not know whether McGregor was part of the corporation to which the year-end sale was made. Shelton filed his schedule in the workpapers and did not call the matter to the attention of Maurer or Isensee since he deemed Melcher's explanation reasonable and the $2.25 million cash which had been received "the best audit proof available." He testified that he did not ask Belcher whether the earlier "sales" had been reflected in the interim reports.

The law judge found that respondents disregarded signs which should have alerted them to make a more careful examination and that a competent audit would have revealed the true nature of the Irving transaction. He specifically noted the following: (1) the size of the transaction, the profit on it, and the fact that, together with only a handful of other transactions, it accounted for Westec's total reported net earnings; (2) Isensee's apparent disregard of the schedule which he caused to be prepared; (3) the statements made by Belcher to Shelton concerning McGregor; (4) Isensee's failure to evaluate Weco's "rather quick success" (Isensee's characterization), and, in a discussion with Belcher in late 1965 concerning the proposed year-end sale, Isensee's satisfying himself as to the *bona fides* of that sale merely with the fact that the sale was to be for cash; and (5) respondents' prior experience with management, particularly in relation to the Weco matter, which should have caused them to be alert for possible misrepresentations.

There appears to be no dispute that respondents took adequate steps to satisfy themselves that the conveyance to Irving was properly effected and that the full purchase price had been received by Westec. And we are cognizant of the testimony of certain of respondents' experts to the effect that they would not have deemed it neces-

sary to inquire further into the purported earlier sales which had
fallen through since the financial statements being audited properly
reflected the year-end transaction. The experts' views, however, were
subject to the caveat that the total audit environment must be considered. In our judgment, respondents should have been alert by
that time to the possibility of improper income inflation. Instead,
they failed to bring to their audit of this transaction the "inquisi-
tiveness" and "healthy skepticism" which are the hallmark of "due
professional care." Respondents were aware of management's desire to generate earnings and its willingness to stretch a point and
conceal material information from them. Here they were presented
with a very large and extraordinarily profitable transaction, involving the sale of the assets of a subsidiary in existence less than a year,
effected just three days before the end of the year. Moreover, considering the audit environment, the circumstances of which Maurer
and Shelton were aware concerning the purported prior "sales" clearly called for further investigation. Yet respondents once again satisfied themselves by relying on the representations of Belcher.

D. *Form of Income Statement*

The administrative law judge found that Westec's consolidated
income statement for 1965 was materially misleading because it failed
to segregate the income from the sales of the Weco properties and the
Camerina production payments, which were nonrecurring and extraordinary items, from ordinary income and that respondents' weaving
of the profits on those sales into ordinary income indicated an intent
to conceal the serious lack of other income.

The income statement—reproduced below—showed the gross income derived from the above sales as two separate items under the
caption "Income," one entitled "Sale of interests in oil and gas properties," the other "Sale of carved-out production payments." The
related costs were shown separately, also as two items, under the
caption "Operating Costs and Expenses."

The form of the income statement was one of the items discussed
at an E&E conference concerning Westec's 1965 financial statements
which was held in Houston in late March 1966. Halvorson came from
Cleveland for the occasion and met with E&E Houston personnel, including Isensee and Maurer. Westec's management had expressed
its preference for a form of income statement in which all revenues
and income would be presented as a single figure. E&E had taken
the position that the different types of income should be reported separately, and that position was supported by Halvorson. As he testified, the participants in the conference did not deem management's
proposed reporting a fair presentation because it would have been a
"mishmash" of various types of revenue and they arrived at a format
substantially the same as that which was ultimately adopted.

CONSOLIDATED STATEMENT OF EARNINGS
WESTERN EQUITIES, INC., AND SUBSIDIARIES
Years ended December 31, 1965, and December 31, 1964

	1965	1964 [After adjustment for subsequent acquisitions]
INCOME		
Sales of manufactured equipment	$31,691,154	$23,426,516
Sales of services	13,279,043	14,080,141
Sale of interests in oil and gas properties—Note 8	2,250,000	– 0 –
Sale of carved-out production payments—Note 7	2,954,628	– 0 –
Sale of ore—Note 6	3,248,601	2,767,051
Sales of oil and gas	434,161	– 0 –
Interest	84,288	70,987
Other, including $350,000 in 1965 from sales of real properties	842,892	720,140
	$54,784,767	$41,064,835
OPERATING COSTS AND EXPENSES		
Cost of manufactured equipment and services sold	$34,371,114	$28,661,720
Cost of interests in oil and gas properties sold—Note 8	207,160	– 0 –
Cost of carved-out production payments sold—Note 7	1,663,237	– 0 –
Mine and oil and gas properties operating expenses	1,738,149	1,151,641
Research and development—Note 9	1,052,926	768,775
Marketing and selling	2,409,750	2,488,856
General and administrative	5,282,577	3,505,055
Amortization of financing costs	238,507	225,961
Interest	855,065	560,195
Other, including $222,354 in 1965 as cost of real properties sold	395,746	111,078
	$48,214,231	$37,473,281
Earnings Before Taxes on Income	$ 6,570,536	$ 3,591,554

TAXES ON INCOME—Note 11

Federal	$ 1,282,425	$ 693,130
Foreign and state	335,827	399,833
	$ 1,618,252	$ 1,092,963
	$ 4,952,284	$ 2,498,591
Minority Interests—Note 1	83,371	70,616
Net Earnings	$ 4,868,913	$ 2,427,975
Special Credit—Note 17	324,000	– 0 –
Net Earnings and Special Credit	$ 5,192,913	$ 2,427,975
Provision for depreciation, depletion and amortization included in operating costs and expenses	$ 3,112,247	$ 2,271,098

See notes to consolidated financial
   statements

A considerable amount of expert testimony was presented on the issue of whether the form of the income statement was misleading. Respondents' expert witnesses all testified that the disclosure in Westec's income statement, including the notes, was proper and that the income statement was not misleading. Certain of them stated that the zero income figures given for the items in question in 1964 disclosed that the 1965 income was nonrecurring. Barr [Chief Accountant of the SEC], on the other hand, testified that the form of the income statement was not proper and that the two items should have been shown separately as extraordinary income. While he indicated that there were different ways of accomplishing this, he testified that one way would have been to add two lines just above "Minority Interests," one labelled "Net income from sale of oil payment" and the other "Net income from sale of oil and gas properties," each of which would show the pertinent net figure.

Respondents' assertion that Barr admitted that the disclosure in the Westec income statement was as complete as the disclosure in "the form of report he favored" is a distortion of the record. True, Barr testified that the format he favored would not have provided more disclosure of fact, but he went on to add the crucial qualification that "the arrangement of the statement makes a difference."

In our judgment, the income statement was misleading. The two transactions were clearly of an extraordinary character, particularly the Weco sale which involved substantially all of that subsidiary's properties. Yet the statement, by lumping the income from these transactions with ordinary operating income and by reporting related costs under "operating costs," tended to convey the impression that these items were ordinary income. The notes contained nothing which would dispel that impression. And the zero figures included for 1964 were at best ambiguous. They did not overcome the inference that, after 1965, a recurrence of these items could be expected.

Chapter 3

INTRODUCTION TO THE CORPORATE
PROPRIETORSHIP ACCOUNTS

1. ACCOUNTING FOR CORPORATE PROPRIETORSHIP

This book deals in the main with the accounting problems of
corporations, rather than those of sole proprietorships and partnerships, which were used for simplicity in Chapter 1. The most important differences occur in accounting for proprietorship interests.
You will recall that for E. Tutt there was a single proprietorship account, or as it is sometimes called, a "capital" account, which reflected
Tutt's original investment in the enterprise and the subsequent changes in his proprietary interest. The proprietorship account for the
Nifty-Novelty partnership resembled that of E. Tutt except that it
was subdivided into separate "capital" accounts for each partner.

When a corporation is formed, cash or property is contributed
to the enterprise by the owners just as in a sole proprietorship or a
partnership, and these contributions constitute the source of the corporation's proprietorship, or capital. As you would expect, these contributions are reflected by debits to the appropriate asset accounts
(e. g., Cash, Inventory, etc.) and credits to a capital account. But
there are some important differences between a corporation's capital accounts and those of a partnership. For one thing, the owners of
a corporation receive stock certificates representing their interests;
in addition, unlike partnership interests, corporate stock is freely
transferable, absent some special restrictions, so that the owners of
a corporation may be constantly changing. Even more important,
these owners—the stockholders—unlike partners or sole proprietors,
are not personally liable for the debts of their enterprise; that is,
the creditors of a corporation can look only to the assets of the corporation for the payment of their claims. Accordingly, the total capital invested in the corporation is a very important figure, since it
represents the amount which the owners have placed at risk in the enterprise.

Historically, in conjunction with the organization of a corporation the total amount of capital to be raised from the stockholders
would be specified, thereby providing notice to prospective creditors
as to what the financial strength of the corporation would be at the
outset. This total capital figure was normally described as divided

145

into a specified number of shares, e. g., "the capital of this corporation shall be $250,000 divided into 2500 shares", to indicate the units into which the ownership interests in the corporation would be divided.

Each share bore the figure designating the aliquot portion of the total capital represented by the share, here $100; this figure came to be referred to as the "par value" of the share. (It is rather unfortunate that this term included the word "value", since except at the very outset this figure bore no necessary relation to the actual value of share.) Obviously, it was essential that no share of stock be issued for any less than the par value, in order to be sure that the full amount of the intended capital would be raised (and that none of the stockholders would get a bargain price).

Today it is no longer necessary for a corporation to state how much capital it intends to raise. But it is still very important to know just how much capital has in fact been raised and is permanently committed to the enterprise, since in effect this amount serves as a substitute for the personal liability of the owners of the enterprise to which creditors could have looked if those owners were members of a partnership rather than stockholders of a corporation. Accordingly, corporation statutes uniformly provide for disclosure of the amount of capital which the stockholders have contributed (and which they are forbidden to withdraw in prejudice to the interests of creditors); this amount is often referred to as the "legal capital". This is often accomplished by the combination of a provision that shares shall have a designated par value (which the incorporators are free to fix at any figure they like), and a prohibition against the issuance of such shares for a consideration, in money or money's worth, less than the par value. The total par value of issued stock having par value then constitutes the legal capital, the amount the corporation is required by law to have received (and which, pursuant to other provisions of the statute discussed below, will not be returned to stockholders against the interests of the creditors). The corporation may of course receive more than par value for its shares, but as we shall see any excess over par value may be free of the constraints on legal capital.

On the corporation's balance sheet, the capital account which is credited upon the issuance of shares is usually called "Stated Capital", or "Capital Stock". That account will record the full par value of all shares issued, and hence prima facia reflects the corporation's legal capital. (As we shall see immediately below, if more than par value is received for shares the excess is credited to a different account.)

To illustrate the foregoing, if 10 shares of $100 par value common stock are issued for $1,000 in cash, the entry for the corporation would be:

Cash	$1,000	
Stated Capital		$1,000

It should be noted that the Stated Capital account in particular, and corporate proprietorship in general, is not subdivided to reflect a separate account for each stockholder. This would hardly be feasible in the case of a corporation with a large number of stockholders, especially in view of the constant changes in ownership which ready transferability facilitates. But even in a small corporation the fact is that stockholders, unlike partners, do not have a claim on any specified amount of the assets of the enterprise, upon liquidation or otherwise; each stockholder merely has the right to share proportionately with all other holders of the same class, after all prior interests have been satisfied. However, when there are separate classes of stock outstanding, representing different interests in the enterprise (e. g., preferred and common stock or class A and class B common stock), a separate Stated Capital account for each class is maintained.

Since it is useful to isolate the contributed capital of a corporation, which constitutes the "legal capital", from other sources of proprietorship, such as earnings, only those changes in proprietorship arising from the issuance (or retirement) of capital stock are recorded in the Stated Capital account. Moreover, when the consideration received by the corporation upon the issuance of stock exceeds the par value of the stock, such excess is normally not recorded in the Stated Capital account, since any excess over par value does not constitute part of the corporation's legal capital. Instead, there are created separate subdivisions of proprietorship, historically called "Surplus" accounts (although as we shall see there is a tendency today to use other terms), and all transactions affecting proprietorship, other than the acquisition (or reduction) or legal capital, are recorded in those accounts. Thus, if 10 shares of $100 par stock are issued for $1,500, the entry might be:

Cash	$1,500	
Stated Capital		$1,000
Surplus		500

Likewise, corporate profit or loss would be closed to a Surplus account. (We will consider shortly the various names given to the separate subdivisions of the Surplus account, in order to disclose the different sources of surplus.)

To summarize, in the case of shares having a par value the Stated Capital account normally shows a figure equal to par times the number of shares outstanding. All other increases and decreases in proprietorship are reflected in a Surplus account, with certain rare exceptions. The sum of the Stated Capital and the Surplus accounts, which together constitute the total corporate proprietorship, was historically called "Net Worth", but is more commonly referred to today as "Stockholders' Equity".

We have already noted that for legal capital to do the job of providing some security for corporate creditors, it is necessary that there be some limitation on voluntary return to the stockholders of their capital contributions. This is normally achieved by provisions in the state corporation statutes limiting the amount a corporation may distribute as dividends to the excess of the total assets of the corporation over the sum of its liabilities plus the figure in its Stated Capital account (which is generally a measure of the legal capital). Such limitations serve to prevent the stockholders from withdrawing the amount of assets representing their original investment of legal capital, thus assuring that this amount will be permanently dedicated to the enterprise (although subject of course to loss in operations). These corporation statutes usually read in terms like dividends "shall not be paid out of capital", or "shall not impair capital", or "shall be paid only out of surplus". The phrase "out of" in these statutory formulas is not to be taken literally. Dividends of course are typically paid from the cash funds of the corporation. These common forms of dividend restriction simply mean that the corporation must have assets in excess of its liabilities plus its stated capital in an amount at least equal to the proposed dividend. Indeed, some statutes are phrased in just these terms: for example, the Delaware statute for many years provided that a corporation could pay dividends only "out of its net assets in excess of its capital". (The term "net assets" is simply a shorthand expression for total assets less liabilities.) This is of course just another way of saying that no dividends may be paid which reduce the assets of the corporation below the amount of its liabilities plus its stated (or legal) capital.

In summary, then, the legal capital of a corporation is reflected in the Stated Capital account, and the amount in that account becomes a measuring rod for determining the propriety of dividends. If total assets less liabilities, i. e., net assets, exceed the stated capital, that excess is not subject to the strict legal rules against withdrawal of assets and hence may well be available for dividend payments.

For many years now corporations have been permitted to issue shares which do not bear any specified par value. Such shares without par value are often referred to as "no-par" shares. The absence of any par figure means that there is no required minimum amount of cash or property that must be received by the corporation for each share issued; instead, shares without par value may ordinarily be issued for such consideration as the board of directors of the corporation may determine. Absent some special action by the board of directors of the corporation, the entire amount of consideration received for no-par shares is credited to the Stated Capital account, and hence would be part of the legal capital; but most corporation statutes permit the board of directors to credit some of the total amount of the consideration received for shares without par value to a Surplus account, in which event only the amount allocated to Stated Capital constitutes legal capital which cannot be returned to the shareholders by way of dividends. (The amount per share allocated to stated capital with respect to no-par shares is sometimes referred to as "stated value", a misnomer which, like the term "par value", does not necessarily bear any relation to the actual value of the shares.)

2. THE BALANCE SHEET AS A STATEMENT OF FINANCIAL POSITION

To understand the role of the balance sheet in stating the financial position of a corporation, it may be helpful to reexamine the relation between the balance sheet and the income statement. Consider, for example, what happens in the balance sheet accounts during the period which the income statement covers. In general, net income is produced by obtaining an amount of cash or other assets in excess of the amount of the assets expended or liabilities incurred. Thus, E. Tutt had net income because the amount of cash and accounts receivable which he obtained from fees during the period exceeded the total of the cash expended and the liabilities incurred for expenses during the same period. Similarly, Jones realized net income by obtaining a total of cash and receivables during the period which exceeded the cost of the shoes which he sold plus the expenses which he paid or became obligated to pay. Notice that whenever net income is earned there will be an increase in net assets, i. e., assets less liabilities; conversely, a net loss for the period will be accompanied by a decline in net assets. This of course is simply another way of saying how net income affects proprietorship, since assets less liabilities, or net assets, always equal proprietorship. To check your understanding of this statement, look at E. Tutt's balance sheets for June 30 and July 31 in the problem which begins at page 36, supra. Net assets were $2,860 on June 30 and $3,670 on July 31. This increase in net assets during July of $810 (ignoring the contribution to and withdrawal from proprietorship during the period of $100 each, which offset one another) was equal to the net income for that period.

Historically, the balance sheet was the only financial statement in practical use. To see how a business was doing, it was considered sufficient merely to compare the change in net assets in successive balance sheets (after eliminating the effects of any direct proprietorship transaction, such as the issuance of more stock). At that time it was common to recognize income and expenses only when cash had been received or paid. With such an unrefined concept of income, an income statement did not add much, and the income and expense items could as well be entered directly in a proprietorship account. As this "cash-basis" method of accounting gave way to the modern technique of accrual accounting, it became possible to show in an income statement a more refined and meaningful picture of what has happened between successive balance sheet dates. A corollary of this development has been a marked shift in emphasis from the balance sheet to the income statement as the significant measure of the progress of a business enterprise. However, the courts have sometimes lagged behind accounting development. You will still occasionally encounter cases which reflect the strong influence of the historical emphasis on the balance sheet. Consider the judicial attitude reflected in this early opinion:

STEIN v. STRATHMORE WORSTED MILLS

Supreme Judicial Court of Massachusetts, 1915.
221 Mass. 86, 108 N.E. 1029.

RUGG, CHIEF JUDGE. The chief question presented by this case is the meaning of the words "net profits" in a contract between the plaintiff and the defendant, whereby the former became a selling agent for the defendant, a textile manufacturer, at a stated annual salary and in addition a percentage of net profits. Net profits has a fairly well-defined significance in law. Profit in a going business implies a comparison between two dates. In the contract between these parties those dates are the beginning and the end of each of the two years as to which the plaintiff seeks to recover his percentage. As applied to these two periods, net profits mean a comparison between the assets of the defendant on these dates. Net profits will be represented by the difference between a sum made up at the end of the year of the receipts from the business, the sums due for goods sold, the value of all stock, materials, machinery, tools, real estate, and plant, on hand, and another sum made up of the value of all similar physical items at the beginning of the year, of all payments made and liabilities incurred for expenses, and of losses sustained by bad debts or otherwise. "In other words, the [net profits] would be what should remain as the clear gain of the venture, after deducting from the net value of all assets on hand the capital invested in the business and all outstanding liabilities" . . . .

In order to ascertain what the difference is between the assets on these two dates, a valuation of approximate correctness ought to be made as of the several material dates . . . .

If the success of an enterprise were going to be measured by computing the change in net assets between successive balance sheet dates, the question of the dollar figure to be put on the assets would become crucial. Recall that we decided to record E. Tutt's assets at cost, on the ground that cost is usually easier to ascertain and more objective than value. But it has often been urged (especially in earlier times, before the advent of accrual accounting) that it would be better to attempt to show the current market value of the assets on the balance sheet, because the balance sheet would thereby present a more meaningful picture of the current condition and worth of the enterprise. And even if the present value of assets were not actually recorded on the balance sheet, one could still take account of any increase (or decline) in the value of those assets when computing the change in net assets between particular dates, as the *Stein* case indicates. Obviously, periodic revaluation of assets could have a significant impact on the picture of the business fortunes of the enterprise portrayed by the financial statements.

Look at E. Tutt's balance sheet for July 31, on page 44, supra. Suppose that on July 31 E. Tutt finds that his office equipment, recorded at $775, has become "worth" $1,000, presumably because of an increase in the price of such equipment in the second-hand market. If he records the asset at that figure, his net assets (and the amount in the Proprietorship account) on July 31 would then be $3,895. Comparison with amount of net assets (and Proprietorship) of $2,860 on June 30 (ignoring the contribution to, and withdrawal from, the enterprise during July of $100 each, which offset one another) would indicate that the enterprise had gained $1,035 since June 30, rather than the $810 shown on the income statement. We will consider shortly whether one of these figures is more meaningful than the other; for the moment it is enough to see how each was derived.

Whenever the balance sheet is being used to judge the financial position of an enterprise, the question of whether assets should be revalued arises. This is of particular importance in dividend law, since, as previously noted, dividend statutes are often phrased in terms of prohibiting dividends "out of capital", or "which impair capital", or "except out of surplus", and all of these tests call for a balance sheet computation. Should the assets be measured at present value, or at a figure based upon cost, in determining the amount by which net assets exceed the legal capital reflected in the Stated Capital account? Even when the dividend statute is phrased in such terms as "dividends may be paid only out of net profits", language which seems to look to the figure on the income statement, a balance sheet valuation approach has sometimes been read into the determination of "net profits", just as the court did in a different context in the *Stein* case. We will consider the practice of revaluation of assets in more detail in Section 6, infra. But you can already see that there are at least two important issues: (1) can value be determined with sufficient accuracy? (2) should even a conceded increase in the value of assets be recorded in the accounts, or considered in determining the propriety of a dividend?

3. THE FINANCIAL CONDITION OF THE ENTERPRISE: RATIOS AND FINANCIAL ANALYSIS

As the foregoing material makes clear, despite the current emphasis on the income statement with its indication of enterprise earning power (and on the statement of changes in financial position, which gives some intimation of the enterprise's capacity to generate cash in the future, see pages 71–76, supra) the balance sheet is not yet ready to be consigned to the financial junk heap. The balance sheet still has a role to play as a statement of what the business owns, what it owes, and the nature of the proprietary interests in it. Moreover, the data on the balance sheet provides a basis for making some relevant judgments about the present financial condition of the enterprise.

The objective of financial statements, as we were informed by FASB Statement of Financial Accounting Concepts No. 1, page 104, supra, is to provide information that is useful to present and potential investors, creditors and other users in reaching rational investment, credit and similar decisions. Normally, these decision-makers are trying to make predictions about the financial future of an enterprise, on the basis of its experience to date as recorded in the accounts. This calls for some analysis of the financial data available, and there are a number of tests and ratios which have proved to be quite instructive. Of course, much depends upon the objective of the decision-maker: a potential buyer of common stock may be expected to focus on different aspects of the financial data from those that will gain the attention of a banker considering a short-term loan, while the holder of a twenty-year bond will have yet a third set of concerns. But these are some common themes, and, as to many of them, ratios derived from information collected on the balance sheet can be quite relevant. Let us look at a few of those ratios, just to get a feel of what is involved.

Consider the following balance sheet for a small corporation.

X Corp.

Assets		Liabilities & Stockholders' Equity	
Cash	$ 2,000	Accounts Payable	$10,000
Accounts Receivable	3,000	Bonds Payable	5,000
Inventory	16,000	Stated Capital	12,000
Plant	19,000	Surplus	13,000
	$40,000		$40,000

Can you say whether this corporation is in good financial shape? You will have noted that X Corp. has a relatively large surplus, although the failure to subdivide that account makes it impossible to tell whether the corporation has had earnings, either recently or at some time in the past. But did you also notice that X Corp. may well have some trouble meeting its accounts payable in the immediate offing? In fact, unless X raises cash through some other means, such as borrowing or issuing more stock, it looks as though X will not be able to pay off its accounts payable until the inventory has been sold and payment has been received. This is the kind of information that is of particular significance to short-term creditors, and it would also be of more than passing interest to long-term creditors and stockholders. Indeed, it is because of the importance of such timing considerations that both assets and liabilities are usually arranged on the balance sheet in the order of their "currentness", with the most current items at the top. Many modern balance sheets go further and expressly classify their assets and liabilities as between "current" and fixed or non-current, as the balance sheet for Colt Industries, on page 52, supra, illustrates. "Current assets" usually include cash and any other assets expected to be converted into cash within a year, which normally means accounts receivable, inventory, probably any marketable securities (and possibly short-term prepaid expenses, although strictly speaking they will not be converted into cash). "Current liabilities" would be those expected to be paid within one year, which would typically include accounts payable (and any expenses payable), plus any portion of a long-term indebtedness falling due within one year. Assuming that none of the $5,000 represented by the bonds is due within a year, X Corp.'s balance sheet might then be recast in classified form as follows:

Current Assets		Current Liabilities	
Cash	$ 2,000	Accounts Payable	$10,000
Acc. Rec.	3,000		
Inventory	16,000	Long-Term Debt	5,000
Total	21,000		
		Stockholders' Equity	
		Stated Capital	12,000
Plant	19,000	Surplus	13,000
	$40,000		$40,000

Because of the importance attached to both current assets and current liabilities, special attention is paid to the excess of current assets over current liabilities, usually referred to as "Working Capital". However, a simple net figure does not tell us a great deal. For example, if one company has $25,000 in current assets and $20,000 in current liabilities, and another has $10,000 in current assets and $5,000 in current liabilities, both have working capital of $5,000, but their financial condition is quite different. Here is where a ratio is more instructive: the first company's ratio of current assets to current liabilities is 1.25 to 1, while the second company's is 2 to 1. This relationship of current assets to current liabilities, known as the "current ratio", is one of the most common tests used in evaluating the financial condition of a business, especially its ability to pay its debts as they mature. It is often said that a current ratio of 2 to 1 or better is satisfactory, a test which X Corp. meets; but of course such rules of thumb must be qualified according to the type of industry, seasonal business factors, and the like. This also points up the fact that any ratio is primarily useful in comparative terms, that is, by way of comparison with the same company's ratio for an earlier year, or with the ratio of some other company, or at least with some rule of thumb.

Because it may take a good deal of time to convert inventory into cash, and short-term creditors are concerned about how they would be paid if the business was suddenly beset by calamity, they often look to a related ratio which ignores the inventory and takes account only of cash and other highly-liquid, or "quick", assets like accounts receivable (and perhaps marketable securities). This ratio of quick assets to current liabilities is known as the "acid test", and it should be in the neighborhood of 1 to 1 to be considered satisfactory (a test which X Corp. does not come close to meeting, thereby providing some confirmation of the concern expressed earlier about its liquidity).

A couple of other relationships involving current assets are worthy of brief mention. The ratio of average accounts receivable to credit sales for the year provides some measure of the liquidity of the accounts receivable. Thus if X Corp.'s credit sales for the year amounted to $30,000 and its average accounts receivable during the year were the same as the year-end figure of $3,000, the ratio is 1 to 10; another way of describing this is to say that the accounts receivable "turn over" 10 times a year. In effect, this means that the average collection period for the receivables is ¹⁄₁₀ of a year or 36.5 days.

The same kind of analysis is commonly made with respect to the relationship between the average inventory figure for the year (often computed by simply averaging the opening and closing inventories) and the total cost of goods sold during the year. Thus if X's average inventory during the year was the same as the year-end figure of $16,000, and the total cost of goods sold for the year (including both cash and credit sales) amounted to $64,000, the inventory would be said to turn over four times a year, meaning that it would normally take approximately 91 days to turn inventory into a sale.

As you might expect, financial analysis is not confined to current assets and liabilities. For example, both investors and lenders are very much interested in the composition of a company's long-term financing, particularly the amount, both absolute and relative, of the long-term debt. Debt financing represents both a special opportunity and a significant risk. The opportunity lies in the fact that if the company can borrow at, say, 12% interest, and earn a return of, say, 15% on the borrowed funds by utilizing them in the business, the excess of 3% redounds to the benefit of the stockholders; under these circumstances, the more debt there is the better the return to the stockholders. This is often described as "leverage": the greater the proportion of debt, the more highly leveraged the company. But the more debt the company has, the greater its risk is, since the interest must normally be paid in all events, even if the company is earning less than the interest rate on the borrowed funds, or perhaps not earning anything at all. In addition, the debtor company must repay the borrowed funds on the agreed date or face the prospect of bankruptcy.

The most common measure of the amount of debt in a corporation's financial structure is in terms of the ratio of the debt to the total stockholders' equity, including surplus (the "debt-equity ratio"), or perhaps to the sum of the debt and equity (the "capitalization ratio"). The relationship of debt to equity provides lenders with some indication of how likely they are to be repaid, in that the amount of assets represented by the stockholders' equity serves as a kind of "cushion" or safety margin for the creditors in case of financial difficulty, because creditors come ahead of stockholders in any liquidation. Hence, the more highly leveraged a company is the greater the risk run by its creditors that they will not receive payment of their principal if the company encounters hard times.

As with any of these financial ratios, judgment about the extent of the leverage depends upon the type of business and other circumstances: for example, a debt-equity ratio of 3 to 2 would be considered quite high for a typical industrial, but relatively normal for many public utilities. Keep in mind too that the balance sheet figures do not necessarily tell the whole story: the amount that the assets would bring upon liquidation may be far less than the figures at which they are recorded. In any event, remember that the various ratios are only as good as the financial statement data from which they are derived.

Some attention is also paid to the ratio of fixed assets to total long-term debt, a kind of non-current counterpart of the current ratio. A ratio of fixed assets, other than intangibles, to debt of 2 to 1 would normally represent a reasonably conservative debt structure.

There are also a number of financial ratios used in connection with the net income figure. The one most frequently encountered is the ratio of net income to sales for the period, usually stated in percentage terms, which provides some index to the efficiency of the enterprise. (In fact, it is not uncommon for the financial statements to include a breakdown showing not only net income but also all of the major expense categories for the period in terms of a percentage of net sales.) Another net income test in common use is the ratio of net income to "invested capital" (that is, the stockholders' equity, representing the amounts contributed by the stockholders, whether directly, upon the purchase of stock, or indirectly, through corporate retention of earnings); this ratio gives a measure of how successfully the management is utilizing the assets of the stockholders under its stewardship.

Bondholders in turn will be much interested in the ratio of earnings to interest charges, which provides some indication of how much the earnings can decline without endangering the interest payments; for this purpose, the earnings figure must be computed by adding back to net income both the interest charges and income taxes, which come after interest. This ratio is usually described in terms of "coverage" of the interest, so that if a company has net income before taxes of $500,000 and interest charges of $250,000, its interest would be covered 3 times.

Of course there are many other ratios of various kinds that can be highly useful in financial analysis, and much more could be said about the way in which such ratios can be helpful. For our purposes it is enough to get some sense of what is involved in these ratios and to be alert to the potential implications of financial analysis, while we turn our primary attention to the accounting processes which underlie the figures recorded on the financial statements.

NOTE ON CLASSIFICATION OF CURRENT
ASSETS AND LIABILITIES

The classification of assets and liabilities into current and non-current categories has provoked substantial comment and criticism over the years. The most recent authoritative analysis is Heath, Financial Reporting and the Evaluation of Solvency, which was published as Accounting Research Monograph No. 3 in 1978. The Monograph takes a very dim view of the present classification system, as the following excerpts from Chapter 4 indicate (while also shedding some additional light on the use and usefulness of financial ratios) *:

Evaluation of Current-Noncurrent Classification
Principles and Practices

Accounting Research Bulletin no. 30 issued by the committee on accounting procedure in 1947 is the only comprehensive pronouncement on current-noncurrent balance sheet classification ever issued by an authoritative body in the United States. In 1953 it was incorporated virtually unchanged as chapter 3A of Accounting Research Bulletin no. 43, a restatement and revision of the first forty-two bulletins issued by the committee. In that form, ARB no. 30 remains in effect today as the authoritative pronouncement of the U.S. accounting profession on the subject of current-noncurrent classification and provides the basis for present practice.

* * *

Accounting Research Bulletin No. 30

The committee on accounting procedure intended that ARB no. 30 would provide a "firm foundation to support a logical body of practice," but the bulletin never achieved that objective. . . .

Faulty Definitions. Current assets and current liabilities are both so poorly defined in the bulletin that it is often difficult if not impossible to determine whether a given asset or liability should be classified as current or noncurrent.

Current Assets. Current assets are defined and described in the bulletin (paragraph 4) as follows:

> For accounting purposes, the term current assets is used to designate cash and other assets or resources commonly identified as those which are reasonably expected to be realized in cash or sold or consumed during the normal operating cycle of the business. Thus the term comprehends in genaral such resources as (a) cash available for current operations and items which are

the equivalent of cash, (b) merchandise or stock on hand, or inventories of raw materials, goods in process, finished goods, operating supplies, and ordinary maintenance material and parts, (c) trade accounts, notes, and acceptances receivable, (d) receivables from officers (other than for loans and advances), employees, affiliates, and others if collectible in the ordinary course of business within a year, (e) installment or deferred accounts and notes receivable if they conform to normal trade practices and terms within the business, (f) marketable securities representing the investment of cash available for current operations, and (g) prepaid expenses such as insurance, taxes, unused royalties, current paid advertising service not yet received, and other items, which, if not paid in advance, would require the use of current assets during the operating cycle.

One of the problems with that definition is that the criterion "realized in cash or sold or consumed during the normal operating cycle" is excessively broad. At least a portion of nearly all assets will be "realized in cash or sold or consumed during the normal operating cycle." Thus, the authors of one leading accounting text argue that—

> In a realistic sense all asset services that will be used in producing revenue during the immediately succeeding operating cycle or accounting period will be realized and converted into liquid resources. Some portion of the investment in plant asset services will be realized in the same sense as will be the investment in raw materials. It may be argued, for example, that standing timber that will be manufactured into plywood in the next operating cycle has as good a claim to inclusion among current assets as a stock of glue that will bind the layers of wood.

The concept of the operating cycle of a business is an integral part of the definition of current assets; to apply the definition, one must first be able to determine the length of the operating cycle of an enterprise. The concept of the operating cycle, however, is also poorly defined. The bulletin (paragraph 5) states—

> The ordinary operations of a business involve a circulation of capital within the current asset group. Cash, when expended for materials, finished parts, operating supplies, labor and other factory services, is accumulated as inventory cost. Inventory costs, upon sale of the products to which such costs attach, are converted into trade receivables and ultimately into cash again. The average time intervening between the acquisition of materials or services entering this process and the final cash realization constitutes an "operating cycle." A one-year time period is to be used as a basis for the segregation of current assets in cases where there are several operating cycles occurring within such time period. However, where the period of the operating cycle is in excess of twelve months, such as in the tobacco, distillery, and lumber businesses, the longer period should be used.

* * *

John W. Coughlan argued that the definitions of the operating cycle and of current assets "involve a complete circle" because "the operating cycle is defined as the time money is 'tied up' in current assets" and current assets are "defined as those that would be converted into cash within the operating cycle." [4]   To illustrate his point, he used a numerical example involving a company that sells a portion of its output on open account with terms of forty-five days and a portion on installment terms payable over four and one-half years. He then reasoned—

> Consider the above attempt to determine whether installment receivables were current assets.   Installment receivables were current if they would be realized in cash within the operating cycle;   but whether they were so realized depended on whether they were included in the computation of this cycle.   Installment receivables are a current asset if, in computing the normal operating cycle, *they are assumed to be current assets.*

*   *   *

Current Liabilities.   Current liabilities are defined and described in the bulletin (paragraph 7) as follows:

> The term current liabilities is used principally to identify and designate debts or obligations, the liquidation or payment of which is reasonably expected to require the use of existing resources properly classifiable as current assets or the creation of other current liabilities.   As a balance-sheet category, the classification is intended to include obligations for items which have entered into the operating cycle, as in the case of payables incurred in the acquisition of materials and supplies to be used in the production of goods or in providing services to be offered for sale, collections received in advance of the delivery of goods or performance of services, and debts which arise from operations directly related to the operating cycle, such as accruals for wages, salaries, commissions, rentals, or royalties.   Other liabilities the regular and ordinary liquidation of which is expected to occur within a relatively short period of time, usually twelve months, are also intended for inclusion, such as short-term debts arising from the acquisition of capital assets, serial maturities of long-term obligations, and agency obligations arising from the collection or acceptance of cash or other assets for the account of a third party.   Income taxes should be included as current liabilities even though the entire amount may not be payable within twelve months.   [Footnotes omitted]

The principal deficiency of that definition is that it is based on an assumed relationship between specific assets and specific liabilities that does not exist.   Most liabilities are paid with cash and most cash is received from collecting receivables that arise from sale of a company's products, merchandise, or services to its customers.   As pointed out in chapter 2, it is meaningless to try to determine which of a company's many assets were the source of the cash used to pay a particular liability;   receivables, inventory, prepaid expenses, plant, equipment, and furniture and fixtures are all used in conjunction with one another to generate cash.   Similarly, it is meaningless to try

---

4.   John W. Coughlan, "Working Capital and Credit Standing," Journal of Accountancy, 110 (November, 1960): 45.

to determine which of a company's liabilities "is reasonably expected to require the use of existing resources properly classifiable as current assets." To try to do so is a futile exercise. . . .

Some accountants have interpreted the phrase "require the use of existing resources properly classifiable as current assets" to mean that the length of a company's operating cycle should be used to classify its current liabilities as well as its current assets. . . .

In practice most liabilities due after one year are classified as noncurrent even if a company uses an operating cycle of several years' duration in classifying current assets. The point here is . . . that the definition is ambiguous—it is subject to disparate interpretations because its application requires accountants to trace a relationship between specific liabilities and specific assets that does not exist.

Itemized Lists. The basic definitions of both current assets and current liabilities in the bulletin are followed by itemized lists of specific assets and liabilities that should be either included in or excluded from the current category. . . .   Some of the assets that the bulletin states should be classified as current do not fit the bulletin's definition of a current asset. For example, installment receivables are required to be classified as current "if they conform to trade practices and terms within the business," not if they "are reasonably expected to be realized in cash or sold or consumed during the normal operating cycle." Similarly, receivables from "officers, employees, affiliates, and others" are to be classified as current only "if collectible in the ordinary course of business within a year" regardless of how long a company's operating cycle may be. Prepaid expenses are declared to be current "not . . . in the sense that they will be converted into cash but in the sense that, if not paid in advance, they would require the use of current assets during the operating cycle."

* * *

Usefulness of Current Practice

There are three basic ways that balance sheet classification of assets and liabilities as current or noncurrent might be useful in evaluating a company's solvency. First, it might be useful as a means of disclosing an important attribute or characteristic of assets and liabilities. If, for example, classification of an asset as current meant that it would be converted into cash within a certain period of time, classification would be useful because when an asset will be converted into cash is an attribute that is relevant in estimating the future cash flows of a company and future cash flows are relevant to the evaluation of a company's solvency. Classification is used as a way of disclosing attributes of items in many areas.

Second, classification might be useful in predicting financial failure through the use of ratios. Thus, even if classification provides financial statement users with no knowledge of the attributes of assets and liabilities, it might still be useful if ratios based on the information provided by the classification bear a predictable relationship to financial failure. The current ratio, in other words, might be associated with a company's ability to pay its debts when due even though at present there may be no accepted theory that explains that relationship. If that is true, it might be argued that classification of assets and liabilities as current or noncurrent is useful simply be-cause it helps predict financial failure.

There is also a third way that current classification practice might be useful. Even if it were found that ratios based on that classification do not actually predict financial failure or that they are poor predictors of financial failure, it might still be argued that if financial statement users do, in fact, calculate current and other ratios that require assets and liabilities to be classified, the practice of having accountants designate which assets and liabilities they believe should be called current is useful because it spares users the need to do their own classification.

Current classification practice is discussed and evaluated in the light of all three of these concepts of usefulness in this section.

Attribute Disclosure.   .   .

The basic point   .   .   . is that current practice fails to com-municate information about the attributes of assets and liabilities ef-fectively.   A prerequisite of effective communication through classi-fication is that all items classified the same way have some attribute in common—the attribute used as the criterion to partition the items into classes.   A user of classified data then knows that if an item is classified in a certain way, it possesses a certain attribute.   Com-munication of attributes is one of the principal functions of nearly all forms of classification.   When Fess refers to the "inconsistency" of classifying a three-year prepaid insurance premium as current while machinery with a three-year life is classified as noncurrent, he is really saying that there is no partitioning attribute that a three-year prepaid insurance premium has in common with other assets classi-fied as current but that machinery with a three-year life does not have.   When Arthur Andersen & Co. questions the "logic" of classify-ing crude oil inventories in tanks [as current] while similar under-ground reserves are classified as noncurrent, it is really saying that there is no partitioning attribute that crude oil inventories in tanks have in common with other assets classified as current but that under-ground reserves do not have.   When Huizingh labels as "irrational" and "inconsistent" the practice of classifying materials and supplies that will be used to maintain fixed assets as current, while the fixed assets themselves are classified as noncurrent, he is really saying that there is no partitioning attribute that spare parts inventories and supplies have in common with other assets classified as current but that fixed assets do not have.

The effect of classifying assets in these "inconsistent," "illogical," and "irrational" ways is that describing an asset as current communi-cates no useful information about that asset to financial statement users because there is no identifiable attribute that all assets classified as current have but all assets classified as noncurrent do not have. The concept of current assets found in practice cannot be described as "those assets that will normally be converted into cash within a year," because many assets that will not be converted into cash within a year are classified as current while others with the same attribute are classified as noncurrent; they cannot be described as assets "reason-ably expected to be realized in cash or sold or consumed during the normal operating cycle" because many assets that will be "realized in cash or sold or consumed" during the next operating cycle (whatever its length) such as a portion of plant and equipment and wasting assets, are excluded; they cannot be described as resources that will be used to pay liabilities classified as current because cash generated from the use of all assets is used to pay both liabilities classified as current as well as those classified as noncurrent. The only attribute that all assets classified as current have in common is that they are the assets that, under current accepted practice, are classified as current—an attribute that has no information content whatever to a user of financial statements concerned with evaluating the solvency of a business enterprise. This same basic criticism applies equally to current practice in classifying liabilities. A current liability can only be described as a liability that is classified as current.

A second prerequisite to effective communication of attributes through classification of data is that the user of classified data know what attribute was used to partition the data. If a user believes that one attribute was used when a different one was used, classification is not merely useless, it is pernicious; it does not just fail to disclose relevant attributes of assets and liabilities, it misleads users of that data.

Many classification rules followed in practice undoubtedly mislead financial statement users because users believe that accountants classify assets and liabilities on the basis of one attribute when, in fact, they use an entirely different criterion. An example is the failure to disclose the length of a company's operating cycle. According to some accounting practitioners, the operating cycles used to classify assets in some companies may be ten or more years. It seems likely that many users, even sophisticated ones, are misled by the practice of classifying receivables due five or more years hence as current because they think of current assets as ones that will normally be converted into cash in the short run. They are unaware of the long operating cycles used as classification criteria for some companies.

There are many other classification practices that undoubtedly mislead users. For example, users who think that current assets are "cash and other assets that are reasonably expected to be realized in cash or sold or consumed during the normal operating cycle of the business or within one year if the operating cycle is shorter than one year" are no doubt misled by the common practice of classifying a three-year prepaid insurance premium as a current asset even though the operating cycle of the insured is less than one year. They are undoubtedly also misled by the classification of underground oil reserves that are "reasonably expected to be . . . sold . . . within one year" as *noncurrent* assets.

Perhaps the most misleading information produced by current classification practice is the classification of deferred income tax debits and credits. Deferred income tax credits, for example, are classified as current on the basis of whether they "relate" to current assets, not on the basis of when they are expected to "reverse" or require the use of cash. It seems likely that many financial statement users believe that current deferred taxes will have to be paid or will "reverse" within a relatively short period of time such as a year, because the one-year rule is followed quite closely in classifying most liabilities. Actually, however, when the will have to be paid or when they "reverse" has nothing to do with how they are classified, and in many, if not most, situations there probably is no basis for assuming they will have to be paid or will "reverse" sooner than even those deferred tax credits classified as noncurrent.

To summarize, present classification is not useful as a means of disclosing an important attribute or characteristic of assets and liabilities. And furthermore, it is misleading because the attributes used to partition current from noncurrent assets and liabilities are not clearly identified, are not understood by users, and are not followed consistently in practice.

Prediction of Financial Failure. One approach to evaluating the usefulness of financial information is to measure its ability to predict the outcome of future events. This approach has been used by several researchers in recent years to evaluate the usefulness of financial ratios in predicting financial failure. Perhaps the best known of those studies and the ones most relevant to this study are those by William H. Beaver.[33]

Beaver's data base for both studies consisted of a paired sample of seventy-nine firms that failed and a similar number of comparable firms that did not fail. In his first study he examined thirty financial ratios. His general findings were as follows:

> Based solely upon a knowledge of the financial ratios, the failure status of firms can be correctly predicted to a much greater extent than would be expected from random prediction. For example, one year before failure the cash flow to total debt ratio misclassified only 13 percent of the sample firms. Five years before failure the same ratio misclassified only 22 percent. Since there was approximately an equal number of failed and nonfailed firms in the sample, the expected error from random prediction was about 50 percent. There is an extremely small probability that random prediction could have done as well as the ratio.

> This evidence, together with other tests conducted, suggested that financial ratios can be useful in the prediction of failure for at least five years prior to the event.

In his second study, Beaver examined the difference in predictive power of fourteen different ratios divided into two groups: those described as liquid asset ratios and those described as nonliquid asset ratios. Those ratios are identified in the table below. The eleven liquid asset ratios all relate some measure of assets described as liquid to total assets, to current liabilities, or to sales. Seven of them are based on current assets, current liabilities, or working capital, all of which depend on current-noncurrent classifications. The three nonliquid asset ratios studied were cash flow to total debt, net income to total debt, and total debt to total assets—none of which depend on current-noncurrent classification. According to Beaver, the

33. William H. Beaver, "Financial Ratios as Predictors of Failure," Empirical Research in Accounting, Selected Studies, 1966, supplement to vol. 4, Journal of Accounting Research, pp. 71–127; and "Alternative Accounting Measures as Predictors of Failure," Accounting Review, 43 (January, 1968): 113–122.

nonliquid ratios studied were selected "because they predicted best among the nonliquid asset ratios in the earlier study." Beaver summarized the findings of his second study as follows:

> The most striking feature of the data is the consistently superior performance of the nonliquid asset ratios. . . . No single liquid asset ratio predicts as well as any of the nonliquid asset ratios.
>
> Surprisingly, the superior predictive power exists not only in the long term but also in the years shortly before failure. . . .

TABLE 4–1

Ratios Used in Beaver Study

I. *Nonliquid asset ratios*
  1. Cash flow to total debt
  2. Net income to total assets
  3. Total debt to total assets

II. *Liquid asset ratios*
A. Total Asset Group
  1. Current assets to total assets
  2. Quick assets to total assets
  3. Net working capital to total assets
  4. Cash to total assets

II. *Liquid asset ratios*
B. Current Debt Group
  1. Current assets to current debt (current ratio)
  2. Quick assets to current debt (quick ratio)
  3. Cash to current debt
C. Net Sales or Turnover Group
  1. Current assets to sales
  2. Quick assets to sales
  3. Net working capital to sales
  4. Cash to sales

Beaver was not specifically concerned with the usefulness of current-noncurrent classification. He did not, therefore, comment on the relative predictive power of ratios based on that classification compared with those not based on it, but his article does contain data showing the predictive power of each of the ratios studied for each of the five years before failure. . . .

* * *

In general, those data show that the ratios based on current-noncurrent classification are not only poorer predictors of financial failure than the three nonliquid asset ratios he studied, but, within the liquid asset group itself, they are among the poorer predictors. The current ratio was found to have the poorest average perdictive power of the three ratios of liquid assets to current debt and, except for the year immediately before failure, was a poorer predictor than the ratio of just plain cash to total assets. The ratio of current assets to total assets had the poorest average predictive power of the four ratios of liquid assets to total assets, and the ratio of current assets to sales had the poorest average predictive power of the four ratios of liquid assets to sales (liquid asset turnover group).

* * *

Calculation Convenience. To a large extent at least, balance sheet classification is a redundant practice. Labeling trade accounts receivable, inventories, and prepaid expenses, for example, as current assets, tells financial statement users nothing about those assets because, with few exceptions, all trade accounts receivable, all inventories, and all prepaid expenses are classified as current.

There is a substantial amount of redundancy in the presentation of all financial statements. If, for example, all of the revenues and expenses of a company are known, presenting the net income figure provides readers with no new information. They could have obtained that figure themselves by merely subtracting the expenses from the revenues. Similarly, the figure labelled total assets on a balance sheet provides no new information if the amounts of all of the individual assets are known.

Redundancy is not necessarily an undesirable attribute of financial statements. Some of it may be quite useful. Presenting an income amount, for example, not only saves the reader time that would otherwise be spent calculating that amount, but it also helps clarify the income statement by directing attention to that amount.

However, the argument that accountants should continue to classify assets and liabilities on the grounds that it is a useful service to financial statement users is not convincing. Although accounting classifications are often used in calculating the current ratio as well as other ratios, accountants should not direct users' attention to the figures generated by a classification system that ignores users' needs.

Many sophisticated financial statement users do not use accounting classifications; they classify assets and liabilities on the basis of their own concepts of what should be called current. Several bankers mentioned this during the interview phase of this study, and Foulke calls attention to it in his book. After pointing out that the definition of current assets in ARB no. 30 begins with the phrase "for accounting purposes" he comments, "This definition as indicated by its first three words is not for credit purposes, management purposes, or analysis purposes; it is solely for 'for accounting purposes.'" [37]

He then lists those assets that he believes should be classified as current and adds, "In this volume, operating supplies and ordinary maintenance material and parts, receivables from officers and employees, no matter how they arose, and prepaid expenses are excluded from current assets."

Summary and Conclusions

ARB no. 30 and current practice based on that bulletin are deficient in many ways. The underlying problem is that the bulletin is based on a fundamental misunderstanding of basic principles of classification and definitions. Although it begins with the statement "The working capital of a borrower has always been of prime interest to grantors of credit," the definitions that follow that opening statement ignore the information needs of credit grantors. Instead of defining current assets and current liabilities in a way that would provide information useful in evaluating a company's solvency, the committee sought instead to define them in a way that would produce

37. Roy A. Foulke, Practical Financial   York: McGraw-Hill, 1968), p. 71n.
Statement Analysis, 6th ed. (New   . . .

a measure of a company's "true" working capital. Since "true" working capital is a meaningless concept, the result is not surprising. The bulletin has been a failure. Although the lists it contains have provided some uniformity to practice, its definitions are not understandable. Current-noncurrent practices based on the bulletin are described as "inconsistent," "illogical," and "irrational." They not only fail to provide information useful in evaluating solvency; they provide misleading information.

Initially it might seem plausible that the solution to present defective current-noncurrent classification practice is to correct the defect by developing a clearer and more helpful current-noncurrent classification, say a simple one-year dividing line (except that for inventories, for example, it is not simple), but that solution is simplistic. It deals with the symptoms and not the cause of the problem. It is unlikely that financial reporting could be improved by trying to redefine current assets and current liabilities in a way that takes into account users' needs in evaluating solvency. The whole approach by financial statement users to the evaluation of solvency has changed since the practice of classifying assets and liabilities was begun. What might have been a useful practice when it was begun shortly after the turn of the century is unlikely to provide the answers needed by today's users.

There are two basic problems with a simple, dichotomous current-noncurrent classification system as a means of communicating information useful in evaluating a company's solvency. First, two classes are inadequate to disclose the information that needs to be disclosed about some assets and liabilities. Receivables and payables, for example, need to be broken down by maturity dates into more than two classes to provide the information needed to estimate a company's cash receipts and required payments for time periods of several different lengths. Second, the same classification criteria cannot be applied to all assets and liabilities. As a practical matter, inventories, for example, cannot be broken down on the same basis as receivables because of uncertainty as to when they will be sold.

Because of the problems just described, a new approach to providing balance sheet information useful in evaluating a company's solvency is needed. . . .

---

4. ISOLATION OF THE RESULTS OF BUSINESS OPERATIONS

As we have seen, proprietorship, and hence net assets, may be increased or decreased by transactions which have nothing to do with operations. For example, when E. Tutt took home a chair from his law office, net assets of his law practice were decreased although the transaction had no relation to his professional (operating) activity. Again, when Tutt received law books for his office, the resulting increase in net assets had nothing to do with the progress of his practice. It is not surprising, then, that comparison of successive balance sheets should have been found to be inadequate for measuring performance of an enterprise, and that the income statement, which isolated those items of increase and decrease in proprietorship resulting from operations, was found necessary.

This segregation of dissimilar types of changes in net assets can be reflected to some extent on the balance sheet. The subdivision of the corporate proprietorship account called "Surplus" can be divided into a number of sub-accounts, each reflecting a different kind of change. For example, a sub-account called "Earned Surplus" might be used to reflect those changes in surplus which result from the earnings (or losses) from operations. Thus, to close $1,000 from "Profit and Loss" at the end of a period, the entry would be:

Profit and Loss	$1,000	
Earned Surplus		$1,000

Now suppose that a stockholder pays $1,500 for 10 shares of $100 par stock. Earlier, when the possibility of segregating the various types of surplus was ignored, it was suggested that the entry might be:

Cash	$1,500	
Stated Capital		$1,000
Surplus		500

If we are going to subdivide the surplus account, we need another sub-account of surplus in which to reflect this $500. Certainly, it should not be credited to Earned Surplus; it does not constitute earnings from operations, any more than the rest of the consideration received by the corporation upon the issue of its stock. Instead, another special subdivision of surplus can be set up to reflect this excess of the amount received over legal capital. Such a sub-account is frequently called "Capital Surplus", or "Paid-in Surplus", connoting that the sum in that account represents an investment of capital which was paid in to the enterprise in exchange for stock but is not subject to the legal limitations imposed upon the legal capital. Thus the full entry might be:

Cash	$1,500	
Stated Capital		$1,000
Capital Surplus		500

The same account would reflect any excess of the consideration received over the amount allocated to the Stated Capital account upon the issuance of no-par stock.

Occasionally, assets are simply donated to a corporation, and no stock is issued for them. In that case, an account called "Donated Surplus" can be created to reflect this increase in net assets (although it could as well simply be included in Capital Surplus). Similarly, if assets were to be revalued on the corporation's books, another special subdivision of the surplus account, which might be called "Revaluation Surplus", or "Appraisal Surplus", could be set up to receive the credit corresponding to the increase in the asset figure.

Segregation of surplus in this way clearly contributes to meaningful disclosure of a corporation's financial position, and the practice is uniformly followed today. In addition, modern state corporation statutes often distinguish among the types of increase in net assets from which dividends may be paid, and this makes separate identification of the various sources of surplus all the more useful. But there has been a distinct shift in the terminology of these subaccounts in recent years, especially away from the word "surplus", pursuant to strong encouragement from official promulgations of the profession, as illustrated by the following excerpts from Accounting Terminology Bulletin No. 1 * :

USE OF THE TERM "SURPLUS"

65. In 1941 the committee [on terminology] suggested a general discontinuance of the use of the term *surplus* in corporate accounting, and a substitution therefor in the proprietorship section of the balance sheet of designations which would emphasize the distinction between (a) legal capital, (b) capital in excess of legal capital, and (c) undivided profits. Extensive discussions of the proposal followed, and in 1949 it was approved "as an objective" by the committee on accounting procedure.

66. A factor of primary importance in the balance-sheet presentation of the stockholders' equity is the status of ownership at the balance-sheet date. Where two or more classes of stockholders are involved, the interests of each must be presented as clearly as possible. These interests include the entire proprietary capital of the enterprise, frequently divided further, largely on the basis of source, as follows:

(1) Capital stock [or stated capital], representing the par or stated value of the shares.

(2) Capital surplus, representing (a) capital contributed for shares in excess of their par or stated value, or (b) capital contributed other than for shares.

(3) Earned surplus, representing accumulated income or the remainder thereof at the balance-sheet date.

67. While the terms *capital surplus* and *earned surplus* have been widely used, they are open to serious objection.

---

* Copyright © 1953 by The American Institute of Certified Public Accountants, Inc. See page 90, supra.

(1) The term surplus has a connotation of excess, overplus, residue, or "that which remains when use or need is satisfied" (Webster), whereas no such meaning is intended where the term is used in accounting.

(2) The terms *capital* and *surplus* have established meanings in other fields, such as economics and law, which are not in accordance with the concepts the accountant seeks to express in using those terms.

(3) The use of the term *capital surplus* (or, as it is sometimes called, *paid-in surplus*) gives rise to confusion. If the word *surplus* is intended to indicate capital accumulated by the retention of earnings, i. e. retained income, it is not properly used in the term *capital surplus;* and if it is intended to indicate a portion of the capital, there is an element of redundancy in the term *capital surplus.*

(4) If the term *capital stock* [or *stated capital*] (and in some states the term *capital surplus*) be used to indicate capital which, in the legal sense, is restricted as to withdrawal, there is an implication in terms *surplus* or *earned surplus* of availability for dividends. This is unfortunate because the status of corporate assets may well be such that they are not, as a practical matter, or as a matter of prudent management, available for dividends.

68.   In seeking terms more nearly connotative of the ideas sought to be expressed, consideration should be given primarily to the *sources* from which the proprietary capital was derived. . . .

69.   In view of the foregoing the committee in 1949 particularized the proposal which had been so long under consideration by recommending that, in the balance-sheet presentations of stockholders' equity:

(1) The use of the term *surplus* (whether standing alone or in such combination as *capital surplus, paid-in surplus, earned surplus, appraisal surplus* etc.) be discontinued.

(2) The contributed portion of proprietary capital be shown as:

   (a) Capital contributed for, or assigned to, shares, to the extent of the par or stated value of each class of shares presently outstanding.

   (b) (i) Capital contributed for, or assigned to, shares in excess of such par or stated value (whether as a result of original issue of shares at amounts in excess of their then par or stated value, or of a reduction in par or stated value of shares after issuance, or of transactions by the corporation in its own shares); and

   (ii) Capital received other than for shares, whether from shareholders or from others.

(3) The term *earned surplus* be replaced by terms which will indicate source, such as *retained income, retained earnings, accumulated earnings,* or *earnings retained for use in the business.* In the case of a deficit, the amount should be shown as

a deduction from contributed capital with appropriate description.

* * *

(6) Any appreciation included in the stockholders' equity . . . should be designated by such terms as *excess of appraised or fair value of fixed assets over cost* or *appreciation of fixed assets.*

70.   As already noted, this proposal was approved "as an objective" by the committee on accounting procedure although it has subsequently used the term *surplus* in certain of its pronouncements where it felt that the avoidance of such usage might seem to border on pedantry. The cogency of the reasons adduced for discontinuing the use of the term in balance-sheet presentations of the stockholders' equity seems obvious, and   .   .   .   the proposal is winning general acceptance   .   .   .   .

Does accounting terminology make a difference to lawyers? Consider the following case:

BURGUIERES v. J. M. BURGUIERES CO., LTD.

Court of Appeal of Louisiana, Fourth Circuit, 1975.
312 So.2d 179, certiorari denied 314 So.2d 735.

REDMANN, J.   La.R.S. 12:102B obliges a corporation to provide annually, upon a shareholder's written request, certain corporate information.[1]

Dissatisfied with defendant corporation's response to his request, plaintiff shareholder sought mandamus, and now appeals from judgment dismissing his demand.

Plaintiff requested "a correct annual report according to law," citing R.S. 12:102B. Specifically, plaintiff requested that the report utilize the exact statutory terms ("stated capital, capital surplus and earned surplus" and "combined statement of income and earned surplus").

In response, the corporation furnished a report signed by its president and secretary containing the information required by R.S. 12:-102A. In a cover letter similarly signed, it advised that it had previously sent to all shareholders its annual consolidated financial report of itself and its subsidiaries (which plaintiff in his written request had admitted receiving). That financial report, the letter advised, contained the statutorily-required items of information: "If you will consult a Certified Public Accountant, he will be able to analyze the report and show you where each of these items are set forth".

1. The statutory wording is "a report signed by the president or vice-president and secretary or assistant secretary, containing the information hereinabove [in § 102A] required to be contained in the last annual report of the corporation preceding said request, together with a condensed balance sheet (showing *inter alia* and separately the amounts of its stated capital, capital surplus and earned surplus) as of the last day of, and a combined statement of income and earned surplus for, the last preceding fiscal year ended more than four months before receipt of such request."

The law does not require a shareholder to hire a certified public accountant in order to be informed of the items specified by R.S. 12:102B. The law unmistakably obliges the corporation to state those items to the requesting shareholder.

Defendant corporation's board chairman (who is also a partner in the corporation's accounting firm) testified he prefers and uses more "modern" accounting terminology than that of the 1968 Louisiana law.[2] We need not inquire whether the difference is in terms only, or in substance as well. A corporation's accounting notions do not exempt it from compliance with R.S. 12:102B: "company rules do not outrank or invalidate state law" . . . .

* * *

The judgment appealed from is reversed. It is ordered that defendant deliver or mail to plaintiff a condensed balance sheet (showing inter alia and separately the amounts of defendant's stated capital, capital surplus and earned surplus) as of the last day of, and a combined statement of income and earned surplus for, the fiscal year ended May 31, 1973. Defendant is to pay all costs.

PROBLEMS

1. Consider for class discussion whether failure to observe the recommendations in paragraphs 65–70 of Accounting Terminology Bulletin No. 1 could give rise to liability. Cf. the full ¶ on page 98, plus f. n. 189.

2. Freidus, the owner of all the stock of Starrett Corporation, which had been issued for $5,000, had also made loans to the corporation totalling $430,000. After the corporation had incurred an operating deficit of $320,000, its balance sheet appeared as follows:

Cash	$ 10,000	Acc. Pay.	$ 35,000
Acc. Rec.	18,000	Loans Pay.	430,000
Invent.	22,000	Stat. Cap.	5,000
Plant	100,000	Surplus (Deficit)	(320,000)

At that point Freidus forgave the corporation's debt to him. Shortly thereafter, the corporation applied to a federal lending agency for a loan, presenting a balance sheet on which the stockholders' equity section showed simply "Stated Capital" of $5,000 and "Surplus" of $110,000. Thereafter, Freidus was indicted under a statute

2. The 1968 revision and recodification, by the Committee of the Louisiana State Bar Association on the Revision of the Corporation Laws, adopted the terminology of the American Bar Association—American Law Institute Model Business Corporation Act; see Himel, Major Changes Made by the New Business Corporation Law, 1968, 16 La.Bar.J. 123; Miller, The 1968 Business Corporation Law of Louisiana, 1969, 29 La.L.Rev. 435. In respect to the modernness of the terms, see also Henn, Corporations (West, 2d ed. 1970), 633–637.

which prohibits the making of a false or fraudulent statement or representation to any agency of the United States. As a court sitting without a jury, how would you decide the case?

5. EXTRAORDINARY ITEMS AND BY–PASSING THE INCOME STATEMENT

The development of the income statement produced some problems of its own with regard to isolating the results of operations. One major difficulty stems from the fact that the income statement is intended to reflect primarily the results of operations *for a particular period.* To take a simple illustration, how should a company's financial statements reflect a recovery in an antitrust suit representing the lost profits of prior years? Obviously, there is no way to recall the statements of those prior years and amend them now; on the other hand, if the amount involved is material its inclusion in income for the current period might give the impression that current operations were more successful than in fact was the case.

One alternative would be to include the item in current income under a separate caption, such as "Income Unrelated to Current Operations", or "Extraordinary Item", which would appear on the income statement after a figure for "Net Income from Current Operations". The latter figure would then provide a picture of current operations unaffected by the special item. However, since the special item would still be reflected in the final "Net Income" figure for the period, this approach would not entirely resolve the problem, especially from the point of view of average, financially unsophisticated investors, who constitute an important group of financial statement users: these investors frequently concentrate (unduly) upon the final "Net Income" figure, particularly since the financial press often publicizes the net income figure, or net income per share, without paying sufficient attention to the presence of special items and the like.

Another alternative is to build on the fact that if these "lost profits" could have been recorded in the earlier years in which they really "belonged", they would have been included in the respective net income figures for those prior years, and hence would now be reflected in earned surplus. Unlike the income statements for prior years, the earned surplus figure can be effectively amended during the current period, simply by making an entry directly to that account. Thus a special item might be credited (or debited) directly to Earned Surplus, and not appear in the income statement for the current year at all. This process of "by-passing" the income statement is often referred to as a "prior period adjustment", connoting the fact that such a direct entry to Earned Surplus actually represents in effect an adjustment of the results of a prior period, on account of an item which was realized currently but really "belongs" in a prior period.

However, this approach too presents difficulties. One obvious question would be how to decide whether a particular item was "special" enough to be omitted entirely from the income statement (and hence from the determination of net income); management might be sorely tempted to err on the side of regarding losses as special, and therefore excludible, while viewing most gains as ordinary and therefore includible. Such a situation would not be calculated to enhance the meaningfulness of the annual income statement. Then too there is the fact that each individual income statement becomes a part of a series of consecutive income statements, which have a special significance because of the importance of discerning trends as a basis for estimating the future prospects of the enterprise. Ideally, any series of consecutive income statements should portray as complete a picture as possible of the fortunes of the business over the total period covered by the series. The effect of by-passing the income statement for any item is to exclude that item from the entire series of income statements, which could impair the validity of the picture presented by the series. It might be better to include every item of gain or loss in the income statement for some year, with an appropriate caption if that year is not the theoretically most "correct" one; the individual reader of the financial statements can then be left to appraise the significance of particular special items.

A related problem is posed by transactions which are only indirectly related to operations (as distinguished from clearly operational matters which, however, "belong" to some prior period). For example, suppose a corporation sells one of its plants. Should the gain or loss from this relatively unusual transaction be included in the income statement for the current period? If such a transaction is to be reflected in any income statement, the income statement for the current period is clearly the proper one. However, once again there is a risk that the inclusion of such an item could lead those unsophisticated investors who rely too heavily on the single "net income" figure to conclude that the enterprise had been considerably more (or less) successful this year than the results of its ordinary, recurring operations would suggest. On the other hand, by-passing the income statement in favor of a direct credit (or debit) to Earned Surplus would exclude this very significant item from the series of income statements and thereby impair the validity of the data obtained therefrom (especially if the enterprise is large enough that sale of a plant is a phenomenon that recurs from time to time).

The conflict between these two objectives—making each individual income statement as meaningful a picture as possible of the operations of the business for that period, and having any series of income statements represent a virtually complete portrayal of the fortunes of the enterprise for the time-span covered by the series—has been a source of continual difficulty. For many years the question of which way to treat any particular unusual item was regarded as pretty much a matter of judgment, to be resolved by each company as it saw fit. Predictably, such flexibility caused a good deal of trouble, both in comparing the company's current performance with its earlier years, and in making current comparisons with other companies which may have treated similar items differently; indeed, sometimes it was difficult just to decide how to describe the current performance, as demonstrated by the following excerpt from Forbes Magazine for May 15, 1967 (which incidentally also illustrates the important role played by the financial press):

```
FAIRCHILD HILLER CORP.
   9 mos Sept 30:    b-1966          1965
   Share earns ....     a-$.88          $.69
   Sales, etc ...... 146,902,000  c-62,111,000
   Net income ..... a-3,910,000     2,064,000
      a-Excludes net gain of $1,630,000 equal to
   37 cents a share, from partial liquidation of
   investment in stock of RAC Corp.  b-includes
   operations of Republic Aviation division.  c-
   Restated by company.
```

```
       FAIRCHILD HILLER CORP.
   9 mos. Sept. 30      1966         1965
   Net income ........ *$5,540,000  $2,064,000
   Shr. earns .........      1.25        69c
      *After a special gain of $1,630,000 from a
   partial liquidation of stock in the RAC Corpo-
   ration.
```

88 CENTS OR $1.25?

Did Fairchild Hiller earn 88 cents or $1.25 per share during the first nine months of 1966? Did Teleprompter earn 29 cents or 81 cents?

It depended on which newspaper you read last Nov. 2. Quite clearly, three of the nation's largest dailies could not get together on the reports.

These clippings from the *New York Times*, the *Wall Street Journal* and the *World Journal Tribune* are not isolated examples, they have occurred with disturbing frequency. The main problem has been the so-called "extraordinary" or "nonrecurring" gains and losses—items like a profit on the sale of a plant or a write-off of a discontinued product line. It was not necessarily the fault of the newspapers; the accountants themselves could not agree on whether or not to include them in net income. So the public, through the press, was left to figure it out.

This year the CPAs are requiring companies to *include* extraordinary items in their "net income" figures, and to identify that part of it that is "extraordinary." Under the new setup, Fairchild's earnings were $1.25 per share, with 37 cents of extraordinary income; Tele-

prompter's were 81 cents with 52 cents of extraordinary income.

Teleprompter Corp. nine months to Sept. 30 net $236,761 or 29 cents a share vs $210,430 or 28 cents a share.

TELEPROMPTER CORP.		
	9 mos. to Sept. 30 1966	1965
Revenues ...	R$14,803,628	$4,006,091
Net Income	663,211	*210,430
Shr. earns	81c	28c
*No provisions were made for Federal income taxes due to tax-loss carryforwards.		

Perhaps, the most dramatic example in American industrial life of differing judgments about how to handle an extraordinary item is illustrated by the following excerpts from the financial statements of General Motors and Standard Oil of New Jersey, indicating the different ways in which the two companies treated the sale of a 50% stock interest in Ethyl Corporation.

1.　FROM THE ANNUAL REPORT OF GENERAL MOTORS CORPORATION FOR 1962:

THE STORY OF ETHYL

On February 2, 1923, a motorist drove up to a Dayton, Ohio, filling station and made the first purchase of a new kind of gasoline called "Ethyl." But the Ethyl story really began with the 1912 Cadillac—the first car offering an electric self-starter coupled with a battery-ignition system. Critics of this new electrical system blamed it when the engine knocked under certain conditions. Experiments made by Charles F. Kettering, inventor of the system, indicated, however, that the difficulty lay in the quality of the fuel, not in the ignition system. Under the direction of Mr. Kettering, an intensive research program was conducted by General Motors, with a young engineer, Thomas Midgely, in charge. At first the experiments were plagued by failure. All evidence, however, pointed to some compound of lead as the cure.

On December 9, 1921, a spoonful of tetraethyl lead (TEL) was poured into the gasoline tank of a test engine operated so as to produce knock. The knock stopped. Further experimentation proved that as little as one part of TEL in 4,000 parts of gasoline would prevent engine knock. Other problems remained, however. It took more than a year of experimenting to produce the right combination—compounds of bromine and chlorine combined with TEL to form Ethyl fluid.

Meanwhile Standard Oil Company (New Jersey) had developed methods for producing TEL in commercial quantities, and in 1924 GM and Standard Oil formed the Ethyl Gasoline Corporation. Prior to 1948 Ethyl fluid was produced for Ethyl under agreements with another manufacturer. Commencing in 1948 Ethyl began producing all of its Ethyl fluid requirements itself.

The new company had more than its share of problems both in processing and marketing its product. By 1926, however, the growing demand indicated that its bromine requirements would shortly exceed the world's annual output. Extraction from sea water proved to be the answer, and Ethyl Corporation, together with Dow Chemical Company, which provided the process, established an extraction plant near Wilmington, N. C. Ethyl was firmly established, and its trademark became familiar to motorists in many countries. As time went by, Ethyl broadened its operations to include more than 50 other chemical products. It built a research laboratory in Detroit and at a later date established other laboratories and research facilities in Baton Rouge, La., for continuing improvement of existing products and development of new ones.

The discovery of TEL as an antiknock compound and its commercial development came about through long and painstaking research. Continued efforts made it possible to improve its quality and lower its cost. Not only was the performance of the automobile improved through higher compression engines made possible by TEL, but operating costs to motorists were reduced through lower gasoline consumption that also contributed to a more economical use of petroleum resources. Seldom has the contribution of research to industrial progress been more dramatically demonstrated. The 40-year Ethyl saga is a striking demonstration of the need for continued energetic effort in the field of research. The work done by the men who developed TEL represented a substantial contribution to General Motors and the economy.

Ethyl Corporation continued to be jointly owned by General Motors and Standard Oil Company, (New Jersey) until November, 1962, when each of these companies sold its interest to Albemarle Paper Manufacturing Company of Richmond, Virginia. GM's decision to accept the Albemarle offer was in line with Corporation policy since the middle 1940's to dispose of investments in partially owned companies and to carry on its operations through divisions or wholly owned subsidiaries.

FINANCIAL REVIEW

* * *

Extraordinary Income From Investment in Ethyl Corporation

In November, 1962, General Motors sold its entire 50% investment in the outstanding capital stock of Ethyl Corporation for $58,-183,132, and received therefor $48,183,132 in cash and $10,000,000 in $5\frac{3}{4}\%$ five-year subordinated notes of the purchaser. The investment in Ethyl Corporation had been carried by the Corporation at a value of $17,519,633, representing the cost of the investment adjusted to include the Corporation's proportion of Ethyl's undivided profits at December 31, 1935. The excess of $40,663,499 in the proceeds from the sale over the carrying value, together with dividends of $60,797,706 received from Ethyl Corporation ($28,000,000 in February out of Ethyl's accumulated earnings of prior years and $32,797,706 in November as a distribution of Ethyl's entire earned surplus through October 31, 1962), resulted in extraordinary income in 1962 amounting to $101,461,205 as shown in the Statement of Consolidated Income. This was equivalent to $0.27 [sic] * per share.

GENERAL MOTORS CORPORATION
and consolidated subsidiaries

STATEMENT OF CONSOLIDATED INCOME
for the years ended December 31, 1962 and 1961

	Year 1962	Year 1961
Net Sales	$14,640,240,799	$11,395,916,826
Equity in earnings of subsidiary companies not consolidated (dividends and interest received amounted to $29,081,483 in 1962 and $32,940,896 in 1961)	50,625,402	58,143,795
Extraordinary income representing special dividends received from, and net proceeds from the sale of the investment in, Ethyl Corporation	101,461,205	—
Other income less sundry income deductions ..	60,133,485	59,008,919
Total	14,852,460,891	11,513,069,540
Less:		
Cost of sales and other operating charges, exclusive of items listed below	10,645,094,732	8,593,215,464
Selling, general, and administrative expenses	718,570,213	656,367,277
Interest and discount on 3¼% debentures	4,678,565	5,940,791
Depreciation and obsolescence of real estate, plants, and equipment	444,639,931	408,547,704
Provision for Bonus Plan and Stock Option Plan	105,000,000	80,976,860
Provision for United States and foreign income taxes	1,475,400,000	875,200,000
Total	13,393,383,441	10,620,248,096
Net Income for the year	1,459,077,450	892,821,444
Dividends on preferred stocks	12,928,290	12,928,292
Amount Earned on Common Stock	$ 1,446,149,160	$ 879,893,152
Average number of shares of common stock outstanding during the year	283,488,664	282,920,050
Amount Earned per Share of Common Stock	$5.10	$3.11

NOTE: Net income and amount earned per share of common stock for 1962 include extraordinary income equivalent to $0.27 per share from General Motors' investment in Ethyl Corporation, which was sold in 1962, as explained on page 34.

* On the 283,488,664 shares of GM stock outstanding, $101,461,205 amounts to approximately $0.36 per share. Excluding the February dividend of $28,000,000 produces a figure of approximately $0.26 per share.

2. FROM THE ANNUAL REPORT OF STANDARD OIL COMPANY (NEW JERSEY) FOR 1962:

FINANCIAL REVIEW

Consolidated earnings of Jersey and its affiliated companies owned more than 50 per cent rose by $82,820,000, or 11 per cent, in 1962 to $840,903,000 or $3.88 a share. This marked the fourth consecutive year of significant gains in earnings. In addition, a nonrecurring gain of $75,298,000 was realized in the last quarter of the year on Jersey's 50 per cent investment in the Ethyl Corporation. This amount, which was added directly to "earnings reinvested and employed in business," consisted of a $32,797,000 dividend out of Ethyl's remaining undistributed earnings of prior years and a $42,501,000 gain on the sale of this investment.

STANDARD OIL COMPANY (NEW JERSEY)

CONSOLIDATED STATEMENT OF INCOME
for the Years 1962 and 1961

	1962	1961
Revenues		
Sales and other operating revenue	$10,326,877,000	$9,148,151,000
Dividends, interest, and other revenue	249,405,000	208,236,000
	10,576,282,000	9,356,387,000
Costs and other deductions		
Crude oil, products, materials, and services ...	4,766,337,000	4,193,377,000
Taxes and other payments to governments (page 21)	3,282,542,000	2,851,711,000
Wages, salaries, and employee benefits	991,623,000	922,970,000
Depreciation, depletion, and retirements	586,467,000	545,696,000
Interest and other financial charges	69,488,000	48,491,000
Income applicable to minority interests	38,922,000	36,059,000
	9,735,379,000	8,598,304,000
Net income	$ 840,903,000	$ 758,083,000

STANDARD OIL COMPANY (NEW JERSEY)

CONSOLIDATED STATEMENT OF SHAREHOLDERS' EQUITY
for the Year 1962

	Capital	Earnings Reinvested	Total
Balances at December 31, 1961	$2,375,657,000	$4,716,177,000	$7,091,834,000
Adjustments arising on consolidation of Esso Standard Eastern (page 20)		139,543,000	139,543,000
Nonrecurring income realized on Ethyl Corporation investment (page 20)		75,298,000	75,298,000
Consolidated net income for 1962		840,903,000	840,903,000
Cash dividends paid in 1962 ...		(537,844,000)	(537,844,000)
Balances at December 31, 1962	$2,375,657,000	$5,234,077,000	$7,609,734,000
Standard Oil Company (New Jersey), parent company	$2,375,657,000	$1,956,828,000	$4,332,485,000
Affiliates operating in Western Hemisphere		2,870,731,000	2,870,731,000
Affiliates operating in Eastern Hemisphere		406,518,000	406,518,000
	$2,375,657,000	$5,234,077,000	$7,609,734,000

3. FROM GILBERT AND GILBERT, TWENTY–FOURTH ANNUAL REPORT OF STOCKHOLDER ACTIVITIES AT CORPORATION MEETINGS (held in 1963): *

Treatment of Sale of Capital Asset—

GM vs. Standard Oil of New Jersey

An article in the Harvard Business Review (May-June 1963) entitled *Showdown On Accounting Principles*, written by Robert N. Anthony stated:

> It is certainly conceivable that the gain on the sale of a capital asset under certain circumstances should be credited to net income, and under other circumstances should be credited directly to owners' equity. But this difference in practice should be consistent with some principle which gives a guide to the action that is appropriate. By contrast, the current situation is illustrated by the following example:

> General Motors and Standard Oil of New Jersey each recently sold its half ownership in Ethyl Corp. at a book gain of many

millions of dollars. GM reported its 50% of the gain as part of its net income for the year. Standard Oil left net income unaffected, crediting its 50% directly to surplus.

From the floor at both the GM and SONJ annual meetings Lewis Gilbert raised the question of accounting treatment of the gain. At GM he received the following reply from Chairman Frederic Donner:

> I think that when we consider these matters of accounting principles that the consistency of the principles followed by an individual company within its own sphere is very important, and I think you will find, certainly over the 36 years that I have been with General Motors, we have followed very consistently the practice of incorporating all these items, whether good or bad, whether pluses or minuses, through the income account, so that if you pick up the summary page, I think it has 20 years results, in the annual report you can tell the changes in our net worth through operations just by adding up the income.

> I personally feel very strongly that there is an accepted practice and that the consistency with which it is followed makes it even more acceptable in a situation.

> What Standard Oil does within its own confines I believe is another matter, for them to consider. I am only speaking of General Motors.

At SONJ Chairman M. J. Rathbone replied:

> A non-recurring gain of about $75,000,000 was realized in the last quarter on Jersey's 50 per cent investment in the Ethyl Corporation.

> We debated this question very carefully in our board and also with our Comptroller, and he in turn discussed it with the outside auditors. We felt that, in view of the size of this item in relation to the total earnings, if we had credited it to current earnings, the reported results for the year would have been materially distorted. We felt it would give a more realistic picture of the progress of the company from the standpoint of comparative figures from year to year if we did not have this sort of distortion in one particular year. For this reason, the $75,000,000 gain was credited as a surplus adjustment on our books.

> Mr. Gilbert—Tell us how many cents a share was involved.

> The Chairman—It was equal to about 35 cents a share.

In the circumstances, it is not surprising that the need for clearer guidelines for dealing with unusual items was perceived by the principle-making arms of the profession. But setting the guidelines has proved to be quite a difficult task, as the following materials indicate:

APB OPINION NO. 9 *

December, 1966.

REPORTING THE RESULTS OF OPERATIONS

I–Net Income and the Treatment of Extraordinary Items
and Prior Period Adjustments

II–Computation and Reporting of Earnings Per Share [Omitted]

INTRODUCTION

1. The American Institute of Certified Public Accountants, through its boards and committees, reviews from time to time the form and content of financial statements to determine how their usefulness may be improved. This Opinion is the result of a review of present practice in the reporting of the results of operations of business entities.

* * *

3. This Opinion (a) concludes that net income should reflect all items of profit and loss recognized during the period except for prior period adjustments, with extraordinary items to be shown separately as an element of net income of the period, (b) specifies the criteria to be used in determining which items, if any, recognized during the current period are to be considered extraordinary items, (c) specifies the criteria to be used in determining which items, if any, recognized during the current period are to be considered prior period adjustments and excluded from net income for the current period and (d) specifies the statement format and terminology to be used and the disclosures to be made when extraordinary items or prior period adjustments are present.

4. This Opinion also specifies the method of treating extraordinary items and prior period adjustments in comparative statements for two or more periods, specifies the disclosures required when previously issued statements of income are restated and recommends methods of presentation of historical, statistical-type financial summaries which include extraordinary items or are affected by prior period adjustments. . . .

5. For convenience, the term *net income* is used herein to refer to either net income or net loss. Similarly, *net income per share* or *earnings per share* is used to refer to either net income (or earnings) per share or net loss per share.

Applicability

6. This Opinion applies to general purpose statements which purport to present results of operations in conformity with generally accepted accounting principles. . . .

I—NET INCOME AND THE TREATMENT OF EXTRAORDINARY ITEMS AND PRIOR PERIOD ADJUSTMENTS

DISCUSSION

General

7.   Business entities have developed a reporting pattern under which periodic financial statements are prepared from their accounting records to reflect the financial position of the entity at a particular date and the financial results of its activities for a specified period or periods.   The statement of income and the statement of retained earnings (separately or combined) are designed to reflect, in a broad sense, the "results of operations."

8.   A problem in reporting the results of operations of a business entity for one or more periods is the treatment of extraordinary items and prior period adjustments.   This Opinion discusses the nature of events and transactions which might be considered "extraordinary," establishes related criteria which the Board feels are reasonable and practicable, and specifies the method and extent of disclosure of such items in the financial statements.   The Opinion also discusses the various types of adjustment which might be considered to be proper adjustments of the recorded results of operations of prior periods and establishes criteria which the Board feels are reasonable and practicable for the relatively few items which should be so recognized.

Historical Background

General

9.   There is considerable diversity of views as to whether extraordinary items and prior period adjustments should enter into the determination of net income of the period in which they are recognized. When Accounting Research Bulletin No. 32 was issued in December 1947, as well as when it was reissued in June 1953 as Chapter 8 of Accounting Research Bulletin No. 43, two conflicting viewpoints had attracted considerable support.   The paragraphs which follow summarize the discussion of these two viewpoints contained in Chapter 8.

Current Operating Performance

10.   Under one viewpoint, designated *current operating performance,* the principal emphasis is upon the ordinary, normal, recurring operations of the entity during the current period.   If extraordinary or prior period transactions have occurred, their inclusion might impair the significance of net income to such an extent that misleading inferences might be drawn from the amount so designated.

11.   Advocates of this position believe that users of financial statements attach a particular business significance to the statement of income and the "net income" reported therein.   They point out that, while some users are able to analyze a statement of income and to eliminate from it those prior period adjustments and extraordinary items which may tend to impair its usefulness for their purposes, many users are not trained to do this.   They believe that management (subject to the attestation of the independent auditors) is in a better posi-

tion to do this, and to eliminate the effect of such items from the amount designated as net income.

12. Advocates of this position also point out that many companies, in order to give more useful information concerning their earnings performance, restate the earnings or losses of affected periods to reflect the proper allocation of prior period adjustments. They believe therefore that items of this type may best be handled as direct adjustments of retained earnings or as "special items" excluded from net income of the current period. They feel that extraordinary items of *all* types may often best be disclosed as direct adjustments of retained earnings, since this eliminates any distortive effect on reported earnings.

All Inclusive

13. Under the other viewpoint, designated *all inclusive*, net income is presumed to include all transactions affecting the net increase or decrease in proprietorship equity during the current period, except dividend distributions and transactions of a capital nature.

14. Proponents of this position believe that the aggregate of such periodic net incomes, over the life of an enterprise, constitutes total net income, and that this is the only fair and complete method of reporting the results of operations of the entity. They believe that extraordinary items and prior period adjustments are part of the earnings history of an entity and that omission of such items from periodic statements of income increases the possibility that these items will be overlooked in a review of operating results for a period of years. They also stress the dangers of possible manipulation of annual earnings figures if such items may be omitted from the determination of net income. They believe that a statement of income including all such items is easy to understand and less subject to variations resulting from different judgments. They feel that, when judgment is allowed to determine whether to include or exclude particular items or adjustments, significant differences develop in the treatment of borderline cases and that there is a danger that the use of "extraordinary" as a criterion may be a means of equalizing income. Advocates of this theory believe that full disclosure in the income statement of the nature of any extraordinary items or prior period adjustments during each period will enable the user of a statement of income to make his own assessment of the importance of the items and their effects on operating results.

Decisions of Committee on Accounting Procedure—Subsequent Developments

15. The committee on accounting procedure (predecessor of the Accounting Principles Board) did not embrace either of these viewpoints in its entirety in issuing its first Accounting Research Bulletin on this subject in December 1947. Instead, the committee stated ". . . it is the opinion of the committee that there should be a general presumption that all items of profit and loss recognized during the period are to be used in determining the figure reported as net income. The only possible exception to this presumption in any case would be with respect to items which in the aggregate are materially significant in relation to the company's net income and are clearly not

identifiable with or do not result from the usual or typical business operations of the period. Thus, only extraordinary items such as the following may be excluded from the determination of net income for the year, and they should be excluded when their inclusion would impair the significance of net income so that misleading inferences might be drawn therefrom: . . . ." The list of items which followed consisted of material charges or credits, other than ordinary adjustments of a recurring nature, (a) specifically related to operations of prior years, (b) resulting from unusual sales of assets not acquired for resale and not of the type in which the company usually deals, (c) resulting from losses of a type not usually insured against, (d) resulting from the write-off of a material amount of intangibles . . . .

16.   Since the issuance of these guidelines for the determination of net income, developments in the business and investment environment have increased the emphasis on, and interest in, the financial reporting format of business entities and the nature of the amount shown as net income therein. As a result of the widespread and increasing dissemination of financial data, often in highly condensed form, to investors and potential investors, suggestions have been made that the criteria for the determination of the amount to be reported as net income, insofar as it is affected by extraordinary items and prior period adjustments, should be re-examined.

OPINION

Summary

17.   The Board has considered various methods of reporting the effects of extraordinary events and transactions and of prior period adjustments which are recorded in the accounts during a particular accounting period. The Board has concluded that net income should reflect all items of profit and loss recognized during the period with the sole exception of the prior period adjustments described below. *Extraordinary items* should, however, be segregated from the results of ordinary operations and shown separately in the income statement, with disclosure of the nature and amounts thereof. The criteria for determination of extraordinary items are described in paragraph 21 below.

18.   With respect to *prior period adjustments*, the Board has concluded that those rare items which relate directly to the operations of a specific prior period or periods, which are material and which qualify under the criteria described in paragraphs 23 and 24 below should, in single period statements, be reflected as adjustments of the opening balance of retained earnings. When comparative statements are presented, corresponding adjustments should be made of the amounts of net income (and the components thereof) and retained earnings balances (as well as of other affected balances) for all of the periods reported therein, to reflect the retroactive application of the prior period adjustments. (See paragraph 26 for required disclosures of prior period adjustments.)

* * *

Income Statement Presentation

20. Under this approach, the income statement should disclose the following elements:

Income before extraordinary items
Extraordinary items
(less applicable income tax)
Net income

If the extraordinary items are few in number, descriptive captions may replace the caption *extraordinary items* and related notes. In such cases, the first and last captions shown above should nonetheless appear. Similarly, even though material extraordinary items may net to an immaterial amount, they should be positioned and disclosed as indicated above, and the first and last captions shown above should appear. If there are no extraordinary items, the caption *net income* should replace the three captions shown above. The amount of income tax applicable to the segregated items should be disclosed, either on the face of the income statement or in a note thereto. . . . Illustrative examples of the treatment of such items in financial statements appear herein as Exhibits A through D.

Criteria for Extraordinary Items Related to the Current Period *

21. The segregation in the income statement of the effects of events and transactions which have occurred during the current period, which are of an extraordinary nature and whose effects are material requires the exercise of judgment. (In determining materiality, items of a similar nature should be considered in the aggregate. Dissimilar items should be considered individually; however, if they are few in number, they should be considered in the aggregate.) Such events and transactions are identified primarily by the nature of the underlying occurrence. They will be of a character significantly different from the typical or customary business activities of the entity. Accordingly, they will be events and transactions of material effect which would not be expected to recur frequently and which would not be considered as recurring factors in any evaluation of the ordinary operating processes of the business. Examples of extraordinary items, assuming that each case qualifies under the criteria outlined above, include material gains or losses (or provisions for losses) from (a) the sale or abandonment of a plant or a significant segment of the business, (b) the sale of an investment not acquired for resale, (c) the write-off of goodwill due to unusual events or developments within the period, (d) the condemnation or expropriation of properties and (e) a major devaluation of a foreign currency. As indicated above, such material items, less applicable income tax effect, should be segregated, but reflected in the determination of net income.

22. Certain gains or losses (or provisions for losses), regardless of size, do not constitute extraordinary items (or prior period adjustments) because they are of a character typical of the customary busi-

---

* [Ed. note] These criteria were significantly narrowed by APB Op. No. 30, set out at page 189 et seq.

ness activities of the entity. Examples include (a) write-downs of receivables, inventories and research and development costs, (b) adjustments of accrued contract prices and (c) gains or losses from fluctuations of foreign exchange. The effects of items of this nature should be reflected in the determination of income before extraordinary items. If such effects are material, disclosure is recommended.

Criteria for Prior Period Adjustments **

23.   Adjustments related to prior periods—and thus excluded in the determination of net income for the current period—are limited to those material adjustments which (a) can be specifically identified with and directly related to the business activities of particular prior periods, and (b) are not attributable to economic events occurring subsequent to the date of the financial statements for the prior period, and (c) depend primarily on determinations by persons other than management and (d) were not susceptible of reasonable estimation prior to such determination. Such adjustments are rare in modern financial accounting. They relate to events or transactions which occurred in a prior period, the accounting effects of which could not be determined with reasonable assurance at that time, usually because of some major uncertainty then existing. Evidence of such an uncertainty would be disclosure thereof in the financial statements of the applicable period, or of an intervening period in those cases in which the uncertainty became apparent during a subsequent period. Further, it would be expected that, in most cases, the opinion of the reporting independent auditor on such prior period would have contained a qualification because of the uncertainty. Examples are material, nonrecurring adjustments or settlements of income taxes, of renegotiation proceedings or of utility revenue under rate processes. Settlements of significant amounts resulting from litigation or similar claims may also constitute prior period adjustments.

24.   Treatment as prior period adjustments should not be applied to the normal, recurring corrections and adjustments which are the natural result of the use of estimates inherent in the accounting process. For example, changes in the estimated remaining lives of fixed assets affect the computed amounts of depreciation, but these changes should be considered prospective in nature and not prior period adjustments. Similarly, relatively immaterial adjustments of provisions for liabilities (including income taxes) made in prior periods should be considered recurring items to be reflected in operations of the current period. Some uncertainties, for example those relating to the realization of assets (collectibility of accounts receivable, ultimate recovery of deferred costs or realizability of inventories or other assets), would not qualify for prior period adjustment treatment, since economic events subsequent to the date of the financial statements must of necessity enter into the elimination of any previously-existing uncertainty. Therefore, the effects of such matters are considered to be elements in the determination of net income for the period in which the uncertainty is eliminated. Thus, the Board believes that prior period adjustments will be rare.

*   *   *

** [Ed. note] Prior period adjustments
were virtually eliminated by FAS No.
16, set out at page 194 et seq.

Disclosure of Prior Period Adjustments and Restatements of Reported Net Income

26. When prior period adjustments are recorded, the resulting effects (both gross and net of applicable income tax) on the net income of prior periods should be disclosed in the annual report for the year in which the adjustments are made. When financial statements for a single period only are presented, this disclosure should indicate the effects of such restatement on the balance of retained earnings at the beginning of the period and on the net income of the immediately preceding period. When financial statements for more than one period are presented, which is ordinarily the preferable procedure, the disclosure should include the effects for each of the periods included in the statements. Such disclosures should include the amounts of income tax applicable to the prior period adjustments. Disclosure of restatements in annual reports issued subsequent to the first such postrevision disclosure would ordinarily not be required.

*   *   *

Capital Transactions

28. The Board reaffirms the conclusion of the former committee on accounting procedure that the following should be excluded from the determination of net income or the results of operations under all circumstances: (a) adjustments or charges or credits resulting from transactions in the company's own capital stock, (b) transfers to and from accounts properly designated as appropriated retained earnings (such as general purpose contingency reserves or provisions for replacement costs of fixed assets) and (c) adjustments made pursuant to a quasi-reorganization.

*   *   *

The Opinion entitled "Reporting the Results of Operations" was adopted unanimously by the twenty members of the Board, of whom five . . . assented with qualification.

Mr. Biegler assents to the issuance of this Opinion because he believes that the usefulness of the income statement to the investor is enhanced when all items of profit and loss relating to the period are included in the determination of net income and the results of the ordinary, recurring operations of a business are reported separately from extraordinary items. He believes that the caption described in paragraph 20 as "Income before extraordinary items" can best meet the needs of investors for an index of the results of and trends in ordinary recurring operations when there is excluded therefrom those gains or losses which are extraordinary because of the combination of rarity in the circumstances giving rise thereto and the abnormal size thereof. Accordingly, he dissents from the conclusion stated in paragraph 22 that certain types of gains or losses, *regardless of size*, must be reflected in the determination of "income before extraordinary items." He believes that the quality of being extraordinary can be derived from rarity or extreme infrequency in size, as well as from the nature of a transaction or event.

*   *   *

EXHIBITS

ILLUSTRATIVE STATEMENTS

The following examples illustrate the treatment of extraordinary items and prior period adjustments in financial statements. The format of the statements is illustrative only, and does not necessarily reflect a preference by the Accounting Principles Board for the format or for the intermediate captions shown. . . .

EXHIBIT A

STATEMENT OF INCOME AND RETAINED EARNINGS
Years Ended December 31, 1967 and December 31, 1966

	1967	1966
Net sales	$84,580,000	$75,650,000
Other income	80,000	100,000
	84,660,000	75,750,000
Cost and expenses—		
Cost of goods sold	60,000,000	55,600,000
Selling, general and administrative expenses	5,000,000	4,600,000
Interest expense	100,000	100,000
Other deductions	80,000	90,000
Income tax	9,350,000	7,370,000
	74,530,000	67,760,000
Income before extraordinary items	10,130,000	7,990,000
Extraordinary items, net of applicable income tax of $1,880,000 in 1967 (Note 1)	(2,040,000)	(1,280,000)
Net Income	8,090,000	6,710,000
Retained earnings at beginning of year—		
As previously reported	28,840,000	25,110,000
Adjustments (Note 2)	(3,160,000)	(1,760,000)
As restated	25,680,000	23,350,000
	33,770,000	30,060,000
Cash dividends on common stock—		
$.75 per share	4,380,000	4,380,000
Retained earnings at end of year	$29,390,000	$25,680,000
Per share of common stock—		
Income before extraordinary items	$1.73	$1.37
Extraordinary items, net of tax	(.34)	(.22)
Net income	$1.39	$1.15

NOTE 1.   During 1967 the Company sold one of its plants at a net loss of $2,040,000, after applicable income tax reduction of $1,880,000. During 1966 the Company sold an investment in marketable securities at a loss of $1,280,-000, with no income tax effect.

NOTE 2.   The balance of retained earnings at December 31, 1966, has been restated from amounts previously reported to reflect a retroactive charge of $3,160,000 for additional income taxes settled in 1967. Of this amount, $1,400,000 ($.24 per share) is applicable to 1966 and has been reflected as an increase in tax expense for that year, the balance (applicable to years prior to 1966) being charged to retained earnings at January 1, 1966.

APB OPINION NO. 30 *

Accounting Principles Board, 1973.

REPORTING THE RESULTS OF OPERATIONS

Introduction

* * *

3.   The purposes of this Opinion are (1) to provide more definitive criteria for extraordinary items by clarifying and, to some extent, modifying the existing definition and criteria, (2) to specify disclosure requirements for extraordinary items, (3) to specify the accounting and reporting for disposal of a segment of a business, (4) to specify disclosure requirements for other unusual or infrequently occurring events and transactions that are not extraordinary items.

* * *

Applicability

7.   This Opinion supersedes paragraphs 20 through 22, paragraph 29 insofar as it refers to examples of financial statements, and Exhibits A through D of APB Opinion No. 9. . . .

* * *

OPINION

Income Statement Presentation and Disclosure

8.   *Discontinued Operations of a Segment of a Business.*   For purposes of this Opinion, the term *discontinued operations* refers to the operations of a segment of a business as defined in paragraph 13 that has been sold, abandoned, spun off, or otherwise disposed of or, although still operating, is the subject of a formal plan for disposal. . . .   The Board concludes that the results of continuing operations should be reported separately from discontinued operations and that any gain or loss from disposal of a segment of a business . . . should be reported in conjunction with the related results of discontinued operations and not as an extraordinary item.   Accordingly, operations of a segment that has been or will be discontinued should be reported separately as a component of income before extraordinary items. . . .

* * *

10.   *Extraordinary Items.*   The Board has also reconsidered the presentation of extraordinary items in an income statement as prescribed in APB Opinion No. 9, and reaffirms the need to segregate extraordinary items. . . .

11.   . . . . .   The caption *extraordinary items* should be used to identify separately the effects of events and transactions, other than

---

the disposal of a segment of a business, that meet the criteria for classification as extraordinary as discussed in paragraphs 19–24. . .

* * *

Criteria for Extraordinary Items

19. Judgment is required to segregate in the income statement the effects of events or transactions that are extraordinary items (as required by paragraph 11). The Board concludes that an event or transaction should be presumed to be an ordinary and usual activity of the reporting entity, the effects of which should be included in income from operations, unless the evidence clearly supports its classification as an extraordinary item as defined in this Opinion.

20. Extraordinary items are events and transactions that are distinguished by their unusual nature *and* by the infrequency of their occurrence. Thus, *both* of the following criteria should be met to classify an event or transaction as an extraordinary item:

a. *Unusual nature*—the underlying event or transaction should possess a high degree of abnormality and be of a type clearly unrelated to, or only incidentally related to, the ordinary and typical activities of the entity, taking into account the environment in which the entity operates. (See discussion in paragraph 21.)

b. *Infrequency of occurrence*—the underlying event or transaction should be of a type that would not reasonably be expected to recur in the foreseeable future, taking into account the environment in which the entity operates. (See discussion in paragraph 22.)

21. *Unusual Nature.* The specific characteristics of the entity, such as type and scope of operations, lines of business, and operating policies should be considered in determining ordinary and typical activities of an entity. The environment in which an entity operates is a primary consideration in determining whether an underlying event or transaction is abnormal and significantly different from the ordinary and typical activities of the entity. The environment of an entity includes such factors as the characteristics of the industry or industries in which it operates, the geographical location of its operations, and the nature and extent of governmental regulation. Thus, an event or transaction may be unusual in nature for one entity but not for another because of differences in their respective environments. Unusual nature is not established by the fact that an event or transaction is beyond the control of management.

22. *Infrequency of Occurrence.* For purposes of this Opinion, an event or transaction of a type not reasonably expected to recur in the foreseeable future is considered to occur infrequently. Determining the probability of recurrence of a particular event or transaction in the foreseeable future should take into account the environment in which an entity operates. Accordingly, a specific transaction of one entity might meet that criterion and a similar transaction of another entity might not because of different probabilities of recurrence. The past occurrence of an event or transaction for a particular entity provides evidence to assess the probability of recurrence of that type of event or transaction in the foreseeable future. By definition, extra-

ordinary items occur infrequently. However, mere infrequency of occurrence of a particular event or transaction does not alone imply that its effects should be classified as extraordinary. An event or transaction of a type that occurs frequently in the environment in which the entity operates cannot, by definition, be considered as extraordinary, regardless of its financial effect.

23. Certain gains and losses should not be reported as extraordinary items because they are usual in nature or may be expected to recur as a consequence of customary and continuing business activities. Examples include:

    a. Write-down or write-off of receivables, inventories, equipment leased to others, . . . or . . . intangible assets.

    b. Gains or losses from exchange or translation of foreign currencies, including those relating to major devaluations and revaluations.

    c. Gains or losses on disposal of a segment of a business.

    d. Other gains or losses from sale or abandonment of property, plant, or equipment used in the business.

    e. Effects of a strike, including those against competitors and major suppliers.

    f. Adjustment of accruals on long-term contracts.

In rare situations, an event or transaction may occur that clearly meets both criteria specified in paragraph 20 of this Opinion and thus gives rise to an extraordinary gain or loss that includes one or more of the gains or losses enumerated above. In these circumstances, gains or losses such as (a) and (d) above should be included in the extraordinary item if they are a direct result of a major casualty (such as an earthquake), an expropriation, or a prohibition under a newly enacted law or regulation that clearly meets both criteria specified in paragraph 20. However, any portion of such losses which would have resulted from a valuation of assets on a going-concern basis should not be included in the extraordinary items. Disposals of a segment of a business should be accounted for pursuant to paragraph 13 and presented in the income statement pursuant to paragraph 8 even though the circumstances of the disposal meet the criteria specified in paragraph 20.

24. *Materiality.* The effect of an extraordinary event or transaction should be classified separately in the income statement in the manner described in paragraph 11 if it is material in relation to income before extraordinary items or to the trend of annual earnings before extraordinary items, or is material by other appropriate criteria. Items should be considered individually and not in the aggregate in determining whether an extraordinary event or transaction is material. However, the effects of a series of related transactions arising from a single specific and identifiable event or plan of action that otherwise meets the two criteria in paragraph 20 should be aggregated to determine materiality.

                    *   *   *

Disclosure of Unusual or Infrequently Occurring Items

26.   A material event or transaction that is unusual in nature or occurs infrequently but not both, and therefore does not meet both criteria for classification as an extraordinary item, should be reported as a separate component of income from continuing operations. The nature and financial effects of each event or transaction should be disclosed on the face of the income statement or, alternatively, in notes to the financial statements. Gains or losses of a similar nature that are not individually material should be aggregated. Such items should not be reported on the face of the income statement net of income taxes or in any manner inconsistent with the provisions of paragraphs 8 and 11 of this Opinion or in any other manner that may imply that they are extraordinary items. Similarly, the earnings per share effects of those items should not be disclosed on the face of the income statement.

* * *

ACCOUNTING INTERPRETATIONS *

The Journal of Accountancy, November, 1973, 82.

The Institute staff has been authorized to issue interpretations of accounting questions having general interest to the profession.

The purpose of the interpretations is to provide guidance on a timely basis without the formal procedures required for an APB Opinion and to clarify points on which past practice may have varied and been considered generally accepted. These interpretations, which are reviewed with informed members of the profession, are not pronouncements of the Board. However, members should be aware that they may be called upon to justify departures from the interpretations.

* * *

Illustration of the Application of APB Opinion No. 30

Question—As stated in paragraph 19 of APB Opinion No. 30, judgment is required to segregate in the income statement the effects of events or transactions that are extraordinary items. What factors must be considered in determining whether the effects of a particular event or transaction are extraordinary items or should otherwise be set forth in the income statement, and how are these factors applied in practice?

Interpretation—The first question which generally should be considered in determining the appropriate classification of profit or loss items which appear to be unusual, infrequently occurring or extraordinary is: Does the event or transaction involve the sale, abandonment or other manner of disposal of a segment of a business as defined in paragraph 13 of the Opinion?

* * *

If it has been determined that the particular event or transaction is not a disposal of a segment of a business, then the criteria for extraordinary items classification should be considered. That is: Does the event or transaction meet both criteria of *unusual nature* and *infrequency of occurrence?*

Discussion—Paragraphs 19–22 of the Opinion discuss the criteria of unusual nature and infrequency of occurrence of events or transactions taking into account the environment in which the entity operates. Paragraph 23 specifies certain gains or losses which should not be reported as extraordinary unless they are the direct result of a major casualty, an expropriation or a prohibition under a newly enacted law or regulation that clearly meets both criteria for extraordinary classification. Events or transactions which would meet both criteria in the circumstances described are:

10. A large portion of a tobacco manufacturer's crops are destroyed by a hail storm. Severe damage from hail storms in the locality where the manufacturer grows tobacco is rare.

11. A steel fabricating company sells the only land it owns. The land was acquired 10 years ago for future expansion, but shortly thereafter the company abandoned all plans for expansion and held the land for appreciation.

12. A company sells a block of common stock of a publicly traded company. The block of shares, which represents less than 10 percent of the publicly held company, is the only security investment the company has ever owned.

13. An earthquake destroys one of the oil refineries owned by a large multinational oil company.

The following are illustrative of events or transactions which do not meet both criteria in the circumstances described and thus should not be reported as extraordinary items:

14. A citrus grower's Florida crop is damaged by frost. Frost damage is normally experienced every three or four years. The criterion of infrequency of occurrence taking into account the environment in which the company operates would not be met since the history of losses caused by frost damage provides evidence that such damage may reasonably be expected to recur in the foreseeable future.

15. A company which operates a chain of warehouses sells the excess land surrounding one of its warehouses. When the company buys property to establish a new warehouse, it usually buys more land than it expects to use for the warehouse with the expectation that the land will appreciate in value. In the past five years, there have been two instances in which the company sold such excess land. The criterion of infrequency of occurrence has not been met since past experience indicates that such sales may reasonably be expected to recur in the foreseeable future.

16. A large diversified company sells a block of shares from its portfolio of securities which it has acquired for investment purposes. This is the first sale from its portfolio of securities. Since the company owns several securities for investment purposes, it should be concluded that sales of such securities are related to its ordinary and typical activities in the environment in which it operates, and thus the criterion of unusual nature would not be met.

* * *

Disposals of part of a line of business . . . . should not be classified as extraordinary items. As discussed in paragraph 13 of the Opinion, such disposals are incident to the evolution of the entity's business, and therefore the criterion of unusual nature would not be met.

STATEMENT OF FINANCIAL ACCOUNTING STANDARDS NO. 16 *

Financial Accounting Standards Board, June, 1977.

PRIOR PERIOD ADJUSTMENTS

Introduction and Background Information

1.   The AICPA Committee on SEC Regulations and others have requested that the FASB consider the criteria for prior period adjustments stated in paragraph 23 of APB Opinion No. 9, "Reporting the Results of Operations," and provide further guidelines for the application of those criteria. . . .

2.   The requests referred to in paragraph 1 were prompted by Securities and Exchange Commission staff administrative interpretations of APB Opinion No. 9 during 1975 limiting prior period adjustments for out-of-court settlements of litigation. The view of the SEC staff was later explained in Staff Accounting Bulletin No. 8 (see Appendix C). In addition, differing interpretations of the criteria of paragraph 23 and of the provisions of paragraph 24 of APB Opinion No. 9 have been cited as a basis for requesting a reconsideration of the concept of prior period adjustments.

* * *

Standards of Financial Accounting and Reporting

10.   Except as specified in paragraph 11 and in paragraphs 13 and 14 with respect to prior interim periods of the current year, all items of profit and loss recognized during a period, including accruals of estimated losses from loss contingencies, shall be included in the determination of net income for that period.

11.   Items of profit and loss related to the following shall be accounted for and reported as prior period adjustments and excluded from the determination of net income for the current period:

(a) Correction of an error in the financial statements of a prior period and

(b) Adjustments that result from realization of income tax benefits of pre-acquisition operating loss carryforwards of purchased subsidiaries.

* * *

* Copyright © by Financial Accounting
Standards Board, 1977. See acknowledgement, page xviii, supra.

This Statement was adopted by the affirmative votes of four members of the Financial Accounting Standards Board. Messrs. Sprouse, Litke, and Walters dissented.

Mr. Sprouse and Mr. Litke dissent primarily because the effect of this Statement is to include in the current year's *income from continuing operations* adjustments related to prior years that previously would have been excluded in the determination of the current year's *net income.* In their opinion this is a quantum leap that detracts from the usefulness of the measure of income from continuing operations and that should not be undertaken without comprehensive consideration of the presentation of information about earnings activities. . . .

Mr. Walters dissents because he does not believe the elimination of prior period adjustments improves financial reporting. To the contrary, he believes that there are clearly valid items, admittedly somewhat rare, whose inclusion in prior periods with which they are specifically identified, enhances the relevance, comparability, and understandability of financial statements and therefore their usefulness. He also does not believe the Board should tinker with this narrow, but basic, issue outside the conceptual framework project. As a minimum, it should be part of a broader project dealing with the meaning and presentation of results of operations.

APPENDIX A

BASIS FOR CONCLUSIONS

18.   This Appendix contains a discussion of the factors deemed significant by members of the Board in reaching the conclusions in this Statement, including various alternatives considered and reasons for accepting some and rejecting others. Individual Board Members gave greater weight to some factors than to others.

Scope

19.   The initial request referred to in paragraph 1 was for clarification of the application of criterion (b)[7] and criterion (c)[8] of paragraph 23 of APB Opinion No. 9 to negotiated settlements of litigation. Paragraph 23 of APB Opinion No. 9 included "settlements of significant amounts resulting from litigation or similar claims" as an example of items that may qualify as prior period adjustments. SEC Staff Accounting Bulletin No. 8 states the SEC staff's conclusion that "litigation is inevitably an 'economic event' and that settlements would constitute 'economic events' of the period in which they occur. Accordingly, it would seem that charges or credits relating to settlements would also not meet" criterion (b).[9] Staff Accounting Bulletin No. 8 also states the view that when litigation is settled, management

---

7.   Criterion (b) of paragraph 23 of APB Opinion No. 9 requires that the adjustments "are not attributable to economic events occurring subsequent to the date of the financial statements for the prior period."

8.   Criterion (c) of paragraph 23 of APB Opinion No. 9 requires that the adjustment "depend primarily on determinations by persons other than management."

9.   See footnote 7.

must make a number of significant judgments, and, hence, criterion (c)[10] has not been met.

*   *   *

Purpose of the Criteria of Paragraph 23 of APB Opinion No. 9

25.   Paragraph 17 of APB Opinion No. 9 states that "net income should reflect all items of profit and loss recognized during the period with the sole exception of . . . prior period adjustments. . ." APB Opinion No. 9 requires restatement of affected prior periods only if the statements of the affected prior periods are presented; otherwise, only the effect on beginning retained earnings of the earliest period presented is required.   The Board believes that a decision to exclude certain items of profit and loss recognized during a period from the determination of net income for that period should be based on a determination that some expected user or class of users would be benefited.   Items of profit and loss clearly related to prior period operations and unrelated to the current period operations, for example, might be excluded from the determination of net income for the current period because existing and potential investors might be misled by their inclusion.   The criteria of paragraph 23 of APB Opinion No. 9 do not serve this purpose because they do not comprehend many other items of profit and loss related to prior periods and unrelated to the current period operations.   The Board concluded that users will not be benefited by special treatment for some items of profit and loss recognized during a period but not for other similar items. . . .

The Matching Concept

26.   A number of respondents to the Exposure Draft noted that adjustments that are reported as prior period adjustments are unrelated to operations of the current period.   In their view, inclusion in net income of the current period of costs or revenues that are directly related to business activities of prior periods distorts net income in the current period by matching revenue of one period with costs of another period.

*   *   *

28.   The Board reviewed items that were reported as prior period adjustments in recent years.   The results of that review are summarized in Appendix B.   Based on that review, the Board concluded that the items that were reported as prior period adjustments were not sufficiently different from other items that were included in the determination of net income in the current period to justify their exclusion.

Relationship to Subsequent Pronouncements

*   *   *

37.   Paragraph 8 of FASB Statement No. 5, issued in March 1975, establishes two conditions for accrual of an estimated loss from a loss contingency and prohibits accrual before those conditions are met.   The Board did not reexamine the concept of prior period adjustments at that time.   Consideration in this Statement of the kinds of items, if any, to be accounted for as prior period adjustments led to

10.   See footnote 8.

the following questions: If pursuant to FASB Statement No. 5 a loss cannot be accrued in the period when it is probable that an asset had been impaired or a liability had been incurred because the amount of loss cannot be reasonably estimated, should the loss be charged retroactively to that period when it can be reasonably estimated in a subsequent period? Does the loss accrue to the earlier period, when it was probable that an asset had been impaired or a liability had been incurred, or to the later period, when the amount of loss can be reasonably estimated? The Board believes that the requirement under APB Opinion No. 9 that certain losses, when they can be reasonably estimated in a later period, be charged retroactively to an earlier period is inconsistent with the intent of FASB Statement No. 5 in prohibiting accrual of an estimated loss when the amount of loss cannot be reasonably estimated, even though it is probable that an asset has been impaired or a liability has been incurred. The Board concluded that all estimated losses for loss contingencies should be charged to income rather than charging some to income and others to retained earnings as prior period adjustments.

* * *

APPENDIX C

EXCERPTS FROM SEC STAFF ACCOUNTING BULLETIN NO. 8
* * *

H. Prior Period Adjustments
Facts:

Accounting Principles Board Opinion No. 9, paragraph 23, limits treatment as a prior period adjustment "to those material adjustments which (a) can be specifically identified with and directly related to the business activities of particular prior periods, and (b) are not attributable to economic events occurring subsequent to the date of the financial statements for the prior period, and (c) depend primarily on determinations by persons other than management and (d) were not susceptible of reasonable estimation prior to such determination."

It is not uncommon for parties to litigation to reach settlement of the matter at issue in an out-of-court settlement.

Question:

Do out-of-court settlements meet the criteria for prior period adjustments?

Interpretive Response:

The staff has been extremely reluctant to permit registrants to charge items to retained earnings as prior period adjustments in the light of the clear intent expressed in APB 9 to limit such charges severely. That opinion effectively adopted an all-inclusive approach to the measurement of periodic income. While such an approach may not result in the best matching of costs and revenues, it does provide assurance that all items will at some time be accounted for as elements of income and it prevents the abuses which were noted prior to the adoption of APB 9 whereby adverse circumstances could be at least partially obscured through the vehicle of a direct charge to retained earnings. If unusual items and items related to matters arising in prior years are properly isolated and described in the income statement, we believe that investors will be able to interpret results in an intelligent fashion. Were the Financial Accounting Standards Board to revise the basic accounting philosophy of the all-inclusive income statement, the staff would, of course, review its position in the light of that revision.

In the meantime, however, the staff intends to continue to apply the four restrictive tests set forth in paragraph 23 of Accounting Principles Board Opinion No. 9 strictly. In this connection, the issue which has arisen most frequently is the treatment of litigation settlements. It is the staff's view that when litigation is settled, the management must make a number of significant judgments and, hence, the test that the amounts must "depend primarily on determinations by persons other than management" (criterion (c) above) has not been met. In addition, in a business world increasingly characterized by litigation to an extent far in excess of that when Accounting Principles Board Opinion No. 9 was adopted (1966), it seems that litigation is inevitably an "economic event" and that settlements would constitute "economic events" of the period in which they occur. Accordingly, it would seem that charges or credits relating to settlements would also not meet the second test (criterion (b) above) set forth in paragraph 23 of Opinion 9 that they not be "attributable to economic events occurring subsequent to the date of the financial statements for the prior period."

PROBLEM

Read the *Kingston* case, which follows this problem, and assume that the Home Life Insurance Company there involved sold its home office building, carried on its books at $1,000,000, for $1,500,000 in cash. How should the resulting gain be reflected in the company's financial statements for the year of the sale? In particular, would it be permissible for the company to treat this transaction in the same way as either General Motors or Standard Oil handled the gain on Ethyl stock? What should the independent accountant do if the company insisted upon adopting either of those approaches?

6. THE PROBLEM OF VALUATION OF ASSETS

KINGSTON v. HOME LIFE INS. CO. OF AMERICA

Delaware Court of Chancery, 1917.
11 Del.Ch. 258, 101 A. 898, affirmed on other issues,
11 Del.Ch. 428, 104 A. 25 (1918).

Bill by shareholders of an insurance company .   .   . to correct irregularities and unlawful acts of officers and directors.

THE CHANCELLOR [CURTIS]. . . . It is also alleged that dividends were paid otherwise than from earnings, and that the capital of the company had been impaired. . . .

Has the investment of the stockholders been jeopardized by the illegal payment of dividends and by an impairment of the capital stock?   Each of these charges is grave and involves serious consequences if sustained by the evidence.

The prayer of the bill on the subject is for an injunction to prevent the officers of the Insurance Company from declaring or paying any dividend upon its stock except out of actual earnings.   This may be granted without much consideration of the facts, because it would be but a declaration of the statute law of the State which permits dividends to be paid only out of surplus or net profits arising from the business of the company.*

It is extremely difficult for anyone who has not had large experience in the practices and book-keeping theories of life insurance companies, or as an expert actuarial accountant, to decide what in a given case constitutes the surplus or net profits of the business of an insurance company.   Some things seem clear, and one is that an estimated increase in the value of the building owned by the Insurance Company and occupied by its officers and employees, however accurately the increase be estimated, is not a net profit arising from the business of the company.   If it is an investment of capital of the company its increased value when realized by a sale may perhaps be treated as a profit, but until realized it is surely unwise, inaccurate and wrong to so regard it and pay out money based on such an estimate, for it is only a guess, and if a correct one it may become incorrect later when the conditions which produced the estimated increase of value change.

Again, a profit of the business of fifteen thousand dollars is not made if an officer of the company authorized to buy for the company with its money real estate for sixty thousand dollars buys it for forty-five thousand dollars.   The assets of the company are not increased, and the saving is not a profit of the business which can be paid out in money as dividends.   .   .   .

a.   THE ACCOUNTING ATTITUDE TOWARD REVALUATION OF ASSETS

Should the Home Life Insurance Co. have revalued its office building on its financial statements (assuming there was some ob-

---

* The Delaware dividend provision has run the gamut over the years: it started, in Delaware's first general corporation statute, in the same form in which it appeared at the time of *Kingston* case, as a prohibition against dividends "except from the surplus or net profits arising from the business" (having been taken over verbatim from the New Jersey statute, which in turn had evolved from a provision prohibiting dividends "except from the surplus profits arising from the business"); then for many years the Delaware statute provided that a corpora-

tion could pay dividends "out of its net assets in excess of its capital" (or, in case of an overall deficit, out of current earnings, subject to certain limitations); in 1967 the statute took its present simple form, permission to pay dividends "out of its surplus" (again with a current earnings alternative).   The question of whether unrealized appreciation can be taken into account in determining the amount of dividends which may be paid seems not to have been decided under either of the latter two versions of the Delaware statute.

jective verification of the unrealized appreciation in value)? At least until rather recently, the response of the profession would have been generally negative (although in earlier times this position seems to have been as often honored in the breach). Particularly in the case of fixed assets, i. e., the buildings, machinery and equipment constituting the plant of a typical industrial, the formal position of the profession has been one of moderate opposition to revaluation. Thus as early as 1940 the AICPA Committee on Accounting Procedure, in ARB No. 5, said:

> "Accounting for fixed assets should normally be based on cost, and any attempt to make property accounts in general reflect current values is both impracticable and inexpedient. Appreciation normally should not be reflected on the books of account of corporations."

However, it is some index to the actual practice at the time that the primary purpose of ARB No. 5 was to deal with cases where such appreciation had in fact been entered on the books, and the question was how the annual depreciation expense on such fixed assets should be computed (with the conclusion being that in such cases depreciation should be computed on the basis of the new and higher recorded figures).

The position on revaluation was even less clear-cut in the subsequent version of ARB No. 5, which appeared as Chapter 9B of ARB No. 43, the 1953 restatement of prior ARB's:

> "Historically, fixed assets have been accounted for on the basis of cost. However, fixed assets in the past have occasionally been written up to appraised values because of rapid rises in price levels, to adjust costs in the case of bargain purchases, etc."

In addition, Accounting Terminology Bulletin No. 1, promulgated in 1953, continued to contemplate at least the possibility of revaluation of fixed assets, as the excerpts from that Bulletin on pages 169–170, supra (paragraphs 69(1) and 69(6)) indicate.

However, any doubts on the matter were laid to rest in 1965 by the Accounting Principles Board, which superseded prior promulgations on the subject with the following statement in paragraph 17 of APB Opinion No. 6:

> "The Board is of the opinion that property, plant and equipment should not be written up by an entity to reflect appraisal, market or current values which are above cost to the entity".

The particular emphasis on fixed assets in this increasingly firm opposition to revaluation should not be taken to suggest a more sympathetic stance toward revaluation of current assets, such as inventory or marketable securities. Rather it is due to the fact that historically fixed assets were often the subject of unsupportable (if not unbelievable) revaluations; the difficulty of determining the value of fixed assets with any precision made them an inviting target for such abuses. But there has been at least as much reluctance to allow recording unrealized appreciation on current assets, despite the fact that, unlike fixed assets, the market value of current assets can often be ascertained with considerable accuracy. Indeed, in the case of some current assets, notably inventory, accountants have gone even further and required such assets to be carried at "lower of cost or market", meaning that any diminution in value must be reflected while unrealized appreciation is ignored. This seemingly inconsistent approach was historically justified by the doctrine of "conservatism", which, as noted back on pages 26–27, sought to offset possible overoptimism on the part of management by requiring that financial statements stretch to reflect all likely losses while not anticipating any gains prior to actual realization. As we shall see shortly, the "lower of cost or market" rule has recently been formally extended to marketable securities, and we will consider its application to inventory in more detail later.

The latest official pronouncement on the general subject of valuation of assets appears in APB Statement No. 4 (1970), entitled "Basic Concepts and Accounting Principles Underlying Financial Statements of Business Enterprises".* In the section dealing with the questions of what events call for recording in the accounts and what dollar amounts should be assigned thereto, the Statement starts with the basic principle that any transfer of resources or obligations by an enterprise to or from another entity should be reflected, and that, in the normal case where an exchange is involved, the figures should reflect the price established in the exchange transactions. Paragraph 183B then contains the following observations which are relevant on the issue of recording unrealized appreciation:

> "*External events other than transfers of resources or obligations to or from other entities.* Examples are changes in specific prices of enterprise assets, changes in interest rates, general price-level changes, technological changes caused by outside entities, and damage to enterprise assets caused by others.
>
> > "*Favorable external events other than transfers generally not recorded.* External events other than transfers that increase market prices or utility of assets . . . are

*Copyright © by the American Institute
of Certified Public Accountants, Inc.

generally not recorded when they occur. Instead their effects are usually reflected at the time of later exchanges.

"*Retention of recorded amounts.* Assets whose prices or utility are increased by external events other than transfers are normally retained in the accounting records at their recorded amounts until they are exchanged. . . ."

The most recent official word from the Financial Accounting Standards Board relating to valuation in the primary financial statements is Statement of Financial Accounting Standards No. 12 (1975), "Accounting for Certain Marketable Securities", which formally adopts the general rule that marketable securities should be carried at the lower of cost or market value, determined as of the balance sheet date. The account to be debited when the securities are in fact written down (i. e., credited) because year-end value is below cost depends upon whether the company classifies its assets as between current and noncurrent on the balance sheet: if it does, then as to those securities classified as current assets (which would presumably include at least those temporary investments management intends to dispose of in the next fiscal year, per an Auditing Interpretation by the AICPA Staff, 139 J. Accountancy (April, 1975, p. 69)), any decline during the year in the overall market value is to be recognized as a current loss and charged against income for the year. For marketable securities classified as noncurrent, as well as for all marketable securities of a company which does not classify as between current and noncurrent, any decline during the year in the overall market value of the portfolio is not charged against income *, but is instead shown as a separate deduction in the stockholders' equity section of the balance sheet—a kind of by-passing of the income statement, except that the amount charged to surplus is shown separately as a deduction from surplus, instead of simply reducing the figure in the surplus account. If there is a subsequent rise in the overall market value of securities previously written down, the securities are to be written up to the higher value ** (but not above the overall cost); the credit is to income in the case of marketable securities classified as current assets, otherwise it goes to reduce the separate deduction from surplus previously created. The Statement also provides that normally no adjustment is made to reflect changes in value of the securities occurring after the date of the

---

* Except when the decline in the value of a noncurrent marketable security is viewed as non-temporary, in which event the decline is charged against income (and the reduced figure is not to be changed for subsequent recoveries in market value). As to what constitutes a non-temporary decline in value, there are no clear guidelines: one likely example is a decline due to specific adverse circumstances affecting only the issuer of the particular security and not the industry or the economy generally.

** Subject to the exception noted in the parenthetical phrase in the preceding footnote.

financial statements, but when such changes are significant they should be disclosed.

There are some explanatory comments in Appendix A to the Statement, captioned "Basis for Conclusions", which also shed light on the Board's views about revaluation in general *:

29.   .   .   .   The Board's conclusion that the lower of cost or market should apply in the determination of carrying amount for such securities was based on the following factors:

(a) The Board excluded from its consideration market value alone as the determinant of carrying value. Consideration of that alternative would raise pervasive issues concerning the valuation of other types of assets, including the concept of historic cost versus current or realizable value. The Board concluded that it could not examine these conceptual issues in a project of such limited scope.

(b) The Board noted that continuance of original cost as the carrying amount of a portfolio of marketable equity securities when its market value is lower has the effect of deferring recognition of the decline in the realizable value of such securities based on the expectation of a future recovery in market value which may or may not occur. Because of the uncertainty of such future recovery, the Board concluded that   .   .   .   a decline in market value below cost should in all cases be reflected in the balance sheet and when such securities are classified as current assets,   .   .   .   the realization of the loss in value of the securities should be regarded as imminent and therefore should be recognized in the determination of net income.

(c) In adopting the lower of cost or market as the determinant for carrying amount, the Board required that when write-downs have been made because the market value of the portfolio has dropped below cost, if market value subsequently rises, the write-down be reversed to the extent that the resulting carrying amount does not exceed cost. The Board does not regard the reversal of the write-down as representing recognition of an unrealized gain. Rather, the Board views the write-down as establishing a valuation allowance representing the estimated reduction in the realizable value of the portfolio, and it views a subsequent market increase as having reduced or eliminated the requirement for such an allowance.   .   .   .

30.   .   .   .   the Board decided not to require in this Statement that declines in the market value below cost of noncurrent marketable equity securities be reflected in net income. In reaching this decision, the Board recognized that the present concepts of income require authoritative clarification with respect to the recognition of unrealized gains and losses on long-term assets. Such clarification, the Board

* Copyright © by Financial Accounting
Standards Board, 1975. See acknowledgement, page xviii, supra.

noted, is beyond the scope of this Statement. For these reasons, the Board concluded that marketable equity securities classified as noncurrent assets should constitute a separate portfolio from those securities classified as current assets for the determination of carrying amount, and that changes in the carrying amount of the noncurrent portfolio should be reflected in the equity section of the balance sheet rather than included in income, provided that the decline in market value is assessed as temporary.

31. An issue inherent in the determination of carrying amount for marketable equity securities was whether the lower of cost or market method adopted by the Board should be applied on the basis of individual security holdings or on a portfolio basis. . . . The Board recognized that the application of the criterion on a portfolio basis may be regarded as having the effect of offsetting the unrealized losses on one security with unrealized gains on another. However, the Board agrees with those respondents who regard the current and noncurrent portfolios of marketable equity securities each as collective assets, hence the determination of the carrying amount on a collective (portfolio) basis is in the Board's view appropriate despite the offsets referred to.

As might be expected, the accounting resistance to reflecting unrealized appreciation in value on the financial statements has not gone without challenge. Consider the following two excerpts which illustrate how sticking to original cost may impede meaningful presentation of financial position:

From Backer, Accounting Theory and Multiple Reporting
Objectives, which appears as chapter 20 of
Modern Accounting Theory (1966) :

Accounting data may be used for diverse purposes. However, the present structure of accounting is rather rigid since both the data collection system and generally accepted principles of accounting are directed toward the two general purpose statements [i. e., the income statement and the balance sheet] rather than to the measurement of defined objectives. As a consequence, the general purpose statements do not and cannot adequately cope with the many demands made on them.

A glaring example of the constraining influence of the present accounting structure took place in the summer of 1964 in connection with the determination of President Johnson's net worth. The following appeared in the *New York Times* on August 18, 1964.

According to *Life* Magazine the L. B. J. family have accumulated a fortune in radio and television stations, Texas real estate and other properties worth nearly $14 million. This estimate exceeds by nearly $10 million the value placed on the Johnson family property by A. W. Moursund, the principal trustee for the family. Mr. Moursund's figures are based on a report prepared by a certified public accountant (Albert W. Caster & Co.). . . . the *Life* article uses the estimated resale value of the various properties whereas Mr. Moursund's estimates were based largely on their so called "book value" which is used for accounting purposes.

Two days later, on August 20, 1964, the *New York Times* contained the following:

> President Johnson and his immediate family own property and liquid assets valued at slightly less than $3.5 million, an independent accounting firm certified today. . . . Haskins and Sells said that the method of accounting was in accord with accepted accounting procedures and was not intended to indicate the values that might be realized if the investment were sold.
>
> . . .
>
> The method of valuation of the Johnson family holdings was immediately attacked by Dean Burch, the chairman of the Republican National Committee. . . . He said that the estimate was "incredibly low", like the City of New York listing the value of Manhattan Island at $24, the price paid, according to legend, to its original Indian residents by the first white settlers.

When accountants are called upon to determine real net worth (i. e., market value of net assets), special circumstances exist, e. g., the purchase or sale of a business, the calculation of an estate tax, or the financial status of a political candidate. The evaluation procedure may involve extremely complex factors, and the result may be subject to a wide margin of error. Nevertheless, this represents a specific objective and the application of "generally accepted principles of accounting" are not apt to produce useful information. In this connection, it is interesting to observe the procedure used by Touche, Ross, Bailey & Smart, another firm of certified public accountants, to determine the net worth of Hubert H. Humphrey, as reported in the *New York Times* of September 22, 1964:

> Because of the nature and purpose of this presentation, the statement value of household goods and of financial condition of the principals has been prepared on the basis of present market value of their assets, which basis of reporting we believe to be appropriate in the circumstances.

From Solow, The Company Twice As Big As Rhode Island, Fortune Magazine, March, 1961, page 138, commenting on the financial picture of the Kern County Land Co. of California in the late 1950's:

> ". . . The profits were around 20 percent of reported net worth, which sounded fine.
>
> "The trouble was that the net-worth figure was meaningless; K. C. L.'s books showed (and still show) 1910 and 1912 values for its huge holdings of land, much of it in a fast-growing region, and show nothing for the company's big oil-royalty reserves. On any fairly realistic appraisal of assets, K. C. L. was earning only about 5 per cent of net worth—about $10 million on something approaching $200 million."

b. THE EFFECTS OF INFLATION

Although the official accounting position confining the primary financial statements to original cost has remained unchanged, in recent years pressure has continued to build in favor of some recognition of current values. Indeed, as early as 1973 the report of the AICPA's blue-ribbon study group on The Objectives of Financial Statements recommended that "current values should also be reported when they differ from historical cost". And of course the galloping inflation rate of recent years provided additional impetus for reflecting assets at figures with more current significance than historical cost.

Obviously, there is room for considerable difference of opinion as to the most meaningful measure of assets on a current basis, particularly in the case of fixed assets. After all, there is normally no ascertainable "market value", in the usual sense, for an aggregation of productive facilities. But a meaningful substitute may be found in determining the current cost of replacing the facilities in their present age and condition (perhaps not with identical assets but rather with assets having the same productive capacity). Alternatively, since the fact that the current replacement cost of assets is higher than the present book value (original cost less depreciation) is often due in large measure to a rise in the price level, and a consequent decline in the purchasing power of the dollar, one might simply restate the book value of the assets in terms of the current purchasing power of the dollar, using an index number reflecting changes in the general price level. The difference between specific replacement costs and general price level adjustments is described in the following excerpts from a 1974 FASB Discussion Memorandum, entitled "Reporting the Effects of General Price-Level Changes in Financial Statements" *:

> The dollar is the unit of measure in which diverse types of items are expressed for financial accounting and reporting purposes in the United States. Although dollar amounts representing many transactions over time are commingled in financial statements, the dollar has not been a stable measuring unit in the sense that its general purchasing power—its command over goods and services in general—has varied over time.
>
> In conventional financial statements, amounts are generally stated on the basis of the actual number of dollars expended or received, regardless of the purchasing power of those dollars. Whether this has been done because purchasing power changes have been regarded as relatively immaterial or simply because

---

* Copyright © by Financial Accounting
Standards Board, 1974. See acknowledgement, page xviii, supra.

accounting has never purported to measure purchasing power is a debatable question. In any event, changes in the purchasing power of the dollar have not been recognized in conventional financial statements.

* * *

General Price-Level Accounting—Historical Perspective

During the past three decades, the purchasing power of the dollar has generally declined from year to year, although the annual amounts of decline have varied considerably. Such declines in purchasing power are commonly known as inflation. The rate of inflation, as measured by the Gross National Product Implicit Price Deflator, has ranged from as much as 12% per year to as little as less than 1%.

* * *

Even when the amount of change in the general purchasing power of the dollar in any given year is relatively small, the cumulative change over a number of years might be regarded as significant for any five or ten year period in recent history. For example, the purchasing power sacrificed in the acquisition of a depreciable asset for 1,000 1958 dollars is the equivalent of an expenditure of nearly 1,600 1973 dollars, a considerable difference even though some might not regard the changes during any one of the intervening years as particularly large. Because conventional financial statements frequently include amounts stated in dollars of a good many years ago, some consider the cumulative effect of changes in the general price level on accounting measurements to be quite significant.

* * *

General Price-Level Adjustments Do Not Measure "Current Value"

. . . . it is important to emphasize that general price-level financial statements are based on historical cost and not "current value". It would only be coincidence if the historical cost of an asset restated for changes in the general purchasing power of the dollar resulted in a measurement which is equivalent to that asset's "current value"—regardless of whether "current value" is thought of in terms of the present value of future cash flows, replacement cost or market value.

In the simplified example above [omitted in these excerpts] the price-level restated cost of the depreciable asset [which cost $1,000 on January 1] was $1,100 in December 31 dollars. From this it cannot be inferred that the asset could be sold or replaced for $1,100 at December 31. All that can be inferred from the $1,100 amount is that the amount of general purchasing power invested in the asset when it was acquired on January 1 was the equivalent of 1,100 December 31 dollars.

As the foregoing indicates, the FASB was at first particularly interested in general price-level adjustments. However the Board ultimately decided to look at all aspects of the measurement process together. No doubt the FASB was much influenced by the fact that the SEC, which had long been a bulwark of resistance to revaluation by virtue of its prohibition against the use of value data in reports filed with Commission, had moved significantly down the road of specific replacement costs, as the following indicates:

SEC STAFF ACCOUNTING BULLETIN NO. 7

March 23, 1976.

TOPIC 6: INTERPRETATIONS OF ACCOUNTING SERIES RELEASES

I. Accounting Series Release No. 190—Relating to Amendments to Regulation S–X Requiring Disclosure of Replacement Cost Data (Rule 3–17)

General Facts:

Accounting Series Release No. 190 amends Regulation S–X by establishing Rule 3–17 thereto which calls for the disclosure of replacement cost data for registrants whose inventories and gross property, plant and equipment exceeds certain amounts. Data required to be disclosed are:

(1) Current replacement cost of inventories;

(2) Cost of sales computed on the basis of the replacement cost of the goods or services at the time of sale;

(3) Gross (new) and depreciated replacement cost of productive capacity; and

(4) Depreciation, depletion and amortization expense on a replacement cost basis.

In addition a description of the methods employed and the presentation of other information of which management is aware and which it believes is necessary to prevent the replacement cost data from being misleading are required. Rule 3–17 is effective for years ending on or after December 25, 1976.

1. Definitions and Concepts

a. Replacement Cost

Facts:

Rule 3–17 requires various replacement cost data.

Question:

What is the definition of replacement cost?

Interpretive Response:

For purposes of this rule, replacement cost is the lowest amount that would have to be paid in the normal course of business to obtain a new asset of equivalent operating or productive capability. In the case of depreciable, depletable or amortizable assets, replacement cost (new) and depreciated replacement cost should be distinguished. Replacement cost (new) is the total estimated current cost of replacing total productive capacity at the end of the year while depreciated replacement cost is the replacement cost (new) adjusted for the already expired service potential of such assets.

b. Productive Capacity

Facts:

Rule 3–17 speaks in terms of "productive capacity."

Question 1:

What is the definition of productive capacity?

Interpretive Response:

Productive capacity is a measurement of a company's ability to produce and distribute. The productive capacity of a manufacturer would be measured by the number of units it can presently produce and distribute within a particular time frame; in the case of a telephone company, for example, it would be a measurement of the number of telephone calls it can presently complete within a certain time frame.

*   *   *

c. Approaches to Replacement Cost

Facts:

The rule requires disclosure of current replacement cost of productive capacity. This concept can be approached in a number of ways.

Question 1:

What approach to replacement cost is contemplated by the rule?

Interpretive Response:

There is no simple concept of replacement cost which will be applicable in every circumstance. In general, replacement cost of productive capacity means the cost of replacing capacity within the existing business framework of the entity. Thus replacement cost does not generally contemplate a single time complete replacement of total capacity while totally ignoring the structure of the business as it exists. Neither does it mean replacement of each of the specific assets currently owned unless that is the way in which the business generally replaces its capacity. Rather, replacement costs should be based on the entity's normal approach to replacement of capacity.

*   *   *

Other Methods of Valuation

Facts:

Replacement cost is one of a number of methods designed to provide financial statement readers with information on the "value to the owners" of properties. Other methods frequently advocated (see the Report of the Inflation Accounting Committee in the U. K., frequently referred to as the "Sandilands Report") are net realizable value (or current disposal value) of the asset and the present value of the expected future earnings from the asset, sometimes referred to as "economic value." Various theoretical systems of financial reporting have been developed using one or more of these methods of valuation.

Question:

Will the staff accept a basis of valuation other than replacement cost?

Interpretive Response:

The staff believes all registrants should disclose replacement cost data. However the staff will not object if these data are supplemented by data setting forth the net realizable value and/or the "economic value" of properties, provided that the basis for such data is fully disclosed.

*   *   *

SEC STAFF ACCOUNTING BULLETIN NO. 12

November 10, 1976.

*   *   *

Question 1:

Is the use of indices an acceptable approach to the determination of replacement cost?

Interpretive Response:

Any logical approach to the estimation of replacement cost is acceptable provided it results in a conclusion which reasonably approximates the replacement cost of productive capacity.

The estimation of the replacement cost of productive capacity is basically a two-step process. Management must first decide if existing capacity would be replaced with assets similar to those presently owned or if different assets would be required because of technology advances, new governmental regulations, or other current economic and operating considerations. The second step is the selection of appropriate methods to price the replacement assets. In many cases, a combination of direct pricing methods and indexing will be required.

Typically, indices do not reflect technological changes to any appreciable extent. Adjusting the original cost of presently owned assets by appropriate indices results in the current cost to reproduce those assets. Reproduction cost may be equivalent to replacement cost if existing productive capacity would be replaced using assets similar to those presently owned. However, if replacement cost is to be estimated on the basis of using assets different from those presently owned, because of technological changes or other factors, measurement techniques other than indexing are usually required. . . .

After a lengthy and careful study of the matter, in 1979 the FASB decided that annual reports (of the largest companies) should include *both* information based upon general changes in the price level, *and* data reflecting specific current costs of inventory and fixed assets, together with a determination of income for the period on both bases. These conclusions were embodied in Statement of Financial Accounting Standards No. 33, "Financial Reporting and Changing Prices", promulgated in September, 1979 (and not long thereafter the SEC withdrew its ASR No. 190, reviewed above, on the ground that its objectives were now achieved by FASB Statement No. 33). The new Statement contains the following summary of its provisions:

STATEMENT OF FINANCIAL ACCOUNTING STANDARDS NO. 33 *

Financial Accounting Standards Board, September, 1979.

Financial Reporting and Changing Prices

SUMMARY

This Statement applies to public enterprises that have either (1) inventories and property, plant, and equipment (before deducting accumulated depreciation) amounting to more than $125 million or (2) total assets amounting to more than $1 billion (after deducting accumulated depreciation).

No changes are to be made in the primary financial statements; the information required by the Statement is to be presented as supplementary information in published annual reports.

For fiscal years ended on or after December 25, 1979, enterprises are required to report:

    a. Income from continuing operations adjusted for the effects of general inflation

    b. The purchasing power gain or loss on net monetary items.

For fiscal years ended on or after December 25, 1979, enterprises are also required to report:

    a. Income from continuing operations on a current cost basis

    b. The current cost amounts of inventory and property, plant, and equipment at the end of the fiscal year

    c. Increases or decreases in current cost amounts of inventory and property, plant, and equipment, net of inflation.

However, information on a current cost basis for fiscal years ended before December 25, 1980 may be presented in the first annual report for a fiscal year ended on or after December 25, 1980.

Enterprises are required to present a five-year summary of selected financial data, including information on income, sales and other operating revenues, net assets, dividends per common share, and market price per share. In the computation of net assets, only inventory and property, plant, and equipment need be adjusted for the effects of changing prices.

Illustrative formats for disclosure of the required information are included in this Summary as Schedules A, B, and C (pages 32–34 of the Statement).

To present the supplementary information required by this Statement, an enterprise needs to measure the effects of changing prices on inventory, property, plant, and equipment, cost of goods sold, and depreciation, depletion, and amortization expense. No adjustments are required to other revenues, expenses, gains, and losses.

In computations of current cost income, expenses are to be measured at current cost or lower recoverable amount. Current cost measures relate to the assets owned and used by the enterprise and not to other assets that might be acquired to replace the assets owned. This Statement allows considerable flexibility in choice of sources of information about current costs: An enterprise may use specific price indexes or other evidence of a more direct nature. This Statement also encourages simplifications in computations and other aspects of implementation: In particular "recoverable amounts" need be measured only if they are judged to be significantly and permanently lower than current cost; that situation is unlikely to occur very often.

The Board believes that this Statement meets an urgent need for information about the effects of changing prices. If that information is not provided: Resources may be allocated inefficiently; investors' and creditors' understanding of the past performance of an enterprise and their ability to assess future cash flows may be severely limited; and people in government who participate in decisions on economic policy may lack important information about the implications of their decisions. The requirements of the Statement are expected to promote a better understanding by the general public of the problems caused by inflation: Statements by business managers about those problems are unlikely to have sufficient credibility until financial reports provide quantitative information about the effects of inflation.

* * *

This Statement calls for two supplementary income computations, one dealing with the effects of general inflation, the other dealing with the effects of changes in the prices of resources used by the enterprise. The Board believes that both types of information are likely to be useful. Comment letters on the Exposure Draft revealed differences of opinion on the relative usefulness of the two approaches. Many preparers and public accounting firms emphasized the need to deal with the effects of general inflation; users generally preferred information dealing with the effects of specific price changes. The Board believes that further experimentation is required on the usefulness of the two types of information and that experimentation is possible only if both are provided by large public enterprises. The Board intends to assess the usefulness of the information called for by this Statement. That assessment will provide a basis for ongoing decisions on whether or not provision of both types of information should be continued and on whether other requirements in this Statement should be reviewed. The Board will undertake a comprehensive review of this Statement no later than five years after its publication.

The adjustment for "the effects of general inflation" required by FASB Statement No. 33 is in effect accomplished by the method referred to in the 1974 FASB Discussion Memorandum, pages 206–207, supra, that is, by restating historical costs in terms of the current purchasing power of the dollar. In Statement No. 33 this is called "historical cost/constant dollar accounting", which is defined as "a method of accounting based on measures of historical prices in dollars, each of which has the same [i. e., constant] general purchasing power". The process is described in the Statement in the following terms:

Historical Cost/Constant Dollar Measurements

39. The index used to compute information on a constant dollar basis shall be the Consumer Price Index for All Urban Consumers, published by the Bureau of Labor Statistics of the U.S. Department of Labor.

40. An enterprise that presents the minimum historical cost/constant dollar information required by this Statement shall restate inventory, property, plant, and equipment, cost of goods sold, depreciation, depletion, and amortization expense . . . in constant dollars represented by the average level over the fiscal year of the Consumer Price Index for All Urban Consumers [unless the figure derived by measuring the asset involved at the amount currently recoverable, as described in paragraphs 62 and 63, infra, is lower, in which event the lower figure should be used. See paragraph 44, infra.] Other financial statement elements need not be restated. An enterprise that chooses to present comprehensive financial statements on a historical cost/constant dollar basis may measure the components of those statements either in average-for-the-year constant dollars or in end-of-year constant dollars.

*   *   *

43. Measurements of historical cost/constant dollar amounts shall be computed by multiplying the components of the historical cost . . . measurements by the average level of the Consumer Price Index for the current fiscal year (or the level of the index at the end of the year if comprehensive financial statements are presented) and dividing by the level of the index at the date on which the measurement of the associated asset was established (i. e., the date of acquisition or the date of any measurement not based on historical cost).

. . . .

44. If it is necessary to reduce the measurements of inventory and property, plant, and equipment, during the current fiscal year from historical cost/constant dollar amounts to lower recoverable amounts, the reduction shall be deducted in the computation of income from continuing operations.

*   *   *

Purchasing Power Gain or Loss on Net Monetary Items

47.   A monetary asset is money or a claim to receive a sum of money the amount of which is fixed or determinable without reference to future prices of specific goods or services.   A monetary liability is an obligation to pay a sum of money the amount of which is fixed or determinable without reference to future prices of specific goods or services.   The economic significance of monetary assets and liabilities (monetary items) depends heavily on the general purchasing power of money, although other factors, such as the credit worthiness of debtors, may affect their significance.

*   *   *

50.   The purchasing power gain or loss on net monetary items shall be equal to the net gain or loss found by restating in constant dollars the opening and closing balances of, and transactions in, monetary assets and liabilities.   An enterprise that presents comprehensive supplementary financial statements on a historical cost/constant dollar basis may measure the purchasing power gain or loss in average-for-the-year constant dollars or in end-of-year constant dollars; other enterprises shall measure the purchasing power gain or loss in average-for-the-year dollars.   .   .   .

Other aspects of the requirements of FASB Statement No. 33, including particularly the determination and recording of "current costs", are described in the following excerpts from the Statement (and, as to paragraphs 148–155, from Appendix C, which sets forth in detail the bases for the Board's conclusions).

Current Cost Measurements

51.   The current cost amounts of inventory and property, plant, and equipment shall be measured as follows:

a.   Inventories at current cost or lower recoverable amount (paragraphs 57–64) at the measurement date.   .   .   .

b.   Property, plant, and equipment (excluding income-producing real estate properties and unprocessed natural resources) at the current cost or lower recoverable amount (paragraphs 57–64) of the assets' remaining service potential at the measurement date.

c.   Resources used on partly completed contracts shall be measured at current cost or lower recoverable amount at the date of use on or commitment to the contracts.

52.   An enterprise that presents the minimum information required by this Statement on current cost income from continuing operations shall measure the amounts of cost of goods sold and depreciation and amortization expense as follows:

a.   Cost of goods sold shall be measured at current cost or lower recoverable amount (paragraphs 57–64) at the date of sale or at the date on which resources are used on or committed to a specific contract.   .   .   .

b. Depreciation and amortization expense of property, plant, and equipment (excluding income-producing real estate properties and unprocessed natural resources) shall be measured on the basis of the average current cost or lower recoverable amount (paragraphs 57–64) of the assets' service potential during the period of use.

Other revenues, expenses, gains, and losses may be measured by such an enterprise at the amounts included in the primary income statement. . . .

*   *   *

Increases or Decreases in the Current Cost Amounts of Inventory and Property, Plant, and Equipment

55. The increases or decreases in the current cost amounts of inventory and property, plant, and equipment represent the differences between the measures of the assets at their "entry dates" for the year and the measures of the assets at their "exit dates" for the year. "Entry dates" means the beginning of the year or the dates of acquisition, whichever is applicable; "exit dates" means the end of the year or the dates of use, sale, or commitment to a specific contract whichever is applicable. For the purposes of this paragraph, assets are measured in accordance with the provisions of paragraph 51.

56. The increases or decreases in current cost amounts of inventory and property, plant and equipment shall be reported both before and after eliminating the effects of general inflation. An enterprise that presents comprehensive supplementary statements on a current cost/constant dollar basis may measure increases or decreases in current cost amounts in average-for-the-year constant dollars or in end-of-year constant dollars; other enterprises shall measure those increases or decreases in average-for-the-year constant dollars. . . .

Information about Current Costs

57. The current cost of inventory owned by an enterprise is the current cost of purchasing the goods concerned or the current cost of the resources required to produce the goods concerned (including an allowance for the current overhead costs according to the allocation bases used under generally accepted accounting principles), whichever would be applicable in the circumstances of the enterprise.

58. The current cost of property, plant, and equipment owned by an enterprise is the current cost of acquiring the same service potential (indicated by operating costs and physical output capacity) as embodied by the asset owned; the sources of information used to measure current cost should reflect whatever method of acquisition would currently be appropriate in the circumstances of the enterprise. The current cost of a used asset may be measured:

a. By measuring the current cost of a new asset that has the same service potential as the used asset had when it was new (the current cost of the asset as if it were new) and deducting an allowance for depreciation;

b. By measuring the current cost of a used asset of the same age and in the same condition as the asset owned;

c.   By measuring the current cost of a new asset with a different service potential and adjusting that cost for the value of the differences in service potential due to differences in life, output capacity, nature of service, and operating costs.

Current cost may be measured by direct reference to current prices of comparable assets or methods such as functional pricing or unit pricing under which the current cost of a unit of service embodied in the asset owned is measured and the current cost per unit is multiplied by the appropriate number of service units.

59.   If current cost is measured in a foreign currency, the amount shall be translated into dollars at the current exchange rate, that is, the rate at the date of use, sale, or commitment to a specific contract (in the cases of depreciation expense and cost of goods sold) or the rate at the balance sheet date (in the cases of inventory and property, plant, and equipment).

60.   Enterprises may use various types of information to determine the current cost of inventory, property, plant, and equipment, cost of goods sold, and depreciation, depletion, and amortization expense.[3]   .   .   .

Depreciation Expense

61.   There is a presumption that depreciation methods, estimates of useful lives, and salvage values of assets should be the same for purposes of current cost, historical cost/constant dollar, and historical cost/nominal dollar depreciation calculations.   However, if the methods and estimates used for calculations in the primary financial statements have been chosen partly to allow for expected price changes, different methods and estimates may be used for purposes of current cost and historical cost/constant dollar calculations.

Recoverable Amounts

62.   The term "recoverable amount" means the current worth of the net amount of cash expected to be recoverable from the use or sale of an asset.   If the recoverable amount for a group of assets is judged to be materially and permanently lower than historical cost in constant dollars or current cost, the recoverable amount shall be used as a measure of the assets and of the expense associated with the use or sale of the assets.   Decisions on the measurement of assets at their recoverable amounts need not be made by considering assets individually unless they are used independently of other assets.

63.   Recoverable amounts may be measured by considering the net realizable values or the values in use of the assets concerned:

a.   Net realizable value is the amount of cash, or its equivalent, expected to be derived from sale of an asset net of costs required to be incurred as a result of the sale.   It shall be considered as a measurement of an asset only when the asset concerned is about to be sold.

---

3. Cost of goods sold measured on a LIFO basis may provide an acceptable approximation of cost of goods sold, measured at current cost, provided that the effect of any decreases in inventory layers is excluded.

b. Value in use is the net present value of future cash flows (including the ultimate proceeds of disposal) expected to be derived from the use of an asset by the enterprise. It shall be considered as a measurement of an asset only when immediate sale of the asset concerned is not intended. Value in use shall be estimated by discounting expected future cash flows at an appropriate discount rate that allows for the risk of the activities concerned.

*   *   *

148. . . . The principal differences between income in the primary financial statements and income under current cost accounting and historical cost/constant dollar accounting will be in the measurements of cost of goods sold and depreciation expense. In both cases, the numbers represent original cost of the related asset adjusted for changes in price levels between the date of acquisition and the date of use or sale. In the case of historical cost/constant dollar accounting, the adjustment is based on an index of general prices; in the case of current cost accounting, the adjustment reflects specific price changes. Similar differences characterize the balance sheet measurements of inventory and property, plant, and equipment under the two systems. It follows that historical cost/constant dollar measurements will approximate current cost measurements only to the extent that general price changes are approximately the same as changes in the specific prices of resources used by the enterprise.

149. The view that historical cost/constant dollar measurements represent an approximation to current cost measurements may be helpful because it focuses attention on differences in the relevance and reliability of information produced under the two systems. The measurement of current cost may be a matter of practical difficulty. If the measurement is based on a specific price index, it will be necessary to choose an appropriate index and accept that the index may fail to reflect the effect of changing technology and the mix of assets used by the enterprise. If the measurement is based on a direct pricing method, it may be difficult to obtain evidence that is unambiguously relevant to the circumstances of the enterprise. Those problems of judgment are avoided in historical cost/constant dollar accounting. Even opponents of historical cost/constant dollar accounting agree that it is verifiable and represents accurately what it purports to represent. Many believe that current cost measurements have greater relevance to the assessment of future cash flows but historical cost/constant dollar measurements have greater reliability. The Board concluded that it should call for the disclosure of income from continuing operations under both historical cost/constant dollar accounting and current cost accounting partly in order to obtain evidence of users' trade-off between relevance and reliability.

The Purchasing Power Gain or Loss on Net Monetary Items

150. An enterprise often needs to hold cash and the effect of doing so may be analyzed according to the concepts of constant dollar accounting. The value of cash is fixed in nominal dollars. If an enterprise holds $100 in cash, it will still have $100 at any later time. Holding cash does not in itself produce a nominal dollar profit or loss;

however, during a period of inflation there is a loss of purchasing power. For example, the holding of $100 for one year, when the inflation rate is 8 percent, involves a loss of $8 of purchasing power (measured in end-of-year dollars): one would need 108 end-of-year dollars to have the purchasing power equivalent of 100 beginning-of-year dollars.

151. The loss of purchasing power from holding cash is one component of the purchasing power gain or loss on net monetary items. Furthermore, if cash loses value, so does a claim to cash (a receivable)—and a payable is associated with a gain of purchasing power: Losses on monetary assets such as receivables, and gains on monetary liabilities such as payables, must be counted in the same way as the loss on holding cash. The reporting of purchasing power gains or losses on net monetary items may provide an improved understanding of some of the implications, in periods of inflation, of the monetary components of working capital and of the amount of debt included in the capital structure of the enterprise.

152. The foregoing discussion has explained the reasons for believing that constant dollar accounting provides a useful basis for assessment of the performance of an enterprise in maintaining the purchasing power of investors. The purchasing power gain or loss on net monetary items is another part of the information that may be useful for that assessment. Suppose, for example, that an enterprise is established with capital of $2,000. It invests $1,500 in inventory and holds $500 in cash. Inventory is sold for $1,950 at the end of the year; general inflation is 10 percent during the year. Cash (and total assets) at the end of the year amount to $2,450 ($1,950 plus $500) and the nominal dollar increase in owners' equity is $450 ($2,450 less $2,000). The adjustment for changes in the purchasing power of owners' equity is $200 ($2,000 times 0.1) and the increase in the purchasing power of the investment in the enterprise is $250 ($450 less $200), measured in "end-of-year dollars." The enterprise will report income from continuing operations, on a historical cost/constant dollar basis, of $300 (sales $1,950 less cost of sales measured at $1,500 times 110/100). However, income overstates the increase in purchasing power because it excludes the loss of purchasing power resulting from the holding of cash. The purchasing power loss on net monetary items will be $50 (cash at the end of the year, $500, less cash at the beginning of the year, in end-of-year dollars, $500 times 110/100). Total increase in purchasing power ($250) is equal to income from continuing operations ($300) less the loss of purchasing power on net monetary assets ($50). Similar results would be obtained under current cost accounting except that historical cost/constant dollar income from continuing operations would be divided between current cost income from continuing operations and the increase or decrease in current cost amounts, net of inflation. Generalization of this kind of reasoning indicates that the total increase or decrease in purchasing power resulting from the activities of an enterprise may be assessed on the basis of the sum of current cost income from continuing operations, the change in current cost amounts of assets net of inflation and the purchasing power gain or loss on net monetary items.

153.   Several commentators on the Exposure Draft argued that it was inappropriate to describe the purchasing power adjustment as a gain or loss. They were particularly critical of the implicit suggestion that an enterprise could gain by borrowing. The Board believes that a gain in purchasing power associated with a prudent amount of debt may be a sign of successful management when the funds have been invested in assets that maintain their purchasing power or lose purchasing power less rapidly than monetary items. The full significance of gains or losses of purchasing power on monetary items can be understood only in the context of a study of all components of income.

154.   Suppose that Enterprise A has $1,000 of equity capital; Enterprise B borrows $1,000 at 15 percent per year. Both enterprises buy inventory at a cost of $1,000 and sell it a year later for $1,500; general inflation is 10 percent per year. Computations of income from continuing operations on a historical cost/constant dollar basis and of the purchasing power gain on debt, in end-of-year dollars, would run as follows:

	Enterprise A	Enterprise B
Sales	$ 1,500	$ 1,500
Cost of goods sold ($1,000 times 110/100)	(1,100)	(1,100)
Gross margin	400	400
Interest expense	–	(150)
Income from continuing operations	$ 400	$ 250
Purchasing power gain on debt	$ 0	$ 100

A comparison of the performance of the two enterprises should take into account the purchasing power gain on debt. Both enterprises need to measure cost of goods sold at $1,100 in order to reflect the amount of general purchasing power invested in the inventory. Both enterprises obtain a gross margin of $400, measured in end-of-year dollars. Enterprise B must pay $150 in interest. However, Enterprise B's income from continuing operations, $250, understates the increase in purchasing power earned for equity investors. Enterprise B has earned a real cash surplus of $350 because it has received $1,500 and needs only $1,150 to repay the borrowing with interest. Another way of looking at the effect of the purchasing power gain on debt would be to regard it as a reduction in the interest expense incorporated in the computation of income. Similar arguments would be applicable when current cost accounting methods are used.

155.   The arguments in paragraphs 150–154 suggest that there is a case for including the purchasing power gain or loss on net monetary items in the computation of income from continuing operations. That treatment would have the advantage that the purchasing power gain on debt could be set against the associated interest expense to produce a measure of interest expense, net of inflation, consistently with the general principles of constant dollar accounting. However, in view of some comments on the Exposure Draft, expressing doubt

about the usefulness of the item, the Board concluded that it would be preferable for it to be displayed separately, pending further experience with its use in practice.

SCHEDULE A

STATEMENT OF INCOME FROM CONTINUING OPERATIONS ADJUSTED FOR CHANGING PRICES
For the year ended December 31, 1980.
(In (000s) of Average 1980 Dollars)

Income from continuing operations, as reported in the income statement		$ 9,000
Adjustments to restate costs for the effect of general inflation		
Cost of goods sold	(7,384)	
Depreciation and amortization expense	(4,130)	(11,514)
Loss from continuing operations adjusted for general inflation		(2,514)
Adjustments to reflect the difference between general inflation and changes in specific prices (current costs)		
Cost of goods sold	(1,024)	
Depreciation and amortization expense	(5,370)	(6,394)
Loss from continuing operations adjusted for changes in specific prices		$(8,908)
Gain from decline in purchasing power of net amounts owed		$ 7,729
Increase in specific prices (current cost) of inventories and property, plant, and equipment held during the year*		$ 24,608
Effect of increase in general price level		18,959
Excess of increase in specific prices over increase in the general price level		$ 5,649

---

* At December 31, 1980 current cost of inventory was $65,700 and current cost of property, plant, and equipment, net of accumulated depreciation was $85,100. [This footnote and the one on the following page is from the original.]

SCHEDULE B

STATEMENT OF INCOME FROM CONTINUING OPERATIONS ADJUSTED FOR CHANGING PRICES

For the year ended December 31, 1980.
(in (000s) of Dollars)

	As Reported in the Primary Statements	Adjusted for General Inflation	Adjusted for Changes in Specific Prices (Current Costs)
Net sales and other operating revenues	$253,000	$253,000	$253,000
Costs of goods sold	197,000	204,384	205,408
Depreciation and amortization expense	10,000	14,130	19,500
Other operating expense	20,835	20,835	20,835
Interest expense	7,165	7,165	7,165
Provision for income taxes	9,000	9,000	9,000
	244,000	255,514	261,908
Income (loss) from continuing operations	9,000	$ (2,514)	$ (8,908)
Gain from decline in purchasing power of net amounts owed		$ 7,729	$ 7,729
Increase in specific prices (current cost) of inventories and property, plant, and equipment held during the year*			24,608
Effect of increase in general price level			18,959
Excess of increase in specific prices over increase in the general price level			5,649

* At December 31, 1980 current cost of inventory was $65,700 and current cost of property, plant, and equipment, net of accumulated depreciation was $85,100.

SCHEDULE C

FIVE-YEAR COMPARISON OF SELECTED SUPPLEMENTARY FINANCIAL DATA ADJUSTED FOR EFFECTS OF CHANGING PRICES

(In (000s) of Average 1980 Dollars)

	Years Ended December 31,				
	1976	1977	1978	1979	1980
Net sales and other operating revenues	265,000	235,000	240,000	237,063	253,000
Historical cost information adjusted for general inflation					
Income (loss) from continuing operations				(2,761)	(2,514)
Income (loss) from continuing operations per common share				$ (1.91)	$ (1.68)
Net assets at year-end				55,518	57,733
Current cost information					
Income (loss) from continuing operations				(4,125)	(8,908)
Income (loss) from continuing operations per common share				$ (2.75)	$ (5.94)
Excess of increase in specific prices over increase in the general price level				2,292	5,649
Net assets at year-end				79,996	81,466
Gain from decline in purchasing power of net amounts owed				7,027	7,729
Cash dividends declared per common share	$ 2.59	$ 2.43	$ 2.26	$ 2.16	$ 2.00
Market price per common share at year-end	$ 32	$ 31	$ 43	$ 39	$ 35
Average consumer price index	170.5	181.5	195.4	205.0	220.9

c. ADDITIONAL EXAMPLES OF JUDICIAL ATTITUDES TOWARD REVALUATION OF ASSETS

RANDALL v. BAILEY *

Supreme Court of New York, New York County, 1940.
23 N.Y.S.2d 173, affirmed 288 N.Y. 280, 43 N.E.2d 43 (1942).

WALTER, JUSTICE. A trustee of Bush Terminal Company, appointed in a proceeding under Section 77B of the Bankruptcy Act, 11 U.S.C.A. § 207, here sues former directors of that company to recover on its behalf the amount of dividends declared and paid between November 22, 1928, and May 2, 1932, aggregating $3,639,058.06. At the times of the declarations and payments, the company's books concededly showed a surplus which ranged from not less than $4,378,554.-83 on December 31, 1927, down to not less than $2,199,486.77 on April 30, 1932. The plaintiff claims, however, that in fact there was no surplus, that the capital was actually impaired to an amount greater than the amount of the dividends, and that the directors consequently are personally liable to the corporation for the amount thereof under Section 58 of the Stock Corporation Law. Defendants claim that there was no impairment of capital and that the surplus was actually greater than the amount which plaintiff concedes as the amount shown by the books.

The claims of the plaintiff, although branching out to a multitude of items, are basically reducible to four:

1. It was improper to "write-up" the land values above cost and thereby take unrealized appreciation into account.

2. It was improper not to "write-down" to actual value the cost of investments in and advances to subsidiaries and thereby fail to take unrealized depreciation into account.

* * *

I next turn to the subject of unrealized appreciation and depreciation.

Until 1915 the company's land was carried upon its books at cost. In 1915 the land was written up to 80% of the amount at which it was then assessed for taxation, and in 1918 it was written up to the exact amount at which it was then so assessed. Those two write-ups totalled $7,211,791.72, and the result was that during the period here in question the land was carried on the books at $8,737,949.02, whereas its actual cost was $1,526,157.30. Plaintiff claims that the entire $7,211,791.72 should be eliminated because it represents merely unrealized appreciation, and dividends cannot be declared or paid on the basis of mere unrealized appreciation in fixed assets irrespective of how sound the estimate thereof may be. That obviously and concededly is another way of saying that for dividend purposes fixed assets must be computed at cost, not value, and plaintiff here plants himself upon that position, even to the point of contending that evidence of value is immaterial and not admissible. If that contention be sound, the company indisputably had a deficit at all the times here

---

* Most of the opinion omitted.

involved in an amount exceeding the dividends here in question. The importance of the question so presented, both to this case and to corporations and corporate directors in general, is thus apparent, and it is, I think, surprising that upon a question so important to and so often occurring in the realm of business there is, not only no decision which can be said to be directly in point, but, also, no discussion in text-book or law magazine which does much more than pose the question without answering it. Even in Halsbury's Laws of England, 2d Ed., Vol. 5, p. 393, note (f), published in 1932, it is stated that the question has not been decided.

It is to be emphasized at the outset that the question is not one of sound economics, or of what is sound business judgment or financial policy or of proper accounting practice, or even what the law ought to be. My views of the business acumen or financial sagacity of these directors, as well as my views as to what the legislature ought to permit or prohibit, are entirely immaterial. The question I have to decide is whether or not an existing statute has been violated. The problem is one of statutory construction.

The words of the statute, as it existed during the period here involved, are: "No stock corporation shall declare or pay any dividend which shall impair its capital or capital stock, nor while its capital or capital stock is impaired, ..."

* * *

In summary, I think that it cannot be said that there is a single case in this State which actually decides that unrealized appreciation cannot be taken into consideration, or, stated in different words, that cost and not value must be used in determining whether or not there exists a surplus out of which dividends can be paid. I think, further, that such a holding would run directly counter to the meaning of the terms capital and capital stock as fixed by decisions of the Court of Appeals construing the earlier statutes, and that such construction of those terms must be deemed to have been adopted by the legislature in enacting the statute here involved. . . . I thus obviously cannot follow decisions to the contrary in other States or any contrary views of economists or accountants. If the policy of the law be bad it is for the legislature to change it.

* * *

. . . I am of the opinion that the same reasons which show that unrealized appreciation must be considered are equally cogent in showing that unrealized depreciation likewise must be considered. In other words, the test being whether or not the value of the assets exceeds the debts and the liability to stockholders, all assets must be taken at their actual value.

I see no cause for alarm over the fact that this view requires directors to make a determination of the value of the assets at each dividend declaration. On the contrary, I think that is exactly what the law always has contemplated that directors should do. That does not mean that the books themselves necessarily must be altered by write-ups or write-downs at each dividend period, or that formal appraisals must be obtained from professional appraisers or even made by the directors themselves. That is obviously impossible in the case of corporations of any considerable size. But it is not impossible nor unfeasible for directors to consider whether the cost of assets continues over a long period of years to reflect their fair value, and the law does require that directors should really direct in the very important matter of really determining at each dividend declaration whether or not the value of the assets is such as to justify a dividend, rather than do what one director here testified that he did, viz. "accept the company's figures." The directors are the ones who should determine the figures by carefully considering values, and it was for the very purpose of compelling them to perform that duty that the statute imposes upon them a personal responsibility for declaring and paying dividends when the value of the assets is not sufficient to justify them. What directors must do is to exercise an informed judgment of their own, and the amount of information which they should obtain, and the sources from which they should obtain it, will of course depend upon the circumstances of each particular case. . . .

* * *

Defendants' motions for judgment at the close of the whole case are granted . . ..

LaBelle Iron Works v. United States, 256 U.S. 377, 41 S.Ct. 528, 65 L.Ed. 998 (1921). Under the excess profits tax applicable in the year 1917, a graduated tax was applied to the annual net income of a corporation in excess of a specified percentage of its "invested capital". "Invested capital" was defined as follows: "(1) Actual cash paid in; (2) the actual cash value of tangible property paid in other than cash, for stock or shares in such corporation . . . at the time of such payment . . .; and (3) paid in or earned surplus and undivided profits used or employed in the business, exclusive of undivided profits earned during the taxable year. . . . " The taxpayer acquired ore land prior to 1904 for which it paid the sum of $190,000. Subsequent extensive exploration disclosed that the lands contained large deposits of ore and were worth not less than $10,150,400. In 1912 the company increased the valuation of these lands upon its books by approximately $10,000,000, and credited its surplus in the same amount. In determining its liability under the excess profits tax for the year 1917, the company sought to include this increase in surplus in its "invested capital". *Held,* "invested capital" within the meaning of the act was limited to the capital actually originally invested in the enterprise and hence appreciation in the market value of the assets acquired could not be included. In answering the contention that the statute as so construed was unconstitutional the court said:

 " . . . The principal line of demarcation—that based upon actual costs, excluding estimated appreciation—finds reasonable support upon grounds of both theory and practice, in addition to the important consideration of convenience in administration, already adverted to. There is a logical incongruity in entering upon the books of a corporation as the capital value of property acquired for permanent employment in its business and still retained for that purpose, a sum corresponding not to its cost but to what probably might be realized by sale in the market. It is not merely that the market value has not been realized or tested by sale made, but that sale cannot be made without abandoning the very purpose for which the property is held, involving a withdrawal from business so far as that particular property is concerned. Whether in a given case property should be carried in the capital account at market value rather than at cost may be a matter of judgment, depending upon special circumstances and the local law. But certainly Congress, in seeking a general rule, reasonably might adopt the cost basis, resting upon experience rather than anticipation. . . . ."

MOUNTAIN STATE STEEL FOUNDRIES, INC.
v. COMMISSIONER

United States Court of Appeals, Fourth Circuit, 1960.
284 F.2d 737.

[The corporate taxpayer agreed to purchase fifty percent of its outstanding stock for $450,000, which was substantially in excess of the surplus shown on the corporation's books. The corporation paid $50,000 in cash, and issued debt obligations for the balance, payable in installments over a number of years, with interest at four percent. The Commissioner disallowed the corporation's deductions for the interest paid on these obligations on the ground that the purchase of the stock impaired the capital of the corporation in violation of a West Virginia statute (referred to below) and that hence the repurchase obligations were unenforceable.]

HAYNSWORTH, CIRCUIT JUDGE.* By statute, West Virginia has authorized a corporation organized under her laws, other than a banking institution, to purchase, hold and sell shares of its own capital stock. There is a proviso, however, that funds and property of the corporation may not be used to purchase its own shares if the use would impair the capital of the corporation.

The Tax Court was apparently of the opinion that the net worth of the corporation should have been reduced by the full amount of the purchase price as soon as the repurchase agreement was entered into and that the question of impairment should be determined by reference to book figures without regard to the real value of the assets. The Circuit Court for Wood County, West Virginia, on the other hand, held that the real value of the assets, which it found to be substantially more than the book figures, was crucial under the statute. The Commissioner finds the entries in the books so authoritarian that he conceded on argument that if the taxpayer had written up the value of its fixed assets on the basis of an appraisal in line with the testimony in this case and in the state court proceeding, there would have been no capital impairment. He does not question the disparity between real and book values; to him, it is the failure to have recorded the real value on the books which occasioned the asserted impairment of the capital.

We think a determination of the substantive rights of creditors, stockholders and the corporation, in the application of this statute,

* Most of the Court's footnotes, and portions of the opinion on other issues, omitted.

should not be so circumscribed by managerial decision to make or withhold particular entries on the books or by the accounting procedures followed by management, procedures which may, or may not, have been realistic or enlightened. Write ups by appraisal are frequently suspect. As a practice they are now usually frowned upon. The suggestion is startling that such a ministerial act, which alters the real situation not in the least, could enlarge corporate power to purchase its stock.

When the legislature spoke of impairment of capital, we think it had a more objective standard than a computation which is the product of years of financial history of an enterprise. If write ups by appraisal be subject to criticism in the world of corporate finance, a blind acceptance of book values as real is much more vulnerable. An overstatement of assets because of a failure to charge off obsolescent equipment should not enlarge the power of the corporation to buy its stock, nor should an understatement because of appreciation in values and the decline in the worth of money restrict it.

Corporate power to purchase its own stock has been frequently abused. Done by corporations conducting faltering businesses, it has been employed to create preferences to the detriment of creditors and of the other stockholders. It was to protect and preserve the margin of safety supplied by the real value of contributed capital that such statutes were enacted. That purpose is not served if the statute is applied in terms of unrealistic values, whether higher or lower than real values. At least until the highest court of West Virginia should otherwise decide, we think for our collateral purpose the statute should be construed as prohibiting the purchase of its own stock if the use of its funds for the purpose would deplete the realizable value of its assets to a point below the total of its liabilities and capital.

What little can be found in decided cases applying similar statutes suggests that actual values, rather than book figures, are critical to the inquiry. Though impressive argument may be made that unrealized gain should not be available justification for dividends, similar language in statutes restricting dividend distributions has been similarly construed. [Citing Randall v. Bailey—Ed.]

If we are to look to actual values in applying the statute, the spirit of the statute requires that they be conservatively determined. Opinion evidence of appreciation should be received with skepticism if insolvency ensues. Here, however, no one questions the fact that the real worth of the plant substantially exceeds its depreciated cost.[7] In subsequent years this small manufacturing enterprise has continued to prosper. Its subsequent earnings have been sufficient to maintain a good current position, meet the obligations to the Millers, pay for

7. For tax purposes, the corporation was required to use as its basis for its fixed assets the depreciated cost of its antecedent partnership. Starting with those figures, it showed on its balance sheet at the end of its fiscal year, 1950, a gross plant account of $543,235.46, a depreciation reserve of $345,355.59 and net book value of fixed assets of $197,879.87. It had approximately $150,000 of current assets to pay $20,000 of current liabilities. It had, according to the books, earned surplus of $132,527.53, which, added to the capital account of $200,000, gave it a net worth of $332,527.53. If, as the testimony indicates, its fixed assets had a realizable sales value of at least $1,000,000, its real net worth was more than $1,100,000.

substantial plant additions and improvements and pay moderate dividends. Its subsequent history is one of prosperity, not of decline. No creditor has suffered loss or delay. . . .

PROBLEM

Frame an argument on appeal from the decision in the *Kingston* case, p. 198, supra. Consider, inter alia, whether there is any issue of statutory construction, and whether the accounting posture on revaluation of assets is relevant in interpreting the statute.

7. REVALUATION OF LONG–TERM STOCK INVESTMENTS

Notice that FAS No. 12, page 202 supra, does not permit recognition of *increases* in the value of marketable securities under any circumstances. Is there room for a different view in the case of securities which represent a relatively permanent investment, perhaps even giving the holder control over the affairs of the issuer? An answer to that question requires a brief look at the process of combining, or, as it is often called, "consolidating", the accounts of two or more affiliated corporations for the purpose of presenting a unified, composite picture of the overall enterprise.

a. CONSOLIDATED ACCOUNTS

Assume that X Corp. plans to purchase all of the stock of Y Corp. Before the purchase, simplified balance sheets for X and Y show the following:

X Corp

Assets		Liabilities & Equity	
Cash	$300,000	Liabilities	$250,000
		Stated Capital	300,000
Plant	400,000	Surplus	150,000
	$700,000		$700,000

Y Corp

Assets		Liabilities & Equity	
Cash	$ 50,000		
Plant	150,000	Stated Capital	$200,000
	$200,000		$200,000

If X purchases all of the stock of Y for $200,000 in cash, X's balance sheet might then be:

X Corp

Assets		Liabilities & Equity	
Cash	$100,000	Liabilities	$250,000
Investment	200,000	Stated Capital	300,000
Plant	400,000	Surplus	150,000
	$700,000		$700,000

Since each share of capital stock in a corporation is a proportionate interest in the equity of the corporation and consequently an indirect interest in its net assets, X's purchase of all of the stock of Y amounts to an indirect purchase of the net assets of Y. If the operations of X and Y are related, it might be desirable to show, both to the outside world and to X's stockholders, a composite picture of the enterprise. A composite or "consolidated" picture of the two corporations is achieved by substituting for the asset "Investment" on X's balance sheet the assets of Y which that investment represents. X's balance sheet would then look like this:

Consolidated Balance Sheet

Assets		Liabilities & Equity	
Cash	$100,000	Liabilities	$250,000
Cash (Y)	50,000		
Plant (Y)	150,000	Stated Capital	300,000
Plant	400,000	Surplus	150,000
	$700,000		$700,000

and, after combining similar items, like this:

Consolidated Balance Sheet

Assets		Liabilities & Equity	
Cash	$150,000	Liabilities	$250,000
		Stated Capital	300,000
Plant	550,000	Surplus	150,000
	$700,000		$700,000

This last statement would be a consolidated balance sheet for X and its affiliated subsidiary, Y. Although the separate entity of each corporation must be maintained for most legal purposes, as a practical matter X could at any time dissolve Y and bring all the assets together under one corporate roof. Even without dissolution or merger, from an accounting point of view consolidation of the accounts of the two corporations may provide a more meaningful picture—both from the point of view of what the stockholders of X actually control and from the point of view of outsiders interested in the enterprise as a whole.

It was assumed, for the sake of simplicity, that Y had no liabilities. The consolidation procedure is about the same if there are liabilities (except for liabilities to X—"intra-family" obligations between X and Y do not belong in the composite picture of X and Y as a unit and should be eliminated in the consolidation procedure by cancelling the receivable on the books of one of the corporations against the payable on the books of the other). Assume that Y's balance sheet at the time of acquisition was as follows:

Y Corp

Assets		Liabilities & Equity	
Cash	$150,000	Liabilities	$100,000
Plant	150,000	Stated Capital	200,000
	$300,000		$300,000

You will note that the net assets of Y are the same as before. Other things being equal, the purchase price might well be the same. To consolidate the accounts of the two corporations, we replace the asset "Investment" on X's balance sheet with the actual assets and liabilities which that investment represents, in order to provide the most meaningful picture of what the composite enterprise owns and owes as a whole. The consolidated balance sheet would look like this:

Consolidated Balance Sheet

Assets		Liabilities & Equity	
Cash	$250,000	Liabilities	$350,000
		Stated Capital	300,000
Plant	550,000	Surplus	150,000
	$800,000		$800,000

The same consolidation procedure applies when the acquired corporation has a surplus at the time of acquisition. Suppose that Y's balance sheet looked like this:

Y Corp

Assets		Liabilities & Equity	
Cash	$ 50,000	Stated Capital	$100,000
Plant	150,000	Surplus	100,000
	$200,000		$200,000

Here again X's purchase of all the stock of Y amounts to an indirect acquisition of the net assets of Y, and it makes no difference whether the source of the net assets of the subsidiary is capital or surplus. Since the net assets are still the same as before, the purchase price for the investment might still be the same, and consolidation would again be effected by replacing the "Investment" asset by the net assets which the investment represents. The consolidated balance sheet would be:

Consolidated Balance Sheet

Assets		Liabilities & Equity	
Cash	$150,000	Liabilities	$250,000
		Stated Capital	300,000
Plant	550,000	Surplus	150,000
	$700,000		$700,000

Note that the consolidated surplus does not include the surplus which Y had at the date of acquisition. Since in a cash purchase X is in effect buying the net assets of Y, it does not matter whether the source of those net assets is capital or surplus; hence the surplus of Y created prior to the acquisition by X does not belong in the composite picture of surplus. (When X issues its own stock to acquire the stock of Y, the accounting is more complex, and in some circumstances it may be appropriate to "pool" the respective surpluses of the two companies, as well as their respective assets and liabilities.)

The price paid by the acquiring corporation would not ordinarily be exactly equal to the net assets of the acquired corporation, as it was in all of these examples. Moreover, consolidation of accounts may be desirable even though the parent corporation owns less than 100% of the stock of the subsidiary. The procedure for consolidation outlined above is equally applicable in such cases, although of course some adjustments would be necessary.

We turn now to the question of how the earnings of the subsidiary subsequent to its acquisition should be reflected in the consolidated accounts. Since the treatment is the same regardless of the make-up of the subsidiary's balance sheet, for the sake of simplicity consider the first balance sheet for Y, which was as follows:

Y Corp

Assets		Liabilities & Equity	
Cash	$ 50,000		
Plant	150,000	Stated Capital	200,000
	$200,000		$200,000

Suppose that during the first year after its acquisition by X, Y earned $50,000 while X was completely inactive. Y's balance sheet might then look like this:

Y Corp

Assets		Liabilities & Equity	
Cash	$100,000	Stated Capital	$200,000
Plant	150,000	Surplus	50,000
	$250,000		$250,000

X's would have remained:

X Corp

Assets		Liabilities & Equity	
Cash	$100,000	Liabilities	$250,000
Investment	200,000	Stated Capital	300,000
Plant	400,000	Surplus	150,000
	$700,000		$700,000

Since the net assets of Y now exceed the original cost of X's investment in Y, the consolidation technique of replacing the asset, "Investment" on X's balance sheet with the net assets of Y appears to make the columns of the consolidated balance sheet unequal:

Consolidated Balance Sheet

Assets		Liabilities & Equity	
Cash	$200,000	Liabilities	$250,000
		Stated Capital	300,000
Plant	550,000	Surplus	150,000
	$750,000		$700,000

What is missing? It would seem that the consolidated surplus must be increased in an amount equal to the $50,000 increase in the subsidiary's surplus after acquisition. This result makes sense, since any increase in Y's surplus after its acquisition is attributable to the consolidated enterprise and properly belongs in the consolidated picture of surplus. The consolidated balance sheet should look like this:

Consolidated Balance Sheet

Assets		Liabilities & Equity	
Cash	$200,000	Liabilities	$250,000
		Stated Capital	300,000
Plant	550,000	Surplus	200,000
	$750,000		$750,000

Notice that a subsequent payment of dividends by Y to X would not affect the consolidated balance sheet. The decrease in the net assets and surplus of Y as a result of the dividend is offset by the equal increase in the net assets and surplus of X.

The foregoing consolidation technique is applicable when the two corporations are sufficiently related in ownership, and perhaps operations, to make a unified, composite financial statement desirable. Suppose, however, that X and Y are not related enough to justify consolidation (an unlikely supposition, given our assumption that X owns all of the stock of Y). The traditional approach was to respect the separate entities of the two corporations, and simply record X's investment in Y as an asset on X's balance sheet, just like an investment in marketable securities. Under this approach, the subsequent earnings of Y would be reflected on X's books only when and to the extent that dividends were actually paid by Y to X, at which time the amount of the dividend would be included in X's income and ultimately in its surplus. There is, however, an intermediate position between this traditional approach and full consolidation, which might be thought of as a kind of "quasi-consolidation": under this technique, although X's balance sheet would show merely its investment in Y (rather than the net assets of Y), the subsequent earnings (or losses) of Y would be reflected each year in X's financial statements whether or not X received dividends from Y, just as would occur under consolidation.

To illustrate, take our last assumption, that Y had earned $50,-000 during the first year after its acquisition by X, while X was completely inactive. Y's balance sheet at the end of that year looked like this:

Y Corp

Assets		Liabilities & Equity	
Cash	$100,000	Stated Capital	$200,000
Plant	150,000	Surplus	50,000
	$250,000		$250,000

Assuming full consolidation was not appropriate, under the traditional view X would have to await the receipt of a dividend from Y before reflecting any of the post-acquisition earnings of Y on X's financial statements. Until then, X's balance sheet would remain the same as it was after its purchase of Y's stock:

X Corp

Assets		Liabilities & Equity	
Cash	$100,000	Liabilities	$250,000
Investment	200,000	Stated Capital	300,000
Plant	400,000	Surplus	150,000
	$700,000		$700,000

Under the quasi-consolidation technique, on the other hand, X would be permitted to write up the investment in Y by the amount of Y's earnings subsequent to acquisition, which would be balanced by an increase in X's surplus. The result would be a special kind of composite balance sheet, which would look like this:

X Corp

Assets		Liabilities & Equity	
Cash	$100,000	Liabilities	$250,000
Investment	250,000	Stated Capital	300,000
Plant	400,000	Surplus	200,000
	$750,000		$750,000

Notice that this quasi-consolidation technique produces a balance sheet very much like the one obtained by consolidation, except that there is no substitution of the net assets of Y for asset "Investment" on X's balance sheet. This treatment of a significant stock investment which is not consolidated is commonly referred to as the "equity method", connoting the fact that the investment is written up on the books of the parent to conform with the increases in the equity of the subsidiary due to its earnings. (As we shall see shortly, under the "equity" method in current practice the write-up of the investment in the subsidiary corresponding to its earnings is included in the parent corporation's income, on its way to being added to the parent's surplus, but this can be ignored for the moment.)

b. THE DU PONT COMPANY'S TREATMENT OF ITS GM INVESTMENT

For an example of the foregoing quasi-consolidation approach, or "equity method", in action (plus some interesting by-play on the subject of segregating the surplus account), consider the following accounting imbroglio involving the manner in which E. I. du Pont de Nemours & Company accounted for its investment in General Motors stock (representing approximately 23% of GM's outstanding stock which du Pont held until a court order under the anti-trust laws compelled complete divestiture, starting in 1962). The du Pont procedure was the same as that in the simplified illustration above, except for two factors: General Motors distributed some of the earnings each year as dividends, and du Pont did not own (anywhere near) 100% of GM's stock. Accordingly, du Pont's annual write-up of its investment in GM was limited to du Pont's proportionate interest in GM's earnings for the year, in excess of dividends paid.

The following excerpts and notes from the financial statements of du Pont come from the prospectus issued May 1, 1947 in connection with a preferred stock offering of $100,000,000:

E. I. DU PONT DE NEMOURS AND COMPANY AND WHOLLY OWNED SUBSIDIARY COMPANIES
Consolidated Balance Sheet December 31, 1946.

Assets
*   *   *

Investment in General Motors Corporation:
10,000,000 shares common stock carried at $26.45 a share (Note 7) ... 264,500,000

*   *   *

Liabilities
*   *   *

Surplus (earned, paid-in, and arising from revaluation of assets) (Notes 5, 7 and 14) 421,931,477

*   *   *

The accompanying notes to the financial statements are an integral part of this consolidated balance sheet.

STATEMENT OF CONSOLIDATED SURPLUS

(Earned, Paid-in, and Arising from Revaluation of Assets)

For the Years Ended December 31, 1944, December 31, 1945,
and December 31, 1946.

	1944	1945	1946
Surplus at Beginning of Year	$335,065,394	$365,510,105	$384,265,043
Add—Net income for the year ...	80,870,106	77,521,007	112,619,706
Adjustment resulting from revaluation of investment in General Motors Corporation (Note 7) ...	15,500,000	7,000,000	10,500,000
Excess of value placed on 12,358 shares of treasury Common Stock, given in exchange for assets of Defender Photo Supply Company, Inc., over cost thereof	....	208,481	....
Total	$431,435,500	$450,239,593	$507,384,749
Less—Dividends (paid or payable in cash):			
Preferred Stock ($4.50 a share each year)	$ 7,599,825	$ 7,599,825	$ 7,599,825
Common Stock $5.25 a share in 1944 and 1945, $7.00 a share in 1946)	58,325,570	58,374,725	77,853,447
Total	$ 65,925,395	$ 65,974,550	$ 85,453,272
Surplus at End of Year (Notes 5, 7 and 14)	$365,510,105	$384,265,043	$421,931,477

NOTES

* * *

5. Other Security Investments:

Other security investments are carried at cost or less with the exception of an investment in the common stock of Canadian Industries Limited. . . . Revaluation of this investment a number of years ago resulted in an increase of $4,364,113 in surplus. . . .

* * *

7. Investment in General Motors Corporation:

General Motors Corporation common stock, in accordance with a practice followed since 1925, has been revalued annually to an amount which closely corresponds to the equity indicated by the consolidated balance sheet of General Motors Corporation at December 31 of the preceding year as reported to its stockholders. The net amount added to consolidated surplus as a result of all such revaluations is $206,-878,242.

The closing market price for General Motors Corporation common stock on the New York Stock Exchange on December 31, 1946, was $52.50 a share which, if multiplied by 10,000,000, would produce a figure of $525,000,000. This amount is not represented to be either the market value or the realizable value of 10,000,000 shares of General Motors Corporation common stock.

* * *

14. Surplus

Since incorporation in 1915, the Company has maintained a single surplus account and has not earmarked or allocated the various charges and credits as falling within any particular class of surplus.

The report of Messrs. Arthur Andersen & Co. . . . states the amounts of the respective classes which, in their opinion, are included in the consolidated surplus as of December 31, 1943, December 31, 1944, and December 31, 1945. The Company cannot accept the opinion of these accountants with respect to the segregation of surplus for the reasons set forth on page 33 in Statement by the Company's Committee on Audit, contained in the Company's 1943 annual report to stockholders, concerning exception stated in certificate of Messrs. Arthur Andersen & Co. for that year with respect to surplus account. Reference is also made to the second paragraph of the report of Messrs. Lybrand, Ross Bros. & Montgomery . . . with respect to segregation of the Company's surplus at December 31, 1946.

REPORTS OF INDEPENDENT PUBLIC ACCOUNTANTS

E. I. DU PONT DE NEMOURS AND COMPANY
Wilmington, Delaware

We have examined the consolidated balance sheet of E. I. du Pont de Nemours and Company and its wholly owned subsidiary companies as of December 31, 1946, and the related statements of consolidated income and surplus, including supplementary profit and loss information, for the year then ended, have reviewed the systems of internal control and the accounting procedures of the companies and, without making detailed audits of the transactions, have examined or tested accounting records of the companies and other supporting evidence, by methods and to the extent we deemed appropriate. Our examination was made in accordance with generally accepted auditing standards applicable in the circumstances and included all procedures which we considered necessary.

The sources of surplus, as noted on the consolidated balance sheet, are "earned, paid-in, and arising from revaluation of assets", but it has not been the practice of the Company to subdivide its surplus account. Lacking a definitive and authoritative basis upon which to predicate retrospective allocations of the various charges and credits which have been made to surplus since incorporation of the Company, we have not derived separate balances for the respective classes of surplus as of December 31, 1946.

In our opinion, the aforementioned consolidated balance sheet and related statements of consolidated income and surplus, including supplementary profit and loss information, present fairly the consolidated position of E. I. du Pont de Nemours and Company and its wholly owned subsidiary companies at December 31, 1946, and the consolidated results of their operations for the year then ended, in conformity with generally accepted accounting principles applied on a basis consistent with that of the preceding year.

We have reviewed, with respect to information shown for the year ended December 31, 1946, the summary of consolidated earnings and other information appearing under the heading "Consolidated Earnings" in this Prospectus and, in our opinion, it presents fairly the consolidated net income and other data shown therein for the year 1946, in conformity with generally accepted accounting principles applied on a basis consistent with that of the preceding year.

LYBRAND, ROSS BROS. & MONTGOMERY

Lybrand, Ross Bros. & Montgomery

Philadelphia, Penna.
  March 14, 1947

To the Board of Directors,

E. I. DU PONT DE NEMOURS AND COMPANY:

We have examined the statements of consolidated income and surplus, including the statement showing supplementary profit and loss information, of E. I. du Pont de Nemours and Company and its wholly owned subsidiary companies, in so far as they relate to the two years ended December 31, 1945, and the summary of consolidated earnings appearing in the Prospectus under the heading "Consolidated Earnings", in so far as it relates to the three years ended December 31, 1945. We previously examined the consolidated financial statements of the Company and its wholly owned subsidiary companies for each of the years ended December 31, 1943, 1944 and 1945, reviewed the system of internal control and the accounting procedures of the companies and other supporting evidence, by methods and to the extent we deemed appropriate. Our examinations were made in accordance with generally accepted auditing standards applicable in the circumstances and included all procedures which we considered necessary. We have not examined the consoldiated financial statements of the Company and its wholly owned subsidiary companies for any period subsequent to December 31, 1945.

The Company maintains a combined surplus account which includes earned surplus, paid-in surplus, and surplus arising from revaluation of assets. In our opinion the respective amounts of these different classes of surplus should be stated separately in the statement of surplus. On the basis of our analysis of the combined surplus account, the balances at December 31, 1943, 1944 and 1945 consisted of the following:

	December 31,		
	1943	1944	1945
Paid-in surplus	$ 39,895,458	$ 39,895,548	$ 40,103,939
Unrealized appreciation of investments, less amount capitalized through stock dividends	141,956,462	157,456,462	164,456,462
Earned surplus	153,213,474	168,158,185	179,704,642
	$335,065,394	$365,510,195	$384,265,043

The foregoing segregation of the surplus account is based on the considerations outlined as follows:

Paid-in surplus credits represent the excess of consideration (cash or other assets) received upon the original issues of securities over the par value thereof and the excess of consideration received in 1933 (cash and preferred stock of Remington Arms Company, Inc.) over the cost of treasury stock issued therefor. Paid-in surplus charges represent premiums paid upon redemption of Debenture Stock and amounts transferred to $4.50 no par cumulative Preferred Stock account to increase the stated value of such stock to $100 per share. These transactions are clearly of a capital nature and accordingly in our opinion are proper paid-in surplus items.

Unrealized appreciation of investments consists of the amounts of the write-ups of investments in General Motors Corporation common stock and Canadian Industries Limited common stock, less the portion of a dividend paid in du Pont Common Stock in 1925 which was charged against the write-up in 1925 in accordance with a resolution of the Board of Directors. In our opinion the balance of unrealized appreciation should not be combined with either paid-in surplus or earned surplus, but should be classified in a separate category.

Earned surplus consists of the net income (together with direct surplus adjustments of income) of the Company since inception, October 1, 1915, and of its subsidiaries since the respective dates of acquisition; less dividends paid in cash or equivalent and in du Pont Common Stock (other than the stock dividend referred to above), discount on Debenture Stock issued, and the write-off of part of the excess of the amount recorded for the assets acquired from The Grasselli Chemical Company (approximately market price at the time of the du Pont Common Stock issued therefor) over the net book value of such assets. At the time of the stock dividends and the discount on Debenture Stock, which in the segregation were charged to earned surplus, the balance in the Company's surplus account consisted only of earned surplus. The write-off of the Grasselli goodwill was reflected in part by elimination of a capital surplus balance which arose in the Grasselli acquisition; the remainder was applied as a reduction of earned surplus, there being no other class of surplus (other than unrealized appreciation) available at the time.

In our opinion the facts surrounding each item are adequate to determine its character and segregation in accordance with generally accepted accounting principles.

With the exception stated above as to the combined surplus account, in our opinion, the accompanying statements of consolidated income and surplus, including the statement showing supplementary profit and loss information, and the summary of consolidated earnings referred to above, present fairly the results of operations and the changes in surplus of E. I. du Pont de Nemours and Company and its wholly owned subsidiary companies, in so far as they relate to the periods stated in the first paragraph of this report, and are in conformity with generally accepted accounting principles consistently applied during the period under review.

ARTHUR ANDERSEN & CO.

Arthur Andersen & Co.

New York, N. Y.
March 10, 1947

THE FOLLOWING STATEMENT BY THE COMPANY'S COMMITTEE ON AUDIT, CONCERNING SEGREGATION OF SURPLUS PROPOSED BY ARTHUR A. ANDERSEN & CO. FOR THE YEAR 1943, APPEARED IN THE COMPANY'S 1943 ANNUAL REPORT TO STOCKHOLDERS

The Surplus Account dates from the organization of the present company in 1915. Over the years there have been many surplus adjustments, and several stock dividends declared, generally without attempt at the time to earmark such items as falling within any particular class of surplus. Moreover, our observation has been that there does not exist sufficient uniformity or consistency of opinion among accountants with respect to the definition of the several classes into which it is suggested that surplus be divided or to the procedure which should be followed in the treatment of many specific items to enable the company to make any segregation of the Surplus Account which would not be subject to question as to its accuracy.

The amounts allocated to the respective classes of surplus by Arthur Andersen & Co. differed from those shown in a similar analysis attempted by another firm of independent public accountants who a number of years ago examined the company's accounts and certified to its financial statements.

The Committee on Audit cannot accept the opinion of Arthur Andersen & Co. as being conclusive for the reason that it believes that certain of the items comprising the Surplus Account are not susceptible of such a segregation except on the basis of arbitrary assumptions or interpretation, and that the company can have no assurance that at some later date the accuracy of the segregation may not be questioned and if found inaccurate the company might not be deemed to have published erroneous information which had served to mislead the stockholders and the investing public.

The company has been advised by counsel for years that, from the standpoint of dividend payments, the law of Delaware recognizes no distinction either in the status or in the availability of any separate parts of surplus. If in the future such a segregation should be required by statute or ruling of some official body, no doubt such action would be accompanied by such instructions as to procedure as will relieve the Directors from the responsibility of making an arbitrary segregation.

The company has consistently maintained the practice of describing in its annual reports the various changes in the Surplus Account as they occur, and we are of the opinion that such practice discloses the material facts.

COMMITTEE ON AUDIT
ELYWN EVANS, *Chairman*

Note—The Committee on Audit is composed of members of the Board of Directors none of whom hold any position in the active management of the company.

NOTE

Du Pont's investment in General Motors originally cost $55,589,-107.

The following table shows the write-ups and write-downs (shown in parentheses) in this asset from the inception of this practice through the end of 1961. Equivalent credits or debits to the surplus account were made with each revaluation.

1925	$ 36,285,893	1944	15,500,000
1926	0	1945	7,000,000
1927	26,184,371	1946	10,500,000
1928	19,962,440	1947	(5,500,000)
1929	24,953,050	1948	32,500,000
1930	22,457,745	1949	52,000,000
1931	(8,484,037)	1950	66,500,000
1932	(9,981,220)	1951	67,000,000
1933	(14,500,000)	1952	32,000,000
1934	2,500,000	1953	45,000,000
1935	5,000,000	1954	55,000,000
1936	14,000,000	1955	79,350,000
1937	8,500,000	1956	131,250,000
1938	6,000,000	1957	72,450,000
1939	6,500,000	1958	66,150,000
1940	5,500,000	1959	22,050,000
1941	5,500,000	1960	75,600,000
1942	8,000,000	1961	91,350,000
1943	15,500,000		

Net Revaluation, 1925–1961	$1,089,578,242
Original Cost	55,589,107
Additional Costs *	77,032,651
Book Value on December 31, 1961	$1,222,200,000

* Almost the entire amount of the additional costs was incurred in 1955 upon the exercise of rights to purchase 1,000,000 shares at $75.00 per share.

In 1952 du Pont altered its practice with respect to presenting the Surplus account in the financial statements. The following is from page 15 of the 1952 Annual Report:

"*Segregation of Surplus*—Historically, the Company has carried its surplus in one account on the books and has followed the practice of describing in its Annual Reports any material facts concerning current changes in the surplus account.

"In order to meet a new requirement of the U. S. Securities and Exchange Commission,* the surplus account was segregated during 1952 into three classes: (1) Earned Surplus, (2) Paid-in Surplus, and (3) Surplus Arising from Revaluation of Security Investments. This retrospective segregation of surplus was set forth in the financial statements made part of the Company's 1951 annual report to the Securities and Exchange Commission, which were certified by the independent public accountants."

The du Pont Company retained Lybrand, Ross Bros. & Montgomery as its independent public accountants until 1954. Since that year Price Waterhouse & Co. have been the independent public accountants. The Surplus account was shown in the following form during the years 1952–1961 (after which the court-ordered divesture of the General Motors stock began):

E. I. DU PONT DE NEMOURS & COMPANY
AND WHOLLY OWNED SUBSIDIARY COMPANIES

Statement of Consolidated Surplus

Earned Surplus

	1961	1960
Balance at Beginning of Year	$1,151,278,492	$1,089,476,650
Add—Net Income for the year	418,162,515	381,403,345
	1,569,441,007	1,470,879,995

* * *

Less—Dividends:

* * *

	1961	1960
Total Dividends	354,694,498	319,601,503
Balance at End of Year	1,214,746,509	1,151,278,492

Paid-in Surplus

	1961	1960
Balance at Beginning of Year	146,981,171	130,221,193
Add—Adjustments arising out of disposition of common stock (Note 6)	19,338,281	16,759,978
Balance at End of Year	166,319,452	146,981,171

* Prior to 1951 Rule 5–02 of Regulation S–X permitted companies with unsegregated surplus on their books to report surplus in unsegregated form in reports required to be filed with the SEC. As amended in 1951, the Rule requires a surplus break-down. See Regulation S–X, Rule 5–02–35. The amendment of the regulations was not accompanied by any instructions as to the procedure for making the segregation.

**Surplus Arising From Revaluation of
Security Investments**

Balance at Beginning of Year	1,002,592,355	926,992,355
Add—Adjustment resulting from revaluation of		
Investment in General Motors Corporation . .	91,350,000	75,600,000
Balance at End of Year (Notes 1–b and 1–c) . .	1,093,942,355	1,002,542,355
Total Surplus at End of Year	$2,475,018,316	$2,300,852,018

c. THE CURRENT VIEW OF THE PROFESSION

Since 1971, the quasi-consolidation, or equity, method has been the approved accounting treatment for significant investments in unconsolidated enterprises, with the further requirement that the annual write-up be included in the income statement of the parent company, as well as its surplus.

APB OPINION NO. 18 *

March, 1971.

The Equity Method of Accounting for Investments in Common Stock

INTRODUCTION

1. The Accounting Principles Board expresses in this Opinion its views on the equity method of accounting for investments in common stock. This Opinion clarifies the applicability of the equity method of accounting (paragraph 6b) to investments in common stock of subsidiaries and extends the applicability of the equity method of accounting to investments in common stock of corporate joint ventures and certain other investments in common stock. The Opinion also applies to investments reported in parent-company financial statements when such statements are prepared for issuance to stockholders as the financial statements of the primary reporting entity.

* * *

3. Several terms are used in this Opinion as indicated:

    a. "Investor" refers to a business entity that holds an investment in voting stock of another company.

    b. "Investee" refers to a corporation that issued voting stock held by an investor.

    c. "Subsidiary" refers to a corporation which is controlled, directly or indirectly, by another corporation. The usual condition for control is ownership of a majority (over 50%) of the outstanding voting stock. The power to control may also exist with a lesser percentage of ownership, for example, by contract, lease, agreement with other stockholders or by court decree.

d. "Corporate joint venture" refers to a corporation owned and operated by a small group of businesses (the "joint venturers") as a separate and specific business or project for the mutual benefit of the members of the group . . .

e. "Dividends" refers to dividends paid or payable in cash, other assets, or another class of stock and does not include stock dividends or stock splits.

f. "Earnings or losses of an investee" and "financial position of an investee" refer to net income (or net loss) and financial position of an investee determined in accordance with accounting principles generally accepted in the United States.

DISCUSSION

4. Paragraph 1 of Accounting Research Bulletin No. 51 states that: "There is a presumption that consolidated statements are more meaningful than separate statements and that they are usually necessary for a fair presentation when one of the companies in the group directly or indirectly has a controlling financial interest in the other companies." Consolidated financial statements combine the assets, liabilities, revenues and expenses of subsidiaries with the corresponding items of the parent company. Intercompany items are eliminated to avoid double counting and prematurely recognizing income. Consolidated financial statements report the financial position and results of operations of the parent company and its subsidiaries as an economic entity. In practice, consolidation has been limited to subsidiary companies, although under certain circumstances valid reasons may exist for omitting a subsidiary from consolidation.

5. Investments are sometimes held in stock of companies other than subsidiaries, namely corporate joint ventures and other noncontrolled corporations. These investments are usually accounted for by one of two methods—the cost method or the equity method. While practice varies to some extent, the cost method is generally followed for most investments in noncontrolled corporations, in some corporate joint ventures, and to a lesser extent in unconsolidated subsidiaries, particularly foreign. The equity method is generally followed for investments in unconsolidated domestic subsidiaries, some corporate joint ventures and some noncontrolled corporations. An adaptation of the cost method, the lower of cost or market, has also been followed for investments in certain marketable securities if a decline in market value is evidently not a mere temporary condition.

6. A summary of the two principal methods of accounting for the investments in common stock discussed in this Opinion follows:

a. *The Cost Method.* An investor records an investment in the stock of an investee at cost, and recognizes as income dividends received that are distributed from net accumulated earnings of the investee since the date of acquisition by the investor. The net accumulated earnings of an investee subsequent to the date of investment are recognized by the investor only to the extent distributed by the investee as dividends. Dividends received in excess of earnings subsequent to the date of investment are considered a return of investment and are recorded as reductions of cost of the investment. A series of operating losses of an investee or other factors may indicate that a decrease in value of the investment has occurred which is other than temporary and should accordingly be recognized.

b. *The Equity Method.* An investor initially records an investment in the stock of an investee at cost, and adjusts the carrying amount of the investment to recognize the investor's share of the earnings or losses of the investee after the date of acquisition. The amount of the adjustment is included in the determination of net income by the investor, and such amount reflects adjustments similar to those made in preparing consolidated statements including adjustments to eliminate intercompany gains and losses, and to amortize, if appropriate, any difference between investor cost and underlying equity in net assets of the investee at the date of investment. The investment of an investor is also adjusted to reflect the investor's share of changes in the investee's capital. Dividends received from an investee reduce the carrying amount of the investment. A series of operating losses of an investee or other factors may indicate that a decrease in value of the investment has occurred which is other than temporary and which should be recognized even though the decrease in value is in excess of what would otherwise be recognized by application of the equity method.

7. Under the cost method of accounting for investments in common stock, dividends are the basis for recognition by an investor of earnings from an investment. Financial statements of an investor prepared under the cost method may not reflect substantial changes in the affairs of an investee. Dividends included in income of an investor for a period may be unrelated to the earnings (or losses) of an investee for that period. For example, an investee may pay no dividends for several periods and then pay dividends substantially in excess of the earnings of a period. Losses of an investee of one period may be offset against earnings of another period because the investor reports neither in results of operations at the time they are reported by the investee. Some dividends received from an investee do not cover the carrying costs of an investment whereas the investor's share of the investee's earnings more than covers those costs. Those characteristics of the cost method may prevent an investor from reflecting adequately the earnings related to an investment in common stock—either cumulatively or in the appropriate periods.

8. Corporations have increasingly established or participated in corporate joint venture arrangements or taken substantial positions (but less than majority ownership) in other corporations. The significant increase in the number of intercorporate investments of less than majority ownership of voting stock has broadened interest in reflecting earnings from investments on a more timely basis than by receipt of dividends. . . .

* * *

10. Under the equity method, an investor recognizes its share of the earnings or losses of an investee in the periods for which they are reported by the investee in its financial statements rather than in the period in which an investee declares a dividend. An investor adjusts the carrying amount of an investment for its share of the earnings or losses of the investee subsequent to the date of investment

and reports the recognized earnings or losses in income. Dividends received from an investee reduce the carrying amount of the investment. Thus, the equity method is an appropriate means of recognizing increases or decreases measured by generally accepted accounting principles in the economic resources underlying the investments. Furthermore, the equity method of accounting more closely meets the objectives of accrual accounting than does the cost method since the investor recognizes its share of the earnings and losses of the investee in the periods in which they are reflected in the accounts of the investee.

11.   Under the equity method, an investment in common stock is generally shown in the balance sheet of an investor as a single amount. Likewise, an investor's share of earnings or losses from its investment is ordinarily shown in its income statement as a single amount.

12.   The equity method tends to be most appropriate if an investment enables the investor to influence the operating or financial decisions of the investee. The investor then has a degree of responsibility for the return on its investment, and it is appropriate to include in the results of operations of the investor its share of the earnings or losses of the investee. Influence tends to be more effective as the investor's percent of ownership in the voting stock of the investee increases. Investments of relatively small percentages of voting stock of an investee tend to be passive in nature and enable the investor to have little or no influence on the operations of the investee.

13.   Some hold the view that . . . the equity method is [not] appropriate accounting for investments in common stock where the investor holds less than majority ownership of the voting stock. They would account for such investments at cost. Under that view the investor is not entitled to recognize earnings on its investment until a right to claim the earnings arises, and that claim arises only to the extent dividends are declared. The investor is considered to have no earnings on its investment unless it is in a position to control the distribution of earnings. Likewise, an investment or an investor's operations are not affected by losses of an investee unless those losses indicate a loss in value of the investment that should be recognized.

OPINION

14.   The Board reaffirms the conclusion that investors should account for investments in common stock of unconsolidated domestic subsidiaries by the equity method in consolidated financial statements, and the Board now extends this conclusion to investments in common stock of all unconsolidated subsidiaries (foreign as well as domestic) in consolidated financial statements. The equity method is not, however, a valid substitute for consolidation and should not not be used to justify exclusion of a subsidiary when consolidation is otherwise appropriate. The Board also concludes that parent companies should account for investments in the common stock of subsidiaries by the equity method in parent-company financial statements prepared for issuance to stockholders as the financial statements of the primary reporting entity.

*   *   *

16. The Board concludes that the equity method best enables investors in corporate joint ventures to reflect the underlying nature of their investment in those ventures. Therefore, investors should account for investments in common stock of corporate joint ventures by the equity method, both in consolidated financial statements and in parent-company financial statements prepared for issuance to stockholders as the financial statements of the primary reporting entity.

17. The Board concludes that the equity method of accounting for an investment in common stock should also be followed by an investor whose investment in voting stock gives it the ability to exercise significant influence over operating and financial policies of an investee even though the investor holds 50% or less of the voting stock. Ability to exercise that influence may be indicated in several ways, such as representation on the board of directors, participation in policy making processes, material intercompany transactions, interchange of managerial personnel, or technological dependency. Another important consideration is the extent of ownership by an investor in relation to the concentration of other shareholdings, but substantial or majority ownership of the voting stock of an investee by another investor does not necessarily preclude the ability to exercise significant influence by the investor. The Board recognizes that determining the ability of an investor to exercise such influence is not always clear and applying judgment is necessary to assess the status of each investment. In order to achieve a reasonable degree of uniformity in application, the Board concludes that an investment (direct or indirect) of 20% or more of the voting stock of an investee should lead to a presumption that in the absence of evidence to the contrary an investor has the ability to exercise significant influence over an investee. Conversely, an investment of less than 20% of the voting stock of an investee should lead to a presumption that an investor does not have the ability to exercise significant influence unless such ability can be demonstrated. When the equity method is appropriate, it should be applied in consolidated financial statements and in parent-company financial statements prepared for issuance to stockholders as the financial statements of the primary reporting entity.

*   *   *

19. *Applying the Equity Method.* The difference between consolidation and the equity method lies in the details reported in the financial statements. Thus, an investor's net income for the period and its stockholders' equity at the end of the period are the same whether an investment in a subsidiary is accounted for under the equity method or the subsidiary is consolidated . . . . .

QUESTIONS

1. To test the significance of the requirement in Opinion No. 18 that the annual write-up of the investment be included in the parent company's income, consider what entry the parent would make upon receipt of a dividend out of the earnings of the subsidiary in a prior year, if those earnings had been reflected in the surplus of the parent in that prior year but not in the parent's income.

2. Was the advice of du Pont's counsel, to the effect that for dividend purposes Delaware law does not distinguish among the various types of surplus, useful on the issue of segregation of surplus on the balance sheet, which is what the independent accountants were concerned about?

Chapter 4

DEFERRAL OF EXPENSE AND INCOME

1. INTRODUCTION

This chapter deals with the use of deferral and accrual techniques to achieve the most informative periodic reflection of expense and income. Although we deal with income and expense items separately at first, it is important to keep in mind that as a practical matter the problems of choosing the appropriate period for reflecting items of income and expense often arise together rather than as separate questions. Business operations consist of a continuous series of transactions in which expenses are incurred in order to produce income, and these transactions give rise to *related* items of income and expense. For the income statement to provide a meaningful picture of operations, the expense items must be included in the same period as the income items they help to produce; in other words, interrelated items of expense and income must be "matched" in some particular period. For example, if Jones sells shoes costing $1,000 for $1,500 it would be a gross distortion to reflect the sales income and the related cost-of-goods sold expense in different periods. This principle of matching plays an essential part in determining the appropriate period for reflecting items of income and expense. Here is another illustration of the principle:

SHELBY SALESBOOK CO. v. UNITED STATES

United States District Court, Northern District Ohio, 1952.
104 F.Supp. 237.

[The plaintiff-taxpayer, a manufacturer of business forms, paid its salesmen commissions immediately on orders written by them which called for shipment within 60 days. The amounts paid to the salesmen on orders not shipped during the current year were deferred until the following year when the goods were shipped and the income was recognized, at which point the related commissions were charged to current expense.]

JONES, CHIEF JUDGE . . . In plaintiff's tax returns for the years in question, it reported as income the selling price of goods shipped and billed to purchasers. It deducted from such income the corresponding commissions to salesmen earned on such orders.

Taxpayer contends that it should have deducted not only the commissions on goods shipped and billed during the tax years in question, but also the commissions paid . . . in those years on orders not shipped until the following year. The Government, on the other hand, takes the position that the method of arriving at net income which was used by taxpayer was proper and clearly reflected its income.

* * *

The Supreme Court of the United States in referring to the change in tax practice permitting taxpayers to prepare their income tax returns on an accrual basis, made this observation in U. S. v. Anderson, 269 U.S. 422, 46 S.Ct. 131, 70 L.Ed. 347:

"It was to enable taxpayers to keep their books and make their returns according to scientific accounting principles, by charging against income earned during the taxable period, the expenses incurred in and properly attributable to the process of earning income during that period; and indeed, to require the tax return to be made on that basis, if the taxpayer failed or was unable to make the return on a strict receipts and disbursement basis." 269 U.S. at page 440, 46 S.Ct. at page 134.

This statement by the Supreme Court reflects the view . . . that expense is to be offset against the income it helps to produce. Only in this way does the return "clearly reflect the income". . . .

Now to straddle the tax years involved by dividing into separate parts the income and the expense of the plaintiff's sales transactions would reflect a sort of imbalance with respect to true income for those years.

After careful consideration, I am of the opinion that the Commissioner was right in not allowing the deductions claimed by the taxpayer. Accordingly, the complaints will be dismissed at plaintiff's costs, and judgment may be entered for defendants.

-----

2. DEFERRED EXPENSES

Given a set of related items which should be matched, that is, reflected in the same period, the question of which is the "right" period can, as we shall see later in this chapter, be quite close. It may be enough that the criteria used in making the decision are reasonable, and are applied consistently to similar transactions. However, in the common case where payment of an expense precedes receipt of the related income, as in the *Shelby* case, the more stringent limitations on recognition of income noted in Chapter One will control the decision, and the expense will have to be deferred until the income can be recognized. The important point is that in any of these situations deferral and accrual of expense or income items provide the mechanics for implementing whatever decision is made.

Many expense items do not relate to any particular transactions, but rather aid generally in the production of revenues. For example, the cost of casualty insurance cannot be matched with any particular income; instead, such an expense is one of the general costs of doing business. Since the benefit of the expense, financial protection against loss, is enjoyed ratably over the duration of the policy, the burden of the expense should be allocated ratably among the periods covered by the policy, and deferral provides the mechanics for accomplishing that objective Thus, if a three-year policy is obtained for $300 on January 1 of year one, $100 should be charged to current expense for year one, while $200 is deferred, to appear on the balance sheet as an asset, Deferred Insurance Expense, at the end of year one. This Deferred Expense asset would be charged off to current expense (or as it is often called, "amortized") ratably over the next two years; that is, $100 would be charged to current expense in year two, with $100 remaining in the Deferred Insurance Expense account at the end of that year, and that remaining $100 would be charged to current expense in year three (just as E. Tutt's prepayment of rent for three years was handled back in Chapter One).

Whenever the benefit of an expense is a function of time, as in the case of insurance, the basis for allocation among the current period and any future periods involved is readily apparent. Thus if a two-year policy was obtained on July 1 of year one for $200, $50 would be charged to expense in year one, $100 in year two, and $50 in year three; again the amount not yet charged to current expense would appear in the Deferred Insurance Expense account on the balance sheet at the end of each of the intervening years.

Occasionally, an expenditure may provide benefits in succeeding periods which are not a function of the passage of time. Suppose an enterprise spends $300 on July 1 of year one for a promotional campaign for one of its products. First, a question of judgment arises as to whether this expenditure will provide any benefit beyond the end of the year. If not, of course, the entire $300 must be charged to current expense in year one. But suppose it is concluded that the company will continue to derive benefit from the promotion through June 30 of year two at which time another promotional expenditure will be made. It does not follow automatically that half of the total expenditure should be charged to expense for each year; rather, another question of judgment is presented, as to how much of the total benefit from the $300 expenditure is enjoyed in each of the two years. If it were determined, on the basis of past experience, professional advice, or otherwise, that the benefits in the first six months after the expenditure were twice as great as those in the next six months, then it would follow that $200 should be charged to current expense in year one, and $100 in year two. Again, the technique of deferral at the end of year one would provide the mechanics for implementing that judgment decision.

The issues referred to thus far in this chapter were summarized as follows by the Accounting Principles Board in its Statement No.

4, promulgated in 1970, which undertook to describe the broad fundamentals of financial accounting:

APB STATEMENT NO. 4 *

Basic Concepts and Accounting Principles Underlying Financial Statements of Business Enterprises

Accounting Principles Board, October, 1970.

* * *

156.   Three pervasive expense recognition principles specify the
bases for recognizing the expenses that are deducted from revenue to
determine the net income or loss of a period.   They are "associating
cause and effect," "systematic and rational allocation," and "immediate
recognition."

157.   *Associating cause and effect.*   Some costs are recognized as
expenses on the basis of a presumed direct association with specific
revenue.

Although direct cause and effect relationships can seldom be conclusively demonstrated, many costs appear to be related to particular
revenue and recognizing them as expenses accompanies recognition of
the revenue.   Examples of expenses that are recognized by associating
cause and effect are sales commissions and costs of products sold or
services provided.

* * *

159.   *Systematic and rational allocation.*   In the absence of a
direct means of associating cause and effect, some costs are associated
with specific accounting periods as expenses on the basis of an attempt
to allocate costs in a systematic and rational manner among the periods
in which benefits are provided.   If an asset provides benefits for
several periods its cost is allocated to the periods in a systematic and
rational manner in the absence of a more direct basis for associating
cause and effect.   The cost of an asset that provides benefits for only
one period is recognized as an expense of that period (also a systematic
and rational allocation).   This form of expense recognition always involves assumptions about the pattern of benefits and the relationship
between costs and benefits because neither of these two factors can
be conclusively demonstrated.   The allocation method used should appear reasonable to an unbiased observer and should be followed systematically.   Examples of items that are recognized in a systematic
and rational manner are depreciation of fixed assets, amortization of
intangible assets, and allocation of rent and insurance.   .   .   .

160.   *Immediate recognition.*   Some costs are associated with
the current accounting period as expenses because (1) costs incurred
during the period provide no discernible future benefits, (2) costs
recorded as assets in prior periods no longer provide discernible benefits or (3) allocating costs either on the basis of association with reve-

nue or among several accounting periods is considered to serve no use-
.ful purpose.

Application of this principle of expense recognition results in charging
many costs to expense in the period in which they are paid or liabilities to pay them accrue. Examples include officers' salaries, most
selling costs, amounts paid to settle lawsuits, and costs of resources
used in unsuccessful efforts. The principle of immediate recognition
also requires that items carried as assets in prior periods that are discovered to have no discernible future benefit be charged to expense, for
example, a patent that is determined to be worthless.

161. *Application of Expense Recognition Principles.* To apply
expense recognition principles, costs are analyzed to see whether they
can be associated with revenue on the basis of cause and effect. If
not, systematic and rational allocation is attempted. If neither cause
and effect associations nor systematic and rational allocations can be
made, costs are recognized as expenses in the period incurred or in
which a loss is discerned. Practical measurement difficulties and consistency of treatment over time are important factors in determining
the appropriate expense recognition principle.

These issues, such as whether an expenditure should be charged
off in the current period, or whether it will provide benefits beyond
the end of the current year, and, if so, for how long and in what
amount, are the kinds of questions of judgment which accountants
constantly face and which are of importance and concern to lawyers.
Before turning to some concrete illustrations posing such questions,
however, let us first consider the analogous question presented in
accounting for fixed assets.

a. DEPRECIATION ON FIXED ASSETS

We have already seen in Chapter One how close a relationship
there is between deferred expenses and fixed assets, like property,
plant and equipment; indeed, such fixed assets (other than land)
really are just another type of deferred expense. The very reason
why the expenditure of, say, $325 for a new sewing machine by X
Corp., a shoe manufacturer, is recorded as an asset is because it is
so clear that the expenditure will provide benefit in future years and
hence should not all be charged to expense in the current year. However, we also noted that such an asset, like most tangible fixed assets other than land, will not last forever; ultimately it will have to
be retired, because it is physically worn out, or has become too inefficient, or perhaps because new developments in the state of the art
have made it desirable to replace the machine. Obviously, one of the
expenses of producing revenues during the time that the machine is
in service, usually referred to as the "useful life" of the machine,
is the $325 spent to acquire it (less any salvage proceeds, that is, any

proceeds received upon the disposition of the machine, for scrap or otherwise, in excess of the costs of disposal). Therefore, this amount should be allocated to expense in some reasonable and systematic manner among the periods of the useful life of the machine, a process referred to as "depreciation" in the case of fixed assets, rather than "amortization", as in the case of intangible deferred expense assets.

Unlike many deferred expense assets, like prepaid insurance, the useful life of a tangible fixed asset cannot be precisely ascertained. Instead, resort must be had to estimation, on the basis of the previous experience of this company (or perhaps others), engineering data, possible technological obsolescence, etc. If a company in fact utilizes machines for less than their normal life, as, for example, an automobile rental company which uses cars for only one or two years and then sells them to a used car dealer, it is the actual useful life to that company over which the cost less salvage should be allocated. (The estimate of salvage, too, should be based upon the actual experience of the company, and generally speaking it is only in the latter type of situation that salvage proceeds are more than nominal.)

Usually it is easiest to calculate the useful life of a tangible fixed asset in units of accounting periods, such as years or months, but occasionally a different unit may prove more convenient. For example, the useful life of a machine might be estimated in terms of hours of running time, in which event the amount charged to expense during each period will depend upon the number of hours of use during each period. Alternatively, the useful life of the machine might be calculated in terms of the total number of items the machine is expected to produce before it is retired, in which event the total charge per accounting period will vary according to the number of items produced.

Assume that in the case of the sewing machine acquired by X Corp. for $325 at the beginning of year one the useful life is estimated in the normal fashion, at ten years, with an estimated salvage value at the end of ten years of $25. In that event, the entry at the end of the first year might be:

Sewing Machine Expense $30

    Sewing Machine $30

Actually, as noted in Chapter One it is more common to use the name "Depreciation Expense" for the expense account which is debited when a portion of the cost (less salvage) of a fixed asset is charged to current expense, connoting the fact that the process is referred to as "depreciation". (Notice that the term "depreciation" in this context has nothing to do with diminution in the value of the asset;

although of course the worth of the asset is probably declining with the passage of time, depreciation does not attempt to measure that.) A general term like "Depreciation Expense" also makes it easier to lump together under one heading all of the expenses of using up fixed assets during the period, an important convenience for a large company which might have thousands or even millions of individual fixed assets.

More important, the credit accompanying the charge to Depreciation Expense would probably not be made directly to the asset account, as it is when an intangible deferred expense asset is being amortized. That is because it is often considered desirable to preserve the original cost of fixed assets on the balance sheet. Instead, the credit would be made to a kind of suspense account, usually called "Accumulated Depreciation", which is carried as an offset to the asset account on the balance sheet. But remember that in general the "Accumulated Depreciation" account at any time simply represents the amount of the cost of the fixed asset charged to expense to date, and that the only reason for creating this account is to make it possible to continue to show the original cost of the fixed asset on the balance sheet. And the net figure, i. e., original cost less accumulated depreciation, often referred to as the "book value" of the asset, represents the amount of the original cost remaining to be allocated to future periods (plus any estimated salvage value).

Thus the sewing machine referred to earlier might appear among the other assets on X's balance sheet at the end of the first year as follows:

Sewing Machine $325

Less: Accumulated Depreciation   30 $295

As a practical matter, however, this machine is likely to be lumped together with all of the company's other machinery and equipment, so that only a single figure showing the total cost of all the machinery and equipment presently in service would appear on the balance sheet, together with an offsetting figure for the total accumulated depreciation to date on that machinery and equipment. (In the past the Accumulated Depreciation account was often called "Reserve for Depreciation", a term which poses some difficulties we will consider later but is still used occasionally today.)

b. DEFERRED EXPENSES AS ASSETS

Returning to the subject of deferred expense assets, we have noted that the result of deferring an expense until it is used up in a subsequent period is to create an asset on the balance sheet. Such assets have had an accounting history quite different from that of the familiar tangible assets, like equipment or inventory, starting back when accounting was still largely on a cash basis and these intangible deferred-expense assets were not created at all, even though expenditures for tangible property were routinely recorded as assets on the balance sheet. But even after accrual accounting came into vogue there was hesitancy about reflecting these intangible assets on the balance sheet, especially for dividend purposes, because these assets so often produced no proceeds to help pay the claims of creditors in the event of a forced liquidation. Hence the view developed in some quarters that these intangible assets should be reflected on the balance sheet only if they had some refund or other realizable value, although this stringent test was not applied to tangible assets, like equipment, which often turned out to have little value upon a forced sale for the benefit of creditors.

Today, there is general agreement that at least as an accounting matter the existence or extent of realizable value is not the controlling consideration for recording an asset on the balance sheet. Prospective creditors are more likely to look to a company's earnings prospects (and perhaps its track record in meeting its obligations) than to the total of its balance sheet assets in judging whether to enter a transaction, and a fortiori existing or prospective shareholders. To be sure, realizable value still plays some role in recording assets. For example, short-term creditors frequently rely on the amount of current assets like accounts receivable or inventory in extending credit, and what such creditors are interested in is the quick realizable value of these assets, as well as their value to the firm as a going concern. However, reliance on realizable value of an asset is today the exception. For most purposes it is proper to view an asset, whether tangible or intangible, as the remaining balance of a previous cash outlay which has not yet been allocated to current expense because some of its usefulness remains to be consumed in the future.

Consider the following excerpts from accounting authorities and judicial opinions on the subject of deferred expenses as assets:

ACCOUNTING TERMINOLOGY BULLETIN NO. 1 (1953)

26. The word *asset* is not synonomous with or limited to property but includes also that part of any cost or expense incurred which is properly carried forward upon a closing of books at a given date. . . . [T]he term *asset*, as used in balance sheets, may be defined as follows:

> Something represented by a debit balance that is or would be properly carried forward upon a closing of books of account according to the rules or principles of accounting (provided such debit balance is not in effect a negative balance applicable to a liability), on the basis that it represents either a property right or value acquired, or an expenditure made which has created a

property right or is properly applicable to the future. Thus, plant, accounts receivable, inventory, and a deferred charge are all assets in balance-sheet classification.

The last named is not an asset in the popular sense, but if it may be carried forward as a proper charge against future income, then in an accounting sense, and particularly in a balance-sheet classification, it is an asset.

APB STATEMENT NO. 4, "BASIC CONCEPTS AND ACCOUNTING PRINCIPLES UNDERLYING FINANCIAL STATEMENTS OF BUSINESS ENTERPRISES" (1970)

132.　　The basic elements of the financial position of an enterprise are assets, liabilities, and owners' equity.

> *Assets*—economic resources of an enterprise that are recognized and measured in conformity with generally accepted accounting principles. Assets also include certain deferred charges that are not resources [26] but that are recognized and measured in conformity with generally accepted accounting principles.[27]

HAMMOND v. CATON, 121 Colo. 7, 212 P.2d 845 (1949). Caton, partner with Hammond in a pet food business, agreed to buy out Hammond's interest for $11,000 plus one-half the inventory value of the stock in trade and accounts receivable. The memoranda of sale provided that "all accounts owing and due said partnership shall be adjusted, . . ." and that the $11,000 to be paid to Hammond was in consideration for "the good will, fixtures, furnishing, machinery, merchandise and other assets of the business . . ." Hammond, dissatisfied with the amount an accountant determined to be due, refused its tender and brought suit for a larger sum. He claimed that the excess over $11,000 to which he was entitled should include, inter alia, one-half the value of the prepaid insurance and prepaid rent, on the ground that these were "accounts owing and due", and hence accounts receivable, within the meaning of the agreement. *Held*, plaintiff is not entitled to any additional payment for the prepaid items. They were assets, not receivables, within the meaning of the contract of sale.

EBBERT v. PLYMOUTH OIL CO., 338 Pa. 272, 13 A.2d 42 (1940). Plaintiff brought a bill on behalf of the nominal defendant corporation to require that its directors account for a sum of $883,146.36, which

---

26. [Footnotes from the original] Deferred charges from income tax allocation are an example of deferred charges that are not resources. The term *deferred charges* is also sometimes used to refer to certain resources, for example, prepaid insurance.

27. This definition differs from that in Accounting Terminology Bulletin No. 1, Paragraph 26, which defines assets as debit balances carried forward upon a closing of books of account that represent property values or rights acquired.

had for eight years been carried as "Deferred Charges" and then charged off to Earned Surplus. Plaintiff claimed the sum in fact represented moneys wrongfully expended by the defendants on their own behalf in the defense of suits against them. The trial court dismissed the bill for laches. *Held,* reversed. Assuming the averments of the bill were true, carrying the amount as "Deferred Charges" amounted to concealment of its true use, and relieved plaintiff of the duty of investigating the item when it first appeared or before it was charged off. While accountants and some others understand the special meaning of a deferred charge entry, "the ordinary person is not to be visited with knowledge of this technical terminology, and so far as plaintiff is concerned, what the statements conveyed to her was that this large sum . . . was an asset of the corporation . . ., and she was not put upon inquiry until its status was changed by being charged to surplus".

WALDHEIM REALTY & INVESTMENT CO. v. COMMISSIONER, 245 F.2d 823 (8th Cir. 1957). Taxpayer, on the cash basis, sought to deduct insurance premiums as a business expense in the year paid although part of such premiums was for insurance covering subsequent years. The Commissioner contended that prepaid insurance constituted an asset whose cost should be amortized over the life of the policy. *Held,* for the taxpayer. "The payment of the insurance premium adds nothing to the taxpayer's plant or equipment or his ability to produce income. In this respect the insurance premiums differ from prepaid rent, lease bonuses, and commissions, as such expenditures are for the purpose of providing the taxpayer the place in which to carry on his business. . . .

"The main reason assigned in . . . [previous] decisions why insurance should be treated as a capital asset is that the unexpired insurance has a surrender value. . . . It is common knowledge that the surrender value of a policy cancelled by the insured is upon a short term rate basis, and considerably less than the prorata return of the premium for the unexpired term. We do not believe that the fact that some salvage value could be realized at the end of the taxable year out of prepaid insurance is sufficient to make the prepaid insurance [an asset for tax purposes]."

Consider also the following significant opinion of the Accounting Principles Board dealing with the accounting for intangible assets; although addressed primarily to good will (a subject we will consider in more detail shortly), the opinion clearly has considerably broader ramifications:

APB OPINION NO. 17: INTANGIBLE ASSETS *

Accounting Principles Board, 1970.

SUMMARY

Problem

1. An enterprise may acquire intangible assets from others or may develop them itself. Many kinds of intangible assets may be identified and given reasonably descriptive names, for example, patents, franchises, trademarks, and the like. Other types of intangible assets lack specific identifiability. Both identifiable and unidentifiable assets may be developed internally. Identifiable intangible assets may be acquired singly, as a part of a group of assets, or as part of an entire enterprise, but unidentifiable assets cannot be acquired singly. The excess of the cost of an acquired company over the sum of identifiable net assets, usually called goodwill, is the most common unidentifiable intangible asset.

2. Accounting for an intangible asset involves the same kinds of problems as accounting for other long-lived assets, namely, determining an initial carrying amount, accounting for that amount after acquisition under normal business conditions (amortization), and accounting for that amount if the value declines substantially and permanently. Solving the problems is complicated by the characteristics of an intangible asset: its lack of physical qualities makes evidence of its existence elusive, its value is often difficult to estimate, and its useful life may be indeterminable.

* * *

Scope and Effect of Opinion

4. The Board has considered the conclusions and recommendations of Accounting Research Study No. 10, the discussions of the appropriateness of accepted methods of accounting for intangible assets, and proposals for alternative accounting procedures. The Board expresses in this Opinion its conclusions on accounting for intangible assets.

5. This Opinion covers the accounting for both identifiable and unidentifiable intangible assets that a company acquires, including those acquired in business combinations. "Company" in this Opinion refers to both incorporated and unincorporated enterprises. The conclusions of the Opinion apply to intangible assets recorded, if any, on the acquisition of some or all of the stock held by minority stockholders of a subsidiary company. This Opinion also covers accounting for costs of developing goodwill and other unidentifiable intangible assets with indeterminate lives.

6. The provisions of this Opinion apply to costs of developing identifiable intangible assets that a company defers and records as assets. Some companies defer costs incurred to develop identifiable in-

tangible assets while others record the costs as expenses as incurred. Certain costs, for example, research and development costs and pre-operating costs, present problems which need to be studied separately. The question of deferral of those costs is beyond the scope of this Opinion.

* * *

Conclusions

9.   The Board concludes that a company should record as assets the costs of intangible assets acquired from others, including goodwill acquired in a business combination.   A company should record as expenses the costs to develop intangible assets which are not specifically identifiable.   The Board also concludes that the cost of each type of intangible asset should be amortized by systematic charges to income over the period estimated to be benefited.   The period of amortization should not, however, exceed forty years.

BACKGROUND

Bases of Classification

10.   Various intangible assets differ in their characteristics, their useful lives, their relations to operations, and their later dispositions. Intangible assets may be classified on several different bases:

Identifiability—separately identifiable or lacking specific identification.

Manner of acquisition—acquired singly, in groups, or in business combinations or developed internally.

Expected period of benefit—limited by law or contract, related to human or economic factors, or indefinite or indeterminate duration.

Separability from an entire enterprise—rights transferable without title, salable, or inseparable from the enterprise or a substantial part of it.

Present Accounting

Accounting for Costs at Acquisition

11.   Present principles of accounting for intangible assets are generally similar to those for tangible, long-lived assets such as property, plant, and equipment.   Intangible assets acquired from other entities are recorded at cost when acquired.   Costs incurred to develop specifically identifiable intangible assets are often recorded as assets if the periods of expected future benefit are reasonably determinable. Costs of developing other intangible assets are usually recorded as expenses when incurred.

Accounting for Deferred Costs After Acquisition

12.   Intangible assets have been divided into two classes for purposes of accounting for their costs: (a) those with a determinable term of existence because it is limited by law, regulation, or agreement, or by the nature of the asset, and (b) those having no limited term of existence and no indication of limited life at the time of acquisition.   The cost of a type (a) intangible asset is amortized by

systematic charges to income over the term of existence or other period expected to be benefited. The cost of a type (b) intangible asset may be treated in either of two ways: (1) the cost may be retained until a limit on the term of existence or a loss of value is evident, at which time the cost is amortized systematically over the estimated remaining term of existence or, if worthless, written off . . ., or (2) the cost may be amortized at the discretion of management by charges to income even though no present evidence points to a limited term of existence or a loss of value.

13. The cost of an intangible asset, including goodwill acquired in a business combination, may not be written off as a lump sum to capital surplus or to retained earnings nor be reduced to a nominal amount at or immediately after acquisition . . ..

Criticism of Present Practice

14. Present accounting for goodwill and other unidentifiable intangible assets is often criticized because alternative methods of accounting for costs are acceptable. Some companies amortize the cost of acquired intangible assets over a short arbitrary period to reduce the amount of the asset as rapidly as practicable, while others retain the cost as an asset until evidence shows a loss of value and then record a material reduction in a single period. Selecting an arbitrary period of amortization is criticized because it may understate net income during the amortization period and overstate later net income. Retaining the cost as an asset is criticized because it may overstate net income before the loss of value is recognized and understate net income in the period of write-off.

Appraisal of Alternative Procedures

Cost of Intangible Assets

15. The cost of intangible assets acquired either singly or in groups, including intangible assets acquired in a business combination, from other businesses or individuals is determined by general principles of the historical-cost basis of accounting. The costs of developing goodwill and other intangible assets with indeterminate lives are ordinarily not distinguishable from the current costs of operations and are thus not assignable to specific assets.

Treatment of Costs

16. Costs of intangible assets which have fixed or reasonably determinable terms of existence are now amortized by systematic charges to income over their terms of existence. Differences of opinion center on the amortization of acquired intangible assets with lives which cannot be estimated reliably either at the date of acquisition or perhaps long after, for example, goodwill and trade names.

17. The literature on business combinations and goodwill, including Accounting Research Study No. 10, *Accounting for Goodwill*, contains at least four possible accounting treatments of goodwill and similar intangible assets:

    a. Retain the cost as an asset indefinitely unless a reduction in its value becomes evident.

b. Retain the cost as an asset but permit amortization as an operating expense over an arbitrary period.

c. Retain the cost as an asset but require amortization as an operating expense over its estimated limited life or over an arbitrary but specified maximum and minimum period.

d. Deduct the cost from stockholders' equity at the date acquired.

18. *Arguments for nonamortization.* The two of the four accounting proposals which do not involve amortization of goodwill as an operating expense are based in part on the contention that goodwill value is not consumed or used to produce earnings in the same manner as various property rights, and therefore net income should not be reduced by amortization of goodwill. Further, net income should not be reduced by both amortization of goodwill and current expenditures that are incurred to enhance or maintain the value of the acquired intangible assets. All methods of amortizing goodwill are criticized as arbitrary because the life of goodwill is indefinite and an estimated period of existence is not measurable.

19. The basis for proposing that the cost of goodwill be retained as an asset until a loss in value becomes evident is that the cost incurred for acquired goodwill should be accounted for as an asset at the date acquired and in later periods. The cost should not be reduced as long as the value of the asset is at least equal to that cost.

20. The basis for proposing that the cost of goodwill be deducted from stockholders' equity at the date acquired is that the nature of goodwill differs from other assets and warrants special accounting treatment. Since goodwill attaches only to a business as a whole and its value fluctuates widely for innumerable reasons, estimates of either the terms of existence or current value are unreliable for purposes of income determination.

Accounting on the Historical-Cost Basis

21. All assets which are represented by deferred costs are essentially alike in historical-cost based accounting. They result from expenditures or owners' contributions and are expected to increase revenue or reduce costs to be incurred in future periods. If future benefit or the period to be benefited is questionable, the expenditure is usually treated as a current expense and not as a deferred cost. Associating deferred costs with the revenue or period to which they are expected to relate is a basic problem in historical-cost based accounting both in measuring periodic income and in accounting for assets. The basic accounting treatment does not depend on whether the asset is a building, a piece of equipment, an element of inventory, a prepaid insurance premium, or whether it is tangible or intangible. The cost of goodwill and similar intangible assets is therefore essentially the same as the cost of land, buildings, or equipment under historical-cost based accounting. Deducting the cost of an asset from stockholders' equity (either retained earnings or capital in excess of par or stated value) at the date incurred does not match costs with revenue.

22. Accounting for the cost of a long-lived asset after acquisition normally depends on its estimated life. The cost of assets with perpetual existence, such as land, is carried forward as an asset without amortization, and the cost of assets with finite lives is amortized by

systematic charges to income. Goodwill and similar intangible assets do not clearly fit either classification; their lives are neither infinite nor specifically limited, but are indeterminate. Thus, although the principles underlying present practice conform to the principles of accounting for similar types of assets, their applications have led to alternative treatments. Amortizing the cost of goodwill and similar intangible assets on arbitrary bases in the absence of evidence of limited lives or decreased values may recognize expenses and decreases of assets prematurely, but delaying amortization of the cost until a loss is evident may recognize the decreases after the fact.

A Practical Solution

23.   A solution to this dilemma is to set minimum and maximum amortization periods. This accounting follows from the observation that few, if any, intangible assets last forever, although some may seem to last almost indefinitely. Allocating the cost of goodwill or other intangible assets with an indeterminate life over time is necessary because the value almost inevitably becomes zero at some future date. Since the date at which the value becomes zero is indeterminate, the end of the useful life must necessarily be set arbitrarily at some point or within some range of time for accounting purposes.

OPINION

Acquisition of Intangible Assets

24.   The Board concludes that a company should record as assets the costs of intangible assets acquired from other enterprises or individuals. Costs of developing, maintaining, or restoring intangible assets which are not specifically identifiable, have indeterminate lives, or are inherent in a continuing business and related to an enterprise as a whole—such as goodwill—should be deducted from income when incurred.

25.   *Cost of intangible assets.* Intangible assets acquired singly should be recorded at cost at date of acquisition. Cost is measured by the amount of cash disbursed, the fair value of other assets distributed, the present value of amounts to be paid for liabilities incurred, or the fair value of consideration received for stock issued . . . .

26.   Intangible assets acquired as part of a group of assets or as part of an acquired company should also be recorded at cost at date of acquisition. Cost is measured differently for specifically identifiable intangible assets and those lacking specific identification. The cost of identifiable intangible assets is an assigned part of the total cost of the group of assets or enterprise acquired, normally based on the fair values of the individual assets. The cost of unidentifiable intangible assets is measured by the difference between the cost of the group of assets or enterprise acquired and the sum of the assigned costs of individual tangible and identifiable intangible assets acquired less liabilities assumed. Cost should be assigned to all specifically identifiable intangible assets; cost of identifiable assets should not be included in goodwill. . . .

Amortization of Intangible Assets

27.   The Board believes that the value of intangible assets at any one date eventually disappears and that the recorded costs of intangible assets should be amortized by systematic charges to income over the periods estimated to be benefited.   Factors which should be considered in estimating the useful lives of intangible assets include:

a.   Legal, regulatory, or contractual provisions may limit the maximum useful life.

b.   Provisions for renewal or extension may alter a specified limit on useful life.

c.   Effects of obsolescence, demand, competition, and other economic factors may reduce a useful life.

d.   A useful life may parallel the service life expectancies of individuals or groups of employees.

e.   Expected actions of competitors and others may restrict present competitive advantages.

f.   An apparently unlimited useful life may in fact be indefinite and benefits cannot be reasonably projected.

g.   An intangible asset may be a composite of many individual factors with varying effective lives.

The period of amortization of intangible assets should be determined from the pertinent factors.

28.   The cost of each type of intangible asset should be amortized on the basis of the estimated life of that specific asset and should not be written off in the period of acquisition.   Analysis of all factors should result in a reasonable estimate of the useful life of most intangible assets.   A reasonable estimate of the useful life may often be based on upper and lower limits even though a fixed existence is not determinable.

29.   The period of amortization should not, however, exceed forty years.   Analysis at the time of acquisition may indicate that the indeterminate lives of some intangible assets are likely to exceed forty years and the cost of those assets should be amortized over the maximum period of forty years, not an arbitrary shorter period.

30.   *Method of amortization.*   The Board concludes that the straight-line method of amortization—equal annual amounts—should be applied unless a company demonstrates that another systematic method is more appropriate.   The financial statements should disclose the method and period of amortization.   Amortization of acquired goodwill and of other acquired intangible assets not deductible in computing income taxes payable does not create a timing difference, and allocation of income taxes is inappropriate.

31.   *Subsequent review of amortization.*   A company should evaluate the periods of amortization continually to determine whether later events and circumstances warrant revised estimates of useful lives.   If estimates are changed, the unamortized cost should be allocated to the increased or reduced number of remaining periods in the revised useful life but not to exceed forty years after acquisition. Estimation of value and future benefits of an intangible asset may indicate that the unamortized cost should be reduced significantly by

a deduction in determining net income. However, a single loss year or even a few loss years together do not necessarily justify . . . [a] charge to income for all or a large part of the unamortized cost of intangible assets. The reason for [any such] deduction should be disclosed.

Disposal of Goodwill

32. Ordinarily goodwill and similar intangible assets cannot be disposed of apart from the enterprise as a whole. However, a large segment or separable group of assets of an acquired company or the entire acquired company may be sold or otherwise liquidated, and all or a portion of the unamortized cost of the goodwill recognized in the acquisition should be included in the cost of the assets sold.

* * *

The Opinion entitled "Intangible Assets" was adopted by the assenting votes of thirteen members of the Board. Messrs. Burger,

Catlett, Davidson, Hellerson, and Horngren dissented.

Mr. Catlett dissents to this Opinion because he believes that goodwill should never be shown as an asset in the balance sheet and should never be amortized as a charge to income. In his view, goodwill, regardless of the form of consideration paid for it, reflects values brought about by investor expectations attributable to a multitude of factors. Such values fluctuate frequently and widely, and the changes do not occur in any rational, predictable manner. Thus, there is no continuing relationship between the value of goodwill and its cost. Goodwill does not have a demonstrable useful life; and its expiration, if any, cannot be related on any logical basis to the operating revenues of particular periods. . . .

Messrs. Burger, Davidson, Hellerson, and Horngren dissent to the required amortization of goodwill and other intangible assets (for example, perpetual franchises) having indeterminate lives. Whether amortization is appropriate depends on the particular circumstances of each case, including the evidence of increases or decreases in the value of such assets. In some cases, the facts may indicate maintenance or enhancement rather than diminution of value of the intangibles. In such cases, amortization is inappropriate. In other cases, the useful life may be determinable; then the cost should be amortized by systematic charges to income over the estimated period of usefulness. In all cases, the amortization of intangible assets should be based on professional judgment, rather than arbitrary rules.

ACCOUNTING INTERPRETATIONS *

The Journal of Accountancy, April, 1971, 70, 74.

The Institute staff has been authorized to issue unofficial interpretations of accounting questions having general interest to the profession. . . . The purpose of the interpretations is to provide guidance on a timely basis without the formal procedures required for an Accounting Principles Board Opinion. . . .

Intangible Assets

Question—APB Opinion No. 17 requires that intangible assets acquired after October 31, 1970 be amortized over a period not exceeding 40 years. Does this Opinion encourage the capitalization of identifiable internally developed intangible assets which have been generally charged to expense in the past?

Interpretation—APB Opinion No. 17 does not change present accounting practice for intangible assets in any way except to require that intangible assets acquired after October 31, 1970 be amortized. Paragraph 6 notes that the costs of some identifiable intangible assets are now capitalized as deferred assets by some companies while other companies record the costs as expenses when incurred. This paragraph also specifies that the question of whether the costs of identifiable internally developed intangible assets are to be capitalized or charged to expense is not covered by the Opinion. Therefore, the Opinion does not encourage capitalizing the costs of a large initial advertising campaign for a new product or capitalizing the costs of training new employees.

COX v. LEAHY

Supreme Court of New York, Appellate Division, 1924.
209 A.D. 313, 204 N.Y.S. 741.

VAN KIRK, J. The plaintiff is the trustee in bankruptcy of Kingsbury-Leahy Company. There were three causes of action stated in the complaint, but of these the cause of action tried and decided was the action under section 28 of the Stock Corporation Law, to recover the loss sustained by the corporation or its creditors by the declaration and payment of a 50 per cent. dividend. . . . The directors of a corporation may declare and pay a dividend, when the corporation has surplus profits equal to or greater than the amount of the dividend paid. The fact that the corporation has not the ready funds sufficient to pay the dividend, and therefore borrows money with which to pay the dividend, does not render the declaration and payment illegal. . . . To what extent the property capital was impaired by the payment of the dividend is the question to be determined, and the dispute is confined to a few of the items in the statement of assets and liabilities. The burden of showing the amount of the impairment on October 18, 1916, rests upon the plaintiff. We will consider the items questioned separately. . . .

Third item—prepaid insurance and taxes: The prepaid insurance, we think, was an asset. It had an actual value belonging to the company. Not only in law is it an asset, but in practice prepaid insurance is uniformly entered as an asset in making the balance sheet of a business. The asset account should be increased by the amount of the unearned premiums, $590.04. We think prepaid taxes rest on a different basis. They are in no wise available for a refund, and are paid for past expenses of government as well as future. . . .

The judgment . . . [is] modified accordingly and, as modified, affirmed, without costs.

PROBLEM

X Corp. had the following balance sheet on January 1:

Assets		Liabilities and Net Worth	
Cash	$11,000	Stated Capital	$100,000
Plant	90,000	Earned Surplus	1,000
	$101,000		$101,000

On February 1, X borrowed $5,000, giving a note due three years later, with interest at 12% per year; the annual interest of $600 was to be paid in two installments each year, $300 on April 30, and $300 on October 31. Assume for simplicity that X Corp. had no income and no other expenses during the calendar year in which the loan was obtained. Work out the entries in the T-accounts required for each month, February through December, to reflect the interest expense and its effect on both the Profit and Loss account and the balance sheet. How large a dividend could X Corp. properly pay at the close of the calendar year, under a statute which permits dividends only "out of net assets in excess of capital"?

Suppose X Corp. had gross income of $1,000 during the calendar year, and no expenses other than the interest on this note. How much should the general manager receive under an employment contract which entitles him to "10% of the net profits, before deduction of such salary, of each calendar year"?

c.　SOME OTHER EXAMPLES: ADVERTISING AND PROMOTION

L. P. LARSON, JR., CO. v. WILLIAM WRIGLEY, JR., CO.

Circuit Court of Appeals of the United States, Seventh Circuit, 1927.
20 F.2d 830.

ALSCHULER, CIRCUIT JUDGE. Both parties appeal from a decree which awarded L. P. Larson, Jr., Company (herein called Larson) $1,384,649.12, as net profits on sales by Wm. Wrigley, Jr., Company (herein called Wrigley) of the latter's brand of "Doublemint" gum sold in package dress held by this court to have infringed Larson's "Wintermint" gum package. . . .

The contested issues on the accounting arise over allowance or rejection of various items claimed by Wrigley in reduction of this gross "Doublemint" profit. The first Wrigley account filed showed items which indicate for the entire accounting period some loss on "Doublemint." A supplemental account, later filed on its behalf, introduced additional items in reduction, which show much greater loss for the period.

Advertising

The item of most importance, and perhaps most sharply controverted, is that of advertising. For years prior to putting out the "Doublemint" brand Wrigley was an extremely heavy advertiser, and before placing "Doublemint" on the market had established a large trade in gum—"Spearmint" being its specially advertised brand. On putting out the "Doublemint" brand, a very heavy and extensive advertising program was inaugurated, and for a considerable time "Doublemint" was greatly stressed. The previously heavily advertised "Spearmint" continued also to be much advertised, and later the policy seemed to be to put special stress on the name "Wrigley," but including both "Doublemint" and "Spearmint" in the advertising matter. Still later in the period Wrigley brought out the "Juicy Fruit" brand, and advertised it with the rest, though not so extensively as "Doublemint." The total expended during the accounting period for advertising, such as newspaper, magazine, billboard, street car advertising, electric signs, and the like, was $6,798,662.73.

Intricate computations of the advertising items were made, each on a different basis, for allocating to "Doublemint" its proper proportion of these items. Wrigley's accountant assigned to "Doublemint" $2,872,844.43, while Larson's accountant fixed it at $1,017,183.59. The master worked out a complicated system whereby a very considerable portion of the advertising was charged up as "institutional," to be amortized in four years; that is, one-fourth of the cost to be charged off for each year as the expense for that year of such advertising. In this way alone much of the advertising expense for the last three years of the period was projected forward; for example, for an "institutional" advertisement for the last year of the accounting period only one-fourth would be charged against the gross profits for that period, and three-fourths projected beyond that period, upon the theory that the advertisement, though contracted and paid for in the first year, will be effective as an advertisement for four years, and that such future benefit will accrue to Wrigley as an institution. We cannot accept as practically probable the proposition that an advertisement is as potent throughout a four-year period as during the year of its publication. And this applies, in large measure, as well to much of the more permanent forms of advertising, such as billboards and electric signs. In time even these become obsolete and stale, and from time to time are renewed or changed, to say nothing of the cost of upkeep. Besides, all of that part of the advertising cost attributable wholly to the infringing "Doublemint," which remained unearned at the close of the accounting period, became lost to Wrigley through the injunction. Nevertheless, the expense for this advertising had been contracted and paid for in good faith, and however it may have been wholly or partly unearned at the close of the accounting period, it was none the less an expense which should be deducted in fixing the net profits on "Doublemint." Where the injured party seeks the profits of an infringer, he takes the chance of their reduction, or even extinguishment, through expenses and losses actually incurred, however unwisely or even improvidently, so long only as they were incurred in good faith.

Our investigation of the record and consideration of the briefs convinces us that far too large a part of the advertising expense was, by the master's report, accredited to the future, and not sufficient to the accounting period, and that much too small a part of the entire advertising costs was attributed to "Doublemint." To undertake the allocation of each of the almost innumerable items of advertising to the various brands, and to "institution," would be indeed a most difficult task, and one wherein certainty would not, in the nature of things, be possible. But laborious examination of the many advertisements appearing in the transcript, and of the numerous tables, charts, graphs, and computations thereon, and the evidence concerning them, together with the very elaborate arguments of counsel submitted on the subject, and the report of the master and the opinion of the District Judge, satisfies us that the conclusions and findings and figures reached by the District Court upon the subject of advertising far more nearly comport with the approximate equity between these parties than those the master reported. Upon this item we quite despair of reaching a result more equitable than that reached by the District Court, and we see no reason for disturbing its conclusions thereon, as carried into the decree.

. . . .

PROBLEM

Assume that a company decides, upon advice of its agency, on a concentrated program of radio advertising once every three years with merely a minor sustaining program in between. The company expects that this program will best support a steady public demand for its products. The cost is estimated to be $1,000,000 during the first year and $100,000 in each of the next two years. What entries should the company make at the close of each year, assuming that costs agree with estimates? Consider also APB Op. No. 17, pages 259–265, supra, particularly ¶ 6, and the Interpretation which follow that Opinion.

What entry should the company make at the close of the third year if the cost for that year turned out to be $130,000? See paragraphs 23 and 24 of APB No. 9, page 186, supra, and FASB No. 16, plus paragraphs 25–28 in Appendix A, pages 194–196, supra.

d. GOODWILL

PROBLEM

Ivy Clothes, a small successful haberdashery proprietorship, had the following balance sheet at the close of its most recent fiscal year:

Assets		Liabilities	
Cash	$50,000	Accounts Payable	$50,000
Inventory	105,000		
Building Fixtures	65,000	Proprietorship	170,000
	$220,000		$220,000

Suppose the proprietor pays off his liabilities and sells all the rest of the assets of his business to a newly-organized corporation, Ivy Corp., for $200,000. Ivy Corp. pays the $200,000 in cash, out of the proceeds of its initial stock issue of $240,000. How should this acquisition be recorded on the books of Ivy Corp.? (If it is relevant, investigation would reveal that the current replacement cost of the inventory is the same as the book value, but it would cost $75,000 to replace the building fixtures in their current condition.) What are the implications of the accounting decisions at the outset on the determination of net income in the future?

In analyzing this problem, consider the following excerpts from accounting and judicial authorities:

FASB DISCUSSION MEMORANDUM: ACCOUNTING FOR BUSINESS COMBINATIONS AND PURCHASED INTANGIBLES *

Financial Accounting Standards Board, 1976, pp. 46–50.

Nature of Goodwill

Determining the nature of goodwill has long been controversial and continues to be perplexing. . . .

Goodwill has not been defined precisely. Most writers generally agree, however about certain characteristics:

    1. Goodwill relates to a business as a whole and, accordingly, is incapable of separate existence and of being sold apart from the identifiable assets of the business.

    2. Individual factors that may contribute to goodwill are not susceptible to independent valuation by any method or formula. Their values can be determined only as an aggregate in relation to a business as a whole.

    3. The future benefits of goodwill recognized in a combination may have no relationship to the costs incurred in the development of that goodwill. Goodwill may exist in the absence of specific costs to develop it.

Accounting literature is replete with divergent opinions about the nature of goodwill. A brief statement of the two broad views that embrace most of those opinions is followed by discussion of each view:

    1. Goodwill represents expected earnings in excess of anticipated normal earnings.

    2. Goodwill represents intangible resources attributable to a company's above-average strength in areas such as technical skill and knowledge, management, and marketing research and promotion that cannot be separately identified and valued.

View 1: Goodwill represents excess future earnings potential

According to this view, a combinor's primary motivation in entering into a combination is to obtain additional future earnings. The aggregate cost reflects an evaluation of the combinee's earning power. Where the aggregate cost exceeds the current value of the combinee's net identifiable assets, the excess must relate to expected additional earning power. Were it not for the expectation of additional future earnings, no amount would be paid for goodwill. Even where goodwill is not evident from past earnings performance, as in companies in bankruptcy or in the development stage, goodwill may exist in terms of expectations about future earnings.

This earning power concept of goodwill is consistent with U. S. Treasury Department, Internal Revenue Service *Revenue Ruling 59–60*, which defines goodwill as an expectation of earnings in excess of a fair return on the capital invested in tangibles or other means of production. . . .

Catlett and Olson concluded in *Accounting Research Study No. 10* that the earning power concept of goodwill is the most relevant one for accounting purposes. They contended that goodwill differs from other elements contributing to the value of a business because (a) it is not a separable resource or property right apart from the business as a whole and (b) its determination generally involves evaluating the business as a whole. . . .

Some have criticized the earning power concept of goodwill, chiefly because they find it of limited help in resolving the accounting for goodwill. According to them, all elements of a company are acquired because of their potential earnings contribution; therefore, to say that goodwill represents superior earnings potential adds nothing substantive about its nature.

View 2: Goodwill represents certain intangible resources

According to this view, if aggregate cost for a combinee exceeds the current value of the net identifiable assets acquired, the combinee presumably possesses some other resources that have value to the combinor. Some have indicated that this view is simply an extension of the earning power concept because even those who emphasize earning power acknowledge that advantageous factors and conditions contribute to that earning power. For example, Catlett and Olson indicated that possible advantageous factors and conditions of a company contributing to its earning power include:

1. Superior management team
2. Outstanding sales manager or organization
3. Weakness in the management of a competitor
4. Effective advertising
5. Secret manufacturing process
6. Good labor relations
7. Outstanding credit rating resulting from an established reputation for integrity (thereby providing a company extra equity "leverage" through more than ordinary borrowings at favorable interest rates)

8. Top-flight training program for employees
9. High standing in a community through contributions to charitable activities and participation in civic activities and by a company's officers
10. Unfavorable developments in operations of a competitor
11. Favorable association with another company
12. Strategic location
13. Discovery of talents or resources
14. Favorable tax conditions
15. Favorable government regulation

IRS *Revenue Ruling 59–60*, which indicates that goodwill, in the final analysis, is based on earning capacity and its value, suggests that other factors may contribute to intangible value, such as prolonged successful operations over a long period of ownership and prestige and renown of the business. A pervasive advantageous factor may be the ability to obtain a "going concern" as opposed to organizing and establishing a new operation. . . .

No exhaustive list of the diverse factors and conditions contributing to goodwill is possible. Some factors may be controlled by management; others may arise from events largely or wholly beyond the control of management. Costs may be incurred in connection with some factors; others may emerge without any incurred cost or managerial effort. Sometimes, the combinor is seeking not only the combinee's existing advantages but also the benefits to be derived by applying the combinor's skills (e. g., management expertise, product knowledge, and good labor relations) to the combinee.

CONCORD CONTROL INC. v. COMMISSIONER *

United States Tax Court, 1976.
35 TCM 1345.

[Petitioner-taxpayer purchased all of the assets of the K–D division of Duplan Corporation for approximately $3,590,000 in cash plus the assumption of K–D's outstanding liabilities amounting to some $237,000, and thereafter continued K–D in operation as a going business. There was evidence that in their negotiations the parties had reached agreement that petitioner would pay book value for K–D's accounts receivable and inventory, and for the fixed assets an amount equal to 89.5% of the appraised values, as determined by Manufacturer's Appraisal Company (MAC); figures derived on this basis were specifically allocated to these various assets in the purchase and sale agreement, accounting for all but a few thousand dollars of the total purchase of some $3,827,000, with the excess being allocated to certain prepaid expenses like insurance, except for "the sum of $1" which was allocated to all other assets purchased. The Commissioner sought to allocate over $1,000,000 of the purchase price to goodwill, which would not be depreciable or otherwise deductible for tax purposes.]

* Findings of fact, portions of the opinion, and all of the footnotes omitted.

STERRETT, JUDGE:

Opinion

The issue before us is the ofttimes litigated and rather vexing question of the proper basis of assets acquired in connection with the purchase of a business. More precisely, in the context of the factual patterns before us, we must decide whether the contract for sale and the allocation of the purchase price therein represent a bona fide reflection of the agreement and intent of the parties to that transaction, or whether the allocation was a device by which petitioner sought to disguise substantial payments for intangible assets, to wit, goodwill.

* * *

We turn first to petitioner's initial contention which, stripped to its bare essentials, is that it purchased the assets of K–D but not K–D itself. . . .

A careful consideration of the evidence convinces us that it cannot be gainsaid that petitioner acquired K–D as a going business in 1964. It is undisputed that Duplan desired to sell and that Stone wished to purchase K–D as an operating entity; that petitioner acquired, with certain minor exceptions, substantially all of K–D's assets and retained, at least, its key personnel; and that the sale caused little or no interruption in the operation of K–D's business. The evidence clearly demonstrates that the shift in K–D's ownership was the sole change emanating from the sale thereof in 1964.

Although not stated in these terms, petitioner's argument equates the relevant transactions with one in which it purchased the same assets from myriad sellers. We simply cannot agree. Evidently petitioner bases this view on the fact that an appraisal of K–D's assets was made and utilized as a basis for negotiations prior to the parties' meeting of the minds on the price ultimately to be paid. Implicit in this reasoning is the notion that this course of conduct is somehow unique, thereby differentiating the transaction herein from the normal purchase of a going business. To the contrary we fail to see an alternative method by which a reasonable businessman, genuinely concerned with his economic future, would acquire a business. A determination of the value of each asset separately is surely a reasonable starting point for a determination of the value of all the assets collectively. We believe that the record supports but one conclusion, that petitioner acquired K–D as a full operating entity.

Turning next to petitioner's second argument, petitioner seeks to have us recognize the contractual allocations as written.

* * *

We agree with petitioner that the contract for sale was the result of arm's-length negotiations and fairly reflects the intention of the parties thereto. Petitioner and Duplan were unrelated corporations and Stone, who owned substantially all of the stock of petitioner, owned no stock in Duplan and had no familial relationship with any of the individuals in control of Duplan. Although Stone was on friendly terms with Kaelin, Kaelin disqualified himself from participation in the negotiations which were in large part conducted between Johnson and Stone. In view of the fact that Johnson was the majority stockholder of Duplan, we think it obvious that out of self-interest alone he would have sought to obtain the best terms and conditions possible.   .   .   .

* * *

Moreover, and most importantly, the portion of the purchase price allocated to the tangible assets was less—not more—than the values placed thereon by MAC. While we recognize that the MAC appraisal is not correct in all respects, it was a *bona fide*, independent appraisal conducted in accordance with accepted appraisal methods without interference on the part of either Duplan or petitioner. Further, it is clear that the negotiating parties accepted the MAC valuations as a genuine reflection of the worth of the assets in question and utilized these values as a basis for the negotiations that followed. Thus, even in these instances in which respondent has demonstrated the MAC appraisal to be in error, the portion of the total purchase price derived from such error nevertheless represents the intended quid pro quo of the parties.

The fact of the matter is that the record is devoid of any evidence that would tend to support a finding of collusion between Duplan and petitioner and fully supports petitioner's contention that the contract for sale reflects the bargain as actually struck by the parties thereto. For this reason we think petitioner tendered payment only for those assets to which a portion of the purchase price was allocated in the contract for sale at the price so allocated, and is entitled to have the intention of the parties, as expressed in their agreement, respected.

In so holding, we recognize that   .   .   .   the tax interests of petitioner and Duplan were not adverse.   .   .   .   As such, we have not attributed to the agreement the weight to which we would otherwise give it had the parties been adverse in the tax sense.

Supporting our conclusion herein are our doubts whether K–D possessed any goodwill in 1964 that petitioner could have purchased had it desired to do so. A precondition to the possession of transferable goodwill is a finding that the seller's business is of such a nature as to provide the purchaser with the expectancy of both continuing excess earning capacity and competitive advantage or continued patronage.   .   .   .   Excess earning capacity in and of itself is insufficient to demonstrate the transfer of goodwill.   .   .   .   Here, K–D at the time of the sale was engaged in an industry fraught with both a high degree of competition and little customer loyalty, manufacturing a product line virtually identical to those of its competitors. In particular, K–D was continually compelled to accede to the demands of NAPA, its largest customer, in order to retain that account. The loss thereof in 1969, despite the rather obsequious role played by K–D and petitioner during the term of their respective relationships with NAPA, amply demonstrates that petitioner had no reasonable expectancy of continued customer patronage flowing from its purchase of K–D.

* * *

Notwithstanding our conclusion that petitioner acquired no goodwill in connection with its purchase of K–D, it clearly did acquire an ongoing business that was earning money, had a trained staff of employees, had a product line presently ready for sale and equipment ready for immediate use. Simply stated, the purchase price paid by petitioner for the various assets acquired in 1964 included substantial going concern value which, as distinguished from goodwill, is the increase in the value of assets due to their existence as an integral part of an ongoing business. The portion of the purchase price for each asset attributable to the going concern value is nondepreciable and must, therefore, be excluded from petitioner's basis therein in computing the depreciation deductions to which it is entitled.

REPUBLIC TECHNOLOGY FUND, INC. v. LIONEL CORP.*

United States Court of Appeals, Second Circuit, 1973.
483 F.2d 540.

OAKES, CIRCUIT JUDGE: This case is the unhappy aftermath of a corporate marriage gone sour, with the bride's family claiming that the groom failed to disclose a number of liabilities at the time of the negotiations leading up to the nuptials. The appeal is from a judgment absolving the appellee from liability under either contractual or securities law in connection with an interim (six months') financial statement, used in proxy materials and in a registration statement, prepared relative to the merger of Hathaway Instruments, Inc. ("Hathaway"), into The Lionel Corporation ("Lionel"). Appellants were stockholders in Hathaway. Their principal claim below and here is that the interim statement (and hence the proxy materials and registration statement) was misleading in that it artificially inflated earnings because it did not reflect $2,221,000 of adjustments that at year's end were ultimately required and also because it contained no write-off of good will of a subsidiary that was losing money at the time. The case essentially involves, therefore, the scope of a corporation's duty to make its interim financial statements accurately reflect the real state of fiscal affairs prior to a merger, or, put another way, the extent to which in an interim statement adjustments that are or should be made at year's end must be anticipated.

* * *

Lionel was the well-known toy and train manufacturer that, after some years of successful operations, entered into a program of corporate acquisitions, one of which was Anton-Imco Electronics Corp., which in turn owned Intercontinental Manufacturing Co., Inc., and Anton Electronics Laboratories Inc. (Anton-Imco and its two subsidiaries are sometimes collectively referred to herein as the "Anton-Imco" or "electronics division" of Lionel.) . . .

. . . unaudited financial statements for the six months' period ending June 20, 1961, had been prepared for Lionel and Hathaway and a combined pro forma for that period had also been prepared. These figures showed a six month's loss for Lionel of $84,000 or $.06 per share and a combined pro forma profit of $245,000 or $.08 per share. It is the omission of the Lionel statement to show certain adjustments made at year's end or to take into account by way of adjustment to Anton-Imco good will that subsidiary's losses that is the crux of the controversy here.

* * *

---

* Portions of the opinion and most of the
footnotes omitted.

There were a number of adjustments recorded as of December 31, 1961, as a result of the year-end audit or of events occurring during the fourth quarter of 1961. Of these, the ones appellants most insistently claim should have been reflected in the June 30 interim statement are:

1. Inventory write-downs: In Lionel's toy and train division $262,830 for inventory obsolescence was written down in the fourth quarter or written off as at December 31; . . . $77,946 was a write-down to lower of cost or market; and the rather remarkable sum of $256,000 was written off as "unlocated difference between December 31, 1961 book and physical inventory".

* * *

4. Deferred selling, advertising and service expense: Lionel wrote off $249,000 of these expenses in its toy and train division at year's end.

The total of the above adjustments which were made at year's end is $2,221,659.

Appellants also claim that the interim statement:

5. Should have reflected a write-off in good will attributable to Lionel's Anton-Imco division, which was carried at $998,-000, despite a $189,000 loss for the first six months of 1961;

* * *

Appellants point out that each $30,000 of adjustments would have reduced profits shown in the proxy materials and registration statement by one cent per share (of the merged company). Indeed, after the year-end adjustments were actually made, without even counting any write-down of Anton-Imco good will, the consolidated profit expected to be shown in the interim statement became a loss in the sum of $1,898,609, and when added to this were $633,668 of special charges, the overall loss totaled over $2.5 million or $1.71 per share.

The district court, sitting without a jury, took testimony both from appellants' accounting expert, Mr. Duchan, and from Mr. Easton, the senior managing accountant for S. D. Leidesdorf & Co. ("Leidesdorf"), independent certified public accountants, who worked on the Lionel audits in 1960 and 1961. Mr. Easton testified both to his preparation of the financial statements in question and as an accounting expert. It may not come as a surprise that while Mr. Duchan testified that in his opinion the June 30 statement should have reflected a substantial portion of the adjustments that were actually made at year's end, Mr. Easton's testimony was to the effect that the interim statement was accurate (in addition to being in accordance with the same generally accepted accounting principles used in Lionel's year-end statements and its prior financial statements).

The district court . . . held that plaintiffs (appellants) had "not established by a fair preponderance of the evidence that the June 30 Financial Statements were materially false or that Lionel omitted to state any material fact necessary to make the statements not false or misleading". . . .

* * *

B. Rule 10b–5, § 17 and Lionel's Interim Accounting. Under both Rule 10b–5 and § 17 of the Securities Act of 1933 . . . it is necessary to determine whether Lionel made "any untrue statement of a material fact" or an omission "to state a material fact necessary in order to make the statements made, in the light of the circumstances under which they were made, not misleading". . . .

Were the interim financial statement and the proxy statement and initial registration statement which utilized the interim statement "misleading" in view of "the circumstances" underlying the transaction? In answering this question we must, of course, give full weight to the district court's findings of fact, even while we are free to look to the application of the securities law to the facts found. . . . Taking the evidence in the light most favorable to the defendant, Lionel, we nevertheless find certain omissions in the interim statement to have been misleading.

1. *Anton-Imco Good Will.* We commence with the $998,000 item for good will of Anton-Imco Electronics Corp., as to which the interim statement of earnings reflected no discount even though this subsidiary had sustained a loss of $188,842 as of June 30.[4] Mr. Easton, Lionel's auditor, acknowledged that the operating loss of Anton-Imco was a "factor to be considered" in deciding whether there was a diminution of the good will. He felt, however, that this single factor was outweighed by the fact that Anton-Imco was only in its first year of operation as a Lionel subsidiary and in his words was "engaged in the development of a new machine—I believe it was a money sensor, a money changing device—and based on all the information that was available at that time the prospects for success seemed very reasonable". Thus, in the opinion of Mr. Easton, credited by the district court, despite Anton-Imco's losses there was no "diminution in value" of its good will.

We cannot accept Mr. Easton's evaluation as a matter of law. The notes to the consolidated interim statements of income contain the following statement:

> This company recently designed and developed a currency recognizing device, several prototype models of which have been built up to this time. The device has not yet been marketed and there is no assurance at this time as to whether it will be a profitable item.

Nowhere do the notes in any way indicate that Anton-Imco had shown a $189,000 loss as of June 30 or that the retention of $998,000 as its good will was based upon the prospects of success of this currency recognizing device which had not yet been marketed. . . . Indeed, since the interim statements do not include a balance sheet but only consolidated statements of income they contained no reference at all to the good will item. This makes them, in our view, all the more misleading. The person viewing the statements would have no reason to suspect that the consolidated earnings were at least subject to question since despite a loss on the part of a major division for the first half-year, its good will was still being carried at a full initial valuation equivalent to about 8 per cent of the Lionel total book value. This is particularly so when the notes emphasize optimistic items, e. g., calling

4. For the full 12-month period the loss was some $724,000 and there was apparently considered at year's end a partial write-down of $307,984 in the good will item, but this was not taken.

attention to the fact that the interim statement did not include certain "special items" (including such things as elimination of a $22,444 reserve for certain employee benefits) that would have improved the earnings by $.10 per share in toto for the first six months of 1961. In other words, the voters on the merger were being shown the frosting on the cake with no allusion in the statements to the fact that a substantial part of the cake itself was dried out, if not mildewed.
. . .

At the very least, good disclosure accounting would have required the notation of some uncertainty regarding the overall interim Lionel profit picture based on this item alone, uncertainty which should have been footnoted, to avoid misleading the stockholder. See SEC Accounting Series Release No. 62, 4 CCH Fed.Sec.L.Rep. ¶ 72,081 at 62,149 (1947) (footnoted explanation must be included in a summary earning statement if the information it would contain is of such "special significance [that] . . . its omission would be likely to give rise to misleading inferences"). Cf. Metropolitan Personal Loan Corp., 7 S.E.C. 234, 239 (1940) (even assuming deferred asset account could be written off in a single year, footnoted explanation required to make income statement not misleading). While stockholders who are voting on a merger are not to be treated like "children in kindergarten", . . . they are entitled to disclosure of the bitter with the sweet. They are at least entitled to assume that the interim financial statements furnished them by their own company or the other party to the merger will give them better than "ballpark" figures and be based on principles of conservatism which the American Institute of Certified Public Accountants speaks of as "a general tendency toward early recognition of unfavorable events and minimization of the amount of net assets and net income". . . . The stockholders are entitled to assume that uncertainty concerning profit or loss should be at least footnoted in the first financial statement issued after the uncertainty arises.

This is, perhaps, another way of saying that in a day and age of mergers and conglomerates—Lionel in the 1960 era was what might be called a baby conglomerate, branching out from toy trains to outboard motors, fishing tackle, electronic and nuclear instruments, and education science toys, among other things, in addition to "currency sensors"—it is as important to shareholders, perhaps more so, that interim statements issued for merger approval purposes accurately reflect corporate events as that the year-end financial statement dressed in the pretty package of an annual report be in accordance with sound or generally accepted accounting principles. Fairly to be able to vote on a merger requires accurate information. Perhaps nothing is more relevant to a vote on whether or not to approve a merger than the [most recent] earnings picture of the acquiring company, at least to the stockholder of the company being acquired. . . . Here . . . the accounting presentation in the summary income statement did not disclose facts of real significance to the voting stockholder. . . .
We hold that the omission by Lionel to make any reference in the interim statement to the substantial good will item and the significant interim loss, when coupled with mention of the unmarketed "currency recognizing device" was misleading as a matter of law.

2. *Inventory Write-downs.* The same does not hold true, however, for the extraordinarily high inventory adjustments made at year's end in reference to the toy and train division and the Lionel Labs. Only a year's end physical inventory was taken; the interim statements point this fact out and indicate that merchandise inventories in the interim statements were "estimated by the management by adding purchases, direct labor and factory overhead . . . and deducting therefrom estimated cost of goods sold", the interim overhead being allocated to the cost of goods sold on the basis of 1960 and 1961 estimated annual production and sales. This disclosure makes virtually unassailable the district court finding that at least as regards the $77,946 "shrinkage" and that $256,000 "unlocated difference" items in the toy and train division there was nothing misleading. To discover a shrinkage or lost (or stolen) merchandise requires a physical inventory, and there is no contention here, nor was there any below, that a physical inventory should have been taken as of June 30.

* * *

5. *Deferred Selling, Advertising and Service Expense.* Some $249,000 of selling, advertising and service expenses were treated as "Deferred Charges" at June 30 and written off at the end of the year. . . . Again, however, it must be remembered that Lionel's business was Christmas seasonal. Over-reporting of deferred expenses early in the year might well not have provided an accurate picture of the company's condition. . . .

* * *

7. *Summary.* In summary, then, we believe that there was a misrepresentation in respect to the $998,000 good will item [and two other items written off at year end], and that on the basis of the evidence adduced the interim statement should have disclosed uncertainty regarding the first and made some adjustment in respect to the other two. Absent further proof we may assume that the adjustment should have equaled 50 per cent of the last two adjustments that were actually made at year end, . . . sums which we find substantial enough to warrant consideration on remand.

C. **Materiality, Scienter and Reliance.** The district court did not consider separately the issues of materiality on the one hand and deceptiveness of the representations in the interim statements on the other hand. Rather, as we have indicated, its findings were basically to the effect that each of the alleged omissions did not involve a "misrepresentation". Since we have found, however, that in certain respects there were misrepresentations, we must remand unless we can say that under no construction of the evidence could the district court find that the misrepresentations were material or that there was established the necessary culpability on the part of Lionel. We by no means can say so.

***

e. ORGANIZATION EXPENSES

BOWE v. PROVIDENT LOAN CORP., 120 Wash. 574, 208 P. 22 (1922). A purchaser of stock from the defendant corporation sued for

rescission of the contract of sale, alleging fraudulent misrepresentations. Among them was the representation by defendant that the
shares were worth $12.50 apiece. This was based on an accountant's
audit in which $45,110 in organizational and promotional expenses
were included as assets of the corporation, which totaled only approximately $150,000. *Held*, plaintiff is entitled to rescission. "This large
item was neither cash, accounts receivable, notes receivable, nor physical property. Obviously, in determining the value of the stock, that
item could not be included as an asset of the company for the purpose
of swelling the paper value of the stock. . . ."

PROBLEM

Y Corp., formed on January 1, paid a bill of $1000 for legal ex-
penses incident to its organization. How should this be reflected in
its financial statements at the close of that year?

---

f. RESEARCH AND DEVELOPMENT EXPENSES

POLIN v. CONDUCTRON CORP.

United States Court of Appeals, Eighth Circuit, 1977.
552 F.2d 797.

[Conductron, a Delaware corporation, was an electronics research
and development firm in Ann Arbor, Michigan, with sales for the year
ending December 31, 1963 of some $5,000,000. McDonnell Douglas
Corporation (MDC) was a St. Louis-based manufacturer of aircraft and aerospace products with sales for the year ending June 30,
1964 of $865,000,000. In 1964 MDC purchased 20% of the outstand-
ing stock of Conductron. On January 7, 1966, MDC and Conductron
entered into an agreement under which Conductron acquired (1) the
business and assets of MDC's Electronic Equipment Division (EED),
engaged in the production of aircraft simulators, (2) all of the stock
of a wholly-owned MDC subsidiary, and (3) $5,000,000 cash, in ex-
change for 1,850,000 shares of newly-issued Conductron stock. At the
same time, MDC purchased 50,000 shares of Conductron stock from its
majority shareholder, giving MDC more than 80% control. A proxy
statement was sent to the Conductron shareholders to secure their approval of the transaction (which was a foregone conclusion because
MDC and the majority stockholder from whom the 50,000 shares were
acquired already controlled more than the necessary votes).

The plaintiff was a stockholder of Conductron at the time of the
transaction with MDC, and he added to his Conductron holdings from
time to time over the next several years. He brought suit against Conductron and MDC and certain of their officers, charging violations of
the federal securities laws. Among other things, he claimed that the
January, 1966 proxy statement, and both Conductron's first 1966 "annual" report (which actually covered just the first six months of 1966,
through June 30) and the second 1966 "annual" report (covering July
1 to December 31), contained false and misleading statements, particularly with reference to the aircraft simulator business Conductron had acquired from MDC.]

TALBOT SMITH, SENIOR DISTRICT JUDGE *:

* * *

In order to analyze properly the frauds allegedly practiced almost throughout Conductron's entire corporate life, it is necessary to acquire some perspective as to the simulator business, its origins, its prospects, and its costs, since all are comprehended, in one form or another, in fraud charges covering the years in question.

The simulator, as the name implies, simulates something else. With respect to aircraft, the simulator duplicates ("simulates") the cockpit of the plane. Through an intricate system of wiring and programming, and with the aid of computers, aircraft operating characteristics may be simulated for various situations both routine and of serious nature. The entire plane performance is duplicated, from take-off, through systems performance, radio navigation and communication, descent, approach and ground operations. The savings accomplished through the use of a simulator are of substantial magnitude. The airplane being simulated, costing from $5,000,000 to $25,000,000 is released for other operations by a simulator costing from $1,000,000 to $2,000,000. Moreover, there is no danger during training to the fledgling pilot or his airplane. The training, in fact, is so detailed that after the simulator work is completed, only "one final flight in the airplane [is required] . . . ."

But the problems involved in simulator manufacture parallel in complexity the operations of the machine itself, since the design, engineering, and manufacture require from two to five years. Since the simulator must match exactly the airplane it is intended to simulate, plane changes require simulator changes, and even between planes of the same general design, such as the Boeing 737, to simulate one is not to simulate all. In addition, different airlines flying the same plane may order different cockpit configurations, as changes are made in equipment, causing unanticipated and substantial losses, arising not only from production design costs but also from changes in the hardware that goes into the simulator cockpit.

The simulator engineers with the Electronic Equipment Division (EED) of MDC did not come to Conductron as novices. A Mr. Toole, then an employee of EED put it, "My feelings were that we had a technical break-through in simulation, one that was worth pursuing as a new line of business. One that had a great deal of potential with the airlines and with the military." The new line of business was anticipated to be profitable, not only because of a large upswing in the purchases of aircraft, but because EED's advanced technology made the competition "rather minimal, in that no large companies who you might say had huge resources behind them were involved." But the roseate future envisioned did not materialize. In fact, the operation foundered.

MDC, through the EED division, obtained contracts for one 737 simulator from Boeing in September, 1965 and for two more 737 simulators from United Airlines the following months. "Everybody was pretty pleased," testified Mr. McDonnell, Chairman of the MDC

* Portions of the text and many of the
footnotes omitted.

Board, in his deposition. In January of 1966 Conductron acquired EED. The contracts for the three 737 simulators were transferred from EED to Conductron, MDC promised Conductron continued business, paid $5,000,000 as part of the agreement, and promised substantial grants for research. It is significant that all parties here recognized the need for additional funds for this purpose.

Increased aircraft purchases were made by the airlines in September of 1966. Conductron felt that its technology would be of great interest to the lines "and it was apparent to us that we would make a lot of sales." But Conductron anticipated achieving a substantial "commonality" among the same aircraft. This did not result. The aircraft (Boeing 737) was itself changed, cockpits were altered, each airline in effect wanted its own simulator with the result that substantial losses were suffered by Conductron. In addition, "competitions were quite vicious," with the result that prices were steadily driven down. Other factors contributed, and in substance, the aircraft market dried up. In addition, special problems developed with the C–5A military aircraft simulator which Conductron was building for Lockheed.

We turn to the matter of costs and the reporting thereof. Obviously, the research and development costs could not be borne by the first model produced. The cost assigned to any unit depended upon the competitive market, cost estimates, and the number of the model to be produced. It is clear that at this point an accounting and disclosure problem is presented.

Conductron made its agreement with MDC for acquisition of EED on January 7, 1966. It is with respect to the representations made, and omitted, in the proxy statement issued in connection therewith that plaintiff's initial charges of misrepresentation arise. The plaintiff's principal challenge is that the proxy statement did not disclose the anticipated losses in the simulator business. The short answer, on the record, is that defendants anticipated substantial profits, not losses. It is true that defendants' roseate economic anticipations were doomed, but economic prognostication, though faulty, does not, without more, amount to fraud. Moreover, the proxy statement gave fair warning that the development and other start-up costs would depend for recovery upon future contracts. The information disclosed with reference thereto stated:

> The Division recently received contract awards from the Boeing Company and United Air Lines to design and build three 737 aircraft transport pilot training simulators for a total of $2,760,966. Expected additional contracts for the Boeing 737 simulator will be necessary to recover development and other start up costs.

It could not reasonably be said that an investor of plaintiff Polin's experience was unaware of the significance of this statement.[26]

26. Cross-examination of Mr. Polin:

Q. And, sir, I take it that you know from your training and your business success that research and development is merely a first stage or first step in making a viable product that will ultimately generate a profit?

A. Yes, sir.

Q. That is the substance of what research and development is all about, isn't it?

A. Yes, sir.

* * *

But beyond the minutiae of the various charges made and behind them as justification therefor, running through the entire series of reports, lies a fundamental accounting problem, namely, when and how Conductron should have written off the design and development costs of the simulator program. These costs were large and could not be charged in their entirety against the first simulators from a competitive standpoint. An amortization over the entire contract life was utilized.[27] If a sufficient number of simulators are sold, amortization presents no problem. If not, due to economic conditions, lack of acceptance of the plane, or other cause, the manufacturer will suffer a loss. The point to be observed here is the fact that a disparity between expenditures and selling price of an early simulator does not result in a "loss." The Conductron Corporation followed a system of accounting employed under these circumstances by its accountants, Ernst & Ernst, under which initial non-recurring costs were allocated pro-rata over the life of the program, rather than being charged off in their entirety at the beginning of the program.

Plaintiff's complaints about the annual reports all revolve around the dates of the reporting of what plaintiff terms "anticipated simulator losses" and the accuracy of the accounting judgments made.[28] As

Q. You also knew, I take it, that it was possible that a company in research and development might strike out completely, didn't you?

A. On any one item, yes, sir.

27. Direct Examination of Mr. Toole, Project Manager for Trainers and Simulators at Conductron:

Mr. Mannino: . . . I think it is important to determine at this point whether or not an amortization procedure as opposed to an instant write-off procedure was used on the simulators . . ..

* * *

The Witness: Well, I was not in the financial side of our company, and I don't know exactly how this was handled from a financial standpoint, but my understanding was that we would spread the development cost over a quantity of simulators. The quantity was predicted based primarily on the number of aircraft that would be purchased. The airlines had a policy of buying one simulator for about every twenty airplanes they bought, and we could look at the aircraft market itself and predict the requirement for simulators at the various airlines.

* * *

28. One of plaintiff's specific charges was that in its Annual Report for the

six months ended June 30, 1966, "Conductron failed to charge off against income or otherwise disclose its anticipated multi-million dollar loss on the existing contracts for the three 737 simulators, instead charging off only $796,195 of the total anticipated loss." Brief for Appellant at 9. Mr. Schumer, a certified public accountant, testified that the $1.2 million after-tax loss written off in the Second Annual Report for 1966, covering the six months ending December 31, 1966, should have been written-off in the First Annual Report for 1966, issued on or about September 6, 1966, because "the same set of facts existed, same situation . . . .." However, Mr. Schumer's assertion that Conductron had the same degree of knowledge regarding losses on its simulator contracts at the time of the First Annual Report of 1966 as at the time of the Second Annual Report is far from convincing, and was contradicted by testimony which will be considered infra, at p. 20. Moreover, on cross examination, Mr. Schumer testified that he had not examined the "commonality" which had been established as of June 30, 1966, as compared with that of December 31, 1966. Failure to achieve expected "commonality" would have an effect upon costs and hence upon anticipated losses. . . .

to the latter, these are matters of judgment,[29] a judgment clearly dependent upon constantly changing factors. It was in recognition by Ernst & Ernst of such variables present in the operation being conducted that no provision for losses was made until the Second 1966 Annual Report, covering the period July 1-December 31, 1966. The Ernst & Ernst Report approving the financial statements in the Second 1966 Annual Report was dated March 17, 1967. Mr. Anderson, the Ernst & Ernst partner in charge of the Conductron auditing, testified that "I would think that there was significantly more information available in March of 1967 than there was in July of 1966," this latter being the date of the Ernst & Ernst report approving the financial statements in the First Annual Report for 1966. Such information required the recognition of certain losses at that time, but Ernst & Ernst cautioned the corporation about the difficulties inherent in making such judgments, stating, in part:

> [It] should be recognized that the estimates of losses referred to herein are subject to considerable revision as the contracts progress, based upon the demonstrated experiences to date.

The financial reports we examine were certified by Ernst & Ernst to be fair and accurate after substantial investigative research. The Court found, moreover:

> [W]e have carefully reviewed each of these reports, as well as the earnings statements and the press releases, in light of plaintiff's complaints and find that none of them are fraudulently misleading either by omissions or by affirmative statements. It is true, of course, that each report painted a gloomier picture of the extent of the losses incurred and anticipated than the preceding one, but there is no substantial basis for the contention that any of the reports withheld material information or fraudulently minimized losses which should have been anticipated.

Under our review of this lengthy record we find no clear error of fact or misapplication of applicable law. There is no sustainable claim for damages or rescission. What we had were, possibly, too-sanguine hopes for the future, as well as differences of opinion between accountants as to the complex problems of financial reporting of the new device, but the elements of fraud, the deceptions, the duplicities and the distortions normally concomitant of false and misleading statements, are completely missing.

---

29. Deposition testimony of Mr. Burke, President of Conductron during most of 1967–70, and an officer and director of MDC during the time in question:

If you have a long-run program, it enables you to help even out the unit costs throughout the life of the program, and that's a factor, I didn't say it is a merit, it is a factor in making such a choice.

Another alternate is examining the market. If you are uncertain of the market, the more conservative approach, then, is to write off start-up and development costs in the earlier part of the contract so that while you have to pay a charge of higher cost per unit, your sales, if successful, will cover your start-up costs even for a short or a small number of units.

There is no what I would call absolute standard for when you do which. It is very much a matter of judgment of the Management.

STATEMENT OF FINANCIAL ACCOUNTING
STANDARDS NO. 2 *

Financial Accounting Standards Board, 1974.

ACCOUNTING FOR RESEARCH AND DEVELOPMENT
COSTS

* * *

Activities Constituting Research and Development

8. For purposes of this Statement, research and development is defined as follows:

(a) *Research* is planned search or critical investigation aimed at discovery of new knowledge with the hope that such knowledge will be useful in developing a new product or service (hereinafter "product") or a new process or technique (hereinafter "process") or in bringing about a significant improvement to an existing product or process.

(b) *Development* is the translation of research findings or other knowledge into a plan or design for a new product or process or for a significant improvement to an existing product or process whether intended for sale or use. It includes the conceptual formulation, design, and testing of product alternatives, construction of prototypes, and operation of pilot plants. It does not include routine or periodic alterations to existing products, production lines, manufacturing processes, and other on-going operations even though those alterations may represent improvements and it does not include market research or market testing activities.

* * *

Accounting for Research and Development Costs

12. All research and development costs encompassed by this Statement shall be charged to expense when incurred.

Disclosure

13. Disclosure shall be made in the financial statements of the total research and development costs charged to expense in each period for which an income statement is presented.

* * *

37. The Board considered four alternative methods of accounting at the time research and development costs are incurred:

(a) Charge all costs to expense when incurred.

(b) Capitalize all costs when incurred.

(c) Capitalize costs when incurred if specified conditions are fulfilled and charge all other costs to expense.

(d) Accumulate all costs in a special category until the existence of future benefits can be determined.

38. In concluding that all research and development costs be charged to expense when incurred (see paragraph 12), Board members considered the factors discussed in paragraphs 39–59. Individual Board members gave greater weight to some factors than to others.

Uncertainty of Future Benefits

39. There is normally a high degree of uncertainty about the future benefits of individual research and development projects, although the element of uncertainty may diminish as a project progresses. Estimates of the rate of success of research and development projects vary markedly—depending in part on how narrowly one defines a "project" and how one defines "success"—but all such estimates indicate a high failure rate. For example, one study of a number of industries found that an average of less than 2 percent of new product ideas and less than 15 percent of product development projects were commercially successful.

40. Even after a project has passed beyond the research and development stage, and a new or improved product or process is being marketed or used, the failure rate is high. Estimates of new product failures range from 30 percent to 90 percent, depending on the definition of failure used.   .   .   .

* * *

Lack of Causal Relationship Between Expenditures and Benefits

41. A direct relationship between research and development costs and specific future revenue generally has not been demonstrated, even with the benefit of hindsight. For example, three empirical research studies, which focus on companies in industries intensively involved in research and development activities, generally failed to find a significant correlation between research and development expenditures and increased future benefits as measured by subsequent sales, earnings, or share of industry sales.

* * *

45. Paragraphs 39–40 indicate that at the time most research and development costs are incurred the future benefits are at best uncertain. In other words, there is no indication that an economic resource has been created. Moreover, even if at some point in the progress of an individual research and development project the expectation of future benefits becomes sufficiently high to indicate that an economic resource has been created, the question remains whether that resource should be recognized as an asset for financial accounting purposes. Although future benefits from a particular research and development project may be foreseen, they generally cannot be measured with a reasonable degree of certainty. According to the research data cited in paragraph 41, there is normally little, if any, direct relationship between the amount of current research and development expenditures and the amount of resultant future benefits to the enterprise. Research and development costs therefore fail to satisfy the suggested measurability test for accounting recognition as an asset.

* * *

49. As noted in paragraph 41, evidence of a direct causal relationship between current research and development expenditures and subsequent future benefits generally has not been found. Also, there is often a high degree of uncertainty about whether research and development expenditures will provide any future benefits. Thus, even an indirect cause and effect relationship can seldom be demonstrated. Because there is generally no direct or even indirect basis for relating costs to revenues, the Board believes that the principles of "associating cause and effect" and "systematic and rational allocation" cannot be applied to recognize research and development costs as expenses. That is, the notion of "matching"—when used to refer to the process of recognizing costs as expenses on any sort of cause and effect basis—cannot be applied to research and development costs. Indeed, the general lack of discernible future benefits at the time the costs are incurred indicates that the "immediate recognition" principle of expense recognition should apply.

* * *

Selective Capitalization

53. Selective capitalization—capitalizing research and development costs when incurred if specified conditions are fulfilled and charging to expense all other research and development costs—requires establishment of conditions that must be fulfilled before research and development costs are capitalized. . . .

54. . . . Considerable judgment is required to identify the point in the progress of a research and development project at which a new or improved product or process is "defined" or is determined to be "technologically feasible," "marketable," or "useful." Nor can the "probability of future benefits" be readily assessed. A "management decision" to proceed with production does not necessarily assure future benefits The Board does not believe that "distortion of net income comparisons," which a few respondents to the Discussion Memorandum suggested, is an operable criterion by which to decide whether research and development costs should be capitalized because the point at which net income comparisons might be "distorted" cannot be defined. Moreover, in assessing risk, financial statement users have indicated that they seek information about the variability of earnings.

55. The Board has concluded that no set of conditions that might be established for capitalization of costs could achieve the comparability among enterprises that proponents of "selective capitalization" cite as a primary objective of that approach.

―――――――

STATEMENT OF FINANCIAL ACCOUNTING STANDARDS NO. 7 *

Financial Accounting Standards Board, 1975.

ACCOUNTING AND REPORTING BY DEVELOPMENT STAGE ENTERPRISES

* * *

Standards of Financial Accounting and Reporting

Guidelines for Identifying a Development Stage Enterprise

8. For purposes of this Statement, an enterprise shall be considered to be in the development stage if it is devoting substantially all of its efforts to establishing a new business and either of the following conditions exists:

(a) Planned principal operations have not commenced.

(b) Planned principal operations have commenced, but there has been no significant revenue therefrom.

9. A development stage enterprise will typically be devoting most of its efforts to activities such as financial planning; raising capital; exploring for natural resources; developing natural resources; research and development; establishing sources of supply; acquiring property, plant, equipment, or other operating assets, such as mineral rights; recruiting and training personnel; developing markets; and starting up production.

* * *

Accounting

30. The Board has concluded that the generally accepted accounting principles that apply to established operating enterprises shall govern the recognition of revenue by a development stage enterprise and shall determine whether a cost incurred by a development stage enterprise is to be charged to expense when incurred or is to be capitalized or deferred. The primary reasons for this conclusion are:

(a) The kinds of transactions engaged in by development stage enterprises are also common to established operating enterprises in expanding their existing businesses. Accounting treatment should be governed by the nature of the transaction rather than by the degree of maturity of the enterprise. Thus, the determination of whether a particular cost should be charged to expense when incurred or should be capitalized or deferred should be based on the same accounting standards regardless of whether the enterprise incurring the cost is already operating or is in the development stage.

(b) Any different standards for a development stage enterprise that would result in deferral of costs that would not be de-

---

* Copyright © by Financial Accounting Standards Board, 1974. See acknowledgement, page xviii, supra.

ferred if the generally accepted accounting principles applicable to established operating enterprises had been applied may cause financial statement users to reach unjustified conclusions about the nature of the costs incurred by a development stage enterprise. The Board believes that adequate financial statement disclosures concerning the costs incurred by a development stage enterprise, both for the current period and cumulatively since its inception, will mitigate that possibility and provide useful financial information for decisions about that kind of enterprise.

31. Established operating enterprises incur costs under various circumstances and with varying degrees of uncertainty about future benefits, especially in expanding their existing businesses. Authoritative accounting literature does not contain general criteria or guidelines for determining when costs should be charged to expense as incurred and when costs should be capitalized or deferred,[15] and this Statement does not attempt to specify such criteria or guidelines.

32. The absence of explicit criteria or guidelines, however, does not provide a free choice to defer costs or to charge them to expense when incurred. The scope of generally accepted accounting principles is broader than the authoritative literature and encompasses practices that have evolved and gained acceptance with time and experience. Many of those practices are described in APB Statement No. 4, "Basic Concepts and Accounting Principles Underlying Financial Statements of Business Enterprises." For example, paragraph 160 of APB Statement No. 4 describes generally accepted accounting principles as calling for immediate recognition as expense when "(1) costs incurred during the period provide no discernible future benefits, (2) costs recorded as assets in prior periods no longer provide discernible benefits or (3) allocating costs either on the basis of association with revenue or among several accounting periods is considered to serve no useful purpose."

33. In concluding that the generally accepted accounting principles applicable to established operating enterprises shall determine whether a cost incurred by a development stage enterprise is to be charged to expense when incurred or is to be capitalized or deferred, the Board is relying primarily on the assessment of recoverability of incurred costs that those principles require. Heretofore, some have felt that generally accepted accounting principles did not apply to the special accounting practices and special financial reporting formats that have been used by some development stage enterprises. The Board's conclusion that the generally accepted accounting principles applicable to established operating enterprises also apply to development stage enterprises, including presentation of the same basic financial statements, eliminates the special practices and formats and

15. Guidance is provided for some specific situations. For example, FASB Statement No. 2 prescribes that the research and development costs encompassed by that Statement shall be charged to expense when incurred and describes the considerations that led to that conclusion. Also, AICPA Industry Audit Guides provide guidance about accounting for costs incurred by enterprises in particular industries. . . .

the question about the applicability of generally accepted accounting principles to them.

> *This Statement was adopted by the affirmative votes of six members of the Financial Accounting Standards Board. Mr. Schuetze dissented.*

Although he agrees with the basic conclusions in this Statement that development stage enterprises should use the same accounting principles and prepare the same basic financial statements as established operating enterprises, Mr. Schuetze dissents because he believes that the Board should have addressed the question of accounting for start-up costs before issuing this Statement. Paragraph 10 states that "capitalization or deferral of costs [in a development stage enterprise] shall be subject to the same assessment of recoverability that would be applicable in an established operating enterprise." A substantial portion of the costs incurred by many development stage enterprises falls into a broad category that most persons would regard as start-up costs. In Mr. Schuetze's view, neither this Statement nor any other authoritative pronouncement furnishes adequate guidance as to how the recoverability of start-up costs should be assessed or as to how those start-up costs that are capitalized or deferred should be accounted for thereafter. . . .

HILL v. INTERNATIONAL PRODUCTS CO., 129 Misc. 25, 220 N.Y.S. 711 (Sup.Ct.1925). In an action to rescind a stock subscription, plaintiff alleged that defendant had misrepresented its financial condition by declaring a dividend when in fact no surplus existed. The company had capitalized many operating expenses, such as for protection, auto repairs, general expenses, charities, gifts and entertainment, by carrying them to the construction account. An accountant called as a witness by defendant testified that the period during which the plaintiffs were negotiating with defendants was part of the development period of defendant company and that during such a period it is customary to capitalize the interest on bonds, losses of various natures and charges for concessions. *Held,* for plaintiff.

". . . He [the accountant] practically admitted that by his method of computation the surplus of the defendant corporation would increase directly with the increase of its losses. . . . There can be no question but that there are certain expenditures which result in assets which are not tangible property, as, for instance, money spent in establishing good will; but I am of opinion there is no legal justification for taking credit in this way for money spent on property dissipated under circumstances which give no corresponding increase to the value of the assets, as, for instance, depreciation and loss due to unprofitable operation."

PROBLEM

An airline company spent $350,000 during the current year to train personnel on new planes before the planes were put into commercial use. How should this be treated in the financial statements of the company? Consider the foregoing material on research and development costs, ABP Op. No. 17 in general and the Interpretation thereof in particular, pages 265–266, supra, and the following FPC Opinion:

FEDERAL POWER COMMISSION ORDER NO. 486

CCH Util. Law Rep. (Fed., 1969 et seq.) ¶ 5503, 1973.

SPECIALIZED TRAINING COSTS

* * *

The purpose of this rulemaking is to establish uniform accounting procedures for the costs of training employees to operate or maintain new and unique facilities. We recognize that training costs of this type are becoming increasingly significant in amount and the existing Uniform Systems of Accounts do not clearly specify whether such costs are to be capitalized or charged to expense currently. The new facilities referred to are those which are constructed under a non-conventional technology where new training is required for their operation and maintenance, and include nuclear power generating plants and other new type generating facilities.

The Commission recognizes that during the construction of such facilities it is necessary that company employees be trained to a degree of competence so as to be able to operate and maintain the facilities when they are ready for service. It is also recognized that the training required under such circumstances usually involves the investment of a considerable amount of time and money.

* * *

. . . . It appears to us that those training costs associated with new or nonconventional facilities are in the nature of a pre-operating cost, and are therefore properly capitalizable as an integral cost of the facility (includable in rate base). This cost would be recoverable through depreciation over the useful life of the facility, and therefore not subject to an artificial amortization period.

Obviously, newly-trained personnel are subject to the same attrition factors as all employees. However, we think that the benefits of the original training in operation and maintenance of the facility provide an input that lasts throughout the life of the project. The original training is as essential to the first year of operation as any other element of the physical plant. This concept incorporates the cost of replacement training being charged to current operations.

* * *

g. INTEREST DURING CONSTRUCTION

HINDS v. BUENOS AYRES GRAND NAT. TRAMWAYS CO., LIMITED

Court of Chancery, [1906].
2 Ch. 654.

The Buenos Ayres Grand National Tramways Company, Limited, . . . borrowed large sums of debentures and preference debentures, and subsequently, for the purpose of converting their undertaking to a system of electric traction, they issued £600,000 conversion debenture stock. They also issued £74,523 income debenture bonds bearing interest at 5 per cent., each year's interest being payable pari passu exclusively out of the profits, if any, of the company made during that year and when such profit should have been ascertained and certified.

On October 19, 1906, the directors passed resolutions to the effect that (it having been ascertained that the cost of the conversion would be about £10,000 per mile) the interest on the conversion debenture stock should be treated as being part of the cost of construction, and as being chargeable to capital account * as from the date at which the company became liable to pay such interest up to the date at which one mile of single track was completed and open for traffic; as from that date to debit the interest charge on the £10,000 conversion debenture stock applicable to that mile of single track to revenue account; and to carry out the work on that system, taking each mile separately and apportioning part of the stock to each section of the line. The result of this arrangement would be that the directors would be able to shew sufficient profit on revenue account to enable them to pay interest on the income debenture bonds.

The company commenced the works, and were carrying them out themselves without employing a contractor. The plaintiff, a shareholder in the company, issued a writ asking for a declaration that the interest on the conversion debenture stock was not part of the cost of the conversion, and ought not to be during any period whatever charged to capital account, but should be considered payable out of revenue; and an injunction to restrain the company from paying any interest on the income debenture bonds except in accordance with that declaration.

He now moved for an injunction in similar terms. . . .

WARRINGTON, J. The Buenos Ayres Grand National Tramways Company, Limited, have issued certain debentures the interest on which is payable out of the profits of each year and the profits only. The question which the Court has to determine is whether the company are bound by law to charge against the profits of the year interest on money which has been borrowed expressly for the purpose of what I may call construction. It is not literally construction—it is the conversion of their horse line into an electrical traction line, but for practical purposes it is the same thing as money borrowed for the purposes of construction. The directors propose, unless they are so bound, to charge during the period of construction as part of the expenses of constructing each mile of the new line not only the money actually expended in paying for that construction, but the interest— the proportionate part of the interest—on the money which they have borrowed. Is there anything that renders it incumbent upon the company to charge that interest to the revenue account? In the first place, it is not contended that there is anything in any of the Companies Acts which in terms compels the company so to charge

---

* [Ed. Note] To "charge to capital account" means to capitalize, i. e., to defer.

this interest. Neither is there any contractual stipulation to that effect in the documents which regulate the constitution of this company. The question therefore is, Is there, independently of statute, or independently of contractual stipulations affecting this company, any general rule of law which compels a company to charge interest on money borrowed for the purposes of construction against revenue, and prohibits it from charging that interest, during construction, to capital account? That really is the question which I have to decide.

In my opinion there is no such principle of law. I think the authorities establish that the principle which regulates all these questions is that which is expressed by Lord Macnaghten in the case of Jamaica Ry. Co. v. Attorney-General of Jamaica. He says in reference to expenditure, which prima facie in that particular case was income expenditure: "Nor is every item of expenditure necessarily to be debited wholly against the income of the period in which it occurs. It may be fair and proper to spread some items over a longer time." [1893] A.C. 127, 136. . . .

. . . That is how the authorities stand. Now, what is it that the company are really proposing to do? They are creating a capital asset by means of which they will hereafter earn, or they hope to earn, profits for the company. They are not simply employing contractors to find the money and do the work. They are finding the money themselves, and they find the money by borrowing it. What does each mile of line cost them under these circumstances—what is it that they expend in constructing each mile of line, taking the amount of the borrowed money expended on that line to be £10,000, that being the company's estimate? The money is borrowed for that particular purpose—the £10,000. They have to pay interest on that £10,000 during the period that construction is taking place. In my opinion that asset which they are so constructing costs them not only the £10,000, but the £10,000 plus the amount of interest during that period of construction; and that is what they are out of pocket during the construction of that mile of line. Now, it seems to me that the company are entitled—I do not say that they are bound to do it— if they think fit to charge in their accounts as the cost of that mile of line not only the £10,000, but the £10,000 and the interest on it during the period of construction. That decides the present case. In my opinion the plaintiff's motion fails. . . .

ACCOUNTING SERIES RELEASE NO. 163

Securities and Exchange Commission, 1974.

CAPITALIZATION OF INTEREST BY COMPANIES OTHER THAN PUBLIC UTILITIES

The Commission has noted with concern an increase in the number of non-utility companies changing their accounting method to a policy of capitalizing interest cost. . . . the Commission has determined to issue the following statement of policy and to adopt certain amendments to Regulation S–X as set forth below. . . .

A. Commentary

The conventional accounting model applicable to companies other than public utilities has not traditionally treated the cost of capital as part of the cost of an asset and, except for two specific industries, no authoritative statement on this subject presently exists. Interest cost on debt is generally treated as a period expense of the period during which debt capital is used, while the cost of equity capital is reflected neither in asset cost nor in the income statement.

This approach has been adopted for a number of reasons. First, it is impossible to follow cash once it has been invested in a firm. Even when a loan is made for a designated purpose and secured by a lien on specific assets, it can be argued that capital made available for one purpose frees other capital for other purposes, and it is therefore unrealistic to allocate the cost of any particular financing to any particular asset. Thus, any allocation of capital cost to particular assets is based on allocation decisions which are inherently arbitrary.

Second, the cost of capital is extremely difficult to measure. While interest rates may be associated with borrowings, any debt normally rests in part on the existence of an equity base which provides borrowing capacity. Suppliers of debt capital almost inevitably look to a borrower's overall economic position in making credit granting decisions. In addition, restrictive covenants and other terms such as compensating balance requirements may make the stated interest rate an unrealistic measure of capital. The cost of common equity capital is even more difficult to measure since it represents the cost of sharing an uncertain future earnings stream rather than a contractual out-of-pocket payment.

Third, it has been felt that interest costs were generally costs of a continuing nature, usually fixed by contract, and that deferral of certain of these costs might leave an erroneous impression as to the level of interest expense (and the cash outlay for interest) that might be expected in the future. Interest would not halt, for example, when an asset constructed with the use of capital funds was completed and placed in service.

For these reasons, interest cost has generally been reflected as an expense of the period during which capital was used rather than associated with the assets acquired by the use of the capital, even though it can be argued that interest cost is a cost which should be allocated to assets like other costs and that expensing interest as accrued is not consistent with the matching model in general use. Two exceptions to this general rule exist in the authoritative accounting literature [the Industry Audit Guide for "Savings and Loan Associations" and the AICPA Industry Accounting Guide "Accounting for Retail Land Sales"]. In addition, electric, gas, water and telephone utilities have traditionally capitalized an allowance for funds used in construction . . . on the basis of rate-making considerations.*

The Commission has recently noted an increasing number of cases where interest has been capitalized by registrants other than electric, gas, water and telephone utilities and the exceptions noted above. This

---

* [Ed. note] In an omitted passage the Release refers to the basis for capitalization of interest by these utilities as "a concept that recovery is virtually assured through the rate-making process".

has created a source of incomparability between financial statements of companies following different practices in this respect.

While the Commission recognizes that arguments can be made for each of the accounting practices in this area, it does not seem desirable to have an alternative practice grow up through selective adoption by individual companies without careful consideration of such a change by the Financial Accounting Standards Board, including the development of systematic criteria as to when, if ever, capitalization of interest is desirable.

Accordingly, the Commission concludes that companies other than [those referred to] above which had not, as of June 21, 1974, publicly disclosed an accounting policy of capitalizing interest costs shall not follow such a policy in financial statements filed with the Commission covering fiscal periods ending after June 21, 1974. At such time as the Financial Accounting Standards Board develops standards for accounting for interest cost, the Commission expects to reconsider this conclusion. Until such time, companies which have publicly disclosed such a policy may continue to apply it on a consistent basis but not extend it to new types of assets. . . .

In addition, the Commission has amended Regulation S–X to require that all companies which capitalize interest costs make disclosure in the face of the income statement of the amount capitalized in each year an income statement is presented and, in addition, that companies other than electric, gas, water and telephone utilities disclose the effect on net income of this accounting policy as compared to a policy of charging interest to expense as accrued. . . .

It is recognized that disclosure as required herein of the effect on net income of capitalizing interest as compared to a policy of charging to expense as accrued is of primary interest to those users of financial statements who wish to undertake a detailed analysis of corporate activities and may not be required in financial disclosure oriented solely to the needs of the average investor.

*　　*　　*

STATEMENT OF FINANCIAL ACCOUNTING STANDARDS NO. 34 *

Financial Accounting Standards Board, 1979.

Capitalization of Interest Cost

INTRODUCTION

1. This Statement establishes standards of financial accounting and reporting for capitalizing interest cost as a part of the historical cost of acquiring certain assets. For the purposes of this Statement, *interest cost* includes interest recognized on obligations having explicit interest rates,[1] [and] interest imputed on certain types of payables in accordance with APB Opinion No. 21 [page 394, infra] . . . .

*　　*　　*

1. Interest cost on these obligations includes amounts resulting from periodic amortization of discount or premium and issue costs on debt. [Footnote from the original.]

3. Some enterprises now charge all interest cost to expense when incurred; some enterprises capitalize interest cost in some circumstances; and some enterprises, primarily public utilities, also capitalize a cost for equity funds in some circumstances. This diversity of practice and an observation that an increasing number of nonutility registrants were adopting a policy of capitalizing interest led the Securities and Exchange Commission to impose, in November 1974, a moratorium on adoption or extension of such a policy by most nonutility registrants until such time as the FASB established standards in this area.

* * *

STANDARDS OF FINANCIAL ACCOUNTING AND REPORTING

6. The historical cost of acquiring an asset includes the costs necessarily incurred to bring it to the condition and location necessary for its intended use. If an asset requires a period of time in which to carry out the activities necessary to bring it to that condition and location, the interest cost incurred during that period as a result of expenditures for the asset is a part of the historical cost of acquiring the asset.

7. The objectives of capitalizing interest are (a) to obtain a measure of acquisition cost that more closely reflects the enterprise's total investment in the asset and (b) to charge a cost that relates to the acquisition of a resource that will benefit future periods against the revenues of the periods benefited.

8. In concept, interest cost is capitalizable for all assets that require a period of time to get them ready for their intended use (an "acquisition period"). However, in many cases, the benefit in terms of information about enterprise resources and earnings may not justify the additional accounting and administrative cost involved in providing the information. The benefit may be less than the cost because the effect of interest capitalization and its subsequent amortization or other disposition, compared with the effect of charging it to expense when incurred, would not be material. In that circumstance, interest capitalization is not *required* by this Statement.

Assets Qualifying for Interest Capitalization

9. Subject to the provisions of paragraph 8, interest shall be capitalized for the following types of assets ("qualifying assets"):

a. Assets that are constructed or otherwise produced for an enterprise's own use (including assets constructed or produced for the enterprise by others for which deposits or progress payments have been made)

b. Assets intended for sale or lease that are constructed or otherwise produced as discrete projects (e. g., ships or real estate developments).

10. However, interest cost should not be capitalized for inventories that are routinely manufactured or otherwise produced in large quantities on a repetitive basis because, in the Board's judgment, the informational benefit does not justify the cost of so doing. In addition, interest shall not be capitalized for the following types of assets:

      a.   Assets that are in use or ready for their intended use in the earning activities of the enterprise

      b.   Assets that are not being used in the earning activities of the enterprise and that are not undergoing the activities necessary to get them ready for use.

    11.   Land that is not undergoing activities necessary to get it ready for its intended use is not a qualifying asset. If activities are undertaken for the purpose of developing land for a particular use, the expenditures to acquire the land qualify for interest capitalization while those activities are in progress. The interest cost capitalized on those expenditures is a cost of acquiring the asset that results from those activities. If the resulting asset is a structure, such as a plant or a shopping center, interest capitalized on the land expenditures is part of the acquisition cost of the structure. If the resulting asset is developed land, such as land that is to be sold as developed lots, interest capitalized on the land expenditures is part of the acquisition cost of the developed land.

The Amount of Interest Cost to Be Capitalized

    12.   The amount of interest cost to be capitalized for qualifying assets is intended to be that portion of the interest cost incurred during the assets' acquisition periods that theoretically could have been avoided (for example, by avoiding additional borrowings or by using the funds expended for the assets to repay existing borrowings) if expenditures for the assets had not been made.

    13.   The amount capitalized in an accounting period shall be determined by applying an interest rate(s) ("the capitalization rate") to the average amount of accumulated expenditures for the asset during the period. The capitalization rates used in an accounting period shall be based on the rates applicable to borrowings outstanding during the period. If an enterprise's financing plans associate a specific new borrowing with a qualifying asset, the enterprise may use the rate on that borrowing as the capitalization rate to be applied to that portion of the average accumulated expenditures for the asset that does not exceed the amount of that borrowing. If average accumulated expenditures for the asset exceed the amounts of specific new borrowings associated with the asset, the capitalization rate to be applied to such excess shall be a weighted average of the rates applicable to other borrowings of the enterprise.

    15.   The total amount of interest cost capitalized in an accounting period shall not exceed the total amount of interest cost incurred by the enterprise in that period. . . .

    16.   For the purposes of this Statement, *expenditures* to which capitalization rates are to be applied are capitalized expenditures (net of progress payment collections) for the qualifying asset that have required the payment of cash, the transfer of other assets, or the incurring of a liability on which interest is recognized (in contrast to liabilities, such as trade payables, accruals, and retainages on which interest is not recognized). However, reasonable approximations of net capitalized expenditures may be used. For example, capitalized costs for an asset may be used as a reasonable approximation of capitalized expenditures unless the difference is material.

The Capitalization Period

17.   The capitalization period shall begin when three conditions are present:

a.   Expenditures (as defined in paragraph 16) for the asset have been made.

b.   Activities that are necessary to get the asset ready for its intended use are in progress.

c.   Interest cost is being incurred.

Interest capitalization shall continue as long as those three conditions are present.   The term *activities* is to be construed broadly.   It encompasses more than physical construction; it includes all the steps required to prepare the asset for its intended use.   For example, it includes administrative and technical activities during the preconstruction stage, such as the development of plans or the process of obtaining permits from governmental authorities;   it includes activities undertaken after construction has begun in order to overcome unforeseen obstacles, such as technical problems, labor disputes, or litigation.   If the enterprise suspends substantially all activities related to acquisition of the asset, interest capitalization shall cease until activities are resumed.   However, brief interruptions in activities, interruptions that are externally imposed, and delays that are inherent in the asset acquisition process shall not require cessation of interest capitalization.

18.   The capitalization period shall end when the asset is substantially complete and ready for its intended use.   Some assets are completed in parts, and each part is capable of being used independently while work is continuing on other parts.   An example is a condominium.   For such assets, interest capitalization shall stop on each part when it is substantially complete and ready for use.   Some assets must be completed in their entirety before any part of the asset can be used.   An example is a facility designed to manufacture products by sequential processes.   For such assets, interest capitalization shall continue until the entire asset is substantially complete and ready for use.   Some assets cannot be used effectively until a separate facility has been completed.   Examples are the oil wells drilled in Alaska before completion of the pipeline.   For such assets, interest capitalization shall continue until the separate facility is substantially complete and ready for use.

19.   Interest capitalization shall not cease when present accounting principles require recognition of a lower value for the asset than acquisition cost;   the provision required to reduce acquisition cost to such lower value shall be increased appropriately.

Disposition of the Amount Capitalized

20.   Because interest cost is an integral part of the total cost of acquiring a qualifying asset, its disposition shall be the same as that of other components of asset cost.   *i*

Disclosures

21.   The following information with respect to interest cost shall be disclosed in the financial statements or related notes:

  a. For an accounting period in which no interest cost is capitalized, the amount of interest cost incurred and charged to expense during the period.

  b. For an accounting period in which some interest cost is capitalized, the total amount of interest cost incurred during the period and the amount thereof that has been capitalized.

*   *   *

This Statement was adopted by the affirmative votes of four members of the Financial Accounting Standards Board. Messrs. Block, Kirk, and Morgan dissented.

Messrs. Block, Kirk, and Morgan dissent to this Statement because, in their opinion, it is founded on a view of interest cost that does not meet the needs of users of financial statements, because it makes the requirement to capitalize interest dependent on meeting an undefined test of materiality, and because it is not evenhanded in the application of its requirements.

Messrs. Block, Kirk, and Morgan consider interest to be a cost of a different order from the costs of materials, labor, and other services in two respects. First, cash—the resource obtained by the payment of interest on debt—has unique characteristics. It is fungible. It is obtained from a variety of sources (principally, earning activities, borrowings, issuance of equity securities, and sales of economic resources), only one of which (borrowings) gives rise to a cost that is recognized in the present accounting framework. The amount of cash (or cash equivalent) given in exchange for a noncash resource provides the basis for measuring the cost of a noncash resource. Because of those characteristics of cash, interest on debt cannot be assigned or allocated to noncash resources in the same way as material, labor, and overhead costs, and association of interest on debt with a particular category of noncash resources, such as assets undergoing a construction or production process, is inherently arbitrary. Second, interest cost is the return to lenders on capital provided by them to an enterprise for a certain period. In the view of Messrs. Block, Kirk, and Morgan, interest cost, like dividends, is more directly associable with the period during which the capital giving rise to it is outstanding than with the material, labor, and other resources into which capital is converted. They acknowledge that the conversion of cash into a nonearning asset entails the sacrifice of the return that the cash could otherwise have earned, but they do not believe that a measure of that sacrifice is a proper addition to the cost of acquiring the asset. In addition, they note that, by attaching an interest cost to all expenditures for a qualifying asset, the prescribed method in this Statement in effect imputes an interest cost to any equity funds that may have been used for it.

Information about the return earned by an enterprise during an accounting period on the capital existing during that period is important to investors and creditors in assessing the enterprise's periodic performance, in assessing the risks of financial leverage, and in assessing their prospects of receiving both return on and return of their investment. Users of financial statements often compute the return earned on the total of debt and equity capital by adding interest expense to reported earnings. Interest capitalization, however, merges interest cost into the costs of assets, with the result that, when the costs of those assets are charged to income in subsequent periods, the interest cost component cannot be distinguished. Thus, the return on total capital in those periods yielded by that computation is misstated. The disclosure requirements of this Statement do not provide the information needed to correct that misstatement.

Messrs. Block, Kirk, and Morgan conclude that charging interest on debt to expense when incurred results in information in the financial statements of all companies that allows the return earned on capital during a period to be readily related on a comparable basis to the capital existing during that period. They believe that information to be more useful in making rational investment, credit, and similar decisions than that provided by including interest cost in the cost of assets.

* * *

Messrs. Block, Kirk, and Morgan believe a goal of standards is similar accounting for similar situations. In their opinion, because this Statement proscribes interest capitalization for certain inventories, even when the effect is material, and does not define those inventories clearly, this Statement will fail to achieve that goal.

Mr. Morgan also dissents because he believes that the application of this Statement may result in unfavorable economic consequences of significance, such as (a) restructuring of analysis models by financial analysts and other users of financial statements, and (b) possible changes in laws and regulations as a result of reaction to the more liberal profitability concept embodied in this Statement.

QUESTIONS

1. How would you have advised the SEC to respond to FASB No. 34?

2. During its recently-ended fiscal year Z Corp. paid $143,000 in real estate taxes, all of which was charged by the bookkeeping department to current tax expense. Analysis at the end of the year revealed that $27,000 of this amount was attributable to a new warehouse which was built during the year but had not yet become operational by the end of the year.

    a. Which of the following year-end adjusting entries, if any, would you recommend?

a.	Warehouse Buildings	$27,000	
	Tax Expense		$27,000
b.	Deferred Expenses	$27,000	
	Tax Expense		$27,000
c.	Prepaid Taxes	$27,000	
	Tax Expense		$27,000

b.   Is there any other information you would like to have in resolving this question?

c.   Would your recommendation be affected by the fact that Z Corp. had outstanding an issue of so-called "income bonds" (that is, bonds on which the specified interest is payable only to the extent earned during the year), and the full amount of the interest was not earned?

d.   Do any of the three authorities in the following section shed any light on these questions?

1.   CHANGES IN ACCOUNTING METHOD

APB OPINION NO. 22: DISCLOSURE OF ACCOUNTING POLICIES *

Accounting Principles Board, 1972.

*   *   *

DISCUSSION

5.   Financial statements are the end product of the financial accounting process, which is governed by generally accepted accounting principles on three levels: pervasive principles, broad operating principles, and detailed principles. Applying generally accepted accounting principles requires that judgment be exercised as to the relative appropriateness of acceptable alternative principles and methods of application in specific circumstances of diverse and complex economic activities. Although the combined efforts of professional accounting bodies, of business, and of the regulatory agencies have significantly reduced the number of acceptable alternatives and are expected to reduce the number further, judgment must nevertheless be exercised in applying principles at all three levels.

6.   The *accounting policies* of a reporting entity are the specific accounting principles and the methods of applying those principles that are judged by the management of the entity to be the most appropriate in the circumstances to present fairly financial position, changes in financial position, and results of operations in accordance with generally accepted accounting principles and that accordingly have been adopted for preparing the financial statements.

*   *   *

OPINION

Applicability

8.   The Board concludes that information about the accounting policies adopted by a reporting entity is essential for financial statement users. When financial statements are issued purporting to present fairly financial position, changes in financial position, and re-

sults of operations in accordance with generally accepted accounting principles, a description of all significant accounting policies of the reporting entity should be included as an integral part of the financial statements. . . .

* * *

Content

12. Disclosure of accounting policies should identify and describe the accounting principles followed by the reporting entity and the methods of applying those principles that materially affect the determination of financial position, changes in financial position, or results of operations. In general, the disclosure should encompass important judgments as to appropriateness of principles relating to recognition of revenue and allocation of asset costs to current and future periods; in particular, it should encompass those accounting principles and methods that involve any of the following:

    a. A selection from existing acceptable alternatives;

    b. Principles and methods peculiar to the industry in which the reporting entity operates, even if such principles and methods are predominantly followed in that industry;

    c. Unusual or innovative applications of generally accepted accounting principles (and, as applicable, of principles and methods peculiar to the industry in which the reporting entity operates).

13. Examples of disclosures by a business entity commonly required with respect to accounting policies would include, among others, those relating to basis of consolidation, depreciation methods, amortization of intangibles, inventory pricing, . . . recognition of profit on long-term construction-type contracts, and recognition of revenue from franchising and leasing operations. This list of examples is not all-inclusive.

* * *

APB OPINION NO. 20: ACCOUNTING CHANGES *

Accounting Principles Board, 1971.

* * *

TYPES OF ACCOUNTING CHANGES

6. The term *accounting change* in this Opinion means a change in (a) an accounting principle, (b) an accounting estimate, or (c) the reporting entity (which is a special type of change in accounting principle classified separately for purposes of this Opinion). The correction of an error in previously issued financial statements is not deemed to be an accounting change.

Change in Accounting Principle

7. A change in accounting principle results from adoption of a generally accepted accounting principle different from the one used previously for reporting purposes. The term *accounting principle* includes "not only accounting principles and practices but also the methods of applying them."

8. A characteristic of a change in accounting principle is that it concerns a choice from among two or more generally accepted accounting principles. However, neither (a) initial adoption of an accounting principle in recognition of events or transactions occurring for the first time or that previously were immaterial in their effect nor (b) adoption or modification of an accounting principle necessitated by transactions or events that are clearly different in substance from those previously occurring is a change in accounting principle.

9. Changes in accounting principle are numerous and varied. They include, for example, a change in the method of inventory pricing, such as from the last in, first out (LIFO) method to the first in first out (FIFO) method; a change in depreciation method for previously recorded assets, such as from the double declining balance method to the straight line method; a change in the method of accounting for long-term construction-type contracts, such as from the completed contract method to the percentage of completion method; . . . . (Paragraph 11 covers a change in accounting principle to effect a change in estimate.)

Change in Accounting Estimate

10. Changes in estimates used in accounting are necessary consequences of periodic presentations of financial statements. Preparing financial statements requires estimating the effects of future events. Examples of items for which estimates are necessary are uncollectible receivables, inventory obsolescence, service lives and salvage values of depreciable assets, warranty costs, periods benefited by a deferred cost, and recoverable mineral reserves. Future events and their effects cannot be perceived with certainty; estimating, therefore, requires the exercise of judgment. Thus accounting estimates change as new events occur, as more experience is acquired, or as additional information is obtained.

11. *Change in estimate effected by a change in accounting principle.* Distinguishing between a change in an accounting principle and a change in an accounting estimate is sometimes difficult. For example, a company may change from deferring and amortizing a cost to recording it as an expense when incurred because future benefits of the cost have become doubtful. The new accounting method is adopted, therefore, in partial or complete recognition of the change in estimated future benefits. The effect of the change in accounting principle is inseparable from the effect of the change in accounting estimate. Changes of this type are often related to the continuing process of obtaining additional information and revising estimates and are therefore considered as changes in estimates for purposes of applying this Opinion.

* * *

OPINION

Justification for a Change in Accounting Principle

15. The Board concludes that in the preparation of financial statements there is a presumption that an accounting principle once adopted should not be changed in accounting for events and transactions of a similar type. Consistent use of accounting principles from one accounting period to another enhances the utility of financial statements to users by facilitating analysis and understanding of comparative accounting data.

16. The presumption that an entity should not change an accounting principle may be overcome only if the enterprise justifies the use of an alternative acceptable accounting principle on the basis that it is preferable. However, a method of accounting that was previously adopted for a type of transaction or event which is being terminated or which was a single, nonrecurring event in the past should not be changed. For example, the method of accounting should not be changed for a tax or tax credit which is being discontinued or for preoperating costs relating to a specific plant. The Board does not intend to imply, however, that a change in the estimated period to be benefited for a deferred cost (if justified by the facts) should not be recognized as a change in accounting estimate. The issuance of an Opinion of the Accounting Principles Board that creates a new accounting principle, that expresses a preference for an accounting principle, or that rejects a specific accounting principle is sufficient support for a change in accounting principle. The burden of justifying other changes rests with the entity proposing the change.

General Disclosure—A Change in Accounting Principle

17. The nature of and justification for a change in accounting principle and its effect on income should be disclosed in the financial statements of the period in which the change is made. The justification for the change should explain clearly why the newly adopted accounting principle is preferable.

* * *

SEC STAFF ACCOUNTING BULLETIN NO. 14

February 3, 1977.

The Division of Corporation Finance and the Office of the Chief Accountant today announced the publication of Staff Accounting Bulletin No. 14. The statements in the Bulletin are not rules or interpretations of the Commission nor are they published as bearing the Commission's official approval; they represent interpretations and practices followed by the Division and the Chief Accountant in administering the disclosure requirements of the federal securities laws.

Staff Accounting Bulletin No. 14 deals with revisions to Staff Accounting Bulletin No. 6 regarding reporting requirements for accounting changes.

Revisions to Staff Accounting Bulletin No. 6

In SAB No. 6, Subsection II, item f, the following statement of "Facts" was given:

f. Reporting Requirements for Accounting Changes

Facts:

Instruction 4(f) to Form 10–Q requires that a registrant who changes its method of accounting shall indicate the date for such changes and the reasons for the changes. The registrant also must include as an exhibit in the "first Form 10–Q filed subsequent to the date of an accounting change, a letter from the registrant's independent accountants . . . indicating whether or not the change is to an alternative principle which in his judgment is preferable under the circumstances." A letter from the independent accountant is not required "when the change is made in response to a standard adopted by the Financial Accounting Standards Board which requires such a change."

The Bulletin then included two questions and interpretive responses related to the above facts. Subsequent to the issuance of the SAB, numerous questions arose regarding the staff's interpretive response to former question No. 1. Discussions indicated that the previous response was misunderstood by some registrants and their independent accountants. The following questions, Nos. 1 through 6, serve as an amplification of the staff's previous views. (The prior question No. 1 and its response are deleted. Prior question No. 2 is redesignated as No. 7 and retained unchanged.)

Question 1:

For some alternative accounting principles, authoritative bodies have specified when one alternative is preferable to another. However, for other alternative accounting principles, no authoritative body has specified criteria for determining the preferability of one alternative over another. In such situations, how should preferability be determined?

Interpretive Response:

In such cases, where objective criteria for determining the preferability among alternative accounting principles have not been established by authoritative bodies, the determination of preferability should be based on the particular circumstances described by and discussed with the registrant. In addition, the independent accountant should consider other significant information of which he is aware.

Question 2: Management may offer, as justification for a change in accounting principle, circumstances such as: their expectation as to the effect of general economic trends on their business (e. g., the impact of inflation); their expectation regarding expanding consumer demand for the company's products; or plans for change in marketing methods. Are these circumstances which enter into the determination of preferability?

Interpretive Response: Yes. Those circumstances are examples of business judgment and planning and should be evaluated in determining preferability. In the case of changes for which objective criteria for determining preferability have not been established by authoritative bodies, business judgment and business planning often are major considerations in determining that the change is to a preferable method because the change results in improved financial reporting.

Question 3: What responsibility does the independent accountant have for evaluating the business judgment and business planning of the registrant?

Interpretive Response: Business judgment and business planning are within the province of the registrant. Thus, the independent accountant may accept the registrant's business judgment and business planning and express reliance thereon in his letter. However, if either the plans or judgment appear to be unreasonable to the independent accountant, he should not accept them as justification. For example, an independent accountant should not accept a registrant's plans for a major expansion if he believes the registrant does not have the means of obtaining the funds necessary for the expansion program.

Question 4: If a registrant, who has changed to an accounting method which was preferable under the circumstances, later finds that it must abandon its business plans or change its business judgment because of economic or other factors, is the registrant's justification nullified?

Interpretive Response: No. A registrant must in good faith justify a change in its method of accounting under the circumstances which exist at the time of the change. The existence of different circumstances at a later time does not nullify the previous justification for the change.

Question 5: If a registrant justified a change in accounting method as preferable under the circumstances, and the circumstances change, may the registrant revert to the method of accounting used before the change?

Interpretive Response: Any time a registrant makes a change in accounting method, the change must be justified as preferable under the circumstances. Thus, a registrant may not change back to a principle previously used unless it can justify that the previously used principle is preferable in the circumstances as they currently exist.

Question 6: As stated in SAB No. 6, question 1 read: "If one client of an independent accounting firm changes its method of accounting and the accountant submits the required letter stating his view of the preferability of the principle in the circumstances, does this mean that all clients of that firm are constrained from making the converse change in accounting (e. g., if one client changes from FIFO to LIFO, can no other client change from LIFO to FIFO)?"

What follows is a revised interpretive response to that question.

Interpretive Response: No. Each registrant must justify a change in accounting method on the basis that the method is preferable under the circumstances of that registrant. In addition, a registrant must furnish a letter from its independent accountant stating that in the judgment of the independent accountant the change in method is preferable under the circumstances of that registrant. If registrants in apparently similar circumstances make changes in opposite directions, the staff has a responsibility to inquire as to the factors which were considered in arriving at the determination by each registrant and its independent accountant that the change was preferable under the circumstances because it resulted in improved financial reporting. The staff recognizes the importance, in many circumstances, of the judgments and plans of management and recognizes that such management judgments may, in good faith, differ. The emphasis contained in the original response in SAB No. 6 on the acceptance by an accounting firm of accounting changes in both directions by different clients was misplaced. As indicated above, the concern relates to registrants in apparently similar circumstances, no matter who their independent accountants may be.

Question 7: If a registrant changes its accounting to one of two methods specifically approved by the FASB in a Statement of Financial Accounting Standards (such as FASB 9), need the independent accountant express his view as to the preferability of the method selected?

Interpretive Response: If a registrant was formerly using a method of accounting no longer deemed acceptable, a change to either method approved by the FASB may be presumed to be a change to a preferable method and no letter will be required from the independent accountant. If, however, the registrant was formerly using one of the methods approved by the FASB for current use and wishes to change to an alternative approved method, then the registrant must justify its change as being one to a preferable method in the circumstances and the independent accountant must submit a letter stating that in his view the change is to a principle that is preferable in the circumstances.

h. "DEFERRED LOSSES" AND THE IMPACT OF RATE REGULATION

FIDELITY–PHILADELPHIA TRUST CO. v. PHILADELPHIA TRANSPORTATION CO.

Supreme Court of Pennsylvania, 1961.
404 Pa. 541, 173 A.2d 109.

COHEN, JUSTICE. Fidelity-Philadelphia Trust Company (Trustee), appellee, brought this action in assumpsit in its capacity as trustee of the mortgage bondholders under a Trust Indenture securing the Consolidated Mortgage 3%–6% bond of Philadelphia Transportation Company (PTC), the defendant-appellant. Under this Indenture, PTC was to pay a fixed 3% interest per annum and up to 3% additional income-interest to the extent that "net income," as defined in the Indenture, was sufficient.

Under the Indenture the Board of Directors of PTC was to apply "accepted principles of accounting" to determine gross income and to make deductions for such items as depreciation and retirement "in accordance with sound accounting practice." The proper interpretation and application of these terms, contained in Article V, Section 2 of the Indenture, represents the major problem in this appeal.

The Trustee attacks PTC's determination that there was no net income for the years 1957 and 1958 and therefore that there was no 3% income-interest available for both of those years. The Trustee claims that these results were arrived at by accounting methods which fall below the standards spelled out in the Indenture. Specifically, the Trustee first claims that extraordinary charges which were allocated by PTC over the years 1956–1959 to the reserve for track depreciation should have been made in full by the end of 1956 by the application of "sound accounting practice," since the PTC had reason to know by the end of 1956 that its mass conversion program (from rail to bus) would render the existing track obsolete. Therefore, the Trustee claims that the charge to depreciation reserve should have been made when the loss occurred sometime before the end of 1956.

Secondly, the Trustee claims that PTC's treatment of the amortization of franchise paving costs was not in accordance with "sound accounting practice" because the paving, which had been eliminated from the rate base in 1953, did not contribute to income during the years in question. The third item involved in the dispute over the accounting methods employed by PTC concerns the treatment of repaving costs owed to the City of Philadelphia in 1957, which costs the PTC deducted completely in 1957 although it was permitted by the Pennsylvania Public Utility Commission (Pa. PUC) to reflect the repaving costs in the rate base for several years thereafter.

The lower court rendered an order on May 9, 1960, finding for plaintiff-Trustee on all of its claims and awarded a total of $1,420,242 with interest to represent the bond income-interest not paid in 1957 and 1958 and an additional $127,507 for costs. PTC appeals from the judgment of the court below.

Before discussion of these three accounting problems it is necessary to dispose of PTC's argument that the lower court erred in not adopting the Pa. PUC's approval of PTC's accounting methods. Three months after this suit was started, PTC instituted proceedings with the Pa. PUC for the sole purposes of obtaining retroactive approval of the PTC's accounting practices. The Pa. PUC approved the PTC methods of accounting but limited its finding to a mere permissive order, apparently recognizing that the Pa. PUC's authority in the public interest to promulgate rules of accounting does not extend to issues involved in a private contract. Therefore, for purposes of determining the rights of these parties under the Indenture the Pa. PUC order is not controlling.

I. *Depreciation for Obsolescence of Track*

Both parties agree that the proper accounting rule on the propriety of the deferred charge method of recognizing a loss is that no deferred charge shall be set up except where costs are involved the benefit of which will inure to the future. The PTC claims that the retirement of track to make way for motor buses falls within the above exception to this rule in that certain benefits did inure to the future in the form of savings in maintenance costs, tax loss carry-over benefits and benefits derived from the new bus system. However, it is obvious that these benefits are at most merely incidental, ancillary outgrowths of the track retirement program and have no direct and continuing dependence on a past capital loss.

The PTC claims, however, that the entire undepreciated book costs should not have been provided for in 1956, as directed by the lower court, since the loss was not "reasonably foreseeable" at that time so as to fall within the rule that a loss should be recognized as such when it is reasonably foreseeable. Notwithstanding PTC's evidence to the contrary, it is nevertheless uncontradicted that by the end of 1956 PTC had made three official unsolicited estimates in rate proceedings and balance sheets of the anticipated track retirement loss, the lowest of which ($7,200,000) both the Trustee and the lower court accepted. In addition, the PTC controller's work papers, which were admitted in evidence, reflect the careful planning of the PTC and the ease with which an estimate of the loss could have been recognized in 1956. Furthermore, by the end of 1956, although only half of the conversion program was actually completed, the new buses were being used on 80% of all the routes which were ultimately converted. From these facts it is evident that the retirement loss in question was reasonably foreseeable by the end of 1956.

We are in accord with the lower court's result that the $7,200,000 track retirement loss should have been recognized and taken by the end of 1956, and that, therefore, the annual $1,200,000 extraordinary appropriations to the reserve for depreciation of track for both 1957 and 1958 were in contravention of the standards contained in the Trust Indenture.

II. *Amortization of Franchise Paving*

These costs represent money expended by predecessor companies at a cost of $15,000,000 to pave and repave streets in order to install and maintain tracks. They were recapitalized by PTC in the amount of $7,500,000 in 1940 under a reorganization plan. When the retirement program was conceived in the mid-1950's, the PTC continued its annual 2% "amortization" of this item and reflected the impact of the retirement program by "amortizing," through a separate account, an additional sum of $300,000 per year for the two years in question.

In a 1953 rate proceeding the Pa. PUC ruled that franchise paving costs should be excluded as a rate base asset. Thereafter, since these "intangible assets," as PTC terms them, no longer contributed to the income of PTC, they were no longer amortizable because at that time it was reasonably foreseeable that the loss had occurred and, since no benefits inured to the future, the entire loss should have been recognized then.

PTC cites authority for the principle that merely because an asset is not included in the company's valuation for rate-making purposes does not necessitate its write-off from the company's books. This may be true, but PTC still does not show that this "intangible asset" continued to benefit the PTC in any manner after 1953. Consequently, since the "asset" was stripped of its only corporate benefit by having been removed from the rate base in 1953 it ceased to be an asset of the corporation at that time.

Thus, we are in accord with the lower court's result that the PTC's amortization of franchise paving in 1957 and 1958 was not in accordance with "sound accounting practice."

III.   *City of Philadelphia Repaving Charges*

Under a set of agreements between the City of Philadelphia and the PTC, the city agreed to repave the streets after PTC's abandonment of the tracks.   Under the last of these agreements, which resulted in a debt of $843,112, PTC charged $177,000 against income in 1956 and the balance of $666,112 in 1957.

In rate proceedings held by the Pa. PUC the PTC was given permission to amortize this latter charge of $666,112 over a period of five years or at the rate of $133,300 per year.   Thus it is obvious that the benefits of this 1957 expense item inured to the future as a result of its inclusion as a rate item for a period of five years.   PTC, however, chose to completely charge off this $666,112 in 1957, a practice which is strangely inconsistent not only with the proper application of the rule governing the propriety of using the deferred charge method, but with the PTC's handling of the track depreciation and franchise paving items.   Thus complete charge-off of the $666,112 by the PTC in 1957 was erroneous.   The sum should have been spread out evenly over a five year period.

Hence, the lower court's disposition of these three accounting items is affirmed.   However, by the application of proper accounting principles it may develop that the PTC sustained a net loss for the year 1956 which would have relieved it of its obligation to make payment of the additional 3% income-interest to the holders of the bonds for that year.   For that purpose and for the determination of that problem we are remanding this case to the court below for further proceedings.   If that court finds that a net loss was sustained in 1956 then it should make provision so that no income-interest is paid for 1957 except to those bondholders who certify to the Trustee and the PTC that they had not held their bonds and received income interest thereon for the year 1956.

* * *

The judgment of the lower court is modified, and as modified, is affirmed and remanded to that court for further proceedings not inconsistent with this opinion.

PROBLEM

Niagara Power Co. is a large public utility.   One of its three main plants, carried on the corporation's books (at original cost less depreciation) at $10,000,000, was located at the head of Niagara Falls.   During the company's most recent fiscal year, a rock slide caused that plant to collapse into the Niagara River.   The company's earned surplus at the beginning of the year was $60,000,000; gross revenues for the year amounted to $180,000,000, and "regular" expenses were $150,000,000.   Should the $10,000,000 book value of the plant be changed against current income for the year?   Past income?   Future income?   Consider, in addition to the Philadelphia Transportation Co. case above, the footnote on page 294, supra, ¶¶ 23 and 24 of APB No. 9, page 186, supra, and FASB No. 16, plus ¶¶ 25–28 in Appendix A, pages 194–196, supra.

3. DEFERRED INCOME

BLACK–CLAWSON CO. v. EVATT

Supreme Court of Ohio, 1941.
139 Ohio St. 100, 38 N.E.2d 403.

[Appellant manufactures machinery on special order. It frequently receives substantial portions of the purchase price from the buyer prior to completion and delivery of the machinery. The appellant sought to deduct these advance receipts as "accounts payable" in listing credits under the Ohio Personal Property Tax, Section 5327 of which provides as follows:

> "The term 'credits' as so used, means the excess of the sum of all current accounts receivable and prepaid items used in business when added together estimating every such account and item at its true value in money, over and above the sum of current accounts payable of the business, other than taxes and assessments. 'Current accounts' includes items receivable or payable on demand or within one year from the date of inception, however evidenced. . . ."

The Board of Tax Appeals held that advanced payments could not be deducted as accounts payable, whereupon this appeal was brought.]

WILLIAMS, JUDGE. Appellant contends that the words "accounts payable" used in Section 5327, General Code, should be given the meaning in which they are used in advanced accounting practice and so should be construed as synonymous with the accounting term "current liabilities"; that the advanced payments on the agreed purchase of a machine to be constructed or in process of construction are sums held for the purchasers and, being payable to them, are accounts payable within the meaning of the statute . . . .

The fallacy which underlies the theory that the payments received and credited constitute accounts payable, is apparent from this language in appellant's brief: "So long as appellant retains in its possession funds which have been advanced to it by customers, and so long as it has not appropriated the completed machine to the discharge of the contract, appellant is in the position of having in its hands money belonging to another party, namely, its customer, and therefore is in the position of owing to that customer the sum of money advanced."

If that assertion is sound, the amounts paid would be held by the seller in trust for the buyer and the seller could not use them in his business. Surely a trust relation does not arise, for the amounts were not received by the seller as deposits; nor does even the relation of debtor and creditor. If there is any liability on the part of the seller to the buyer, it is assuredly contingent. Yet we must ever hark back to the reality that there is no liability until the contingency arises. That contingency is the breach of the sale contract by the seller and the resulting liability is founded not on an account but on the breach. What boots it that the measure of recovery may be based in whole or in part upon the total amount paid on the contract price? Obviously there is no subsisting liability until the breach occurs, for normally the seller's contractual obligation is to be discharged by the delivery of the finished product and not by cash. Even though the payment be set up on the books of the seller as an account, there would be nothing payable on it, as such, at any time.

After all the test is not what is good accounting practice but what is the meaning and intent of the taxational provision. . . .

What, then, is the correct interpretation? What is the plain meaning of the statute when viewed in the light of the object to be accomplished? When the machine is partially completed and partially paid for there is still payable to the seller the balance at the specified time or times. Such balance must be listed by the buyer as accounts payable if due on demand or within one year. Then, are the payments previously made also accounts receivable which the buyer must list? Certain it is that if the advance payments be accounts payable, as claimed by the appellant, they are payable to the buyer and must be listed in the buyer's return as accounts receivable. The result would be that the buyer would be listing the part of the price paid as owing to and receivable by him. An interpretation which leads to that result would be an anomaly. When the language of the statute is considered in its fullness and at the same time in its plain meaning, it admits of but one interpretation. The advance payments cannot be listed as accounts payable and deducted from the sum of accounts receivable and prepaid items in determining credits.

For the reasons given the decisions of the Board of Tax Appeals are affirmed.

Decisions affirmed. . . .

TURNER, JUDGE (concurring). . . . "Current accounts" is defined to include all items receivable or payable on demand within one year from the date of inception, however evidenced. What the appellant is contending for in this case is an interpretation of the term "current accounts payable" which would make that term synonymous with all current liabilities.

Counsel for appellant say in their brief: "In its broad, general sense, the term 'accounts payable' is synonymous with the more commonly used accounting term of 'current liabilities,' . . . ." However, on the same page, counsel quote Budd and Wright, The Interpretation of Accounts, page 340: " 'Accounts Payable' should include only debts which arise through the purchase of goods or services from outsiders; it should not include such items as accrued wages, accrued taxes or similar debts of the business. . . ."

Counsel also quote from Accountants' Handbook (Rev.Ed.), page 839, as follows: "In the narrowest usage this term may be restricted to trade creditors' accounts, consisting primarily of liabilities created through the purchase of merchandise, materials and supplies on account."

Counsel for appellant state their position in their brief as follows: "In present day accounting practice, the obligation represented by advancements of customers is generally treated as a current liability." I agree with that statement without reservation, but "current liability" is a wider term than "current account payable."

Counsel cite seven leading authorities on accounting practices, not one of whom, with possibly a single exception, treats advance payments as current accounts payable. The one possible exception is Professor Saliers, who lists "deposits" under accounts payable. However, the term "deposits" is usually used to indicate such items as meter deposits, water deposits, and other public utility deposits, although sometimes used to describe payments in advance. . . .

In counsel's quotation from Paton, who relies on Bliss as an authority, it is said at page 247 of "Accountants' Handbook": "Where advances are made by customers for a considerable time in advance of delivery, as often happens in manufacturing, it is not good practice to treat the transaction as a sale in the accounting records. Instead the amount received should be credited to the customer's account and to a special account entitled 'advances on sales contracts,' 'unfilled paid orders,' or by other appropriate caption."

I am not unmindful that there is a real and subsisting liability on the part of the manufacturer to the customer who has made advance payments for machinery to be delivered, which liability should be reflected on the manufacturer's books as a liability and on the customer's books as an asset.

Whether the manufacturer sets up a reserve against inventory or work in process, or uses the method pursued in the instant case, is a matter of accounting practice but does not change the fact that the Legislature has limited the liabilities which may be deducted from current accounts receivable and prepaid items to current accounts payable.

These advance payments are not recoverable in the ordinary course by the customer. Where a customer has made an advance payment and the manufacturer has failed to deliver or has breached any warranty of the sales contract, the customer has (a) a cause of action for damages for nondelivery (Section 8447, General Code), (b) a cause of action for specific performance (Section 8448, General Code), or (c) a cause of action for a breach of warranty (Section 8449, General Code), which includes rescission.

By the great weight of accounting authority, none of these rights of action may be classed as a current account payable by the manufacturer. The fact that the books of the parties should reflect the respective contingent asset or liability does not alter the situation.

* * *

MATTHIAS, JUDGE (dissenting). I dissent from the decision of the majority. Deposits or advance payments made to and accepted by the appellant became liabilities of that company, and the decision of the court that they are not liabilities disregards the opinion of the Board of Tax Appeals to the contrary. An obligation arises on the part of the company to either cancel this indebtedness by delivery of the machine or return the money advanced. It is not correct to assume that the liability of the appellant is one arising in an action for breach of contract, for clearly the purchaser for good cause could rescind the contract and recover back the money advanced, in an action not based on a contract breached, but upon a rescission.

. . . . In my opinion, the construction of the statute by the majority is clearly erroneous and results in an injustice to the taxpayer.

BOISE CASCADE CORP. v. UNITED STATES *

United States Court of Claims, 1976.
530 F.2d 1367, certiorari denied, 429 U.S. 867,
97 S.Ct. 176, 50 L.Ed.2d 147 (1977).

OPINION

PER CURIAM:

These are consolidated cases, in which plaintiffs seek the recovery of nearly $2,400,000 in income taxes plus interest thereon, paid for the years 1955 through 1961. They now come before the court on exceptions by the parties to the recommended decision filed by Trial Judge Lloyd Fletcher, on September 20, 1974, pursuant to Rule 134(h), having been submitted to the court on the briefs and oral argument of counsel. He held for the plaintiffs on all the significant issues. After briefing and oral argument, the court agrees with the trial judge in part, and disagrees in part.

* * *

We agree substantially with the portions of the recommended opinion that hold the Commissioner of Internal Revenue to have abused his discretion under IRC § 446(b), in determining that Ebasco's method of accounting failed to reflect income clearly for Federal Income Tax purposes and in requiring a change in such method as set forth below. The portions of the said trial judge's opinion that deal with this subject are set forth below and are adopted as our opinion with some modifications made by the court.

* * *

Trial Judge Fletcher's opinion, as modified by the court, follows:

The plaintiffs are Boise Cascade Corporation and several of its subsidiary companies. The original petition was filed by Ebasco Industries Inc. and its subsidiary companies which had filed consolidated tax returns for the taxable years 1955 through 1958. Later, Ebasco Industries was merged with Boise Cascade in a non-taxable transaction, and the necessary steps were taken thereafter to consolidate the actions now before the court.

Ebasco Industries was engaged in holding various investments during the years 1955 through August 31, 1969, the date of its merger into Boise Cascade. These investments included marketable securities, short-term investments, and ownership interests in various operating subsidiaries which were (and continue to be) engaged primarily in rendering engineering, construction, architectural, and consulting services. Two of such subsidiaries were Ebasco Services,

---

* Portions of the text and some of the
footnotes omitted.

Inc. (Ebasco) and Chemical Construction Corporation (Chemical Construction). Ebasco Industries owned stock possessing at least 80 percent of the voting power of all classes of stock of those subsidiary corporations.

The plaintiffs' annual shareholder reports included a certification by independent accountants that the financial statements were prepared in conformity with generally accepted accounting principles applied on a basis consistent with that of the preceding year.

In its business, Ebasco Services enters into contracts to perform engineering and similar services. Under the various terms of these contracts, Ebasco is entitled to bill fixed sums either in monthly, quarterly, or other periodic installments, plus such additional amounts as may be provided for in a particular contract. Depending on the terms of the different contracts, payments may in some cases be due prior to the annual period in which such services are to be performed, and in some cases subsequent thereto.

For a number of years prior to 1959 and continuing to the time of trial, Ebasco included in its income for both book and tax purposes amounts attributable to services which it performed during the taxable year, a procedure accepted by the Internal Revenue Service on prior audits. Ebasco determined the amounts so earned by dividing the estimated number of service hours or days required to complete the particular contract into the contract price. The resulting quotient represents an hourly or daily rate which is then multiplied by the number of hours or days actually worked on the contract during the taxable year. As the contract is performed, the rate is adjusted to reflect revised estimates of the work required to complete the contract.

Where Ebasco billed for services prior to the tax year in which they were performed, it credited such amounts to a balance sheet account called "Unearned Income". Where the services were performed in a subsequent period, the "Unearned Income" account was debited, and such amounts were included in an income account called "Service Revenues." The amount recorded in the latter account was included in income for both book and tax purposes. In determining the amount which was to be included in the "Unearned Income" account, the costs of obtaining the contract were not taken into account; [1] and, with the exception of prepaid insurance and similar items, all such amounts were expensed in the tax year during which they were incurred. The amounts in the "Unearned Income" account were treated as liabilities and were excluded from gross income for each tax year consistently in Ebasco's books, records, and shareholder reports, as well as in its tax returns. All of the amounts included in the account during one tax year were earned through the performance of services during the following year and were included in income for such following tax year. When the amounts credited to the "Unearned Income" account were collected, Ebasco had an unrestricted right to the use of such funds.

During the three tax years in issue, an average of over 94 percent of the amounts included in the "Unearned Income" account was

---

1. These amounts included the cost of preparing bids, proposals, and estimates, overhead, advertising, and selling expenses.

received by Ebasco under contracts which obligated it to perform engineering services in connection with the design and construction of electric generating plants.   These contracts either required that services be performed by a specified date or required that Ebasco should perform those services "with all reasonable dispatch and diligence," as "expeditiously as possible," or some comparable requirement.   The small remaining amounts in the account were received either under contracts which required Ebasco to perform specific services in connection with a specific project of a client, or required Ebasco to provide consultation and advice on an annual basis for an annual fee.

In addition to its "Unearned" account, Ebasco maintained an "Unbilled Charges" account computed in the same manner as the "Unearned Income" account.   The balance in such account represented amounts earned through the rendering of services, or on partially completed contracts, or earned prior to contracting, under all of which payment was not then due by the terms of a contract or was not billable and due prior to execution of a future contract. Stated another way, the amounts included in this account were those which Ebasco was not entitled to bill or receive until a year subsequent to the year in which the services were actually rendered. Such amounts were recorded in "Service Revenues" and included in income for tax as well as book purposes in the taxable year in which the services were rendered.   Likewise, the costs attributable to the rendering of services which produced the year-end balance in the "Unbilled Charges" account were deducted from gross income in the year such services were rendered.   In 1959, 1960, and 1961 there were approximately $405,000, ($56,000), and $179,000 of such net amounts, respectively, carried in the "Unbilled Charges" account.

Plaintiffs' consolidated income tax returns for 1959 through 1961 were audited by the Government, and the amounts in the "Unearned Income" account were included in taxable income for Federal tax purposes.   These adjustments were made pursuant to section 446(b) of the 1954 Code under which the Commissioner determined that plaintiffs' deferral method of accounting did not clearly reflect income.   During the same examination for the same tax years, no adjustments were made to the "Unbilled Charges" or the "Service Revenues" accounts.

At trial Ebasco presented expert testimony related solely to the accounting practices described above.   The sole witness was a qualified certified public accountant and a partner in a major accounting firm.   Based on his broad experience with comparable service companies and his personal familiarity with the accounting practices of Ebasco, he expressed his expert opinion with respect to the accounts in issue and the changes made by the Commissioner.

He testified that the method of accounting used by Ebasco which employs both an "Unearned Income" account and an "Unbilled Charges" account and is based on accruing * amounts as income at

---

* [Ed. note]   The word "accruing" is here used not in the limited, technical sense of recording of income (or expense) before cash has moved (which would render the word inapt, to the extent payment of the Unearned Income had already been received), but rather simply as a synonym for "recognizing".

the time the related services are performed is in accordance with recognized and generally accepted accounting principles and clearly reflects Ebasco's income. He indicated that this method properly matched revenues with costs of producing such revenues and is particularly appropriate in this case because almost all of Ebasco's income is derived from the performance of services by its own personnel. He further testified that this method of accounting was widely used by companies engaged in rendering engineering and similar services, and that such method clearly reflected the income of Ebasco.

With respect to costs incurred in obtaining contracts, such as bid preparation, overhead, advertising, and other selling expenses, the witness considered them to be properly deducted in the year incurred as continuing costs of doing and developing business.[2] He explained that these costs should not properly be amortizable over the life of any particular contract since they were costs connected with new business development and were unrelated to performance of the contract.

The accounting method proposed by the Commissioner requires Ebasco to accrue as income the amounts included in the "Unearned Income" account and also requires the accrual, consistent with plaintiffs' accounting method, of amounts in the "Unbilled Charges" account. In the opinion of plaintiffs' expert, this method of accounting was not in accordance with generally accepted accounting principles and did not clearly reflect Ebasco's income. To him, the Commissioner's method was erroneous in that it required the inclusion in income of amounts billed but not yet earned on contracts in one accounting period without at the same time acknowledging the obligations and costs to be incurred by Ebasco in the future performance of such contractual commitments. He termed such method as "hybrid" in that while it recognized the accrual method with respect to unbilled charges which were earned but not yet billable, it had the effect of imposing a cash basis method as to the billed but unearned charges in the "Unearned Income" account.

Finally, the witness testified that if Ebasco were to use a method of accounting under which amounts in the "Unearned Income" account would be accrued as income and amounts in the "Unbilled Charges" account would *not* be accrued as income, such method would more clearly reflect the income of Ebasco than the method of accounting proposed by the Commissioner. He stated that, while such method was not technically in accordance with generally accepted accounting principles, it was a more logical and consistent approach to use in determining the income of Ebasco than the Commissioner's method.

* * *

These issues present but another facet in the continuing controversy over the proper timing for Federal income tax purposes of various income and expense items incurred by an accrual basis tax-

2. The witness distinguished such costs from commissions which in some instances may properly be amortized where they relate directly to the contract involved and thus reduce the amount realizable under such contract.

payer. Based on expert accounting testimony presented by Ebasco at trial, it can hardly be disputed that Ebasco's system for deferral of unearned income is in full accord with generally accepted accounting principles as that phrase is used in financial or commercial accounting. But such a showing alone is not determinative for income tax purposes. The taxpayer must also show that its method clearly reflects income for the purposes of the Internal Revenue Code. Thus, while generally accepted methods of accounting are of probative value and are treated with respect by Treas.Reg. § 1.446–1 (a)(2), they are not necessarily synonymous with the proper tax accounting to be afforded an accrual item in a given situation. . . .

This variance is especially noticeable in cases where the taxpayer's accounting method results in the deferment of income. The taxpayer in such a situation is generally relying on well-known accounting principles which essentially focus on a conservative matching of income and expenses to the end that an item of income will be related to its correlative expenditure. Tax accounting, on the other hand, starts from the premise of a need for certainty in the collection of revenues and focuses on the concept of ability to pay. Thus, under this theory, where an item of income has been received even though as yet unearned, it should be subject to taxation because the taxpayer has in hand (or otherwise available) the funds necessary to pay the tax due. . . .

* * *

Thus, it can readily be seen that, under Ebasco's system, all amounts reported as income were determined with reference to the related services performed within the annual accounting period. The record clearly establishes that such system is a generally accepted accounting method for a business such as Ebasco's. Does it clearly reflect income as required by section 446 of the Code?

Defendant stoutly responds to that question in the negative. It relies heavily on the decisions of the Supreme Court in American Automobile Ass'n v. United States, 367 U.S. 687, 81 S.Ct. 1727, 6 L.Ed.2d 1109 (1961) and Schlude v. Commissioner of Internal Revenue, 372 U.S. 128, 83 S.Ct. 601, 9 L.Ed.2d 633 (1963), which cases defendant contends have firmly established the rule that, in the absence of a specific statutory exception, a taxpayer has no right to defer recognition of income received or accrued under a contract for the performance of services.

Counsel for Ebasco respond with equal vigor that Ebasco's accounting system does, in fact, clearly reflect income. To them, the Supreme Court in the above-cited decisions only held that the Commissioner of Internal Revenue did not abuse his discretion under section 446 by rejecting what the Court referred to as a "purely artificial" accounting method. Ebasco's counsel are astonished that defendant could in this case interpret *American Automobile* and *Schlude* as preventing any income deferral when, as recently as 1971, the Commissioner, in Rev.Proc. 71–21, 1971–2 C.B. 549 has held that taxpayers may defer the inclusion in income of payments received in one taxable year for services to be performed in the next succeeding year.

Although one can hardly speak with complete confidence in this troublesome and confusing area of tax law as affected by modern accounting methods, I think it fair to conclude that, on balance, Ebasco's position in this litigation is the reasonable one of the conflicting viewpoints.

The starting point, of course, must involve a close look at the trilogy of Supreme Court decisions dealing with the problem of income deferral.   Those cases are Automobile Club of Michigan v. Commissioner of Internal Revenue, 353 U.S. 180, 77 S.Ct. 707, 1 L. Ed.2d 746 (1957); American Automobile Ass'n v. United States, supra, and Schlude v. Commissioner, supra.

In *Michigan*, the Court sustained the action of the Commissioner of Internal Revenue in rejecting the taxpayer's method of deferral accounting pursuant to the authority of section 41 of the 1939 Code, the predecessor of 1954 Code section 446(b), supra.   The taxpayer was engaged in performing various services to the automotive industry including the rendition of services to members of the club but only upon their specific request.   Under its method of accounting, the club deferred taking into income the full amount of annual membership dues which the club required to be paid in advance, irrespective of whether the dues-paying member might call upon the club for any services during the 12-month period.   Upon collection, these prepaid amounts were deposited in the club's regular bank account and used for general corporate purposes.   In its books, the club entered these prepaid amounts into a liability account titled "Unearned Membership Dues," and thereafter for each of the 12 months of membership, one-twelfth of the amounts so paid was credited to an account called "Membership Income."   In sustaining the Commissioner's rejection of this accounting method as not clearly reflecting income, the Court held:

> The pro rata allocation of the membership dues in monthly amounts is *purely artificial and bears no relation to the services which petitioner may in fact be called upon to render for the member.*   Section 41 vests the Commissioner with discretion to determine whether the petitioner's method of accounting clearly reflects income.   We cannot say, in the circumstances here, that the discretionary action of the Commissioner, sustained by both the Tax Court and the Court of Appeals, exceeded permissible limits   .   .   .   353 U.S. 189, 77 S.Ct. 712. [Emphasis supplied.]

Four years later, the issue returned to the Court in the *American Automobile case.*   While the facts were essentially similar to those in *Michigan*, it was contended in *American Automobile* that the earlier case did not control because the Court had before it at last a full record containing expert accounting testimony that the system used was in accord with generally accepted accounting principles, that proof of membership service cost was detailed, and that the correlation between such cost and the period of time over which the dues were credited as income was shown and justified by proof of experience.

The Court, however, was unimpressed.   Unable to perceive any significant difference between the methods of operation and accounting employed by the two automobile clubs, the Court held that, just as in *Michigan*, the American Automobile Association's system of accounting was "purely artificial" because "substantially all services are performed only upon a member's demand and the taxpayer's performance was not related to fixed dates after the tax year." 367 U.S. 691, 81 S.Ct. 1729. The Court explained at 692, 81 S.Ct. at 1729:

> It may be true that to the accountant the actual incidence of cost in serving an individual member in exchange for his individual dues is inconsequential, or, from the viewpoint of commercial accounting, unessential to determination and disclosure of the overall financial condition of the Association. That "irregularity," however, is highly relevant to the clarity of an accounting system which defers receipt, as earned income, of dues to a taxable period *in which no, some, or all of the services paid for by those dues may or may not be rendered.* The Code exacts its revenue from the individual member's dues which, no one disputes, constitute income. When their receipt as earned income is recognized ratably over two calendar years, *without regard to correspondingly fixed individual expense or performance justification,* but consistently with overall experience, their accounting doubtless presents a rather accurate image of the total financial structure, but fails to respect the criteria of annual tax accounting and may be rejected by the Commissioner. [Emphasis supplied.]

The third of this trilogy of cases is Schlude v. Commissioner, supra, where the Court again rejected an attempt by an accrual basis taxpayer to defer prepaid amounts for future services. The taxpayers there operated a dance studio and offered dancing lessons under contracts which required the students to pay their tuition in advance with no right to refund, *i. e.,* the studio was entitled to receive the advance payments under the contracts irrespective of whether the studio was ever called upon to render any teaching services.[5] At the end of each fiscal period, the total number of actually taught hours were multiplied by the applicable hourly rate. The resulting sum was then deducted from the deferred income account and reported as earned income on taxpayers' financial statements and income tax returns.

The Court held that the case was "squarely controlled by *American Automobile Association,*" (372 U.S. 134, 83 S.Ct. 604) and sustained the Commissioner's rejection of Schlude's accounting method. Said the Court at 135–136, 83 S.Ct. at 605:

> The *American Automobile Association* case rested upon an additional ground which is also controlling here. Relying upon Automobile Club of Michigan v. Commissioner, 353 U.S. 180, 77 S.Ct. 707, 1 L.Ed.2d 746, the Court rejected the taxpayer's system as *artificial since the advance payments related to services which were to be performed only upon customers' demands without relation to fixed dates in the future. The system employed here suffers from that very same vice,* for the studio sought to defer its cash receipts on the basis of contracts which

---

5. No dates for dancing lessons were fixed but simply left to a mutually agreeable arrangement between student and teacher. Significant amounts of income flowed from cancellations resulting in no performance of services.

did not provide for lessons on fixed dates after the taxable year, but left such dates to be arranged from time to time by the instructor and his student.   Under the contracts, the student could arrange for some or all of the additional lessons or could simply allow their rights under the contracts to lapse.   But even though the student did not demand the remaining lessons, the contracts permitted the studio to insist upon payment in accordance with the obligations undertaken and to retain whatever prepayments were made without restriction as to use and without obligation of refund.   At the end of each period, while the number of lessons taught had been meticulously reflected, the studio was uncertain whether none, some or all of the remaining lessons would be rendered.   *Clearly, services were rendered solely on demand in the fashion of the American Automobile Association and Automobile Club of Michigan cases.*   [Emphasis supplied.]

It seems clear to me that, despite defendant's vigorous contention to the contrary, this trilogy of Supreme Court decisions cannot be said to have established an unvarying rule of law that, absent a specific statutory exception, a taxpayer may never defer recognition of income received or accrued under a contract for the performance of future services, no matter whether such deferral clearly reflects income.

Defendant persuasively argues, however, that its interpretation of the cases is justified by the Court's additional ground for decision in both *American Automobile* and *Schlude*.   In both cases, it is true, the Court's majority and minority opinions gave close consideration to the legislative history of sections 452 and 462 of the 1954 Code.   These sections contained the first explicit legislative sanctions of deferral of income (§ 452) and deduction of future estimated expenses (§ 462).   In the next year, however, both sections were retroactively repealed.   Ch. 143, 69 Stat. 134.   To the majority in *American Automobile*, this repealer action constituted "clearly a mandate from the Congress that petitioner's system was not acceptable for tax purposes."   367 U.S. 695, 81 S.Ct. 1731.   The dissent, of course, viewed the legislative history in different perspective.[7]

To me, the dilemma and its likely solution, have been gracefully and accurately stated by the able and comprehensive opinion of the Fifth Circuit Court of Appeals in Mooney Aircraft, Inc. v. United States, 420 F.2d 400, 408–409 (5th Cir., 1969) where the court observed:

7.   For example, in his *Schlude* dissent, Mr. Justice Stewart observed at 372 U.S. 139–140, 83 S.Ct. 607:
  "For the reasons I have elsewhere stated at some length, to rely on the repeal of §§ 452 and 462 as indicating congressional disapproval of accrual accounting principles is conspicuously to disregard clear evidence of legislative intent.   The Secretary of the Treasury, who proposed the repeal of these sections, made explicitly clear that no inference of disapproval of accrual accounting principles was to be drawn from the repeal of the sections.   So did the Senate Report.   The repeal of these sections was occasioned solely by the fear of temporary revenue losses which would result from the taking of "double deductions" during the year of transition by taxpayers who had not previously maintained their books on an accrual basis."   [Footnotes omitted.]

This alternative ground, based on legislative intent, would seem to dispose of the entire question: *all* deferrals and accruals are bad unless specifically authorized by Congress. But the Court was careful to discuss the legislative history as dictum and restricted its holding to a finding that the Commissioner did not abuse his discretion in rejecting the *AAA's* accounting system. It specifically refrained from overruling *Beacon* [Beacon Publishing Co. v. Commissioner of Internal Revenue, 218 F.2d 697 (10th Cir. 1955) (deferral of prepaid subscriptions)] and *Schuessler* [Schuessler v. Commissioner of Internal Revenue, 230 F.2d 722 (5th Cir. 1956) (accrual of expenses of 5-year service period)], distinguishing them on the ground that future performance was certain. *AAA*, supra, 367 U.S. at 692, n. 4, 81 S.Ct. 1727. It seems, then, that the Court is for the present taking a middle ground pending Congressional reform and clarification in this extremely confused area of the law: While the repeal of §§ 452 and 462 does not absolutely preclude deferrals and accruals, it indicates that the Commissioner should have very broad discretion to disallow such accounting techniques when there is any reasonable basis for his action.

The *Mooney Aircraft* approach was foreshadowed by the Seventh Circuit's decision in Artnell Company v. Commissioner of Internal Revenue, 400 F.2d 981 (7th Cir., 1968). There, Chicago White Sox, Inc. had received and accrued in a deferred unearned income account amounts attributable to advance ticket sales and revenues for other services related to baseball games to be played thereafter during the 1962 season. Prior to such performance, however, Artnell acquired Chicago White Sox, Inc., liquidated it, and continued operation of the team. In the final short-year return filed as transferee by Artnell in behalf of White Sox, Inc., Artnell excluded the deferred unearned income previously received by White Sox. The Commissioner required such amounts to be accrued as income to White Sox on receipt, and the Tax Court sustained him. In reversing and remanding, the Seventh Circuit analyzed the Supreme Court's trilogy, supra, and said at 400 F.2d 984–985:

> Has the Supreme Court left an opening for a decision that under the facts of a particular case, the extent and time of future performance are so certain, and related items properly accounted for with such clarity, that a system of accounting involving deferral of prepaid income is found clearly to reflect income, and the commissioner's rejection deemed an abuse of discretion? Or has it decided that the commissioner has complete and unreviewable discretion to reject deferral of prepaid income where Congress has made no provision? The tax court apparently adopted the latter view, for it concluded "that the Supreme Court would reach the same decision regardless of the method used by the taxpayer for deferring prepaid income."

> It is our best judgment that, although the policy of deferring, where possible, to congressional procedures in the tax field will cause the Supreme Court to accord the widest possible latitude to the commissioner's discretion, there must be situations where the deferral technique will so clearly reflect income that

the Court will find an abuse of discretion if the commissioner rejects it.

Prior to 1955 the commissioner permitted accrual basis publishers to defer unearned income from magazine subscriptions if they had consistently done so in the past. He refused to allow others to adopt the method. In 1955 his refusal was held, by the tenth circuit, in *Beacon,* to be an abuse of discretion. In *Automobile Club of Michigan,* the Supreme Court distinguished *Beacon,* on its facts, because "performance of the subscription, in most instances, was, in part, necessarily deferred until the publication dates after the tax year." The Court, however, expressed no opinion upon the correctness of *Beacon.* In 1958, Congress dealt specifically with the *Beacon,* problem. It is at least arguable that the deferral as income of prepaid admissions to events which will take place on a fixed schedule in a different taxable year is so similar to deferral of prepaid subscriptions that it would be an abuse of discretion to reject similar accounting treatment.

In any event the prepaid admission situation approaches much closer to certainty than the situations considered in *Automobile Club of Michigan, American Automobile Association,* or *Schlude.* [Footnotes omitted.]

Judicial reaction to *Artnell* has been mixed.

. . . Defendant's reaction, of course, is simply that "*Artnell* was wrongly decided." Df's Br. p. 33.

Out of this mélange, one must choose a path. To use one of Justice Holmes' favorite expressions, I "can't help" but conclude that what Ebasco is pleased to call its "balanced and symmetrical" method of accounting does in fact clearly reflect its income. It achieves the desideratum of accurately matching costs and revenues by reason of the fact that the costs of earning such revenues are incurred at the time the services are performed. See, *Mooney Aircraft,* supra, 420 F.2d at 403. Entirely unlike the factual situations before the Supreme Court in the automobile club and dance studio cases, Ebasco's contractual obligations were fixed and definite. In no sense was Ebasco's performance of services dependent solely upon the demand or request of its clientele.[8]

Based upon the foregoing considerations, it is necessary to conclude that Ebasco's method of accounting under which income is ac-

8. By way of illustrating the point, the overwhelming majority of the amounts carried in the "Unearned Income" account were paid to Ebasco pursuant to contracts for the performance of engineering services in the design and construction of electric generating plants. The construction of such a plant is, of course, a vast and complicated project involving many contractors and suppliers whose activities must be closely coordinated under rigid schedules. Therefore, as pointed out by Ebasco, there was never any question but that Ebasco had to perform its engineering services all of which were absolutely necessary to completion of the project. Many contracts contained fixed and specific dates for Ebasco's performance; others simply required Ebasco to proceed as "expeditiously as possible" or similar language. Thus, unlike the taxpayers in the Supreme Court decisions, Ebasco had a fixed obligation to perform its services without the uncertainty as to performance so prominent in those cases.

crued as the related services are performed clearly reflects its income, and, accordingly, the Commissioner is not authorized by § 446 (b) to impose another method of accounting. That this is true becomes particularly obvious when it is realized that the accounting method imposed upon Ebasco by the Commissioner is a classic example of a hybrid system combining elements of the accrual system with a cash system, a mixture generally viewed with disfavor. . . Thus, where Ebasco's billing precedes the rendition of its contracted-for services, the Commissioner proposes to tax as income amounts billed even though such amounts have not then been earned by performance. On the other hand, where the performance of services precedes billing, the Commissioner would tax amounts as income at the time the services are rendered even though, under such contracts, Ebasco has no present right to bill, or receive payment of such amounts. The inconsistency within the Commissioner's method is strident.

His method would appear to the ordinary mind to distort income instead of clearly reflecting it. Judging both by what he has rejected and what he would impose he has abused his discretion within the meaning of the authority cited, *Mooney Aircraft* and *Artnell*. Ebasco has demonstrated not only that its method of accounting is in accordance with generally accepted accounting principles but, in addition, clearly reflects its income, treating these issues to be discrete, as we must. Therefore, the amounts accrued in Ebasco's "Unearned Income" account are not taxable until the year in which Ebasco performs the services which earn that income.

QUESTIONS

1. Assume that early in its most recent calendar year Ebasco (E) learned that a large utility, P Corp., might be interested in obtaining engineering and consultative services in connection with construction of a new generating plant. One of E's three sales representatives, who work full-time soliciting this kind of business for E, on a straight salary of $27,000 per year each, without commissions, spent all of his time for four months trying to land a contract with P. In addition, since P was considering a number of unusual features for its new plant, E retained a well-known scientist to work with its regular staff during the spring on the preparation of a proposal to P Corp., for which the scientist was paid $19,000. In July E got the contract, which called for specified engineering and other consultative services over the following 15–18 months in connection with building the new plant. Under the contract, E was to receive a total of $500,000, payable at the rate of $100,000 every three months, starting on September 15, regardless of when E's services were actually performed. Due to delays in P's construction schedule, E had in fact performed no services for P by the close of the calendar year. How should these facts be reflected in E's financial statements for the year?

2. Would your views on the foregoing be affected by either (a) the fact that E's sales representatives had been urged to concentrate on getting contracts which, like the one with P, were likely to produce substantial advance payments, and hence would provide E with additional working capital, or (b) the fact that in order to encourage such contracts E generally charged approximately 10% less than its normal prices for similar work?

3. Would your answer to Question 1 be different if it turned out that by the end of the first year E had performed one-tenth of its total expected services under the contract with P?

a. SPECIAL PROBLEMS OF INCOME RECOGNITION ON LONG–TERM CONTRACTS

GRAESE AND DeMARIO, REVENUE RECOGNITION FOR LONG TERM CONTRACTS *

142 J. Accountancy (Dec., 1976) 54.

In recent years the forms of contracts under which goods and services are delivered have become markedly more complex, and the range of products and services delivered under contractual arrangement has greatly expanded. At one time contracting transactions were limited to the physical construction of major goods, such as an office building or large ship, and did not generally include services. However, the range of items that is delivered under contractual arrangements today includes research, computer software services, sophisticated weapons delivery systems and space hardware and software. Further, at one time it was unusual to encounter contracts other than straightforward fixed-price or cost-plus-fixed-fee contracts. However, the form of contracts has also changed as evidenced by the AICPA's 1965 industry audit guide, *Audits of Government Contractors*, which enumerated 14 types of fixed-price and cost contracts in a list confined to the "more common" variations of such contracts. These changes in practices in contracting make it appropriate to reconsider the basis and application of relevant accounting principles to the new business environment. This article examines the problems of revenue recognition on long term contracts and provides guidelines for using the percentage-of-completion method (percentage method) of revenue recognition.

Scope of This Article

The accounting concepts addressed in this article apply to those contracting transactions where (a) revenue recognition at the time the contract is entered into is not appropriate because the earning process is incomplete and (b) the individual contract serves as the basis for revenue recognition, cost accumulation and cost estimation because the earning process and costs incurred are inextricably bound up with the seller's obligations under the contract.

Such contracting situations are frequently referred to as "long term," but the distinguishing feature of the transactions to which this article applies is not any specific duration of the period of performance under the contract. Rather, the distinguishing feature is that the transaction is not completed at the time the contract is entered into and that the contract appropriately serves as the cost and profit center. Accordingly, the term "long term contracts" as used in this article is not restricted to contracts with a specified minimum performance period, nor is any such restriction provided in authoritative literature on revenue recognition for long term contracts.

* * *

The Basic Accounting Issue

The principal problem in accounting for long term contracts is determining the period in which revenue should be recognized. A key consideration in the determination of the appropriate accounting period for revenue recognition is an evaluation of the uncertainties which arise because performance on a given contract extends over a period of time. The uncertainties include the buyer's ability to make the payments required by the contract, the seller's ability to complete his performance obligations under the contract and the seller's ability to make reasonable estimates of the stage of completion and of future costs to complete the contract at the end of any accounting period.

The need to make estimates is present in many aspects of the accounting process, but it is of particular concern in contract accounting. The fact that performance extends over a period of time makes predictions of future costs and estimates of the stage of completion difficult. This difficulty tends to increase as the length of the performance period increases, although even in relatively shorter term contracts, circumstances can be such that estimates of the percentage of completion and of future costs can be difficult to make.

The nature of work to be performed under the contract also contributes to the difficulty of making estimates. For example, it may be a relatively simple matter to estimate the percentage of completion and the costs to complete where the contract calls for the construction of a type of equipment normally constructed by the contractor. A more difficult estimating problem would be involved in a contract for the construction of an underwater tunnel where unforeseen technical problems could arise, including those resulting from inaccurate geological surveys. Still more difficulty is encountered in estimates involving a new product, particularly one involving technology that extends beyond the present state of the art. Examples of this are frequently found in the aerospace-defense industry.

Authoritative literature provides for two acceptable methods for recognizing revenue on long term contracts, one of which recognizes revenue over the period of contract performance based on estimates where such estimates are reasonably reliable and the other of which postpones revenue recognition until the ultimate profit is known, thereby recognizing all the revenue in the period when the performance is completed or substantially completed. Both of these methods are widely employed in accounting practice. They are the percentage-of-completion method and the completed-contract method.

The Two Methods of Revenue Recognition

Accounting literature states that revenue is generally recognized when the earning process is complete or virtually complete and an exchange has taken place. The completed-contract method conforms to this realization principle in that income is recognized only when the contract is completed, or substantially so. (However, consistent with generally accepted accounting principles, anticipated losses are recognized as soon as they become evident.) The percentage-of-completion method, also provided for in authoritative accounting literature, is an acknowledged exception to the realization principle; revenue is recognized as work progresses, i. e., before the earning process is complete.

The principal advantage of the completed-contract method is that it does not rely on estimates for revenue recognition purposes and therefore eliminates the risk of recognizing revenue that does not materialize or that is subject to substantial subsequent adjustment. A major disadvantage of the method is that periodic reported income can be erratic when, for example, a few large contracts are completed in one accounting period but no contracts are completed in the previous or subsequent period even though the level of performance activity has been relatively constant throughout. When numerous contracts are regularly completed in each accounting period, periodic income may not be erratic, but there is a continuous lag between the time when work is performed and when the related revenue is recognized.

The disadvantage of the percentage-of-completion method is that it is subject to the risk of error in estimating the portion of contract performance completed and the costs to be incurred. When conditions are present that permit reasonable estimates to be made, the percentage-of-completion method has the advantage of recognizing revenue each period, based on the contracting efforts that took place in that period.

The AICPA committee on accounting procedure indicated in Accounting Research Bulletin No. 45 that the advantage of reflecting in the financial statements the revenue from business activity on long term contracts in periods prior to their completion should take precedence over the greater degree of certainty of results reported under the completed-contract method—provided the estimates necessary to apply the percentage method are sufficiently dependable. This all-important caveat enables us to redefine the basic issue in accounting for long term contracts: What are the circumstances that indicate that the estimates necessary to apply the percentage method will be sufficiently dependable to produce reliable results? This question has important implications for both the completed-contract method and the percentage method because, if the circumstances indicate that the percentage method cannot be used, the completed-contract method must be applied.

ARB No. 45 also sets forth the dependability of estimates as the criterion for determining when it is appropriate to use the percentage method as opposed to the completed-contract method. Accounting Principles Board Statement No. 4 (par. 152) in referring to the percentage method states, "This exception to the realization principle is based on the availability of evidence of the ultimate proceeds and the consensus that a better measure of periodic income results." The conditions that satisfy the requirements for the use of the percentage method are presented below. We believe that if the requirements are met, the percentage method is clearly preferable for accounting for revenue on long term contracts because it reflects income in the accounting period during which the effort was expended to earn that income. In certain situations the seller may meet the requirements for the use of the percentage method but may wish to account for all contract revenues consistently by the completed-contract method. We recognize that accounting literature permits the completed-contract method to be used even if all criteria for the use of the percentage method are met. So long as authoritative standard setting bodies permit the continuation of this accounting alternative for recognizing contract revenue, the use of the percentage method, although preferred, cannot be considered mandatory even though the requirements for its use are met.

Requirements for Use of the Percentage Method

The percentage method produces reliable results if there is available adequate evidence of ultimate proceeds and if the estimates of future costs and the extent of contract performance completed are reasonably dependable. Compliance with these key requirements for each contract is essential to justify the use of the percentage method for that contract. Thus, certain contracts could appropriately be accounted for by the use of the percentage method while others are appropriately accounted for only by the completed-contract method. We believe the requirements for the use of the percentage method on long term contracts can be presumed to be fulfilled if all of the following conditions are present:

- There is a written contract executed by the parties that clearly specifies the goods or services to be provided and received by the parties, the consideration to be exchanged and the manner and terms of settlement.
- The buyer has the ability to satisfy his obligations under the contract.
- The seller has the ability to perform his contractual obligations.
- The seller has an adequate estimating process and the ability to estimate reliably both the cost to complete and the percentage of contract performance completed.
- The seller has a cost accounting system that adequately accumulates and allocates costs in a manner consistent with the estimates produced by the estimating process.

Let us expand on these conditions and show how we might determine if the requirements for the use of the percentage method have been met.

* * *

Ability to estimate. The seller must have the ability to reliably estimate costs to complete and should also have established methods to provide reasonable assurance of a continuing ability to estimate. . .

It should be noted that the degree of accuracy required of the estimating process is greater than that required under the completed-contract method. Under the percentage method, the seller must not only be able to estimate that costs will not exceed contract revenues but he must also be able to reasonably determine the amount of profit that will result. Previous reliability of a seller's estimating process can be indicative of continuing estimating ability, particularly if the circumstances in the situation in question are similar to those of the past. However, new or changing circumstances may raise doubts about the continuing reliability of a previously demonstrated estimating ability.

* * *

Measurement of the Percentage of Completion

Authoritative literature, such as the AICPA's *Audits of Construction Contractors*, provides for the use of the ratio of aggregate cost to date to the most recent estimate of total costs at completion (cost-to-cost) for the measurement of the percentage of completion. However, it also recognizes the possibility of using other methods of measuring the percentage of completion where such methods appropriately measure the portion of work performed. For example, labor hours, labor dollars, machine hours or architectural estimates may provide an appropriate measure of work performed.

In measuring contract performance, the method used must, because of the nature of contracting, give recognition to the risks of contract performance. Inherent in the seller's obligation under the contract are risks of performance which can affect the cost of the contract. For example, suppose a contract calls for the construction of a machine that the seller has had previous experience in manufacturing but requires that the machine perform a function which is not provided for by the existing design and requires that the contractor develop modifications in design which enable the machine to perform that function. In this case, an appropriate measure may be manufacturing labor hours since contract revenue recognition should not begin until the performance risks inherent in developing modifications (e. g., all engineering design costs) have been eliminated. The seller's risks of performance should be carefully evaluated and taken into account in selecting the measure of contract performance and in determining the percentage of completion appropriate in the circumstances.

In practice the predominant method of measurement of the percentage-of-contract performance completed is the cost-to-cost method. In applying the cost-to-cost method, adjustments must be made for the following:

- Materials purchased that have not been installed or used during the contract performance, if such materials are significant to costs incurred to date.
- Subcontractor costs, to the extent that the timing of payments to the subcontractor differs significantly from the amount of work performed under the subcontract.
- Types of costs included in costs incurred to date but not included in the total cost estimate.

Some contend that, when using the cost-to-cost method, the full amount of the subcontract price should be included in the seller's incurred costs to date at the date the subcontract is entered into. Those who support this treatment generally take the position that the seller's performance with respect to the subcontract is complete at the time of entering into the subcontract. However, the objective of the measurement of the percentage of completion is to provide a basis for recognition of revenue as work is performed, and the signing of a subcontract does not constitute performance. Therefore, we believe subcontracts should not be included in the seller's incurred costs to date unless these subcontract costs are adjusted in the same manner as the seller's other incurred costs to date (e. g., major purchases by the subcontractor that are not installed or utilized should be deducted from subcontract costs included in the seller's costs incurred to date for purposes of the cost-to-cost computation). Many sellers do not have direct access to the subcontractor's records for purposes of such adjustment. However, sellers generally have available other sources of information regarding subcontractor performance (e. g., reports of seller personnel involved in supervising the subcontractor) and should carefully consider those available sources of information for possible adjustment of costs billed by the subcontractor and included in the seller's cost-to-cost computation.

Care must be exercised to ensure that costs included in contract costs to date are appropriately reflected in both the numerator and the denominator of the cost-to-cost calculation of the percentage of completion. Examples of the types of cost that might be found in the numerator on a total-to-date basis and not fully estimated in the denominator are general and administrative costs associated with contract effort and certain purchased services. If such costs are included as contract costs to date for the purpose of the cost-to-cost computation, the total anticipated amount of such costs must be included in total estimated contract costs. Failure to include the estimated amount of these costs in the total estimated contract costs, while including the currently incurred portion in contract costs to date, results in an erroneous determination of contract performance and a disproportionate recognition of profit.

Certain sellers, although using the percentage method for contract revenue recognition, defer any recognition of revenue until a specified percentage-of-contract performance is complete (in practice the percentages noted ranged from 5 percent to 40 percent). Those sellers who defer revenue recognition under the percentage method until a specified level of performance is reached take the position that, although they generally meet all the criteria for the application of the percentage method at the outset of the contract, completion to the specified level gives additional assurance of the dependability of the estimating process. We believe that the practice of deferring revenue recognition until a specified contract performance level is reached is acceptable if the specified performance level is reasonable in the circumstances, if the practice is applied consistently to all contracts and if full disclosure of the method is made in the financial statements.

Deferral of Costs in Anticipation of Future Sales

* * *

In some instances, sellers incur precontract costs (e. g., the cost of engineering, estimating or architectural effort or other costs for work begun on goods or services before any contracts are received).

The decision to incur these costs may be based on commitments or other indications of interest in negotiating a contract. We believe that precontract costs, whether based on a commitment or not, should not be included in contract costs or inventory prior to receipt of the contract. Such costs, however, may be deferred subject to evaluation as to probable recoverability. We believe that such precontract costs may be deferred only if the costs can be directly associated with a specific anticipated future contract and it is probable that the costs will be recovered from that contract.

Other costs may be incurred which relate to the purchase of materials, production equipment or supplies that are expected to be used in connection with anticipated future contracts. We believe that such costs may be deferred if it is probable that the costs will be recovered from future contract revenue or other disposition.

In some cases, sellers will produce goods in excess of the amounts required by a contract in anticipation of future orders. The costs that are appropriately related to producing those goods may be deferred if it is probable that the costs deferred will be recovered. In considering recovery, special consideration must be given to the uniqueness of the goods involved.

Frequently, learning or startup costs are incurred in connection with the performance of a contract. In some circumstances, the seller anticipates that follow-on or future contracts will be received for the same goods or services. He therefore considers it appropriate to spread such costs over both existing and anticipated future contracts. Under this approach, aggregate total revenues expected to be received for the product or service under both existing and anticipated future contracts and aggregate total costs expected to be incurred in relation to those revenues are estimated, and the average of total costs is matched with current contract revenues. This results both in averaging the net profit of current and anticipated future contracts and in a higher profit ratio for the current contract than if accounted for singly. This accounting, frequently referred to as the program method, is most often used in the aerospace-defense industry.

Such learning or startup costs are generally labor, overhead, rework or other unique costs that must be incurred in order to complete the existing contract in progress. It is difficult to establish a direct relationship between such costs and the anticipated future contracts. More importantly, because receipt of future contracts cannot reasonably be anticipated, we believe it is not appropriate to aggregate revenues and costs from both existing and anticipated future contracts. Further, because future revenues and the related incremental costs generally cannot be estimated, the recovery of such costs from anticipated contracts is in such doubt that we believe they should not be deferred but should be charged to the contracts under which they were incurred.

Costs that were expensed when incurred because their recovery was not considered probable should not be reinstated by a credit to earnings if a contract is subsequently obtained. Costs that were appropriately deferred may be included in contract costs upon receipt of the contract. As required by FASB Statement No. 2, research and development costs must be charged to expense when incurred. . . .

Chapter 5

ACCRUAL OF EXPENSE AND INCOME

1. ACCRUAL OF EXPENSE

As the court in the Boise Cascade Corporation case observed, at least for financial accounting purposes the critical element is "matching", so that "an item of income will be related to its correlative expenditure". See page 318, supra. It should be observed, however, that deferring the advance receipts until the related expenses were incurred was not the only way of accomplishing such matching. Matching could also have been achieved even though the advance receipts were recognized as income in the year received, by accruing the related future expenses in that year—that is, determining what the amount of those expenses was likely to be and charging that amount to current expense in the year of the receipts.

We have already seen the mechanics for accruing expenses in a period prior to payment. The debit is to the appropriate current expense account, and the credit is to an Expense Payable (or Accrued Expense) liability account, to reflect the fact that the expense has not been paid yet but there is an obligation to pay it in the future. This accrual technique might have been used by Ebasco in the Boise Cascade case to match the related future expenses with the advance receipts in the year in which the latter were received. To be sure, Ebasco would presumably not know exactly what the amount of those expenses would be, whereas in all of our prior examples of accrual of expense, like E. Tutt's telephone expense for March, or Nifty-Novelty's storage expense for February, the amount of the expense allocable to the month was fixed and certain. However, the inability to determine the amount precisely is no more of a bar to reflecting an expense in the current period than the fact that cash has not moved; if an expense belongs in the current period although the amount is uncertain, an estimate should be made as accurately as possible, and the estimated figure is then accrued in the usual manner. (As indicated in some of the tax cases set out later, there was often resistance to accruing an expense for tax purposes unless the amount was certain; but this is less true today, and in any event, as we have noted repeatedly, what is permissable for tax purposes does not govern what is appropriate for financial accounting purposes.)

Actually, such estimation may well be the norm rather than the exception, as it is quite common to have to resort to estimating the

332

amount of an expense which is to be reflected currently, prior to payment. Thus, suppose that in the Boise Cascade case it was expected that the prospective performance covered by the advance receipts would include some work which would require the services of outside consultants, at an estimated cost of $50,000. Then this estimated expense could be accrued in the year of the advance receipts with the following entry:

Consultant Expense	$50,000	
Consultant Expense Payable		$50,000

There is one other significant distinction between this Ebasco hypothetical and the accruals in E. Tutt and Nifty-Novelty. In the latter cases the services for which the expense was accrued had already been performed, and the benefit of those services had been enjoyed in the current period—Tutt had had the use of the telephone during March, and Nifty-Novelty had utilized the storage space during February. As a corollary, there was nothing conditional, or any other doubt, about the obligation to pay reflected by the Expense Payable liability created. The same was true of that $100 worth of services by Tutt's secretary which had not been paid for by the end of March, but was accrued so that March would bear the burden of all the secretarial services which had benefited the month by aiding in the production of revenues. In the Ebasco hypothetical, on the other hand, the consultants would not have performed any of their expected services by the end of the year of the advance receipts; therefore, Ebasco would not have enjoyed any of the benefit of these services as yet, and presumably Ebasco's liability to pay for the services would be conditioned upon their actual performance.

Nevertheless, if the income to which such prospective expenses are related is going to be recognized in the current period, then those expenses must also be reflected (i. e., accrued) in that period, in order to achieve the necessary matching. In effect, Ebasco would be viewed as having enjoyed the benefit of these expenses, even though they have not yet been performed, because performance of the services is a necessary condition to the earning of the income involved. As a corollary, Ebasco would be regarded as obligated to pay for these services, in an accounting sense even if not legally speaking, thus justifying the creation of an Expense Payable type of liability account.

However, unlike the mere fact that payment has not yet been made, or the inability to ascertain the precise amount of the expense, the fact that services representing the expense in question have not yet been performed *is* a reason for substantial reluctance to accrue the expense, even though it is not an absolute bar. Among other things, it is often much more difficult to estimate the cost of services that have not been performed than those that have been. Fortunately, this problem is avoided in large measure by the application of the rule that the income from a transaction should not be recognized until there has been substantial completion of the required performance. By hypothesis, when overall performance has been substantially completed there can not be much in the way of related services still unperformed, and hence there should not be much occasion for accruing an expense reflecting services not yet performed. In other words, delaying recognition of income until substantial completion of the work to be done, in order to be as sure as reasonably possible that the income will not be lost by virtue of a default in performance, assures that practically all of the services related to the income will have been completed; as a result, any expenses to be accrued are likely to be for services already performed, which means that the corresponding liability created will represent an unconditional obligation (as well as that any needed estimation is likely to be facilitated).

However, note that the rule for recognition of income does not require absolute completion of performance, only *substantial* completion. The very meaning of substantial completion is that there may be some relatively unimportant matters remaining to be finished; hence in cases of this kind the occasion may still arise to accrue expenses for services before they have been performed. For example, assume that a manufacturer of machinery has completed the machines for a particular order and shipped them to the customer by the end of the current period, but the manufacturer's performance is not totally completed because of a remaining obligation to install the machines in the customer's plant. In such a case, there first arises a question of judgment as to whether performance is sufficiently close to completion to call for recognition of the income on the transaction (and we will look at some examples involving resolution of this issue later in this chapter). If the decision is to recognize the income, that normally means, as we have seen, recognition of *all* the income from the transaction; as a corollary, all related expenses, regardless of whether the services involved have been performed as yet, should be accrued, in order to achieve a proper matching with the income being recognized.

It might be observed that the Ebasco situation does not quite fit this analysis, since under a literal application of the rule for recognition of income it would seem that none of the income from a particular contract should be recognized until performance under the whole contract has been substantially completed. But as discussed in connection with the Boise Cascade case, contracts for the delivery of goods or services which take a long time to perform, commonly referred to as "long-term" contracts, are often treated as an exception to the recognition of income rule: in order to give a more meaningful picture of operations in each period, income from such contracts may be recognized in each period in an amount proportionate to the percentage of the total expected work on the contract which was actually performed in the particular period. It was this kind of "percentage of completion" method of recognizing income on a long-term contract which Ebasco seemed to be using in the Boise Cascade case.

One other point about accrual of expenses is worth a brief mention here. It has sometimes been suggested that in any cases where it is necessary to estimate the amount of an expense being accrued (particularly when the services involved have not been performed yet, so that there may be less confidence in the estimate, and in any event the accompanying liability is inherently conditional), it may be desirable to use a different name for the liability created in the accrual process, in order to separate such liabilities from those which are unconditional (whether or not due yet) and certain in amount. Sometimes the term "Estimated Liability" is used for this purpose: thus the liability created in conjunction with accrual of an expense for future installation of machines might be called "Estimated Liability for Installation" rather than Installation Expense Payable (or Accrued Installation Expense). Today, there seems to be no uniform practice on the matter, and many companies lump all their accrued expense liabilities under a single heading like Accrued Expenses.

However, there is a bit of history on this subject that is worth knowing about. Another name often used in the past to signify estimated or conditional liabilities was "Reserve", i. e., "Reserve for Installation Expenses", or just "Reserve for Installation", and this term still appears in accounting and legal materials, particularly in some of the older cases. It was not a happy choice of name, since it seemed to connote the reservation of something, presumably assets, to pay the liability. Of course any accrual of an expense lowers net income for the period; hence earned surplus at the end of the period, and the amount of dividends that could be paid (if the company wanted to make a distribution equal to its entire earned surplus) is less than it would have been, and so the accrual of the expense and corollary creation of a liability might be viewed as preserving assets in a general sense. But it is also possible to set aside cash (or other assets) and specifically earmark it for a particular purpose, like discharging an indebtedness (or paying for a new plant), either by setting up a formal escrow arrangement, or less formally by simply opening a special bank account. The problem with the term "Reserve" was that it suggested the existence of some such arrangement (or other special provisions for the payment of the liability) whereas in fact calling the liability a "Reserve" meant no more than that the liability had been created in conjunction with the accrual of an expense which was uncertain in amount (and perhaps represented services not yet performed).

In addition, the use of the term "Reserve" in this context has often been accompanied by rather loose terminology. For example, you may encounter references, particularly in judicial opinions, to "deducting the reserve from income", or "reserves out of income". Such phrases can be confusing, since as we know a Reserve is a liability which appears on the balance sheet and does not itself affect the determination of net income; probably this terminology was intended simply to express the fact that a Reserve account is created in conjunction with a charge against income in exactly the same amount.

Accordingly, it is not surprising that the same Accounting Terminology Bulletin No. 1 which recommended elimination of the term "Surplus", see pages 168–170, supra, also urged that the word "Reserve" be narrowly confined, and that its use in connection with accrual of expenses be discontinued.

Note that we have now developed a kind of hierarchy of credits accompanying the recognition of an expense in the current period. The credit is to:

a. A Prepaid or Deferred
    Expense account ....if the expense has been prepaid in a prior period.

b. Cash ....if the expense is paid in the current period.

c. An Expense Payable
    (or Accrued Expense)
    account.......................if the expense has not been paid yet, but there is a fixed liability to pay a fixed amount of money.

d. An Estimated Liability
    account (or, formerly,
    a Reserve account) ....if the expense has not been paid yet, but there is a fixed liability to pay money in an amount which can only be estimated, or a liability to perform or provide services (and a segregation of these kinds of liabilities is desired).

Whatever the name given to the liability created in connection with the accrual of an expense, when it is paid the bookkeeping treatment is the same as when any other liability, such as an Account Payable, is paid: the debit is to the liability account to show that it has been discharged, and the credit is of course to cash. The expense originally estimated is not reflected in the income statement for the period in which the liability is discharged, which is as it should be since that expense has already been recognized in an earlier period.

When the size of the liability could only be estimated at the time the expense was accrued, the amount actually required to discharge the liability will rarely prove exactly equal to the figure originally estimated and charged against income. Any difference should be reflected in the income statement for the period in which the liability is discharged: such normal, recurring corrections, which are inherent in the use of estimates were expressly ruled out of prior period adjustment treatment under ¶ 24 of APB Op. No. 9, even before FASB No. 16 practically abolished all prior period adjustments (and of course they certainly do not qualify as extraordinary under APB No. 30). So if in the foregoing hypothetical Ebasco had accrued an estimated $50,000 of expense for consultants' services in the year of the advance receipts, with an accompanying credit to an Estimated Liability Account, and in the later year of performance it turned out to cost $60,000, the entry in that latter year would be:

Estimated Liability for Consultants	$50,000	
Consultant Expense	10,000	
Cash		$60,000

The foregoing illustrates the mechanics of recognizing an expense or loss before it is paid or incurred. The more important question of judgment as to the extent to which a future expected expenditure or loss should be charged against the current period calls for application of the same criteria as those considered earlier in connection with the deferral of expenses: expenses should be matched with related items of revenue; if an expense is not related to any particular revenue-producing transaction, it should be charged against the period or periods in which it contributes generally to the production of revenues.

a. RELATION BETWEEN ACCRUAL OF EXPENSE AND DEFERRAL OF INCOME

Notice that whenever the liability account created in conjunction with accrual of an expense reflects an obligation to perform or provide services, as it often does, it bears some resemblance to a "Deferred Income" account, which also reflects an obligation to perform services (or deliver goods). The following material may shed some further light on the relation between these accounts:

CAPITAL WAREHOUSE CO. v. COMMISSIONER *

United States Court of Appeals, Eighth Circuit, 1948.
171 F.2d 395.

THOMAS, CIRCUIT JUDGE.   The petitioner is a Minnesota corporation engaged in the public warehouse business at St. Paul, Minnesota. It keeps its books and files its Federal income tax returns on the accrual basis.   . . .

The sole question presented is whether the respondent was right in his determination that the petitioner could not for the taxable years involved exclude from its gross income that portion thereof which it had set aside on its books as a reserve fund to cover its contractual liability to its customers to remove merchandise from its warehouse at the end of the storage period.

The Tax Court held that respondent was right (9 T.C. 966), and the petitioner seeks a review and reversal of that decision.

The controlling facts are not in dispute. Upon receipt of merchandise for storage, customers, designated depositors, were required to pay, in a single amount, a charge in accordance with the terms of various contracts, for the handling into and out of the warehouse. The charges thus made for handling were credited on petitioner's books to an account designated "handling revenue." This account included the cost of moving goods when received from the cars into the warehouse, loading the goods from the warehouse back into cars when they were ordered out, and various incidental charges.

For the purpose of determining its liability to its customers for "handling out" charges at the end of each fiscal year, petitioner set up on its books an account designated "Reserve for Handling Out." To determine the amount of such liability an inventory was taken of stored merchandise on hand at the end of the year and not delivered but for which a handling charge had been made and collected. Of the total handling charge which had been made and collected on the merchandise shown on such inventory 60% thereof was allocated to the estimated cost of handling out and 40% to the cost of handling in. The division so made was based upon experience within the industry. This allocation, the Tax Court found, was made by other warehouse concerns because merchandise came into their warehouses in carload lots and left in less than carload lots, thus requiring a greater expenditure for handling out than for handling in. The merchandise stored by petitioner, however, later developments disclosed, was shipped out in carload lots. On the basis of the allocation so made the petitioner, after taking the inventory at the end of the fiscal year, adjusted its books to show petitioner's liability to its customers for merchandise then in storage and for which it had not performed its contract to handle out upon order.

The unearned handling out charges thus determined at the end of each fiscal year were claimed as deductions by the petitioner on its Federal income tax returns for each of the fiscal years under review and denied by the respondent. In his notice of deficiency, the respondent determined that the amounts placed in the reserve in each of the

* Portions of the opinion omitted.

taxable years did not represent deferred income and that said amounts should be included in gross income.

The petitioner contends that under . . . the Internal Revenue Code a public warehouse company may accrue as a deductible item of expense the cost of removing from its warehouse goods stored therein for which removal it had previously been paid, and that the Tax Court erred in denying its right to do so.

* * *

. . . there is no basis for the contention that the Tax Court erred in its decision. Certainly the amount of the taxpayer's liability to its customers for the expense of loading out their merchandise in future years was not "fixed" in the taxable year nor did the particular event upon which the amount depended occur in the taxable year. That event was the determination of the actual cost of loading out at the time the merchandise was ordered out by the customer. Here the petitioner has only estimated such cost. . . .

It is true petitioner's liability, that is its obligation to pay the cost of "handling out", had become final during the taxable years in the sense that it was not a contingent liability; but the amount of the liability or cost of handling out was not definite or fixed. . . .

PROBLEMS

1.　Assume that in year 1 Capital Warehouse received $60 from a customer to cover the handling out of certain goods received for storage in that year. Under the company's normal practice, upon receipt of the $60 the bookkeeper would credit that amount to "Handling Revenue", an income account which is closed to Profit and Loss at the end of each year. Assume also that the company expected that the cost of handling these goods out would be $50, thus producing a $10 profit on this handling activity. If the goods were not handled out until sometime in year 2, which of the following entries should the company have made at the end of year 1 for ordinary financial reporting purposes?

1. — Handling Expense	$50	
Estim. Liab. (Reserve) for Handling		$50
2. — Handling Revenue	$60	
Deferred Handling Revenue		$60
3. — No Entry.		

In reaching your conclusion, work out the effect which each alternative would have on the net income of years 1 and 2, assuming that the actual cost of handling these goods out in year 2 proved to be $50.

Consider also in this connection the following case:

SCHUESSLER v. COMMISSIONER *

United States Court of Appeals, Fifth Circuit, 1956.
230 F.2d 722.

TUTTLE, CIRCUIT JUDGE. This is a petition for review of a decision by the Tax Court disallowing a deduction in 1946 of an item of $13,300.00, representing a reserve set up by taxpayers while keeping their books on the accrual basis, to represent their estimated cost of carrying out a guarantee, given with each of the furnaces sold by them during the year, to turn the furnace on and off each year for five years.

The opinion of the Tax Court treats the matter as though ample proof was offered by the taxpayer (hereafter the husband will be called "taxpayer") to raise the legal issue and we find the record warrants this treatment. Taxpayer was in the gas furnace business in 1946, during which he sold 665 furnaces, each with a guarantee that he would turn the furnace on and off each year for five years. The fact that such service, if performed, would cost $2.00 per call was amply established. The taxpayer, himself a bookkeeper and accountant prior to entering this business, testified to his keeping his books on the accrual method and claimed that the only way his income could be accurately reported was by charging against the cost of furnaces sold in 1946 the reserve representing the amount which he became legally liable to expend in subsequent years in connection with the sales. The proof was clear that he actually sold the furnaces for $20.00 to $25.00 more than his competitors because of his guarantee, which they did not give.

We think it quite clear that petitioner's method of accounting comes much closer to giving a correct picture of his income than would a system in which he sold equipment in one year and received an inflated price because he obligated himself, in effect, to refund part of it in services later but was required to report the total receipts as income on the high level of the sales year and take deductions on the low level of the service years. The reasonableness of taxpayer's action, however, is not the test if it runs counter to requirements of the statute.

We find that not only does it not offend any statutory requirement, but, in fact, we think it is in accord with the language and intent of the law. Clearly what is sought by this statute is an accounting method that most accurately reflects the taxpayer's income on an annual accounting basis.

The decisions of the Tax Court and of the several Courts of Appeals are not uniform on this subject, some circuits requiring a mathematical certainty as to the exact amount of the future expenditures that cannot be satisfied in the usual case. Other circuits, seemingly more concerned with the underlying principle of charging to each year's income reasonably ascertainable future expenses necessary to earn or retain the income, have permitted the accrual of restricted items of future expenses.

* * *

* Portions of the opinion and footnotes
omitted.

The case of Beacon Publishing Co. v. Commissioner is considered by both parties here and was noted by the Tax Court as of especial significance. That case involved the treatment of prepaid income received by the Beacon Publishing Co. covering subscriptions to be furnished in subsequent years. The Tax Court in its decision here said:

> ". . . This is essentially the same problem as the reporting of prepaid income in the year in which received for services to be performed in following years. The petitioner in fact, on brief, recognizes that the two problems are identical and cites Beacon Publishing Co. v. Commissioner, 10 Cir., 1955, 218 F.2d 697, in support of his argument that the reserve here in issue was a proper deduction in computing his income in 1946."

The Tax Court then simply declined to follow the Court in the Beacon case, preferring to adhere to its own views as expressed in Curtis A. Andrews v. Commissioner, 23 T.C. 1026. We prefer the reasoning as well as the conclusion reached by the Court in the Tenth Circuit. There the opinion correctly, we think, disposed of the "claim of right" theory advanced by the Commissioner and adopted by the Tax Court in this type of case.

Finally we think the enactment in 1954 of Section 462 of the Internal Revenue Code of 1954 * and its subsequent repeal constitute no legislative history bearing on the construction of the provisions of the Internal Revenue Code of 1939.

The record below amply supports the contention of the taxpayer that there was a legal liability created in 1946, when the purchase price was paid for the gas furnaces, for the taxpayer to turn the furnaces on and off for the succeeding five years; that the cost of such service [was] reasonably established at a minimum of $2.00 per visit; and that the payment of $20.00 to $25.00 extra by the purchasers fully proved their intention to call upon the taxpayer each year for the service. These facts authorized the setting up of a reserve out of the 1946 income to enable the taxpayer to meet these established charges in future years. The decision of the Tax Court is therefore in error and must be reversed.

b.　CONTINGENT EXPENSES AND LIABILITIES

Perhaps the most troublesome questions in the area of accrual arise in connection with contingent losses and expenses, i. e., those which are conditional and hence may or may not ever occur. Should such an item be reflected currently despite the uncertainty? This poses a real dilemna, particularly when the contingent loss or expense is one which contributed to the production of revenues in the current period, and therefore is clearly chargeable to the current period (provided it is ultimately incurred). If and when the loss or expense occurs in some later period, the company will be sorry

---

* See the reference to § 462 in the Boise
Cascade case, page 321, supra.

if it was not charged to the earlier period to which it "belonged", but if it turns out never to be incurred, the company will regret having charged it to the earlier period; and often there is simply no way of telling how it will turn out. If the decision is to accrue the expense or loss in the current period, then as usual the debit would be to a current expense account, and the credit to a liability, which might be given a special name, like "Contingent Liability", to distinguish it on the balance sheet from those liabilities which are not conditional in this same way.

To illustrate, suppose that X is a shipbuilding corporation which usually builds and sells one ship a year. X's practice is to guarantee that the ship will be able to maintain a certain speed for a specified number of years, with the commitment that $25,000 of the purchase price will be refunded if the ship does not live up to the guaranty. Certainly if X has to make good in some future period on such a guaranty made in the year of sale, that cost would be a proper charge against the revenue received in the year of sale; but there is substantial doubt that X will ever have to pay. A question of judgment arises: is the likelihood that this expense or loss will ultimately be incurred sufficient to justify making a charge against income in the year of sale? If so, the entry might be:

Guaranty Expense	$25,000	
Contingent Liability on Guaranty		$25,000

Even if the likelihood of having to pay this liability is small enough that a charge against current income is not warranted, a question remains whether the contingent liability should be reflected in some other way in the financial statements, perhaps simply by disclosing the existence of the contingent liability in a footnote. If no charge against current income is made but it turns out later that the expense or loss is actually incurred in some later year, it would be charged against income in that year (since qualification as a prior period adjustment under FAS No. 16 is out of the question).

Notice the difference between this kind of truly contingent liability, where there is uncertainty as to whether any expense or loss at all will be incurred, and the situation where it is clear that some expense or loss attributable to the current period will ultimately be incurred but there is uncertainty as to the amount. As we have seen, the latter is usually handled by making as accurate an estimate of the likely amount as possible. Occasionally, however, the amount is so incapable of being ascertained with any reasonable accuracy that there is reluctance to make any charge against current income, in which event some method of simply disclosing the liability, perhaps by a footnote, might be used. Of course if a contingent expenditure or loss is also very uncertain as to amount, that simply represents another factor against charging the contingent item against current income.

Sometimes a number of related contingent expenses or losses arise in the same year. Actually this fact serves to simplify the accounting treatment. Suppose, for example, that our shipbuilding corporation, X, sells many ships per year, each with the same guaranty assumed above. Although each particular guaranty is entirely contingent, there is now practically a statistical certainty that there will have to be some refunds, and the previous experience of X or some similar shipbuilder is likely to provide a fairly sound guide as to the percentage of the total potential refunds which will have to be made. In other words, the situation becomes more like a fixed liability which is simply uncertain in amount, rather than a truly contingent liability. Therefore if, as is often the case, the amount can be ascertained with reasonable accuracy, a charge against current income should be made, with a credit to an estimated liability account. Keep an eye out for cases of this kind in the following materials.

PIERCE ESTATES, INC. v. COMMISSIONER, 195 F.2d 475 (3d Cir. 1952). The taxpayer issued 30 year notes, in the face value of $150,000, which provided for interest of 6% per year, but payable only if and to the extent that the taxpayer had net income for the year, before the deduction of such interest. If the net income of the taxpayer was insufficient in any year to pay the entire interest, any excess of net income over current interest in a later year was to be applied to make up the deficiency. After being unable to pay the full interest on the notes for a number of years, in 1946 the taxpayer earned sufficient net income to pay both current interest and a substantial part of the deficiency from the prior years. The Commissioner denied the taxpayer's right to deduct the entire interest paid in 1946 on the ground that the excess over current interest had accrued in prior years. *Held*, for the taxpayer. "In the case of a taxpayer on the accrual basis of accounting an item of expense is to be regarded as incurred, and hence deductible as accrued, only in the year when the taxpayer's liability to pay it becomes definite and absolute, whether or not it is presently paid or payable. On the other hand if the liability to pay the item of expense is wholly contingent upon the happening of a subsequent event the item cannot be regarded as incurred or deductible as accrued until the year in which by the occurrence of the event the contingent liability becomes an absolute one. Because interest is compensation for the use or forbearance of money it ordinarily accrues as an item of expense from day to day even though its payment may be deferred until a later date. But this is not true if the payment is not merely deferred but the obligation to pay at all is wholly contingent upon the happening of the later event as, for example, the subsequent earning of profits. In the latter case, the interest may not be regarded as an accrued expense until the year in which, by the earning of the profits, the contingency is satisfied and the obligation to pay becomes fixed and absolute."

WATKINS v. ILLINOIS CENT. R. CO., 232 F. 691 (6th Cir. 1916). The defendant-vendors sold the capital stock of the Tennessee Railroad to the plaintiff-purchasers under an agreement which provided that "all income and all accrued liabilities . . . [prior to January 1, 1913] shall be borne by and belong to the vendors, . . . while all income and liabilities accruing . . . after the said date . . . shall be borne by and belong to the purchaser". A tariff of the railroad provided that a shipper who shipped raw material via the railroad into certain named cities would be entitled to a refund of a portion of the freight paid on such shipments if he thereafter presented satisfactory evidence that he had shipped out the manufactured products over the Tennessee's lines. During the early months of 1913, a shipper presented the required evidence and received refunds against the freight he had paid on inbound shipments of raw materials prior to January 1, 1913. The plaintiffs claimed that the defendants should bear this expense.

Held, for the plaintiffs. "The vendors insist that the liability cannot properly be called 'accrued,' so long as it remains contingent, and that since, on January 1st, the duty of the Tennessee Railroad to make refund was contingent upon the action of the shipper in thereafter manufacturing the logs in a different form and shipping the product out over this railroad, it is a perversion of the contract to charge this liability upon the vendors. We cannot think the word 'accrued' or the phrase 'accrued liability' has any such fixed and established, hard and fast meaning that the question is settled as soon as the statement is made. Some of the dictionary definitions of 'accrued' are ample to cover such a liability as this; the parties did not say 'matured,' or 'fixed and definite,' or use other unambiguous language. They selected a word which may be applied in more than one way to the circumstances that later arose; but they are presumed to have intended its use in a particular sense, and that intent is to be determined from all parts of the contract and from the situation existing when it was made. . . .

"Considering all parts of the contract and the existing course of business, we think the natural inference is that this liability is to be charged against the operations of 1912. The vendors were reserving for themselves the 1912 income; that is, they were appropriating this very . . . [original freight charge] which it later developed could not be collected to the [full] extent . . . if it was unpaid, or to that extent must be refunded if it had been paid. This refund was not charged upon or in reduction of the outbound freight rate accruing in 1913. It was, in effect, a correction of the erroneous inbound charge made in 1912. . . . Adopting the parties' broad idea of drawing the line of January 1st between what the vendors transferred and what they kept, we think this item belonged on the 1912 side of the line, and that the language does not clearly show their intent to put it on the other side. . . .

"Another consideration leading to the same conclusion is that according to the course of business from month to month the refunds which might later become owing on account of these inbound shipments, were entered upon the books of the Tennessee Railroad under an account titled 'Freight Claims—Suspense' and charged against 'Freight Earnings.' This seems to be a declaration that the liability was expected to develop into something which must be paid, and it apparently implies (although the bookkeeping is not fully disclosed) that the amount of the suspense claims was cut out of the 1912 net operating revenue shown by the books. Certainly it indicates a recognition by the parties that these refund claims constituted a liability which might arise on account of the transactions before January 1st."

L. P. LARSON, JR., CO. v. WILLIAM WRIGLEY, JR., CO., 20 F.2d 830 (7th Cir. 1927). [The facts and another portion of the opinion in this case appear at pages 267–269, supra.]

"Contingent Liability for Unredeemed United Profit-Sharing Coupons

"On this item the master charged against 'Doublemint' gross profits $98,519.06, which the District Court increased by $64,715.60. With each 5-cent package of gum there was enclosed a profit-sharing coupon good for one-fifth of a cent, and also coupons of larger denomination with cartons of gum packages. The coupons were exchangeable either for cash or merchandise, and unlimited as to time of presentation. Many millions were put out each year. Their redeemability in articles of merchandise of various kinds was an incentive for saving them until sufficient quantities accumulated to effect a desirable exchange. Of course, many became lost and will never be redeemed. As to those actually redeemed, no question arises. The dispute comes respecting those not redeemed, which continue to be a potential liability of Wrigley, since Wrigley must pay the profit-sharing company on the basis of $3 for each 1,000 of one-fifth cent coupons presented. Evidence was offered of the experience of others who had for many years given out such coupons with their merchandise. There was evidence of very substantial redemptions for many years after their issuance. It appears that the government, in the computation of profits, allowed Wrigley 60 per cent. of the face value of the coupons issued in each year as fairly representing this liability. The master's allowance was based on a 33⅓ per cent. of such redemption, which the District Judge raised by 5 per cent. From a careful review of the situation, we are satisfied that the percentage of redemption allowed by the court is still too low, and ought to be somewhat further increased. In our judgment an additional 6⅔ per cent. over and above the further allowance by the District Court, making in all 45 per cent. probably would not overestimate Wrigley's ultimate liability upon the unredeemed coupons, and we are of opinion that this charge against 'Doublemint' gross profits should be increased accordingly."

WARREN CO. v. COMMISSIONER, 135 F.2d 679 (5th Cir. 1943). The Undistributed Profits Tax applicable to the years 1937 and 1938 imposed a tax on the net income of a corporation not distributed as dividends except to the extent that dividends were prohibited by law or by contract. During the years in question the taxpayer had outstanding an issue of bonds under an indenture which provided that no dividends could be paid unless the taxpayer's current assets remained equal to at least twice the amount of its current liabilities. The taxpayer was in the business of selling household merchandise at retail. It normally received only a portion of the purchase price at the time of the delivery to the customer, taking the remaining balance in the form of a note payable in installments. The taxpayer's practice was to sell these notes to a finance company, under an agreement which required the taxpayer, in the event of default by the maker, to repurchase the notes at the price paid by the finance company less any collections obtained by it. The taxpayer had net income during the years in question but it did not pay any dividends, and the Commissioner asserted a deficiency under the Undistributed Profits Tax. The taxpayer contended that its contingent liability to repurchase the notes from the finance company in the event of default by the maker constituted a "current liability", in which event the prohibition against payment of dividends in the bond indenture was in operation. *Held*, for the Commissioner. "We are unable to conclude that the so-called contingent liabilities can be, or were intended to be, classified as current liabilities under the [bond issue]. . . . The phrase 'current liability' carries with it the idea of a liability that is presently enforceable. The phrase 'contingent liability' connotes a liability that may or may not accrue. 'Contingent' is the antithesis of 'current'."

SIBLEY, CIRCUIT JUDGE (dissenting). ". . . A liability, in the vocabulary of accounting, is anything which you will or may have to pay. If you will certainly have to pay it, it is an absolute liability. If you may or may not have to pay it, it is contingent. Thus as respects the quality of certainty, all liabilities are divided into absolute and contingent liabilities. From another standpoint, all liabilities are divided into 'current' and 'fixed' liabilities. Current means literally 'running', 'flowing'. Current liabilities are those which are in the run or flow of the business, changing as business is done. Fixed liabilities are those which do not so change. Bonds and plant mortgages are fixed liabilities. All others, arising out of the business done, are current liabilities. . . .

"That a liability is contingent has no bearing on whether it is current or not. The classification as current has nothing to do with the classification as contingent. The liability before loss on every insurance policy is a contingent liability but it is a current liability. The guaranty of a friend's conduct or account outside of the course of your business would be a contingent liability, but if running over a long period it might be a fixed rather than a current liability. The Warren Company had no fixed liability except these bonds. All its other liabilities, whether absolute or contingent, were current liabilities, by definition and in fact."

STATEMENT OF FINANCIAL ACCOUNTING STANDARDS NO. 5 *

ACCOUNTING FOR CONTINGENCIES

Financial Accounting Standards Board, 1975.

INTRODUCTION

1. For the purpose of this Statement, a contingency is defined as an existing condition, situation, or set of circumstances involving uncertainty as to possible gain (hereinafter a "gain contingency") or loss [1] (hereinafter a "loss contingency") to an enterprise that will ultimately be resolved when one or more future events occur or fail to occur. Resolution of the uncertainty may confirm the acquisition of an asset or the reduction of a liability or the loss or impairment of an asset or the incurrence of a liability.

2. Not all uncertainties inherent in the accounting process give rise to contingencies as that term is used in this Statement. Estimates are required in financial statements for many on-going and recurring activities of an enterprise. The mere fact that an estimate is involved does not of itself constitute the type of uncertainty referred to in the definition in paragraph 1. For example, the fact that estimates are used to allocate the known cost of a depreciable asset over the period of use by an enterprise does not make depreciation a contingency; the eventual expiration of the utility of the asset is not uncertain. Thus, depreciation of assets is not a contingency as defined in paragraph 1, nor are such matters as recurring repairs, maintenance, and overhauls, which interrelate with depreciation. Also, amounts owed for services received, such as advertising and utilities, are not contingencies even though the accrued amounts may have been estimated; there is nothing uncertain about the fact that those obligations have been incurred.

3. When a loss contingency exists, the likelihood that the future event or events will confirm the loss or impairment of an asset or the incurrence of a liability can range from probable to remote. This Statement uses the terms *probable, reasonably possible*, and *remote* to identify three areas within that range, as follows:

(a) *Probable.* The future event or events are likely to occur.

(b) *Reasonably possible.* The chance of the future event or events occurring is more than remote but less than likely.

(c) *Remote.* The chance of the future event or events occurring is slight.

4. Examples of loss contingencies include:

(a) Collectibility of receivables.

(b) Obligations related to product warranties and product defects.

---

[1] The term *loss* is used for convenience to include many charges against income that are commonly referred to as *expenses* and others that are commonly referred to as *losses*.

(c) Risk of loss or damage of enterprise property by fire, explosion, or other hazards.

(d) Threat of expropriation of assets.

(e) Pending or threatened litigation.

(f) Actual or possible claims and assessments.

*   *   *

5. Some enterprises now accrue estimated losses from some types of contingencies by a charge to income prior to the occurrence of the event or events that are expected to resolve the uncertainties while, under similar circumstances, other enterprises account for those losses only when the confirming event or events have occurred.

6. This Statement establishes standards of financial accounting and reporting for loss contingencies (see paragraphs 8–16) and carries forward without reconsideration the conclusions of Accounting Research Bulletin (ARB) No. 50, "Contingencies," with respect to gain contingencies (see paragraph 17) . . . . .

STANDARDS OF FINANCIAL ACCOUNTING AND REPORTING

Accrual of Loss Contingencies

8. An estimated loss from a loss contingency (as defined in paragraph 1) shall be accrued by a charge to income if *both* of the following conditions are met:

    (a) Information available prior to issuance of the financial statements indicates that it is probable that an asset had been impaired or a liability had been incurred at the date of the financial statements.[4] It is implicit in this condition that it must be probable that one or more future events will occur confirming the fact of the loss.

    (b) The amount of loss can be reasonably estimated.

Disclosure of Loss Contingencies

9. Disclosure of the nature of an accrual made pursuant to the provisions of paragraph 8, and in some circumstances the amount accrued, may be necessary for the financial statements not to be misleading.

10. If no accrual is made for a loss contingency because one or both of the conditions in paragraph 8 are not met, or if an exposure to loss exists in excess of the amount accrued pursuant to the provisions of paragraph 8, disclosure of the contingency shall be made when there is at least a reasonable possibility that a loss or an additional loss may have been incurred.[6] The disclosure shall indicate the nature of the

---

4. *Date of the financial statements* means the end of the most recent accounting period for which financial statements are being presented.

6. For example, disclosure shall be made of any loss contingency that meets the condition in paragraph 8(a) but that is not accrued because the amount of loss cannot be reasonably estimated (paragraph 8(b)). Disclosure is also required of some loss contingencies that do not meet the condition in paragraph 8(a)—namely, those contingencies for which there is a *reasonable possibility* that a loss may have been incurred even though information may not indicate that it is *probable* that an asset had been impaired or a liability had been incurred at the date of the financial statements.

contingency and shall give an estimate of the possible loss or range of loss or state that such an estimate cannot be made. Disclosure is not required of a loss contingency involving an unasserted claim or assessment when there has been no manifestation by a potential claimant of an awareness of a possible claim or assessment unless it is considered probable that a claim will be asserted and there is a reasonable possibility that the outcome will be unfavorable.

11. After the date of an enterprise's financial statements but before those financial statements are issued, information may become available indicating that an asset was impaired or a liability was incurred after the date of the financial statements or that there is at least a reasonable possibility that an asset was impaired or a liability was incurred after that date. The information may relate to a loss contingency that existed at the date of the financial statements, e. g., an asset that was not insured at the date of the financial statements. On the other hand, the information may relate to a loss contingency that did not exist at the date of the financial statements, e. g., threat of expropriation of assets after the date of the financial statements or the filing for bankruptcy by an enterprise whose debt was guaranteed after the date of the financial statements. In none of the cases cited in this paragraph was an asset impaired or a liability incurred at the date of the financial statements, and the condition for accrual in paragraph 8(a) is, therefore, not met. Disclosure of those kinds of losses or loss contingencies may be necessary, however, to keep the financial statements from being misleading. If disclosure is deemed necessary, the financial statements shall indicate the nature of the loss or loss contingency and give an estimate of the amount or range of loss or possible loss or state that such an estimate cannot be made. Occasionally, in the case of a loss arising after the date of the financial statements where the amount of asset impairment or liability incurrence can be reasonably estimated, disclosure may best be made by supplementing the historical financial statements with pro forma financial data giving effect to the loss as if it had occurred at the date of the financial statements. It may be desirable to present pro forma statements, usually a balance sheet only, in columnar form on the face of the historical financial statements.

* * *

General or Unspecified Business Risks

14. Some enterprises have in the past accrued so-called "reserves for general contingencies." General or unspecified business risks do not meet the conditions for accrual in paragraph 8, and no accrual for loss shall be made. No disclosure about them is required by this Statement.

Appropriation of Retained Earnings

15. Some enterprises have classified a portion of retained earnings as "appropriated" for loss contingencies. In some cases, the appropriation has been shown outside the stockholders' equity section of the balance sheet. Appropriation of retained earnings is not prohibited by this Statement provided that it is shown within the stockholders' equity section of the balance sheet and is clearly identified as an appropriation of retained earnings. Costs or losses shall not be

charged to an appropriation of retained earnings, and no part of the appropriation shall be transferred to income.

* * *

Gain Contingencies

17.   The Board has not reconsidered ARB No. 50 with respect to gain contingencies.   Accordingly, the following provisions of paragraphs 3 and 5 of that Bulletin shall continue in effect:

    (a)   Contingencies that might result in gains usually are not reflected in the accounts since to do so might be to recognize revenue prior to its realization.

    (b)   Adequate disclosure shall be made of contingencies that might result in gains, but care shall be exercised to avoid misleading implications as to the likelihood of realization.

* * *

APPENDIX A

EXAMPLES OF APPLICATION OF THIS STATEMENT

21.   This Appendix contains examples of application of the conditions for accrual of loss contingencies in paragraph 8 and of the disclosure requirements in paragraphs 9–11.   Some examples have been included in response to questions raised in letters of comment on the Exposure Draft.   It should be recognized that no set of examples can encompass all possible contingencies or circumstances.   Accordingly, accrual and disclosure of loss contingencies should be based on an evaluation of the facts in each particular case.

Collectibility of Receivables

22.   The assets of an enterprise may include receivables that arose from credit sales, loans, or other transactions.   The conditions under which receivables exist usually involve some degree of uncertainty about their collectibility, in which case a contingency exists as defined in paragraph 1.   Losses from uncollectible receivables shall be accrued when both conditions in paragraph 8 are met.   Those conditions may be considered in relation to individual receivables or in relation to groups of similar types of receivables.   If the conditions are met, accrual shall be made even though the particular receivables that are uncollectible may not be identifiable.

23.   If, based on available information, it is probable that the enterprise will be unable to collect all amounts due and, therefore, that at the date of its financial statements the net realizable value of the receivables through collection in the ordinary course of business is less than the total amount receivable, the condition in paragraph 8(a) is met because it is probable that an asset has been impaired.   Whether the amount of loss can be reasonably estimated (the condition in paragraph 8(b)) will normally depend on, among other things, the experience of the enterprise, information about the ability of individual debtors to pay, and appraisal of the receivables in light of the current economic environment.   In the case of an enterprise that has no experience of its own, reference to the experience of other enterprises in the same business may be appropriate.   Inability to make a reasonable

estimate of the amount of loss from uncollectible receivables (i. e., failure to satisfy the condition in paragraph 8(b)) precludes accrual and may, if there is significant uncertainty as to collection, suggest that the installment method, the cost recovery method, or some other method of revenue recognition be used (see paragraph 12 of APB Opinion No. 10, "Omnibus Opinion—1966"); in addition, the disclosures called for by paragraph 10 of this Statement should be made.

Obligations Related to Product Warranties and Product Defects

24. A warranty is an obligation incurred in connection with the sale of goods or services that may require further performance by the seller after the sale has taken place. Because of the uncertainty surrounding claims that may be made under warranties, warranty obligations fall within the definition of a contingency in paragraph 1. Losses from warranty obligations shall be accrued when the conditions in paragraph 8 are met. Those conditions may be considered in relation to individual sales made with warranties or in relation to groups of similar types of sales made with warranties. If the conditions are met, accrual shall be made even though the particular parties that will make claims under warranties may not be identifiable.

25. If, based on available information, it is probable that customers will make claims under warranties relating to goods or services that have been sold, the condition in paragraph 8(a) is met at the date of an enterprise's financial statements because it is probable that a liability has been incurred. Satisfaction of the condition in paragraph 8(b) will normally depend on the experience of an enterprise or other information. In the case of an enterprise that has no experience of its own, reference to the experience of other enterprises in the same business may be appropriate. Inability to make a reasonable estimate of the amount of a warranty obligation at the time of sale because of significant uncertainty about possible claims (i. e., failure to satisfy the condition in paragraph 8(b)) precludes accrual and, if the range of possible loss is wide, may raise a question about whether a sale should be recorded prior to expiration of the warranty period or until sufficient experience has been gained to permit a reasonable estimate of the obligation; in addition, the disclosures called for by paragraph 10 of this Statement should be made.

26. Obligations other than warranties may arise with respect to products or services that have been sold, for example, claims resulting from injury or damage caused by product defects. If it is probable that claims will arise with respect to products or services that have been sold, accrual for losses may be appropriate. The condition in paragraph 8(a) would be met, for instance, with respect to a drug product or toys that have been sold if a health or safety hazard related to those products is discovered and as a result it is considered probable that liabilities have been incurred. The condition in paragraph 8(b) would be met if experience or other information enables the enterprise to make a reasonable estimate of the loss with respect to the drug product or the toys.

Risk of Loss or Damage of Enterprise Property

27. At the date of an enterprise's financial statements, it may not be insured against risk of future loss or damage to its property by fire,

explosion, or other hazards. The absence of insurance against losses from risks of those types constitutes an existing condition involving uncertainty about the amount and timing of any losses that may occur, in which case a contingency exists as defined in paragraph 1. . . .

28.   The absence of insurance does not mean that an asset has been impaired or a liability has been incurred at the date of an enterprise's financial statements.   Fires, explosions, and other similar events that may cause loss or damage of an enterprise's property are random in their occurrence.   With respect to events of that type, the condition for accrual in paragraph 8(a) is not satisfied prior to the occurrence of the event because until that time there is no diminution in the value of the property.   There is no relationship of those events to the activities of the enterprise prior to their occurrence, and no asset is impaired prior to their occurrence.   Further, unlike an insurance company, which has a contractual obligation under policies in force to reimburse insureds for losses, an enterprise can have no such obligation to itself and, hence, no liability.

Risk of Loss from Future Injury to Others, Damage to the Property of Others, and Business Interruption

29.   An enterprise may choose not to purchase insurance against risk of loss that may result from injury to others, damage to the property of others, or interruption of its business operations.   Exposure to risks of those types constitutes an existing condition involving uncertainty about the amount and timing of any losses that may occur, in which case a contingency exists as defined in paragraph 1.

30.   Mere exposure to risks of those types, however, does not mean that an asset has been impaired or a liability has been incurred.   The condition for accrual in paragraph 8(a) is not met with respect to loss that may result from injury to others, damage to the property of others, or business interruption that may occur after the date of an enterprise's financial statements.   Losses of those types do not relate to the current or a prior period but rather to the *future* period in which they occur.   Thus, for example, an enterprise with a fleet of vehicles should not accrue for injury to others or damage to the property of others that may be caused by those vehicles in the future even if the amount of those losses may be reasonably estimable.   On the other hand, the conditions in paragraph 8 would be met with respect to uninsured losses resulting from injury to others or damage to the property of others that took place prior to the date of the financial statements, even though the enterprise may not become aware of those matters until after that date, if the experience of the enterprise or other information enables it to make a reasonable estimate of the loss that was incurred prior to the date of its financial statements.

Write-Down of Operating Assets

31.   In some cases, the carrying amount of an operating asset not intended for disposal may exceed the amount expected to be recoverable through future use of that asset even though there has been no physical loss or damage of the asset or threat of such loss or damage.   For example, changed economic conditions may have made recovery of the carrying amount of a productive facility doubtful.   The question of whether, in those cases, it is appropriate to write down the

carrying amount of the asset to an amount expected to be recoverable through future operations is not covered by this Statement.

Threat of Expropriation

32.   The threat of expropriation of assets is a contingency within the definition of paragraph 1 because of the uncertainty about its outcome and effect. If information indicates that expropriation is imminent and compensation will be less than the carrying amount of the assets, the condition for accrual in paragraph 8(a) is met. Imminence may be indicated, for example, by public or private declarations of intent by a government to expropriate assets of the enterprise or actual expropriation of assets of other enterprises. Paragraph 8(b) requires that accrual be made only if the amount of loss can be reasonably estimated. If the conditions for accrual are not met, the disclosures specified in paragraph 10 would be made when there is at least a reasonable possibility that an asset has been impaired.

Litigation, Claims, and Assessments

33.   The following factors, among others, must be considered in determining whether accrual and/or disclosure is required with respect to pending or threatened litigation and actual or possible claims and assessments:

(a) The period in which the underlying cause (i. e., the cause for action) of the pending or threatened litigation or of the actual or possible claim or assessment occurred.

(b) The degree of probability of an unfavorable outcome.

(c) The ability to make a reasonable estimate of the amount of loss.

34.   As a condition for accrual of a loss contingency, paragraph 8(a) requires that information available prior to the issuance of financial statements indicate that it is probable that an asset had been impaired or a liability had been incurred at the date of the financial statements. Accordingly, accrual would clearly be inappropriate for litigation, claims, or assessments whose underlying cause is an event or condition occurring after the date of financial statements but before those financial statements are issued, for example, a suit for damages alleged to have been suffered as a result of an accident that occurred after the date of the financial statements. Disclosure may be required, however, by paragraph 11.

35.   On the other hand, accrual may be appropriate for litigation, claims, or assessments whose underlying cause is an event occurring on or before the date of an enterprise's financial statements even if the enterprise does not become aware of the existence or possibility of the lawsuit, claim, or assessment until after the date of the financial statements. If those financial statements have not been issued, accrual of a loss related to the litigation, claim, or assessment would be required if the probability of loss is such that the condition in paragraph 8(a) is met and the amount of loss can be reasonably estimated.

36.   If the underlying cause of the litigation, claim, or assessment is an event occurring before the date of an enterprise's financial statements, the probability of an outcome unfavorable to the enterprise must be assessed to determine whether the condition in paragraph 8

(a) is met. Among the factors that should be considered are the nature of the litigation, claim, or assessment, the progress of the case (including progress after the date of the financial statements but before those statements are issued), the opinions or views of legal counsel and other advisers, the experience of the enterprise in similar cases, the experience of other enterprises, and any decision of the enterprise's management as to how the enterprise intends to respond to the lawsuit, claim, or assessment (for example, a decision to contest the case vigorously or a decision to seek an out-of-court settlement). The fact that legal counsel is unable to express an opinion that the outcome will be favorable to the enterprise should not necessarily be interpreted to mean that the condition for accrual of a loss in paragraph 8(a) is met.

37. The filing of a suit or formal assertion of a claim or assessment does not automatically indicate that accrual of a loss may be appropriate. The degree of probability of an unfavorable outcome must be assessed. The condition for accrual in paragraph 8(a) would be met if an unfavorable outcome is determined to be probable. If an unfavorable outcome is determined to be reasonably possible but not probable, or if the amount of loss cannot be reasonably estimated, accrual would be inappropriate, but disclosure would be required by paragraph 10 of this Statement.

38. With respect to unasserted claims and assessments, an enterprise must determine the degree of probability that a suit may be filed or a claim or assessment may be asserted and the possibility of an unfavorable outcome. For example, a catastrophe, accident, or other similar physical occurrence predictably engenders claims for redress, and in such circumstances their assertion may be probable; similarly, an investigation of an enterprise by a governmental agency, if enforcement proceedings have been or are likely to be instituted, is often followed by private claims for redress, and the probability of their assertion and the possibility of loss should be considered in each case. By way of further example, an enterprise may believe there is a possibility that it has infringed on another enterprise's patent rights, but the enterprise owning the patent rights has not indicated an intention to take any action and has not even indicated an awareness of the possible infringement. In that case, a judgment must first be made as to whether the assertion of a claim is probable. If the judgment is that assertion is not probable, no accrual or disclosure would be required. On the other hand, if the judgment is that assertion is probable, then a second judgment must be made as to the degree of probability of an unfavorable outcome. If an unfavorable outcome is probable and the amount of loss can be reasonably estimated, accrual of a loss is required by paragraph 8. If an unfavorable outcome is probable but the amount of loss cannot be reasonably estimated, accrual would not be appropriate, but disclosure would be required by paragraph 10. If an unfavorable outcome is reasonably possible but not probable, disclosure would be required by paragraph 10.

39. As a condition for accrual of a loss contingency, paragraph 8(b) requires that the amount of loss can be reasonably estimated. In some cases, it may be determined that a loss was incurred because of unfavorable outcome of the litigation, claim, or assessment is probable (thus satisfying the condition in paragraph 8(a)), but the range of possible loss is wide. For example, an enterprise may be litigating an

income tax matter. In preparation for the trial, it may determine that, based on recent decisions involving one aspect of the litigation, it is probable that it will have to pay additional taxes of $2 million. Another aspect of the litigation may, however, be open to considerable interpretation, and depending on the interpretation by the court the enterprise may have to pay taxes of $8 million over and above the $2 million. In that case, paragraph 8 requires accrual of the $2 million if that is considered a reasonable estimate of the loss. Paragraph 10 requires disclosure of the additional exposure to loss if there is a reasonable possibility that additional taxes will be paid. Depending on the circumstances, paragraph 9 may require disclosure of the $2 million that was accrued. . . .

ABA STATEMENT OF POLICY
REGARDING LAWYERS' RESPONSES
TO AUDITORS' REQUESTS FOR INFORMATION *
American Bar Association, 1975. 31 Bus.Law. 1709.

Preamble

The public interest in protecting the confidentiality of lawyer-client communications is fundamental. The American legal, political and economic systems depend heavily upon voluntary compliance with the law and upon ready access to a respected body of professionals able to interpret and advise on the law. The expanding complexity of our laws and governmental regulations increases the need for prompt, specific and unhampered lawyer-client communication. The benefits of such communication and early consultation underlie the strict statutory and ethical obligations of the lawyer to preserve the confidences and secrets of the client, as well as the long-recognized testimonial privilege for lawyer-client communication.

Both the Code of Professional Responsibility and the cases applying the evidentiary privilege recognize that the privilege against disclosure can be knowingly and voluntarily waived by the client. It is equally clear that disclosure to a third party may result in loss of the "confidentiality" essential to maintain the privilege. Disclosure to a third party of the lawyer-client communication on a particular subject may also destroy the privilege as to other communications on that subject. Thus, the mere disclosure by the lawyer to the outside auditor, with due client consent, of the substance of communications between the lawyer and client may significantly impair the client's ability in other contexts to maintain the confidentiality of such communications.

* Copyright © 1975 by the American Bar Association. The Board of Governors of the American Bar Association on December 8, 1975, approved this ABA Statement of Policy on this subject. (The Statement had been approved in principle by the Section Council in Montreal in August 1975 and, as revised, in early December 1975). A Statement on Auditing Standards, which coordinates with the approach set forth in the revised ABA Statement, was approved on January 7, 1976, by the AICPA Auditing Standards Executive Committee.

Under the circumstances a policy of audit procedure which requires clients to give consent and authorize lawyers to respond to general inquiries and disclose information to auditors concerning matters which have been communicated in confidence is essentially destructive of free and open communication and early consultation between lawyer and client. The institution of such a policy would inevitably discourage management from discussing potential legal problems with counsel for fear that such discussion might become public and precipitate a loss to or possible liability of the business enterprise and its stockholders that might otherwise never materialize.

It is also recognized that our legal, political and economic systems depend to an important extent on public confidence in published financial statements. To meet this need the accounting profession must adopt and adhere to standards and procedures that will command confidence in the auditing process. It is not, however, believed necessary, or sound public policy, to intrude upon the confidentiality of the lawyer-client relationship in order to command such confidence. On the contrary, the objective of fair disclosure in financial statements is more likely to be better served by maintaining the integrity of the confidential relationship between lawyer and client, thereby strengthening corporate management's confidence in counsel and encouraging its readiness to seek advice of counsel and to act in accordance with counsel's advice.

Consistent with the foregoing public policy considerations, it is believed appropriate to distinguish between, on the one hand, litigation which is pending or which a third party has manifested to the client a present intention to commence and, on the other hand, other contingencies of a legal nature or having legal aspects. As regards the former category, unquestionably the lawyer representing the client in a litigation matter may be the best source for a description of the claim or claims asserted, the client's position (e. g. denial, contest, etc.), and the client's possible exposure in the litigation (to the extent the lawyer is in a position to do so). As to the latter category, it is submitted that, for the reasons set forth above, it is not in the public interest for the lawyer to be required to respond to general inquiries from auditors concerning possible claims.

It is recognized that the disclosure requirements for enterprises subject to the reporting requirements of the Federal securities laws are a major concern of managements and counsel, as well as auditors. It it submitted that compliance therewith is best assured when clients are afforded maximum encouragement, by protecting lawyer-client confidentiality, freely to consult counsel. Likewise, lawyers must be keenly conscious of the importance of their clients being competently advised in these matters.

Statement of Policy

NOW, THEREFORE, BE IT RESOLVED that it is desirable and in the public interest that this Association adopt the following Statement of Policy regarding the appropriate scope of the lawyer's response to the auditor's request, made by the client at the request of the auditor, for information concerning matters referred to the lawyer during the course of his representation of the client:

(1) *Client Consent to Response.* The lawyer may properly respond to the auditor's requests for information concerning loss contingencies . . . to the extent hereinafter set forth, subject to the following:

(a) Assuming that the client's initial letter requesting the lawyer to provide information to the auditor is signed by an agent of the client having apparent authority to make such a request, the lawyer may provide to the auditor information requested, without further consent, unless such information discloses a confidence or a secret or requires an evaluation of a claim.

(b) In the normal case, the initial request letter does not provide the necessary consent to the disclosure of a confidence or secret or to the evaluation of a claim since that consent may only be given after full disclosure to the client of the legal consequences of such action.

(c) Lawyers should bear in mind, in evaluating claims, that an adverse party may assert that any evaluation of potential liability is an admission.

(d) In securing the client's consent to the disclosure of confidences or secrets, or the evaluation of claims, the lawyer may wish to have a draft of his letter reviewed and approved by the client before releasing it to the auditor; in such cases, additional explanation would in all probability be necessary so that the legal consequences of the consent are fully disclosed to the client.

(2) *Limitation on Scope of Response.* It is appropriate for the lawyer to set forth in his response, by way of limitation, the scope of his engagement by the client. It is also appropriate for the lawyer to indicate the date as of which information is furnished and to disclaim any undertaking to advise the auditor of changes which may thereafter be brought to the lawyer's attention. *Unless the lawyer's response indicates otherwise, (a) it is properly limited to matters which have been given substantive attention by the lawyer in the form of legal consultation and, where appropriate, legal representation since the beginning of the period or periods being reported upon, and (b) if a law firm or a law department, the auditor may assume that the firm or department has endeavored, to the extent believed necessary by the firm or department, to determine from lawyers currently in the firm or department who have performed services for the client since the beginning of the fiscal period under audit whether such services involved substantive attention in the form of legal consultation concerning those loss contingencies referred to in Paragraph 5(a) below but, beyond that, no review has been made of any of the client's transactions or other matters for the purpose of identifying loss contingencies to be described in the response.*

(3) *Response may be Limited to Material Items.* In response to an auditor's request for disclosure of loss contingencies of a client, it is appropriate for the lawyer's response to indicate that the response is limited to items which are considered individually or collectively material to the presentation of the client's financial statements.

(4) *Limited Responses.* Where the lawyer is limiting his response in accordance with this Statement of Policy, his response should so

indicate (see Paragraph 8). If in any other respect the lawyer is not undertaking to respond to or comment on particular aspects of the inquiry when responding to the auditor, he should consider advising the auditor that his response is limited, in order to avoid any inference that the lawyer has responded to all aspects; otherwise, he may be assuming a responsibility which he does not intend.

(5) *Loss Contingencies.* When properly requested by the client, it is appropriate for the lawyer to furnish to the auditor information concerning the following matters if the lawyer has been engaged by the client to represent or advise the client professionally with respect thereto and he has devoted substantive attention to them in the form of legal representation or consultation:

(a) *overtly threatened or pending litigation,* whether or not specified by the client;

(b) *a contractually assumed obligation* which the client has specifically identified and upon which the client has specifically requested, in the inquiry letter or a supplement thereto, comment to the auditor;

(c) *an unasserted possible claim or assessment* which the client has specifically identified and upon which the client has specifically requested, in the inquiry letter or a supplement thereto, comment to the auditor.

With respect to clause (a), overtly threatened litigation means that a potential claimant has manifested to the client an awareness of and present intention to assert a possible claim or assessment unless the likelihood of litigation (or of settlement when litigation would normally be avoided) is considered remote. With respect to clause (c), where there has been no manifestation by a potential claimant of an awareness of and present intention to assert a possible claim or assessment, consistent with the considerations and concerns outlined in the Preamble and Paragraph 1 hereof, the client should request the lawyer to furnish information to the auditor only if the client has determined that it is probable that a possible claim will be asserted, that there is a reasonable possibility that the outcome (assuming such assertion) will be unfavorable, and that the resulting liability would be material to the financial condition of the client. Examples of such situations might (depending in each case upon the particular circumstances) include the following: (i) a catastrophe, accident or other similar physical occurrence in which the client's involvement is open and notorious, or (ii) an investigation by a government agency where enforcement proceedings have been instituted or where the likelihood that they will not be instituted is remote, under circumstances where assertion of one or more private claims for redress would normally be expected, or (iii) a public disclosure by the client acknowledging (and thus focusing attention upon) the existence of one or more probable claims arising out of an event or circumstance. In assessing whether or not the assertion of a possible claim is probable, it is expected that the client would normally employ, by reason of the inherent uncertainties involved and insufficiency of available data, concepts parallel to those used by the lawyer (discussed below) in assessing whether or not an unfavorable outcome is probable; thus, assertion of a possible claim would be considered probable only when the prospects of its being asserted seem reasonably certain (i. e., supported by extrinsic evidence strong enough to establish a presumption that it will happen) and the prospects of non-assertion seem slight.

It would not be appropriate, however, for the lawyer to be requested to furnish information in response to an inquiry letter or supplement thereto if it appears that (a) the client has been required to specify unasserted possible claims without regard to the standard suggested in the preceding paragraph, or (b) the client has been required to specify all or substantially all unasserted possible claims as to which legal advice may have been obtained, since, in either case, such a request would be in substance a general inquiry and would be inconsistent with the intent of this Statement of Policy.

The information that lawyers may properly give to the auditor concerning the foregoing matters would include (to the extent appropriate) an identification of the proceedings or matter, the stage of proceedings, the claim(s) asserted, and the position taken by the client.

In view of the inherent uncertainties, the lawyer should normally refrain from expressing judgments as to outcome except in those relatively few clear cases where it appears to the lawyer that an unfavorable outcome is either "probable" or "remote;" for purposes of any such judgment it is appropriate to use the following meanings:

(i) *probable*—an unfavorable outcome for the client is probable if the prospects of the claimant not succeeding are judged to be extremely doubtful and the prospects for success by the client in its defense are judged to be slight.

(ii) *remote*—an unfavorable outcome is remote if the prospects for the client not succeeding in its defense are judged to be extremely doubtful and the prospects of success by the claimant are judged to be slight.

If, in the opinion of the lawyer, considerations within the province of his professional judgment bear on a particular loss contingency to the degree necessary to make an informed judgment, he may in appropriate circumstances communicate to the auditor his view that an unfavorable outcome is "probable" or "remote," applying the above meanings. No inference should be drawn, from the absence of such a judgment, that the client will not prevail.

The lawyer also may be asked to estimate, in dollar terms, the potential amount of loss or range of loss in the event that an unfavorable outcome is not viewed to be "remote." In such a case, the amount or range of potential loss will normally be as inherently impossible to ascertain, with any degree of certainty, as the outcome of the litigation. Therefore, it is appropriate for the lawyer to provide an estimate of the amount or range of potential loss (if the outcome should be unfavorable) only if he believes that the probability of inaccuracy of the estimate of the amount or range of potential loss is slight.

The considerations bearing upon the difficulty in estimating loss (or range of loss) where pending litigation is concerned are obviously even more compelling in the case of unasserted possible claims.

In most cases, the lawyer will not be able to provide any such estimate to the auditor.

As indicated in Paragraph 4 hereof, the auditor may assume that all loss contingencies specified by the client in the manner specified in clauses (b) and (c) above have received comment in the response, unless otherwise therein indicated. The lawyer should not be asked, nor need the lawyer undertake, to furnish information to the auditor concerning loss contingencies except as contemplated by this Paragraph 5.

(6) *Lawyer's Professional Responsibility.* Independent of the scope of his response to the auditor's request for information, the lawyer, depending upon the nature of the matters as to which he is engaged, may have as part of his professional responsibility to his client an obligation to advise the client concerning the need for or advisability of public disclosure of a wide range of events and circumstances. The lawyer has an obligation not knowingly to participate in any violation by the client of the disclosure requirements of the securities laws. The lawyer also may be required under the Code of Professional Responsibility to resign his engagement if his advice concerning disclosures is disregarded by the client. The auditor may properly assume that whenever, in the course of performing legal services for the client with respect to a matter recognized to involve an unasserted possible claim or assessment which may call for financial statement disclosure, the lawyer has formed a professional conclusion that the client must disclose or consider disclosure concerning such possible claim or assessment, the lawyer, as a matter of professional responsibility to the client, will so advise the client and will consult with the client concerning the question of such disclosure and the applicable requirements of FAS 5.

(7) *Limitation on Use of Response. Unless otherwise stated in the lawyer's response, it shall be solely for the auditor's information in connection with his audit of the financial condition of the client and is not to be quoted in whole or in part or otherwise referred to in any financial statements of the client or related documents, nor is it to be filed with any governmental agency or other person, without the lawyer's prior written consent. Notwithstanding such limitation, the response can properly be furnished to others in compliance with court process or when necessary in order to defend the auditor against a challenge of the audit by the client or a regulatory agency, provided that the lawyer is given written notice of the circumstances at least twenty days before the response is so to be furnished to others, or as long in advance as possible if the situation does not permit such period of notice.*

(8) *General.* This Statement of Policy, together with the accompanying Commentary (which is an integral part hereof), has been developed for the general guidance of the legal profession. In a particular case, the lawyer may elect to supplement or modify the approach hereby set forth. If desired, this Statement of Policy may be incorporated by reference in the lawyer's response . . ..

Consider the following examples, from recent financial statements, of current accruals of contingent expenses, as reflected in the accompanying notes, as well as cases involving simply disclosure of contingencies without any charge against current income:

THE LODGE & SHIPLEY COMPANY

Notes to Financial Statements

9. Loss contingencies

In accordance with Financial Accounting Standards Board Statement No. 5 issued in March 1975, the Company will be required in 1976 to change its method of accounting for obligations related to product warranties and product defects, and to restate its consolidated financial statements for prior years. Changes from previously reported amounts will result principally from the new requirement to accrue estimated costs of product warranties and product defects at the time of the product sale: previously, such costs were expensed when incurred. The Company estimates (1) that the approximate effects at December 31, 1975 will be to increase (decrease) current assets $187,000, current liabilities $389,000 and stockholders' equity ($202,000) and (2) that the effect on net income for 1975 and 1974 will be immaterial.

NATIONAL DISTILLERS AND CHEMICAL CORPORATION

Notes to Financial Statements

Note 3 Extraordinary Charge

In December 1975, a settlement agreement was submitted for approval to the Federal District Court in New York which provides for termination of a class action against the Company and others alleging violations of the Federal Securities Laws in connection with the 1973 exchange offer under which National shares owned by the class plaintiffs were exchanged for shares, owned by the Company, of the Company's subsidiary Almaden Vineyards, Inc. Under the settlement agreement National has paid $3,000,000 into a fund which, after deduction of fees and expenses approved by the Court, will be disbursed to eligible members of the class who submit and substantiate claims. No tax recoveries are anticipated with respect to the settlement.

If the settlement agreement is approved by the Court the cost to the Company, including legal expenses and after giving effect to recovery on insurance, would be $2,568,000, which has been provided in 1975 as an extraordinary charge. In December 1973, the Company credited to income an extraordinary gain of $25,868,000 as a result of the exchange offer.

Note 13 Contingencies

The Company has claims against others, and there are claims by others against it, in a variety of matters arising out of the conduct of the Company's business. Actions against the Company include a class action entitled Kors vs. National Distillers and Chemical Corporation, et al. pending in the Federal District Court in New York. In

December 1975, a settlement agreement was submitted for approval to the Court which provides for termination of this action (see Note 3). The Company's management has no reason to believe the settlement agreement will not be approved as submitted. However, if the proposed settlement is not approved, the ultimate liability, if any, which might arise in this action would not, in the opinion of the Company's management, have a materially adverse effect on the Company's financial position.

THE GOODYEAR TIRE & RUBBER COMPANY

Notes to Financial Statements

Contingent Liability and Related Subsequent Event

In November of 1974, Big O Tire Dealers, Inc. instituted a lawsuit alleging the infringement of a trademark by Goodyear's use of the term "Bigfoot" in connection with a line of tires, and seeking injunctive relief and actual and punitive damages. In September 1975, a jury awarded damages to Big O in the amount of $19.6 million and on February 13, 1976 the trial judge affirmed the jury verdict and granted injunctive relief.

Goodyear denies liability and will vigorously appeal the decision of the trial court. Accordingly, no provision for the contingent liability associated with this litigation has been made in the financial results for 1975.

THE LODGE & SHIPLEY COMPANY

Notes to Financial Statements

2. Litigation

The Company is defendant in a lawsuit seeking damages of $900,000 for alleged breach of warranty arising out of the sale of a product for approximately $52,000. Although the outcome of the lawsuit cannot presently be determined, the Company has filed a third party complaint for indemnification, an answer denying liability, and plans to defend the claim vigorously.

Auditor's Opinion

The Board of Directors and Stockholders,

The Lodge & Shipley Company

We have examined the accompanying consolidated balance sheet of The Lodge & Shipley Company at December 31, 1975 and the related consolidated statements of operations and retained earnings and changes in financial position for the year then ended. Our examination was made in accordance with generally accepted auditing standards, and accordingly included such tests of the accounting records and such other auditing procedures as we considered necessary in the circumstances. We have previously made a similar examination of the financial statements for the prior year.

As discussed in Note 2 to the consolidated financial statements, the Company is defendant in a lawsuit, the ultimate outcome of which cannot presently be determined.

In our opinion, the statements mentioned above present fairly the consolidated results of operations and changes in financial position of The Lodge & Shipley Company for the year ended December 31, 1975 and, subject to the effects, if any, on the financial statements of the ultimate resolution of the matter referred to in the preceding paragraph, the consolidated financial position at December 31, 1975 and 1974, and the consolidated results of operations and changes in financial position for the year ended December 31, 1974, in conformity with generally accepted accounting principles applied on a consistent basis during the period.

————

Sat. Evening Post

PROBLEM

X Corp. is the publisher of a magazine which until a few years ago was a rather placid periodical. Four years ago (year 1), in an effort to boost lagging sales, X adopted a new policy of featuring more exciting, even sensational articles. The following year (year 2), the magazine published an alleged exposé in which the coach of a major football team was accused of fixing a game. A year later (year 3), the coach brought suit for libel, claiming damages of $5,-000,000. X was advised by counsel that (1) there was a good chance X would be held liable, and (2) if so, the damages were most likely to run between $50,000 and $100,000, with an outside possibility that the amount would be much greater, perhaps even in seven figures. During X's most recent fiscal year (year 4), which ended a couple of months ago, the case was tried before a jury, which found against X and awarded general damages of $60,000 plus punitive damages of $3,000,000. The trial court reduced the total damages to $460,000. Pursuant to the advice of counsel, X appealed, primarily on the ground that it was error to award the plaintiff any punitive damages; but just last week the judgment of $460,000 was affirmed, and that amount was paid by X.

X's earnings for the past four years, without taking any account of this lawsuit, have been as follows:

Year 1	Year 2	Year 3	Year 4 (recently ended)
$375,000	$600,000	$700,000	$750,000

X's balance sheet at the close of year 4 (recently-ended) was as follows:

Cash	$ 800,000	A/P	$1,250,000
A/R	1,100,000	Note Pay.	600,000
Inventory	1,300,000	Stat. Cap.	4,000,000
Plant	5,800,000	Earn. Surp.	3,150,000
	$9,000,000		$9,000,000

X has faced libel suits from time to time in the past, but never one as large as this. In all of the prior actions X either defended successfully or settled for some modest amount, the largest being some $30,000 two years ago.

How, if at all, should the events relating to the coach's libel claim have been reflected in X's financial statements in each of the last four years? Consider, in addition to the foregoing material, FASB No. 16, including both Appendices A and C, pages 194–198, supra.

Would an appropriation of earned surplus ("retained earnings" in the modern accounting terminology) be useful in these circumstances? Consider the following:

c. APPROPRIATION OF RETAINED EARNINGS

The "appropriation" of retained earnings (earned surplus under the older terminology *) referred to in ¶ 15 of FASB No. 5 is simply a bookkeeping device for giving more publicity than a footnote alone would to a potential loss or expense not yet ripe for a charge against current income. Mechanically, this is accomplished by a debit to the Retained Earnings account in an amount equal to the estimated possible loss, and a credit to a new account variously referred to as *Appropriated* Retained Earnings, or *Segregated* Retained Earnings, (or, as we shall see shortly, a "Reserve"), which appears in the Stockholders' Equity section of the balance sheet, usually immediately adjacent to Retained Earnings.

Originally the notion seems to have been that such segregation would reduce the amount of retained earnings available to support the payment of dividends, and thereby serve to prevent a possible future deficit in retained earnings which could result if that account was exhausted by the payment of dividends and thereafter the po-

---

* Although the casebook generally used the older term "Earned Surplus" (as lawyers commonly do, probably because that is the one uniformly employed in the corporation statutes), it seems appropriate to shift to "Retained Earnings" in this section to conform to the modern accounting usage utilized in FASB No. 5.

tential loss or expense was in fact incurred. However, from the company's point of view it is hardly necessary to segregate a portion of retained earnings in order to restrict the payment of dividends, since whether to pay a dividend, and in what amount, is a matter within the discretion of the board of directors anyway. Conversely, the question of how large a dividend can lawfully be paid is not controlled by whether some otherwise available surplus has been segregated as an accounting matter; rather that rests upon a construction of the governing corporation statute, in the light of all the circumstances (including the existence of a possible future loss or expense). Moreover, today dividends are normally based upon current earnings; stockholders would not view a corporation's entire retained earnings as available for dividends as a practical matter, so segregation of a portion of the retained earnings would not have much impact upon the dividend expectations of the stockholders (and, anyway, a message about dividends is likely to be communicated to the stockholders more directly by way of the dividend action (or non-action) of the board of directors, presumably accompanied by some public announcement on the matter).

Accordingly, the usefulness of this segregation approach rests primarily upon whether it constitutes a more meaningful form of disclosure about pending contingencies than a footnote. In this connection, note that such segregation is not likely to be utilized in connection with a specific identifiable claim, at least if it is being resisted by the company, because the company's litigation or settlement position could be adversely affected by such public acknowledgment, as the ABA Statement of Policy, in ¶ 1(c), page 357, supra, warns may be true of any "evaluation" of a claim. Hence, such a segregation or appropriation of retained earnings is more likely to be used to identify general contingencies, as, for example, "Reserve for Foreign Business Risks", the caption of an appropriation of retained earnings (in the nice round sum of $5,000,000) which appears in one recent balance sheet.

The fact that such an appropriation or segregation is often termed a "Reserve" deserves some further comment. This kind of reserve created out of retained earnings is a very different animal from the type of estimated liability which used to be called a "Reserve" until the practice was discouraged by Accounting Terminology Bulletin No. 1, as described at pages 335–336, supra (which should be reviewed at this point). Those estimated liabilities arise in conjunction with accruing an expense (which is uncertain in amount) by a charge to a current expense account; and when the expense is actually paid subsequently, the charge is to the estimated liability account. A reserve which constitutes an appropriation of retained earnings, on the other hand, is of course created by a reduction of retained earnings, and no charge against current income is involved; moreover, as ¶ 15 of FASB No. 5 takes pains to emphasize, if and when the loss subsequently materializes it would not be charged to this reserve account but rather would be charged against current income at that time, thereby lowering net income for the period, and ultimately retained earnings (but this reduction in retained earnings would be offset by the restoration of the reserve, or appropriation of retained earnings, to the regular retained earnings account).

It is to this type of appropriation of retained earnings that Accounting Terminology Bulletin No. 1 suggests the word "Reserve" should be confined, and that is pretty much the present terminology posture. It might have been as well to abandon the use of "Reserve" even for that purpose; after all, a similar potential for confusion exists, since segregating a portion of retained earnings does not in and of itself "reserve" assets, just as is true of accrual of an expense, as discussed at page 335, supra. However, since segregation of retained earnings has only the function of reducing the apparent dividend—paying capacity, perhaps it can be viewed as conveying a kind of conservation-of-assets message which justifies the use of the term "Reserve".

2. ACCRUAL OF INCOME

PEOPLE v. SAN FRANCISCO SAVINGS UNION

Supreme Court of California, 1887.
72 Cal. 199, 13 P. 498.

SEARLS, C. This cause was submitted to the court below upon an agreed statement. Defendant had judgment, from which plaintiff appeals. The defendant is a banking corporation. . . .

During the six months commencing June 30, 1883, the surplus profits arising from the business of the corporation, including the interest arising from its capital stock and deposits, amounted to the sum of $280,092. In this amount of surplus profits, and as a part thereof, is included—*First*, the sum of $5,825 for interest which has accrued for the months of November and December, in the year 1883, upon the coupons of bonds of the United States held by the defendant, but which, by the terms of said coupons, is not payable until February 1, 1884; *second*, the sum of $23,917 for interest that has matured since thirtieth of June, 1883, but which has not been collected, upon a portion of the loans made by the defendant upon real-estate security. The value of the real estate held by the defendant as security for the said loans, and for each thereof, is more than double the amount of the respective loans and the matured interest thereon. . . .

The question in difference and point of controversy upon which the decision and judgment of the court is sought, is the following: "Is the defendant authorized by law to appropriate and pay, as a dividend to its stockholders and depositors on the profits arising from its business, any portion of the interest upon its loans or investments that may have matured or accrued, but which have not been actually collected and received in money?" What are the *surplus profits* arising from the business of the corporation? The word "profits" signifies an excess of the value of returns over the value of advances. The excess of receipts over expenditures; that is, net earnings. Connolly v. Davidson, 15 Minn. 519 (Gil. 428.) The receipts of a business deducting current expenses; it is equivalent to net receipts. Eyster v. Centennial Board of Finance, 94 U.S. 500, 24 L.Ed. 188. . . .

Under these definitions, it is not easy to comprehend how *profits, or surplus profits,* can consist of earnings never yet received. The term imports an excess of *receipts* over *expenditures,* and without *receipts* there cannot properly be said to be profits. Money earned as interest, however well secured, or certain to be eventually paid, cannot in fact be distributed as dividends to stockholders, and does not constitute *surplus profits* within the meaning of the statute. To hold the contrary would, we think, tend to open the door to a practice under which the assets of corporations would be liable to distribution as dividends upon no surer basis than the judgment of their directors as to the value of their bills receivable. Such is not and should not be the policy of the law. . . .

It follows that the judgment of the court below nonsuiting plaintiff should be reversed, and the cause remanded, with directions to the court below to enter judgment in favor of plaintiff as provided in the agreed statement contained in the record.

ELHARD v. ROTT

Supreme Court of North Dakota, 1917.
36 N.D. 221, 162 N.W. 302.

BRUCE, C. J. This is an action for the specific performance of a contract to sell bank stock. The defendant had agreed to sell the plaintiff the stock in question at its "book value" at the time of the purchase, and the only question which we need to consider is the meaning of the term "book value." In arriving at the book value of the stock, was it necessary to compute the accrued interest on the notes which were held by the bank, even though such notes were not due? And did the books include all of the books of the bank, or merely the ledger? In other words, should a note for $500 which drew 10 per cent. interest and was due six months from date be figured merely at its face value if only three months had run since the note was executed, or, in estimating its value, should the accrued interest for the three months be taken into consideration? The learned trial court held that in view of all the circumstances, the parties intended that in arriving at the book value of the stock such interest should be taken into consideration. We are satisfied that he was justified in this conclusion. We believe, indeed, that the term "book value" has an established meaning in so far as the capital stock of a banking corporation is concerned. It means value as predicated on the face value of the assets of the corporation after deducting its liabilities. . . .
The assets, of course, must appear upon the books of the company, and must be able to be estimated therefrom, but it does not follow

that the computation must have been made on such books and appear
on the ledger. The book value of stock is determined by the face
value of the assets as they appear upon the books. The bills receivable of every bank contain not merely the record of the notes and of
the face value of the principal thereof, but of the interest which they
draw and the dates of their making and maturity. If these notes
were sold or discounted, it is very clear that the interest already
earned would be taken into consideration. A note, for instance, of
$500, which draws interest at the rate of 10 per cent., and which has
run for three months, is surely worth more than its face value of $500,
even though it has some three months yet to run before it reaches
maturity and the interest can be collected. This conclusion disposes
of the case, and the other questions raised need not be considered.

The judgment of the district court is affirmed.

H. LIEBES & CO. v. COMMISSIONER OF
INTERNAL REVENUE

Circuit Court of Appeals of the United States, Ninth Circuit, 1937.
90 F.2d 932.

[Petitioner's vessel was prevented from catching seals in the
Bering Sea by a U. S. cutter in 1893. In 1896 a federal court decided
that the action of the cutter was wrongful but that there was no remedy for the owner. Not until 1924 did Congress provide a means of
recovering damages from the U. S. for such interference. Petitioner
obtained judgments in three separate actions against the U. S. in 1928,
the right to appeal from which expired in 1929. The . . . judgments were paid by virtue of a special appropriation in 1929. In an
appeal from an assessment of a deficiency for failure to report the
judgments as income during the 1929 fiscal year (ending January 31,
1930), the court affirmed. Portions of the opinion follow.]

    . . . [I]t is apparent that the general definition of accrued
is limited when taken in connection with income returns. We may
conclude that income has not accrued to a taxpayer until there arises
to him a fixed or unconditional right to receive it.

So far, only the right to receive has been considered. Must we also consider the prospect of realization on that right by the taxpayer?
In other words, when the right to receive arises, should the fact that
the right is or is not collectible be taken into consideration in determining whether income has accrued? We believe that no income accrues unless there is a reasonable expectancy that the right will be
converted into money or its equivalent.* . . .

The complete definition would therefore seem to be that income
accrues to a taxpayer, when there arises to him a fixed or unconditional right to receive it, if there is a reasonable expectancy that the right
will be converted into money or its equivalent.

* * *

With respect to the action in which petitioner recovered judgment, it seems to be conceded that income therefrom accrued to peti-

---

* [Ed. note] See page 34, supra.

tioner in the fiscal year prior to the one ending January 31, 1930, unless the right to receive, fixed by the judgment, was conditional. Respondent contends that the right was conditional, because (1) the judgment might be reversed on appeal, and, therefore, it was not unconditional until the time for appeal had expired, which in such case was in the fiscal year ending January 31, 1930; and (2) there was no appropriation to satisfy the judgment until during the fiscal year ending January 31, 1930.

Did the right to receive become fixed or unconditional at the time judgment was entered, or when the time within which an appeal might be taken had expired?

It is clear that where a claim exists, no income may accrue, in the absence of a settlement, so long as a judgment has not been entered. . . . This rule seems to coincide with what is considered to be proper accounting practice, Ronald, Accountant's Handbook (2d Ed.) p. 298.

Approaching the other end of the process of litigation, we have for consideration the case where the claim has been reduced to judgment but an appeal has been taken. United States v. Safety Car Heating & Lighting Co., supra, 297 U.S. 88, 99, 56 S.Ct. 353, 358, 80 L.Ed. 500, we believe establishes the rule, namely that no income accrues until the appeal is determined. . . .

As to the situation lying between the two mentioned, that is where judgment is entered, and no appeal has been taken, but the time within which an appeal might be taken has not expired, we find no cases directly in point. If appeal is taken the right is not fixed until determination of the appeal; and if no appeal is taken, the right is fixed. We believe in the latter situation that the right becomes fixed on termination of the appeal time. This seems to coincide with the actual practice of the government, as shown by provisions regarding payment of judgments rendered against the United States. It is usually provided that payment will not be made until the time for appeal has expired. . . .

With respect to the contention that the absence of an appropriation makes the right conditional, we believe that such fact does not affect the right, but the realization of the right. Even if the judgment remained unpaid, the right would not be impaired. But the absence of an appropriation may be considered in connection with the condition in the general definition hereinabove mentioned, that there must be a reasonable expectancy that the right will be converted into money or its equivalent. . . . It is inconceivable that Congress would go through the idle ceremony of enacting a statute authorizing the suits in question, and subsequently render it nugatory by the failure to make an appropriation. We believe that when the appeal time expired, there was a reasonable expectancy that the right would be converted into money.

In conformity with the foregoing, we hold that income from petitioner's claim, on which it recovered judgment, accrued to petitioner during the fiscal year ending January 31, 1930.

PROBLEMS

1. Assume that the B Bank was organized on January 1 last year with $2,000,000 of paid in capital. B immediately began to accept deposits from the public and had accumulated $3,000,000 in deposits by the end of the year. On July 1 of that year B made a loan of $500,000 to the Y Manufacturing Corporation, taking a one-year note with interest of 8% payable at maturity (on the following June 30). On August 1 B invested $1,000,000 in 6%, 20-year, $1,000 government bonds. The annual interest of $60 per bond was payable in quarterly installments, represented by 80 coupons in the face amount of $15 each, attached to each bond and maturing serially every three months. The first of these coupons matured on October 31 of that year, and B collected $15,000. B also invested $2,800,000 in listed marketable securities, on which B received $250,000 in cash dividends during the year. B's total expenses for the year, including interest on its deposits, amounted to $180,000, and all but $40,000, representing accrued interest owed to depositors, was paid in cash during the year.

a. How large a dividend could the B Bank properly pay at the end of the year under a statute which provides that "dividends may be paid out of net assets in excess of capital"?

b. To how much additional compensation is the president of B entitled under a contract which provides for a bonus of "10% of annual net profits, computed without deduction of the bonus"?

2. Wootton Real Estate, Inc., a concern which traded in real estate, owned some obsolete housing in East Cambridge. It desired to expand its operations by acquiring land suitable for new residential construction. Paulus and Company, a manufacturing concern, owned some land in Lincoln on which it had intended to erect a factory if the zoning boundaries could be changed. When a citizens' committee in Lincoln was formed to oppose the Paulus project, Paulus decided to build in East Cambridge. An even exchange was arranged between Wootton and Paulus. Wootton estimated the value of the Lincoln land at $50,000. The East Cambridge property had cost Wootton $40,000.

Wootton's book entries were:

Lincoln Land	$50,000	
East Cambridge Property		$40,000
Income		10,000

The independent accountants objected to the credit to income where there had been no "receipt of cash or its equivalent, to evidence earnings." They argued that since Wootton's risk was the same as before—the risk of loss of value of land held in portfolio—there had been no "realization."

Wootton replied that if all its holdings were liquidated the next day the transaction would show a profit of at least $10,000. Wootton had already received a bid of $27,000 for half of the Lincoln property.

Are the accountants or Wootton right? Consider APB No. 29, set out below. What about the accounting for Paulus and Company, assuming that Paulus' cost of the Lincoln land was $35,000? Suppose Paulus had made the swap with Wootton because it had abandoned plans for a new plant and was instead interested in the East Cambridge property as a land speculation?

APB OPINION NO. 29: ACCOUNTING FOR NONMONETARY TRANSACTIONS *

Accounting Principles Board, 1973.

* * *

OPINION

Basic Principles

18. The Board concludes that in general accounting for nonmonetary transactions should be based on the fair values of the assets (or services) involved which is the same basis as that used in monetary transactions. Thus, the cost of a nonmonetary asset acquired in exchange for another nonmonetary asset is the fair value of the asset surrendered to obtain it, and a gain or loss should be recognized on the exchange. The fair value of the asset received should be used to measure the cost if it is more clearly evident than the fair value of the asset surrendered. Similarly, a nonmonetary asset received in a nonreciprocal transfer should be recorded at the fair value of the asset received. . . .

* * *

Modifications of the Basic Principle

20. *Fair Value Not Determinable.* Accounting for a nonmonetary transaction should not be based on the fair values of the assets transferred unless those fair values are determinable within reasonable limits . . . .

21. *Exchanges.* If the exchange is not essentially the culmination of an earning process, accounting for an exchange of a nonmonetary asset between an enterprise and another entity should be based on the recorded amount (after reduction, if appropriate, for an indicated impairment of value) of the nonmonetary asset relinquished. The

Board believes that the following two types of nonmonetary exchange transactions do not culminate an earning process:

   a.   An exchange of a product or property held for sale in the ordinary course of business for a product or property to be sold in the same line of business to facilitate sales to customers other than the parties to the exchange, and

   b.   An exchange of a productive asset not held for sale in the ordinary course of business for a similar productive asset or an equivalent interest in the same or similar productive asset [Ed. Note: Examples given earlier in paragraph 7 include the trade of player contracts by professional sports organizations, exchange of leases on mineral properties, exchange of one form of interest in an oil producing property for another form of interest, exchange of real estate for real estate.]

*   *   *

26.   Fair value should be regarded as not determinable within reasonable limits if major uncertainties exist about the realizability of the value that would be assigned to an asset received in a nonmonetary transaction accounted for at fair value. An exchange involving parties with essentially opposing interests is not considered a prerequisite to determining a fair value of a nonmonetary asset transferred; nor does an exchange insure that a fair value for accounting purposes can be ascertained within reasonable limits. If neither the fair value of a nonmonetary asset transferred nor the fair value of a nonmonetary asset received in exchange is determinable within reasonable limits, the recorded amount of the nonmonetary asset transferred from the enterprise may be the only available measure of the transaction.

*   *   *

When should the income from sales or services in the ordinary course of business be recognized?

HUTCHINSON v. CURTISS

Supreme Court of New York, 1904.
45 Misc. 484, 92 N.Y.S. 70.

CLARKE, J. . . . This is an action brought by plaintiffs as stockholders on behalf of themselves and all other stockholders similarly situated against the defendant Curtiss, as director of the company, to compel him to account for and pay to the company the amount of the dividends declared and paid as not having been paid out of the profits, but out of the capital. The board of directors having upon demand refused or neglected to bring suit in the name of the company, it was joined as a party defendant. . . . By virtue of the statutes, this state allows the recovery of dividends unauthorized by the state of New Jersey from directors of a New Jersey corporation in the same manner and to the same extent as the directors of a domestic corporation. That is, it is the New Jersey statute which makes the dividend unauthorized, but the recovery is to be had according to the New York statute. What, then, is unauthorized? "No corporation shall make dividends except from the surplus or net profits arising from its business." Net profits are defined in the Century Dictionary as "what remains as the clear gain of any business after deducting the capital invested in the business, the expenses incurred in its management, and the losses sustained by its operation." And the controlling question of fact is, were these dividends paid from "net profits?" The 21 branches, located in many places and in different states, which were actually engaged in the business of manufacturing the malt from the barley, sent in to the general office in New York daily, weekly, and monthly statements in great detail of their business. From these statements branch books were made, and from these a general set of books was prepared. All of the books and papers from the general office, which were used in the accounting department, were produced in court, identified, and marked in evidence. The defendant objects to the summaries made up from these books and from any and all conclusions of fact to be drawn from said books and said summaries upon the ground that concededly the contracts and the contract books were not produced and were not considered. It was in evidence that malt was always oversold; that contracts for future deliveries, running over many months, were entered into, and the claim is that such contracts were required to be taken into consideration when it came to be determined whether any particular dividend was warranted or not. Such claim, in my opinion, is unfounded. The law is that "no corporation shall make dividends except from the surplus or net profits." These contracts were to deliver at a future time a product not yet made from raw material, not yet purchased, with the aid of labor not yet expended. The price agreed to be paid at that future time had to cover all the possible contingencies of the market in the meanwhile, and might show a profit, and ran the chance of showing a loss. When the sales actually took place they were entered in the books. But to calculate months in advance on the result of the future transactions, and on such calculations to declare dividends, was to base such dividends on paper profits—hoped for profits, future profits—and not upon the surplus or net profits required by law. It does not seem to me that you can "divide"—that is, make a dividend of—a hope based on an expectation of a future delivery at a favorable price of what is not yet in existence, under the statute. . . . There was entered on the books on the 31st of December, 1898, an item of $388,063.36 of the anticipated or estimated future profits on contracts for future deliveries running over many months. This entry, for the reasons stated in regard to the contracts for future deliveries, was unjustifiable. The company subsequently removed this entry. The actual transactions—that is, the deliveries of the malt called for by the contracts and the receipts in payment therefor—being reported from time to time as they occurred, resulting in double credits, the cancellation or reversal of the entry was absolutely required.

Judgment for the plaintiffs as indicated, with costs and extra allowance of $2,000.

PROBLEM

Suppose that in year 1 the company entered into a contract calling for the manufacture and delivery of goods in year 2 for $1,000,000.

The company estimated that it would cost $612,000 to perform the contract. What entries would the company make at the close of year 1 if it wanted to reflect the profit on this contract in year 1? Would that be proper?

Was there an argument available to defendants in Hutchinson v. Curtiss akin to the one we considered on behalf of the defendants in the *Kingston* case, page 198, supra?

NATIONAL CASH REGISTER COMPANY

Annual Report, 1948

* * *

During the year a change was made in the basis of recording domestic sales. Sales to customers were previously recorded at the time shipment was made from the factory. The sales shown during the year 1948, however, were recorded at the time installation of the equipment was made. Had this change in the method of recording sales not been made, net sales for the year 1948 would have been approximately $7,000,000 greater than shown above. Accounts receivable would have increased the same amount, while inventories would have decreased an amount equal to the cost of these sales.

Income Statement, 1948

Notes:

(1) During 1948 the Company changed its method of recording sales, from a basis under which sales were taken up at the time shipments were made from the factories on customers' orders, to a basis under which sales are taken up at the time of installation by local branch offices. Under the former basis net income for the year 1948 would have been approximately $2,000,000 greater.

PACIFIC GRAPE PRODUCTS CO. v. COMMISSIONER

United States Court of Appeals, Ninth Circuit, 1955.
219 F.2d 862.

Pope, Circuit Judge. Petitioner is a canner of fruit and fruit products. It regularly billed its customers for all goods ordered by them, but not yet shipped and remaining in petitioner's warehouse, on December 31 in each year. It accrued upon its books the income from the sales of such unshipped goods in the taxable years ending on the days of such billing. On the same date it also credited to the accounts of brokers the brokerage due on account of sales of such unshipped goods, and accrued the cost of such unshipped goods including therein the anticipated cost of labeling, packaging and preparing the same for shipment. For many years the petitioner reported its income accordingly. (It filed its returns on the calendar year, accrual basis.)

The Commissioner, in determining deficiencies for the years 1940 to 1944, held petitioner's method of accounting did not clearly reflect its income and made adjustments by excluding from the computation of income for the years 1939, 1940 and 1941, the sales prices of unshipped goods billed on December 31 of those years, and included such amounts in the computations of income for the years 1940, 1941 and 1942 respectively. He likewise transferred to these later years the brokerage fees and the estimated costs mentioned which related to these goods. The result was a deficiency in income tax for the years 1940 and 1943, and in excess profits tax for the years 1940, 1941, 1942 and 1944, and in declared value excess profits tax for the year 1944. The determinations mentioned were upheld by the Tax Court on petition for redetermination.

Since its organization in 1926 petitioner has operated its cannery at Modesto, California. Its product was limited to fruit and fruit products. Its canning season in each year extends from about July 1st to November 1st. During such season it enters into numerous contracts for the sale of its current pack. . . .

The contracts described the quantity, price, grade, size of cans, and variety of fruit or fruit products to be sold. Some provided for labels bearing petitioner's name; others provided for the use of labels bearing the buyer's trade name, in which case the labels were furnished by the buyer to whom an allowance was made for the labels. A large portion of the goods covered by the contracts are shipped during the calendar year in which the fruits are packed. On occasion some buyers request petitioner to withhold shipment of all or part of their contract amounts until the following year and petitioner normally complies with such request. In that connection the contract form used provides: "Goods to be shipped in seller's discretion as soon as practicable after packing. . . . If seller shall elect to withhold shipment at buyer's request, then the goods unshipped shall be billed and paid for on the following dates respectively hereinafter specified. . . . Fruits, Fruit Products or Sundry Vegetables, December 31." Accordingly goods remaining unshipped on December 31 of each year were billed by the petitioner to their respective buyers on that date.

On December 31 of each year the petitioner always has on hand a sufficient quantity of goods of every variety, grade and size of can to fill all contracts. . . . The fruits of different varieties, grades and sizes of cans were separately arranged in separate stacks with no commingling of variety, grade or size in any one stack. It was stipulated in the Tax Court that all of the canned fruits and fruit products here involved were fungible goods within the meaning of the Uniform Sales Act. . . . The evidence showed that in accruing and entering upon its books in these years the expense of brokerage fees, petitioner calculated the amount of such fees in accordance with the customary trade practice of the California canning industry. That practice was to accrue the expenses of such fees as of the dates the unshipped goods were billed. With respect to the expenses of shipment of the goods, that is, the cost of labeling, packing and freight, it accrued and entered upon its books as an item of deduction the anticipated cost of these items. What the cost would be was known from the petitioner's past experience with such expenditures.

The Tax Court, six judges dissenting, upheld the Commissioner's determination that the method employed by the petitioner of computing accrued income from its sales did not clearly reflect its income. 17 T.C. 1097. The court based its conclusion entirely upon its determination that title to the goods in question did not pass to the buyers on the billing dates. . . . In this we think that the Tax Court was in error. . . .

It is true that the goods here had to be labeled, packed and shipped at a subsequent date. Such a circumstance is a matter to be taken into consideration in ascertaining the intention of the parties as to when the property in the goods is to pass under Rule 2 of the California Civil Code, § 1739, § 19 of the Uniform Sales Act. But that circumstance is not controlling, for all of the rules specified in that section are subject to the initial qualification of the section,—"unless a different intention appears", etc. Not only is the different intention indicated by the proof of the custom here referred to, but the language of the contract provides that the goods unshipped shall be billed and paid for on December 31. While there is no evidence to show that the buyers actually paid for those goods on December 31 (the implication is quite otherwise), yet the contract clearly specifies that payment was due on that date, which would further confirm an understanding that title had then passed.

Since title had thus passed to the buyers, it is plain that petitioner's method of accounting and accruing in such years its gross income from sales of such merchandise clearly reflected its income. Consistently, and to make reflection of income complete, it properly accrued its shipping expenses relating to this merchandise as part of its cost of goods sold in the respective years billed. The record shows that the items making up these expenses were either precisely known or determinable with extreme accuracy. Labels and cases for packing were on hand. The expenses of labor in labeling and casing were determinable on the basis of petitioner's past experience. Freight costs were available from published rate schedules. . . .

We think also that petitioner correctly treated the brokerage fees relating to the goods billed on the December 31 dates as deductible expenses in those years. The Tax Court disapproved this procedure on the ground that it thought there was a failure to introduce evidence of the contracts with the brokers to show that there was any fixed liability for the brokerage fees prior to the payment of the purchase price for the goods. The evidence, however, showed that the brokers doing business with the industry contracted in accordance with the established trade practice of considering that title to the unshipped goods passed on the billing dates, and that the brokerage fees accrued to the broker on those dates. In our view the finding that there was want of proof on this point is clearly erroneous. . . .

Finally, we are of the view that the petitioner's method of accounting clearly and accurately reflected its income wholly apart from the question whether title to the goods did or did not pass to the buyers on the dates of billing. Upon this aspect we are agreed with what the six dissenting judges said in this case.[14]

14. "Opper, J. dissenting: The practice of disapproving consistent accounting systems of long standing seems to me to be exceeding all reasonable bounds.

Not only do we have here a system of accounting which for years has been adopted and carried into effect by substantially all members of a large industry, but the system is one which appeals to us as so much in line with plain common sense that we are at a loss to understand what could have prompted the Commissioner to disapprove it. Contrary to his suggestion that petitioner's method did not reflect its true income it seems to us that the alterations demanded by the Commissioner would wholly distort that income. It is reasonable that both the taxpayer and the Government should be able accurately to ascertain the income accruing to the taxpayer on account of each annual pack. The Commissioner would break up the petitioner's product for the year 1940 and throw the receipts from the portion shipped before December 31 into gross income for that year and the receipts from the unshipped portion into the following year. If in a succeeding year there arose a market shortage which led to a demand which brought about almost complete shipment of the pack before December 31, the Commissioner's accounts for that succeeding year would cover one nearly complete pack and portions of the income and deductions relating to the preceding pack. We see no reason for any such requirement on the part of the Commissioner.

The judgment of the Tax Court is reversed and the cause is remanded with directions to modify the judgment in accordance with this opinion.

PROBLEM

Assume that at the close of its fiscal year just ended the Pacific Grape Products Company had on hand $300,000 of completed canned goods inventory which had been ordered by customers but not yet labelled or shipped, and that the sales price of these goods was $420,000, the brokers' commissions were 5% of sales price, and the estimated cost of labelling and shipping the goods was $15,000. Assume further that if the company had treated these goods as not having been sold during the year just ended, and hence had not recognized the income and related expenses during that year (the accounting

. . . Methods of keeping records do not spring in glittering perfection from some unchangeable natural law but are devised to aid business men in maintaining sometimes intricate accounts. If reasonably adapted to that use they should not be condemned for some abstruse legal reason, but only when they fail to reflect income. There is no persuasive indication that such a condition exists here. On the contrary, a whole industry apparently has adopted the method used by petitioner.

"It will not do to say that respondent should not have disturbed petitioner's accounting method, but that since he has done so, we are powerless to do otherwise. As long as we continue to approve the imposition of theoretical criteria in so purely practical a field, respondent will go on attempting to seize on such recurring fortuitous occasions to increase the revenue, even though he may actually accomplish the opposite. . . . I think it evident that petitioner's generally recognized accounting system did not distort its income and that it should be permitted to continue to use it. . . ." [17 T.C. at 1110.]

[Other footnotes by the court omitted.]

approach urged by the Commissioner for tax purposes), its balance sheet as of the close of that year would have appeared as follows:

Cash		$ 90,000	Liabilities	$ 334,000
Acc. Rec.	$700,000		Note Pay.	500,000
Less Allowance for			Expenses Payable	75,000
Uncollect. Acc.	14,000	686,000	Estim. Liab.	12,000
Inventory		580,000		
Fixed Assets (after			Stat. Cap.	1,500,000
depreciation)		1,634,000		
Deferred Expenses		10,000	Earn. Surp.	579,000
		$3,000,000		$3,000,000

How would the company's balance sheet have looked if these goods had been treated as sold during the year just ended? What would the difference have been in the company's income statement? Which of the two approaches would you favor?

a. THE PROBLEM OF UNCOLLECTIBLE ACCOUNTS

As we have seen, revenue from a sales transaction is normally recognized at the point when the seller has substantially completed its required performance, and it does not matter that the buyer has not paid as yet (unless there is some special doubt about the ultimate ability of the buyer to pay). So if S Corp. completes a sale of goods in year 1 to Jones Company for $1,000 on credit, the entry would be:

A/R Jones Co.	$1,000	
Sales Income		$1,000

Suppose that in year 2 S learns that Jones has become insolvent and there is no prospect of recovering anything on the claim against him. Since that account receivable is now worthless, it ought to be "written off", i. e., eliminated from S's books, which can be done simply enough by crediting the account receivable; as for the corresponding debit, unless some steps have been taken earlier to pave the way for a different alternative the only possibility would be a charge to a current loss or expense account (since even before prior period adjustments were virtually eliminated by FASB No. 16 there would have been no warrant for according that treatment to a constantly recurring business phenomenon like the failure of some credit customers to pay what they owe). But query, does charging the loss due to an uncollectible account against the year in which the account happens to become uncollectible represent meaningful matching of related expense and income items? It seems not, since losses stemming from uncollectible accounts are really part of the cost of selling goods on credit, and therefore should be matched, like all other related expenses, with the revenues from the sales which gave rise to the losses. What is needed is an entry each year reflecting the likely future losses resulting from credit sales made during that year. Of course, as already noted, if there is a special risk that the revenue from a particular credit transaction will not be forthcoming—for example, where the solvency of the buyer is doubtful—income should not be recognized until payment is actually received. But in fact in the great majority of cases payment is received in the ordinary course of business; moreover, the amount of the defaults which will occur is reasonably predictable, on the basis of prior experience or the like. Accordingly, each year the expected losses on credit sales made during the year should be estimated and accrued, thereby matching those losses with the revenues to which they are related.

The technique for reflecting these future expected losses as an expense of the current year is much the same as the process for accruing any expense before it has been paid. The debit is to a current expense account, often called "Bad Debt Expense", or perhaps "Uncollectible Accounts Expense", in the amount of the estimated future credit losses on the credit sales made during that year. The corresponding credit is to an account which might be thought of as a kind of estimated liability, paralleling the normal practice of crediting an estimated liability account when an expense or loss is accrued prior to payment. There are, however, a couple of differences. For one thing, unlike the other estimated liability accounts with which we have dealt, this one does not represent a liability to pay money (or perform services), but rather represents the fact that some money projected to be received in the future (through the recording of an account receivable) will in fact not be forthcoming. Second, as we shall see this estimated-liability-type account used in connection with estimated losses on credit sales is usually shown on the balance sheet as an offset to Accounts Receivable, rather than separately as a liability on the right-hand side, in order to give a more immediate picture of how much cash is actually expected to be obtained from the receivables. Perhaps for these reasons, the usual "Estimated Liability" caption is not used for this account; instead it is commonly called something like "Allowance for Uncollectible Accounts".

As we have already noticed with other accounts of this sort,* in the past it was common to call this type of liability account, created in conjunction with accrual of a conditional expense (or one requiring estimation of the amount), a "Reserve"; here the term often used was "Reserve for Bad Debts", or "Reserve for Uncollectible Accounts". This terminology is still used in much of the literature, in connection with potential credit losses; you should recognize

---

* See pages 335–336, supra.

that it means exactly the same thing as "Allowance for Uncollectible Accounts".

Again paralleling estimated liability accounts, an Allowance for Uncollectible Accounts makes it possible to handle an account receivable which becomes uncollectible without affecting current income in the later period when that occurs. Upon determining that a particular account receivable has become either wholly or partly uncollectible, the debit balancing the credit to the account in the amount which has become uncollectible would be to the Allowance for Uncollectible Accounts, and the current P & L would be unaffected. This differs from the normal practice with liability accounts only in the fact that the credit is to the worthless account receivable rather than to cash. So if S in the example above had previously created an Allowance for Uncollectible Accounts, upon discovering in year 2 that the account receivable from Jones had become totally uncollectible S would make the following entry:

Allowance for Uncollectible Accounts $1,000
     A/R Jones Co. $1,000

Occasionally some payment is received on an account receivable which was previously written off. Suppose, for example, that in year 3 the Jones Company had some unexpected good fortune and was able to make a payment of $100 on its account with S. Since the write-off of the account receivable did not affect current income, such a recovery should not affect current income either. Instead, this receipt would be viewed as an indication that the previous total write-off of the account was erroneous, calling for a pro tanto reversal of that earlier entry, plus an entry reflecting the receipt of cash:

A/R Jones Co. $100
     Allowance for Uncollectible Accounts $100
Cash $100
     A/R Jones $100

These two entries might well be combined into a single entry reaching the same end point, as follows:

Cash $100
     Allowance for Uncollectible Accounts $100

Incidentally, no attempt is made to isolate the credit losses from different years in separate accounts; rather a single continuing Allowance for Uncollectible Accounts is used. The Allowance account is increased each year by the credit, corresponding to the debit to current expense, in the amount of the year's credit sales which are expected to become uncollectible (plus a credit for any receipts on accounts theretofore written off as worthless), and decreased by the amount of accounts receivable which actually become worthless and are written off during the year.*

Estimation of the amount which should be credited to the Allowance for Uncollectible Accounts each year is somewhat more complicated than in the usual case of estimating the amount of an expense which is to be reflected in the current year although it has not been paid yet. That is because this Allowance account serves *two* important functions. One, as we have already seen, is to reflect the expense of doing business on a credit basis in the respective years in which the related credit sales are made; in this respect, the Allowance for Uncollectibles is much like the ordinary estimated liability accounts with which we have dealt. As with these other estimated liability accounts, experience is normally the best guide for determining the proper amount; and in fact the past experience of the company itself or some similar enterprise is usually available to help reach a fairly accurate estimation of the percentage of credit sales made in any period which will result in uncollectible accounts. This figure, then, might be considered the *prima facie* cost of doing business on credit for the period.

But the Allowance for Uncollectible Accounts performs a second function not served by ordinary estimated liability accounts. The accounts receivable on a balance sheet are second only to cash, and perhaps marketable securities, in liquidity, which makes them of great significance to investors of all kinds, and most particularly short-term creditors. Accordingly, in recording this asset on the balance

---

* Reference to one mechanical bookkeeping refinement may be in order at this point. It is perfectly appropriate to write off worthless accounts receivable directly against the Allowance for Uncollectible Accounts, and likewise to credit receipts from accounts receivable previously written off directly to that account. But bookkeepers like to have a separate account to reflect the amount of accounts receivable which have become uncollectible during the period, and also a separate account to show the amount of receipts on accounts receivable previously written off. Accordingly, bookkeepers often set up special temporary sub-accounts of the Allowance for Uncollectible Accounts account, called "Bad Debts Charged Off", and "Bad Debts Collected" respectively, to reflect these items. In that event, when an account receivable is written off as uncollectible, the debit would be to the "Bad Debts Charged Off" account; at the end of the period that account would be closed to the left-hand side of the Allowance for Uncollectible Accounts. Similarly, payments received on accounts receivable previously written off as uncollectible would be credited to the "Bad Debts Collected" account, and at the end of the period the total in that account would be closed to the right-hand side of the Allowance for Uncollectible Accounts. While these sub-accounts may be useful to management in analyzing the overall credit picture of the enterprise, they represent mechanical refinements which we can easily dispense with.

sheet consideration must be given to the real value of the accounts receivable, that is, the amount that is actually expected to be collected. Certainly it would be misleading to show on a company's balance sheet the gross amount of accounts receivable outstanding, without in some way indicating the likelihood that not all of those receivables will prove collectible. This is confirmed as an accounting matter by FASB No. 5, particularly ¶'s 22 and 23, pages 350–351, supra, and it is principally for this reason that the Allowance for Uncollectible Accounts normally appears on the balance sheet as a deduction from Accounts Receivable, rather than on the right-hand side of the balance sheet as a liability account.

This vital role played by the Allowance for Uncollectible Accounts in reducing the gross amount of accounts receivable to the net amount actually expected to be collected also means that the size of the Allowance account should not be left entirely to the annual additions to the account based upon the percentage of credit sales during the period which previous experience indicates are likely to become uncollectible. Instead, a detailed analysis of the existing accounts receivable should be made at the end of each year, to determine whether the figure in the Allowance account represents the best possible estimate of the amount of those receivables which will prove uncollectible. In particular, business experience confirms that the collectibility of accounts is largely a function of the "age" of the outstanding receivables, since the likelihood of non-payment increases as a receivable becomes progressively overdue; hence the estimate of the likely amount of uncollectibles should pay careful attention to how old the existing accounts receivable are (i. e., how the total breaks down among such categories as, say, less than three months old, between three and six months, between six and twelve months, and more than twelve months old), as well as any other special circumstances that may affect particular accounts. The figure arrived at by this process is the amount which should appear in the Allowance account at the end of the year, and a corresponding increase or decrease in the charge to current expense (Bad Debt Expense) for the year is made to fix the amount in the Allowance account at the desired level.

PROBLEMS

1. Returning to the Pacific Grape Products Co. problem on page 377, supra, suppose that it was the practice of the company to charge Bad Debt Expense each month in the amount of $\frac{1}{4}\%$ of the credit sales made during the month, with a corresponding credit to Allowance for Uncollectible Accounts. On $5,000,000 of sales during the year (not including, it will be recalled, the $420,000 relating to the goods ordered but not shipped at year end), this had produced

$12,500 of Bad Debt Expense for the year. The $14,000 in the Allowance account was the product of $12,000 in the account at the beginning of the year, plus the $12,500 charged to current expense and $1,000 received during the year on accounts previously written off, less $11,500 of accounts receivable written off during the year and charged against the Allowance account.

The company follows the practice of fixing the amount in the Allowance account at year end on the basis of "aging" its account receivables. Under the company's credit terms payment is due within thirty days, and the company's experience is that once thirty days has passed without payment the percentage of loss rises steeply, the older the accounts. This past experience indicates that the figure in the Allowance account should be at least equal to the sum of the following percentages of the respective age categories: ¼% of the existing receivables less than one month old; 2% of the receivables between one and three months; 7% of the receivables between three and six months old; 25% of those between six and twelve months old; and 75% of those over a year old. The following table shows the breakdown of the company's receivables among the various age categories at the end of its recent fiscal year, and the percentage of each category which should be reflected in the allowance account:

Age Category	Amount of Receivables	Percentage
Less than one month old	$440,000	¼%
One to three months	200,000	2%
Three to six months	40,000	7%
Six to twelve months	16,000	25%
Over twelve months	4,000	75%

What entry should the company make at the close of the year as a result of this aging procedure? Consider in this connection FASB No. 5 on Accounting for Contingencies, particularly ¶'s 22 and 23, pages 350–351, supra.

Would your answer be the same if the issue arose in the context of applying an employee bonus provision based upon "annual net profits from operations"? Suppose instead the question was the propriety of a dividend under a "net assets in excess of capital" provision? Cf. the *Vogtman* case, which appears immediately after problem 3 below.

2. What effect would it have on the Allowance account, if any, to recognize in the year just ended the sale of those goods ordered but not shipped at year end?

3. Suppose that a couple of months after the close of the year, while the financial statements for the year are being prepared, the

company learns that a customer who had purchased goods for $10,000 on credit in the next to the last month of the year has unexpectedly become insolvent and there is substantial doubt about collecting any of the amount due. How, if at all, should this information be reflected in those financial statements? Consider FAS No. 5, supra, particularly ¶ 11.

VOGTMAN v. MERCHANTS MORTGAGE & CREDIT CO., 20 Del.Ch. 364, 178 A. 99 (1935). Under the corporate charter the preferred shareholders had sole voting power in case dividends had not been paid for two semi-annual periods. The court held that the charter referred to lawful dividends. It then dealt with the claim that certain dividend payments had been unlawful so that voting power had shifted to the preferred shareholders and consequently that an election of directors by the common shareholders was invalid. The court said:

"The dividend is sought to be justified by the defendants as having been paid out of net assets in excess of capital, that is to say, out of surplus. The complainant insists there was no surplus out of which the dividend could be paid. . . .

"Was there a surplus? A point of pronounced divergence in view between the parties exists as to whether or not assets for dividend purposes may be counted at cost regardless of present worth. The defendants insist that they may. The complainant insists that they must be reconciled to present value either by appropriate write-downs or by the equivalent of an appropriate reserve liability. It may be conceded that an estimated increase in the market value of a fixed asset in the from of a parcel of real estate which houses the offices of a corporation cannot be treated as a profit until the same has been realized by sale. Kingston v. Home Life Ins. Co., 11 Del.Ch. 258, 101 A. 898. But this is far from saying that assets consisting of loans and investments which constitute the business turn-over of such a corporation as the defendant, may not be regarded as having suffered a shrinkage below cost when it is sought to ascertain whether there is a surplus of assets over liabilities for purposes of a dividend. American Steel & Wire Co. v. Eddy, 138 Mich. 403, 101 N.W. 578. The Pennsylvania Supreme Court in Loan Society of Phila. v. Eavenson, 248 Pa. 407, 94 A. 121, appears to have been of like view with respect to worthless loans. If so, assets of that general type which are only partially bad, should suffer an appropriate reduction. It is a question of degree only. In Hubbard v. Weare, 79 Iowa 678, 44 N.W. 915, it was held that where dividends may be paid out of the excess of assets over liabilities, on accounts due from agents and customers a proper deduction should be made for shrinkage or loss in collection. If they are good accounts they should be credited at face value. . . .

"Looking at the balance sheet of the defendant corporation as of December 31, 1932, we find an asset of loans receivable of $86,580.09. This figure represents the full amount invested by the company in such loans. The testimony shows that some of the loans were unsecured, others of them which the defendants describe as 'slow' were far in arrears, and others of them were secured by liens on automobiles and by junior liens on real estate. Yet in the face of these facts the defendant corporation carried the loans receivable at cost. If this corporation could realize cost on December 31, 1932, out of loans of $86,580.09 made on the type of collateral it accepted and in part on no collateral at all, its management possessed a financial shrewdness which no other concern in like business I dare say could demonstrate. The complainant contends that something like $22,000.00 should be depreciated on the item of loans receivable. That would be about a twenty-seven per cent write-off. That may or may not be too much. Certainly it seems to me a ten per cent. depreciation would be as generous a compliment to the integrity of those accounts as the most sanguine hopes could reasonably extend. An accountant, I venture to say, would consider the suggested ten per cent. depreciation as too little. A reduction of at least $8,650.00 should be made in the item of loans receivable. . . ."

b. INSTALLMENT PAYMENTS OVER A LENGTHY
PERIOD

The principles governing recognition of income have been sorely tested in situations where the receipt of payment is stretched out over a long period. One illustration is that of land development companies which subdivide tracts of land into individual house lots for sale to retail customers. Quite often, especially in the boom of the early 1970's, only a small cash down payment was required upon the execution of the contract, with payment of the balance due in installments over an extended period. High pressure sales tactics were all too common, and a substantial amount of these receivables proved uncollectable. Nevertheless, the major land developers usually recognized full profit based upon the face amount of the sales contract at the time of execution, despite the small equity of the buyer in the property and the high risk that full payment would not be completed. Also largely ignored by developers were two other important factors: (1) the interest rate provided in the buyer's installment obligation was frequently a good deal below the appropriate "market" rate, so that the obligation was worth substantially less than face (a problem obviously not unique to land development companies, as is made clear by APB Op. No. 21, pages 394–399, infra, which should be read at this point); and (2) developers often had an obligation to perform additional development work well into the future, but there was no deferral of any revenue or profit relating to this performance requirement, nor any accrual of the expenses involved.

The problems of retail land companies and the response of the profession are thoughtfully reviewed in the following article:

KLINK & WHITE, THE ACCOUNTANTS RESHAPE THE RETAIL LAND SALES INDUSTRY *

3 Real Estate Review No. 1, 47 (Spring, 1973).

Recent years have been difficult for the retail land developers. . . . Not the least of their problems has been the continuing attack on their accounting practices fostered primarily by the fact that little cash is received when a contract is signed by a land purchaser, with payments for the remaining sales price due over many years. The accounting controversy has now quieted down with the release by the American Institute of Certified Public Accountants (AICPA) of the new Accounting Guide for retail land sales, with the support of the SEC for the new rules assured.

* * *

Previous Accounting Practices in the Industry

The land development industry has mushroomed since the 1950s. As the industry became more complex and diversified, the accounting problems also became more difficult. There have been few guidelines to use in accounting for real estate sales; the accounting profession has therefore applied general accounting principles to a very specialized industry. The paucity of authoritative literature has meant a wide variation in principles employed and many abuses. Most major land developers recognized full profit on the basis of the face amount of the sales contract *regardless* of the following factors:

- There may have been no cash down payment or it may have been so small that the buyer had virtually no equity in the property.
- The stated interest rate on the receivable may have been considerably less than the "market" rate, and in fact there may have been no stated interest at all.
- Development work may not have begun, may have been scheduled for the distant future, or may not have been planned at all. In fact, the land may not have been usable. In addition, no revenue or profit relating to future performance requirements was deferred by the developer.

It should be noted that most or all of the buyer's initial payments go to pay salesmen's commissions, and do not immediately benefit the land developer in terms of cash flow. Much criticism arose from these accounting practices as well as from various court cases involving retail land developers. It became obvious that something had to be done.

Ad Hoc Accounting Committee Created

As a result of the criticism, the AICPA established an ad hoc committee to study these significant accounting problems. The committee worked for almost three years on an Accounting Guide which has now finally been issued, substantially changing the guidelines for

---

* Reprinted from Real Estate Review, Volume 3, Spring, 1973. Copyright   1973, Warren, Gorham & Lamont, Inc. All rights reserved.

income recognition for retail land developers. (Partly as a result of the uncertainty regarding the guidelines which would ultimately become effective, the market prices of land development securities during this period suffered drastic declines.)

* * *

In August 1972 an exposure draft of the Guide was released for public comment. The draft was rejected at the November 1972 meeting of the Accounting Principles Board (APB), after a major industry group presented its objections. John C. Burton, chief accountant of the SEC, then strongly urged the committee to adopt the installment accounting method of reporting. This method, also endorsed by the New York Stock Exchange and the Financial Analysts Federation, recognizes profit proportionately as cash is received, whereas the *accrual method* recognizes profits at the time of sale. The SEC did indicate (reluctantly) that it would reconsider its position on installment accounting if a satisfactory alternative were passed by a two-thirds majority of the APB.

* * *

Principles Adopted in the New Accounting Guide

The final version of the Accounting Guide had the approval of five of the six members of the ad hoc committee, one of whom approved with qualification, and fifteen of the eighteen members of the APB, two of whom approved with qualification.

The Guide is similar to an industry audit guide, but it deals with accounting matters and not with auditing aspects. It is effective for 1972 and, because the provisions of the Guide have such a material impact, it requires that financial statements for prior periods be restated on a comparable basis.

The Accounting Guide is applicable to retail lot sales on a volume basis, ...

When to Recognize a Sale

The Guide sets stringent criteria for the recognition of contracts as sales for accounting purposes based on the premise that a contract is not a sale (1) unless the customer has a serious intent to complete the contract, and (2) until the company is capable of fulfilling its obligations. Specifically, contracts should be recorded as sales *only* if the following conditions are met:

- The customer has made the down payment plus all regular payments until the refund period has expired. The refund period should be the longest of the one required by local law, the one established by company policy, or the one set by the contract.
- The aggregate payments made, including interest, must equal or exceed 10 percent of the contract sales price.
- The selling company must clearly be financially capable of providing the land improvements and off-site facilities as promised.

Until these conditions are met, cash collected must be recorded as deposits.

These criteria, particularly the 10 percent requirement, will have a material impact on land developers as many have been recording profits with much less down payment.

The ad hoc committee's original down payment requirement was only 5 percent but was changed to 10 percent at the time of the August 1972 exposure draft. The 10 percent requirement is clearly an arbitrarily determined percentage designed to provide an amount that would represent a sufficient equity commitment on the part of the buyer so that he could be expected to complete the remaining payments under the terms of the sales contract.

When to Apply the Accrual Method

The Guide enumerates certain requirements for the use of the accrual method; otherwise the more conservative installment method must be used. The choice of accounting method must be based on the company's own experience with each individual project. The accrual method is to be used if *all* of the following criteria are met:

- The properties clearly will be useful for residential or recreational purposes at the end of the normal payment period.

- The project's improvements have progressed beyond preliminary stages, and there is evidence that the improvements will be completed according to plan.

- The receivable is not subject to subordination to new loans on the property except for home construction purposes where collection experience is the same as on contracts not subordinated.

- Collection experience for the project indicates that collectibility of receivable balances is reasonably predictable and that 90 percent of the contracts in force six months *after sales are recorded* will be collected in full. Down payments sufficient to record a sale if it were a casual sale (say 20–25 percent) are an acceptable substitute for this test of collection experience.

The company's collection experience must provide the information to support a reasonable prediction of whether the required percentage of contracts will pay out to maturity. In order to predict collection results, a company must have had sufficient experience as to prior sales of the type of land being currently marketed in the project and a sufficiently long collection period, as well as information by sales method. This requirement, of course, will have a material impact on new, untried companies. They will either have to use the installment method initially or collect down payments of 20–25 percent if they wish to use the accrual method.

When the criteria are met for the accrual method, revenue should be recognized in the amount of the contract price, exclusive of the portion applicable to (1) any discount required through valuation of the receivable, and (2) deferred revenue related to improvement work not yet performed. Provision for estimated contract cancellations is required and selling expenses should, of course, be charged to expense as incurred.

What will these requirements for the recording of sales and use of the accrual method mean to the land developer? First, new companies will show a much slower rate of earnings growth than did their counterparts during the 1960s since they will have to apply the installment method until they develop a sales history. But their earnings should be better quality earnings. The investor should be able to buy shares of land developers with more confidence than in the past. On the other hand, it is going to be more difficult for the land developer to obtain financing. For the untried company, the Guide will have a major impact. For the seasoned, stable developer who applied rather conservative accounting practices in the past, there will be little impact on operating results, although there may be major adjustments to stockholders' equity.

When to Apply the Installment Method

When *all* the criteria for use of the accrual method are not met, the installment method should be used until the *entire project* meets all such criteria. Application of the installment method is described in detail in the Guide. When the requirements for use of the accrual method for a particular project are met, the income adjustment resulting from the change should be reflected as a one-line item in the income statement.

Imputation of Interest on Contract Receivables

The committee considered at great length the question of what value should be ascribed to a long-term receivable where the stated interest rate is less than the prevailing current rate for an obligation similar in terms, security, and risk. The valuation problem is very difficult as there is no market for such receivables and virtually no opportunity for discounting without recourse.

The appropriate interest rate to be used was the subject of a great deal of discussion over the past two years. . . .

The committee ultimately concluded that while a fully comparable lending situation does not exist, the credit ratings of purchasers from retail land developers approximate those of users of retail consumer installment credit provided by commercial banks and established retail organizations. Accordingly, under the Guide, the effective annual yield on the receivable should not be less than the minimum annual rate charged locally by commercial banks and established retail organizations to borrowers financing the purchase of consumer personal property with installment credit. A footnote [1] in the Guide eliminates the possible use of interest rates on auto loans (which may be at effective rates less than 10 percent).

Application of this imputation-of-interest concept will result in a reduction in the amount of revenue initially recognized, since the difference between the stated rate (frequently 6 or 7 percent) and the retail installment rate (of at least 12 percent) will be deferred and amortized to income over the life of the contract.

---

1. The footnote in the Guide is as follows: "The rate to be applied should be the one which is predominantly used in installment financing of soft goods and appliances. The Committee believes that for 1972 and recent prior years a rate of not less than 12 percent is appropriate."

Income Related to Future Performance Requirements

At the time a sale is recorded on the accrual basis, revenue that is recognized should be based on the stage of completion of the required performance and be measured by cost incurred in relation to total estimated costs to be incurred, including direct costs of the marketing effort on the project. The portion of the revenue related to costs not yet incurred is to be deferred and recognized subsequently as the costs are incurred. In developing estimated costs, consideration should be given to the following factors.

- Adequate engineering studies, including reasonable provision for unforeseen costs;
- Cost inflation;
- Unrecoverable costs of off-site improvements.

This requirement for deferral of revenue on improvement work yet to be done will, of course, go a long way toward eliminating the "front-ending" of income. There was a great deal of discussion on the appropriate means of applying this concept or whether this concept should be applied at all. In the August 1972 exposure draft, it was stated that "The percentage relationship that the average future performance costs bear to the average total costs and expenses should be applied to net sales to determine the amount of sales to be deferred." The December 1972 draft provided for no allocation of profit to the improvement process, but the final Guide reinstated the cost relationship concept. There was much discussion of an alternative, the imputed-profit method, which would impute a construction industry profit on the future improvement costs, but the committee specifically rejected this concept.

Capitalized Costs

The question of which costs should be capitalized in property inventories is also an important one to the retail land developer. Under the Guide, costs directly related to inventories of unimproved land or to construction required to bring land and improvements to a salable condition should be capitalized until a salable condition is reached. Such costs would usually include real estate taxes and interest on loans directly related to the land and construction in process; however, the carrying amount may not exceed net realizable value. Other interest, selling expenses (except those specifically deferrable under the deposit or installment accounting methods), and general and administrative expenses should be expensed as incurred.

With respect to allocation of costs to parcels sold, any reasonable method may be used, but the value approach is considered to be preferable. This position opens the door to a diversity of practices, but it is apparent that the committee did not wish to take a stand on this point even though there were comments on the exposure draft recommending only the value approach.

Disclosure

Numerous disclosures are recommended by the Guide and such disclosures are stated to be applicable to (1) retail land sales companies, (2) diversified companies with significant retail land sales operations, and (3) statements of investors deriving significant portions of their income from investees engaged in retail lands sales operations. This may cause some difficulties for companies involved in a number of businesses in addition to real estate.

* * *

The new Accounting Guide must be followed by retail land developers unless they are prepared to justify a departure. . . .

As noted in the foregoing article, the Chief Accountant of the SEC pressed (unsuccessfully) for the adoption of the installment method of accounting for all retail land development operations, with the following letter to the AICPA Committee:

Gentlemen:

The Commission has directed me to make the following comments on the paper "Accounting for Retail Land Sales" which you issued for comment. Prior to developing these comments, we have carefully reviewed the draft, read the letters received by the committee, held discussions with you, with a group representing a significant segment of the industry and with a number of financial analysts concerned with the area. We have also received letters addressed directly to us on this subject.

On the basis of these inputs, we have concluded that the method of revenue recognition set forth in the paper is not an appropriate one and, therefore, that the adoption of the paper in its present form would not serve the interests of the investing public. It is our view that the many letters opposing the paper successfully make the case that the percentage of completion approach as developed in the draft does not reflect the business of the companies involved, is subject to a significant degree of manipulation, requires the establishment of arbitrary rules and will result in a set of financial statements that are difficult to justify within the framework of accounting theory. Most important, it appears that the accounting procedures set forth would be virtually impossible for the average informed investor to understand. The suggestions made by the industry committee to amend the draft would further complicate the paper's proposals.

Financial statements which can be understood by investors are an essential ingredient if the industry hopes to re-establish its credibility in the market place. If the investor feels that the accounting model represents a "black box" out of which financial statements spring by some unknown, complicated and mysterious process, it is unlikely that he will develop much faith in the model or its end product.

We all recognize the need for continuous improvement in financial reporting. We believe that the present accounting methods of the industry, which in our judgment are inappropriately labeled "accural accounting," no longer meet the necessary tests of fair presentation and conformity with the common sense accounting approach understood by users of the financial statements. The basic canons of accrual accounting theory require revenue to be recognized when the essential ingredients of the earning process are complete. In the case of land sales companies, revenue has been recorded at the point where a potential customer signs an agreement to buy land. At that time the customer receives neither title to nor use of the land, the contract is generally cancellable by the customer at any time on surrender of his rights to the payments made and the land developer has generally not begun the development process. To say that the earning process has been completed at this point requires imagination indeed.

Beyond the theory involved, there are major practical difficulties with both current practice and with the committee's suggested approach. Under both systems, many estimates must be made of cancellations, collections and costs which will occur over a period of ten years or more. Such estimates are inherently unreliable and have caused significant adjustments on the books of many companies in the industry with accompanying loss of investor faith. The committee's approach also requires the determination of a rate of discount which may be difficult to determine empirically as well as difficult to defend conceptually.

For more than two years the committee has struggled valiantly to try to develop appropriate accounting principles for this industry but in our judgment it has not succeeded in doing so. At the same time, we have concluded that current practice is deficient. It is apparent, however, that some solution on principles must be promptly reached if the industry and its investors are not to suffer unreasonably from accounting uncertainty as well as from business uncertainty.

Under these unusual conditions, it seems appropriate that the Commission indicate to you its judgment as to the proper application of accrual accounting in this industry. We believe that if we outline our views as to the general solution, you will be able to deal promptly with the many related problems and to develop a revised paper which will be most helpful to the industry, accountants and the public.

We believe that in this industry, revenue should be recognized as cash payments are received from customers and that the cost of land and direct selling and developments costs should be deferred and matched against revenue on a proportionate basis. General and administrative expenses and indirect selling costs should be charged to expense as incurred.

While this method is generally called "installment accounting," we believe that in this industry it represents good accrual accounting as well as having a number of practical benefits. In an industry where cancellation of a contract can take place by simply halting payment, a strong argument can be made that the receipt of cash represents the transaction which is necessary to legitimatize the realization of revenue. It is also apparent that under these conditions, the collection process represents an important part of the work to be done in the earning process.

In addition to its theoretical merit, revenue recognition on the basis of cash receipts also has the benefit of significantly reducing the uncertainties in the income statement due to both estimation and measurement problems. The impact of the estimate of future cancellations on income will be sharply reduced and the importance of the estimated cost of development on the financial statements will also be much less. Finally, the problem of selecting an appropriate rate of discount will no longer affect the income statement.

Beyond this, our suggested approach meets the important test of understandability. Investors will be aware of what the financial statements mean and they will be able to use them with increased confidence. The increased congruence between cash and income will also decrease the likelihood of unpleasant surprise which can easily arise when liquidity is totally unrelated to reported income.

While we believe that the basic financial statements for land sales companies should be prepared on the basis we have outlined, it is also apparent that the balance sheet and income statement prepared in this fashion will not tell the entire story of such a company's economic activity. Accordingly, we feel that it is most important that a format be developed for supplemental footnote disclosure which will reflect both current sales of land and a measure of the value created through such sales. We believe that the committee could productively address itself to such disclosure problems. In addition, supplemental disclosure relating to the assets and liabilities may well be desirable. The disclosure required for receivables in the paper is a worthwhile example.

. . . .

Sincerely,
/s/ John C. Burton
Chief Accountant

The installment method of accounting urged by the Chief Accountant of the SEC has generally been resisted by the profession, except in special circumstances, on the ground that it is inconsistent with the fundamental tenets of accrual accounting. In APB Op. No. 10 (1966), the Board put it this way:

INSTALLMENT METHOD OF ACCOUNTING

12. Chapter 1A of ARB No. 43, paragraph 1, states that "Profit is deemed to be realized when a sale in the ordinary course of business is effected, unless the circumstances are such that the collection of the sale price is not reasonably assured." The Board reaffirms this statement; it believes that revenues should ordinarily be accounted for at the time a transaction is completed, with appropriate provision for uncollectible accounts. Accordingly, it concludes that, in the absence of the

circumstances [8] referred to above, the installment method of recognizing revenue is not acceptable.

Substantially the same position was taken by the Board in APB Statement No. 4 (1971):

"Revenue is usually recognized at the time of exchanges in which cash is received or new claims arise against other entities. . . .

"[However, the] terms of an exchange transaction or other conditions related to receivables collectible over a long period may preclude a reasonable estimate of the collectibility of the receivables. Either an installment method or a cost recovery method of recognizing revenue and expenses may be used as long as collectibility is not reasonably assured. . . . Under both installment and cost recovery methods the proceeds collected measure revenue. Under an installment method expenses are measured at an amount determined by multiplying the cost of the asset sold by the ratio of the proceeds collected to the total selling price."

APB OPINION NO. 21

INTEREST ON RECEIVABLES AND PAYABLES *

Accounting Principles Board, 1971.

INTRODUCTION

1. *Problem.* Business transactions often involve the exchange of cash or property, goods, or service for a note or similar instrument. The use of an interest rate that varies from prevailing interest rates warrants evaluation of whether the face amount and the stated interest rate of a note or obligation provide reliable evidence for properly recording the exchange and subsequent related interest. This Opinion sets forth the Board's views regarding the appropriate accounting when the face amount of a note does not reasonably represent the present value [1] of the consideration given or received in

---

8. The Board recognizes that there are exceptional cases where receivables are collectible over an extended period of time and, because of the terms of the transactions or other conditions, there is no reasonable basis for estimating the degree of collectibility. When such circumstances exist, and as long as they exist, either the installment method or the cost recovery method of accounting may be used. (Under the cost recovery method, equal amounts of revenue and expense are recognized as collections are made until all costs have been recovered, postponing any recognition of profit until that time.)

1. Present value is the sum of the future payments discounted to the present date at an appropriate rate of interest. The Appendix contains a description of the valuation process.

the exchange. This circumstance may arise if the note is noninterest bearing or has a stated interest rate which is different from the rate of interest appropriate for the debt at the date of the transaction. Unless the note is recorded at its present value in this circumstance the sales price and profit to a seller in the year of the transaction and the purchase price and cost to the buyer are misstated, and interest income and interest expense in subsequent periods are also misstated. The primary objective of this Opinion is to refine the manner of applying existing accounting principles in this circumstance. Thus, it is not intended to create a new accounting principle.

2. *Applicability.* The principles discussed in this Opinion are applicable to receivables and payables which represent contractual rights to receive money or contractual obligations to pay money on fixed or determinable dates, whether or not there is any stated provision for interest, except as stated in paragraphs 3 and 4. Such receivables and payables are collectively referred to in this Opinion as "notes." Examples are secured and unsecured notes, debentures, bonds, mortgage notes, equipment obligations, and some accounts receivable and payable.

3. Except that paragraph 16 covering statement presentation of discount and premium is applicable in all circumstances, this Opinion is not intended to apply to:

(a) receivables and payables rising from transactions with customers or suppliers in the normal course of business which are due in customary trade terms not exceeding approximately one year;

(b) amounts which do not require repayment in the future, but rather will be applied to the purchase price of the property, goods, or service involved (e. g., deposits or progress payments on construction contracts, advance payments for acquisition of resources and raw materials, advances to encourage exploration in the extractive industries);   .   .   ..

4. This Opinion is also not intended to apply to, and the Board is not presently taking a position as to, the application of the present value measurement (valuation) technique to estimates of contractual or other obligations assumed in connection with sales of property, goods, or service, for example, a warranty for product performance.
.   .   .

DISCUSSION

6. *Note received or issued for cash.* The total amount of interest during the entire period of a cash loan is generally measured by the difference between the actual amount of cash received by the borrower and the total amount agreed to be repaid to the lender. Frequently, the stated or coupon interest rate differs from the prevailing rate applicable to similar notes, and the proceeds of the note differ from its face amount. As the Appendix to this Opinion demonstrates, such differences are related to differences between the present value upon issuance and the face amount of the note. The difference between the face amount and the proceeds upon issuance is

shown as either discount or premium, which is amortized over the life of the note.[5]

* * *

8. *Note received or issued in a noncash transaction.* A note exchanged for property, goods, or service represents two elements, which may or may not be stipulated in the note: (1) the principal amount, equivalent to the bargained exchange price of the property, goods, or service as established between the supplier and the purchaser and (2) an interest factor to compensate the supplier over the life of the note for the use of funds he would have received in a cash transaction at the time of the exchange. Notes so exchanged are accordingly valued and accounted for at the present value of the consideration exchanged between the contracting parties at the date of the transaction in a manner similar to that followed for a cash transaction. The difference between the face amount and the present value upon issuance is shown as either discount or premium, which is amortized over the life of the note.

9. *Determining present value.* If determinable, the established exchange price (which, presumably, is the same as the price for a cash sale) of property, goods, or service acquired or sold in consideration for a note may be used to establish the present value of the note. When notes are traded in an open market, the market rate of interest and market value of the notes provide the evidence of the present value. The above methods are preferable means of establishing the present value of the note.

10. If an established exchange price is not determinable and if the note has no ready market, the problem of determining present value is more difficult. To estimate the present value of a note under such circumstances, an applicable interest rate is approximated which may differ from the stated or coupon rate. This process of approximation is frequently called imputation, and the resulting rate is often called an imputed interest rate. Nonrecognition of an apparently small difference between the stated rate of interest and the applicable current rate may have a material effect on the financial statements if the face amount of the note is large and its term is relatively long.

OPINION

11. *Note exchanged for cash.* When a note is received or issued solely for cash and no other right or privilege is exchanged, it is presumed to have a present value at issuance measured by the cash proceeds exchanged. . . .

5. For example, if a bond is issued at a discount or premium, such discount or premium is recognized in accounting for the original issue. The coupon or stated interest rate is not regarded as the effective yield or market rate. Moreover, if a long-term noninterest bearing note or bond is issued, its net proceeds are less than face amount and an effective interest rate is based on its market value upon issuance. As the Appendix illustrates, the coupon or stated rate of interest and the face amount of a note or bond may *not* be the appropriate bases for valuation. The presumption that market values provide the evidence for valuation must be overcome before using coupon or stated rates and face or maturity amounts as the bases for accounting.

12. *Note exchanged for property, goods, or service.* When a note is exchanged for property, goods, or service in a bargained transaction entered into at arm's length, there should be a general presumption that the rate of interest stipulated by the parties to the transaction represents fair and adequate compensation to the supplier for the use of the related funds. That presumption, however, must not permit the form of the transaction to prevail over its economic substance and thus would not apply if (1) interest is not stated, or (2) the stated interest rate is unreasonable (paragraphs 13 and 14) or (3) the stated face amount of the note is materially different from the current cash sales price for the same or similar items or from the market value of the note at the date of the transaction. In these circumstances, the note, the sales price, and the cost of the property, goods, or service exchanged for the note should be recorded at the fair value of the property, goods, or service or at an amount that reasonably approximates the market value of the note, whichever is the more clearly determinable. That amount may or may not be the same as its face amount, and any resulting discount or premium should be accounted for as an element of interest over the life of the note (paragraph 15). In the absence of established exchange prices for the related property, goods, or service or evidence of the market value of the note (paragraph 9), the present value of a note that stipulates either no interest or a rate of interest that is clearly unreasonable should be determined by discounting all future payments on the notes using an imputed rate of interest as described in paragraphs 13 and 14. This determination should be made at the time the note is issued, assumed, or acquired; any subsequent changes in prevailing interest rates should be ignored.

13. *Determining an appropriate interest rate.* The variety of transactions encountered precludes any specific interest rate from being applicable in all circumstances. However, some general guides may be stated. The choice of a rate may be affected by the credit standing of the issuer, restrictive covenants, the collateral, payment and other terms pertaining to the debt, and, if appropriate, the tax consequences to the buyer and seller. The prevailing rates for similar instruments of issuers with similar credit ratings will normally help determine the appropriate interest rate for determining the present value of a specific note at its date of issuance. In any event, the rate used for valuation purposes will normally be at least equal to the rate at which the debtor can obtain financing of a similar nature from other sources at the date of the transaction. The objective is to approximate the rate which would have resulted if an independent borrower and an independent lender had negotiated a similar transaction under comparable terms and conditions with the option to pay the cash price upon purchase or to give a note for the amount of the purchase which bears the prevailing rate of interest to maturity.

14. The selection of a rate may be affected by many considerations. For instance, where applicable, the choice of a rate may be influenced by (a) an approximation of the prevailing market rates for the source of credit that would provide a market for sale or assignment of the note; (b) the prime or higher rate for notes which are discounted with banks, giving due weight to the credit standing of the maker; (c) published market rates for similar quality bonds; (d) current rates for debentures with substantially identical terms and risks that are

traded in open markets; and (e) the current rate charged by investors for first or second mortgage loans on similar property.

15. *Amortization of discount and premium.* With respect to a note which by the provisions of this Opinion requires the imputation of interest, the difference between the present value and the face amount should be treated as discount or premium and amortized as interest expense or income over the life of the note in such a way as to result in a constant rate of interest when applied to the amount outstanding at the beginning of any given period. This is the "interest" method . . . .

However, other methods of amortization may be used if the results obtained are not materially different from those which would result from the "interest" method.

16. *Statement presentation of discount and premium.* The discount or premium resulting from the determination of present value in cash or non-cash transactions is not an asset or liability separable from the note which gives rise to it. Therefore, the discount or premium should be reported in the balance sheet as a direct deduction from or addition to the face amount of the note. It should not be classified as a deferred charge or deferred credit. The description of the note should include the effective interest rate; the face amount should also be disclosed in the financial statements or in the notes to the statements. Amortization of discount or premium should be reported as interest in the statement of income. Issue costs should be reported in the balance sheet as deferred charges.

* * *

APPENDIX

18. *Present value concepts.* Upon issuance of a note or bond, the issuer customarily records as a liability the face or principal amount of the obligation. Ordinarily, the recorded liability also represents the amount which is to be repaid upon maturity of the obligation. The value recorded in the liability account, however, may be different from the proceeds received or the present value of the obligation at issuance if the market rate of interest differs from the coupon rate of interest. For example, consider the issuance of a $1,000, 20-year bond which bears interest at 10% annually. If we assume that 10% is an appropriate market rate of interest for such a bond the proceeds at issuance will be $1,000. The bond payable would be recorded at $1,000 which represents the amount repayable at maturity and also the present value at issuance which is equal to the proceeds. However, under similar circumstances, if the prevailing market rate were more (less) than 10%, a 20-year 10% bond with a face amount of $1,000 would usually have a value at issuance and provide cash proceeds of less (more) than $1,000. The significant point is that, upon issuance, a bond is valued at (1) the present value of the future coupon interest payments *plus* (2) the present value of the future principal payments (face amount). These two sets of future cash payments are discounted at the prevailing market rate of interest (for an equivalent security) at the date of issuance of the debt. As the 8% and 12% columns show, premium or discount arises when the prevailing market rate of interest differs from the coupon rate:

	Assume prevailing market rate of		
	10%	8%	12%
1. Present value of annual interest payments of $100 (the coupon rate of 10% of $1,000) for 20 years	$ 851	$ 982	$747
2. Present value of payment of the face amount of $1,000 at the end of year 20	149	215	104
Present value and proceeds at date of issuance	$1,000	$1,197	$851

19. In the case of a $1,000, noninterest bearing 20-year note, where the prevailing market rate for comparable credit risks is 10%, the following valuation should be made:

1. Present value of no annual interest payments .... $ 0
2. Present value of payment of the face amount of $1,000 at the end of year 20   149

   Present value and proceeds at date of issuance $149

Comparison of the results of the illustrations in paragraph 18 with the illustration above shows the significant impact of interest.

20. *Illustrations of balance sheet presentation of notes which are discounted.*

	December 31	
	1970	1969
Example 1—Discount presented in caption		
NOTE RECEIVABLE FROM SALE OF PROPERTY:		
$1,000,000 face amount, noninterest bearing, due December 31, 1975 (less unamortized discount based on imputed interest rate of 8%—1970, $320,000; 1969, $370,000)	$ 680,000	$ 630,000
Example 2—Discount presented separately		
NOTE RECEIVABLE FROM SALE OF PROPERTY:		
Noninterest bearing note due December 31, 1975	$1,000,000	$1,000,000
Less unamortized discount based on imputed interest rate of 8%	320,000	370,000
Note receivable less unamortized discount ..	$ 680,000	$ 630,000

BAUMEL v. ROSEN *

United States District Court, District of Maryland, 1968.
283 F.Supp. 128.

[Action by plaintiffs Baumel and Weiner alleging that their sales of stock of Gulf American Company to the defendants had been induced by misrepresentations and omissions, in violation of SEC Rule 10b–5. In July, 1957 the defendant Rosen brothers had organized Gulf American to sell land lots in Florida, paying $52,000 for 26,000 shares, which represented 52% of the total authorized stock of 50,000 shares. To raise additional funds, in the fall of 1957 Gulf American sold "units", consisting of a $10,000 debenture and 500 shares of stock, for $11,000 per unit to friends and acquaintances of the Rosens, and the plaintiffs each bought one unit. All of the buyers had received a prospectus containing a projection of land sales for the years 1958–1961 in the respective amounts of $2,000,000 for 1958, $3,000,000 for 1959, $4,000,000 for 1960, and $3,000,000 for 1961, with net profit after taxes for the four-year period of several million dollars. These figures were in fact substantially exceeded.

In 1959 the Rosens set out to acquire all of the Gulf American stock held by outsiders, and in August of that year they purchased the plaintiffs' units for $20,000 each, $10,000 for the debenture and $10,000 for the 500 shares of stock.]

WINTER, CIRCUIT JUDGE (by designation):

*   *   *

An issue in the case is the proper method of accounting to determine the income from the sale of lots sold under installment contracts. The dispute revolves around whether the gross selling price of a lot should be treated as income in the fiscal period in which the contract of sale of the lot is executed (the "accrual" method of accounting), or whether there should be included in income only the installment payments made under such a contract, with an appropriate entry treating payments yet to be made as a species of deferred income (the "installment" method of accounting).

*   *   *

The results of operations, including Gulf American sales, cancellations and collections, were known on a day-to-day basis to Leonard and Julius Rosen. Both were actual and self-acknowledged experts in making installment sales, and both had full appreciation of the fact, implicit in such business, that the greater the volume of sales the greater the need for additional capital to purchase land, to make improvements thereon, and to pay expenses in connection with such sales until such time as the total purchase prices under the installment contracts of sale were paid in full. Leonard Rosen also fully understood the difference between installment and accrual methods of accounting for a

---

* Portions of the opinion and most of the footnotes omitted. The decision on liability was affirmed by the Court of Appeals for the Fourth Circuit, but the decree of rescission was reversed (because the plaintiffs did not move expeditiously enough to disavow their sales) in favor of damages measured as of the date of Gulf American's first public offering, in 1961. 412 F.2d 571 (1969).

business of the type in which Gulf American was engaged. Conversely, Milton J. Baumel, who had experience only as a prize fighter and the operator of a restaurant, and Earl R. Weiner, who is a dentist, lacked this sophisticated business knowledge. In the operation of his restaurant, Baumel relies on Mrs. Baumel and an outside accountant to keep his books and records.

[The Court then detailed the circumstances under which the Rosens had purchased units from stockholders other than the plaintiffs.]

Against this background, the specific acquisitions from the plaintiffs will be considered. First, consideration should be given to the extent of knowledge which the plaintiffs had of Gulf American's operations. Plaintiffs' business knowledge, or lack thereof, implicit from the business and profession in which each had theretofore been engaged, has been stated. The plaintiffs were furnished with a copy of the "Proposal" which set forth the anticipated results of Gulf American's operations. Additionally, a stockholders meeting was held March 31, 1958, the minutes of which recite that the plaintiffs were present. At the meeting it was announced that Gulf American had sold over $1,000,000 worth of lots by March 26, 1958, and that the level of sales should attain a minimum of $3,000,000 worth of sales by August 30, 1958.

A second stockholders meeting was held December 17, 1958, at which Leonard Rosen stated that Gulf American "had projected sales" in the amount of $8,000,000 during the year 1959. George London, an accountant, who had been associated with Rosen enterprises for many years, made a financial report on operations for the fiscal year ended August 31, 1958 and stated that a copy of the financial report containing a balance sheet and profit and loss statement would be mailed out within several days. Milton J. Baumel was present at this meeting; the record does not disclose whether Dr. Weiner was also present. The report which was mailed contained a balance sheet as of August 31, 1958 showing an impairment in the stockholders' investment of $1,496.42 as a result of a net loss in like amount from operations for the year ended August 31, 1958. The statement of profit and loss employed the installment method of accounting and, while it showed net sales of lots in the amount of $6,368,597.42 with gross profit thereon of $3,519,725.30, the last-named figure was reduced by unrealized gross profit on installment sales amounting to $2,661,248.98, thus leaving a gross profit realized on lots sold of $858,476.32. While the minutes of the December 17, 1958 stockholders meeting do not corroborate the fact, there was testimony that, at that meeting, George London explained the difference between installment and accrual accounting. The report, prepared by Bogue and Taylor, certified public accountants, of Fort Myers, Florida, contained no such explanation, although it did state that Gulf American had elected for accounting purposes and for federal income tax reporting to take into income each year "only that portion of gross profit on installment sales that the ratio of gross profit bears to the cash received," and that this method of reporting was "consistent with accepted accounting practices within the industry as well as for federal income tax purposes."

In connection with the semi-annual payment of interest on debentures, debenture holders were advised by letter dated January 2, 1959 that Gulf American had "gone over the $9 million sales figure in spite of the fact that business has been very slow during the last sixty days of the year." A similar letter, dated July 10, 1959, succinctly stated, "Business and progress continue satisfactorily."

On or about August 24, 1959, Leonard Rosen telephoned Baumel to arrange a meeting with him. When they met, Rosen told Baumel that Gulf American was badly in need of financing and that he (Rosen) needed Baumel's stock and other stock that Rosen had or was going to get to make a substantial loan to keep Gulf American going. Rosen did not disclose, nor did Baumel ask, the person or source from which the loan could be made. While Baumel had received the Bogue and Taylor report of August 31, 1958, he was impressed only by the net loss figure of $1,496.42. Baumel did not actually know that sales were consistently running ahead of projections. He was impressed by Rosen's statement that Gulf American needed money and could get money only with Baumel's stock and the stock of others, so that Baumel concluded " . . . I thought if I wouldn't do it, I was going to lose my investment so that the best thing to do would be to sell it to him." Notwithstanding this belief, Baumel traded the price for his stock from $8,000 up to $10,000, and, on the day of settlement, further negotiated the sale of his debenture.

* * *

Because of the claim that Rule 10b–5 was violated by the failure to disclose certain other events concerning Gulf American which occurred prior to the acquisition of plaintiffs' stock, it is necessary to state these events. There is no question on this record that plaintiffs neither knew nor were advised of them, although they were well known to Leonard and Julius Rosen and to Bernard Herzfeld. Plaintiffs have testified that knowledge of any one of these facts would have had a material bearing on their decision to sell.

Gulf American sales had increased from approximately $6,000,000 for the fiscal year ended August 31, 1958 to $14,000,000 for the fiscal year ended August 31, 1959. Leonard Rosen paid strict attention to the volume of sales on a day-to-day basis, as well as cancellations and collections, and this information was communicated to his brother and his close financial advisers.

Early in 1959, Leonard Rosen commenced negotiations with Meadow Brook National Bank of Nassau County, Long Island, for a loan to Gulf American. The loan, in the amount of $600,000, was forthcoming on June 3, 1959. It was the first large outside financing that Gulf American had obtained and Leonard Rosen viewed the loan as "substantial" and "important," not only as advancing Gulf American's business but as a mark of lender confidence in Gulf American. In connection with negotiating the loan, Leonard Rosen obtained a statement of accounts for Gulf American as of March 31, 1959, prepared by London and Selenkow, a firm of which George London was a partner, *employing the accrual basis of accounting*, which showed an estimated profit for the seven months of operations ended March 31, 1959, after taxes, of $1,539,174—*an estimated profit of $15,000 per unit of stock outstanding*.

The statement compared the results of operations under the installment method of accounting also, but made the significant statement " . . . this method [installment method of accounting] in the early and formative stages of a business does not truly reflect the results of the activities. . . . This is entirely proper for Income Tax reporting, but management desires to show the activities of the company as reflected on the Accrual basis, setting up certain reserves for future Administration and Collection Costs."

As originally represented in the "Proposal" Gulf American had acquired 280 acres of land and had an option for an additional 1,500 adjacent acres. Prior to the acquisition of plaintiffs' stock, Gulf American had substantially increased its inventory of salable acreage.

At some time in the period August 12 to August 25, 1959, Leonard Rosen met with representatives of Shields & Co. for the purpose of inducing Shields to effect a public offering of Gulf American securities. Leonard Rosen made disclosure to Shields & Co. of financial information concerning Gulf American, including sales, cancellations and profits, and Shields & Co. expressed interest in arranging for public or private financing, but made no commitment in that regard. Shields & Co. tentatively valued the equity of Gulf American at more than $5,000,-000.[6]

* * *

APPLICATION OF LEGAL PRINCIPLES

The Court finds that Leonard and Julius Rosen, beginning in February, 1959, formulated and embarked on a plan to acquire stock of Gulf American. . . .

The plan to acquire stock of Gulf American was not in itself illegal, but the manner of execution and the misrepresentation and the material non-disclosures made to the plaintiffs in connection therewith, in the context of the plan, violated Rule 10b–5. First, the misrepresentations and non-disclosures to Baumel will be commented on:

Baumel was told that Gulf American needed money. The statement was literally true, but the making of this representation and the context in which it was made in the view of the Court created a duty to make a specific disclosure why Gulf American needed money and, in particular, to disclose that Gulf American's sales were exceeding all expectations so that, because the sales were made on an installment basis, Gulf American needed additional funds to acquire more land and to develop that which had been sold. It is true that the record discloses that Baumel had some knowledge of a rising trend of sales, but the full extent of the rise was not known to him. Conversely, Leonard and Julius Rosen and, through them, Rosen Investment Corporation, knew on a day-to-day basis net land sales, exclusive of cancellations, and the extent of collections. The non-disclosure of the volume of sales, under the circumstances, was in itself a violation of Rule 10b–5.

Rule 10b–5 was also violated by the defendant's failure to disclose deferred profits during the part of fiscal 1959 to the date that the purchase of Baumel's stock was negotiated. On the basis of the expert accounting testimony, the Court does not find that the accrual method of accounting was proper for all circumstances, but the Court is in full agreement with Gulf American's accountants (London and Selenkow)

---

6. If this estimate is accepted a "unit" of stock (500 shares) would have a value of approximately $50,000.

that the installment method of accounting tended to conceal the real success of the Gulf American enterprise in its beginning stage. While the use of the accrual method of accounting would not be provident for income tax purposes and other usual business purposes, a purchase of stock by an insider would, in the view of the Court, require a specific disclosure to an unsophisticated outsider of deferred profits which had accrued since the last financial statement. It should be noted that the last financial statement was only a few days short of a year old when the Baumel purchase was effected. Under these circumstances, and in the context of the affirmative statement that Gulf American needed money, disclosure of the report on which a $600,000 bank loan had been obtained and which showed that deferred profits of $15,000 had accrued on the stock purchased from Baumel for $10,000, should have been made.

Disclosure should also have been made of the fact of the bank loan as such. . . .

Notwithstanding his testimony to the contrary, the Court does not conclude that acquisition of additional land by Gulf American was material to Baumel; nor was the identity of the purchaser material. The Court also concludes that Gulf American's negotiations with Shields & Co. were too speculative to require disclosure.

* * *

The record shows that Baumel realized a handsome profit when he sold stock for which he paid $1,000 for $10,000, after having held the stock for a period of approximately 21 months, but the substantiality of this profit pales when the share of the deferred profits attributable to this stock interest in fiscal 1959, and the tentative valuation of Shields & Co. on this stock interest are considered. The Court concludes that Baumel's profit was not the only motivating factor causing him to sell, and the Court further concludes that he was influenced by the material non-disclosures and the material misrepresentation to which reference has been made.

———

Compare May v. Wilcox Furniture Downtown, Inc., 450 S.W.2d 734 (Tex.Civ.App.1969), sustaining an auditor's determination of the "book value" of the stock of two furniture corporations, under a stock repurchase agreement, on the basis of the installment method of accounting regularly used by the corporations for both financial accounting and tax purposes; the court accepted the auditor's characterization of the installment basis as "an acceptable method of computing income for financial purposes even though it may not have been the preferred method," rejecting the plaintiff's contention that the accrual basis "is the most reasonable, equitable and logical method."

PROBLEM

Culinary Corporation (CC) is a large, publicly-owned corporation operating a chain of rapid service restaurants under the name "Chicken Counter" throughout the country. CC keeps its books of account on a fiscal year basis, and its most recent fiscal year just ended last month. After considerable growth earlier, a few years ago CC's net income levelled out at around $3,000,000, on sales revenues of approximately $50,000,000. In an effort to expand its operations, CC's management decided to embark on a franchising program, under which local entrepreneurs would be awarded a permanent franchise to conduct a restaurant under the name and distinctive style of "Chicken Counter". The cost of a franchise was set at $50,000, payable $10,000 down and $10,000 per year for each of the next four years; in case of default in such payments, CC reserved the right to cancel the franchise and treat payments made to date as liquidated damages. In addition, the franchisee is required to pay CC annual royalties in the amount of 2% of the franchisee's sales. The franchise agreements also required that the enterprise be conducted in strict accordance with CC's rules and regulations, and many of the items sold in the restaurant were expected to be purchased from CC.

The new franchise program was formally adopted by CC's board of directors about eighteen months ago, with sales of the franchises to start a couple of months later. The management believed that for the foreseeable future the optimum number of franchises which CC could properly service and supervise would be about 120, and they planned to award about forty new franchises a year until that number was reached. It was expected that cost of getting forty franchises started, consisting of such things as site selection, start-up advertising and promotion, and pre-operation training of franchise personnel, would amount to approximately $720,000.

The new franchise program got off to a slow start in that first year (year 1), and no franchises had been sold by the beginning of CC's most recent fiscal year (year 2). While there was no dearth of applicants for franchises, it proved to be more difficult than expected to screen the applicants and decide which ones should receive franchises. In fact, CC's initial lack of regularized procedures for selecting applicants had led to substantial controversy with some of the applicants, who claimed that they had been promised franchises by certain of CC's representatives. Several lawsuits had been commenced or threatened by the end of year 1, with damages sought in amounts ranging from $30,000 to $70,000 per claim. In the opinion of CC's counsel, ten of the disappointed applicants had strong claims for breach of contract against CC, for amounts ranging from $20,000 to $30,000 each; CC's financial statements for that fiscal year contained a footnote making general reference to the company's possible liability on this account. However, by the beginning of year 2 CC had substantially improved its procedures for dealing with applicants for franchises, and no additional claims of this sort were expected.

Early last year CC's management decided that a substantial promotional campaign should be undertaken to publicize the new franchise program. After consulting with its long-time advertising firm about the most effective promotion program for the sale of franchises, CC adopted a plan under which $800,000 was expended last year (year 2) in promoting the sale of franchises, and another $400,000 is to be spent during the current year (year 3); no further franchise advertising is expected to be needed next year (year 4) to sell the last 40 franchises.

As the sale of new franchises began to pick up momentum last year, CC's management decided that it would be advisable not to incur the risk of unfavorable publicity that might result from trial of the claims of the disappointed applicants for franchises. Accordingly, CC instructed its counsel to settle all of these claims on as favorable terms as possible, which counsel succeeded in doing well before the end of the year (year 2), at a total cost of $240,000. By the close of the year (year 2), CC had sold its first forty franchises for $2,000,-000, of which it had received downpayments totalling $400,000.

CC's management is aware that franchise companies have been the subject of special attention in the stock market, with a good deal of concern expressed about not only the picture of current operations for such companies but also their long-term growth rate. Accordingly, the management wants to be very careful about how the facts relating to the franchise program are reflected in the company's financial statements for last year, which are already in the process of preparation. The CC management had consulted the senior partner in your office, who in turn has asked for your views on the matter, particularly with regard to whether income should be recognized on the sale of the forty franchises, and, if so, in what manner.

3. REFLECTING THE OBLIGATION TO MAKE A FUTURE PAYMENT AS A LIABILITY BEFORE IT IS CHARGED TO CURRENT EXPENSE

Review pages 30–31, supra, particularly footnote 2 which suggests that under some circumstances an obligation to pay an expense in the future may call for recording as a liability on the balance sheet even though the expense involved is not being charged against current income. Take the brokers' commissions in the Pacific Grape Products Co. problem, page 377, supra. As we noted, if the $300,000 of goods ordered but not shipped at the end of the year are treated as not sold during that year then the principles of matching dictate that these commissions should not be charged to expense for that year; it would normally follow that no Expense Payable would be created, and the liability for the brokers' commissions would not appear on the balance sheet at the close of that year. However, suppose, as suggested in the *Pacific Grape* case, at page 376, supra, that the brokers had earned their commissions as of the end of the year: might it not be misleading to fail to disclose this liability on the balance sheet? If the liability is to be recorded, there must be a corresponding debit, and, as that footnote 2 on page 31 suggests, creation of a deferred expense asset would seem to be the only possibility, despite the fact that cash has not moved.

QUESTION

Suppose that two months before the end of year 1 Pacific Grape had contracted for four months of spot advertising on radio for $10,000 per month, designed to pave the way for a new product to be introduced to the market early in year 2. Payment of the entire $40,000, covering the last two months of year 1 and the first two months of year 2, became due on the last day of year 1, but nothing had been paid as of that date. How should this transaction be reflected in Pacific Grape's financial statements for year 1?

Similar issues may arise with regard to reflecting receivables prior to recognition of the related income. For example, take the $420,000 which the customers had contracted to pay for those goods ordered but not shipped at year end, in the Pacific Grape problem on page 377. Although traditional accounting would seem to point in the direction of not reflecting the company's right to receive this amount until the income from the transaction is recognized, see page 33, supra, notice how Ebasco, in the *Boise Cascade* case, accounted for amounts billed for services not yet performed, as described in the last full paragraph on page 315, supra. See also the treatment of the "sale" price for the nursing homes in the *Herzfeld* case, at pages 129–130, supra.

A. LEASES

The question of when and how to reflect commitments for future expenses is presented in dramatic fashion in the case of long-term leases; the issues involved are analyzed in the following article, and the subsequent resolution of the problem by the FASB is set out immediately thereafter.

WYATT, ACCOUNTING FOR LEASES *

1972 Illinois Law Forum 497.

Controversies over the accounting for and reporting of leases have persisted for years. Disagreement among accountants on the under-

---

lying issues plus pressures from imbedded business interests have made resolution of these controversies difficult. Still, however, most accountants are anxious to resolve the divergencies in practice, for until uniformity is achieved investors and creditors will be forced to make their own adjustments to the financial reports of companies significantly involved in leasing.

I.   Nature of Leases in Accounting

Accountants generally agree that leases are executory contracts; at the time a lease agreement is signed one party agrees to pay a sum at future dates in return for the right to use a specified resource over a specified future period. In accounting, executory contracts are typically accounted for as the resources are used and the agreed payments are earned; no accounting entries are generally recorded at the time the agreements are signed. Likewise, for many leases no accounting entries are made at the agreement date. Accounting entries are made periodically either at the start of a period in which leased resources are available for use and a payment is made for those services, or, less frequently, following the period of use.

The recognition of lease contracts in accounting records in this manner is similar to the accounting for other types of executory contracts, such as personal services of salaried or hourly rated employees, and discount (interest) payments for the use of money. Many accountants contend that recognition of lease obligations in this manner for accounting purposes is not only appropriate but is the only permissible approach. Other accountants agree that many lease obligations are properly accounted for in this manner but that some lease contracts have essentially the same economic and legal substance as installment purchases and should be accounted for as installment purchases. Still other accountants believe the right to use property constitutes an asset that requires accountability.

A.   *Leases as Installment Purchases*

For various business reasons contracts to grant a party the right to use property owned by another (leases) are sometimes drawn so that the lessee is making a noncancellable commitment to pay rent for the use of the property for its entire economic life. Various conditions may exist with regard to the conveyance of title at the end of the lease term. The important point, however, is that while the business document underlying the agreement is called, and may legally be, a lease, it nonetheless has the economic attributes of an installment sale (purchase) contract.

Accountants are inclined to focus more closely on economic substance than legal form. In practice, therefore, these leases are recorded in the same manner as installment purchases. The lessee records the property subject to the lease as a fixed asset based upon the present value of the lease commitment. This amount (cost of the property) is then depreciated over the useful life of the property. Also, upon execution of the lease, a liability is recorded to offset the cost. Rental payments are then charged partly to interest expense and partly to a reduction of the liability recorded.

B. *Operating Leases and Financing Leases*

As the economic substance of the lease agreement becomes less like an installment sales contract, the accounting issue becomes more complicated. The lease terms become wide ranging and complex and thus less clear from both a legal and accounting view. Accountants have developed only two basic methods to account for leasing transactions. The problem, therefore, is to fit each of the wide range of transactions bearing the label "lease transaction" into one of the two methods. The fit results in considerable straining at times, particularly when a document which has been painstakingly structured to appear to be at one extreme of the lease spectrum is in economic substance at the opposite end.

Accountants have come to classify leases for accounting purposes as either operating leases or financing leases. Operating leases are those determined to be principally in the nature of a "true" lease. The lessee is generally committing himself on a noncancellable basis for a period less than the life of the property being leased. The lessor is generally retaining significant rights in connection with the leased property so that when the lease term expires he will have control of the property either for releasing or other disposition. Under an operating lease the lessee recognizes the lease rental payments as an expense in the period in which the property is used. The lessee may additionally disclose in a financial statement footnote the commitments existing at a balance sheet date for existing leases. The lessor of an operating lease will recognize the lease rentals receivable in a period as revenue and will charge against income depreciation on the leased property, maintenance, and other related costs.

Financing leases are those determined to be essentially in the nature of installment purchases. The lessee is generally committing himself on a noncancellable basis for substantially all the economic life of the property under lease, or possibly for a shorter period when the payments under the noncancellable commitment cover the full purchase price of the property. In either case the lessor generally expects to receive under the lease terms the full normal sales price of the property after giving effect to the interest element in the lease rentals. The value of any future rights of the lessor at the time he enters into a financing lease are generally nominal.

Under a financing lease the lessee recognizes as a long-term asset (Property Used Under Lease Arrangement) the present value of the noncancellable lease commitments. Likewise, the lessee will recognize a similar amount as a long-term liability. The rental payments are partly a reduction of the liability and partly a charge to income for interest expense. The amount assigned to the long-term asset is depreciated over its useful life. The lessor of a financing lease will recognize a sale at the time the lease is entered into and charge the cost of the leased property to cost of sales. The receivable recognized to offset the sale will be reduced when rentals are received. Interest income will also be recognized for a portion of each rental.

II. ACCOUNTING FOR LEASES—LESSEE

Once a lessee has determined whether he has a "true" lease or an effective installment purchase, his method of accounting is relatively clear. The existing controversy centers primarily on the determination of the nature of the lease and not on the mechanics of accounting once its nature is determined. Before examining the methods used to distinguish the nature of a leasing transaction, however, the accounting entries to effect recognition of the transaction should be discussed briefly.

Assume a lessee enters into a lease arrangement on January 2, 1972, that provides for annual rental payments of $100,000 for each of the next 10 years. Assume further that the applicable borrowing rate for the lessee is 6 per cent.

If this lease is determined to be an operating lease by the lessee, he will make the following entry each period:

Dr. Rent Expense $100,000
   Cr. Rent Payable (Cash) $100,000

Thus, the charge against income would be $100,000 each year. In addition, the lessee would disclose pertinent details of the lease arrangement in notes to the financial statements.

If this lease is determined to be a financing lease by the lessee, he will make the following entry when the lease agreement becomes effective:

Dr. Property Used Under Lease
    Arrangement $780,169
   Cr. Lease Rentals Payable $780,169

The amount of $780,169 represents the present value at 6 per cent of 10 rental payments of $100,000 due annually, the first payment due upon the effective date of the lease agreement. An additional entry would be made for payment of the first rental:

Dr. Lease Rentals Payable $100,000
   Cr. Cash $100,000

The lessee would also make the following entries for the first year of use of the leased property, assuming the depreciable life is 10 years, no salvage is anticipated, and straight line depreciation is used. Each of these assumptions should be based upon the specific circumstances of the lessee and the property, and the lease terms are not significant to decisions on these assumptions.

Dr. Depreciation Expense $ 78,017
   Cr. Property Used Under
      Lease Agreement $ 78,017
Dr. Interest Expense $ 40,810
   Cr. Lease Rentals Payable $ 40,810

The first of these entries reflects the cost of the use of the property, while the second is necessary to record the interest expense related to the obligation due under the lease arrangement. It represents the cost of borrowing $680,169 ($780,169 the original amount due, less $100,000 paid) for one year at 6 per cent.

Thus, the total charge to income would be $118,827 for the first year, or $18,827 greater than the charge to income under the operating method. This excess will diminish as the years pass because of lower charges to interest expense as the lease rental liability is liquidated. In the ninth year the charge to income will be $83,-677 (the depreciation charge of $78,017 and an interest charge of $5,660). In the tenth year the final rental will be paid at the start of the year, so no interest would be incurred and the total charge to income would be $78,017 for depreciation.

. . .

Lessees generally tend to favor the operating lease designation for two reasons: (1) charges to income are lower in the early years of use, and (2) no liability for the lease rentals is recorded and reported on the lessee's balance sheet.

III. ACCOUNTING FOR LEASES—LESSOR

The lessor has the same problem of determining whether a given lease transaction is a "true" lease or is, in effect, a sale of the asset being leased. While it might seem logical that only one judgment is necessary for a given lease, and that both lessee and lessor would account for the lease based on that judgment, this is not the case. For practical reasons lessees and lessors do not necessarily account for a given lease in the same manner.* Judgments differ based upon different perspectives. Furthermore, existing guides in accounting are not consistent. Thus, for example, a substantial number of jet aircraft presently in use are not reported as assets on the financial statements of any company. The airline lessees view them as true leases (operating), while lessors view the leases as substantive sales, at least for accounting purposes.

As an illustration of lessor accounting, assume the same lease facts as in the preceding examples for a lessee: a lease arrangement that provides for annual rental payments in advance of use of $100,000 for each of the next 10 years; an applicable borrowing rate for the lessor of 6 per cent.

If the lessor determines this lease to be an operating lease, the rental receipts will be accounted for as revenue in the period they become receivable.

> Dr. Rent Receivable (Cash) $100,000
>   Cr. Rental Income $100,000

Thus, the revenue from the leasing of the asset will be level over the 10-year period. Against this revenue the lessor will charge depreciation based on the cost of the leased asset, any maintenance and other operating costs he must bear under the terms of the

---

* [Ed. note] The differences in treatment by lessors and lessees have been substantially curtailed by FAS No. 13, set out immediately below. See paragraphs 61 and 62, page 418, infra.

lease, and interest on any amounts borrowed to finance the construction or acquisition of the asset. Thus, even assuming straight line depreciation, the lessor will report decreasing costs and thus an increasing amount of net income from this lease since the interest costs will decline as the investment in the asset is recovered from the rental receipts.

If the lessor determines the lease to be a financing lease, he will recognize the lease transaction as equivalent to a sale. Thus, if the lessor is a manufacturer, he will recognize his manufacturing profit at the time the lease agreement becomes effective. If the lessor is not a manufacturer, the amount of profit would generally be smaller since the lessor's cost for the asset when acquired from the manufacturer would have included the manufacturer's profit. The lessor's entries for the lease used in previous examples would be as follows if the lessor concluded the lease was a financing lease:

Dr. Lease Rentals Receivable	$780,169	
Cr. Sales		$780,169
Dr. Cost of Sales	$650,000 [1]	
Cr. Inventory		$650,000

In addition, the lessor would make the following entries in the first year:

Dr. Cash	$100,000	
Cr. Lease Rentals Receivable		$100,000
(Receipt of first year's rent)		
Dr. Lease Rentals Receivable	$ 40,810	
Cr. Interest Income		$ 40,810

The latter entry represents the interest earned by the lessor for permitting the lessee to take 10 years to pay for the property. A similar entry would be made each year, but in declining amounts as the rent receipts reduce the amount "borrowed" by the lessee.

The above entries are based on the lessor's also being a manufacturer. If the lessor is basically a financier, the lessor will report as income only the interest earned on the funds provided. Thus, decreasing amounts of income would be reported as the years pass and the initial year would not include any noninterest profit element.

In many situations manufacturer-lessors favor the financing lease designation because it permits them to recognize their manufacturing profit in the year the equipment goes on lease rather than periodically over the term of the lease. Likewise, nonmanufacturer-lessors favor the financing method since periodic net income tends to be higher in early years and, therefore, tends to relate better to the relatively higher unrecovered investment that lessors have in the early years. The operating lease designation, on the other hand, tends to give a pattern of increasing net income even though unrecovered investment is declining. . . .

---

1. The $650,000 cost of the leased asset is an assumed amount.

IV. RATIONALE FOR OPERATING LEASE CLASSIFICATION

As noted earlier, many accountants tend to classify most if not all leases as operating leases because the legal form of the agreement is a lease, and title to the leased property remains with the lessor. Other accountants, as well as many lessors, believe many leases are financing leases and should be capitalized as long-term assets by lessees and considered to be receivables by lessors.

Generally, three reasons are put forth for the hesitancy of lessees to classify lease transactions as financing leases: (1) A desire to minimize the amount of debt reported on the balance sheet by not capitalizing lease obligations; (2) a legal distinction between direct debt and lease obligations; and (3) a position that leased facilities are not assets of the lessee.

Undoubtedly, the most compelling reason historically for lessees not desiring a financing method of classification is a desire to present a favorable picture of debt position in the balance sheet. Even today some bankers apparently consider the fixed commitments under noncancellable lease agreements to be of a nature different from debt. Indentures and loan agreements still sometimes do not include prohibitions against leasing, although this condition is changing. Casual analyses of debt-equity relationships obviously lead to more favorable conclusions if lease obligations are not shown as liabilities.

Increasingly today, bankers recognize that lease obligations are equivalent to direct debt, although indications continue to exist that companies receive better credit ratings if their obligations are for leased facilities rather than for mortgaged facilities. . . .

Lease obligations, however, are virtually identical to direct debt when financial adversity hits. Thus, an investment of $16 million by General Foods in its Burger Chef chain became an $83 million loss largely because of long-term lease commitments. . . .

Another reason lease obligations are not included as liabilities in financial statements of lessees is the emphasis on the legal distinction between a lease and a direct debt. There is no doubt that in law a lease is an executory contract, an agreement that services will be provided in the future. Both the performance of the services and the payment under the contract are based on contingencies, so that the lease obligation is different from the obligation on a conventional debt. However, accountants do not restrict their reports to legal distinctions. Many other "liabilities" in accounting have no status as such in the law. Unless accounting is to narrow existing practice and limit its financial statements to strict legalities, the real question is whether the lease obligation is too uncertain or too conjectural to appear as debt on a balance sheet.

Finally, many believe leased facilities are not assets of the lessee, since the lessee lacks ownership and merely has use of the facilities as long as he makes rental payments. Again, the issue is one of legal form in comparison to economic substance. Some lease agreements are virtually identical to installment purchase agreements, and the issue for accountants is whether legal status or economic substance should govern.

Many who object to the inclusion of leased facilities as assets and liabilities of lessees argue just as strongly that full and complete disclosure of the lease arrangements should be made in the notes to financial statements. Apparently the view is that the lease arrangement is important enough to require full disclosure but not important enough to require accountability in the financial statements. For many accountants the distinction is unacceptable. Independent certified public accountants bear the same responsibility (and legal liability) for representations in the financial statements and representations in the footnotes. The lower status some accord to footnote disclosures is not warranted in terms of reporting responsibility.

*   *   *

Income Statements

Whereas the principal concern up to the present time in lease accounting has been with the need to capitalize leases on the balance sheet, increasing interest is centered in the income statement effects. The exhibits presented earlier indicate that operating leases provide level rental costs for lessees and level revenue credits for lessors. However, for lessors the net revenues would show an increasing pattern after deduction of depreciation (generally straight line), operating costs, and interest on the unrecovered investment.

Financing leases, on the other hand, result in higher charges to income for lessees in the early years than if the lease were an operating lease. In later years this pattern reverses as the interest charges decline. For lessors the financing pattern may result in significant profit in the first year, particularly if the lessor is a manufacturer, and declining income over the lease term.

Thus, lessees have two reasons to classify leases as operating leases. First, such classification will prevent balance sheet capitalization and reporting of the lease commitments as liabilities. Second, such classification results in a level charge to income, and avoids the higher charges to income in early years that the financing method produces. While some interest has been expressed in using sinking-fund approaches to depreciation accounting (lower charges in early years, increasing as time passes), accountants have traditionally opposed such a depreciation pattern because of its relative lack of conservatism and the possibility that asset book values will exceed realizable values in early years.

Lessors, on the other hand, are generally motivated to have leases classified as financing leases for accounting purposes. Manufacturers and dealers are particularly so motivated in order to recognize their manufacturing or trading profit in the year the lease agreement is signed, rather than periodically over the lease term. Other lessors also generally prefer the financing method because the pattern of income recognition more closely relates to the unrecovered investment in the property than does the operating method.

*   *   *

STATEMENT OF FINANCIAL ACCOUNTING
STANDARDS NO. 13

Financial Accounting Standards Board, November, 1976.

ACCOUNTING FOR LEASES

* * *

Classification of Leases for Purposes of this Statement

6. For purposes of applying the accounting and reporting standards of this Statement, leases are classified as follows:

   a. Classifications from the standpoint of the lessee: *

      i. *Capital Leases.* Leases that meet one or more of the criteria in paragraph 7.

      ii. *Operating Leases.* All other leases.

* * *

Criteria for Classifying Leases . . .

7. The criteria for classifying leases set forth in this paragraph and in paragraph 8 derive from the concept set forth in paragraph 60. If at its inception . . . a lease meets one or more of the following four criteria, the lease shall be classified as a capital lease by the lessee. Otherwise, it shall be classified as an operating lease.

   a. The lease transfers ownership of the property to the lessee by the end of the lease term · . . . .

   b. The lease contains a bargain purchase option . . . . .

   c. The lease term . . . is equal to 75 percent or more of the estimated economic life of the lease property . . . . . However, if the beginning of the lease term falls within the last 25 percent of the total estimated economic life of the leased property, including earlier years of use, this criterion shall not be used for purposes of classifying the lease.

   d. The present value at the beginning of the lease term of the minimum lease payments . . . ., excluding that portion of the payments representing executory costs such as insurance, maintenance, and taxes to be paid by the lessor, including any profit thereon, equals or exceeds 90 percent of . . . the fair value of the leased property [less any related investment tax credit]. However, if the beginning of the lease term falls within the last 25 percent of the total estimated economic life of the leased property, including earlier years of use, this criterion shall not be used for purposes of classifying the lease. . . . A lessee shall compute the present value of the minimum lease

---

* Copyright © by Financial Accounting Standards Board, 1976. See acknowledgement, page xviii, supra. Substantial portions of the Statement, particularly those dealing with treatment of leases by lessors, omitted. However, see ¶'s 60–62, infra.

payments using his incremental borrowing rate [except in special circumstances].

* * *

Accounting and Reporting by Lessees

Capital Leases

10.   The lessee shall record a capital lease as an asset and an obligation at an amount equal to the present value at the beginning of the lease term of minimum lease payments during the lease term, excluding that portion of the payments representing executory costs such as insurance, maintenance, and taxes to be paid by the lessor, together with any profit thereon.   However, if the amount so determined exceeds the fair value of the leased property at the inception of the lease, the amount recorded as the asset and obligation shall be the fair value.   If the portion of the minimum lease payments representing executory costs, including profit thereon, is not determinable from the provisions of the lease, an estimate of the amount shall be made.   The discount rate to be used in determining present value of the minimum lease payments shall be that prescribed for the lessee in paragraph 7(d).

11.   Except . . . with respect to leases involving land, the asset recorded under a capital lease shall be amortized as follows:

a.   If the lease meets the criterion of either paragraph 7(a) or 7(b), the asset shall be amortized in a manner consistent with the lessee's normal depreciation policy for owned assets.

b.   If the lease does not meet either criterion 7(a) or 7(b), the asset shall be amortized in a manner consistent with the lessee's normal depreciation policy except that the period of amortization shall be the lease term.   The asset shall be amortized to its expected value, if any, to the lessee at the end of the lease term. . . .

12.   During the lease term, each minimum lease payment shall be allocated between a reduction of the obligation and interest expense so as to produce a constant periodic rate of interest on the remaining balance of the obligation. . . .

13.   Assets recorded under capital leases and the accumulated amortization thereon shall be separately identified in the lessee's balance sheet or in footnotes thereto.   Likewise, the related obligations shall be separately identified in the balance sheet as obligations under capital leases and shall be subject to the same considerations as other obligations in classifying them with current and noncurrent liabilities in classified balance sheets.   Unless the charge to income resulting from amortization of assets recorded under capital leases is included with depreciation expense and the fact that it is so included is disclosed, the amortization charge shall be separately disclosed in the financial statements or footnotes thereto.

* * *

Operating Leases

15.   Normally, rental on an operating lease shall be charged to expense over the lease term as it becomes payable.   If rental pay-

ments are not made on a straight-line basis, rental expense nevertheless shall be recognized on a straight-line basis unless another systematic and rational basis is more representative of the time pattern in which use benefit is derived from the leased property, in which case that basis shall be used.

Disclosures

16. The following information with respect to leases shall be disclosed in the lessee's financial statements or the footnotes thereto . . . .

    a. For capital leases:

       i. The gross amount of assets recorded under capital leases as of the date of each balance sheet presented by major classes according to nature or function. This information may be combined with the comparable information for owned assets.

       ii. Future minimum lease payments as of the date of the latest balance sheet presented, in the aggregate and for each of the five succeeding fiscal years, with separate deductions from the total for the amount representing executory costs, including any profit thereon, included in the minimum lease payments and for the amount of the imputed interest necessary to reduce the net minimum lease payments to present value (see paragraph 10).

       iii. The total of minimum sublease rentals to be received in the future under noncancelable subleases as of the date of the latest balance sheet presented.

       iv. Total contingent rentals (rentals on which the amounts are dependent on some factor other than the passage of time) actually incurred for each period for which an income statement is presented.

    b. For operating leases having initial or remaining noncancelable lease terms in excess of one year:

       i. Future minimum rental payments required as of the date of the latest balance sheet presented, in the aggregate and for each of the five succeeding fiscal years.

       ii. The total of minimum rentals to be received in the future under noncancelable subleases as of the date of the latest balance sheet presented.

    c. For all operating leases, rental expense for each period for which an income statement is presented, with separate amounts for minimum rentals, contingent rentals, and sublease rentals. Rental payments under leases with terms of a month or less that were not renewed need not be included.

    d. A general description of the lessee's leasing arrangements including, but not limited to, the following:

       i. The basis on which contingent rental payments are determined.

    ii. The existence and terms of renewal or purchase options and escalation clauses.

   iii. Restrictions imposed by lease agreements, such as those concerning dividends, additional debt, and further leasing.

*   *   *

APPENDIX B

BASIS FOR CONCLUSIONS

*   *   *

60.   The provisions of this Statement derive from the view that a lease that transfers substantially all of the benefits and risks incident to the ownership of property should be accounted for as the acquisition of an asset and the incurrence of an obligation by the lessee and as a sale or financing by the lessor.   All other leases should be accounted for as operating leases.   In a lease that transfers substantially all of the benefits and risks of ownership, the economic effect on the parties is similar, in many respects, to that of an installment purchase.   This is not to say, however, that such transactions are necessarily "in substance purchases" as that term is used in previous authoritative literature.

61.   The transfer of substantially all the benefits and risks of ownership is the concept embodied in previous practice in lessors' accounting   .   .   .   as a basis for determining whether a lease should be accounted for as a financing or sale or as an operating lease.   However, a different concept has existed in the authoritative literature for lessees' accounting, as evidenced by APB Opinion No. 5, "Reporting of Leases in Financial Statements of Lessee." That Opinion required capitalization of those leases that are "clearly in substance installment purchases of property," which it essentially defined as those leases whose terms "result in the creation of a material equity in the property."   Because of this divergence in both concept and criteria, a particular leasing transaction might be recorded as a sale or as a financing by the lessor and as an operating lease by the lessee.   This difference in treatment has been the subject of criticism as being inconsistent conceptually, and some of the identifying criteria for classifying leases, particularly those applying to lessees' accounting, have been termed vague and subject to varied interpretation in practice.

62.   The Board believes that this Statement removes most, if not all, of the conceptual differences in lease classification as between lessors and lessees and that it provides criteria for such classification that are more explicit and less susceptible to varied interpretation than those in previous literature.

63.   Some members of the Board who support this Statement hold the view that, regardless of whether substantially all the benefits and risks of ownership are transferred, a lease, in transferring for its term the right to use property, gives rise to the acquisition of an asset and the incurrence of an obligation by the lessee which should be reflected in his financial statements.   Those members nonetheless support this Statement because, to them, (i) it clarifies

and improves the guidelines for implementing the conceptual basis previously underlying accounting for leases and (ii) it represents an advance in extending the recognition of the essential nature of leases.

Chapter 6

INVENTORY

---

1. INTRODUCTION

Review the introductory materials on accounting for inventories in Chapter 1, section 7. As those materials suggest, inventory accounting is just a specialized problem of deferral, under which some of the total inventory costs incurred during a given year are charged to current expense for the year and some are deferred to future years. The process can be expressed in the form of an equation, as follows:

1		2		3
total inventory costs incurred	=	costs allocable to current year	+	costs deferred to later years

The difficulty lies in the fact that items 2 and 3 are both unknowns. While it is possible to determine the costs allocable to the current year by keeping a careful record of the cost of each item sold during the year, normally this would prove too time-consuming and expensive. Instead, the most practical way of approaching the problem is to attempt to ascertain item 3 by "taking inventory" at the end of the period. So the above equation is in effect rewritten as follows:

1		3		2
total inventory costs incurred	—	costs deferred to later years	=	costs allocable to current year

In this form, the equation states the operation of the Cost of Goods Sold account. In other words, the amount by which the total of inventory costs incurred during the year, consisting of the sum of the opening inventory and the purchases, exceeds the costs to be deferred to later years, represented by the closing inventory, is the figure obtained as the net debit balance in the Cost of Goods Sold account, constituting the cost of goods sold expense applicable to the current period.

Accounting for inventories, like accounting for bad debts, has both an income statement and a balance sheet objective. From the income statement point of view, it is important that the inventory costs related to current revenues be matched with those revenues in the current period. The balance sheet role of inventory stems from

420

the fact that inventory is one of the most liquid (i. e., readily convertible into cash) of a company's assets, ranking right after accounts receivable in this respect, and so the inventory figure receives close attention from those financially interested in the company, particularly short-term creditors concerned about the immediate financial resources of the enterprise; under the accounting principle of conservatism, there is much to be said for the proposition that Inventory, like Accounts Receivable, should not be carried on the balance sheet at anymore than the current realizable value. These respective balance sheet and income statement objectives may sometimes point in opposite directions, and we shall be considering shortly how any conflict between the two should be resolved.

Since the closing inventory for any period is the unknown item which is to be ascertained in order to determine the cost of goods sold, and is also the figure which will appear as "Inventory" on the balance sheet, this is the pivotal item. The principal questions revolve around the basis on which the closing inventory should be "priced", that is, translated into a dollar figure. But before we can grapple with the problems of pricing closing inventory, we must deal first with the question of what is included in closing inventory. You should recall that we have already considered one aspect of this problem in connection with the Pacific Grape Products Co. case. There we saw that a necessary corollary to the recognition of income from the "sale" of certain goods still in the company's warehouse was that those goods must be excluded from closing inventory. We turn now to the beginning of the cycle of operations, to consider at what point purchased goods first become included in inventory.

2. WHAT TO INCLUDE IN INVENTORY

The important twin roles of the closing inventory figure, to distribute inventory costs between present and future periods, and to represent an asset which is particularly significant because of its relative liquidity, underscore the need for an accurate physical check. When the company makes this check, i. e., "takes inventory", troublesome questions arise as to whether to include in the count goods "belonging" to the company but in the possession of someone else, or goods in the company's possession which "belong" to someone else. The following excerpt from Accountants' Handbook 12.21–12.23 (4th ed. by Wixon and Kell, 1956) * states accepted practice:

SPECIAL INVENTORY ITEMS. At the end of an accounting period, questions often arise as to what constitutes proper treatment of the following items:

1. Goods in transit on the inventory date, either from vendors or to customers.

2. Goods on hand which have been segregated for certain customers, or goods on order which have been segregated by the vendor.

3. Goods on order and advances on orders.

4. Merchandise either acquired or delivered on approval or under conditional sales contracts.

5. Goods consigned to agents or acquired on consignment.

6. Pledged or hypothecated merchandise.

Whether such items should be included in, or excluded from, inventory is usually determined by applying a legal test—the *passage of title*. There are a number of limitations to the legal rule as a practical solution to inventory questions, and where there is no legal controversy, present or imminent, other more practical criteria are often employed. It is important, however, for the accountant to remember that the utilization of a criterion other than the legal rule rests on the assumption that no significant information is concealed by failure to apply the legal rule.

Goods in Transit. Where goods are shipped F.O.B. shipping point and are in the hands of the common carrier on the last day of the period, strict application of the legal rule requires inclusion in inventory of in-transit purchases and exclusion of customer shipments. Occasionally, however, accountants object to the application of this rule to purchases on the grounds that it is impractical, preferring instead to employ the *criterion of receipt* on or before the last day of the period. Although the use of the receipt criterion, consistently applied, does not in most instances seriously distort the statement of financial position, the ease with which in-transit purchases can ordinarily be segregated by reviewing the receiving reports for the first few days of the new period leaves little support for the use of any other than the legal criterion. In the case of goods shipped F.O.B. destination, application of the legal rule requires exclusion of in-transit purchases and inclusion of in-transit merchandise sold to customers. Common accounting procedure, however, while adhering to the legal rule for purchases, employs the more practical *criterion of shipment* to exclude the merchandise shipped. Consistent application of the shipment rule causes little distortion of income and its usage eliminates the difficult task of locating merchandise en route to customers.

Segregated Goods. Where goods for filling customers' orders have been segregated by the vendor, title may pass upon segregation. If title has passed and the purchaser is aware of it, cost of the goods should be included in the purchaser's inventory and the payable recognized. Obviously, however, if the purchaser is unaware of the passage of title, such goods will be overlooked in the compilation of his inventory. The small error caused by failure to include these goods in inventory is usually considered preferable to the adoption of a procedure for surveying vendors to determine the legal status of goods on order. From the *legal point of view*, merchandise segregated by the vendor for customers is not a portion of the vendor's inventory. Inclusion of such goods in the inventory of the vendor means that neither the receivable nor the sale is recognized; on the other hand, exclusion of the goods means that revenue and the receivable are to be recognized before shipment. The effect of segregation upon the passage of title is often dependent upon legal technicalities difficult for even a lawyer to decide. For this reason many accountants are inclined to adopt the practice of recognizing revenue upon shipment of goods, a practice resulting in the inclusion of segregated goods in the inventory of the vendor.

Purchase Orders and Advances. In general, goods on order are not included in inventory. Although the purchase contract is binding on both parties, the goods either do not exist, or, if they do, title has not passed. Ordinarily, no entry should be made upon the books of the purchaser until actual delivery takes place. This, however, should not be construed as prohibiting the use of *statement footnotes* in order to call attention to any unusual conditions with respect to purchase commitments. . . .

Advances on purchase contracts are not inventory items. They are more in the nature of *prepayments*, being cash payments in advance for services (i. e., goods) to be received in the future. Since the advance is realized upon in the form of goods, not cash, it is the first step in the *investment-disbursement cycle* of working capital. It constitutes the working capital element furthest removed from the cash realization point, i. e., it must pass through the successive phases of inventory and accounts receivable before disinvestment. For this reason, treatment of the item as a receivable is as poor practice as considering it inventory. Byrnes-Baker-Smith (Auditing) suggest, as a reasonable treatment of this item, placing it directly below the inventory on the financial statements. Care should be taken by vendors receiving advances to see that they are properly recorded as liabilities.

Conditional and Approval Purchases and Sales. The treatment accorded approval and other conditional sales is largely a matter of expediency. A great deal depends upon the probability of the return of such goods. Legally, title to the goods is vested in the vendor until the customer accepts, makes payment, or otherwise performs on the contract in the manner specified for the passage of title. As a matter of convenience, where returns on goods sold on approval are small proportionate to total shipments, the simplest procedure is to consider shipment equivalent to sale. If this *expedient procedure* is adopted, a further refinement is possible. At the end of the accounting period an allowance can be created for the amount of anticipated returns on outstanding goods shipped on approval. This allowance should be treated as a valuation account for the receivables and a *special inventory account* should be established for the cost of the goods outstanding and expected to be returned. Where the more conservative practice of deferring revenue recognition until receipt of the customer's approval is adopted, the cost of the goods shipped conditionally, and now in the hands of customers, should be displayed in the financial statement as a separate inventory element.

Where goods are sold conditionally on *instalment contracts,* the cost of the goods held on such contracts, less the buyers' equity in such goods, should be carried as a special inventory account.

Consignments. The title to goods shipped or received on consignment remains with the consignor while possession of such goods is transferred to the consignee who acts as the agent of the consignor. Goods on consignment should be included in the inventory of the consignor as a special type of inventory and should be excluded from the inventory of the consignee. Where arbitrary markons are added to the cost of goods shipped on consignment, they must be deducted from the dollar amount of consigned goods before inclusion in the final inventory. Shipping and other appropriate charges for transfer of the goods to the consignee are legitimate additions to the cost of goods shipped on consignment and are therefore a proper portion of inventory. Care should be taken to see that shipping and other charges added to the manufacturing cost of the goods on consignment are reasonable and do not include charges for double freight, etc. . . .

Pledged or Hypothecated Goods. Where goods have been pledged or hypothecated as security on a contract, title is not transferred by the pledge or hypothecation. Such goods should be included in the inventory of the owner, with the special conditions indicated in a *footnote* to the financial statements.

EMPIRE LABORATORIES, INC. v. GOLDEN DISTRIBUTING CORP.

Supreme Judicial Court of Massachusetts, 1929.
266 Mass. 418, 164 N.E. 772.

CARROLL, J. This is a suit in equity under G.L. c. 156, §§ 36, 38, to enforce the liability of the officers of the Golden Distributing Corporation, hereafter called the Golden Company, for the debts of the corporation, the defendants being charged with making a false return.

The plaintiff alleged that the annual report of the corporation was false in respect to the item of merchandise, $51,534.55. By this item the sum $4,822.90 appears as office furniture, equipment, stationery, and the like. This sum of $4,822.90 was found to be correct, that the corporation had tangible assets to this extent. The controversy concerns the remainder of the item of $51,534.55, namely $46,711.65.

The Golden Company was in the business of distributing moving picture prints to theaters in New England. It obtained these prints as lessee from national distributors. The national distributors remained the owners. They were to receive sixty-five per cent. of the gross rentals received for the prints by the Golden Company. It was the practice of the national distributors to receive from the Golden Company when the prints were delivered to it, advances on account of the sixty-five per cent. royalties which were expected to become due under the contract. These advances were treated by the Golden Company as assets. On December 31, 1925, the account of advances to the national distributors under the contracts showed a balance of $46,711.65. This balance or asset was treated as "merchandise" and described as such in the annual report.

The judge ruled that these advance payments, "coupled with the possession of the prints as lessee but not as owner, were not properly described as 'merchandise'; and that as to the asset in question 'merchandise' was a material false representation, although not known to be false by the individual defendants in the sense that they were conscious of any wrong-doing in describing it as 'merchandise.'" He found . . . that this false representation was one which the defendants could have known was false on reasonable examination, within the meaning of G.L. c. 156, § 36.

G.L. c. 156, § 47, requires an annual report of a corporation to be submitted to the commissioner, the report to contain a statement of assets and liabilities of the corporation to be made substantially in the form set out in this section; and, under section 36 of this chapter, the officers shall be liable for the debts of the corporation "if any statement or report required by this chapter is made by them which is false in any material representation and which they know, or on reasonable examination could have known, to be false."

The purpose of the statute requiring an annual return or statement of the condition of the corporation is to give the public information of the character and condition of the corporation, so that those dealing with it may know the facts and its financial condition. . . . The advances made by the Golden Company to the national distributors under the contract were not merchandise and could not correctly be described as such. "Merchandise" is, it has been said, a word of large signification. . . . It is however limited to "subjects of commerce," goods, wares, commodities, having "a sensible, intrinsic value." . . .

The word "merchandise" in the certificate of the condition of the corporation would lead a creditor to believe that the corporation had actual tangible assets to the amount of $51,534.55. The return stated that the Golden Company possessed merchandise to this amount. The natural inference would be that this amount could be reached if necessary to satisfy the debts by the corporation. The portion representing advance payments to the national distributors was a mere bookkeeping asset, which could not be sold; it was not a tangible asset. Calling it merchandise would mislead a creditor, and it was correctly ruled that it was not merchandise; that, within the meaning of the statute, it was a false representation which on reasonable examination the defendants could have known to be false.

An examination of the evidence shows that the defendants acted in good faith and were not conscious they were making a false return in describing this asset as merchandise; and they may have been misled by information they received from accountants and others. But we are satisfied that the return was false, and the individual defendants could have known this if they had made a reasonable examination.   .   .   .

Decree affirmed with costs.

PROBLEMS

1.   A large cotton mill company contemplated a public issue of its securities and ordered a sudden audit of its books by auditors designated by the would-be underwriters.   The accounting firm retained over many years by the company assisted in the audit.   Although there were no disputes as to the physical counts of goods on hand or as to methods of pricing, the bankers' auditors concluded that the company's inventories were overstated by more than one million dollars.   On the other hand, the company's accountants asserted that the new auditors were understating accounts payable by the same amount.

The dispute turned on the analysis of the transactions whereby the company acquired its raw cotton.   In essence they were as follows: the company's cotton buyer would place an order for a firm amount and grade of cotton at a certain price (based on the New York cotton market) with one of several firms of cotton brokers in Boston.   The broker would promptly segregate specific cotton in warehouses in the South and direct its shipment to the company. Title to this cotton was in the broker, subject to pledge evidenced by warehouse receipts in the hands of banks.   The cotton arrived on the company's siding, but the shipping documents, including the receipts or bills of lading, went to the bank in Boston.   By arrangement with the bank, the company unloaded the cotton, mingled it in its warehouse and sometimes started to process part of it immediately upon arrival.   The company "classed" the cotton to see if it was up to contract specifications and on the ninth day after its arrival would give a check to the broker from whom the purchase had been made.   The broker then paid the bank which surrendered the documents to the broker who then turned them over to the company.

The dispute hinged on whether cotton in the company's warehouse, or, in some cases, tumbling through its opening machinery, should or should not have been included in inventory while "title" to it remained in the bank.

In your opinion, what should be the "cut-off" point in such transactions, and how much if any of this cotton should appear in inventory on the company's financial statements?

Suppose that the company decided to acquiesce in the viewpoint of the auditors for the underwriters.   If under this view opening inventory was overstated by $900,000 and closing inventory was overstated by $1,100,000, the journal entries to implement the changed policy would be:

Purchases	$900,000	
Opening Inventory		$900,000

(To record as purchases in the current year goods previously treated as purchased in the prior year.)

A/P	$1,100,000	
Purchases		$1,100,000

(To reverse an earlier entry which erroneously treated these goods as purchased in the current year.)

Assuming that the price of cotton has remained constant throughout, to what extent would the change in policy affect the net income of the company for the period involved?

2. On December 24 of year 1, X Corp. ordered goods in the amount of $10,000 from one of its suppliers for delivery in late January of year 2. In accordance with its business practice with its suppliers, X included a check in the amount of 10% of the purchase price with its order. On December 29, X learned that its order had been accepted and its check cashed. How should this transaction be recorded in the financial statements of X for year 1?

3. PRICING OF INVENTORY: FIFO AND AVERAGE COST

Once it is determined what goods are included in inventory for the particular year, we reach the more complicated question of how the closing inventory should be priced. As we have already seen, pricing of the closing inventory performs the double function of determining what amount of the total inventory costs for the period will be treated as an expense of the current period, to be matched against current revenues, and what amount will be deferred as closing inventory to be matched against the revenues of some later period. This process is neatly performed by the cost of goods sold account. Opening inventory and purchases for the period are added together on the left-hand side of this account as the tentative expense for the period; the sum of these two items is then reduced by a right-hand entry in the amount of the closing inventory, with a corresponding debit to the asset "Closing Inventory". This process of cutting down the expense applicable to the current period and creating an asset is exactly the same as we have commonly used on other occasions to defer a portion of an expense. Indeed, as was suggested in Chapter 1, section 7, the asset "Closing Inventory" could just as appropriately be called "Deferred Cost of Goods Sold Expense".

You may recall that in Chapter 1 it was also suggested that this so-called periodic method of inventory pricing is utilized because in general it is not feasible to identify the cost of particular items as they are sold. It should be evident that it is equally difficult to identify the actual cost of the items still on hand at the end of the period when the physical count of the closing inventory is taken. However, a company's purchase records do indicate the cost of the various lots of goods purchased during the year. For example, suppose that the Jones Shoe Company is a wholesaler of shoes in a single style and price line. During its first year of operations Jones purchases 8,000 pairs of shoes in four equal lots at different prices and sells 5,000 pairs. At the end of the year Jones' purchase records would show the dates and prices of the various lots, which might have been as follows:

Date	Amount	Unit Price	Total Price
Jan. 1	2,000	$2.00	$4,000
March 1	2,000	$2.20	$4,400
June 1	2,000	$2.30	$4,600
Nov. 1	2,000	$2.10	$4,200

In view of the difficulty of determining which lots the 3,000 pairs of shoes still on hand at the end of the year actually came from, at least without prohibitively expensive record keeping, it becomes necessary to find some other basis for pricing these shoes in closing inventory. Since businessmen normally expect to sell their oldest goods first, in order to minimize spoilage or obsolescence, one obvious alternative is to assume that the goods are sold in the order of their purchase, in which event the goods on hand at the end of a period would be the ones most recently obtained. This method is often called "fifo", which is shorthand for the "first-in, first-out" assumption which underlies the method. On the fifo method, Jones' closing inventory of 3,000 pairs of shoes would be carried at $6,500, consisting of the last lot of 2,000 at $2.10 per pair and 1,000 from the next to the last lot purchased at $2.30 per pair.

The fifo method is also used in pricing the inventory of manufacturing companies. Of course determination of the cost of various lots of manufactured goods is somewhat more complicated, since cost includes not only the purchase price of the component raw materials but also labor expense and a portion of the general overhead expense for the period. But once the cost of the various lots is computed, pricing of the goods on hand at the end of the period can be based on the assumption that they were the goods most recently produced.

Another method used is "average cost". Under the most common variant of this method the average cost of all inventory during the period is determined by dividing the total cost of all inventory for the period by the total number of items; this average cost is then used to price the goods still on hand at the end of the period to obtain the figure for closing inventory. For the Jones Shoe Company the average cost of shoes was $2.15; the price of closing inventory on the basis of average cost would therefore be $6,450.

In outlining the fifo and average cost inventory methods, we have dealt with the first year of operations to avoid the problem of opening inventory. Actually, however once one of these methods is adopted, the pricing of closing inventory for one period determines the figure for opening inventory the next period; that opening inventory then becomes part of the total inventory costs for the next period, to be handled in accordance with whichever method has been selected. Thus for the Jones Shoe Company, on fifo the 3,000 pairs priced at $6,500 in closing inventory at the end of year one would be regarded as the first shoes sold in year two; on average cost the 3,000 pairs at $6,450 would be included in the computation of average cost for year two.

4. LOWER OF COST OR MARKET

Fluctuating market prices may produce problems in the pricing of closing inventory. Suppose that due to a drop in the price level, or for any other reason, prices have declined by the end of a period to a figure below the fifo or average cost figure for closing inventory. As we have seen, the pricing of closing inventory performs an important balance sheet function, which makes the current market value or realizable value of inventory at the date of the balance sheet an important figure.

In view of the general historical tendency to stress balance sheet valuation, it is perhaps not surprising that this balance sheet aspect of pricing inventory became paramount, leading to the classic doctrine of "lower of cost or market", which ordains that inventory should be carried on the balance sheet at market value (as of the balance sheet date) whenever that figure is below original cost. It should be noted that the result of pricing closing inventory at the lower value figure in such circumstances is to increase the cost of goods sold expense for the period (since the smaller the closing inventory figure on the right-hand side of the Cost of Goods Sold account, the greater the net debit balance in that account). As a consequence, the cost of goods sold expense for the period would exceed the cost of the inventory actually used up during the period, which arguably interferes with the matching of related costs and revenues.

But this impact of the "lower of cost or market" doctrine has generally been defended on the ground that a diminution in the value of inventory below its cost constitutes a "loss" which should be recognized in the current period under traditional principles of conservatism.

Incidentally, although one often encounters the term "writing down" inventory from cost to market, you should be able to see that there is no need to make a separate entry reducing closing inventory from the fifo or average cost figure to market. It is simply a matter of pricing the closing inventory at the lower market figure at the time the entry is made debiting Closing Inventory and crediting the Cost of Goods Sold account. The "write-down" notion arises from the fact that these same goods will have been included in the Purchases account, and hence will be closed to the left-hand side of the Cost of Goods Sold account, at cost. The net result is an increase in the cost of goods sold expense, and a reduction in net income, by the amount of the difference between cost and market. (However, sometimes a separate write-down entry is desired, in order to highlight a significant inventory loss: in that event, closing inventory is priced at cost in the first instance, and then is actually written down by a credit to the asset (Closing Inventory) account, and a debit to a Loss on Inventory account which is closed to the left-hand side of the current Profit and Loss account.)

Adoption of the lower of cost or market basis for pricing closing inventory leads immediately to the question of what constitutes "market", or realizable, value. Where the goods are of a type for which an actual market price quotation can be obtained, the appropriate quotation at the close of the period, i. e., the current replacement cost, is the figure most often used. Thus in the case of the Jones Shoe Company, if the current cost of shoes was $2.00 per pair at the close of year one, the closing inventory of 3,000 pairs would be carried at $6,000 on the basis of lower of cost or market.

The use of replacement cost as the measure of "market" ignores the fact that in all likelihood there will be no involuntary liquidation and the goods will be sold in the normal course of the company's business rather than in the replacement market. Hence it has often been argued that the relevant "market" is not the replacement market but the market in which the company sells. Under this view, the appropriate "market" figure is the estimated selling price of the goods less the estimated costs of sale. For example, assume that Jones estimates that it will be able to sell the shoes included in closing inventory for at least $2.50 per pair, after spending an additional 20 cents per pair for such expenses of sale as packaging, shipping and the like. The argument is that the figure for estimated selling price less costs of sale, often called *net realizable value*, constitutes a more meaningful guide to market value than replacement cost; thus in the above example since the net realizable value of $2.30 is higher than actual cost, as determined by either fifo or average cost, there would be no need to carry inventory at less than actual cost.

Using net realizable value as the measure of "market" is premised on the notion that no "loss" on closing inventory has been incurred so long as a company can sell its inventory the following year at a price which will at least cover the original cost plus expenses of sale. On the other hand, when it is estimated that the selling price of closing inventory will not cover the sum of cost plus estimated expenses of sale, then some loss on the inventory is clearly in prospect, and pricing the closing inventory at net realizable value instead of the higher cost figure serves to charge this loss to the current period while reflecting inventory on the balance sheet at a figure no higher than the amount that is actually expected to be realized (an importance objective, as we have seen, in the case of this highly liquid asset). So if the selling price of the shoes in Jones' closing inventory as of the end of year one was estimated to be only $2.00 per pair, and the expenses of sale were estimated at 20 cents per pair, using net realizable value as the controlling "market" would mean that the inventory would be carried at $1.80 per pair (even if replacement cost was equal to or greater than the original cost of the shoes).

One argument against using net realizable value instead of replacement cost as the test for market value is that since the principal objective of inventory pricing at lower of cost or market is balance sheet conservatism, such pricing should be on the basis of forced and speedy liquidation, of which replacement cost is a better measure. However, in any event it generally is conceded that replacement cost is of doubtful validity as a guide to market value for the uncompleted work-in-process in the inventory of a manufacturing company. The "replacement cost" of these kinds of goods, presumably determined on the basis of the current costs of component raw materials and labor, would by no means approximate potential liquidation proceeds. In fact it would seem more likely that a potential buyer of uncompleted work in process would base his offer on the net realizable value of the goods, which in this case would consist of the estimated selling price of the completed product less the costs of completion and sale.

One other school of thought as to the "market" value of inventory deserves mention here. It has been urged in some quarters that since the economic significance or utility of inventory lies in the fact that it can be sold for a profit, the proper guide to whether the market value of inventory has fallen below cost is whether the profit-making potential of the inventory has decreased: in other words, the question would be whether the profit which was expected to be derived from the inventory when it was acquired can still be realized. For example, assume that the Jones Company originally acquired a pair of shoes for $2.00 which it expected to be able to sell for $2.50 after spending an additional 20 cents. If the estimated selling price for such shoes still on hand at the end of the year had dropped to $2.30, then according to this school of thought such shoes would have to be purchased at $1.80 to have the same profit-making or economic utility, and hence the "market" value of the shoes would be $1.80. Thus the market value of inventory under this theory, for the purpose of applying the principle of lower of cost or market, would be the estimated selling price less both the costs of sale and the normal profit. This figure is usually called "Net Realizable Value Less Normal Profit".

Read Statements 1–6 of ARB No. 43, Chapter 4, pages 438–442, infra, plus paragraph 14 on page 443.

As we have already observed, the principle of inventory pricing at the lower of cost or market is largely based on the historical emphasis on conservative balance sheet valuation. The current stress on the meaningfulness of the income statement, and particularly a series of consecutive income statements, invites some reconsideration of the doctrine of lower of cost or market, especially when "market" is taken to mean replacement cost. There is now increasing concern that a by-product of the conservative balance sheet valuation produced by pricing closing inventory at the lower of cost or market may be a less meaningful or even misleading periodic picture of business operations. Consider the following excerpt from Finney and Miller, Principles of Accounting—Intermediate, pages 251–255 (Prentice-Hall, Inc., 5th ed. 1958) *, one of the most thoughtful of the accounting texts:

General discussion of cost or market. The cost or market basis of inventory pricing conforms with an old rule of accounting conservatism often stated as follows: Anticipate no profit and provide for all possible losses. If market purchase prices decline, it is assumed that selling prices will decline with them; reducing the inventory valuation to market purchase price reduces the profit of the period when the cost price decline took place, and transfers the goods to the next period at a price which will presumably permit the earning of a normal gross profit on their sale. If the market purchase price increases, the inventory is valued at cost so that a profit will not be anticipated.

The cost or market basis has been, in the past, one of the most generally accepted applications of conservative accounting principles. It was developed and widely accepted during the long period when bankers and other creditors were primarily concerned with the balance sheet and when relatively little consideration was given to the income statement. With the emphasis thus placed on the balance sheet, the primary essential was a conservative valuation of the assets shown therein. The valuation of the inventory at the lower of cost or market is unquestionably conservative from the balance sheet standpoint.

To obtain this balance sheet conservatism, all other considerations were ignored or their importance was minimized. It was recognized that the cost or market approach was subject to question on the ground of consistency; to absorb against current gross profits an unrealized and even problematical loss on unsold merchandise, while ignoring an unrealized potential increase in gross profit which might result from a rising market, was recognized as inconsistent; but such an inconsistency was regarded as of no concern when questions of conservatism were at issue. It was recognized that, even from the balance sheet standpoint, the cost or market rule resulted in inconsistencies and in valuations which were not comparable. Different items in an inventory might be priced on different bases —some at cost and some at market; the inventories of the same concern at two dates might be priced on different bases—at cost on a rising market and at market on a falling market—and a comparison of the balance sheet valuations might therefore lead to incorrect interpretations; the inventories of two concerns might be priced on different bases, because acquired at different dates, and therefore not be comparable. But all such inconsistencies were considered unimportant in comparison with considerations of conservatism in the valuation of each inventory.

Recently, however, the income statement has become increasingly recognized as a significant measure of debt-paying ability and investment desirability. As a consequence, bankers, other creditors, business management, and stockholders are becoming increasingly concerned with the income statement—and not only with the income statement for a single period, but with the trend of earnings as shown by a series of income statements. For this reason the propriety of the cost or market approach is becoming a subject of question.

Accountants are now raising the question as to whether, giving consideration to the income statements for a series of periods, the cost or market rule is as conservative as it seemed to be. If, at the close of one period, the market value of the inventory is less than its cost, the reduction of the inventory valuation to market undoubtedly produces a conservative balance sheet valuation and a conservative computation of income in the statements for that period. But what is the effect on the income statement of the subsequent period? The effect may be so great a distortion of stated profits of successive periods as to render a series of income statements definitely misleading.

To illustrate, assume that, at the beginning of January, merchandise was purchased at a cost of $100,000; that half of the goods were sold in January for $75,000; that the remaining half were sold in February for $73,000; and that the inventory at the end of January, which cost $50,000, had a market value (replacement cost) of $40,000. The statement . . . [below] shows:

In the first column, the computation of gross profits for the first two months under the cost or market rule.

In the second column, the computation of gross profits for the two months with the inventory valued at cost.

	With Inventory Valued At	
	Cost or Market	Cost
January:		
Sales..	$75,000	$75,000
Cost of goods sold ($100,000 of purchases, minus the inventory)	60,000	50,000
Gross profit	$15,000	$25,000
February:		
Sales..	$73,000	$73,000
Cost of goods sold (consisting of the opening inventory) ..	40,000	50,000
Gross profit	$33,000	$23,000

The balance sheet valuation of the inventory at the end of January on the cost or market basis instead of on the cost basis ($40,000 instead of $50,000), and the resulting statement of gross profit for January ($15,000 instead of $25,000), may be accepted as conservative. But is the February income statement on the cost or market basis (showing $33,000 of gross profit instead of $23,000) conservative? And would not the statements for the two months on the cost or market basis give a misleading impression as to the trend of operations to anyone who did not realize that the increase in profit shown by the statements was caused by the write-down of the inventory and the consequent transfer of profits from January to February?

The cost or market inventory-pricing basis is founded on the assumption that a decrease in market purchase costs will be accompanied by a decrease in selling prices before the disposal of the inventory. This was not the case in the foregoing illustration, and in the actual conduct of business affairs it frequently is not the case. Therefore, there is a trend toward the opinion that it is not necessary or desirable to reduce the inventory valuation to market if there is no probability that sales prices will also decrease; there is also some trend of opinion in favor of the idea that reduction to market is unnecessary if, even though some decline in selling prices has occurred or can be expected, the inventory can probably be disposed of at a selling price which will include the cost and some profit. And there is even some opinion that reduction to market is unnecessary if the inventory can probably be disposed of without loss.

Some accountants, therefore, believe that, instead of assuming that a decrease in selling prices will promptly follow a decrease in cost, consideration should be given to the trend in selling prices, and that the inventory valuation should not be reduced unless selling prices have decreased at the balance sheet date or it is expected that they will decrease sufficiently after that date and before the disposal of the inventory to cause a loss.

If a decrease in the realizable value of the inventory is in prospect, balance sheet conservatism undoubtedly requires a reduction in the inventory valuation; however, bearing in mind the importance of the income statement, there still remains the question as to whether the customary procedure of reducing the inventory valuation by an accounting method which also reduces the gross profit of the period in which market costs declined is desirable. The question of distortion of profits between periods still remains. To illustrate, let us return to the foregoing case in which the inventory at the end of January cost $50,000 and had a market cost value of $40,000. In that illustration it was assumed that the selling prices in February did not decline, notwithstanding the decrease in market costs. Let us now assume that the selling prices decreased $10,000 —an amount equal to the decrease in inventory valuation. Statements on the cost or market basis and on the cost basis are presented below:

	With Inventory Valued At	
	Cost or Market	Cost
January:		
Sales	$75,000	$75,000
Cost of goods sold	60,000	50,000
Gross profit	$15,000	$25,000
February:		
Sales	$65,000	$65,000
Cost of goods sold	40,000	50,000
Gross profit	$25,000	$15,000

The figures in the "Cost" column seem to reflect the facts more truly: The company made less profit in February than in January because of the decrease in selling prices. The "Cost or Market" column tells a very strange story: The company made more profit in February than in January, notwithstanding the decrease in selling prices.

It seems to the authors that accountants might expect that the shift in emphasis from the balance sheet to the income statement would produce a similar shift in emphasis in the accounting approach to inventory pricing. When the emphasis was on reporting financial position, the approach to the inventory problem was one of valuation for purposes of properly reflecting financial position. Under these conditions cost or market, whichever is lower, seemed well suited. With the emphasis currently on the measurement of net income, the accountant logically gives preeminent consideration to those procedures associated with the assignment or "matching" of costs against related revenues. With the emphasis on a matching of costs and revenues, it would seem that the approach should be shifted to one of determining the portion of the total merchandise cost outlay for a period that should be charged against current revenues and the portion that should be assigned to future periods. The emphasis, thus, would not be one of inventory "valuation," but of cost assignment, the residue being carried forward to apply to future periods.

To some extent, this shift in approach to inventory pricing has occurred. Cost or market, whichever is lower, is receiving less support from accountants and is being refined in a number of ways, all in the direction of not reducing the cost figure unless a loss on the inventory investment is clearly in prospect. . . .

BRANCH v. KAISER

Supreme Court of Pennsylvania, 1928.
291 Pa. 543, 140 A. 498.

FRAZER, J. Defendants appealed from a decree entered by the court below on a bill in equity, filed by a trustee in bankruptcy, to compel repayment by respondents of moneys paid out as dividends alleged to have been wrongfully declared by the directors of the bankrupt corporation. Hearing was had in the court below by the court in banc on bill and answer.

The corporation in question, known as the Girard Grocery Company, was incorporated in 1908 under the laws of this commonwealth, for the purpose of carrying on a wholesale business principally in groceries and food products. The stockholders were confined to retail grocers to whom the company sold goods, the business accordingly being carried on in the nature of a co-operative organization. The original capital was $175,000, later increased to $1,000,000, divided into 10,000 shares of $100 each, of which there was issued and outstanding at the time of the bankrupt proceedings, stock to the aggregate value of $441,800. The business was prosperous from the start and by the year 1920 the corporation had accumulated a surplus of assets over liabilities of approximately $171,000, and for a number of years, up to 1920, had declared and paid dividends. In that year, however, it met with financial disaster, suffering a loss of $1,000,000, due, as claimed by respondents and admitted by the trustee, not to mismanagement, neglect, or wrongful practices on the part of the directors, but to a condition in the market for certain commodities, chiefly sugar and food products, which, to supply the demands of customers, it had bought outright and contracted for future deliveries, at the then prevalent high prices, but these suddenly enormously slumped, particularly sugar, large quantities of which the company had bargained for, in addition to immediate purchases, at prices ranging from 26 to 28 cents a pound, and which suddenly dropped to as low as 5½ cents a pound, entailing in this one item a loss of $500,000. A similar amount was lost on purchases of food products. This occurrence culminated during the fiscal year of the company between July 1, 1920, and June 30, 1921. It was a post war condition in the market which the directors could neither foresee nor prevent. . . . .

. . . At this point respondents, who had the active management and control of the business, committed error disastrous to them in every respect. Instead of acquainting the stockholders with the actual unstable financial condition of the corporation, for which they were blameless, facing the publicity of the unquestioned insolvency, of which they certainly had knowledge, and setting about for a legal adjustment of affairs, they deliberately adopted and put into practice a bold and reprehensible system of deception, designed to conceal the insolvency from the stockholders and the public with the expectation of recouping, by means of future business, the loss of the $1,000,000, and thereby again place the company upon a sound financial standing. The situation was desperate, of course. There was practically no longer a surplus, and a manifest impairment of capital existed.

Respondents exercised a practically exclusive supervision over and management of the company's business and financial transactions, and in this situation appear to have experienced no difficulty in putting into effect their plans for an effective concealment of the loss of 1920 and to enable the company, as they hoped, to emerge financially rehabilitated from its troubles. These plans included false overvaluation of assets, refraining from notice of the $1,000,000 loss in their reports, a presentation of false annual statements, and a diversion into dividends of profits that should have been applied to lessening the capital's impairment. A summary of these practices will show the extent and method of their operations. Beginning with the close of the fiscal year of 1921, they made no record in the company's books of the $1,000,000 loss, gave no notice of it in their annual report, and merely noted in that report a deficit of $22,756.87. In addition, they presented inflated inventory sheets, giving to the actual merchandise the company had on hand a cost valuation, when in fact the value had enormously decreased. The same methods of concealment, misrepresentation, and fictitious inventories were continued during the years down to and including 1925.

These methods and practices, as set forth in detail in the bill, are frankly admitted in respondents' answer, with the explanation, or excuse, that "the increase in the item of inventory was made with the intent and purpose of carrying on the business of the said Girard Grocery Company for the benefit of its stockholders." It is doubtless true that such was the actuating motive impelling respondents to resort to their fraudulent misrepresentations and concealments; it was, however, a practice which safe and honest business methods will not support and which the law will not tolerate. . . .

In our opinion, we need not enter further into this discussion. It is undisputed that respondents by illegal methods made and continued concealment, from both the stockholders of the company and the public, of the precarious financial standing of the corporation, repeatedly inflating inventories of goods on hand, thus presenting a fraudulent overvaluation of assets, and, lastly, declared dividends, at the time the corporation was insolvent and its capital seriously depleted and impaired, out of profits that should have been used for its stabilization. The court below found the disbursements were illegal, under the Act of May 23, 1913 (P.L. 336; Pa.St.1920, § 5786), and that the directors are personally liable for the dividends so declared. We concur in that judgment.

The decree of the court below is affirmed at appellants' costs.

On the issue of the extent to which inventory write-downs should be reflected in interim financial statements, see the Lionel Corporation case, supra, at page 279.

The principal authoritative promulgation of the profession on the matter of inventory pricing, now some twenty-five years old, is as follows:

ACCOUNTING RESEARCH BULLETIN NO. 43 *

Committee on Accounting Procedure, American Institute of Accountants, 1953.

* * *

CHAPTER 4

INVENTORY PRICING

1. Whenever the operation of a business includes the ownership of a stock of goods, it is necessary for adequate financial accounting purposes that inventories be properly compiled periodically and recorded in the accounts.[1] Such inventories are required both in the statement of financial position and for the periodic measurement of income.

2. This chapter sets forth the general principles applicable to the pricing of inventories of mercantile and manufacturing enterprises. Its conclusions are not directed to or necessarily applicable to noncommercial businesses or to regulated utilities.

STATEMENT 1

The term *inventory* is used herein to designate the aggregate of those items of tangible personal property which (1) are held for sale in the ordinary course of business, (2) are in process of production for such sale, or (3) are to be currently consumed in the production of goods or services to be available for sale.

Discussion

3. The term *inventory* embraces goods awaiting sale (the merchandise of a trading concern and the finished goods of a manufacturer), goods in the course of production (work in process), and goods to be consumed directly or indirectly in production (raw materials and supplies). This definition of inventories excludes long-term assets subject to depreciation accounting, or goods which, when

---

* Copyright © 1953 by the American Institute of Certified Public Accountants, Inc.

1. Prudent reliance upon perpetual inventory records is not precluded.

put into use, will be so classified. The fact that a depreciable asset is retired from regular use and held for sale does not indicate that the item should be classified as part of the inventory. Raw materials and supplies purchased for production may be used or consumed for the construction of long-term assets or other purposes not related to production, but the fact that inventory items representing a small portion of the total may not be absorbed ultimately in the production process does not require separate classification. By trade practice, operating materials and supplies of certain types of companies such as oil producers are usually treated as inventory.

STATEMENT 2

A major objective of accounting for inventories is the proper determination of income through the process of matching appropriate costs against revenues.

Discussion

4. An inventory has financial significance because revenues may be obtained from its sale, or from the sale of the goods or services in whose production it is used. Normally such revenues arise in a continuous repetitive process or cycle of operations by which goods are acquired and sold, and further goods are acquired for additional sales. In accounting for the goods in the inventory at any point of time, the major objective is the matching of appropriate costs against revenues in order that there may be a proper determination of the realized income. Thus, the inventory at any given date is the balance of costs applicable to goods on hand remaining after the matching of absorbed costs with concurrent revenues. This balance is appropriately carried to future periods provided it does not exceed an amount properly chargeable against the revenues expected to be obtained from ultimate disposition of the goods carried forward. In practice, this balance is determined by the process of pricing the articles comprised in the inventory.

STATEMENT 3

The primary basis of accounting for inventories is cost, which has been defined generally as the price paid or consideration given to acquire an asset. As applied to inventories, cost means in principle the sum of the applicable expenditures and charges directly or indirectly incurred in bringing an article to its existing condition and location.

Discussion

5. In keeping with the principle that accounting is primarily based on cost, there is a presumption that inventories should be stated at cost. The definition of cost as applied to inventories is understood to mean acquisition and production cost,[2] and its determination involves many problems. Although principles for the determination of inventory costs may be easily stated, their application, particularly to such inventory items as work in process and finished goods,

---

2. In the case of goods which have been written down below cost at the close of a fiscal period, such reduced amount is to be considered the cost for subsequent accounting purposes.

is difficult because of the variety of problems encountered in the allocation of costs and charges. For example, under some circumstances, items such as idle facility expense, excessive spoilage, double freight, and rehandling costs may be so abnormal as to require treatment as current period charges rather than as a portion of the inventory cost. Also, general and administrative expenses should be included as period charges, except for the portion of such expenses that may be clearly related to production and thus constitute a part of inventory costs (product charges). Selling expenses constitute no part of inventory costs. It should also be recognized that the exclusion of all overheads from inventory costs does not constitute an accepted accounting procedure. The exercise of judgment in an individual situation involves a consideration of the adequacy of the procedures of the cost accounting system in use, the soundness of the principles thereof, and their consistent application.

STATEMENT 4

Cost for inventory purposes may be determined under any one of several assumptions as to the flow of cost factors (such as first-in first-out, average, and last-in first-out); the major objective in selecting a method should be to choose the one which, under the circumstances, most clearly reflects periodic income.

Discussion

6. The cost to be matched against revenue from a sale may not be the identified cost of the specific item which is sold, especially in cases in which similar goods are purchased at different times and at different prices. While in some lines of business specific lots are clearly identified from the time of purchase through the time of sale and are costed on this basis, ordinarily the identity of goods is lost between the time of acquisition and the time of sale. In any event, if the materials purchased in various lots are identical and interchangeable, the use of identified cost of the various lots may not produce the most useful financial statements. This fact has resulted in the development of general acceptance of several assumptions with respect to the flow of cost factors (such as *first-in first-out, average,* and *last-in first-out*) to provide practical bases for the measurement of periodic income. In some situations a reversed mark-up procedure of inventory pricing, such as the retail inventory method, may be both practical and appropriate. The business operations in some cases may be such as to make it desirable to apply one of the acceptable methods of determining cost to one portion of the inventory or components thereof and another of the acceptable methods to other portions of the inventory.

7. Although selection of the method should be made on the basis of the individual circumstances, it is obvious that financial statements will be more useful if uniform methods of inventory pricing are adopted by all companies within a given industry.

STATEMENT 5

A departure from the cost basis of pricing the inventory is required when the utility of the goods is no longer as great as its cost. Where there is evidence that the utility of goods, in their disposal in the ordinary course of business, will be less than cost, whether due to physical deterioration, obsolescence, changes in price levels, or other causes, the difference should be recognized as a loss of the current period. This is generally accomplished by stating such goods at a lower level commonly designated as *market*.

Discussion

8. Although the cost basis ordinarily achieves the objective of a proper matching of costs and revenues, under certain circumstances cost may not be the amount properly chargeable against the revenues of future periods. A departure from cost is required in these circumstances because cost is satisfactory only if the utility of the goods has not diminished since their acquisition; a loss of utility is to be reflected as a charge against the revenues of the period in which it occurs. Thus, in accounting for inventories, a loss should be recognized whenever the utility of goods is impaired by damage, deterioration, obsolescence, changes in price levels, or other causes. The measurement of such losses is accomplished by applying the rule of pricing inventories at *cost or market, whichever is lower*. This provides a practical means of measuring utility and thereby determining the amount of the loss to be recognized and accounted for in the current period.

STATEMENT 6

As used in the phrase *lower of cost or market* [4] the term *market* means current replacement cost (by purchase or by reproduction, as the case may be) except that:

(1) Market should not exceed the net realizable value (i. e., estimated selling price in the ordinary course of business less reasonably predictable costs of completion and disposal); and

(2) Market should not be less than net realizable value reduced by an allowance for an approximately normal profit margin.

Discussion

9. The rule of *cost or market, whichever is lower* is intended to provide a means of measuring the residual usefulness of an inventory expenditure. The term *market* is therefore to be interpreted as indicating utility on the inventory date and may be thought of in terms of the equivalent expenditure which would have to be made in the ordinary course at that date to procure corresponding utility. As a general guide, utility is indicated primarily by the current cost of replacement of the goods as they would be obtained by purchase or reproduction. In applying the rule, however, judgment must always be exercised and no loss should be recognized unless the evidence indicates clearly that a loss has been sustained. There are therefore exceptions to such a standard. Replacement or reproduction prices would not be appropriate as a measure of utility when the estimated sales value, reduced by the costs of completion and

---

4. The terms *cost or market, whichever is lower* and *lower of cost or market* are used synonymously in general practice and in this chapter. The committee does not express any preference for either of the two alternatives.

disposal, is lower, in which case the realizable value so determined more appropriately measures utility. Furthermore, where the evidence indicates that cost will be recovered with an approximately normal profit upon sale in the ordinary course of business, no loss should be recognized even though replacement or reproduction costs are lower. This might be true, for example, in the case of production under firm sales contracts at fixed prices, or when a reasonable volume of future orders is assured at stable selling prices.

10. Because of the many variations of circumstances encountered in inventory pricing, Statement 6 is intended as a guide rather than as a literal rule. It should be applied realistically in the light of the objectives expressed in this chapter and with due regard to the form, content, and composition of the inventory. The committee considers, for example, that the retail inventory method, if adequate markdowns are currently taken, accomplishes the objectives described herein. It also recognizes that, if a business is expected to lose money for a sustained period, the inventory should not be written down to offset a loss inherent in the subsequent operations.

STATEMENT 7

Depending on the character and composition of the inventory, the rule of *cost or market, whichever is lower* may properly be applied either directly to each item or to the total of the inventory (or, in some cases, to the total of the components of each major category). The method should be that which most clearly reflects periodic income.

Discussion

11. The purpose of reducing inventory to *market* is to reflect fairly the income of the period. The most common practice is to apply the *lower of cost or market* rule separately to each item of the inventory. However, if there is only one end-product category the cost utility of the total stock—the inventory in its entirety—may have the greatest significance for accounting purposes. Accordingly, the reduction of individual items to *market* may not always lead to the most useful result if the utility of the total inventory to the business is not below its cost. This might be the case if selling prices are not affected by temporary or small fluctuations in current costs of purchase or manufacture. Similarly, where more than one major product or operational category exists, the application of the *cost or market, whichever is lower* rule to the total of the items included in such major categories may result in the most useful determination of income.

12. When no loss of income is expected to take place as a result of a reduction of cost prices of certain goods because others forming components of the same general categories of finished products have a market equally in excess of cost, such components need not be adjusted to market to the extent that they are in balanced quantities. Thus, in such cases, the rule of *cost or market, whichever is lower* may be applied directly to the totals of the entire inventory, rather than to the individual inventory items, if they enter into the same category of finished product and if they are in balanced quantities, provided the procedure is applied consistently from year to year.

13.   To the extent, however, that the stocks of particular materials or components are excessive in relation to others, the more widely recognized procedure of applying the *lower of cost or market* to the individual items constituting the excess should be followed. This would also apply in cases in which the items enter into the production of unrelated products or products having a material variation in the rate of turnover.   Unless an effective method of classifying categories is practicable, the rule should be applied to each item in the inventory.

14.   When substantial and unusual losses result from the application of this rule it will frequently be desirable to disclose the amount of the loss in the income statement as a charge separately identified from the consumed inventory costs described as *cost of goods sold*.

STATEMENT 8

The basis of stating inventories must be consistently applied and should be disclosed in the financial statements; whenever a significant change is made therein, there should be disclosure of the nature of the change and, if material, the effect on income.

Discussion

15.   While the basis of stating inventories does not affect the over-all gain or loss on the ultimate disposition of inventory items, any inconsistency in the selection or employment of a basis may improperly affect the periodic amounts of income or loss.   Because of the common use and importance of periodic statements, a procedure adopted for the treatment of inventory items should be consistently applied in order that the results reported may be fairly allocated as between years.   A change of such basis may have an important effect upon the interpretation of the financial statements both before and after that change, and hence, in the event of a change, a full disclosure of its nature and of its effect, if material, upon income should be made.

STATEMENT 9

Only in exceptional cases may inventories properly be stated above cost.   For example, precious metals having a fixed monetary value with no substantial cost of marketing may be stated at such monetary value;   any other exceptions must be justifiable by inability to determine appropriate approximate costs, immediate marketability at quoted market price, and the characteristic of unit interchangeability.   Where goods are stated above cost this fact should be fully disclosed.

Discussion

16.   It is generally recognized that income accrues only at the time of sale, and that gains may not be anticipated by reflecting assets at their current sales prices.   For certain articles, however, exceptions are permissible.   Inventories of gold and silver, when there is an effective government-controlled market at a fixed monetary value, are ordinarily reflected at selling prices.   A similar treatment

is not uncommon for inventories representing agricultural, mineral, and other products, units of which are interchangeable and have an immediate marketability at quoted prices and for which appropriate costs may be difficult to obtain. Where such inventories are stated at sales prices, they should of course be reduced by expenditures to be incurred in disposal, and the use of such basis should be fully disclosed in the financial statements.

STATEMENT 10

Accrued net losses on firm purchase commitments for goods for inventory, measured in the same way as are inventory losses, should, if material, be recognized in the accounts and the amounts thereof separately disclosed in the income statement.

Discussion

17. The recognition in a current period of losses arising from the decline in the utility of cost expenditures is equally applicable to similar losses which are expected to arise from firm, uncancelable, and unhedged commitments for the future purchase of inventory items. The net loss on such commitments should be measured in the same way as are inventory losses and, if material, should be recognized in the accounts and separately disclosed in the income statement. The utility of such commitments is not impaired, and hence there is no loss, when the amounts to be realized from the disposition of the future inventory items are adequately protected by firm sales contracts or when there are other circumstances which reasonably assure continuing sales without price decline.

> *One member of the committee, Mr. Wellington, assented with qualification, and two members, Messrs. Mason and Peloubet, dissented to adoption of chapter 4.*

Mr. Wellington objects to footnote (2) to statement 3. He believes that an exception should be made for goods costed on the *last-in first-out* (LIFO) basis. In the case of goods costed on all bases other than LIFO the reduced amount (market below cost) is cleared from the accounts through the regular accounting entries of the subsequent period, and if the market price rises to or above the original cost there will be an increased profit in the subsequent period. Accounts kept under the LIFO method should also show a similar increased profit in the subsequent period, which will be shown if the LIFO inventory is restored to its original cost. To do otherwise, as required by footnote (2), is to carry the LIFO inventory, not at the lower of cost or current market, but at the lowest market ever known since the LIFO method was adopted by the company.

Mr. Mason dissents from this chapter because of its acceptance of the inconsistencies inherent in *cost or market whichever is lower*. In his opinion a drop in selling price below cost is no more of a realized loss than a rise above cost is a realized gain under a consistent criterion of realization.

Mr. Peloubet believes it is ordinarily preferable to carry inventory at not less than recoverable cost, and particularly in the case of manufactured or partially manufactured goods which can be sold only in finished form. He recognizes that application of the *cost or market* valuation basis necessitates the shifting of income from one period to another, but objects to unnecessarily accentuating this shift by the use, even limited as it is in this chapter, of reproduction or replacement cost as *market* when such cost is less than net selling price.

———————

Notice that Statement 6 of the foregoing ARB No. 43, Ch. 4, sets up a formula for determining the "market" value of inventory which incorporates all three of the bases discussed at pages 430–432 above. Under this formula market value is a figure lying somewhere between a maximum of net realizable value and a minimum of net realizable value less expected or normal profit. It might be conceived of graphically as follows:

—————————————————————
net realizable value
—————————————————————

—————————————————————
net realizable value less normal profit

Whenever replacement cost is somewhere between the maximum and the minimum, replacement cost is the proper test of market value. However, if replacement cost is higher than net realizable value, then net realizable value is the appropriate figure for market value. If replacement cost is lower than net realizable value less normal profit, then the latter is the figure for market value. And of course do not overlook the fact that only when the market value as so determined is lower than cost does the principle of lower of cost or market have any application.

PROBLEMS

1. Assume the following facts as to an item to be included in a closing inventory:

Cost	$5.00
Replacement Cost	$3.50
Estimated Selling Price	$6.00
Additional Cost of Disposal	$2.00
Normal Profit	$1.00

What is the appropriate figure at which this item should be carried in inventory:

(a) under the formula of Statement 6 of chapter 4, ARB No. 43?

(b) in accordance with the view expressed by Mr. Peloubet in his partial dissent to chapter 4?

(c) in accordance with the views expressed by Finney and Miller in the excerpt quoted above?

(d) under the decision in Branch v. Kaiser, supra? With which do you agree?

2. If a company decided not to apply the principle of lower of cost or market, how should the company carry inventory on its balance sheet when market value by every test is below cost?

3. Assume that the appropriate market value of the goods ordered in Problem 2, on page 427, supra, is only $9,200 at the end of year 1. In the light of Statement 10 of ARB No. 43, ch. 4, above, which of the following entries would you make to reflect this fact in X's financial statements on that date?

(a) No entry

(b) Loss on Inventory Commitment $800
       Advance on Inventory Commitment $800

(c) Loss on Inventory Commitment $800
       Estimated Loss on Inventory
         Commitment $800

a. INVENTORY APPRECIATION

As to the converse situation when the market value of inventory is above cost, consider the *Hill* case which follows, together with statement 9 of ARB No. 43, ch. 4, above. Was there an argument available to the defendants in the *Hill* case akin to the one we considered on behalf of the defendants in the *Kingston* case, page 198 supra, and Hutchinson v. Curtiss, page 372, supra?

HILL v. INTERNATIONAL PRODUCTS CO.

Supreme Court of New York, 1925.
129 Misc. 25, 220 N.Y.S. 711.

[This was an action to rescind brought by a purchaser of a large block of preferred stock of the defendant corporation against the corporation and its directors. The complaint alleged misrepresentation by the latter as to the affairs of the defendant corporation. Although the defendants' defense of laches on the part of the plaintiff was sustained, the following portion of the opinion indicates the court's adverse reaction to certain accounting practices indulged in by the company.]

MAHONEY, J. . . . The $349,000, however, as I understand it, is alleged surplus carried over from 1918, and was not earnings for 1919.

The dividend declared on August 19, 1919, was, as above noted, $356,452.25, away in excess of the surplus net profits on June 30,

1919, from a very favorable calculation of defendant's assets. A careful reading, however, of the reports of Price, Waterhouse & Co. and W. B. Peat, in evidence, made on Central Products Company and International Products Company for the period to the close of the year 1918, Defendant's Exhibits H–8 and I–8, have convinced me that the assumed surplus of $349,000 did not actually exist. Plaintiffs' Exhibit 51, which is Exhibit A attached to Defendant's Exhibit H–8, shows a surplus in Central Products Company at the close of 1918 of $798,672.48, Argentine paper. The notation appearing on said Exhibit A is as follows:

"Surplus on Live Stock, etc., as per Profit and Loss Account, Exhibit B, $798,672.48."

It is this figure translated into United States gold which is the $349,000, the assumed surplus carried over from 1918. The reports of the accountants, upon even a most casual analysis, show that as a result of the operations of Central Products Company up to the close of 1918 there was no such surplus. Defendant's Exhibit H–8 is entitled:

"Report, Balance Sheet, and Profit and Loss Account, August 1, 1917, to December 30, 1918, of Central Products Company."

The report is dated August 1, 1919. This alleged surplus apparently arises almost entirely from book entries respecting the alleged increase in the value of cattle on the hoof. It is not claimed that the cattle were actually weighed. They were apparently assumed to be heavier, because they had grown older and their weight increased. At the trial, moreover, the following testimony was given by Mr. Farquhar:

"Q. Now, you realize, do you not, that in making up this estimated surplus and undivided profits of June 28, 1919, of $527,951.58, that that was composed of surplus and net earnings, December 28, 1918, of $349,000? A. Yes.

"Q. And the other figure, that makes up that total of $178,951.-58, was the estimated profits for the first six months? A. Yes; on canned meat and quebracho extract.

"Q. And this item of $349,000—that was the item carried over to the fattening of cattle, as surplus from 1918, wasn't it? A. Breeding—the business of the cattle department—breeding and fattening of cattle.

"Q. Well, except for a very small portion, that was an item due, wasn't it, as you understood, to the fattening of cattle? A. And breeding.

"Q. What? A. And breeding; increased age and weight.

"Q. Exactly; increased age and weight. You didn't understand that that profit had accrued from sales actually made, but from an estimate of the increased value of the cattle? A. And inventory of the increase.

"Q. Well, an inventory of the increased value of the cattle? A. Yes.

"Q. Not from actual sales of cattle made and money taken in? A. No.

"Q. So that, in voting for this dividend in August, 1919, you regarded these inventory estimates or valuations of the profits of the cattle department as an earning actually made, didn't you? A. Breeding; increased weight; fattening inventory.

"By the Court: Q. Did you consider that as earnings of the company? A. Based on the chartered accountant's reports and the lawyers' advice.

"Q. Irrespective of what it was based on, did you yourself consider it as earnings of the company? That is what the judge wants to know. A. Yes.

"By Mr. Seabury: Q. And you realized, did you not, when you voted for this dividend, if that item of $349,000 was not properly to be regarded as earnings, that then you did not have earnings sufficient to pay the dividends of $356,000? A. But we did regard it as earnings."

It would seem to me that this alleged increase in value of cattle not realized by an actual sale of cattle is not a proper item to be taken into consideration in determining actual surplus of a going concern. Hutchinson v. Curtiss, 45 Misc. 484, 92 N.Y.S. 70; . . . Kingston v. Home Life Ins. Co. of America, 11 Del.Ch. 258, 101 A. 898.

. . . Irrespective of what causes may have been instrumental in bringing about this alleged surplus of $349,000, which was carried over from 1918, the facts indicate to me that such surplus did not exist. The representation of the company, made through the declaration of such dividend, that the surplus and net profits were at least equal to the dividend declared, was therefore, in my opinion, a material misrepresentation. . . .

5. PRICING OF INVENTORY: LIFO

As we have seen, the current stress on the income statement raises questions about whether and how to apply the lower of cost or market doctrine, when inventory prices have fallen below fifo or average cost. There is also reason to question whether in times of rising inventory prices fifo and average cost might not themselves be inconsistent with the modern emphasis on meaningful periodic reporting. For example, suppose that in year 1 the Jones Shoe Company's inventory and purchase records show the following:

Date	Quantity	Unit Price	Total
Open. Inv.	3,000	fifo	$6,500
February	2,000	$2.20	4,400
April	2,000	2.30	4,600
July	2,000	2.40	4,800
October	2,000	2.60	5,200
December	2,000	2.80	5,600

Suppose further that Jones sold 4,000 pairs of shoes during the first half of year 1 at an average price of $3.00 per pair, and 4,000 pairs during the second half of the year at an average price of $3.50 per pair, for total sales revenues of $26,000. If Jones continued to carry closing inventory on the fifo basis, Jones' gross profit, i. e., sales less cost of goods sold, would be computed as follows:

Sales			$26,000
Less: Cost of Goods Sold			
Opening Inventory		$ 6,500	
Purchases		24,600	
		$31,100	
Less:			
Closing Inventory of 5,000			
pairs on Fifo		$13,200	$17,900
Gross Profit			$ 8,100

It should be evident that under this approach some of the lower inventory costs incurred before the middle of year 1 are being matched with the higher revenues obtained in the latter part of year 1. In other words, a substantial part of the gross profit is due simply to the rising price level rather than to improvement of the company's competitive position or increased efficiency of operations. This component resulting from inflation must now be disclosed in the supplementary statements required by FASB No. 33, page 211 et seq., supra. See particularly paragraphs 40 and 60. The matter was even more directly addressed by the SEC a couple of years earlier in the following Release:

ACCOUNTING SERIES RELEASE NO. 151

Securities and Exchange Commission, 1974.

DISCLOSURE OF INVENTORY PROFITS REFLECTED IN INCOME IN PERIODS OF RISING PRICES

The year 1973 was a period of rapidly increasing prices in the United States when compared to historical economic norms for this country. During the year consumer prices rose by about 8 percent, wholesale prices by about 16 percent and the crude industrial materials component of the wholesale price index by about 30 percent. There were wide fluctuations in the prices of individual items.

Under such conditions the usefulness of the traditional accounting measurement model based upon historical cost is significantly reduced. The process of matching costs against revenues is less likely to produce meaningful economic information if the costs were incurred at a time when the price level associated with such goods and services differed significantly from that at the time when revenues were realized.

While a continuation or acceleration of the rate of price-level change might require a fundamental change in the basic accounting measurement model used in preparing financial statements, it would be premature for the Commission to suggest such a change at this time. Careful consideration of the many implications of such a major step would be necessary both by the Financial Accounting Standards Board and by the Commission. At the same time, it does not seem appropriate that registrants and accountants should simply ignore the impact of rapidly changing prices on financial statements.

The most significant and immediate impact of price fluctuations on financial statements is normally felt in cost of goods sold in the income statement. In periods of rising prices, historical cost methods result in the inclusion of "inventory profits" in reported earnings. "Inventory profit" results from holding inventories during a period of rising inventory costs and is measured by the difference between the historical cost of an item and its replacement cost at the time it is sold. Different methods of accounting for inventories can affect the degree to which "inventory profits" are included and identifiable in current income, but no method based upon historical cost eliminates or discloses this "profit" explicitly. Such "profits" do not reflect an increase in the economic earning power of a business and they are not normally repeatable in the absence of continued price-level increase. Accordingly, where such "profits" are material in income statements presented, disclosure of their impact on reported earnings and the trend of reported earnings is important information for investors assessing the quality of earnings.

In recognition of the need for additional disclosure in regard to inventories and cost of goods sold, the Commission recently proposed amendments to Regulation S–X (Securities Act Release No. 5427, October 4, 1973) which would require registrants to indicate "the effect on net income, if significant, of using current replacement cost [for valuing inventories] in the computation of cost of sales." To date the Commission has received a large number of comments on this proposed disclosure and the effectiveness of that requirement in eliciting information about "inventory profits." The comments also indicated that problems of implementation existed. The Commission has given careful consideration to these comments and has concluded that it would not be desirable to adopt final requirements in this area which would be effective for 1973 financial statements. At the same time, the Commission recognizes that the impact of "inventory profits" on currently reported earnings appears to be signicant in many cases and that failure to make appropriate disclosure may result in investors being inadequately informed as to the source and replicability of earnings.

The Commission therefore believes that it would be in the best interest of both statement preparers and users to disclose the extent to which reported earnings are comprised of potentially unrepeatable and usually unsegregated "inventory profits." Accordingly, the Commission urges registrants to make disclosure of such amounts prior to the adoption of final requirements by the Commission. Such disclosure may be made in the financial statements, the notes thereto or in textual material accompanying financial statements.

The Commission recognizes that registrants usually do not compute cost of goods sold on both an historical cost and current value basis so that computation of such amounts may often require estimation by the registrant. It is also recognized that computational methods or bases of valuation other than current replacement cost for each item sold might be used in developing useful information about such "profits." For example, computing the cost of goods sold for each month using a price-level adjusted inventory amount might produce a reasonable and useful estimate of such "profits" in some cases. Until final requirements are established, registrants are encouraged to use any method or basis deemed appropriate by management in exhibiting the impact of such "profits" along with a statement of the method or basis used and the reasons for adopting it.

The determination of cost of sales on a current replacement cost basis, however, provides only partial information regarding the effects of inflation on a company's operations. A second factor is the responsiveness of a company's selling prices to changes in costs. If a company is able to raise selling prices immediately upon realizing cost increases (or in anticipation of cost increases), its net income in dollar terms benefits from inflation. On the other hand, as price increases lag behind cost increases the benefit of inventory "profits" is offset and the net inflation effect on income may be negative. Because of various regulatory restraints on prices, many companies may have experienced significant pricing lags in the current year.

The impact of price-level changes does not fall equally among companies. Some firms operate in sectors of the economy, where prices of goods purchased are more volatile than selling prices. Accordingly, the Commission urges registrants to discuss the relationship of costs and prices experienced in the current year in connection with disclosing inventory profits.

By the Commission.

————

A more pervasive approach to so-called inventory profits resulting from a rising price level affecting both sales revenues and inventory costs is to try to match with a company's current revenues during the year its most current inventory costs, rather than the oldest ones, as fifo tends to do. One way of accomplishing this objective is simply to adopt an assumption which is the converse of that underlying fifo. Under this approach it is assumed that the goods are sold "off the top of the pile", or, in other words, in the inverse order from that in which they are purchased; the last goods purchased during the year are considered to have been the first goods sold, and the goods on hand at the end of the year are priced in closing inventory as if they were the goods acquired earliest in the year. This means that whenever the number of items in closing inventory does not exceed the number of similar items in the opening inventory for the same year, the items in closing inventory are priced at the same figure as was used in opening inventory; any excess of the number of items in closing inventory over the number in opening inventory is priced according to the cost of the earliest acquisitions during the year. In this way, the cost of goods sold expense for the current year is made to consist of the most current inventory costs. This method of inventory pricing is called "lifo", which is shorthand for the last-in, first-out assumption which underlies it.

Applying lifo to the Jones Company in the above example would result in a closing inventory of $10,900, arrived at by pricing 3,000 pairs at the opening inventory figure of $6,500 and the remaining 2,000 pairs at the cost of the first 2,000 pairs purchased during the year, $4,400. The gross profit on lifo would be computed as follows:

Sales			$26,000
Less: Cost of Goods Sold			
Opening Inventory		$ 6,500	
Purchases		24,600	
		$31,100	
Less:			
Closing Inventory of 5,000			
pairs on Lifo		$10,900	$20,200
Gross Profit			$ 5,800

As you should expect, the increase in the current cost of goods sold expense which results from pricing the closing inventory on lifo produces a lower gross profit figure. This lower figure may well be a better indication of the success of the company's operations in the rising price market.* Similarly, in a falling market a strict application of lifo would enable a company to match the current lower inventory costs against revenues which are likely also to be declining, and hence to avoid showing the loss which would result from matching the older higher inventory costs against such revenues.

It should be observed that the lifo assumption is in general an unrealistic one, and indeed would be an accurate reflection of the physical flow of goods only in a case, for example, where goods are piled as received and issued from the top of the pile, as perhaps would be true of a supplier of coal. And even in that case, it would be perfectly clear that goods acquired during a given year after the date of the last sale could not in fact have been sold during that year. But the lifo method does not purport to be an accurate reflection of the flow of goods; rather it presumes that the physical flow is of no real significance, and it instead stresses the importance of matching related current costs with current revenues. Note particularly that lifo nevertheless involves no departure from the principle of using cost

---

* See footnote 3 to paragraph 60 of FASB No. 33, page 216, supra.

as the primary basis of inventory pricing; it seeks only to provide a sound answer to the question of which of the inventory costs incurred during the current year should be treated as "used up" during the current year, and hence charged to current expense.

The lifo method received a considerable boost in popularity in 1939 when it was accepted for federal income tax purposes, subject to two conditions which still obtain today: (1) lifo may be used for tax purposes only if it is also used by the company for general financial reporting purposes; and (2) the figure at which inventory is carried under lifo may not be reduced for tax purposes through application of the conventional lower of cost or market rule. Lifo has received renewed impetus in recent years because of the high rate of inflation (and the very substantial tax savings that lifo provides); today over half of the country's largest public corporations have adopted the lifo method for at least part of their inventories. Here's an example of one company that shifted over to lifo during that period:

ETHYL CORPORATION

	1975	1974
Current assets:		
Inventories	$124,864,000	$149,367,000

Notes to Financial Statements

Note 1 (in part): Summary of Significant Accounting Policies:

Inventories—Inventories are stated at the lower of cost or market with cost determined on the last-in, first-out basis for substantially all domestic inventories and on either average cost or first-in, first-out for other inventories. Cost elements included in work in process and finished goods inventories are raw materials, direct labor and manufacturing overhead. Raw materials and stores and supplies include purchase and delivery costs.

Note 5: Inventories:

	1975	1974
Inventories include:		
Finished goods	$ 55,910,000	$57,964,000
Raw materials and work in process	48,804,000	71,931,000
Stores, supplies, etc.	20,150,000	19,472,000
	$124,864,000	$149,367,000

Inventories stated on the last-in, first-out basis amounted to $70,587,000 at December 31, 1975, and $105,601,000 at December 31, 1974, which are below replacement cost by approximately $45,600,000 and $50,900,000 respectively.*

In 1975, the inventory reductions resulted in liquidations of LIFO inventory quantities carried at lower costs prevailing in prior years as compared with 1975 costs, the effect of which increased net income by approximately $6,873,000 or 73 cents per share.

In 1974, the last-in, first-out method of valuing inventories was extended to substantially all the domestic inventories which were accounted for previously on first-in, first-out or average cost. The effect of this change was to reduce net income for 1974 by $6,509,000, or 68 cents per share, from what it would have been if the former inventory valuation methods had been continued.

The change in inventory method was made to minimize the impact of price level changes on inventory valuations and to achieve a better match of current costs with current revenues for determining profits. There is no cumulative effect of this change on prior years reported earnings.

But among the accounting authorities LIFO has had as many critics as fans. Consider the following excerpts from Statement No. 6, "Inventory Pricing and Changes in Price Levels", promulgated by the Committee on Accounting Concepts and Standards of the American Accounting Association ** (reprinted in 29 Acc.Rev. 188 (1954)):

> The so-called FIFO method of inventory valuation possesses three attractive characteristics: First, in the great majority of cases it so nearly approximates the physical movement of goods that the actual differences in flow can be ignored; second, it eliminates all possibility of influencing profits through selection of individual items from a homogeneous inventory or

---

* Under Rule 5–02–6(b) of SEC Regulation S–X, companies using the lifo method must disclose, either parenthetically on the balance sheet or, as here, in a note, the excess of replacement cost over the lifo figure, if material. FASB statement No. 33 in effect provides the same kind of information by way of its supplementary statement showing current costs.

** Reprinted by permission of the American Accounting Association. The AAA is composed principally of teachers of accounting, although anyone interested in accounting may join. The primary objective of the Association is "To develop accounting principles and standards, and to seek their endorsement or adoption by business enterprises, public and private accountants, and governmental bodies." The status of statements by the Committee on Accounting Concepts and Standards is described in the following note accompanying Statement No. 6:

"Statements of the Committee on Accounting Concepts and Standards represent the reasoned judgment of at least two-thirds of its members. They are not official pronouncements of the American Accounting Association or of its Executive Committee.

"They shall not necessarily be viewed as stating rules of current professional conduct or procedure. Rather, they state objectives in the development of accounting principles. Some are intended to have immediate applicability, while others forecast the general direction in which accounting may develop."

through the mere expansion or contraction of inventory quantities; third, the method produces a balance-sheet quantum which is, in general, a reasonable reflection of the current market.

The principal objection to FIFO is its failure to compensate for changes in the price level. It is observed that in those cases where inventories are a material factor in the determination of annual earnings the costs charged against the year's revenues may, when prices change, produce an effect upon profits which appears erratic. Thus, low costs may be matched against relatively high selling prices and vice versa. The effect produced during periods of steeply rising prices is often described as one *of* "fictitious inventory profits."

With respect to this point, it should first be noted that, in the absence of changes in the *general* level of prices, the so-called inventory profits are as real as are the profits under any conceivable set of circumstances. Clearly such profits may not be disbursable as dividends if the business is to maintain its level of physical stock. The fact, however, that a portion of the profits must be retained in the business because of higher costs of inventory in no way denies the validity of the profits as such. *To argue otherwise is to confuse profit determination on the one hand with financial management on the other.*

When, on the other hand, the general price level has undergone change it is evident that historical FIFO has distinct limitations. Significantly, however, the defect is not implicit in the FIFO assumption but rather in the adherence to historical dollar symbols.

* * *

The effect of LIFO is to charge against the revenues of the year the historical cost of goods purchased from the time of the year-end back through a period long enough to encompass acquisition of goods equal to the quantity sold during the year.

In an appraisal of LIFO certain points are especially to be noted:

(1) To the extent that price changes of the goods under consideration match changes in the general level of prices, the resulting profit figures are theoretically superior to those attained by realistic flow assumptions unadjusted for price-level changes. To the extent, however, that the price changes do not so move in parallel fashion, the *artificial LIFO* method may easily exaggerate, conceal, or even show in reverse, real gains and losses.

(2) The inventory valuation which results from *artificial LIFO* may become so far out of date as to be seriously misleading especially when no disclosure is made of the current market value of the inventory. For this reason the Committee has proposed that when LIFO is used there be reported in the financial statements figures showing the inventory valuation and the operating costs (including tax effects) on a realistic basis.

(3) The LIFO method is peculiarly open to the charge that through its use the periodic profits can be influenced to a sub-

stantial extent by the expedient of contracting or expanding the inventory quantities. Otherwise stated, it is literally true that up to the end of the year, management, under LIFO, has considerable leeway in deciding what the cost-of-goods-sold figure for the year shall be. In an extreme case, at the very end of the year, a quantity of goods equal to the entire quantity sold during the year could be acquired and such last-minute purchases would, under this artificial flow assumption, be treated as if they were the goods actually sold during the past twelve months. In reverse, the inventories are subject to intentional depletion for the purpose of influencing the profit figure.

While the opportunity to influence profits in this way does exist under LIFO, it is reasonable to assume that management ordinarily would not risk putting the inventories in an unbalanced condition simply for the purpose of achieving a better income statement result; however, it should be noted that the opportunity in this respect is far greater than is alleged to exist in the use of identified cost.

CHRYSLER CORPORATION

TEXT OF COMMENTS AT A PRESS CONFERENCE FEBRUARY 9, 1971

Remarks by Lynn Townsend, Chairman.

Gentlemen:

I'd like to make some informal comments, if I may, first on the results for the year ended December 31, 1970. As you know at this point, our unit sales for 1970 were 2,459,336 units world wide, compared with 2,446,605 units world wide in 1969. Our U. S. unit sales were down, reflecting the depressed condition in the United States automobile market. Our U. S. sales amounted to 1,504,678 units compared with 1,559,263 units in 1969. Our dollar sales were almost exactly equal to 1969, amounting to $7 billion in 1970, compared with $7.1 billion in 1969. We recorded a loss in 1970 of $7.6 million or $.16 a share, compared with a profit in 1969 of $99 million or $2.09 a share.

We of course do not like to report a loss, but I think when you put it in perspective and realize the recession that our economy has been going through for the past year—when you realize the high cost of money and the negative consumer confidence that we have had in this country, and the reorganization that Chrysler has gone through during this period—we are very proud that we have reported a profit for the last nine months of the year.

Our entire loss, of course, was incurred in the first three months and we were not able to recoup that loss entirely by December 31, 1970.

I'd also like to make a few comments about our change from the Last In First Out (LIFO) method of inventory evaluation to the First In First Out (FIFO) method of inventory evaluation. Chrysler Corporation converted from FIFO to LIFO in 1957. We were the only company in our industry to convert to the LIFO basis. Our three competitors have traditionally been on FIFO and have so reported, all through their period of existence.

Up until 1968, the greatest effect in any one year that this inventory method had on our net earnings had been $.15 (per share). But then we came into the 1967 contract negotiations, and inflation began to move in this country. In 1968 the effect of this inventory method reduced our net earnings on a per share basis by $.26. So this is the year that we first began to be concerned. It was the first year that we inserted in our annual report's financial review section the effect on earnings of using the LIFO method. You will find the $.26 in that document. The next year, 1969, we had almost as big a reduction—$.22 a share. We treated the $.22 as we had in 1968, by commenting on it in our financial review. We had hoped in this way to point out the different accounting practice we were following and the effect on our earnings as we went through the years. So we came into 1970, where this amount of understatement was compounded because of the rate of inflation in this country.

In 1970, had we continued to use the LIFO method, it would have resulted in an understatement of our results in the amount of $.40 a share. And as we projected 1971, it would have become an even more significant item. So we felt we had no alternative but to convert back to FIFO, so that our reported numbers would be comparable with those reported by our competitors. We have restated all of our results for the previous years on the FIFO basis. We have also included in our shareholders letter the restated amounts for the first, second, third and fourth quarters of 1970.

QUESTIONS

1. Review Branch v. Kaiser, pages 436–438, supra. Assuming that the selling prices for the company's goods in that case must have declined in an amount paralleling the sharp decline in the replacement cost, once the company refused to recognize the inventory loss in the year of the price drop shouldn't that loss have shown up in the income statement for the following year?

2. Assume that Company X, in its first year of operation, purchased three units of inventory in a rising market, at prices of $5, $6 and $7 successively, and sold two of them during the year for a total of $16. Compute X's gross profit on sales under both fifo and lifo.

3. Assuming that X adopted lifo in year 1, and that during its second year X purchased two more units of inventory, at $8 and $9 successively, while selling two units for a total of $20, what would its gross profit be in year 2? Would the gross profit be different if X purchased a third item of inventory during that year, also at $9, which still selling only two items for a total of $20? How about if X purchased only one item during the year, at $8, while still selling two for $20? On this last question, read Section 6 below, following question 4.

4. Now suppose that in year 3 X, still on lifo, starts with a single item of inventory, at a cost of $5, and during the year prices peak and turn downward, so that X purchases three items during the year, at successive costs of $10, $8, and $6, while selling two items for a total price of $18. Compute X's gross profit for the year. Is there a lower of cost or market problem lurking here? Does anything in Statements 4 and 5 of Chapter 4 of ARB No. 43, or the dissents thereto, pages 440–441 and 444, supra, shed any light on the matter? If lower of cost or market does apply, consider the impact of Statement 7 of Ch. 4, ARB No. 43.

6. INVOLUNTARY LIQUIDATION OF LIFO INVENTORY

As we have seen, under the lifo method the earliest inventory costs of the period in which lifo is adopted (starting with the opening inventory of that period, if any) make up the original lifo cost figure. That lifo cost figure is in effect thereafter frozen on the balance sheet as a part of the asset Inventory, so long as the physical quantity of inventory at year-end in subsequent periods does not fall below the quantity at the end of the year in which lifo was adopted. For example, if in the year a company adopts lifo its closing inventory consists of ten units, and on lifo for that period the cost of those ten units is $1 each, then as long as the company has at least ten units on hand at year-end in each succeeding year it will have ten units priced in its closing inventory at that original lifo cost of $1. (If the physical quantity on hand at year-end expands, the excess over ten will be priced according to the lifo principle as applied in the respective years in which the increase in volume occurred.)

For a company which has been on lifo for a long time, this can result in reflecting the asset Inventory on the balance sheet on the basis of some very out-of-date costs; and when there has been a period of sustained inflation the lifo cost figure may be far below the current market value of the inventory. This very conservative representation of inventory on the balance may not bother creditors, who could only be pleasantly surprised to find, in case of financial difficulty, that the inventory is worth more than might have been expected on the basis of the figure at which it is recorded; but, as we have noted, undue conservatism may give a misleadingly pessimistic view of the state of the company's affairs.

Of course, this preservation of old costs on the balance sheet does not affect the income statement, so long as the quantity of goods in the inventory at the end of each year is at least as great as the quantity on hand at the close of the prior year (and the beginning of the current year). When this is the case, the costs that are matched against revenues for the current year are costs incurred during that year. But suppose that the quantity on hand at the end of the year is less than it was at the beginning, perhaps because of a voluntary reduction in the scope of the company's operations, or an involuntary shortage due to war, strikes, or the like. Then some of those old lifo costs imbedded in the Opening Inventory figure will be matched with current revenues, and in the typical case where the lifo costs are much lower than current costs, the result will be a much higher current net income figure than would have been the case if the inventory quantity at year end had not fallen below the quantity at the beginning of the year.

To illustrate this problem raised by liquidation of so-called lifo inventory stocks, suppose that the Jones Company had adopted lifo at the time of its organization and that the cost of shoes was $1.00 per pair throughout that year. Suppose further, for simplicity, that the company bought 3,000 more pairs of shoes than it sold in that year, but that in each of the next eight years it purchased only exactly as many pairs of shoes as it sold. Accordingly, closing inventory for year 9, and of course opening inventory for year 10, would be 3,000 pairs of shoes, priced under lifo at $1.00 per pair, making a total of $3,000. If Jones' purchases and sales for year 10 were exactly the same as indicated in the illustration on page 448, supra, gross profit for the year computed on the lifo basis would be the same $5,800 it was in the illustration on page 452, supra:

Sales		$26,000
Less: Cost of Goods Sold		
Opening Inventory (on Lifo)	$ 3,000	
Purchases	24,600	
	$27,600	
Less:		
Closing Inventory of 5,000		
pairs on Lifo	$ 7,400	20,200
Gross Profit		$ 5,800

This should cause no surprise: since the closing inventory in both cases is equal to the sum of opening inventory (whatever it may be) plus $4,400 (the cost of the first 2,000 pairs of shoes purchased during the year), the cost of goods sold remains the same.

But suppose that the Jones Company did not make any purchases in October and December, so that total purchases for the year amounted to only 6,000 pairs.   In that event, the gross profit would be computed as follows:

Sales		$26,000
Less: Cost of Goods Sold		
Opening Inventory (Lifo)	$ 3,000	
Purchases	13,800	
	$16,800	
Less:		
Closing Inventory of 1,000		
pairs on Lifo	$ 1,000	15,800
Gross Profit		$10,200

Thus although the company's operations still consisted of selling 8,000 pairs of shoes for $26,000, a much higher net income is reflected. This higher income figure results from the fact that the older, much lower, lifo inventory costs, which would have remained on the balance sheet, and would not have entered into the determination of net income, if the quantity of inventory at year-end had not fallen below the quantity in opening inventory, were here matched against current revenues (of this higher price-level era).

It may well be argued that to show such an inflated net income figure for the period in which the liquidation of some of the lifo inventory happens to occur will distort the picture of both current operations and the trend of the company's fortunes.   There is force in this argument, whether the reduction in inventory was entirely involuntary, as for example in the case of war scarcity, or simply inadvertent, or was intentional, as for example if the company decided to reduce the scope of its operations.   Yet it seems clear that this extra net income which results from liquidation of some (or all) of the low-cost lifo inventory can not be kept off the current income statement. Would it qualify for extraordinary item treatment?   See APB Op. No. 30, page 189, supra, particularly paragraph 23.

For an example of this kind of gain, see the second paragraph of note 5 to the Ethyl statement on page 454, supra; consider also the following view expressed in SEC Staff Accounting Bulletin No. 1 (1975):

H.   LIFO LIQUIDATIONS

Facts: Registrant on a LIFO basis of accounting liquidates a substantial portion of its LIFO inventory and as a result includes a material amount of income in its income statement which would not have been recorded had the inventory liquidation not taken place.

Question: Is disclosure required of the amount of income realized as a result of the inventory liquidation?

Interpretive Response: Yes. Such disclosure would be required in order to make the financial statements not misleading. Disclosure may be made either in a footnote or parenthetically on the face of the income statement.

7. ACCOUNTING FOR THE INVENTORY OF A MANUFACTURER: A BRIEF INTRODUCTION TO COST ACCOUNTING

Accounting for the inventory of a manufacturing enterprise presents some special problems, in part because there are really three separate inventories, consisting of raw materials, goods in the process of being completed, and finished goods ready for sale. While the raw material inventory creates no particular difficulty, goods in process and finished goods certainly do. Obviously, the cost of these assets at year end must at a minimum include not only the raw material used but also the cost of the labor employed in bringing the goods to their present condition. The costs of material and the expense of labor directly involved in the production process, which together are usually referred to as *direct*, or *prime*, costs, can often be determined from the manufacturing records, which will typically show the amount and kind of raw materials used and the number of hours and type of labor expended. But there are also so-called factory overhead costs, that is, the normal expenses of operating the factory, such as light, heat, depreciation, insurance and property taxes, which may be viewed as being as much a part of production expense as the prime costs of raw material and labor, even though these overhead costs are not readily assignable to any particular goods. In accounting terms, there seems no more reason to charge as an expense of the period the portion of these overhead costs allocable to the inventory of goods in process and finished goods on hand at the end of the period than there would be to charge off the raw material (or direct labor) incorporated in that inventory; rather the appropriate amount of overhead expense should be deferred and added to the cost of the goods in process and finished goods included in closing inventory. The difficulty comes in deciding what portion of the total factory overhead for the period should be allocated to the goods in process and finished goods on hand at the end of the period.

Factory overhead costs are often described as "fixed", to distinguish them from the "variable" costs like raw material and direct labor which are only incurred as a result of the production of particular goods. (General administrative expenses, like executive salaries, or interest on debt, are also examples of fixed costs, although unlike factory overhead such costs are not allocated to inventory but are charged off entirely as expenses of the period in which they were incurred.) Notice, however, that not all factory overhead expenses are absolutely fixed, that is, entirely independent of the amount and type of goods produced. Some costs may vary with the total, or the mix, of production—depreciation, for example, if the machines wear out more rapidly in one type of manufacturing process than another. Similarly, a single foreman may be able to supervise a particular manufacturing process at one level of production, but require assistance if the level of production is expanded beyond that point. (The same is true of general administrative expenses— e. g., additional executives may be needed at higher levels of operation, and more borrowed funds resulting in greater interest expenses might be required as well.)

The process of allocating these overhead, or indirect, costs is one of the functions of *cost accounting*. Like most accounting processes, this is an art, not a science, and the objective is to find a reasonable and practical approach rather than to look for some precisely accurate solution. Especially is this true when a company has a number of different products, rather than just one, in various stages of manufacture; but even for a relatively simple, one-product enterprise it can prove exceedingly difficult to allocate costs between goods still in process and those which have been completed during the period (of which most have been sold but some of course remain on hand at the end of the period).

PHOTO–SONICS, INC. v. COMMISSIONER *

United States Court of Appeals, Ninth Circuit, 1966.
357 F.2d 656.

ELY, CIRCUIT JUDGE:

We face a petition for review of a Tax Court decision upholding the assessment of a deficiency in the payment of income taxes.

The controversy stems from taxpayer's method of accounting for its inventory of goods which it manufactured. Under the method, generally described as "prime costing" or "prime cost", only the cost of direct labor and materials were allocated to inventory value. No portion of factory-overhead expense, variable or fixed, was included.

The key to validity of an accounting method is, in accounting terms, a matching of costs and revenues and, in terms of the taxing statute, a clear reflection of income. . . . The Government urges that, just as labor and materials cannot be expensed in the year in which such expenses are incurred without giving due regard to wheth-

* Footnotes by the Court omitted.

er the manufactured product remains on hand, factory-overhead expenses which constitute a portion of the cost of unsold manufactured products cannot be expensed as they are incurred but rather should be allocated to the manufactured products and deducted, as a cost of sale, when the goods are sold. It contends that proper allocation of factory-overhead expenses, both fixed and variable, to the inventory is the only manner by which the taxpayer's income for a given period may be clearly reflected.

It may be that "direct costing", the allocation to inventory of labor, materials, and variable factory overhead, is an accurate method by which to account for inventory. If consistently applied, it would not seem to be less satisfactory than the method advanced by the Government, i. e., the "absorption costing" method under which labor, material, and both fixed and variable factory overhead are allocated. Both methods are accepted, although "absorption costing" seems now to be preferred by most American accountants. The Tax Court arrived at its determination "without attempting to lay down any broad principles applicable to inventories." 42 T.C. at 936. We, exercising similar restraint, are concerned with a particular accounting method only as it relates to the particular facts which are before us.

Here, the taxpayer allocated no portion of its factory-overhead expense to inventory. The regulations clearly specify that such be done. Treas.Reg. § 1.471–3(c) (1964). A method which excludes all factory-overhead costs is not an acceptable accounting practice. See American Institute of Certified Public Accountants, Accounting Research Bull. No. 43.* The significance of failure to allocate any of such costs to inventory is emphasized by looking in this case, as an example, to one of the items of unallocated factory overhead, shop and tool expense. This expense represented items purchased during the year which were either too inexpensive to depreciate or were consumed during the year. The Tax Court found that it amounted to $8,215.34 in 1958, $40,397.22 in 1959, and $103,896.18 in 1960. Thus, in an expanding business in which some of the products manufactured in one fiscal period are sold in a subsequent fiscal period, the expenses which are attributable to the cost of sales in a subsequent year are matched against the lower sales revenues of a prior year. The effect of such a practice, if allowed, would obviously permit taxpayer to report less income than the amount which was truly earned. It would not be an "accounting practice * * * clearly reflecting the income" as required by section 471.

In reviewing the proceedings below, it is seen that certain testimony of accountants produced by the taxpayer cast doubt upon the validity of taxpayer's accounting method. One such witness admitted, in the Government's cross examination, that an opinion given by a Certified Public Accountant as to the accuracy of financial statements prepared by taxpayer's method would require qualification if factory-overhead expense were material; otherwise, an examiner of the financial statement would be misled. It cannot be denied that, here, factory-overhead expense was significantly material.

* [Ed. note]. Statement 3 of Chapter 4, pages 439–440, supra.

We are not persuaded that the Commissioner's determination was arbitrary. It follows that the Tax Court's decision, not clearly erroneous, must be Affirmed.

The actual process for allocating factory overhead costs to inventory will vary from company to company, and we need not pause here to consider the intricacies involved. It is sufficient simply to note that one common approach is to allocate the total overhead on the basis of some relevant feature of the company's various products, such as direct labor cost. Thus, if the total direct labor expended in all production during a period was $100,000, and the total factory overhead was $50,000, then the overhead might be allocated among the company's products (including those in process at year end) at the rate of 50 cents for each $1.00 of direct labor expended. On the other hand, in an industry where, perhaps by virtue of automated equipment, labor is not as significant a factor, machine hours might be used as the basis of allocation instead. Consider the following approach to the allocation of costs in a non-inventory setting:

RE WASHINGTON GAS LIGHT CO.

District of Columbia Public Utilities Commission, 1949.
83 P.U.R. (N.S.) 4.

By the Commission:

Nature of Proceeding

On July 14, 1949, the Washington Gas Light Company (hereinafter referred to as the "Company") filed an application with this Commission for an emergency increase of its rates to produce additional operating revenues of $900,000 in the aggregate on an annual basis, the over-all effect of which would be an increase of approximately 7 per cent.

In support of its application, the Company stated that the additional revenues requested are needed to enable the Company to comply with its obligation "to furnish service and facilities reasonably safe and adequate." The application sets forth that revenues derived from the rates now in effect are not sufficient to pay all of the costs of operation and to provide an adequate return on the property used in supplying gas to customers. It is further stated that the rate of return realized by the Company from its sales to District of Columbia customers has declined from approximately 6 per cent in 1941 to approximately 3.25 per cent in the current year; and that after adjusting for normal temperatures, to offset the adverse effect of the mild weather during the heating season of 1948, 1949, the current return would not exceed 3.68 per cent.

* * *

Description of the Company

The Washington Gas Light Company distributes and sells straight natural gas in the District of Columbia. Its wholly owned subsidiaries, the Washington Gas Light Company of Maryland, Inc. (Washington Maryland Company) and the Rosslyn Gas Company (Rosslyn Company) also distribute and sell straight natural gas in near-by areas of Maryland and Virginia. The rates charged for gas service in these latter areas are fixed by the Public Service Commission of Maryland and the State Corporation Commission of Virginia, respectively. . . .

* * *

Allocation of Certain Sales Promotion Expenses to Subsidiary Company

One of the divisions of the sales department of the Company is known as the promotional division. The primary function of this division is to promote the sale of gas in new construction. During the twelve months ended May 31, 1949, the total cost of this division, including direct supervision, amounted to $91,079.20 for the Company and its two distributing subsidiaries, namely, Washington Maryland Company and Rosslyn Company. During the month of June, 1948, all such salaries were charged on the books of the Washington Company and prorated to the two subsidiaries on the basis of therms of gas sold. From July, 1948, through May, 1949, such costs were charged directly on the books of each of the three companies. The Rosslyn Company maintained its own organization, and no question of allocation was involved. A single organization, however, performed this work for both the Washington Company and the Maryland Company, and the charges made on the books of these two companies, while made directly from a time sheet distribution, nevertheless approximated the ratio of therm sales in the District and Maryland to the total therm sales in these two jurisdictions. As a result, the total costs set forth above were apportioned among the three companies as follows:

Washington	$48,859.84
Washington Maryland	14,870.62
Rosslyn	27,348.74
	$91,079.20

The Company's witness contended that the apportionment of these costs among the three companies on the basis of therm sales in the three areas represented a reasonable allocation. The Commission's witness, however, testified that, since the major activity of this division had to do with new construction, and that since new construction in both Maryland and Virginia was substantially greater than in the District, the therm sales basis did not produce a reasonable allocation. As for eleven months of the year, when the direct charges made on the books of the Rosslyn Company covered the salaries of the promotional salesmen working in that territory, the witness made no adjustment to Rosslyn. However, by reason of the single organization working in both the District and Maryland, he made an adjustment in the amount of $29,362.33, which resulted in a reduction of District expenses and an increase in the expenses of the Washington

Maryland Company. This adjustment was arrived at by determining the cost per meter of additional meters installed in the Rosslyn territory during the twelve months ended May 31, 1949, and applying this cost per meter to the increase in meters in the Maryland territory; and by deducting from the resulting amount the charges actually recorded on the Maryland books under the method used by the Company. Using the Commission witness' method of allocating these costs, the total amount involved would be apportioned as follows:

Washington	$19,497.51
Maryland	44,232.95
Virginia	27,348.74
	$91,079.20

The revised District of Columbia figure represents a cost of $9.35 per meter installed in the District during the twelve months ended May 31, 1949, compared with the actual cost of $8.59 in Rosslyn, which was the figure used in arriving at the revised Maryland figure. The witness stated that while he believed this method to be reasonable for the purposes of this proceeding, he would not advocate its adoption for future use in apportioning costs of this character among the three jurisdictions. He did, however, express the opinion that a change should be made in the present procedure and recommended that a direct time sheet allocation, representing the employees' best estimate of the time spent between the two jurisdictions, be adopted.

The allocation of costs between jurisdictions always presents a difficult problem, and, in the case of promotional expenses, it is doubly difficult by reason of the absence of definite yardsticks to measure the results accomplished.

It does not appear that either the therm-sales basis used by the Company's witness or the increase-in-meters method used by the Commission's witness produces results which can be relied upon with any degree of certainty. By reference to Exhibit 23, it appears that during the month of June, 1948, the use of the therm-sales ratio resulted in an inadequate charge to the Rosslyn Company in comparison with the actual costs incurred during the eleven months of the year ended May 31, 1949. To elaborate, on a therm-sales basis, Rosslyn was charged with approximately 10 percent of the costs of the promotional division for all three companies during the month of June, 1948. The costs of Rosslyn's promotional division on an actual basis for the eleven months ended May 31, 1949, amounted to approximately 32 percent of the costs of the promotional divisions for all three companies.

The increase-in-meters method may also produce distorted results between the two jurisdictions by reason of the fact that the activities of the promotional division occur well in advance of the time of the actual installation of the meter. In view of the foregoing, the Commission believes that the amount charged the Maryland Company is well below a reasonable amount, but it is not convinced that the adjustment made by the Commission's witness is sufficiently well supported to justify its unqualified acceptance. In the final conclusion, recognition will be given to the fact that expenses of the promotional division charged to District of Columbia operations are well in excess of a reasonable amount.

As to the future treatment of these costs, the Commission is firmly convinced that the therm-sales basis of allocation should be discarded and replaced by an actual time sheet distribution of costs of this character. This conclusion is adequately supported by the comparison of the two methods cited above with respect to the Rosslyn Company.

While cost accounting has important implications in the preparation of the financial statements, as in connection with the valuation of closing inventory, its role in the financial affairs of an enterprise is a good deal broader than that. For one thing, some reasonable system for recording and measuring both fixed and variable costs is indispensable to an acceptable system of internal control over the operations of the enterprise, as is now specifically required by the Foreign Corrupt Practices Act of 1977. See page 118, supra. Equally important, distinctions between fixed and variable costs, and a sensible method of allocating these costs to the production process, are essential to sound pricing decisions, as well as determination of whether to undertake production of a new product. For example, there may be room for argument over whether a new product is "profitable" only if it can be sold at a price which covers both all direct costs and a proportionate share of the factory overhead costs (and maybe some portion of the general administrative expenses as well), since as long as the new product makes some contribution to the fixed expenses it will reduce the amount of those expenses allocable to the existing products and hence might be viewed as increasing the profit on those items; but it seems indisputable that taking on a new product which does not hold promise of at least covering its direct costs plus any variable overhead costs is likely to be a losing play. In any event, it is clear that management must have detailed information on cost allocation in order to make decisions of this kind.

Cost accounting is also of considerable importance in a number of other contexts of special concern to lawyers. Look back at the *Larson* case on page 267, supra, involving a suit to recover the profits of an infringer. Since the plaintiff was only entitled to the profits realized on the infringing product, counsel (and the court) were faced with an exercise in cost accounting, in trying to establish just what costs of the infringing company were allocable to that product for the period in question. The same kind of issues can arise in simple cases of suit for damages for breach of contract by a seller against a buyer who has refused to perform. E. g., Vitex Mfg. Corp. v. Caribtex Corp., 377 F.2d 795 (3d Cir. 1967) (in a claim for lost profits the seller is entitled to recover the difference between the selling price and the direct, variable costs, thereby realizing the contribution to fixed overhead which the transaction would have made). And of course in cases under the Robinson-Patman Act, which in effect outlaws quantity discounts unless justified by "differences in the cost of manufacture, sale or delivery", the manner in which various costs are allocated is crucial.

Here is another example of cost accounting at work, in a context of considerable current significance:

UNITED STATES v. RESERVE MINING CO.

United States District Court, District of Minnesota, 1976.
423 F.Supp. 759.

Memorandum and Order

DEVITT, CHIEF JUDGE.

In order to guarantee safe drinking water to residents of communities on the North Shore of Lake Superior, the court ordered a temporary water filtration program, pending construction of permanent filtration facilities, and, because of its expertise in the area, the United States Army Corps of Engineers was ordered to initially finance and manage this program. . . . Last February this court concluded that defendants Reserve, Republic and Armco were liable for the costs of this interim filtration program and ordered them to reimburse the Corps for expenses it incurred in this project. The parties were ordered to meet to determine the exact amount due the Corps. If the parties were unable to agree, the court indicated that, upon proper motion, it would take evidence to determine the exact amount due. United States v. Reserve Mining Co., 408 F.Supp. 1212, 1219 (D.Minn.1976).

The parties have not been able to agree upon the exact amount due but have filed a stipulation which, they contend, makes an evidentiary hearing unnecessary. This stipulation indicates that representatives of the parties met and agreed on the amount of expenses incurred by the Corps in connection with this program and divided these expenses into two categories, "direct" and "indirect." Defendants have agreed to reimburse the Corps for the direct expenses which include costs incurred in letting contracts for filter design and actual filter purchase, installation and maintenance but they have refused to be responsible for those expenses defined as indirect. Although the stipulation does not clearly state and explain all items included in the indirect expense category, it seems that the parties are talking about overhead, broadly defined. Among the items included in this category are the following:

> 1. a pro rata portion of the salaries of regular Corps employees who have worked on the filtration program, determined by reference to time cards, work sheets and other documents;

2. a pro rata portion of the government's contributions to employee life and health insurance plans, social security (for temporary employees) etc.;

3. overhead, defined to include administrative salaries, materials and supplies.

Defendants contend that, because these indirect expenses would have been substantially incurred by the Corps even in the absence of the water filtration program, they should not be liable for them. The Corps counters by arguing that if the court had required defendants to operate the filtration program through contracts with private companies, they would have paid these overhead expenses as part of the contract costs. Therefore, to allow defendants to escape this obligation would allow them an unearned windfall at the expense of the taxpayers of this country. Finally, at oral argument on this motion, counsel for the Corps stated that because of the expense it has incurred to date in administering this program, it has had to defer until next fiscal year a number of functions it would have done this year.

Thus, the issue presented for resolution is may a service agency, such as the Corps, when it is ordered because of its expertise and resources to correct a problem, recover from those causing the problem, in addition to its direct costs, its overhead. The only case on point cited by either party is United States v. Denver & R. G. R. R., C74–145 (D.Utah 1975). In that case, the court allowed the Bureau of Land Management to recover the costs, including "overhead or indirect costs," incurred in suppressing a forest fire negligently started by defendant.

The logic of this holding and the government's position in this case is compelling. Were it not for defendants' discharges into Lake Superior, the filtration program would not be necessary. United States v. Reserve Mining Co., supra, at 1219. Therefore, the court ordered defendants to reimburse the Corps for expenses incurred in this project. Id. Although it is true that many of these indirect costs would have incurred regardless of defendants' discharges, they are real costs and are part of the total cost of providing clean, safe water to the residents of the affected communities. . . .

Therefore, the court declares that defendants must reimburse the Corps of Engineers for the indirect costs detailed in the Stipulation, Clerk's entry #1713.

QUESTIONS

1. Is there any inconsistency between insisting upon allocation of factory overhead to inventory for accounting (and tax) purposes while ignoring overhead when computing the lost profits of a seller in a contract action against a defaulting buyer?

2. M Corp., a manufacturer of electronic business equipment, and D Co., which operates a large department store, have reached a tentative agreement that M will design and build a special computer for D to provide better inventory control. Because of D's unique requirements, the machine will be different from any that M has built before, and hence the parties have agreed that the price

for the new machine should be equal to M's costs of building it plus a flat fee of $50,000. Your law firm is general counsel for D Co. and you have been asked to consider how the computation of M's costs should be approached in the formal contract, and whether there are any problems calling for special attention.

M maintains the following expense accounts:

Employment Costs

    Wages & salaries, including vacation pay and sick leave

    Social security taxes

Plant and Machinery Costs

    Depreciation

    Repair and maintenance

    Plant protection

Selling

    Advertising expense

    Bad debt expense

    Sales force compensation

General and Administration

    Insurance

    Property taxes

    Utilities expense

    Legal and accounting fees

    Stockholder relations (meetings, annual reports, etc.)

    Contributions & donations

    Amortization of patents

Financing

    Interest expense

Chapter 7

DEPRECIABLE FIXED ASSETS

1. HISTORICAL BACKGROUND

At pages 253–255, supra (which should be reviewed at this point) we were introduced to depreciation accounting, that is, the process of allocating the cost of a tangible fixed asset (less any estimated salvage value) ratably among the periods of the asset's useful life. One authoritative description of depreciation is the following, from paragraph 56 of Accounting Terminology Bulletin No. 1 (1953):

> *Depreciation accounting* is a system of accounting which aims to distribute the cost . . . of tangible capital assets, less salvage (if any), over the estimated useful life of the unit (which may be a group of assets) *in a systematic and rational manner.* It is a *process of allocation*, not of valuation. *Depreciation for the year* is the portion of the total charge under such a system that is allocated to the year. Although the allocation may properly take into account occurrences during the year, it is not intended to be a measurement of the effect of all such occurrences.

Notice that this definition of depreciation does not require that the cost of fixed assets (less salvage value) be apportioned *ratably* over the useful life, i. e., allocation of an equal amount to each period (or to each hour of running time, or to each unit produced, if useful life happens to be calculated on either of those bases); systems involving non-ratable allocation of cost, for example larger amounts in the early years than in the later years, may also be rational, as we shall see. But ratable allocation is the most common practice, and that is the system referred to by the term "straight-line" depreciation, connoting the fact that the cost is apportioned evenly over the asset's useful life.

A brief historical review of accounting for fixed assets may be useful at this point. Prior to the modern emphasis on the proper matching of expenses and revenues, only rudimentary efforts were made to allocate the cost of fixed assets among the periods in which such assets contributed to the production of revenues. Occasionally, account would be taken during the life of a fixed asset of so-called "observed depreciation", that is, physical deterioration as indicated by an engineering appraisal; this corresponded as much to asset re-valuation as to depreciation accounting, which is not surprising in view of the emphasis in that earlier era on balance sheet valuation. Otherwise, no account was taken of the "using up" of a fixed asset over time until the asset was finally retired (whether because it was completely worn out or for any other reason), at which point recognition of the consumption of the asset could no longer be postponed and so the entire balance sheet figure for the asset (less any salvage proceeds) would be written off.

As accounting emphasis shifted from balance sheet valuation to meaningful periodic reflection of income, the deficiencies in this "retirement method" of accounting for fixed assets became readily apparent. The principal one of course was the failure to allocate some ratable share of the cost of a fixed asset to each of the years of its useful life, thus overstating income in each of those years. In addition—really as a corollary—income in the year of retirement was substantially understated, because the entire book value of the asset (less any salvage proceeds) was charged to that year.

In defense of the retirement method it was sometimes pointed out that, at least under conditions of relatively stable prices and a uniform rate of retirement of assets, this method could roughly approximate the cost allocation obtained under depreciation accounting. For example, assume for simplicity that a particular taxicab company uses each of its cabs for exactly five years and then disposes of it without salvage proceeds. If the company starts year 1 with a new cab costing $2,000, and thereafter buys one new cab every year for $2,000, from the fifth year on there would always be five cabs in service and the retirement expense would be $2,000 each year. Depreciation accounting would produce the same annual expense of $2,000, on five cabs costing $2,000 each and having a useful life of five years with no salvage value. But obviously, the assumed situation is far from typical; normally, the retirement method would be a haphazard substitute for a more orderly method of cost allocation. Certainly the start-up years of an enterprise, and any other years in which a company is expanding, would be undercharged by the retirement method. Further, the balance sheet would show the fixed assets at full cost, here $10,000 for the five cabs, rather than at book value, i. e., cost less depreciation to date, of perhaps $6,000 (the precise figure depending upon how long each cab had been owned). (This balance sheet overstatement was sometimes regarded as an advantage of the retirement method, particularly by a public utility allowed to include the assets at $10,000 in the rate base on which it was entitled to earn a fair return.)

These deficiencies in the retirement method led to the development of the so-called "Retirement Reserve" method, under which future retirements were viewed as an expense which should be allocated among at least some of the years prior to the year of retirement. Each year a charge would be made to a current expense account, which might be called Retirement Expense, with a corresponding credit to a kind of Estimated Liability account, but which in fact, pursuant to the old practice we have noted before, was called a "Reserve", here "Reserve for Retirements". When an asset was in fact retired, the amount at which it was carried on the balance sheet (typically the full cost) was charged to the Reserve account, just as a particular account receivable which becomes worthless is charged against the Allowance for Uncollectible Accounts (which also used to be called a "Reserve"), and the year of the retirement was not affected.

The problem with this approach was that the annual charge to current income was not based on a rational system of cost allocation. For example, a common method of determining the charge to be made in any given year was to estimate the amount of the retirements which would be made in the next few years; the amount charged to Retirement Expense for the current year would then be fixed as the amount necessary to build up the Reserve account to that level. In addition, the absence of any fixed schedule of annual charges meant that companies could increase these charges in good years and decrease them in bad years, thus in effect leveling out net income over a series of years, contrary to the objectives of meaningful periodic reporting. Also, the Reserve account was ordinarily carried on the right-hand side of the balance sheet rather than as an offset to the asset account, and thus failed to make clear that some of the total benefit to be derived from the asset had already been consumed.

DETROIT EDISON COMPANY

Annual Report, 1926.

.　.　.

Retirement Reserve—Depreciation

Another question which has been asked is what our policy is with respect to depreciation. The Uniform Classification of Accounts provides for our charging a monthly item of Retirement Expense as part of the cost of doing business, which item is transferred into a Retirement Reserve. Against that Retirement Reserve there is written off, at the time of retirement, the book value of each item of plant or property retired from service for any cause whatsoever. There is no mandate by the Commission as to the amount which shall be put into the Reserve monthly. We, of course, observe literally the rule about writing off all retired property, and we have exercised our best judgment as to the amounts which should be put into reserve to provide for prospective retirements. But we have refrained from setting up any mathematical rule which would bind us to make monthly charges according to the estimated life of any piece or part of our plant. We have increased or supplemented our monthly appropriations to Retirement Reserve,

(a) when we foresaw earlier retirement of any large item or class of property,

(b) when and as the total investment in depreciable property was increased, and further,

(c) when we had good years we have made further supplemental additions to the Reserve.

Conversely, we have revised our estimates of requirements in the direction of a decrease when apparatus in service proved to be more durable than we had expected, and we have made smaller appropriations when net earnings for the time being were definitely less than we had anticipated.

The condition of affairs at the end of 1926 is that the Retirement Reserve has a balance of $14,078,828.41 which, when compared to the observed condition of our depreciable property, is enough to take care of the retirements expected in the next few years, even though we should be unable to make intended additions to the Reserve in those same years.

We are aware of a theory which would require us to make a calculated addition to a Reserve as a yearly or monthly expense item, whether the net earnings for the period were adequate or otherwise. That theory provides a reserve to meet the Retirement charges as they actually arrive, but it does not allow the Reserve to serve its equally useful purpose of allowing the fat years of business to make provision against the lean years. Instead of a Reserve, that theory sets up an Encumbrance. . . .

EDITORIAL

91 Journal of Accountancy 840 (June 1951).

From time to time we have been asked for our opinion on the important question whether the retirement reserve method of accounting for fixed assets is still considered to be in accord with generally accepted accounting principles. . . .

In our opinion, the retirement reserve method of accounting ceased to be a generally accepted accounting principle among commercial and industrial companies many years ago. . . .

Within the compass of a short discussion such as this we cannot contrast to any extent the retirement reserve and depreciation accounting methods, but perhaps it should be said that the most commonly cited inadequacies of the retirement reserve method include the following:

1. The reserve ordinarily does not measure, in terms of cost, the expired portion of the economic life or usefulness of fixed assets at any given time, the reserve being considered sufficient if large enough to absorb any plant retirements contemplated currently or within a relatively few years. . . .

4. The method is fraught with the danger of giving rein to the making of inconsistent provisions as between accounting periods and

does violence to the concept that utilization of service capacity of plant is a regularly recurring cost entering into a determination of net income. . . .

ATTORNEY GENERAL v. TRUSTEES OF BOSTON ELEVATED RY. CO.

Supreme Judicial Court of Massachusetts, 1946.
319 Mass. 642, 67 N.E.2d 676.

RONAN, JUSTICE. This is an information in equity, . . . against the trustees of the Boston Elevated Railway Company . . seeking a declaratory decree as to the manner in which the trustees should keep the books, accounts and balance sheets of the company, and defining the authority of the said trustees to include certain charges as a part of the cost of service rendered by the company under their management and operation, and praying for an injunction to restrain the trustees from charging in the future against the cost of service such items as may be determined in this suit to be beyond their authority to charge. . . .

The principal specific complaints of the Attorney General and of the city of Boston, which was allowed to intervene, are . . . that charges to the cost of service for depreciation have been made which were not made upon any estimates of actual depreciation of the property but were made for the purpose of securing funds to purchase new capital assets or for the purpose of building up a reserve for depreciation; that the charges for depreciation were in excess by several million dollars of the amounts necessary to restore and maintain the property in good operating condition and to return it to the company in that condition—which was all that the trustees were required to do—and will give to the company, in addition to its property in this condition, additions and improvements constituting capital assets, which were provided by the trustees without right from the operating revenue of the company; and that such charges have adversely affected not only the amounts due as deficiency payments by the Commonwealth but also the interests of the Commonwealth in the reserve fund. . . .

The trustees are expressly authorized by section 6 of the public control act to include allowances for depreciation and obsolescence in the cost of service. The meaning of each of these terms is well understood, and so are their nature and purpose. Regard must be given to the matter of depreciation in ascertaining the financial condition of a going concern. . . .

Depreciation represents the consumption of physical assets, resulting from the manufacture of goods or the furnishing of services, which is not restored by current maintenance in making repairs or by the substitution of new minor or small parts which have become worn. Depreciation is the deterioration of physical assets due to wear and tear, decay and age. Another form of depreciation is obsolescence. This we understand to mean a loss in the service value of a fixed or capital asset which has become useless or inefficient on account of advances in the art, new inventions, inadequacy, the shift-

ing of business centers, the loss of trade or some governmental ruling. . . . Nothing in this opinion depends on any distinction between these forms of depreciation. We refer to both as depreciation. The service life of a machine or plant is shortened by use, and the depreciation if correctly estimated and properly entered upon the books will reflect the lessened value of this capital asset. This lessened value which has occurred in a year is the basis for making a charge against income for annual depreciation as a part of the operating expenses. The purpose and methods for keeping accounts of depreciation and also reserves for depreciation have been frequently stated in decisions dealing with reviews of rate making controversies.
. . .

As far as possible, a customer ought not to be charged with depreciation as a part of the service to him where the depreciation did not arise from the production of that service but had occurred years previous thereto. The charge for depreciation as a part of the cost of service is at best only an estimate. If enough is not charged the company furnishing the service must bear the loss, but if too much is charged the customers have been compelled to contribute to the capital investment of the company. The purpose of a charge for depreciation is to protect the integrity of the investment, and the cost of service ought not to be burdened with any item that yields the company more than is required to offset the loss due to depreciation. . .

. . . We are not primarily concerned with methods adopted by the trustees in keeping the books of the company. Our inquiry is not so much concerned with what the books show or how certain transactions have been recorded, but rather with what items were included by the trustees in ascertaining the cost of service. The allegations based upon the claim that the trustees had no power to use the straight line method of depreciation state no cause for relief. We have no power to decide what is the best method of accounting with reference to depreciation. The choice lies with the trustees. We cannot say they were wrong in employing the method which they did and which appears from decisions of the Supreme Court of the United States and of this court to be one of the recognized methods of good accounting. . . . There is no just ground of complaint that the trustees did not have an appraisal made of the company's property when they took possession on July 1, 1918, and did not ascertain by an examination of the properties the amount they had then been depreciated. The theory that the determination of depreciation by observation of the property is preferable to the estimates of experts based upon judgment and experience finds support in [some early cases], but it has since been pointed out that one method as matter of law is not entitled to more weight than the other. . . .

2. BALANCE SHEET PRESENTATION OF FIXED ASSETS

As indicated at page 255, supra, the uniform practice today is to state fixed assets at cost on the balance sheet, and to carry the Accumulated Depreciation account as an offset thereto; the net figure resulting, i. e., the book value of the fixed assets, represents the amount of the original cost of the assets remaining to be allocated to future periods (plus any estimated salvage value). APB Op. No. 12 (1967) confirms this practice (while mandating some other disclosures about depreciation as well):

CLASSIFICATION AND DISCLOSURE OF ALLOWANCES

2. Although it is generally accepted that accumulated allowances for depreciation and depletion and asset valuation allowances for losses such as those on receivables and investments should be deducted from the assets to which they relate there are instances in which these allowances are shown among liabilities or elsewhere on the credit side of the balance sheet.

3. It is the Board's opinion that such allowances should be deducted from the assets or groups of assets to which the allowances relate, with appropriate disclosure.

DISCLOSURE OF DEPRECIABLE ASSETS AND DEPRECIATION

4. Disclosure of the total amount of depreciation expense entering into the determination of results of operations has become a general practice. The balances of major classes of depreciable assets are also generally disclosed. Practice varies, however, with respect to disclosure of the depreciation method or methods used.

5. Because of the significant effects on financial position and results of operations of the depreciation method or methods used, the following disclosures should be made in the financial statements or in notes thereto:

a. Depreciation expense for the period,

b. Balances of major classes of depreciable assets, by nature or function, at the balance-sheet date,

c. Accumulated depreciation, either by major classes of depreciable assets or in total, at the balance-sheet date, and

d. A general description of the method or methods used in computing depreciation with respect to major classes of depreciable assets.

Nevertheless, there have been occasional spokesmen for a different view about how to reflect the Accumulated Depreciation account on the balance sheet:

SIMON, THE RIGHT SIDE FOR ACCUMULATED DEPRECIATION *

34 Acc.Rev. 101–103 (1959).

. . . . Now what justification may be given for the suggestion that accumulated depreciation might better be shown on the right side of the balance sheet? . . .

In the first place, the accumulated depreciation account, under today's industrial conditions, can be thought of as more of a reserve for obsolescence than merely for depreciation. It may therefore be considered, to a significant extent, somewhat in the nature of a reserve for contingencies. When queried as to why it displayed the account among liabilities and capital, an official of the DuPont Company based his reply almost entirely on this point, and insisted that this concept would seem to provide a fundamental basis from the standpoint of accounting theory for showing the reserve on the right-hand side of the balance sheet.

* * *

One of the ways of emphasizing the obsolescence problem in the replacement of assets might indeed be to place accumulated depreciation with other reserves for contingencies on the right-hand side of the statement of financial position. This is especially true where accelerated methods of computing annual depreciation have been employed, because much of the argument to justify acceleration is based on the anticipation of substantial plant retirements at some unknown date in the future as a result of obsolescence of processes and products due to advancing technology.

This uncertainty of the life of fixed assets appears in none of the other assets subject to periodic cost allocation, such as prepaid insurance, bond discount, and others. The amortization of these items is certain, regular, and can be accurately computed. They are not subject to the unpredictability to which depreciable assets are addicted, so that their treatment as contingencies, as is suggested for accumulated depreciation, could not be justified on the basis of this argument.

Depreciation was always an estimate—it is even more of an uncertainty in the dynamic industrial world of today. Deducting depreciation from cost to give a net figure which has an illusion of value to the lay reader can present a definitely false impression. It might indeed be more realistic to show the original cost of the asset on the one hand, and the amount of that cost that has been recovered, or cash flow being retained from net profits and surplus, to cushion the shock of the asset's ultimate obsolescence and retirement, among the sources of funds on the other, or right-hand, side of the statement.

This leads into the next point. The balance sheet not only fails to display the value of fixed assets, but can no longer truly be said to show the net worth of the business. The financial condition of an enterprise, as shown on this statement, was always suspect because of the many estimates necessarily involved in the figures shown for assets. But that estimation is today compounded by such accounting methods as LIFO, direct costing, original rather than replacement cost, etc., so that the balance sheet figures have little relation with actual values.

Rather, the statement of financial condition can be said to be in the main a summary at a given date of the effect of previous changes in its component parts—assets, liabilities and proprietorship. Put in another way, it displays, as of a certain moment of time, a cumulative compilation of the ways in which its funds have been employed and the sources from which these funds have been derived in the past.

When viewed as a statement of funds received and applied, from the date of the inception of the business to the date of the report, the placement of accumulated depreciation among the sources of funds is quite reasonable. Indeed this was cited by officials of the Cleveland Electric Illuminating Company as a major justification for their corporation's support of the position favoring right-hand display of the account.

The basic accounting principle of showing fixed assets at cost on the balance sheet * can readily be explained by considering the asset figures as showing how the funds of the business have been used or invested. Similarly, viewing the right-hand side of the statement as disclosing the sources of funds makes the overall purpose of the balance sheet much more clear. The liability items show how much of the funds were obtained from creditors, short or long term, and the contributed capital figure indicates the extent to which funds were derived from stockholder investment. Retained earnings, accumulated from profits of past periods not dissipated in dividends, is another source of the funds employed by the enterprise. In a somewhat similar manner, accumulated depreciation has resulted in the retention of funds, not considered as profits and dispersed in dividends, and should be shown on the right-hand side among the sources of funds.

It is true that depreciation involves the cost allocation of long term assets, a problem of matching revenues of a period with the charges against those revenues. It is equally true, technically, that the charging of depreciation does not actually provide the funds. They are provided by the revenues from the sales of goods or services to customers. But if the revenues were sufficient to cover all costs,

---

* [Ed. note] The following observations, made earlier in this article, are relevant at this point:

" . . . The cost shown alone in the assets side, were the "right-side" method adopted, would be consistent with a showing of other long term assets, permanent investments and intangibles at cost. Perhaps it might eventually lead to the discarding of the highly questionable cost or market rule for the valuation of current assets so that these assets also could be shown at cost. It then should not take too long to educate even the lay reader to understand that balance sheet asset figures are costs only, and to discard the present misconception that they represent values.

"If the net plant figure must be known, the reserve on the right-hand side could be connected with its related asset by . . . [some appropriate notation so that] by a quick mental subtraction the unamortized cost could easily be ascertained by anyone actually wanting that figure."

the depreciation reserve results in the retention or provision of funds because it prevents their disbursement as dividends.

*   *   *

While academicians may argue that depreciation does not provide any funds, business firms nevertheless make considerable use of the dollars so obtained. Over the past twelve years, for instance, the American Telephone & Telegraph Company has paid for some five billion dollars out of its sixteen billion dollar construction program out of accumulated depreciation. Indeed, depreciation allowances, or the funds they make available when earned, account for about half of the capital expenditures of American industry.

Certainly in the common parlance of the businessman, who must wrestle with the problem of obtaining capital, accumulated depreciation is very much a source of funds. Evidence of this can be seen in the increasing number of presidents' letters and numerous charts in annual reports that now stress the importance of cash flow and point to a combination of earnings and depreciation charges as an indication of business success. . . .

*   *   *

PROBLEM

A state statute requires that the officers and directors of every corporation file annually a "report of condition" of the corporation, which must include a statement of assets and liabilities as of the end of the corporation's most recent fiscal year, in such form as the secretary of state may require. The prescribed form, as described by the court in one reported case, is a balance sheet, showing, on one side, "Assets", subdivided according to their nature, and, on the other side, "Liabilities", including indebtedness of various kinds, "Capital Stock", "Reserves" and "Surplus". A companion statute provides that if officers and directors make any required statement or report "which is false in any material representation and which they know to be false", they shall be liable "to persons who shall have relied upon such false report to their damage".

Some years ago E Transport Corp. filed a report of condition which included a balance sheet showing on the asset side, "Autos, trucks and teams", carried at $14,735. The liability side showed "Reserves" at $13,833. The $14,735 represented the original purchase price of the equipment, which had been purchased about ten years ago and was currently worth about $1,000. The $13,833 in "Reserves" consisted of about $13,535 charged to expense over the years on account of depreciation on the equipment, plus approximately $300 for bad debts.

A creditor who extended credit to E after the above report of condition had been filed brought an action against the officers and directors of E on the ground that the report of condition was false in a material representation "with reference to the value of the autos, trucks and teams owned by the corporation". What judgment? In considering your answer, suppose that E's balance sheet, except for the figure of $13,833 for "Reserves", appeared in the report of condition as follows:

Assets		Liabilities	
Cash	$ 198	Acc. Pay	$8,000
Acc. Rec.	2,000		
Autos, trucks,		Cap. Stock	7,000
and teams	14,735		
Good will	12,900	Surplus	1,000

Could a judgment about whether to lend, say, $1,000, to or invest in E Corp. be affected by where the figure for Reserves was carried on the balance sheet? Cf. pages 335–336 and 364–366, supra.

3. ACCOUNTING FOR RETIREMENTS

As might be expected, the switch from retirement reserve and similar methods to depreciation accounting led to a different view of how to account for asset retirements. Depreciation accounting does not produce a "reserve" against which the cost of a retired asset (less salvage proceeds) can be charged; instead, an "Accumulated Depreciation" account is created to reflect the total depreciation taken on the asset to date, and that account appears separately on the balance sheet, as an offset to the asset account, in order to preserve the original cost figure. Upon retirement of the asset, however, there is obviously no longer any need to preserve the original cost figure. Therefore, a sensible starting point is to actually credit the amount in the Accumulated Depreciation account against the original cost in the asset account, thereby reducing the figure in the asset account to book value (which is what it would have been if depreciation had been credited directly to the asset account all along, as in fact is done in connection with the amortization of an intangible asset). This could be thought of as a simple mathematical step of subtraction; but actually the bookkeeper is likely, as usual, to make an entry to accomplish this, consisting of a debit to the Accumulated Depreciation account, to close it out, and a credit to the asset account. To illustrate, assume that at the beginning of year 1 a company acquires a cab, with an expected useful life of five years and an estimated salvage value of $500, for $5500. At the end of year 5, the cab would have a book value of $500, represented by the original cost of $5,500 standing in the asset account, offset by $5,000 in the Accumulated Depreciation account. Assuming that the cab is to be retired at the close of year 5, the entry closing out the Accumulated Depreciation account and reducing the figure in the asset account to the $500 book value would be:

Accumulated Depreciation	$5,000	
Cab		$5,000

If the original estimate of salvage value proves to be as accurate as the estimate of useful life was in this simple illustration, the salvage proceeds upon disposition of the cab at the end of year 5 will be $500, and the entry reflecting this transaction would be:

Cash	$500	
Cab		$500

However, since the closing out of the Accumulated Depreciation account occurs at the same time as (indeed, is occasioned by) the disposition of the asset upon retirement, normally the bookkeeper would not make the separate entries shown above, but rather would use a single composite entry:

Cash	$500	
Accumulated Depreciation	$5,000	
Cab		$5,500

Notice that in form this entry appears much the same as the one that used to be made under the old retirement reserve method, where the difference between the original cost of the asset and the salvage proceeds was charged against the reserve, and perhaps as a result of the similarity this entry is sometimes described in terms of "charging the asset (less salvage proceeds) to the Accumulated Depreciation account"; but as we have seen the theory of the entry is very much different, being simply a reduction of the asset account to its book value (plus a reflection of the disposition of the asset for cash).

Now suppose that only $200 is obtained when the cab is disposed of at the end of year 5. When the bookkeeper comes to make the composite entry, there is a missing debit of $300:

Accumulated Depreciation	$5,000	
Cash	200	
?	300	
Cab		$5,500

One way of looking at the situation is to say that salvage value was originally overestimated, with the result that the depreciation expense for each of the intervening years was understated; that is, instead of allocating among the years in which the cab was used the full $5,300 of cost actually consumed, which would have required a charge of $1,060 per year, only $1,000 was charged to each year. Even if viewed in this light, however, there would be no escape from a charge against current income, since a prior period adjustment would obviously not be available; and the same is true if the transaction is regarded as a simple sale of an asset for less than book value, giving rise to a current loss. Thus the entry here would be:

Accumulated Depreciation	$5,000	
Cash	200	
Loss on Disposition of Cab	300	
Cab		$5,500

Is the same approach applicable when an asset is retired before the end of its useful life? Suppose that the cab with which we have been dealing is disposed of at the end of year 3 for $1,900. At that point, there would be $3,000 in the Accumulated Depreciation account, making the book value of the asset $2,500. Here it is less easy to say that the three years during which the cab was used have been undercharged in the amount of the $600 gap between the book value of the asset and the disposition proceeds; it is *not* a function of straight-line depreciation to produce a book value for the asset equal to its market value at any particular point in time during the life of the asset. On the other hand, again the transaction may be seen as reducing the asset to its book value, and then selling the asset for less than book value, producing a loss in the amount of the difference. So the same form of entry as above would be utilized:

Accumulated Depreciation	$3,000	
Cash	1,900	
Loss on Disposition of Cab	600	
Cab		$5,500

4. GROUP METHOD OF DEPRECIATION

As a practical matter, treating every fixed asset as a separate unit for depreciation (and retirement) purposes can produce rather onerous bookkeeping burdens, at least for a company of substantial size. It is often more sensible to deal with a number of individual items together, treating the group as if it constituted a single unit and applying a single depreciation rate to the total cost of the assets in the group (less the total estimated salvage value). This is called the "group method", or sometimes the "composite method", of depreciation accounting. For example, an obvious cases for application of the group method would be presented if a cab company owned ten cabs of exactly the same type, all purchased at the same time and for the same $5,500 price. In such a case, it would be far more convenient to treat the ten cabs as a group, viewing the group as though it constituted a single unit which cost $55,000 and had an estimated useful life of five years and an estimated salvage value of $5,000. Thus the journal entry for annual depreciation on this group of cabs would be:

Depreciation Expense	$10,000	
Accumulated Depreciation		$10,000

If more cabs are purchased, they would simply be added to the group, and the group depreciation rate would thereafter be applied to the new total cost (less salvage). For example, suppose at the beginning of the second year five more cabs are purchased for $6,000 apiece. This would constitute an addition to the asset "Cabs" of $30,000. Assuming that the estimated salvage value of these new cabs is $500 each, the group would then be regarded as a single asset with a total original cost of $85,000 and a salvage value of $7,500. In that event, the charge for depreciation for the second year, one-fifth of the new cost-less-salvage figure for the group, would be $15,-500:

Depreciation Expense	$15,500	
Accumulated Depreciation		$15,500

One of the advantages of the group method is that it dispenses with the necessity for reflecting gain or loss upon the retirement of each individual machine. For example, assume that one of the ten original cabs in the group is retired at the end of the fourth year and disposed of for $1,000. On the unit method that cab would have had a book value at the end of the fourth year of $1,500 and hence its disposition for $1,000 would have required charging a loss of $500 to the current year. The theory of the group method, however, is that in a group of related fixed assets any underdepreciation on some of the assets will be balanced by overdepreciation on others; in other words, while some assets will be retired prematurely or disposed of for less than the anticipated salvage value, some other assets in the group will prove useful for longer than the estimated useful life, or will bring more than the expected salvage value. Accordingly, upon the retirement of an asset in the group it is not necessary to determine what the book value of the asset standing alone would have been, and then charge (or credit) the difference between that amount and the salvage proceeds against current income; instead any such difference is in effect charged (or credited) to the Accumulated Depreciation account, through the simple expedient of charging the entire cost of the asset to the Accumulated Depreciation account while crediting that account with any disposition proceeds, and the current income statement is not affected. The entry:

Accumulated Depreciation	$5,500	
Cabs		$5,500
Cash	$1,000	
Accumulated Depreciation		$1,000

or simply:

Accumulated Depreciation	$4,500	
Cash	$1,000	
Cabs		$5,500

(Occasionally, an exception is made for a so-called "abnormal retirement", i. e., an unusually early and unexpected retirement well outside the company's normal experience; in such cases, the company may in effect revert pro tanto to the unit method and charge against the Accumulated Depreciation account only as much of the cost of the retired asset as is equal to the amount of depreciation which would have been taken on the asset to date under the unit method, while reflecting separately the loss (or gain) measured by the difference between the salvage proceeds, if any, and the remaining cost of the retired asset.)

Note that under the group method the figure in the Accumulated Depreciation account at any point in time does not necessarily reflect, as it does under the unit method, the exact amount of the depreciation to date, because in effect gains and losses upon previous retirements of assets from the group have also been included in that account. But since it is expected that the gains will balance the losses in the long run, it is not considered inappropriate to continue to describe the account as "Accumulated Depreciation".

As the foregoing example shows, it is not a necessary condition for use of the group method that all the units in a group be purchased at the same time or for the same price; nor is it necessary that all of the units be similar items, or even that they all have the same useful life. It is necessary only that the group include assets which are sufficiently homogeneous or related to permit the computation of a single average or composite rate of depreciation to be applied to the total cost (less salvage) of the assets in the group. Of course determination of the appropriate rate may involve difficult mathematical computations when the group includes assets of varying useful lives, but we need not be concerned with such complications since the function of the group method remains the same. Once the appropriate rate for the group has been established, it is applied annually to the total cost (less salvage) of the assets then included in the group, unless changes in the composition of the assets in the group result in a change in the average life, requiring the use of a different rate. Of course the figure for the total cost of the group will constantly change as the costs of new assets acquired are added to the group total and the costs of assets retired are eliminated.

PROBLEMS

1.   M Co. uses the group method of depreciation. One group consists of 100 machines (with no expected salvage value) depreciated at a rate of 10% per annum. The total cost of the group is $200,000. Twenty of the machines were purchased at the beginning of the most recent fiscal year. At the end of that year twenty of the machines were five years old, thirty were ten years old, and thirty were fifteen years old. What would the entry for depreciation on this group be for the year? Would you have any comment to make to the company? In considering the latter question, assume for simplicity that (1) all of the machines in this group are identical, (2) the cost of these machines has remained stable at $2,000 throughout the fifteen year period, and (3) these are all the machines of this type that the company has ever owned. What would the figure in the Accumuated Depreciation account be in these circumstances? Can you determine what that figure would be if instead the company had started with 100 such machines in the group fifteen years ago and had maintained 100 machines in operation continuously throughout the fifteen year period?

2.   Consider whether each of the following statements is true or false:

   a.   Under the group method of depreciation an asset may be depreciated for longer than its useful life.

   b.   Under the group method of depreciation, an asset may be depreciated for more than its actual cost.

3.   Upon its organization at the beginning of year 1 Red Cab, Inc., acquired five identical cabs for $5,500 apiece. The estimated useful life of the cabs was five years, and the expected salvage value was $500 per cab. At the close of year 2, Red Cab disposed of one of its cabs for $2,000, and obtained a new cab for $6,000. Since the corporation used the group method of depreciation for its cabs, the entire cost of the old cab less the cash received for it was charged to Accumulated Depreciation. Red Cab's balance sheet at the close of year 2, after the sale of the old cab and the purchase of the new one, was as follows:

Red Cab, Inc.

Cash		$ 6,000	Accounts Payable	$ 3,500
Cabs	$28,000			
Less: Accum. Depr.	6,500	21,500	Capital Stock	20,000
Supplies		400	Earned Surplus	4,400
		$27,900		$27,900

How large a dividend could Red Cab, Inc. legally pay under a statute which permits dividends "only out of net assets in excess of capital"? (Consider what Red Cab's balance sheet would have looked like if the unit method of depreciation had been used, and whether that is relevant in answering the foregoing question.)

5.   FULLY-DEPRECIATED ASSETS

Suppose that M Co. in Problem 1 on page 486, supra, had been using the unit method of depreciation instead of the group method. How much would the total charge for depreciation have been on those machines for the year in question? Is this an appropriate reflection of depreciation on those machines for the year? Is there any accounting step which could be utilized to achieve a more meaningful depreciation figure for the year under the unit method? If M Co. switched to the group method of depreciation at the beginning of the year, should the fully-depreciated machines be included in the group?

In connection with these questions, consider the following paragraph which appeared in Accounting Research Bulletin No. 27 (1946):

> 6.   In special situations in which material amounts of depreciable assets are determined to have a substantially longer or shorter life than was originally anticipated, a more adequate assignment of cost to the future revenues to be derived from such assets during their useful lives may result from an adjustment or restatement of the accumulated depreciation previously recorded. Such a re-allocation of the cost of assets between past and future operations and revenues may be desirable when there have been circumstances which prevented the determination of an ordinary and reasonable approximation of the useful lives of assets and when the amounts of such assets and the annual depreciation charges thereon are large in relation to the total property in use and to the annual net income. In general, useful financial statements are not achieved by an understatement or an overstatement of asset carrying value which is to be accompanied

by an overstatement or understatement of future income because of materially excessive or deficient prior allocations of costs.

ARB No. 27 was addressed to so-called "emergency facilities", which, because of their importance to the war effort, were permitted to be depreciated for income tax purposes over a short period (typically 5 years). Many companies had used the same five-year period for financial accounting purposes and accordingly found themselves with, or facing the prospect of, fully-depreciated facilities in active service. The Bulletin did also observe that "under most circumstances, costs once identified and absorbed through amortization or depreciation charges are not considered subject to further accounting, and corrections of estimates affecting the allocations are commonly reflected in revised charges during the remaining life of the property", especially since normally any "overestimate or underestimate of the useful life of a facility is recognized before a major proportion of the service life has elapsed". In ARB No. 43, which was a compilation of all the prior ARB's, the restatement of ARB No. 27 in Chapter 9(C) omitted any reference to adjustment of accumulated depreciation, or revision of depreciation charges during the remaining life of an asset; instead, Chapter 9(C) emphasized the fact that the useful life allowed for tax purposes was not controlling for financial accounting, and that for the latter purpose the estimate should, as always, be made on the basis of all the circumstances (of which, of course, one important one was the special war-time role of such facilities).

It does not appear that any authoritative accounting promulgation since ARB No. 27 has specifically addressed the question of fully-depreciated facilities still in service. There have, however, been references to the treatment of changes in the estimated remaining useful life of fixed assets, as for example in the first two sentences of ¶ 24 of APB Op. No. 9, page 186, supra (no longer operative, of course, by virtue of FASB No. 16, page 194, supra), and perhaps it has been supposed that the possibility of revising estimated remaining useful life from time to time would avoid the phenomenon of fully-depreciated facilities still in service. Any such supposition has not been borne out in fact, as is indicated by the following excerpts from SEC Staff Accounting Bulletin No. 7, dealing with the disclosure of replacement cost data required for large companies by the SEC in ASR No. 190. See pages 208–210, supra. (Although ASR No. 190 was withdrawn as no longer necessary in the light of FASB No. 33, page 211, supra, the observations made may still be instructive.)

REPLACEMENT COST OF PRODUCTIVE CAPACITY

* * *

b. FULLY DEPRECIATED ASSETS

Facts:

Registrant has assets which are still in use although fully depreciated.

Question 1:

.   .   .   [S]hould the replacement cost of fully depreciated assets be disclosed?

Interpretive Response:

Yes. .   .   .   [S]ince these assets are still a part of productive capacity, their replacement cost (new) should be disclosed.

Question 2:

Should depreciation expense computed on a replacement cost basis be adjusted to reflect depreciation for fully depreciated assets still in use?

Interpretive Response:

The disclosure required .   .   .   of "the amount of depreciation which would have been accrued if it were estimated on the basis of current replacement cost" would not be changed but if such assets were significant in amount, the registrant presumably would conclude that supplemental information should be given .   .   . .   Such disclosure might include an estimate of the amount of depreciation which would have been accrued if fully depreciated assets were still being depreciated at a rate reflecting current estimates of their economic life.

---

a. CHANGES IN ACCOUNTING ESTIMATES

The latest word on how to deal with changes in accounting estimates in general, and revisions of estimated remaining useful life of fixed assets in particular, appears in APB No. 20 (1971), portions of which are set out at pages 302–304, supra, and should be reviewed at this point, especially paragraphs 10 and 11. The treatment of changes in accounting estimates in that opinion must be viewed in the context of what is said about changes in accounting principles, which comes first in the following excerpts:

VIEWS ON REPORTING CHANGES IN ACCOUNTING PRINCIPLES

14.   An essential question in reporting a change in accounting principle is whether to restate the financial statements currently

presented for prior periods to show the new accounting principle applied retroactively. A summary of differing views bearing on that question is:

a. Accounting principles should be applied consistently for all periods presented in comparative financial statements. Using different accounting principles for similar items in financial statements presented for various periods may result in misinterpretations of earnings trends and other analytical data that are based on comparisons. The same accounting principle therefore should be used in presenting financial statements of current and past periods. Accordingly, financial statements presented for prior periods in current reports should be restated if a reporting entity changes an accounting principle.

b. Restating financial statements of prior periods may dilute public confidence in financial statements and may confuse those who use them. Financial statements previously prepared on the basis of accounting principles generally accepted at the time the statements were issued should therefore be considered final except for changes in the reporting entity or corrections of errors.

c. Restating financial statements of prior periods for some types of changes requires considerable effort and is sometimes impossible. For example, adequate information may not be available to restate financial statements of prior periods if the method of recording revenue from long-term contracts is changed from the completed contract method to the percentage of completion method.

d. Restating financial statements of prior periods for some changes requires assumptions that may furnish results different from what they would have been had the newly adopted principle been used in prior periods. For example, if the method of pricing inventory is changed from the FIFO method to the LIFO method, it may be assumed that the ending inventory of the immediately preceding period is also the beginning inventory of the current period for the LIFO method. The retroactive effects under that assumption may be different from the effects of assuming that the LIFO method was adopted at an earlier date.

[paragraphs 15–17 are set out on page 304, supra.]

Reporting a Change in Accounting Principle

18. The Board believes that, although they conflict both (a) the potential dilution of public confidence in financial statements resulting from restating financial statements of prior periods and (b) consistent application of accounting principles in comparative statements are important factors in reporting a change in accounting principles. The Board concludes that most changes in accounting should be recognized by including the cumulative effect, based on a retroactive computation, of changing to a new accounting principle in net income of the period of the change . . . but that a few spe-

cific changes in accounting principles should be reported by restating the financial statements of prior periods .   . ..

19.　For all [but those latter few specific] changes in accounting principle . . .　the Board therefore concludes that:

   a.　Financial statements for prior periods included for comparative purposes should be presented as previously reported.

   b.　The cumulative effect of changing to a new accounting principle on the amount of retained earnings at the beginning of the period in which the change is made should be included in net income of the period of the change.

   c.　The effect of adopting the new accounting principle on income before extraordinary items and on net income (and on the related per share amounts) of the period of the change should be disclosed.

   d.　Income before extraordinary items and net income computed on a pro forma basis should be shown on the face of the income statements for all periods presented as if the newly adopted accounting principle had been applied during all periods affected.

Thus, income before extraordinary items and net income (exclusive of the cumulative adjustment) for the period of the change should be reported on the basis of the newly adopted accounting principle. . . .

20.　*Cumulative effect of a change in accounting principle.* The amount shown in the income statement for the cumulative effect of changing to a new accounting principle is the difference between (a) the amount of retained earnings at the beginning of the period of a change and (b) the amount of retained earnings that would have been reported at that date if the new accounting principle had been applied retroactively for all prior periods which would have been affected and by recognizing only the direct effects of the change and related income tax effect.　The amount of the cumulative effect should be shown in the income statement between the captions "extraordinary items" and "net income."　The cumulative effect is not an extraordinary item but should be reported in a manner similar to an extraordinary item.　The per share information shown on the face of the income statement should include the per share amount of the cumulative effect of the accounting change.

* * *

Reporting a Change in Accounting Estimate

31.　The Board concludes that the effect of a change in accounting estimate should be accounted for in (a) the period of change if the change affects that period only or (b) the period of change and future periods if the change affects both.　A change in an estimate should not be accounted for by restating amounts reported in financial statements of prior periods or by reporting pro forma amounts for prior periods.

32.　A change in accounting estimate that is recognized in whole or in part by a change in accounting principle should be reported as a change in an estimate because the cumulative effect attributable to the change in accounting principle cannot be separated from the current or future effects of the change in estimate (paragraph 11). Although that type of accounting change is somewhat similar to a change in method of amortization . . ., the accounting effect of a change in a method of amortization can be separated from the effect of a change in the estimate of periods of benefit or service and residual values of assets. A change in method of amortization for previously recorded assets therefore should be treated as a change in accounting principle, whereas a change in the estimated period of benefit or residual value should be treated as a change in accounting estimate.

33. *Disclosure.* The effect on income before extraordinary items, net income and related per share amounts of the current period should be disclosed for a change in estimate that affects several future periods, such as a change in service lives of depreciable assets or actuarial assumptions affecting pension costs. Disclosure of the effect on those income statement amounts is not necessary for estimates made each period in the ordinary course of accounting for items such as uncollectible accounts or inventory obsolescence; however, disclosure is recommended if the effect of a change in the estimate is material.

Although not immediately relevant for our purposes, the following additional excerpts from Op. No. 20, using a change in depreciation method to illustrate the normal operation of the opinion, and pinpointing a change from lifo to some other method of inventory pricing as one of those above-mentioned "few specific changes" representing an exception to the normal rule, are included here for completeness:

22. The principal steps in computing and reporting the cumulative effect and the pro forma amounts of a change in accounting principle may be illustrated by a change in depreciation method for previously recorded assets as follows:

    a.   The class or classes of depreciable assets to which the change applies should be identified. (A "class of assets" relates to general physical characteristics.)

    b.   The amount of accumulated depreciation on recorded assets at the beginning of the period of the change should be recomputed on the basis of applying retroactively the new depreciation method. Accumulated depreciation should be adjusted for the difference between the recomputed amount and the recorded amount. Deferred taxes should be adjusted for the related income tax effects.

    c.   The cumulative effect on the amount of retained earnings at the beginning of the period of the change resulting from the adjustments referred to in (b) above should be shown in the income statement of the period of the change.

    d.   The pro forma amounts should give effect to the pro forma provisions for depreciation of each prior period presented and to the pro forma adjustments of nondiscretionary items, computed on the assumption of retroactive application of the newly adopted method to all prior periods and adjusted for the related income tax effects.

23. *Change in method of amortization and related disclosure.* Accounting for the costs of long-lived assets requires adopting a systematic pattern of charging those costs to expense. These patterns are referred to as depreciation, depletion, or amortization methods (all of which are referred to in this Opinion as methods of amortization). Various patterns of charging costs to expenses are acceptable for depreciable assets; fewer patterns are acceptable for other long-lived assets.

24. Various factors are considered in selecting an amortization method for identifiable assets, and those factors may change, even for similar assets. For example, a company may adopt a new method of amortization for newly acquired, identifiable long-lived assets and use that method for all additional new assets of the same class but continue to use the previous method for existing balances of previously recorded assets of that class. For that type of change in accounting principle, there is no adjustment of the type outlined in paragraphs 19–22, but a description of the nature of the change in method and its effect on income before extraordinary items and net income of the period of the change, together with the related per share amounts, should be disclosed. If the new method of amortization is however applied to previously recorded assets of that class, the change in accounting principle requires an adjustment for the cumulative effect of the change and the provisions of paragraphs 15 to 22 should be applied.

* * *

26. *Cumulative effect not determinable.* Computing the effect on retained earnings at the beginning of the period in which a change in accounting principle is made may sometimes be impossible. In those rare situations, disclosure will be limited to showing the effect of the change on the results of operations of the period of change (including per share data) and to explaining the reason for omitting accounting for the cumulative effect and disclosure of pro forma amounts for prior years. The principal example of this type of accounting change is a change in inventory pricing method from FIFO to LIFO for which the difficulties in computing the effects of that change are described in paragraph 14–d.

27. *Special changes in accounting principle reported by applying retroactively the new method in restatements of prior periods.* Certain changes in accounting principle are such that the advantages of retroactive treatment in prior period reports outweigh the disadvantages. Accordingly, for those few changes, the Board concludes that the financial statements of all prior periods presented should be restated. The changes that should be accorded this treatment are: (a) a change from the LIFO method of inventory pricing to another method, (b) a change in the method of accounting for long-term construction-type contracts, and (c) a change to or from the "full cost" method of accounting which is used in the extractive industries.

6. PROBLEMS RAISED BY THE HIGH COST
OF REPLACEMENT

Consider the following excerpts from an address delivered on October 18, 1977 by Harold M. Williams, Chairman of the SEC, entitled "Corporate Profits: Illusion and Reality":

* * *

Public Perceptions of Corporate Profits

It is common-place to read in the press that particular well-known corporations have reported "record" or "all-time high" earnings. In terms of the absolute number of dollars involved, these statements are, of course, true. It is, however, useful and important to put those figures in perspective. And when the perspective is business's ability to generate required new capital, "record" earnings figures may, in my judgment, prove to be distressingly low.

In 1974, economist George Terborgh wrote an interesting article which appeared in the *Financial Analyst Journal,* and which forcefully illustrates this point. Terborgh studied corporate profits, the impact of inflation on those profits, and the ability of corporate earnings to generate the capital required by industry. The year to which he directed his attention was 1973. That year saw the highest corporate earnings in history, as of that time—reported after-tax profits of $50 billion. Terborgh noted that this compared with $38 billion in 1965, an increase of about 32% over a period of 8 years.

Terborgh performed two adjustments in order to transform the $50 billion of 1973 reported profits into a figure more closely representing the costs and revenues, in terms of real purchasing power, resulting from business operations. First, he recomputed earnings based on current-cost, double-declining balance depreciation. The objective of this step was to charge against earnings a figure which more accurately reflects both the manner in which capital equipment is consumed and the cost—in inflated, current dollars—of replacing it. Second, he converted inventory consumption charges, as reflected in the cost of goods sold, from historical to current cost. In both cases, then, the adjustments were designed to produce an income figure which reflected current, inflation enhanced costs of doing business rather than the historical costs on which traditional accounting methods rely. Adjusting for the effects of under-depreciation and one time inventory profits, Terborgh found that 1973 after-tax profits were $23 billion, less than half as large as the $50 billion figure on a reported basis. Profits for 1965 comparably adjusted were $36 billion. This converted a reported 32% increase between 1965 and 1973 to a 30% decrease. Finally, adjusting for inflation by converting earnings to 1965 constant dollars resulted in a decline in profits from $36 billion in 1965 to $18 billion on a comparable basis in 1973.

Terborgh also directed his attention to the share of its profits which business retains as a source of capital for re-investment. He found that retained earnings comparably adjusted fell from $19 billion in 1965 to $2 billion in 1973, a drop of 90%. Business had, in effect, paid its dividends and taxes out of capital. During the same period GNP grew 88%.

The effect of adjusting corporate earnings to allow for inflation is equally startling from the perspective of federal tax policy. In 1965, after-tax profits, both as reported and as adjusted by Terborgh, were nearly identical. By the mid-1970's, however, reported after-tax profits were just about double the figures adjusted for under-depreciation and inventory gains. Naturally, this has led to higher and higher effective tax rates on the profits that remain. As pointed out by Terborgh, the effective tax rate on "real" earnings has risen from a little more than 43% in the mid-1960's to almost 66% in the mid-1970's. Thus inflation, and the failure of the tax system to recognize its distortion of corporate profits, have resulted, in effect, in a 50% increase over the last decade. This increase has, of course, been accomplished without congressional action of any sort and, consequently, with no opportunity for debate over the effects on capital formation—a debate which would certainly occur if a legislative increase of 50% in the corporate tax rate were proposed.

As each dollar of corporate income or in the corporate stream of cash flow becomes less potent in terms of real purchasing power, business profits—which the man in the street, with the acquiescence of the news media, may perceive as astronomical—dwindle in terms of their ability to meet capital needs. The distortions in financial reporting which inflation spawns are not, of course, confined to income statements. Balance sheets which reflect the historical costs of corporate assets are similarly unrealistic, both because they reflect assets at figures which may far understate current values and, correspondingly, because the equity side of balance sheet omits any recognition of the impact on retained earnings which results from inflation-induced changes in depreciation levels and asset values. Without attempting to challenge the underlying assumptions with which accountants have traditionally dealt, I would suggest that a balance sheet which was "up-graded" to reflect replacement value of assets would look considerably different than do the statements which capital-intensive industries are today disseminating.

The most unfortunate consequence, in my view, of current corporate disclosure practices, particularly with regard to depreciation, is that those practices lull both policy-makers and the public—and perhaps more importantly corporate managers—into a false sense of security regarding investment needs. The tax system, in turn, reenforces these misperceptions, and the net result is likely to be over-taxation, skewed balance sheets, and ultimately, a handicapping of the corporate sector's ability to raise the capital which it must have to play the role we demand of it. In my judgment, if we are to meet our need for adequate new investment, the disclosure and taxation systems must be converted into tools which will aid the effort rather than obstacles which frustrate it.

* * *

The Role of the Press

I want to conclude by relating my theme briefly to those whose profession it is to inform the public concerning the business and economic environment. As I have explained already, I believe that, as long as reported earnings continue to fail to take into account an accurate assessment of the impact of inflation, investors, managers, government policy-makers, and the general public will all necessarily remain uncertain of the level, expected growth, and rate of change in profits. The press has, I believe, an important role to play in correcting this situation.

.   .   . For example, the undependable nature of reported earnings subtly affects confidence in the securities markets. To the extent that the investor doubts the relevance of reported earnings, he will be less willing to hold corporate shares and less willing to acquire new equity issues. To put it simply, if reported earnings fail accurately to reflect economic and financial realities, investor confidence is eroded.

The effect of traditional methods of financial disclosure on the securities markets can also be viewed from another perspective. The current average price-earnings ratio of the companies composing the Dow Jones industrial average is around 10. A recent study by one investment research organization indicates, however, that, if depreciation based on replacement cost is taken into account in computing earnings, the over-all average P/E ratio rises to almost 34. It might, I suppose, be argued from this that the market as a whole does take the effects of inflation into account in pricing securities to a greater degree than is generally assumed. Indeed, a P/E ratio of 34 would suggest that—rather than being depressed—the stock market is, at present, unrealistically high.

*   *   *

In the long run, the solutions to the problems which stem from the failure to recognize the inflation components in corporate profits lie, I suppose, primarily with those who establish accounting principles, disclosure requirements, and—perhaps most importantly—federal tax policy. I believe, however, that the press also has an important role to play in helping the public and businessmen themselves to understand the function of corporate earnings in our society, and the importance—not simply, or even primarily, to stockholders but to all of us—of profits which are adequate to permit investment in our industrial future.   .   .   .

The concern expressed by Chairman Williams about the dangers of failing to adjust depreciation charges to reflect current price levels is by no means a new one. As long ago as 1947 U. S. Steel not only recognized the problem (in terms that are quite reminiscent of the current scene), but decided to do something about it:

UNITED STATES STEEL CORPORATION

Annual Report 1947.

Financial Summary

Enders M. Voorhees
Chairman Finance Committee

REAL COSTS

The extent of real costs may be seriously obscured in periods of rapidly rising or falling wages and prices. Failure to establish and record the real costs in such periods weakens and may ultimately destroy the ability of a business to continue its job of profitably producing products and services for exchange. The period of 1940–1947 has been one of such marked increases in wages and prices.

Increased Wage Costs—In 1947, wages, salaries and other employment expenses accounted for 45 per cent of U. S. Steel's total costs. Since 1940 there has been a continual increase in the average hourly earnings of U. S. Steel's employees until—in December 1947—the increase over 1940 was 80 per cent, as shown in the following table:

	Increases Over 1940			
	5 War Years	1946	1947	December 1947
Average Hourly Earnings	29%	59%	78%	80%

Increased Cost of Products and Services Bought—In 1947, products and services bought accounted for 42 per cent of U. S. Steel's total costs. Since by far the major part of the total cost of all products and services in the nation is for wages and salaries, the advance from 1940 to the end of 1947 in general wage rates has been translated into higher prices for the things U. S. Steel must buy. Since 1940, it has been U. S. Steel's experience that every increase in hourly earnings has been followed shortly by a nearly equal percentage increase in the cost of products and services it must buy for its operations.

Increases in the costs of a few of the important items purchased by U. S. Steel are indicated by the following table:

	Per Cent Increases Over 1940			
	5 War Years	1946	1947	December 1947
Zinc Ore	24	31	54	62
Copper	–2	30	69	77
Tin	8	27	71	96
Fuel Oil	22	36	89	130
Scrap	7	32	75	93
Coke	28	58	91	111

Increased Cost of Replacing and Adding Facilities—Current construction costs likewise reflect the wage-price spiral. Merely to replace the tools of production (machinery, plants and mines) as they wear out requires, at present prices, an annual expenditure very much greater than the depreciation recovered on the basis of their original cost. The following table, based on virtually identical facilities acquired by U. S. Steel in 1940 and 1947, gives specific indication of how such costs have increased:

	Per Cent Increase **1947 Over 1940**
Wire Drawing Machine	91
Standard Electric Crane	105
Reheating Furnace	108
Blast Furnace	105
By-Product Coke Ovens	150
Mine Locomotive	44
Large Electric Motor	50
Continuous Rolling Mill	84
Concrete Construction	124
Brick Construction	250

The cost of replacing existing tools and adding to plants and facilities continues to increase. For example, a new cold reduced sheet mill, authorized late in 1945 at an expenditure of $25,250,000 to expand capacity, is currently estimated to have a final cost of $43,220,-000, or 71 per cent more than planned. Again, additional tin plate capacity authorized late in 1945 at an expenditure of $13,250,000, is currently estimated to have a final cost of $19,542,000, or 47 per cent more than planned. The increase since 1940 in construction costs, as measured by the *Engineering News-Record* index shown in the accompanying chart, has been as follows:

	5 War Years	**1946**	**1947**	**December 1947**
		Increases Over 1940		
Cost of Construction	18%	43%	68%	79%

Construction costs continue to advance. Because of the upward trend of such costs it is necessary continuously to revise upward the amounts initially estimated to complete projects under way. Thus merely to meet the increase in construction costs since original authorizations of facilities under way at December 31, 1947, U. S. Steel had to add $77 million to the amounts estimated initially. The amount necessary to complete all authorizations for additions to and replacements of facilities, including the $77 million, was $350 million at December 31, 1947.

Recording These Increases—These rising wages and prices mean that sums greater than originally expended must be spent currently to replace short-term inventories (stocks of goods) and long-term inventories (machinery, plants and mines) used up in production. Such additional amounts for replacement, required to be spent if production is to be sustained, must be recorded as a cost of doing business if overstatement of profits and dissipation of capital are to be avoided.

Short-Term Inventories—An accepted procedure for determining the cost of short-term inventories is the last-in, first-out method. This method recognizes fluctuations in the purchasing power of the dollar by reflecting current costs of employment and purchases—whatever the price change—in the cost of products currently sold. It is the most acceptable method yet developed of recording in costs purchasing power equivalent to that originally expended. It became a generally accepted accounting practice, legislatively recognized for tax purposes, many years after the heavy inventory losses experienced following World War I—a previous period of marked price changes.

U. S. Steel in 1941 substituted the last-in, first-out method of determining the cost of its major classifications of inventories for the average cost method previously used when prices were relatively stable. In 1942 and 1947, as it became practicable to do so, this method was extended to certain other inventories. Thus U. S. Steel's inventories, for the most part, are priced in 1940 dollars. By this change in method, rising wages and prices currently incurred by U. S. Steel to reproduce what is sold are recorded as cost and not as increased inventory valuation and seeming profit.

Long-Term Inventories—Believing that the same principle of recording the cost of short-term inventories consumed is applicable to recording the cost of long-term inventories consumed (wear and exhaustion of machinery, plants and mines), U. S. Steel in 1947 increased its provisions for wear and exhaustion from $87.7 million based on original cost to $114.0 million, or by 30 per cent. This was a step toward stating wear and exhaustion in an amount which will recover in current dollars of diminished buying power the same purchasing power as the original expenditure.

If a business is to continue, it is necessary to recover the purchasing power of sums originally invested in tools so that they may be replaced as they wear out. Therefore, this added amount is carried as a reserve for replacement of properties. It is a simple truth that to buy similar tools of production takes many more dollars today than formerly; to count as profits, rather than as cost, the added sums required merely to sustain production is to retreat from reality into self-deception.

The 30 per cent increase in the provision for wear and exhaustion was determined partly through experienced cost increases and partly through study of construction cost index numbers. Although it is materially less than the experienced cost increase in replacing wornout facilities, it was deemed appropriate in view of the newness of the application of this principle to the costing of wear and exhaustion. The use of index numbers for cost purposes gained recognition early in 1947 in a Tax Court decision in Hutzler Brothers Company, Petitioner v. Commissioner of Internal Revenue, Respondent. Although this case deals only with costing short-term inventories, the principles set forth are just as applicable to costing the wear and exhaustion of long-term inventories.

While awaiting accounting and tax acceptance, U. S. Steel believed that it was prudent for it to give some recognition to these increased replacement costs rather than to sit idly by and witness the unwitting liquidation of its business should inadequate recording of costs result in insufficient resources to supply the tools required for sustained production.

Cost-Price Balance—The discovery and measurement of real costs are not the end of the story. Knowing costs and covering costs are not the same thing. It is the balancing of real costs with competitive prices that determines whether the production and exchange of products and services in the end are to walk in step with the depreciation of the dollar.

CONSOLIDATED STATEMENT OF INCOME

	1947	1946
* * * * * * * * *	* * *	* * *
Wear and Exhaustion of Facilities		
Based on Original Cost	$ 87,745,483	$ 68,739,174
Added to Cover Replacement Cost †	26,300,000	—
	$ 114,045,483	$ 68,739,174
* * * * * * * * *	* * *	* * *
INCOME	$ 127,098,148	$ 88,622,475

* * *

CONSOLIDATED STATEMENT OF FINANCIAL POSITION

	Dec. 31, 1947	Dec. 31, 1946
* * * * * * * * *	* * *	* * *
Plant and Equipment, less depreciation	$ 940,486,342	$ 826,873,347
* * * * * * * * *	* * *	* * *
Total Assets Less Current Liabilities	1,746,267,520	1,677,957,057
Deduct		
Long-Term Debt	77,229,313	81,197,155
Reserves		
For estimated additional costs arising out of war	25,420,807	27,961,425
For replacement of properties † ...	26,300,000	—
For insurance, contingencies and miscellaneous expenses	106,557,221	114,224,696
Excess of Assets Over Liabilities and Reserves	$1,510,760,179	$1,454,573,781

† [Ed. note] Price Waterhouse took exception to this treatment in its certificate.

From U. S. Steel Annual Report, 1948:

Wear and Exhaustion—In its accounts for 1947, U. S. Steel reflected in the total wear and exhaustion for the year an amount of $26.3 million in addition to the normal depreciation based on original cost of its facilities. This added amount, which represented 30 per cent of the normal depreciation, was determined partly through experienced cost increases and partly through study of construction cost index numbers. Although it was materially less than the experienced cost increase in replacing worn-out facilities, it was a step toward stating total wear and exhaustion in an amount which would recover in current dollars of diminished buying power the same purchasing power as the original expenditure.

This principle was continued during the first three quarters of 1948. In view of the continued increase in the cost of goods and facilities during 1948, the additional charge for wear and exhaustion was advanced, effective as of January 1, 1948, to 60 per cent of the depreciation based upon original cost, because the 30 per cent initially adopted was not sufficient to cover the true cost of property currently consumed.

In the release of the accounts for the third quarter of 1948, it was stated that, in view of the position taken by the American Institute of Accountants and the discussions between the Corporation and the Securities and Exchange Commission, further study was being made in an effort to agree upon principles satisfactory to the Commission for determining and reflecting additional wear and exhaustion cost.

U. S. Steel believes that the principle which it adopted in 1947 and continued in 1948 is a proper recording of the wear and exhaustion of its facilities in terms of current dollars as distinguished from the dollars which it originally expended for those facilities. However, in view of the disagreement existing among accountants, both public and private, and the stated position of the American Institute of Accountants, which is supported by the Securities and Exchange Commission, that the only accepted accounting principle for determining depreciation is that which is related to the actual number of dollars spent for facilities, regardless of when or of what buying power, U. S. Steel has adopted a method of accelerated depreciation on cost instead of one based on purchasing power recovery. This method is made retroactive to January 1, 1947. The amount of the accelerated depreciation for the year 1948 is $55,335,444, including a deficiency of $2,675,094 in the amount reported in 1947 as depreciation added to cover replacement cost. Such accelerated depreciation is not presently deductible for Federal income tax purposes.

* * *

The accelerated depreciation is applicable to the cost of postwar facilities in the first few years of their lives, when the economic usefulness is greatest. The amount thereof is related to the excess of current operating rate over U. S. Steel's long-term peacetime average rate of 70 per cent of capacity. The annual accelerated amount is 10 per cent of the cost of facilities in the year in which the expenditures are made and 10 per cent in the succeeding year, except that this amount is reduced ratably as the operating rate may drop, no acceleration being made at 70 per cent or lower operations. The accelerated depreciation is in addition to the normal depreciation on such facilities but the total depreciation over their expected lives will not exceed the cost of the facilities.

* * *

CONSOLIDATED STATEMENT OF INCOME

	1948	1947
* * * * * * * * *	* * *	* * *
Wear and Exhaustion of Facilities	$145,986,681	$114,045,483
* * * * * * * * *	* * *	* * *
INCOME	$129,627,845	$127,098,148

CONSOLIDATED STATEMENT OF FINANCIAL POSITION

	Dec. 31, 1948	**Dec. 31, 1947**
* * * * * * * * *	* * *	* * *
Plant and Equipment, less depreciation	$1,300,816,762	$ 914,186,342 †
* * * * * * * * *	* * *	* * *
Total Assets Less Current Liabilities	2,030,116,022	1,720,078,678
Deduct		
Long-Term Debt	71,554,196	77,229,313
Reserves		
For estimated additional costs arising out of war	20,562,262	25,420,807
For insurance, contingencies and miscellaneous expenses	104,939,571	106,557,221
Excess of Assets Over Liabilities and Reserves	$1,833,059,993	$1,510,871,337

As indicated in U. S. Steel's 1948 Annual Report, the accounting profession turned a deaf ear to proposals for depreciation based upon current costs. The formal rejection came in Accounting Research Bulletin No. 33,* promulgated by the AICPA's Committee on Accounting Procedure in December, 1947:

> 1. The American Institute of Accountants committee on accounting procedure has given extensive consideration to the problem of making adequate provision for the replacement of plant facilities in view of recent sharp increases in the price level.

---

† [Ed. note] After reclassification of reserve for replacement of properties as additional accumulated depreciation.

The problem requires consideration of charges against current income for depreciation of facilities acquired at lower price levels.

2. The committee recognizes that business management has the responsibility of providing for replacement of plant and machinery. It also recognizes that, in reporting profits today, the cost of material and labor is reflected in terms of 'inflated' dollars while the cost of productive facilities in which capital was invested at a lower price level is reflected in terms of dollars whose purchasing power was much greater. There is no doubt that in considering depreciation in connection with product costs, prices, and business policies, management must take into consideration the probability that plant and machinery will have to be replaced at costs much greater than those of the facilities now in use.

3. When there are gross discrepancies between the cost and current values of productive facilities, the committee believes that it is entirely proper for management to make annual appropriations of [retained earnings] in contemplation of replacement of such facilities at higher price levels.

4. It has been suggested in some quarters that the problem be met by increasing depreciation charges against current income. The committee does not believe that this is a satisfactory solution at this time. It believes that accounting and financial reporting for general use will best serve their purposes by adhering to the generally accepted concept of depreciation on cost, at least until the dollar is stabilized at some level. An attempt to recognize current prices in providing depreciation, to be consistent, would require the serious step of formally recording appraised current values for all properties, and continuous and consistent depreciation charges based on the new values. Without such formal steps, there would be no objective standard by which to judge the propriety of the amounts of depreciation charges against current income, and the significance of recorded amounts of profit might be seriously impaired.

5. It would not increase the usefulness of reported corporate income figures if some companies charged depreciation on appraised values while others adhered to cost. The committee believes, therefore, that consideration of radical changes in accepted accounting procedure should not be undertaken, at least until a stable price level would make it practicable for business as a whole to make the change at the same time.

6. The committee disapproves immediate write-downs of plant cost by charges against current income in amounts believed to represent excessive or abnormal costs occasioned by current price levels. However, the committee calls attention to the fact that plants expected to have less than normal useful life can properly be depreciated on a systematic basis related to economic usefulness.

In 1953, ARB No. 33 was republished as Chapter 9A of ARB No. 43 (a recompilation of all the prior Accounting Research Bulletins); but there were six dissenters, and they particularly challenged the assertion in paragraph 4 that formal recording of appraised current value of fixed assets was a necessary precondition to reflecting current price levels in depreciation:

> "[The dissenters] believe that plant may continue to be carried in the balance sheet at historical cost with deduction for depreciation based thereon. In addition to historical depreciation, a supplementary annual charge to income should be permitted with corresponding credit to an account for property replacements and substitutions, to be classified with the stockholders' equity. This supplementary charge should be in such amount as to make the total charge for depreciation express in current dollars the exhaustion of plant allocable to the period. The supplementary charge would be calculated by use of a generally accepted price index applied to the expenditures in the years when the plant was acquired. The last sentence of paragraph [4] would then be no longer valid; the usefulness of financial statements would be enhanced without sacrifice of presently existing comparability."

Adjusting depreciation expense for the effects of inflation is now governed by FASB No. 33, page 211, supra (which of course only requires that such depreciation information be disclosed in supplementary schedules, leaving the regular financial statements to follow the traditional historic cost approach). The following excerpts from SEC Staff Accounting Bulletin No. 7 (although no longer operative because of the withdrawal of ASR No. 190, under which they were promulgated, as noted on page 211, supra) may serve to illuminate some of the issues involved in computing depreciation on the basis of current cost.

7.   Depreciation on Replacement Cost Basis

* * *

b.   Economic Lives

Question:

Should estimates of economic life be changed for purposes of computing replacement cost depreciation when it appears that the estimates being used for historical cost depreciation are no longer accurate?

Interpretive Response:

Generally accepted accounting principles require that when the original estimate of economic life used for purposes of calculating depreciation no longer reflects the current estimate of the useful life of the asset, the life used in the calculation should be changed to reflect up-to-date estimates and the remaining undepreciated cost of the asset should be allocated on a systematic and rational basis over the remaining life. Therefore, any change in economic life should not result from replacement cost requirements but from changing estimates of economic conditions relating to the asset. . . .

* * *

c. Example of Depreciation Computations

Facts:

Assume the following:

	Year		
	1	2	3
Replacement cost of new asset having three year life:			
Beginning of year	$100	$140	$160
End of year	140	160	200
Average for the year	120	150	180

Question:

What are replacement cost depreciation expense and accumulated depreciation for each of the three years?

Interpretive Response:

The amounts are as follows:

	Year		
	1	2	3
Depreciation expense . . . (computed as ⅓ of average replacement cost for the year)	$40	$ 50	$ 60
Accumulated depreciation (computed as proportion of end of year replacement cost which has expired i. e., ⅓, ⅔, ³⁄₃)	47	107	200
Depreciated replacement cost . . . (end of year replacement cost less accumulated depreciation)	93	53	–0–

It should be noted that in the example given depreciation expense does not total to accumulated depreciation; in year 1 there is a $7 difference and in years 2 and 3 there is a cumulative difference of $17 and $50, respectively. These amounts, frequently referred to as "backlog depreciation," are not includable in replacement cost depreciation expense . . . . .

In considering the foregoing material, it may be helpful to review the function and effect of depreciation accounting. At the outset, note that although the term "provision for depreciation" is often used, in fact accounting for depreciation does not "provide" anything; much less does it guarantee that there will be funds sufficient to replace the fixed assets at the end of their useful lives. For example, assume that X Corp. was organized on January 1 of year one, with stated capital of $100,000 and a plant which cost the same amount. Its balance sheet at that time would be:

Plant	$100,000	Stated Capital	$100,000

Assuming that the plant is estimated to have a 50-year useful life, without salvage value, the straight-line depreciation expense for year one would be $2,000. If X has no income and no other expenses for the year, the Profit and Loss account for the year would show a loss of $2,000, and the balance sheet at the end of year one would look like this:

Plant	$100,000		Stated Capital	$100,000
Accum. Deprec.	2,000	98,000	Deficit	(2,000)
		$98,000		$98,000

It should be perfectly evident that, given 49 more years like this, even the most scrupulous application of depreciation accounting would not provide any funds to replace the plant at the end of its useful life. Only the realization of receipts in excess of expenditures can provide the funds necessary for replacement of fixed assets (or any other purpose). The role of depreciation accounting in this context, like the allocation of any other deferred-expense asset to current expense, is simply to indicate that the excess of receipts over actual cash expenditures does not constitute net income for accounting purposes.

The same is true of any depreciation technique designed to charge against current revenues an amount of depreciation expense based on the current replacement cost of the asset rather than its original cost. For example, assume for simplicity that immediately after X acquired its plant on January 1 of year one the replacement cost of the plant rose to $200,000, due to a sudden increase in the price level which thereafter remains stable for 50 years. If X decided to charge current depreciation expense on the basis of the replacement cost of the plant, the annual depreciation expense would be $4,000. Query whether the extra $2,000 would be credited to the regular Accumulated Depreciation account, since the Accumulated Depreciation account computed on that basis would no longer bear any rational relationship to the original cost of the asset, against which it appears as an offset on the balance sheet, and eventually could even exceed the original cost figure. On the other hand, setting up an "Expense Payable" or "Estimated Liability" account to reflect this extra depreciation, in accordance with the usual practice when an expense is charged against current income before it is paid, would be troublesome because extra depreciation on the basis of current replacement cost does not in fact represent a liability which will ever have to be paid. U. S. Steel in 1947 fell back on the old catch-all term "Reserve", labeling the credit account "Reserve for Replacement of Properties", but as we have seen use of the term "Reserve" has gone out of fashion for expenses charged against income. So it might be best, in order to pursue our illustration, simply to invent a new account, called, say, "Accrued Depreciation on Replacement Cost" ("Accrued Depreciation" for short), which would appear on the right-hand side of the balance sheet. Now if X again had no income or other expenses in year one, the Profit and Loss account would show a loss of $4,000, and the balance sheet at the end of the year would look like this:

Plant	$100,000		Accrued Deprec.	$ 2,000
			Stated Capital	100,000
Accum. Deprec.	2,000	98,000	Deficit	(4,000)
		$98,000		$98,000

Obviously, merely increasing the depreciation expense and creating a corresponding Accrued Depreciation account does not provide any funds for subsequent replacement.

Now assume instead that in year one X has revenues of $4,000 and no expenses other than depreciation. The revenues received will be reflected on the balance sheet as an increase in liquid assets, which for simplicity we will assume to be cash. If X makes a normal straight-line charge for depreciation, the Profit and Loss account would show net income of $2,000, and the balance sheet at the end of the year would look like this:

Cash		$ 4,000	Stated Capital	$100,000
Plant	$100,000			
Accum. Deprec.	2,000	98,000	Earned Surplus	2,000
		$102,000		$102,000

Notice that the receipt of revenues in excess of expenditures does provide a source of funds which could be used to finance replacement; after another 49 years just like year one, X would have $200,000 in assets available to finance replacement of the plant or for any other purpose (assuming of course, no other use of these liquid assets in the meantime). Notice too that the amount of the cash (or other increase in assets) generated in the foregoing example is not limited to the amount of the net income for the period, but rather is equal to the sum of net income plus the depreciation expense for the period, since depreciation does not constitute an actual expenditure during the year even though it is an expense which decreases net income. Thus if X's annual revenues amounted to only $2,000, so that after depreciation expense it would merely break even each year, and its earned surplus over the 50 year period would amount to $0, X would still have accumulated $100,000 during the 50 years, which could be applied to replacement of plant or any other purpose. It is in this sense that depreciation accounting may be thought of as a "source" of funds for use in the business, along with any retained earnings, as suggested by Mr. Simon in his article at pages 478–480, supra; that is, if an enterprise at least breaks even, so that its revenues cover all expenses for the period including depreciation, assets equal to the depreciation expense will be generated and will be available for use in the business.

In the same vein, it would make no difference so far as funds available for replacement are concerned if in the example above X decided to charge current depreciation expense each year in the amount of $4,000, based upon an assumed current replacement cost for the plant of $200,000. In that event, the Profit and Loss account for year one would show a zero balance, and X's balance sheet at the end of that year would look like this:

Cash		$ 4,000	Accrued Deprec.	$ 2,000
Plant	$100,000		Stated Capital	100,000
Accum. Deprec.	2,000	98,000	Earned Surplus	0
		$102,000		$102,000

Notice that the amount of the increase in liquid assets is the same as it was in the previous example—obviously, increasing the depreciation charge does not affect the amount of the assets on hand (although it does reduce net income, and ultimately earned surplus, producing an increase in Accrued Depreciation instead). Hence, in this case also, after another 49 years just like year one X would have $200,-000 in liquid assets available for replacement of plant or any other purpose (assuming, as before, no other use of these liquid assets in the meantime).

There is, however, one important difference between these two situations which could have an important impact upon the amount of X's liquid assets at any point in time. One common use of such assets by a corporation is the payment of dividends to shareholders. Since, as we have seen, corporation statutes normally permit dividends to be paid at least to the extent of earned surplus, in the first case X could pay dividends of up to $2,000 per year, or a total of $100,000 over the 50 year period; in the second case, when depreciation expense is based upon current replacement cost, X's net income each year would be zero, resulting in no earned surplus, and hence no dividends could be paid. This would suggest that charging the higher depreciation expense can serve to limit dividends and thereby assure a larger amount of accumulated liquid assets on hand. To be sure, since the payment of dividends is a matter within the discretion of the directors, it is not necessary to use an accounting device to hold down the amount of dividends; regardless of how much is legally available for distribution, the directors can and should set the actual dividend policy with an eye to the corporation's requirements of liquid funds to finance its business needs, including replacement of fixed assets. On the other hand, stockholders do tend to pin their dividend hopes on the current earnings of the enterprise, and reducing that figure by charging depreciation expense on the basis of current replacement cost may well deflate dividend expectations and thereby avoid disappointment. But perhaps this is more a matter of financial management than accounting, to be dealt with in the chief executive's letter to the stockholder or whatever other text may accompany the financial statements, rather than in the statement figures themselves.

At bottom what is at issue here is whether charging depreciation expense on the basis of current replacement cost provides a more meaningful (or, as Chairman Williams suggested above, a more realistic) net income figure than results from depreciation based on original cost. This goes to the fundamental question of what the accounting process is trying to measure, a question right now receiving the principal attention of the FASB. Is it relevant that a lower net income figure resulting from depreciation based on current replacement cost may make it easier to respond to labor requests for higher wages, or conversely could lead to a decline in the market price of the corporation's securities, to the great dismay of the stockholders? And what about the role of federal income taxes? There seems little doubt that a major objective of the proponents of depreciation based upon current replacement cost is, as Chairman Williams indicated above, to eliminate the taxation of "income" which in fact must be plowed back in the business simply to maintain present plant capacity; but of course this question is not necessarily controlled by generally accepted accounting principles.

One final note relates to the suggestion in the 1947 Annual Report of United States Steel Corporation, page 499, supra, that the practice of charging depreciation expense on the basis of current replacement cost can be supported by analogy to the lifo method of accounting for inventories, in that both methods attempt to match current costs against current revenues. However, there is an important difference between the two situations, in that the lifo inventory method is based upon inventory costs which have actually been incurred during the current period, whereas this method of depreciation accounting really amounts to what might be called a "nifo", next-in-first-out, system, since the annual depreciation expense is based upon a current replacement "cost" which has not yet been incurred. Indeed, the very nature of long-term fixed assets precludes application of true lifo system. However, the critical question is whether this method of measuring depreciation expense provides a more meaningful measure of the consumption of fixed assets, and ultimately net income, for the period, and not whether the method differs from recognized procedures used in other areas.

PROBLEM

D Corp. is a manufacturer of pollution control equipment with its plant located in the Northeast. A couple of years ago, in anticipation of a likely increase in demand for its products, at least in the near term, D decided to expand and commenced construction of a new facility in the Southeast, having approximately half the capacity of its existing plant. The new plant cost $2,500,000 and was expected to have a twenty-year life, with no salvage value; it was completed some fourteen months ago, in time for operations to get underway in earnest at the beginning of D's most recent fiscal year (which ended a couple of months ago). D's Northeastern plant was built ten years ago, at a cost of $3,000,000, and its estimated useful life was twenty years, without salvage value.

Over the last several years the D management has often. discussed the impact of inflation on both its operations and its financial statements, but this 67% increase in cost brought home the point in dramatic fashion. Accordingly, the management has insisted that in D's financial statements for the fiscal year just ended the depreciation on the Northeastern plant should be computed on the basis of current replacement cost (new) of $5,000,000 rather than the $3,000,000 actual cost, producing a charge to depreciation expense on account of that plant of $250,000 instead of $150,000. In addition, the management decided to charge extra depreciation of 3% per year for each of the first three years of useful life of the new plant because of the expected intensive use of the new plant for at least that long; this produced a total charge to depreciation expense on account of the new plant of $200,000.

Partly as a result of this additional depreciation expense, D's operating results in the recently-ended fiscal year were somewhat disappointing, with net income after taxes of only $600,000, down from almost $1,000,000 the year before. But there were other reasons for this sharp decline in profitability. Although D's production during the year was at record levels, fully utilizing the added capacity of the new plant, there was a distinct softening in the price for D's products, engendered by a very considerable increase in competition due to the entry of a large number of new firms into the industry. Thus D was able to maintain its share of a growing market only by accepting significantly lower prices and profit margins.

D has outstanding 100,000 shares of preferred stock, under an Article provision calling for dividends of up to $8 per share to be paid each year to and only to the extent earned. The Articles also provide that D's "earnings shall be determined for each year in accordance with currently accepted accounting principles, after making all necessary charges for consumption of resources and other costs accrued and losses incurred during the year". The directors of D have declared a dividend of $6 per share on the preferred stock for the year just ended, and a group of preferred stockholders has consulted your law office as to whether they are entitled to a larger dividend. (In advising them, keep in mind the possible implications of APB Op. No. 20, at pages 302–304 and 489–493, supra.)

7. ACCELERATED DEPRECIATION METHODS

In paragraph 6 of ARB No. 33, page 503, supra, it was suggested that depreciation methods other than straight-line could be utilized if justified by the expected economic usefulness of the asset. This led a number of companies, including United States Steel, as noted at page 501, supra, to experiment with various forms of accelerated depreciation, designed to charge a greater share of the total cost of the asset to the earliest years of its life when its usefulness will be greatest (or at least most predictable). These efforts ultimately led to more formal "declining charges" methods, under which the depreciation charge is highest in the first year and declines progressively each year thereafter.

Among the reasons advanced in support of accelerated depreciation methods was the fact that annual maintenance costs usually rise as an asset grows older and therefore declining depreciation charges result in the total expenses associated with an asset being reasonably level over the full useful life. Another justification suggested is that heavier depreciation charges at the outset tend to correspond with the decline in the realizable value of the asset, which is usually greatest in the earliest years of use; such parallelism is viewed as a plus by all who favor having balance sheet figures correspond as closely to value as possible, though of course it is acknowledged that depreciation accounting does not seek to reflect diminution in realizable value as such. Finally, there is the point that most decisions about expansion of capacity, and maybe even ordinary replacement, are made on the basis of relatively short-term needs, because projections beyond that are regarded as too speculative to be useful; since the anticipated benefits are more certain in the earliest years, it is appropriate to allocate a greater portion of the total cost of the asset to those years.

Accelerated depreciation received a substantial boost in 1954 when Congress approved declining charges methods for tax purposes in the Internal Revenue Code. The two most commonly used accelerated depreciation systems, the "declining-balance" method, and the "sum-of-the-years-digits" method, are described as follows in the Regulations:

§ 1.167(b)–2. *Declining balance method*—(a) *Application of Method.*—Under the declining balance method a uniform rate is applied each year to the unrecovered cost or other basis of the property. . . . The declining balance rate may be determined without resort to formula. Such rate determined under section 167(b)(2) shall not exceed twice the appropriate straight line rate computed without adjustment for salvage. While salvage is not taken into account in determining the annual allowances under this method, in no event shall an asset (or an account) be depreciated below a reasonable salvage value.

. . .

(b) *Illustrations.* The declining balance method is illustrated by the following example:

Example (1). A new asset having an estimated useful life of 20 years was purchased on January 1, 1954, for $1,000. The normal straight line rate (without adjustments for salvage) is 5 percent, and the declining balance rate at twice the normal straight line rate is 10 percent. The annual depreciation allowances for 1954, 1955, and 1956 are as follows: *

Year	Basis	Declining Balance Rate	Depreciation Allowance
1954	$1,000	10%	$100
1955	900	10%	90
1956	810	10%	81

§ 1.167(b)–3. *Sum of the years-digits method*—(a) *Applied to a single asset*—(1) *General rule.*—Under the sum of the years-digits method annual allowances for depreciation are computed by applying changing fractions to the cost or other

---

* Notice that the rate under the declining-balance method is applied to the gross cost of the asset rather than to cost less salvage value. This is probably due to the fact that the traditional formula for determining the rate which under the declining-balance method will reduce an asset to salvage value at the end of its useful life assumes that the rate will be applied to gross cost. The computation of the rate under this formula is extremely complicated and the rate so computed is generally higher than twice the straight-line rate. This complicated computation is usually avoided and instead the maximum rate of twice the straight-line rate permitted for tax purposes is generally used for ordinary financial reporting as well.

basis of the property reduced by estimated salvage. The numerator of the fraction changes each year to a number which corresponds to the remaining useful life of the asset (including the year for which the allowance is being computed), and the denominator which remains constant is the sum of all the years digits corresponding to the estimated useful life of the asset.

. . .

(i) *Illustrations.*—Computation of depreciation allowances on a single asset under the sum of the years-digits method is illustrated by the following example:

Example (1). A new asset having an estimated useful life of five years was acquired on January 1, 1954, for $1,750. The estimated salavage is $250. For a taxpayer filing his returns on a calendar year basis, the annual depreciation allowances are as follows:

Year	Cost of Other Basis Less Salvage	Fraction **	Allowable Depreciation	Depreciation Reserve
1954	$1,500	$5/15$	$500	$ 500
1955	1,500	$4/15$	400	900
1956	1,500	$3/15$	300	1,200
1957	1,500	$2/15$	200	1,400
1958	1,500	$1/15$	100	1,500

Unrecovered value (salvage) .... $ 250

Shortly after, the AICPA Committee on Accounting Procedure added its official imprimatur of approval to declining charges methods of depreciation, in ARB No. 44 (1954) (revised in 1958 in connection with accounting for differences in tax treatment not here material):

DECLINING–BALANCE DEPRECIATION

1. The declining-balance method of estimating periodic depreciation has a long history of use in England and in other countries including, to a limited extent, the United States. Interest in this method has been increased by its specific recognition for income tax purposes in the Internal Revenue Code of 1954.

2. The declining-balance method is one of those which meets the requirements of being "systematic and rational".[1] In those cases where the expected productivity or revenue-earning power of the asset is relatively greater during the earlier

---

** The denominator of the fraction is the sum of the digits representing the years of useful life, i. e., 5, 4, 3, 2, and 1, or 15. [Footnote from the original.]

1. [From the original.] Accounting Terminology Bulletin No. 1, par. 56 [page 471, supra].

years of its life, or where maintenance charges tend to increase during the later years, the declining-balance method may well provide the most satisfactory allocation of cost. The conclusions of this bulletin also apply to other methods, including the "sum-of-the-years-digits" method, which produce substantially similar results.

3. When a change to the declining-balance method is made for general accounting purposes, and depreciation is a significant factor in the determination of net income, the change in method including the effect thereof, should be disclosed in the year in which the change is made.

* * *

From the 1976 edition of the AICPA's ACCOUNTING TRENDS & TECHNIQUES (Annual Survey of Accounting Practices Followed in 600 Stockholders' Reports) :

TABLE 3–10: DEPRECIATION METHODS

	Number of Companies			
	1978	**1977**	**1976**	**1975**
Straight-line	560	559	567	567
Declining balance	67	67	66	80
Sum-of-the-years digits	35	34	37	46
Accelerated method-not specified	67	60	71	73
Unit of production	44	40	41	38

QUESTION

In the problem on page 510, supra, suppose D Corp. had adopted the declining balance depreciation method (using twice the straight-line rate) on its new plant. How would that affect your conclusions?

Chapter 8

ALLOCATION OF INCOME TAXES

---

1. INTRODUCTION

Read paragraphs 8, 10, 11 and 14 of APB Opinion No. 11, which begins at page 520, infra. Paragraphs 8 and 11 indicate that, just as is true of other expenses, the amount of income tax allocable to a particular period is not necessarily determined by how much was actually paid (or became due) during the period. It may be that some of the income tax paid during a particular period should be deferred, to be charged as expense in a future period; conversely, there may be occasions when some of the taxes expected to be paid in a future period should be accrued and charged to expense in the current period.

2. TAX ALLOCATION WITHIN THE SAME PERIOD

It may help in getting started on this subject to look first at the special type of situation referred to in paragraph 10 of APB Op. No. 11. Note, by the way, that this category of cases has been greatly diminished since the date of Op. No. 11, by the tightening of the standards for extraordinary treatment in APB No. 30, page 189, supra, and the virtual elimination of prior period adjustments in FASB No. 16, page 194, supra. (The third type of case mentioned in paragraph 10, direct entries to other stockholders' equity accounts, usually do not involve any tax consequences anyway.)

Consider the case of L Corp., with income before taxes for the year in the amount of $5,000,000. Assuming for simplicity a tax rate of 50%, L's taxes for the year would be $2,500,000, and its net income would be $2,500,000. Suppose that during the year L suffers a catastrophe resulting in the loss of property carried on L's books at $2,000,000, for which there is no insurance. This loss would be reflected by a credit eliminating the property and a debit to some "Loss" account, which, as we have seen, is akin to an expense account and would be closed to Profit and Loss. As a result, L's income before taxes for the year would be $3,000,000, and, since the loss would presumably be deductible for tax purposes, L's taxes would be $1,500,000. But suppose this catastrophe loss qualified for extraordinary item treatment under APB No. 30: then on L's income statement the loss should be shown separately from the income from regular operations, so that a reader of the financial statements can get a picture of how the enterprise would have fared without this unusual and non-recurring item. The theory of separating out such extraordinary items, it may be recalled, is that the reader of the financial statements may be helped to make a more meaningful comparison of this year's performance with that of prior years (in which, presumably, such an item did not occur), or to make a judgment about the prospects of the enterprise in future years (in which in all likelihood such an item will not occur).

How should L's income statement portray this data? There are two obvious possibilities:

(a)

Income before Extraordinary Loss and Taxes	$5,000,000
Less: Extraordinary Loss	2,000,000
Income before Taxes	3,000,000
Less: Taxes	1,500,000
Net Income	$1,500,000

(b)

Income before Extraordinary Loss and Taxes	$5,000,000
Less: Taxes	1,500,000
Income before Extraordinary Loss	3,500,000
Less: Extraordinary Loss	2,000,000
Net Income	$1,500,000

Both of these approaches appear to separate out the extraordinary loss, and both of course reach the appropriate net income figure. However, in fact neither one completely disengages the extraordinary item from the results of ordinary operations. Under alternative (a) the extraordinary loss is combined with the pretax income from ordinary operations, to produce the penultimate "Income before Taxes", from which the tax figure is then deducted. But the investor who wants to make some judgments about the future on the basis of how the enterprise fared during the current year in its ordinary operations will presumably want an after-tax figure to work with, and will not find it readily available if alternative (a) is used.

Alternative (b) is even more troubling. Although it does purport to provide an after-tax figure for income before extraordinary items (which in effect is income from regular operations), that figure is of doubtful significance, if not downright misleading, because it is based upon a tax figure which is substantially affected by the existence of the extraordinary loss, being $1,000,000 lower than it would have been had no such loss occurred. In other words, the extraordinary item, though reflected separately itself, is still exerting a significant impact upon the after-tax income from regular operations because of the tax effects of the extraordinary loss, and the result is a figure for after-tax income from regular operations which is not indicative of how the company would have performed in the absence of such an extraordinary loss.

What seems called for is an approach which will separate out not only the extraordinary loss itself but also its related tax effect, and associate that tax effect directly with the extraordinary item. That is exactly what is recommended in paragraphs 51 and 52 of APB No. 11, page 529, infra, which should be read at this point.

Now look at Exhibit A, APB No. 9, page 188, supra. How much did the company actually lose on the sale of the plant recorded as an extraordinary item in 1967? Is this an important figure? (Note that this loss would presumably no longer qualify for extraordinary treatment, as a result of APB No. 30.) How much was the company's actual tax bill for 1967? Is that an important figure? Assuming that the company initially debited its book loss on the plant to a current Loss (or Expense) account, and initially debited the amount of its actual tax bill to the current Tax Expense account, what entry did the company make to produce the figures for "Income Tax" and "Extraordinary Items" shown in the 1967 income statement? As the outside auditor, would you approve the company's treatment of these items, and the manner in which they are reflected on the income statement?

In considering these questions, compare the position taken in Op. No. 11 with (1) the following observations made back in 1945 in the SEC's Accounting Series Release No. 53, in criticizing the allocation of income tax effects to a loss which was treated as a prior period adjustment, and (2) the *Levy* case, which immediately follows the excerpt from ASR No. 53:

> It is also sometimes pointed out that "cost" in the case of securities or property acquired is generally considered to be the sum of the purchase price plus incidental costs such as brokerage and any specific taxes paid by the buyer and that on sale the proceeds are computed as the selling price less incidental deductions such as commissions or any specific taxes paid by the seller. By analogy and in justification of the proposed treatment of income taxes it is frequently urged that a so-called "tax saving" must be allocated or attributed to or ultimately associated with particular losses or expenses because the tax consequences of the transaction involving the loss or expense were a motivating factor in arriving at the decision to consummate it. Thus, it is claimed that a property would not have been sold out but for the "tax saving" thereby effected and that for this reason it is proper to consider that the true "loss" on the sale is not the excess of cost over selling price but is equal instead to the difference between cost on the one hand and selling price plus "tax saving" on the other. We do not believe such an analogy is sound and we cannot accept that analysis as a basis for reporting

the results of actual operations. It is undoubtedly true that the tax consequences of selling a property often are an important consideration in arriving at the decision to sell, and may in some cases have been a deciding factor. However, tax consequences undoubtedly play an important role in the making of a great variety of decisions involving the incurrence and amounts of purely operating expenses such as advertising, wage rates and bonus plans. Yet it can hardly be argued that wages or bonuses or advertising are to be reported as less in amount because income taxes would have been higher if the amounts spent on such items were less. We see no basis for adopting a different approach in figuring the "loss" involved in sale of property. We feel instead that there has been a loss of the full difference between cost and selling price coupled with a tax benefit which is properly reflected in the lower taxes actually paid. We feel that the proposed treatment of income taxes tends to obscure these facts and that the treatment of income taxes required by our rules and heretofore almost universally followed clearly discloses what has taken place. Where the tax paid for the year is unusual in amount because of unusual conditions, an appropriate explanation would be called for as is now required in the case of other unusual events.

As to this last principal contention urged by the certifying accountants (that income taxes are an expense that should be allocated as other expenses are allocated) we feel, first, that there is grave doubt whether income taxes can properly be considered as an expense in the same category as the cost of materials or wages, and, second, that the treatment proposed does not result in the allocation of income taxes "as other expenses are allocated." We feel instead that the proposed treatment is purely an effort to have items shown in the income statement at what is considered to be a "normal" amount.

LEVY v. DOUGLAS AIRCRAFT CO.

United States District Court, Southern District of New York, 1974.
374 F.Supp. 341.

[Action for damages under a provision of the federal securities law prohibiting material misrepresentations or omissions in connection with a sale of new securities to the public. One of the complaints was that Douglas' reference in its selling literature to the results of its operations for the most recent quarter did not mention the full loss of $7,517,000, but only the so-called "net loss" of $3,463,000 (that is, the loss figure adjusted for the tax carryback to which Douglas was entitled as a result of the loss). The opinion of the court (MOTLEY, J.) on that issue follows.]

III. *Failure to Disclose Pre-Tax Loss of $7,517,000*

Plaintiffs have emphasized defendant's failure to explicitly state in the prospectus that there was a pre-tax loss of $7,517,000 for the second quarter of fiscal 1966. Since the prospectus stated that there was a net loss of $3,463,000 recorded for the three months ended May

31, 1966, failure to disclose the pre-tax loss would be material if 1) a reasonably prudent investor could not readily have ascertained the size of the pre-tax loss if he were told the size of the net loss and 2) an investor would be misled if he knew only the size of the net loss.

With regard to the first requirement, the court finds that it would have been difficult for the ordinary investor to figure out the size of the pre-tax loss.[18]

The court further finds that the average, prudent investor would be interested in the size of the pre-tax loss and, if informed of the large size of that loss, for the single quarter, might have been deterred from purchasing the debentures.

An investor would want to know the size of pre-tax losses because the tax credits which permit pre-tax losses to be reduced are exhaustible.

While the court cannot find that reasonable investors would necessarily have concluded that these credits would be exhausted in the foreseeable future, Douglas' prospects were sufficiently uncertain that investors might have concluded that the credits could be depleted in the near future. Such reasonable investors, had they been informed of the extent of the pre-tax loss, might have been deterred from purchasing debentures since they might have concluded that the $7,517,000 pre-tax loss was more ominous than the $3,463,-000 net loss, which was disclosed, since the $7,517,000 loss would have resulted in a substantial depletion of the available tax credits.

Moreover, the post-tax loss takes advantage of *prior* tax events which for one reason or another have given the corporation a tax credit. In contrast, pre-tax loss more accurately reflects the *current* financial health of the corporation. An investor is rightly concerned with the current profits and losses being sustained by the corporation.

Therefore, the court finds that the fact omitted, i. e., the $7,517,-000 pre-tax loss, was material since a reasonable bond investor would have considered the fact important in the making of his decision whether to invest.

3. INTER–PERIOD TAX ALLOCATION

Somewhat more complex questions are presented when the differences between tax and financial accounting call for the allocation of income tax expense over two or more periods. It is to these issues that APB Op. No. 11 is primarily directed, and that opinion should now be read in its entry.

---

18. See Tr., Oct. 17, 1973, pp. 1379–80.

The court disagrees that it would have been "fairly evident" to the ordinary, prudent investor that Douglas was in a 50 per cent tax bracket and that investors could, accordingly, have readily ascertained the pre-tax loss.

APB OPINION NO. 11 *
Accounting Principles Board, 1967.

Accounting for Income Taxes

CONTENTS

INTRODUCTION
* * *

APPLICABILITY

6. This Opinion applies to financial statements which purport to present financial position and results of operations in conformity with generally accepted accounting principles.

7. The Board emphasizes that this Opinion, as in the case of all other Opinions, is not intended to apply to immaterial items.

SUMMARY OF PROBLEMS

8. The principal problems in accounting for income taxes arise from the fact that some transactions affect the determination of net income for financial accounting purposes in one reporting period and

the computation of taxable income and income taxes payable in a different reporting period. The amount of income taxes determined to be payable for a period does not, therefore, necessarily represent the appropriate income tax expense applicable to transactions recognized for financial accounting purposes in that period. A major problem is, therefore, the measurement of the tax effects of such transactions and the extent to which the tax effects should be included in income tax expense in the same periods in which the transactions affect pre-tax accounting income.

9. The United States Internal Revenue Code permits a "net operating loss" of one period to be deducted in determining taxable income of other periods. This leads to the question of whether the tax effects of an operating loss should be recognized for financial accounting purposes in the period of loss or in the periods of reduction of taxable income.

10. Certain items includable in taxable income receive special treatment for financial accounting purposes, even though the items are reported in the same period in which they are reported for tax purposes. A question exists, therefore, as to whether the tax effects attributable to extraordinary items, adjustments of prior periods (or of the opening balance of retained earnings), and direct entries to other stockholders' equity accounts should be associated with the particular items for financial reporting purposes.

11. Guidelines are needed for balance sheet and income statement presentation of the tax effects of timing differences, operating losses and similar items.

SUMMARY OF CONCLUSIONS

12. The Board's conclusions on some of the problems in accounting for income taxes are summarized as follows:

a. Interperiod tax allocation is an integral part of the determination of income tax expense, and income tax expense should include the tax effects of revenue and expense transactions included in the determination of pretax accounting income.

b. Interperiod tax allocation procedures should follow the deferred method [described in paragraph 19, infra,—Ed.].

. . .

c. The tax effects of operating loss carry*backs* should be allocated to the loss periods. The tax effects of operating loss carry*forwards* usually should not be recognized until the periods of realization.

d. Tax allocation within a period should be applied to obtain fair presentation of the various components of results of operations.

e. Financial statement presentations of income tax expense and related deferred taxes should disclose (1) the composition of income tax expense as between amounts currently payable and amounts representing tax effects allocable to the period and (2) the classification of deferred taxes into a net current amount and a net noncurrent amount.

DEFINITIONS AND CONCEPTS

13. Terminology relating to the accounting for income taxes is varied; some terms have been used with different meanings. Definitions of certain terms used in this Opinion are therefore necessary.

a.   *Income taxes.* Taxes based on income determined under provisions of the United States Internal Revenue Code and foreign, state and other taxes (including franchise taxes) based on income.

b.   *Income tax expense.* The amount of income taxes (whether or not currently payable or refundable) allocable to a period in the determination of net income.

c.   *Pretax accounting income.* Income or loss for a period, exclusive of related income tax expense.

d.   *Taxable income.* The excess of revenues over deductions or the excess of deductions over revenues to be reported for income tax purposes for a period.

e.   *Timing differences.* Differences between the periods in which transactions affect taxable income and the periods in which they enter into the determination of pretax accounting income. Timing differences originate in one period and reverse or "turn around" in one or more subsequent periods. Some timing differences reduce income taxes that would otherwise be payable currently; others increase income taxes that would otherwise be payable currently.

f.   *Permanent differences.* Differences between taxable income and pretax accounting income arising from transactions that, under applicable tax laws and regulations, will not be offset by corresponding differences or "turn around" in other periods.

g.   *Tax effects.* Differentials in income taxes of a period attributable to (1) revenue or expense transactions which enter into the determination of pretax accounting income in one period and into the determination of taxable income in another period, (2) deductions or credits that may be carried backward or forward for income tax purposes and (3) adjustments of prior periods (or of the opening balance of retained earnings) and direct entries to other stockholders' equity accounts which enter into the determination of taxable income in a period but which do not enter into the determination of pretax accounting income of that period. A permanent difference does not result in a "tax effect" as that term is used in this Opinion.

h.   *Deferred taxes.* Tax effects which are deferred for allocation to income tax expense of future periods.

i.   *Interperiod tax allocation.* The process of apportioning income taxes among periods.

j. *Tax allocation within a period.* The process of apportioning income tax expense applicable to a given period between income before extraordinary items and extraordinary items, and of associating the income tax effects of adjustments of prior periods (or of the opening balance of retained earnings) and direct entries to other stockholders' equity accounts with these items.

14. Certain general concepts and assumptions are recognized by the Board to be relevant in considering the problems of accounting for income taxes.

a. The operations of an entity subject to income taxes are expected to continue on a going concern basis, in the absence of evidence to the contrary, and income taxes are expected to continue to be assessed in the future.

b. Income taxes are an expense of business enterprises earning income subject to tax.

c. Accounting for income tax expense requires measurement and identification with the appropriate time period and therefore involves accrual, deferral and estimation concepts in the same manner as these concepts are applied in the measurement and time period identification of other expenses.

d. Matching is one of the basic processes of income determination; essentially it is a process of determining relationships between costs (including reductions of costs) and (1) specific revenues or (2) specific accounting periods. Expenses of the current period consist of those costs which are identified with the revenues of the current period and those costs which are identified with the current period on some basis other than revenue. Costs identifiable with future revenues or otherwise identifiable with future periods should be deferred to those future periods. When a cost cannot be related to future revenues or to future periods on some basis other than revenues, or it cannot reasonably be expected to be recovered from future revenues, it becomes, by necessity, an expense of the current period (or of a prior period).

TIMING DIFFERENCES

Discussion

Nature of Timing Differences

15. Four types of transactions are identifiable which give rise to timing differences; that is, differences between the periods in which the transactions affect taxable income and the periods in which they enter into the determination of pretax accounting income. Each timing difference originates in one period and reverses in one or more subsequent periods.

a. Revenues or gains are included in taxable income later than they are included in pretax accounting income. For example, gross profits on installment sales are recognized for accounting purposes in the period of sale but are reported for tax purposes in the period the installments are collected.

b.   Expenses or losses are deducted in determining taxable income later than they are deducted in determining pretax accounting income. For example, estimated costs of guarantees and of product warranty contracts are recognized for accounting purposes in the current period but are reported for tax purposes in the period paid or in which the liability becomes fixed.

c.   Revenues or gains are included in taxable income earlier than they are included in pretax accounting income. For example, rents collected in advance are reported for tax purposes in the period in which they are received but are deferred for accounting purposes until later periods when they are earned.

d.   Expenses or losses are deducted in determining taxable income earlier than they are deducted in determining pretax accounting income. For example, depreciation is reported on an accelerated basis for tax purposes but is reported on a straight-line basis for accounting purposes.

Additional examples of each type of timing difference are presented in Appendix A to this Opinion.

16.   The timing differences of revenue and expense transactions entering into the determination of pretax accounting income create problems in the measurement of income tax expense for a period, since the income taxes payable for a period are not always determined by the same revenue and expense transactions used to determine pretax accounting income for the period. The amount of income taxes determined to be payable for a period does not, therefore, necessarily represent the appropriate income tax expense applicable to transactions recognized for financial accounting purposes in that period.

17.   Interperiod tax allocation procedures have been developed to account for the tax effects of transactions which involve timing differences. Interperiod allocation of income taxes results in the recognition of tax effects in the same periods in which the related transactions are recognized in the determination of pretax accounting income.

Differing Viewpoints

18.   Interpretations of the nature of timing differences are diverse, with the result that [different] methods of interperiod allocation of income taxes have developed and been adopted in practice.
.   .   .

19.   Interperiod tax allocation under the *deferred method* is a procedure whereby the tax effects of current timing differences are deferred currently and allocated to income tax expense of future periods when the timing differences reverse. The deferred method emphasizes the tax effects of timing differences on income of the period in which the differences originate. The deferred taxes are determined on the basis of the tax rates in effect at the time the timing differences originate and are not adjusted for subsequent changes in tax rates or to reflect the imposition of new taxes. The tax effects of

transactions which reduce taxes currently payable are treated as deferred credits; the tax effects of transactions which increase taxes currently payable are treated as deferred charges. Amortization of these deferred taxes to income tax expense in future periods is based upon the nature of the transactions producing the tax effects and upon the manner in which these transactions enter into the determination of pretax accounting income in relation to taxable income.

* * *

21. Interperiod tax allocation under the *net of tax method* is a procedure whereby the tax effects (determined by either the deferred or liability methods) of timing differences are recognized in the valuation of assets and liabilities and the related revenues and expenses. The tax effects are applied to reduce specific assets or liabilities on the basis that tax deductibility or taxability are factors in their valuation.

22. In addition to the different methods of applying interperiod tax allocation, differing views exist as to the extent to which interperiod tax allocation should be applied in practice.

23. Some transactions result in differences between pretax accounting income and taxable income which are permanent because under applicable tax laws and regulations the current differences will not be offset by corresponding differences in later periods. Other transactions, however, result in differences between pretax accounting income and taxable income which reverse or turn around in later periods; these differences are classified broadly as timing differences. The tax effects of certain timing differences often are offset in the reversal or turnaround period by the tax effects of similar differences originating in that period. Some view these differences as essentially the same as permanent differences because, in effect, the periods of reversal are indefinitely postponed. Others believe that differences which originate in a period and differences which reverse in the same period are distinguishable phases of separate timing differences and should be considered separately.

24. In determining the accounting recognition of the tax effects of timing differences, the first question is whether there should be any tax allocation. One view holds that interperiod tax allocation is never appropriate. Under this concept, income tax expense of the period equals income taxes payable for that period. This concept is based on the presumption that income tax expense of a period should be measured by the amount determined to be payable for that period by applying the laws and regulations of the governmental unit, and that the amount requires no adjustment or allocation. This concept has not been used widely in practice and is not supported presently to any significant extent.

25. The predominant view holds that interperiod tax allocation is appropriate. However, two alternative concepts exist as to the extent to which it should be applied: partial allocation and comprehensive allocation.

Partial Allocation

26. Under partial allocation the general presumption is that income tax expense of a period for financial accounting purposes should

be the tax payable for the period. Holders of this view believe that when recurring differences between taxable income and pretax accounting income give rise to an indefinite postponement of an amount of tax payments or to continuing tax reductions, tax allocation is not required for these differences. They believe that amounts not reasonably expected to be payable to, or recoverable from, a government as taxes should not affect net income. They point out in particular that the application of tax allocation procedures to tax payments or recoveries which are postponed indefinitely involves contingencies which are at best remote and thus, in their opinion, may result in an overstatement or understatement of expenses with consequent effects on net income. An example of a recurring difference not requiring tax allocation under this view is the difference that arises when a company having a relatively stable or growing investment in depreciable assets uses straight-line depreciation in determining pretax accounting income but an accelerated method in determining taxable income. If tax allocation is applied by a company with large capital investments coupled with growth in depreciable assets (accentuated in periods of inflation) the resulting understatement of net income from using tax allocation is magnified.

27. Holders of the view expressed in paragraph 26 believe that the only exceptions to the general presumption stated therein should be those instances in which specific nonrecurring differences between taxable income and pretax accounting income would lead to a material misstatement of income tax expense and net income. If such nonrecurring differences occur, income tax expense of a period for financial accounting purposes should be increased (or decreased) by income tax on differences between taxable income and pretax accounting income provided the amount of the increase (or decrease) can be reasonably expected to be paid as income tax (or recovered as a reduction of income taxes) within a relatively short period not exceeding, say, five years. An example would be an isolated installment sale of a productive facility in which the gross profit is reported for financial accounting purposes at the date of sale and for tax purposes when later collected. Thus, tax allocation is applicable only when the amounts are reasonably certain to affect the flow of resources used to pay taxes in the near future.

28. Holders of this view state that comprehensive tax allocation, as opposed to partial allocation, relies on the so-called "revolving" account approach which seems to suggest that there is a similarity between deferred tax accruals and other balance sheet items, like accounts payable, where the individual items within an account turn over regularly although the account balance remains constant or grows. For these other items, the turnover reflects actual, specific transactions—goods are received, liabilities are recorded and payments are subsequently made. For deferred tax accruals on the other hand, no such transactions occur—the amounts are not owed to anyone; there is no specific date on which they become payable, if ever; and the amounts are at best vague estimates depending on future tax rates and many other uncertain factors. Those who favor partial allocation suggest that accounting deals with actual events, and that those who would depart from the fact of the tax payment should show that the modification will increase the usefulness of the reports to management, investors or other users. To do this requires a demon-

stration that the current lower (or higher) tax payments will result in higher (or lower) cash outflows for taxes within a span of time that is of significant interest to readers of the financial statements.

Comprehensive Allocation

29.   Under comprehensive allocation, income tax expense for a period includes the tax effects of transactions entering into the determination of pretax accounting income for the period even though some transactions may affect the determination of taxes payable in a different period.   This view recognizes that the amount of income taxes payable for a given period does not necessarily measure the appropriate income tax expense related to transactions for that period. Under this view, income tax expense encompasses any accrual, deferral or estimation necessary to adjust the amount of income taxes payable for the period to measure the tax effects of those transactions included in pretax accounting income for that period.   Those supporting comprehensive allocation believe that the tax effects of initial timing differences should be recognized and that the tax effects should be matched with or allocated to those periods in which the initial differences reverse.   The fact that when the initial differences reverse other initial differences may offset any effect on the amount of taxable income does not, in their opinion, nullify the fact of the reversal.   The offsetting relationships do not mean that the tax effects of the differences cannot be recognized and measured.   Those supporting comprehensive allocation state that the makeup of the balances of certain deferred tax amounts "revolve" as the related differences reverse and are replaced by similar differences.   These initial differences do reverse, and the tax effects thereof can be identified as readily as can those of other timing differences.   While new differences may have an offsetting effect, this does not alter the fact of the reversal;   without the reversal there would be different tax consequences.   Accounting principles cannot be predicated on reliance that offsets will continue.   Those supporting comprehensive allocation conclude that the fact that the tax effects of two transactions happen to go in opposite directions does not invalidate the necessity of recognizing separately the tax effects of the transactions as they occur.

30.   Under comprehensive allocation, material tax effects are given recognition in the determination of income tax expense, and the tax effects are related to the periods in which the transactions enter into the determination of pretax accounting income.   The tax effects so determined are allocated to the future periods in which the differences between pretax accounting income and taxable income reverse. Those supporting this view believe that comprehensive allocation is necessary in order to associate the tax effects with the related transactions.   Only by the timely recognition of such tax effects is it possible to associate the tax effects of transactions with those transactions as they enter into the determination of net income.   The need exists to recognize the tax effects of initial differences because only by doing so will the income tax expense in the periods of initial differences include the tax effects of transactions of those periods.

31.   Those who support comprehensive allocation believe that the partial allocation concept in stressing cash outlays represents a departure from the accrual basis of accounting.   Comprehensive alloca-

tion, in their view, results in a more thorough and consistent association in the matching of revenues and expenses, one of the basic processes of income determination.

32.   These differences in viewpoint become most significant with respect to the tax effects of transactions of a recurring nature—for example, depreciation of machinery and equipment using the straight-line method for financial accounting purposes and an accelerated method for income tax purposes.   Under partial allocation the tax effects of these timing differences would not be recognized under many circumstances; under comprehensive allocation the tax effects would be recognized beginning in the periods of the initial timing differences. Under partial allocation, the tax effects of these timing differences would not be recognized so long as it is assumed that similar timing differences would arise in the future creating tax effects at least equal to the reversing tax effects of the previous timing differences.   Thus, under partial allocation, so long as the amount of deferred taxes is estimated to remain fixed or to increase, no need exists to recognize the tax effects of the initial differences because they probably will not "reverse" in the foreseeable future.   Under comprehensive allocation tax effects are recognized as they occur.

Permanent Differences

33.   Some differences between taxable income and pretax accounting income are generally referred to as permanent differences. Permanent differences arise from statutory provisions under which specified revenues are exempt from taxation and specified expenses are not allowable as deductions in determining taxable income.   (Examples are interest received on municipal obligations and premiums paid on officers' life insurance.)   Other permanent differences arise from items entering into the determination of taxable income which are not components of pretax accounting income in any period.   (Examples are the special deduction for certain dividends received and the excess of statutory depletion over cost depletion.)

Opinion

34.   The Board has considered the various concepts of accounting for income taxes and has concluded that comprehensive interperiod tax allocation is an integral part of the determination of income tax expense.   Therefore, income tax expense should include the tax effects of revenue and expense transactions included in the determination of pretax accounting income.   The tax effects of those transactions which enter into the determination of pretax accounting income either earlier or later than they become determinants of taxable income should be recognized in the periods in which the differences between pretax accounting income and taxable income arise and in the periods in which the differences reverse.   Since permanent differences do not affect other periods, interperiod tax allocation is not appropriate to account for such differences.

35.   The Board has concluded that the deferred method of tax allocation should be followed since it provides the most useful and practical approach to interperiod tax allocation and the presentation of income taxes in financial statements.

36.   The tax effect of a timing difference should be measured by the differential between income taxes computed with and without in-

clusion of the transaction creating the difference between taxable income and pretax accounting income. The resulting income tax expense for the period includes the tax effects of transactions entering into the determination of results of operations for the period. The resulting deferred tax amounts reflect the tax effects which will reverse in future periods. The measurement of income tax expense becomes thereby a consistent and integral part of the process of matching revenues and expenses in the determination of results of operations.

37. In computing the tax effects referred to in paragraph 36, timing differences may be considered individually or similar timing differences may be grouped. The net change in deferred taxes for a period for a group of similar timing differences may be determined on the basis of either (a) a combination of amounts representing the tax effects arising from timing differences originating in the period at the current tax rates and reversals of tax effects arising from timing differences originating in prior periods at the applicable tax rates reflected in the accounts as of the beginning of the period; or (b) if the applicable deferred taxes have been provided in accordance with this Opinion on the cumulative timing differences as of the beginning of the period, the amount representing the tax effects at the current tax rates of the net change during the period in the cumulative timing differences. If timing differences are considered individually, or if similar timing differences are grouped, no recognition should be given to the reversal of tax effects arising from timing differences originating prior to the effective date of this Opinion unless the applicable deferred taxes have been provided for in accordance with this Opinion, either during the periods in which the timing differences originated or, retroactively, as of the effective date of this Opinion. The method or methods adopted should be consistently applied.

TAX ALLOCATION WITHIN A PERIOD

Discussion

51. The need for tax allocation within a period arises because items included in the determination of taxable income may be presented for accounting purposes as (a) extraordinary items, (b) adjustments of prior periods (or of the opening balance of retained earnings) or (c) as direct entries to other stockholders' equity accounts.

Opinion

52. The Board has concluded that tax allocation within a period should be applied to obtain an appropriate relationship between income tax expense and (a) income before extraordinary items, (b) extraordinary items, (c) adjustments of prior periods (or of the opening balance of retained earnings) and (d) direct entries to other stockholders' equity accounts. The income tax expense attributable to income before extraordinary items is computed by determining the income tax expense related to revenue and expense transactions entering into the determination of such income, without giving effect to the tax consequences of the items excluded from the determination of income before extraordinary items. The income tax expense attributable to other items is determined by the tax consequences of transactions involving these items. If an operating loss exists before ex-

traordinary items, the tax consequences of such loss should be associated with the loss.

FINANCIAL REPORTING

Discussion

*   *   *

Income Statement

55.   Interperiod tax allocation procedures result in income tax expense generally different from the amount of income tax payable for a period.   [A]lternative approaches have developed for reporting income tax expense:

*   *   *

    b.   *Combined amount plus disclosure (or two or more separate amounts)*.   In this presentation the amount of income taxes reported on the tax return is considered significant additional information for users of financial statements.   The amount of taxes payable (or the effect of tax allocation for the period) is, therefore, disclosed parenthetically or in a note to the financial statements.   Alternatively, income tax expense may be disclosed in the income statement by presenting separate amounts—the taxes payable and the effects of tax allocation.

    c.   *"Net of tax" presentation*.   Under the "net of tax" concept the tax effects recognized under interperiod tax allocation are considered to be valuation adjustments to the assets or liabilities giving risk to the adjustments.   For example, depreciation deducted for tax purposes in excess of that recognized for financial accounting purposes is held to reduce the future utility of the related asset because of a loss of a portion of future tax deductibility.   Thus, depreciation expense, rather than income tax expense, is adjusted for the tax effect of the difference between the depreciation amount used in the determination of taxable income and that used in the determination of pretax accounting income.

Opinion

Balance Sheet

56.   Balance sheet accounts related to tax allocation are of two types:

    a.   Deferred charges and deferred credits relating to timing differences; and

    b.   Refunds of past taxes or offsets to future taxes arising from the recognition of tax effects of carry*backs* and carry*forwards* of operating losses and similar items.

57.   Deferred charges and deferred credits relating to timing differences represent the cumulative recognition given to their tax effects and as such do not represent receivables or payables in the usual sense.   They should be classified in two categories—one for the net current amount and the other for the net noncurrent amount.   This

presentation is consistent with the customary distinction between current and noncurrent categories and also recognizes the close relationship among the various deferred tax accounts, all of which bear on the determination of income tax expense. The current portions of such deferred charges and credits should be those amounts which relate to assets and liabilities classified as current. Thus, if installment receivables are a current asset, the deferred credits representing the tax effects of uncollected installment sales should be a current item; if an estimated provision for warranties is a current liability, the deferred charge representing the tax effect of such provision should be a current item.

* * *

59.   Deferred taxes represent tax effects recognized in the determination of income tax expense in current and prior periods, and they should, therefore, be excluded from retained earnings or from any other account in the stockholders' equity section of the balance sheet.

Income Statement

60.   In reporting the results of operations the components of income tax expense for the period should be disclosed, for example:

    a.   Taxes estimated to be payable

    b.   Tax effects of timing differences

    c.   Tax effects of operating losses.

These amounts should be allocated to (a) income before extraordinary items and (b) extraordinary items and may be presented as separate items in the income statement or, alternatively, as combined amounts with disclosure of the components parenthetically or in a note to the financial statements.

61.   When the tax benefit of an operating loss carry*forward* is realized in full or in part in a subsequent period, and has not been previously recognized in the loss period, the tax benefit should be reported as an extraordinary item in the results of operations of the period in which realized.

62.   Tax effects attributable to adjustments of prior periods (or of the opening balance of retained earnings) and direct entries to other stockholders' equity accounts should be presented as adjustments of such items with disclosure of the amounts of the tax effects.

General

63.   Certain other disclosures should be made in addition to those set forth in paragraphs 56–62:

* * *

    c.   Reasons for significant variations in the customary relationships between income tax expense and pretax accounting income, if they are not otherwise apparent from the financial statements or from the nature of the entity's business.

The Board recommends that the nature of significant differences between pretax accounting income and taxable income be disclosed.

64.   The "net of tax" form of presentation of the tax effects of timing differences should not be used for financial reporting. The

tax effects of transactions entering into the determination of pretax accounting income for one period but affecting the determination of taxable income in a different period should be reported in the income statement as elements of income tax expense and in the balance sheet as deferred taxes and not as elements of valuation of assets or liabilities.

* * *

APPENDIX A

EXAMPLES OF TIMING DIFFERENCES

The following examples of timing differences are taken from Accounting Research Study No. 9, *Interperiod Allocation of Corporate Income Taxes*, by Homer A. Black, pages 8–10. They are furnished for illustrative purposes only without implying approval by the Board of the accounting practices described.

(A) *Revenues or gains are taxed after accrued for accounting purposes:*

Profits on installment sales are recorded in accounts at date of sale and reported in tax returns when later collected.

Revenues on long-term contracts are recorded in accounts on percentage-of-completion basis and reported in tax returns on a completed-contract basis.

Revenue from leasing activities is recorded in a lessor's accounts based on the financing method of accounting and exceeds rent less depreciation reported in tax returns in the early years of a lease.

Earnings of foreign subsidiary companies are recognized in accounts currently and included in tax returns when later remitted.

(B) *Expenses or losses are deducted for tax purposes after accrued for accounting purposes:*

Estimated costs of guarantees and product warranty contracts are recorded in accounts at date of sale and deducted in tax returns when later paid.

Expenses for deferred compensation, profit-sharing, bonuses, and vacation and severance pay are recorded in accounts when accrued for the applicable period and deducted in tax returns when later paid.

Expenses for pension costs are recorded in accounts when accrued for the applicable period and deducted in tax returns for later periods when contributed to the pension fund.

Current expenses for self-insurance are recorded in accounts based on consistent computations for the plan and deducted in tax returns when losses are later incurred.

Estimated losses on inventories and purchase commitments are recorded in accounts when reasonably anticipated and deducted in tax returns when later realized.

Estimated losses on disposal of facilities and discontinuing or relocating operations are recorded in accounts when anticipated and determinable and deducted in tax returns when losses or costs are later incurred.

Estimated expenses of settling pending lawsuits and claims are recorded in accounts when reasonably ascertainable and deducted in tax returns when later paid.

Provisions for major repairs and maintenance are accrued in accounts on a systematic basis and deducted in tax returns when later paid.

Depreciation recorded in accounts exceeds that deducted in tax returns in early years because of:

> accelerated method of computation for accounting purposes

> shorter lives for accounting purposes

Organization costs are written off in accounts as incurred and amortized in tax returns.

(C) *Revenues or gains are taxed before accrued for accounting purposes:*

Rent and royalties are taxed when collected and deferred in accounts to later periods when earned.

Fees, dues, and service contracts are taxed when collected and deferred in accounts to later periods when earned.

Profits on intercompany transactions are taxed when reported in separate returns, and those on assets remaining within the group are eliminated in consolidated financial statements.

Gains on sales of property leased back are taxed at date of sale and deferred in accounts and amortized during the term of lease.

Proceeds of sales of oil payments or ore payments are taxed at date of sale and deferred in accounts and recorded as revenue when produced.

(D) *Expenses or losses are deducted for tax purposes before accrued for accounting purposes:*

Depreciation deducted in tax returns exceeds that recorded in accounts in early years because of:

Accelerated method of computation for tax purposes.

Shorter guideline lives for tax purposes.

Amortization of emergency facilities under certificates of necessity.

Unamortized discount, issue cost and redemption premium on bonds refunded are deducted in tax returns and deferred and amortized in accounts.

Research and development costs are deducted in tax returns when incurred and deferred and amortized in accounts.

Interest and taxes during construction are deducted in tax returns when incurred and included in the cost of assets in accounts.

Preoperating expenses are deducted in tax returns when incurred and deferred and amortized in accounts.

In order to have a concrete example to illustrate the operation of APB Op. No. 11, let us return to the problem at pages 510–511, supra, and examine more closely the treatment of the claims for breach of contract against CC that arose in year 1 and were settled by the payment of $240,000 in year 2. Assume for this purpose (although it seems somewhat unlikely) that as of the close of year 1 those potential claims were regarded as probable within the meaning of FASB No. 5, and that the amount of those claims could be reasonably estimated at $240,000. In that event, under FASB No. 5 CC would be required to accrue those claims as an expense (or loss) in year 1, with a debit in the amount of $240,000 to a current Expense (or Loss) account (which we might call "Franchise Claims Expense"), and a credit in the same amount to an estimated liability account, such as "Contingent Liability on Franchise Claims". Assume also that because of the contingent nature of this expense it would not be deductible for federal income tax purposes in year 1, in which event the $240,000 actually paid to settle these claims in year 2 would be deductible for tax purposes in that year. Assume further for simplicity that apart from this item CC's revenues and expenses in years 1 and 2 were identical, say, $60,000,000 in gross revenues and $52,000,000 in expenses other than income taxes. For its own accounting purposes CC would show $52,240,000 of expenses in year 1, after inclusion of the accrued expense for the franchise claims, resulting in net income before taxes of $7,760,000 for the year; in year 2 CC would show $52,000,000 of expenses, resulting in net income before taxes of $8,000,000. However, since the $240,000 of franchise claims expense would not be deductible for tax purposes in year 1, CC's taxable income that year would be $8,000,000 ($60,000,000 of revenues less $52,000,000 in expenses) and its tax bill (at an assumed 50% rate) would amount to $4,000,000. On the other hand, in year 2 the $240,-000 paid to settle the franchise claims would be deductible for tax purposes, so that taxable income in year 2 would be $7,760,000, and the tax bill for the year would be $3,880,000.

The following chart summarizes the foregoing computations (with the franchise claims expense focused separately only for illustrative purposes since, not being an extraordinary item, it would normally be included with the other expenses for the year rather than being detailed separately) :

	Year 1	Year 2
Income before Franchise Claims and Taxes	$8,000,000	$8,000,000
Less: Franchise Claims	240,000	——
Income before Taxes	7,760,000	8,000,000
Less: Tax Expense	4,000,000	3,880,000
Net Income	$3,760,000	$4,120,000

This is an example of a timing difference, as defined in paragraph 13(e) of Op. No. 11, since the franchise claims expense affects taxable income in a different period from the one in which it affects pretax accounting income. (An example of this very kind of timing difference is given in the seventh paragraph of Section B of Appendix A to Op. No. 11, page 533, supra.) Unless some further step is taken, the impact of recognizing the franchise claims expense in year 1 is exaggerated, and the difference in net income between years 1 and 2 is exacerbated, because year 1 bears the burden of the franchise claims expense while the "tax effect" of that expense (that is, the tax saving it produces) is reflected in year 2. The solution adopted in Op. No. 11 is to allocate tax expense between the two years, so that the tax expense in each year will, in the words of paragraph 34 of Op. No. 11, "include the tax effects of revenue and expense transactions included in the determination of pretax accounting income" in the respective years. In the instant situation this means that the tax expense in year 1 should be reduced, to reflect the tax saving of $120,000 associated with the franchise claims expense, since that expense is deducted in determining pretax accounting income in year 1; as a corollary, tax expense in year 2 should be increased (by $120,000) to $4,000,000, consistent with the pretax accounting income of $8,000,000 shown in that year.

The mechanics for implementing this allocation are the same as in any case when it is determined that an expenditure in one year should not be charged to current expense until a later year; that is, the expense should be deferred until the later year. Here, then, $120,000 of the taxes incurred in year 1 should be deferred in that year, and then charged to current tax expense in year 2. The effect of that step on the two years is reflected in the following chart:

	Year 1	Year 2
Income before Franchise Claims and Taxes	$8,000,000	$8,000,000
Less: Franchise Claims	240,000	—
Income before Taxes	7,760,000	8,000,000
Less: Tax Expense	3,880,000	4,000,000
Net Income	$3,880,000	$4,000,000

Notice that now the difference in net income between years 1 and 2 is only $120,000, equal to the amount of the franchise claims expense less the tax effects, as it should be under the assumption that the two years were identical except for the franchise claims; before, without this tax allocation, the difference was $360,000, which certainly gave a distorted picture of the comparison between the two years and the performance trend from year 1 to year 2. The figure for tax expense in year 1 is made up of the $4,000,000 tax liability actually incurred in year 1, less the $120,000 deferred until year 2 (by a debit to Deferred Tax Expense, usually called simply "Deferred Taxes"). The entry in year 1, assuming for simplicity that the entire tax liability for the year was paid in cash at one time, would be as follows:

Tax Expense	$3,880,000	
Deferred Taxes	120,000	
Cash		$4,000,000

In year 2, the tax expense would be composed of the tax liability incurred for the year of $3,880,000 plus the $120,000 deferred from year 1:

Tax Expense	$4,000,000	
Deferred Taxes		$ 120,000
Cash		3,880,000

a. *"Net of Tax" Presentation*

Mention should be made of one other technique for taking account of the fact that the franchise claims expense enters into the determination of pretax accounting income in a year prior to the one in which it affects taxable income. If the only objective were to "correct" the net income figures in these two years by eliminating the distortion resulting from this timing difference, that could be accomplished as well by accruing in year 1 not the full amount of the estimated franchise claims expense of $240,000, but rather only the amount of that estimated expense less the expected tax saving, or $120,000. Then in year 2 when the franchise claims are actually paid in the full amount of $240,000, $120,000 would have to be charged to expense in year 2, since the estimated liability created in year 1 would only amount to $120,000, and hence would only be available to absorb $120,000 of the expenditure. Taxes, on the other hand, would be reflected in each year in the amount actually incurred. Under this approach, the income statements for the two years would look like this:

	Year 1	Year 2
Income before Franchise Claims and Taxes	$8,000,000	$8,000,000
Less: Franchise Claims	120,000 *	120,000 **
Income before Taxes	7,880,000	7,880,000
Less: Tax Expense	4,000,000	3,880,000
Net Income	$3,880,000	$4,000,000

* Net of future tax saving.

** Portion equal to tax saving; balance charged to year 1.

This method does produce the same corrected net income figures in the two years; in addition, as noted, the figure for taxes in each of the two years corresponds to the actual tax liability incurred in each of the two years. This is an example of the "net of tax" presentation referred to in paragraphs 54(d) and 55(c) of Op. No. 11: the accrual of the expense in year 1 is limited to the amount of the expense "net of tax", i. e., the amount of the expense less the expected future reduction in taxes due to the expense, based on the notion that this net figure is the true measure of the actual burden of this expense. The trouble with this approach is that it attempts to solve a problem stemming from a difference in tax timing by allocating the underlying expense which gives rise to the timing difference, instead of allocating the tax expense. And this allocation of the underlying expense is quite questionable, since there is no basis under traditional accounting principles for allocating any of the franchise claims expense to year 2; under FASB No. 5 the entire amount of this liability should be accrued in year 1, on the basis of the assumption that the liability was both probable and capable of being reasonably estimated in amount by the end of year 1. The only justification for allocating a portion of this expense to year 2 is to correct for the tax effects, and it is solely on this basis that the amount allocated to year 2 is determined. Hence the substance of this approach is an allocation of tax expense, and it seems more realistic, and more meaningful, to adopt that form directly. Accordingly, paragraph 64 of Op. No. 11 categorically rejects the "net of tax" method, in favor of allocation of tax expense. (For an example of the "net of tax" presentation in the depreciation area, see pages 541–543, infra.)

PROBLEMS

1. In the problem at pages 510–511, supra, suppose that CC decides that the promotion expenditures of $800,000 in year 2 and $400,000 in year 3 will provide level benefits in years 2, 3, and 4, and that accordingly $400,000 of promotion expense should be allocated to each of those three years. For tax purposes, however, CC will deduct the amount actually expended in each year, i. e., $800,000 in year 2, $400,000 in year 3, and zero in year 4. What tax adjustment, if any, would be called for in each of years 2, 3 and 4? (For illustrative purposes, assume that in each of those three years CC's net income before promotion expense and taxes equals $8,000,000, and the tax rate is 50%.)

2. Acme Transportation Corporation is engaged in the trucking business. Acme has outstanding 10,000 shares of preferred stock pursuant to a provision which calls for the payment of dividends of up to $8 per share for each fiscal year, to the extent covered by net income for that year. During its fiscal year just ended Acme's rate

schedule included a provision that any customer who shipped raw materials into certain named cities via Acme's trucks during that year would be entitled to a refund of twenty percent of the freight paid to Acme on those shipments if the manufactured products were subsequently shipped out of those cities via Acme's trucks. This arrangement was applicable only to shipments into the named cities during last year, and Acme did not renew it for the current year.

Last year Acme's net income was $70,000, after deduction of all refunds paid (or owed) by year end because the manufactured goods had been shipped out via Acme's trucks by the close of the year. However, on the basis of Acme's experience last year it is probable that another $20,000 of freight charges received by Acme on raw materials shipped into the named cities last year will have to be refunded because the manufactured products will be shipped out via Acme's trucks during the current year. (Assume that no portion of the $20,000 would be deductible for tax purposes last year.)

How much should be paid to the preferred stockholders for last year? (Assume a 50% tax rate.)

4. ALLOCATION OF TAX IN CONNECTION WITH DEPRECIATION

a. RAPID DEPRECIATION ON "EMERGENCY FACILITIES"

By far the most important incident of tax allocation occurs in connection with depreciation, when the method used for financial accounting purposes differs from that utilized for tax purposes. A good way to start on the tax allocation issues relating to depreciation is to look at a case involving a so-called "emergency facility", that is, an asset which, as described on page 488, supra, is permitted to be depreciated over a five-year period for tax purposes even though its useful life may actually be expected to be a good deal longer. For example, assume that on January 1 of year 1 X Corporation acquired for $1,000,000 a new plant which qualified in full for "emergency facility" treatment, with no expected salvage value, and hence could be written off at $200,000 per year for tax purposes. However, X's best estimate of the actual useful life of the new plant was ten years, with no net salvage value, so for financial accounting purposes the new plant would be depreciated at the rate of $100,000 per year. Assume further that during year 1 X's income before both depreciation on the emergency facility and income taxes was $1,200,000, and that the tax rate was a flat 50%. Since X would deduct depreciation of $200,000 on the emergency facility for tax purposes, its taxable income would be $1,000,000 and the tax bill would be $500,000:

INCOME FOR TAX PURPOSES

Income before Depreciation on Emergency Facility	$1,200,000
Less: Depreciation	200,000
Taxable Income	1,000,000
Income Taxes (at assumed 50% rate)	$ 500,000

Absent some additional step, X's net income on its own financial statements would be computed as follows:

INCOME ON X'S OWN BOOKS

Income before Depreciation on Emergency Facility and Taxes	$1,200,000
Less: Depreciation	100,000
Income before Taxes	$1,100,000
Less: Income Taxes	500,000
Net Income	600,000

The actual tax expense for year 1 is thus $50,000 less than would be expected on the basis of X's pretax accounting income, and the resulting figure for net income after taxes is $50,000 higher than would be expected. The same would be true for each of the next four years, while the rapid write-off for tax purposes was continuing. On the other hand, in the years after completion of the rapid write-off of the emergency facility for tax purposes the situation would be reversed: then the actual tax expense on X's income statement would be higher than would be expected on the basis of X's pretax accounting income, and the resulting figure for net income after taxes would be lower, since X would still be deducting depreciation on the emergency facility for financial accounting purposes but would no longer be getting any deduction for tax purposes.

Assuming that income before depreciation on the emergency facility, and the tax rate, both remain constant for the full ten years, the following table indicates how X's financial net income would be computed for each of the first five years (the period of the rapid write-off for tax purposes), and for each of the second five years (the rest of the facility's depreciable life for financial accounting); for comparison, the table also shows how X's financial net income would have been computed for all the ten years if the new facility had not qualified for special tax treatment and had simply been depreciated over a ten-year life for both tax and financial accounting purposes.

	First five years with rapid depreciation for tax purposes	Second five years with rapid depreciation for tax purposes	All ten years if no rapid depreciation for tax purposes
Income before Depreciation and Taxes	$1,200,000	$1,200,000	$1,200,000
Less: Depreciation	100,000	100,000	100,000
Income before Taxes	1,100,000	1,100,000	1,100,000
Less: Income Taxes	500,000	600,000	550,000
Net Income	$ 600,000	$ 500,000	$ 550,000

It does not seem meaningful for X to show a higher net income for each of the first five years and a lower net income for each of the last five years, when it is assumed that X carried on the same volume of business and had the same earning performance in each of the ten years. A review of this ten-year series of income statements might suggest that X's business had taken a turn for the worse during years 6–10, when in fact it remained exactly the same over the whole ten-year period. Further, in each year the figure for income taxes is different from what would be expected on the basis of X's pretax accounting income.

What is needed, of course, is an interperiod allocation of tax expense so that the income tax expense for each year will be based upon the amount of depreciation expense included in the determination of pretax accounting income for that year—and that is exactly what APB Op. No. 11 calls for. Thus in each of the first five years income tax expense should be increased by $50,000, consistent with the fact that the amount deducted for depreciation in computing pretax accounting income is $100,000 less than the amount deducted in determining taxable income, and the tax effect of this difference (at an assumed 50% rate) is $50,000. This debit to current income tax expense each year would be balanced by a credit to a liability-type account a kind of estimated liability reflecting the fact that a tax expense being charged currently will not actually be incurred until some time in the future — an account which is usually called simply "Deferred Income Taxes". Notice that the term Deferred Income Taxes standing alone might well suggest an asset, a deferred expense type of asset, and indeed the very same term is used to describe the asset which results when the timing difference requires that some of the taxes actually paid currently should be deferred until a subsequent year, as occurred in the case of the franchise claims expense analyzed above, at pages 534–536. However, there is little danger of confusion as to when the term Deferred Income Taxes connotes an asset and when a liability, since its location on either the left-hand side or the right-hand side of the balance sheet will make clear which is involved. (Of course sometimes a company will have *both* an asset and a liability resulting from accounting for tax effects, when there have been two or more transactions giving rise to timing differences of both kinds.)

With the application of Op. No. 11, the income statement each year would look the same as if the emergency facility had not been the subject of rapid depreciation over a five-year period for tax purposes *:

	First five years with rapid depreciation for tax purposes	Second five years with rapid depreciation for tax purposes	All ten years if no rapid depreciation for tax purposes
Income before Depreciation and Taxes	$1,200,000	$1,200,000	$1,200,000
Less: Depreciation	100,000	100,000	100,000
Income before Taxes	1,100,000	1,100,000	1,100,000
Less: Tax Expense	550,000	550,000	550,000
Net Income	$ 550,000	$ 550,000	$ 550,000

The tax expense in columns one and two respectively is computed as follows:

First five years		**Second five years**	
Taxes actually payable	$500,000	Taxes actually payable	$600,000
Add: Tax effects of timing differences in depreciation on emergency facility	50,000	Less: Tax effects of timing differences in depreciation on emergency facility	50,000
Tax expense	$550,000	Tax expense	$550,000

Thus Tax Expense during each of the first five years is $50,000 higher than the actual tax payable by virtue of an added charge in that amount each year, balanced by a credit to a Deferred Taxes liability account; and in each of the last five years Tax Expense is $50,000 less than the taxes actually payable because $50,000 of the taxes paid in each of those years will be charged to the Deferred Taxes liability account (set up in the first five years) rather than to current tax expense.

To complete this picture, let us examine briefly how the "net of tax" approach, rejected in Op. No. 11, would operate in this depreciation case. Under that method, instead of increasing the tax expense in each of the first five years, depreciation expense would

---

* Actually, given the assumption of exactly level business operations over the ten-year period, X's net income from year 2 on would probably be higher than it would have been without the rapid depreciation for tax purposes, since by postponing the payment of taxes of $50,000 per year from the first five years to the second five years X has the benefit of the use of that money, which should enable it to either earn interest or save interest charges by reducing its borrowings.

be increased by $50,000 in each of those years. The justification for charging $150,000 to depreciation expense in each of the first five years, rather than just $100,000, would be that this will produce, after offsetting the $100,000 "tax saving" in each of those years resulting from the deduction of $200,000 of depreciation for tax purposes, the same after-tax, or "net of tax", burden of $50,000 per year which would result from a simple, straight-line deduction of $100,000 of depreciation expense in each of those years for financial accounting and for tax purposes (the latter producing a "tax saving" of $50,000 each year). Under this alternative, no separate entry would be required, merely the following entry for depreciation expense in each of the first five years:

Depreciation Expense	$150,000	
Accumulated Depreciation		$150,000

At the end of the first five years the total accumulated depreciation would then amount to $750,000 rather than $500,000, and only $250,000 of the original cost would remain to be written off over the last five years for financial accounting purposes. Accordingly, depreciation expense in each of the last five years would be only $50,000 a year, which again would produce the desired "net of tax" burden of $50,000 in each of those years, since there would be no depreciation deduction for tax purposes in those years and hence no offsetting tax saving. Under this alternative, the tables would appear as follows:

	First five years with rapid depreciation for tax purposes	Second five years with rapid depreciation for tax purposes	All ten years if no rapid depreciation for tax purposes
Income before depreciation and taxes	$1,200,000	$1,200,000	$1,200,000
Less: Depreciation	150,000	50,000	100,000
Income before Tax Expense	1,050,000	1,150,000	1,100,000
Less: Tax Expense	500,000	600,000	550,000
Net Income	$ 550,000	$ 550,000	$ 550,000

Note that this approach too produces a net income figure each year which is the same as it would have been if the emergency facility had not been the subject of rapid depreciation over a five-year period for tax purposes; and the figure for tax expense each year corresponds to the actual tax liability each year. But like the "net of tax" approach analyzed above in conjunction with the franchise claims expense, pages 536–537, supra, this is not a meaningful allocation of the expense involved, from the financial accounting point of view; charging three times as much depreciation expense in each of the first five years as in each of the last five years does not represent a rational allocation of the cost of the emergency facility over its useful life. It can be justified only as an effort to correct for the tax effects, which is why APB No. 11 rejects such a "net of tax" approach in favor of a direct and express allocation of the tax expense itself.

b. ACCELERATED DEPRECIATION

Similar tax allocation issues arise when a company uses an accelerated depreciation method for tax purposes while determining pretax accounting income on the basis of straight-time depreciation. This has been the most controversial incident of tax allocation, and is probably the primary reason for the sharp dispute between partial and comprehensive allocation focused in paragraphs 26–32 of APB Op. No. 11. In opting for comprehensive allocation the APB in effect adopted the view that when accelerated depreciation is used for tax purposes while straight-line is employed in determining pretax accounting income, the situation should be viewed as essentially analogous to the foregoing case of writing off an emergency facility over five years for tax purposes while depreciating it over its longer actual expected life in determining pretax accounting income.

In theory, the analogy is sound enough. Depreciation of an asset on an accelerated basis produces more depreciation expense than the straight-line method during the early years of the asset's life; therefore, during those years taxable income resulting from accelerated depreciation will be lower than the pretax accounting income based upon straight-line depreciation, and taxes actually payable will be lower than would be appropriate on the basis of the pretax accounting income. This situation is reversed in the later years of the asset's life, when accelerated depreciation produces a lower annual expense than straight-line: then taxable income computed on the basis of accelerated depreciation will be greater than the pretax accounting income derived by the use of straight-line depreciation, and the taxes actually payable will be greater than would be appropriate on the basis of pretax accounting income. As with other timing differences, Op. No. 11 calls for an additional charge to the Tax Expense account in those early years, to increase the total tax expense for the year to the amount which is appropriate on the basis of pretax accounting income (with a corresponding credit to a Deferred Taxes liability account in the amount of the additional charge to Tax Expense). Then in the later years of the asset's life, when the taxes actually payable are in excess of the amount which would be appropriate on the basis of pretax accounting income, that excess is charged to the Deferred Taxes liability account, instead of to the current Tax Expense account, so that the figure for current tax expense is based upon the amount of depreciation expense included in the determination of pretax accounting income for the year. As noted earlier, this process parallels the tax allocation procedure used when an emergency facility is written off over only five years for tax purposes while being depreciated over a longer period in computing pretax accounting income.

However, as indicated in paragraph 26 of Op. No. 11, the objections to this application of comprehensive allocation have special force in the case of timing differences arising from the use of accelerated depreciation for tax purposes. The reason is that in most cases of this kind, where accelerated depreciation is being utilized for tax purposes on substantially all of the company's tangible assets, and the company is continually adding new assets, at least to replace existing capacity, if not to expand, the increase in taxes predicted to occur in the later years of a particular asset's useful life is not really encountered, because it is offset by the reduction in taxes due to the application of accelerated depreciation for tax purposes to newly-acquired assets. In fact, as long as a company's annual replacement expenditures at least maintain its plant at a stable dollar level (and remember that in the current era of steady inflation an increasing dollar amount of investment is needed just to maintain the same capacity), the additional tax expense projected by the process of comprehensive tax allocation will never actually occur; as a corollary, the Deferred Taxes liability account will never be reduced, and indeed that account will steadily increase in proportion to the increased dollar investment in plant resulting from the increasing cost of replacement due to inflation, plus any additional investment reflecting an expansion of capacity.

Consider the following illustration (set out in tabular form below), which for simplicity assumes a company with five similar depreciable assets, each with a five-year life and no salvage value, and one of which is retired and replaced on January 1 of each year. Assuming further that each unit costs $150, and that the price level remains steady, under the straight-line method depreciation expense on each unit will be $30 per year, and the total depreciation expense will be $150. Under accelerated depreciation, using the sum-of-the-years-digits method, the annual depreciation expense per unit would be $50, $40, $30, $20 and $10 respectively, in the five years of its useful life. At the start of the year in which the sum-of-the-years-digits method is elected for tax purposes, there would be, we will assume, one unit (E) purchased on January 1, and units D, C, B, and A, with ages of 1, 2, 3, and 4 years respectively. For that first year, which we will assume to be 1978, the depreciation for tax purposes on the new unit E under accelerated depreciation would be $50, while on D, C, B, and A the depreciation, under the straight-line method, would continue at $30 each, so that the total annual depreciation for 1978 would be $50 + 4 \times \$30 = \$170$, or $20 more than under straight-line. On January 1 of 1979, unit A would be replaced by unit F, which would be depreciated for tax purposes that year at $50, with E (now one year old) at $40, and D, C, and B at $30 each, for a total deduction in 1979 of $50 + 40 + 3 \times 30 = \$180$. The deduction for tax purposes in 1980 would be $50 + 40 + 30 + 2 \times 30 = \$180$; in 1981, $50 + 40 + 30 + 20 + 30 = \$170$; and in 1982, and succeeding years, $50 + 40 + 30 + 20 + 10 = \$150$, the same as under straight-line.

In the following table, the individual assets are listed in order of their age in the first column. The next column shows the basis of depreciation used for tax purposes for that asset, and the following columns show how much depreciation expense that asset contributed to the total annual depreciation expense for tax purposes for each year. Thus, to see how the total annual depreciation for each year is computed, read down the columns for each year.

ASSET	DEPRECIATION METHOD	1978	1979	1980	1981	1982
(Year in which acquired, on Jan. 1, shown in parentheses)						
A (1974)	Straight-line	$30	retired			
B (1975)	Straight-line	30	$30	retired		
C (1976)	Straight-line	30	30	$30	retired	
D (1977)	Straight-line	30	30	30	$30	retired
E (1978)	Sum/yrs./digs.	50	40	30	20	$10
F (1979)	Sum/yrs./digs.		50	40	30	20
G (1980)	Sum/yrs./digs			50	40	30
H (1981)	Sum/yrs./digs.				50	40
I (1982)	Sum/yrs./digs.					50
Total Annual Depreciation		$170	$180	$180	$170	$150

In the years from 1983 on, the computation would be the same as it is for 1982. Thus it appears that even with the unrealistic assumption of a steady price level the tax "saving" resulting from the use of accelerated depreciation for tax purposes may be permanent, subject to being lost only if the price level declines or there is a contraction in the size of the business. Nevertheless, pursuant to the decision in favor of comprehensive allocation Op. No. 11 requires tax allocation, or as it is sometimes called, "tax normalization" (connoting the fact that the amount charged to tax expense each year is the "normal" tax liability which would be consistent with the company's pretax accounting income determined on the basis of straight-line depreciation).

Tax normalization in connection with the use of accelerated depreciation for tax purposes has been a very important issue in the field of public utility rate regulation. Until the middle 1960's the Federal Power Commission permitted utilities subject to its jurisdiction to practice tax normalization, thereby increasing the amount of tax expense allowed as a deduction in computing the rates needed to permit the company to earn a fair return. The FPC's position was sustained on appeal in a number of cases as a permissible exercise of regulatory discretion, against the argument that current customers were being charged higher rates to cover an expense that would not in fact be incurred in the forseeable future. E. g., El Paso Natural Gas Co. v. Federal Power Commission, 281 F.2d 567 (5th Cir. 1960). Then in 1964, with very little advance fanfare (but after a very substantial change in the membership of the Commission), the FPC reversed itself and by 3 to 2 vote rejected normalization in favor of the "flow-through" approach (so-called because only the taxes actually payable for the year are charged to current expense, and hence the tax saving from the use of accelerated depreciation for tax purposes flows through directly to, and increases, net income). Alabama-Tennessee Natural Gas Co., 31 F.P.C. 208, 52 P.U.R.3d 118 (1964). On appeal, the Commission's adoption of the flow-through method was affirmed by the Court of Appeals for the 5th Circuit. Alabama-Tennessee Natural Gas Co. v. Federal Power Commission, 359 F.2d 318 (5th Cir. 1966). The following excerpts from Judge Wisdom's opinion for the court may shed some further light on the issues:

> D. *Tax Savings from Normalization.* For any given tax year, a utility's depreciable properties include assets of various ages. Consequently, so the Commission found, "below normal" depreciation on older assets is counterbalanced by "above normal" depreciation on new assets as long as the company continues the use of liberalized depreciation and continues to make at least some capital additions. Under these conditions, liberalized tax depreciation will always exceed straight-line tax depreciation and the accumulations established under the normalized rate and deferred tax accounting will continue to increase until the dollar value of gross plant stabilizes. Even if the composite plant of a company remains stable, where the dollar value of retirements equals the cost of replacements, annual liberalized depreciation will not be lower than straight-line depreciation and the reserve established under normalization will not decline.
>
> A regulated utility, therefore, will *never* be required to pay higher income taxes because of its election to claim liberalized depreciation *unless* its gross plant declines in dollar value as a result of lower demand or lower plant construction cost. Normalization during a period of growth or stability would force

the ratepayers to provide funds for a hypothetical tax liability that might never become payable or, at the very least, to provide funds many years in advance of the time they are needed. The Commission's records show that the deferred tax accounts of Alabama-Tennessee and other pipeline companies have increased substantially since the accelerated depreciation election became available.*

Petitioner argues that under [IRC] Section 167, liberalized depreciation is applied to facilities constructed during the period covered by the tax return and it is necessary that the taxpayer maintain the identity of individual units of property in order to know what deductions may be made each year for depreciation. Moreover, the Commission's Uniform System of Accounts requires this. That the reserve for deferred taxes may continue to increase for an indefinite period the petitioner deems of no consequence. The petitioner would hold the Commission in its ratemaking process to the same computation of depreciation on specific assets as required by the Internal Revenue Service under Section 167 for tax accounting. It would have the Commission disregard the cumulative reserve for accelerated depreciation for the utility's total assets. The Commission's error, according to petitioner, is that it refuses to recognize the mechanics of determining the taxes to be paid. The short answer is that accounting for tax purposes and even the Commission's present Uniform System of Accounts may be valuable tools, but they cannot dictate ratemaking policies. . . .

*   *   *

Alabama-Tennessee and amici supporting the petitioner argue persuasively that the Commission fails to give adequate consideration to future risks.[39] In the depression the public

---

* [Ed. note] Earlier in the opinion the Court observed: "In 1960 when the Commission held its first hearing on the issue, the aggregate total of the accumulated tax reserves of natural gas pipeline companies was about $150 million. December 31, 1963, it was $304 million."

39. In a notable opinion, Judge Schaefer, for the Illinois Supreme Court, said: "The assumption of a continuous deferral of taxes due to accelerated depreciation may be justified in many cases and the Commission would be justified in acting on this assumption if it saw fit. [citations omitted] Experience may show that proper results can only be achieved by this approach. However, several not unlikely events might occur which would prove the assumption erroneous. A war, a general depression or a decline in the local market might curtail a

utility's capital expenditures, and prevent further tax deferrals. As a result, taxes might increase just at the time when economic circumstances would make the added expense most burdensome. It is also possible that section 167 will be repealed, thus ending further tax deferrals.

If we could see clearly into the future and say with certainty that continuing expansion was certain, and countervailing considerations were nonexistent, we would hold that the Commission may not permit current charges for a liability that will never arise. Predictions of future developments, however, are unsure estimates at best. The problem is a new one; that factual and policy considerations that bear upon its solution have not as yet been fully developed. Even the future of accelerated depreciation in the Federal tax structure is not entirely settled. If for any reason continued in-utility industry was the victim of misguided theories of depreciation and retirement reserve accounting. The petitioner insists that it cannot be assumed that the cash requirements in the future to pay deferred tax expenses will be offset by other items of tax deduction from other properties. The basic reality is that taxes deferred must be paid in the future; the permanence of deferrals or the equation of deferrals with savings is an illusion; deferred accounting is a necessity in order to meet future increases in taxes. Flow-through, so petitioner asserts, must necessarily have an adverse effect upon the financial standing and credit. And an overhanging burden of unfunded deferred taxes imposes additional risks which will be reflected in the cost of equity and debt-financing.

It is true that the Commission's decision rests on its reading of the future. But clairvoyance is part of the daily grind of a regulatory agency. Whether flow-through or normalization is the rule, the agency must base the rule on some projection into the future. As we see it, the case for normalization requires more speculation than the case for flow-through. And it is at the expense of consumers.

On the record before us and the facts outside of the record which the Commission properly notices, the Commission's ruling is based on substantial evidence of present conditions and a fair guess as to future conditions in the pipeline industry. If the Commission is wrong, the pipelines will still have paid only actual taxes; these will be recouped in full as part of the cost of service. Besides, as a hedge against the risk of a "payback", the Commission has allowed Alabama-Tennessee to retain tax reserves accumulated since 1954. Should the future support the Commission's competency in clairvoyance and should normalization be allowed, consumers will have made enormous contributions to the pipelines' capital funds at no cost to the pipelines. The Commission must, of course, concern itself with the possibility of having misread the future and with the future's taking a turn without benefit of advice from the Commission. All things change. But we should expect agency policy to be sufficiently flexible to attempt to change with changing times. Sufficient unto the day is the evil thereof.

In final analysis, putting to one side the issue of congressional intent, the petitioner's challenge to the FPC order addresses itself to the competency of the Commission to choose between the competing accounting theories and competing economic guesses. We see nothing irrational in the Commission's choice.

———————

vestment in utility plant at current levels should cease, or accelerated depreciation be denied, the financial stability of utilities might be jeopardized if some provision had not been made for the increased taxes that would result. Rate regulation is a continuing process; greater experience may bring greater wisdom in dealing with these problems. At this time, we think it permissible for the Commission to safeguard the financial integrity of utilities by recognizing as present expenses those tax liabilities which are deferred by use of accelerated depreciation for Federal tax purposes." City of Alton v. Commerce Commission, 1960, 19 Ill. 2d 76, 165 N.E.2d 513, 521.

The SEC has followed the lead of the accounting profession in supporting tax allocation, after some early reluctance which included an explicit ruling to the effect that the amount shown as tax expense for the year "should reflect only actual taxes believed to be payable under the applicable tax laws". See ASR No. 53 (1945), an excerpt from which appears at pages 517–518, supra. In 1960 the SEC approved the stand taken in ARB No. 44, a predecessor of APB Op. No. 11, in favor of tax normalization when accelerated depreciation is used for tax purposes, in the following release, which seems principally concerned with prohibiting the treatment of the Deferred Taxes liability account as part of stockholders' equity (a prohibition similarly reflected in paragraph 59 of APB Op. No. 11):

ACCOUNTING SERIES RELEASE NO. 85 *

Securities and Exchange Commission, 1960.

STATEMENT OF ADMINISTRATIVE POLICY REGARDING BALANCE SHEET TREATMENT OF CREDIT EQUIVALENT TO REDUCTION IN INCOME TAXES

. . . This statement of policy is designed to advise all interested persons of the Commission's views as to the presentation in financial statements filed with the Commission of the credit arising when deferred tax accounting is employed. It pertains to the propriety of designating as earned surplus (or its equivalent) or in any manner as a part of equity capital, in financial statements filed with this Commission, the accumulated credit arising from accounting for reductions in income taxes for various items, including those under Section 167 (liberalized depreciation) and Section 168 (accelerated amortization of emergency facilities) of the Internal Revenue Code of 1954. . . .

The problem arises from the deduction of costs for income tax purposes at a faster rate than for financial statement purposes where the difference is material. The amount of income tax payable for any period is affected by the amount of costs deducted in determining taxable income. In a year in which costs are deducted for tax purposes in amounts greater than those used for financial statement purposes, then, unless corrected, there is a failure properly to match costs and revenues in the financial statements by the amount of the tax effect of the cost differential. To correct the resultant distortion in periodic net income after taxes, it is therefore necessary to charge income in earlier years with an amount equal to the tax reduction and to return this amount to income in subsequent years when the amount charged for financial statement purposes exceeds the amount deducted for tax purposes. It is our understanding that such deferred tax accounting is in accordance with generally accepted accounting principles.

With specific reference to depreciation, since the total deduction allowed over the life of an asset is limited to its cost and hence is not

* All but one of the footnotes omitted.

affected by the method by which it is deducted from income, acceleration of tax deductions in earlier years results in deferring to later years the payment of taxes on an amount equivalent to the cost differential. Because of the interrelationship between income taxes and depreciation, the Commission is of the view that in the earlier years the charge equivalent to the tax reduction should be treated . . . as a provision for future taxes in the income statement with a corresponding credit in the balance sheet to a non-equity caption such as a deferred tax credit . . . .** In the Commission's view it is improper to charge income with an item required for the proper determination of net income and concurrently to credit earned surplus.

* * *

The Committee on Accounting Procedure of the American Institute of Certified Public Accountants agrees with the position expressed above. Accounting Research Bulletin No. 44 (Revised) states, in connection with the deduction of depreciation for income tax purposes at a more rapid rate than for financial accounting purposes, that the accounting company should employ deferred tax accounting ["crediting a deferred tax account to recognize the related tax effect"]. A difference of opinion arose among certifying accountants whether the language of this bulletin permitted the deferred tax account to be classified as earned surplus restricted for future income taxes. To resolve the controversy, the Committee on Accounting Procedure sent a letter dated April 15, 1959, to all members of the Institute in which it clarified the bulletin on the point. The pertinent portion of the letter reads:

"Question has been raised with respect to the intent of the committee on accounting procedure in using the phrase 'a deferred tax account' in Accounting Research Bulletin No. 44 (revised), *Declining-balance Depreciation*, to indicate the account to be credited for the amount of the deferred income tax. . . .

"The committee used the phrase in its ordinary connotation of an account to be shown in the balance sheet as a liability or a deferred credit. A provision in recognition of the deferral of income taxes, being required for the proper determination of net income, should not at the same time result in a credit to earned surplus or to any other account included in the stockholders' equity section of the balance sheet."

* * *

. . . Arguments have been advanced, particularly on behalf of public utility companies, to the effect that from analytical and rate-making viewpoints the treatment prescribed herein might have undesirable results upon investors and consumers. However, it is entirely appropriate that regulatory agencies treat the accumulated credit arising from deferred tax accounting in whatever manner they deem most relevant to their purposes.[11]

* * *

** In this release the SEC also condoned the net-of-tax method of charging additional depreciation (described at pages 541–543, supra), but the Commission appears to have accepted the profession's rejection of that method in APB Op.No. 11.

11. So far as this Commission is concerned, since it believes that classifying the item as a component part of common stock equity is misleading for financial statement purposes, it does not intend to consider the item as a part of common stock equity for

For the foregoing reasons, on and after the effective date of this statement of administrative policy, any financial statement filed with this Commission which designates as earned surplus (or its equivalent) or in any manner as a part of equity capital (even though accompanied by words of limitation such as "restricted" or "appropriated") the accumulated credit arising from accounting for reductions in income taxes resulting from deducting costs for income tax purposes at a more rapid rate than for financial statement purposes will be presumed by the Commission to be misleading or inaccurate despite disclosure contained in the certificate of the accountant or in footnotes to the statements, provided the amounts involved are material.

QUESTION

In the problem on page 510, supra, suppose that D Corp. adopted declining balance depreciation on its new plant for tax purposes while using straight-line for determining pretax accounting income. Assuming for simplicity a flat corporate income tax rate of 50%, what effect would this have on the amount due the preferred stockholders? How would it affect the amount which could be distributed as a dividend to common stockholders under a corporate statute which permits dividends "out of net assets in excess of capital"?

c. THE INVESTMENT CREDIT

Perhaps the most troublesome tax allocation issue of all has been the question of how to account for the investment credit provided by IRC § 38, which allows a credit reducing federal income taxes in the amount of a specified percentage (generally 7% today) of a taxpayer's cost investment in tangible business personal property during the year. So strong have the feelings run on the choice between the two competing accounting alternatives that back in the early 1960's the Accounting Principles Board was forced to retreat from its choice of one of the two and instead to permit both (despite the Board's general mandate to narrow the areas of difference and inconsistency in accounting treatment). Similarly, an effort to deal with the subject in a tentative draft of APB Op. No. 11 provoked such opposition that the matter was omitted from the final version of Op. No. 11 in favor of "further study" (which never was concluded). Here is the draft treatment of the investment credit omitted from Op. No. 11, followed by a Treasury Department promulgation on the subject:

analytical purposes, although it may give consideration to the item as one of a number of relevant factors in appraising the overall financial condition of a company. The Commission, of course, does not have jurisdiction over rate-making, although under the Public Utility Holding Company Act of 1935 it is concerned with the interests of consumers. Alleged adverse results as to investors and consumers are no different from those complained of whenever any requirement designed to assure financial stability is imposed.

INVESTMENT CREDIT

Discussion

50.   The United States Internal Revenue Code provides for "investment credits" which, in general, are equivalent to specified percentages of the costs of certain depreciable assets acquired.   The credits are subject to certain statutory limitations.   The amounts available in any one year are used to reduce the amount of any income tax payable for that year.   Although they do not result in timing differences or permanent differences as these terms are used in this Opinion, investment credits create another situation in which interperiod tax allocation may be applicable.

51.   The Board previously has considered the problems in accounting for investment credits.   Its views are found in APB Opinions Nos. 2 and 4, issued in December 1962 and March 1964.   The Board stated in Opinion No. 2 that "there can be but one useful conclusion as to the nature of the investment credit and that it must be determined by the weight of pertinent factors."   After identifying alternative views as to the nature of the investment credit, the Board concluded that the investment credit "should be reflected in net income over the productive life of acquired property and not in the year in which it is placed in service."   This conclusion was based, in part at least, on the Board's analysis of the substance of the investment credit "as a reduction in or offset against a cost otherwise chargeable in a greater amount to future accounting periods."

52.   In Opinion No. 4, the Board reaffirmed its preference for the conclusion on accounting for the investment credit as expressed in Opinion No. 2 (generally referred to as the *deferral method*), but stated additionally that "the alternative method of treating the credit as a reduction of Federal income taxes of the year in which the credit arises is also acceptable."   This alternative method (generally referred to as the *flow-through method*) is supported in part at least by the view that the investment credit is in substance a selective reduction in taxes related to the taxable income of the year in which the credit arises.

*   *   *

54.   The investment credit provisions of the Internal Revenue Code become applicable upon existence of two conditions:

   a.   the taxpayer acquires qualifying property in a period, which property will have a useful term of life, and be held or used, at least as long as certain time periods specified in the Code, and

   b.   the taxpayer has taxable income resulting in taxes payable against which the investment credit may be fully or partly offset.   .   .   .

55.   Under the *flow-through method* the tax effect of the investment credit is recognized in determining income tax expense in the period in which the credit is used in the determination of income taxes payable.   The investment credit is considered to be a selective tax reduction in the year in which taxes otherwise payable are reduced by the credit.   Thus, the investment credit is not viewed as a determi-

nant of the cost of any asset or of the cost of using assets but is a reduction of income tax expense of the period when it is obtained.

56.   Under the *deferral method* the tax effect of the investment credit is recognized in determining income tax expense in those periods in which the cost of the property acquired is amortized and thereby enters into the determination of results of operations of these periods.   The investment credit is considered to be related both to the property acquired, which serves as the basis for the credit, and to income tax expense.   The reduction in income tax expense which results from the investment credit is viewed as being related to the periods in which the cost of the property that gave rise to the credit is amortized by charges to income.

57.   The advocates of the flow-through method as well as many of those who favor the deferral method generally agree that the investment credit represents an income tax benefit arising from a reduction of current taxes payable rather than a reduction in the cost of the asset or a temporary tax advantage that must be repaid at a future date.   Thus, the difference in views concerns primarily the period in which the credit should be reflected in income.   Advocates of the flow-through method believe, for several reasons, that the investment credit should be reflected in results of operations in the same period that the benefit is used to reduce income taxes payable:

a.   The investment credit is both earned and realized by the occurrence of two events: (1) making an investment in newly acquired facilities and (2) the existence of current taxable income arising for the most part from revenues earned currently through the use of facilities previously installed. Therefore, the investment credit currently realized does not depend on or relate to revenues earned during subsequent periods.   Since there is no relationship between this element of income tax expense and future revenues there is no basis for deferral of the investment credit under the matching concept and amortization of it over subsequent accounting periods; instead it is earned in the same period in which it is realized.

b.   The investment credit arises from transactions reflected in the same period for both financial accounting and tax purposes.   .   .   .   [T]he principles of interperiod allocation discussed elsewhere in [Op. No. 11] are not applicable.

c.   Advocates of current recognition regard the opinion in paragraph 60, that the investment credit should be spread over the same asset life and by the same method as depreciation of the asset is determined for financial accounting purposes, as a contradiction of the Board's opinion that the investment credit is an element of income tax expense.   This spreading requirement implies that the credit is a reduction in the cost of the asset, not an adjustment of income tax expense.

d.   Finally, by instituting or suspending the investment credit as desired to attempt the stimulation or curtailment of business activity, the Federal government uses the investment credit as an instrument of fiscal policy.   The credit results in "cash in hand" in the period it enters into the determination of the final tax bill, available without restraint for any business purpose that management may elect. Accounting should not obscure the resulting impact on corporate earnings.

58.   Advocates of the deferral method likewise offer several arguments to support reflecting the investment credit in financial accounting income in those periods and on the same basis as the cost of the acquired property giving rise to the investment credit enters into the determination of net income:

a.   The investment credit arises from the simultaneous existence of two sets of conditions: (1) the acquisition of property qualifying for the credit and (2) the incurrence of income taxes otherwise payable from operations or events unrelated to the investment credit.   The incentive which the investment credit contains, as well as the genesis of the investment credit and its magnitude, are directly related to the acquisition of qualifying property.   Further, the holding of the property during a stipulated time period is also required . . . .   The investment credit is, therefore, primarily associated with the property which gives rise to the credit. Deferral of the investment credit and amortization of it over the periods of useful life of the property which gives rise to the credit result in associating the credit with those time periods with which the use of such property is associated. The matching thereby achieved is consistent with the objectives of income measurement.

b.   Permitting the investment credit to flow through to net income in the period the benefit is used to reduce income taxes payable may result in increasing or decreasing reported net income solely by reason of the timing of acquisitions, rather than by the use, of property.   The result is inconsistent with the accepted concept that income results from the use and not from the acquisition of assets.   Allocation of the investment credit to those periods in which the property which gave rise to the credit is utilized associates the income effects of the credit with the use of the property, not its acquisition.   This does not result in normalization of income as some have asserted, but results in the elimination of fluctuations in income arising from voluntary actions unrelated to the production of current income.

c.   A conclusion that the investment credit should flow through to income in the same year the benefit is used to reduce taxes payable places this one element of income tax expense on the cash basis of accounting.   Inasmuch as income taxes are an expense which involves accrual, deferral, and estimation concepts in much the same manner as these concepts apply to other expenses, all components of income tax expense should be subject to these accrual, deferral, and estimation concepts.   The investment credit is no different from many other transactions that affect cash inflow or outflow in a period but enter into the determination of income in different periods.

d. Many transactions of a business have a tax effect which (1) is reflected in income tax expense, but (2) is dependent upon some other transaction insofar as allocation and timing of the effect on income is concerned. The close association of the investment credit with the property which gives rise to such credit carries no implication that the credit is an element of the the cost of the property. Rather, it recognizes the investment credit for what it is—an element of income tax expense whose allocation and timing relate primarily to the item which gave rise to the credit, the property acquired.

e. To the extent that the Federal government has used the suspension and reinstatement of the investment credit as a matter of fiscal policy, there may be some effect on the decisions of corporate management with respect to the acquisition of qualifying property. Decisions as to property acquisitions, however, have no bearing on how periodic income should be determined and thus have no bearing on how the investment credit should be accounted for in financial statements. Property acquisitions have a prospective influence on earnings, whereas current earnings result from successful operations of the business of which the use of property, not its acquisition, is an integral part.

Opinion

59. The Board recognizes that each of the differing viewpoints expressed concerning the manner in which the investment credit should be accounted for possesses merit. However, it has concluded that the circumstances surrounding the investment credit do not justify alternative treatments. It also is aware that at present many, perhaps a majority of, companies account for the credit on a flow-through basis. However, the flow through method, because it reflects the entire effect of the credit in the year in which it is obtained, can result in substantial fluctuations in net income unrelated to current revenue-producing activities. The recent statutory increase in the amount of allowable credit may result in a significant increase in the magnitude of these fluctuations.

60. The Board concludes that allowable investment credits should be applied in the determination of income tax expense in the same periods and on the same basis as the costs of the acquired properties giving rise to the investment credits enter into the determination of pretax accounting income through provisions for depreciation or amortization. This conclusion recognizes that the investment credit is essentially an element of income tax expense, and that it additionally derives accounting significance from the *utilization* of the property to which it relates.

TREASURY DEPARTMENT RELEASE F–1075
November 8, 1967.

The Treasury Department today released a copy of a letter to the Accounting Principles Board of the American Institute of Certified Public Accountants expressing Treasury's views on the Board's proposed Opinion on accounting for income taxes. The Institute recently solicited views from interested parties on the APB's proposed Opinion, and Stanley S. Surrey, Assistant Secretary for Tax Policy, replied for the Treasury Department.

We submit the following comments in response to your solicitation of views on the Exposure Draft of the proposed APB Opinion on accounting for income taxes.

The Treasury Department has a substantial interest in the manner in which American business concerns report their Federal income tax liabilities. While the statutory corporate income tax rate is 48 percent, it is clear that the effective corporate tax rate on American business as a whole is considerably less than this. The reduction results from conscious decisions on the part of the Congress to achieve this lower effective tax rate on American business in general and on special industries in particular. The accounting approach suggested in the proposed APB Opinion would, however, in the aggregate, substantially overstate the tax liability of American business and present an inaccurate picture of our tax system. Since the tax liability would be substantially overstated in the aggregate, it would obviously also be overstated individually for the vast majority of United States corporations.

Congress has achieved this lower effective tax rate by a variety of means—artificial deductions structured to achieve a rate reduction (e. g., Western Hemisphere trade corporations), expensing of capital costs (e. g., intangible drilling expenses and certain research and development costs), fast tax write-offs (e. g. amortization of emergency facilities), expensing in excess of cost (e. g., depletion), creation of excessive reserves (e. g., financial institutions), capital gains rates (e. g., timber and livestock), special deferrals (e. g., shipping companies and life insurance companies), and credits (e. g., investment credit). The financial accounting treatment for each of these items of tax reduction are all facets of a single problem. Moreover, it appears that the treatment of these items does not readily fall within the framework of traditional accounting concepts. The proposed Opinion recognizes this fact. Thus, paragraph 37 of the Exposure Draft enumerates some of these items as presenting accounting problems still to be resolved.

The effect of the various deductions in these areas still to be resolved, as well as the intention behind their presence in the tax system, is to reduce the effective tax rate on companies in the particular industries involved (e. g., financial institutions, oil and gas exploration, stock life insurance companies, and certain United States steamship companies). For example, in the case of savings institutions, the tax reduction is achieved by what is recognized to be an unrealistic deduction for additions to reserves for bad debts.

The financial accounting of these institutions does not recognize these additions as charges to income. (While it may be contended that it is always possible that loss experience could utilize the reserve, this is so unlikely that prudent accounting does not take the possibility into account in reflecting current income.) This provision, once devoid of its technical characterization in the Internal Revenue Code, is seen to be simply a preferential tax rate made applicable to these institutions through the device of a bad debt reserve. A substantially identical tax result could have been achieved by a reduction in tax rates applicable to these institutions. Under this approach there would have been no doubt as to the accounting treatment of this reduction—it would have been recognized immediately.

In many of the preference situations mentioned above, the particular means of, achieving tax reduction is less important than the fact that there is a reduction. Most deductions could be structured as credits and, in turn, most deductions and credits could equally well be rate reductions. The financial accounting treatment of the tax reduction arising from the investment credit is a part of this broad problem. In this regard, the investment credit is designed to give a lower effective tax rate to companies modernizing or expanding their machinery and equipment.

When originally proposed the investment credit was to be allowed only on the excess of current investment over current depreciation charges on the theory that new investment equal to annual depreciation was normal investment necessary simply to maintain a company's status quo and would not represent a new level of investment effort. Under this form of the credit it would be difficult to say that' the investment credit would be associated with any particular asset. It would represent, rather, a selective tax reduction to those corporations engaged in modernization or expansion. The fact that the provision as finally enacted provided for an investment credit measured by a percentage of gross investment should not be viewed as determinative of the nature and accounting treatment of the credit.

The basic question to be resolved in the case of the investment credit, as well as in the case of the other preferences, is whether the financial accounting treatment of a tax reduction should depend on the mechanical method by which the reduction is measured or implemented in the statute. To seek a solution to the accounting treatment by following the manner in which these reductions are characterized within the Internal Revenue Code will surely lead to accounting inconsistencies because of the variation in the legislative approaches used in achieving these reductions. For example, the tax benefits enjoyed by Western Hemisphere trade corporations, certain cattle and timber sales, dividends received by corporations, etc., are also tax reduction measures. Yet, the benefits arising from these particular measures are recognized immediately for accounting purposes, because the technique by which they are implemented in the statute is regarded as relating more closely to a tax rate reduction. It appears basically inconsistent to recognize immediately the benefits of these tax reduction measures but then to defer the benefits of certain other tax reduction measures because they are artificially associated with assets or because it is possible under some circumstances they may "turn-around" in a later period. In many of these situations the "turn-around" was not viewed by the legislature as a real possibility. While we recognize that under traditional accounting concepts the future prospects of a particular corporation should be viewed with a degree of caution, given the present dynamic economy of this country and the commitment of our society to continued economic growth, such a view is not cautious, but unrealistically pessimistic.

In total, the preferences incorporated within the tax law clearly result in an effective corporate tax rate that is less than 48 percent. We believe that financial accounting should recognize this—both because it is the fact and because the stimulative effects resulting from the tax reduction should not be obscured.

The essential question is whether the characterization of a tax reduction in the Internal Revenue Code should control the accounting treatment of that reduction, when following such a ritualistic approach has these unfortunate consequences. It appears to us that an accounting approach must be developed that is capable of dealing appropriately and consistently with each item of tax reduction regardless of how it is implemented in the statute.

Special care must be exercised with respect to the investment credit because of its magnitude and because most companies would have to change their existing practice in response to the position taken in the APB Exposure Draft. Presumably, this will result in a massive restatement of earnings whose effects on the economy, while difficult to measure, could be serious. Furthermore, a mandate to defer the benefit arising from the investment credit could well blunt its effectiveness as an incentive to modernization and expansion.

The Treasury Department has said many times that it would like to look to the accounting profession for leadership in the computation of income for tax purposes, for these problems are essentially and historically accountants' problems. Obviously, there are areas where the tax law differs, and indeed must differ, from the accounting approach but in each such case there should be a compelling nonaccounting reason for this. We would view it as an unfortunate reversal for the accounting profession to be bound in its determination of income for financial reporting by the ad hoc characterizations and structures of tax benefits adopted in the Internal Revenue Code for the purpose of achieving selective tax reductions.

Chapter 9

LONG–TERM INDEBTEDNESS

1. INTRODUCTION

We have already dealt to some extent with long-term indebtedness, that is, debt which is not due to be repaid for an extended period of time, like the bonds in the *Hinds* case, page 291, supra. As a corollary of the extended maturity date, such indebtedness almost always contains some provision for the payment of interest, as both types of bonds involved in *Hinds* did.

We have also previously considered accounting for interest costs in a variety of contexts, including the question of whether in some circumstances interest paid during one year should be deferred and charged to expense in later years. The starting point is of course the normal rule that the cost of borrowing should be charged to current expense in each period in which the company has the benefit of the use of the borrowed funds. It is worth underscoring the difference in this regard between funds obtained by borrowing and amounts received upon the issuance of capital stock (often referred to as "equity"): unlike interest on debt, dividends paid on stock do not constitute an expense (and hence do not reduce net income), but rather are viewed as a return to the equity owners out of net income (or surplus). This dichotomy in treatment makes the distinction between debt and equity of considerable importance. However, while it is easy enough to distinguish between, say, a demand loan from a bank and an investment in common stock, there is a good deal less difference between, say, long-term bonds and preferred stock where the two have similar rates of return, and still less between an "income bond", i. e., one on which the interest is payable only if earned, and a mandatory preferred stock, i. e., one where the dividend must be paid if earned. Another borderline kind of case is debt which is convertible into stock, that is, can be exchanged for shares of stock on some specified exchange ratio, a hybrid security which presents its own special problems.

Generally speaking, the ingredients of a valid debt instrument are a promise to pay a sum certain (the "principal"), on demand, or on a specific date (or dates, if payable in installments), with a specified rate of interest during the interim. When the debt instruments are to be held by the public, they are typically divided into units of $1,000 of principal, and it is to these instruments that the term

559

"bonds" is usually applied, although when they are not secured, by a mortgage on fixed assets or otherwise, the instruments are often referred to as "debentures". Relatively short-term obligations, whether held by the public, a small group, or even a single private lender, are usually called "notes". "Registered" debt obligations are issued to named holders, like shares of stock, and the specified interest is mailed to the holders, annually or more often, according to the terms of the obligations. "Coupon" instruments are simply payable to whoever holds them (the "bearer"), and the right to interest is represented by a series of coupons attached to the obligation, which are detached seriatim on the specified dates and turned in to the debtor or its agent for payment.

2.　DISCOUNT (AND PREMIUM) ON DEBT

The problems arising in accounting for such indebtedness may be best approached by considering a concrete example. Assume that on January 1, 1980 a corporation issues 20-year, $1,000 bonds in the total amount of $1,000,000, bearing interest at 10%. Normally the price paid by the public buyers will not be exactly $1,000 per bond, because the specified interest rate, which is generally set at a reasonably round figure for administrative convenience, usually does not represent the precise rate that the market "sets" at the moment of issue. In order to adjust for this difference, the actual price paid by the buyers will be either a little less than $1,000 per bond, reflecting the need for a higher interest rate, or a little more than $1,000 per bond, reflecting the fact that the buyers are willing to accept a lower rate of interest. Thus if the bonds bring only $950 each (which in market parlance would be referred to as an issuance "at 95", since bonds are usually quoted in terms of $100, even though the bonds themselves are normally in units of $1,000 each), it means that the market demanded a higher rate of interest than 10%, and of course the $100 per year which will be paid on each bond represents more than 10% on the $950 per bond actually invested by the buyer. In addition, there is the extra $50 which the company must pay at maturity when the full $1,000 principal amount of the bonds comes due, and this excess of the principal amount due at maturity over the amount actually received from the lender, normally referred to as "discount", is simply another element of cost to the borrower (and income to the lender) for the use of the borrowed funds—in other words, additional interest. (In the converse case, when the buyer pays more for a bond than the principal amount due at maturity, thereby producing a lower interest rate than the one specified, this spread is referred to as "premium".)

The foregoing is a capsule description of the subject addressed in APB Op. No. 21, supra at pages 394–399, which should be reviewed at this point. Although Opinion No. 21 applies to a wide spectrum of receivables and payables, it is of particular importance in dealing with bonds and other relatively long-term liabilities.

In pursuing the issues involved, let us use an example with terms paralleling those referred to in Example 2 in the Appendix to Op. No. 21: hence, assume that our 20-year 10% bonds bring only $851 per bond upon issuance, resulting in a discount of $149 per bond (a total of $149,000 on the full $1,000,000 of bonds issued). Obviously, the market demanded an interest rate substantially higher than 10%, and the actual rate of interest can be determined by using present value tables to compute the interest rate implicit in a transaction in which the creditor "lends" $851 to obtain an annual return of $100 on the loan for 20 years, plus an additional $149 at the end of the 20 years when he receives the full $1,000 at maturity. As Example 2 in the Appendix to Op. No. 21 indicates, the interest rate is 12%, because that is the interest rate at which the sum of (1) the right to receive $100 per year for 20 years, plus (2) the right to receive $1,000 at the end of 20 years, has a present worth of $851. As noted above, the discount of $149 per bond, or $149,000 on the entire bond issue, really constitutes additional interest in the transaction; therefore, the true nature of the deal is a loan of $851,000 for 20 years, with interest payable at the rate of $100,000 per year for 20 years plus an additional $149,000 of interest payable at the end of the twentieth year.

How should this transaction be treated in the financial statements of the borrower? One alternative would be simply to record the liability on the company's balance sheet at the true amount of the borrowing, $851,000, thereby exactly balancing the amount of the cash received. While this would mean that the balance sheet would not reflect the full face amount of the bonds, for which the company is liable at maturity, the maturity date is after all many years away (at least absent any default which would accelerate the maturity of the bonds), and disclosure of the face amount in a footnote might be regarded as sufficient. Regardless of how the liability is initially recorded, it is necessary to account each year not only for the annual interest of $100,000 actually paid but also for an appropriate portion of that extra $149,000 of interest which must be paid at maturity; each of the twenty years should bear its fair share of that additional interest cost, rather than leaving it all to be charged to interest expense at the end of the twentieth year. This is simply one more variant of the basic theme that recognition of expense (or income) is not controlled by when cash moves; hence, the usual entry for accruing an expense before cash is paid, a debit to Interest Expense and a credit to Interest Expense Payable, could be made each year. More likely, the credit would be made to the Bonds Payable account: increasing that account each year would help to underscore the fact that each passing year brings closer the maturity date of the bonds when that additional $149,000, along with the $851,000 originally invested, will be due and payable.

As to the amount of interest expense to be accrued each year (in addition to the $100,000 actually paid), the simplest approach would be to charge one-twentieth of the total $149,000 to each of the twenty years, thereby allocating the total discount equally among the twenty years involved. However, this simple "straight-line" method does not take account of the fact that this additional interest component does not have to be actually paid until the end of the twenty years, so that the true burden of this additional interest cost is smaller at the beginning of the term when the need to actually pay is furthest away, but rises with each successive year as the time for making the payment draws closer. (Just as the value of $1 in hand today is greater than the value of $1 to be received a year from now, so the burden of having to pay $1 a year from now is less than the burden of paying $1 today.) It should also be noted that the liability on the bonds would be increasing each year, by virtue of the annual accrual of this additional interest component (assuming that the annual accrual, however measured, is being added to the Bonds Payable account); this too would suggest that the annual interest expense should be higher each year. Accordingly, the preferred approach is to use an "increasing-charges" method of allocating the total discount (a kind of converse of the declining-charges method of allocating depreciation), under which the amount of additional interest accrued each year would increase, conforming to the increase in the Bonds Payable account at the beginning of the year. Specifically, the figure for the additional interest to be accrued each year would be that amount which, when added to the $100,000 of interest expense for the year, would equal the product of the "real" interest rate in the transaction, here 12%, times the amount in the Bonds Payable account at the beginning of that year. To illustrate, assuming that during the first year the Bonds Payable account would show $851,000, the total interest expense for the first year should be 12% times $851,000 or $102,120; therefore, $2,120 should be accrued as additional interest expense and credited to the Bonds Payable account. At the beginning of the second year, the Bonds Payable account would show $853,120, so the total interest for the year should be $102,374 (12% x $853,120); accordingly, $2,374 should be accrued as additional interest expense, and added to the Bonds Payable account. For the third year the total interest expense should be 12% x $855,494, or $102,659, so $2,659 should be accrued as additional interest expense and added to the Bonds Payable account. This same process would continue throughout the twenty year period.

In actual practice the accounting for long-term debt is usually somewhat different from the foregoing description, largely because it is thought desirable for the Bonds Payable account on the balance sheet to show the full amount for which the company will ultimately be liable. Hence the most common approach is to credit the Bonds Payable account with the full principal liability at the outset, and to carry the discount as a direct deduction from this figure. Thus in our illustration the balance sheet representation at the outset would be as follows:

Bonds Payable (at face)	$1,000,000
Less: Discount (based on original issue price of $851,000)	149,000
Bonds Payable less Discount	$851,000

Note that just as the Allowance for Uncollectibles account, though carried on the left-hand side of the balance sheet as an offset to Accounts Receivable, is the functional equivalent of a right-hand estimated liability account, so the Discount account, carried on the right-hand side of the balance sheet as an offset to Bonds Payable, is the functional equivalent of a left-hand deferred interest expense asset. (Although the discount has not actually been paid in advance, in accounting effect it is viewed as though it had been, as a corollary of recording the full liability on the bonds.) Indeed, under earlier practice discount was often actually carried on the left-hand side of the balance sheet, but ¶ 16 of Op. No. 21 unqualifiedly rejects that treatment, in favor of the direct deduction approach.

Pursuant to this mode of presentation, when the additional interest expense, representing the allocation of the discount, is accrued each year, the credit is to the Discount account rather than to Bonds Payable; but of course the result is exactly the same, since the reduction of an offsetting subsidiary account produces the same net result as an increase in the principal account. This process further points up the similarity of a Discount account to a deferred expense asset, since such an asset is normally charged off against income over time by charges to a current expense, with corresponding credits to the deferred expense asset; hence, it is not surprising that the process of accruing additional interest expense each year with a credit to the Discount account, is often referred to as "amortization" of the discount, as it is in ¶ 15 of Op. No. 21 (and of course the "interest" method of amortization mentioned there is the increasing-charges mode of allocating discount detailed above). At the end of year 3, then, the

Bonds Payable item in our illustration would appear on the company's balance sheet as follows:

Bonds Payable (at face)	$1,000,000
Less: Unamortized Discount	141,847
Bonds Payable less Unamortized Discount	$858,153

PROBLEM

X Corp. was an insolvent tobacco company being administered in federal bankruptcy proceedings. Y Co., a large publicly-held corporation, offered to purchase X's principal asset, its inventory of tobacco, for $4,000,000, payable in unsecured ten-year notes bearing interest at 8% per year. When X's creditors, who had become in effect the owners of X's property, appeared hesitant about accepting, Y offered them the alternative of 90% in cash, in lieu of the face amount of the notes to which they would be entitled. One-half of the X creditors elected the cash option, receiving $1,800,000. The remaining half accepted the notes, receiving $2,000,000 in face amount. How should Y Co. have recorded those notes on its financial statements? Is it relevant that the notes traded in the over-the-counter market at prices ranging from $90 to $100 during the first few months after they were issued?

3. ISSUE EXPENSE

Obviously, the issuance of bonds or notes, especially to the public, can cost substantial sums, for legal, accounting, and printing expenses, as well as for underwriting or other selling commissions. If in our illustrative example the underwriting commissions on the issuance of the $1,000,000 (in face amount) of bonds amounted to $50,000, and the rest of the expenses totaled $30,000, the company would end up with only $771,000 in net proceeds from the offering. It would be no more appropriate to charge all of this expense to the year of issuance than it would to charge the entire discount to that year (or to the year the bonds mature); instead, these issue expenses too should be allocated over the term of the bonds. The appropriate method is to set up the total issue costs as a deferred expense asset, as the last sentence of ¶ 16 of Op. No. 21 indicates, and then amortize the asset over the twenty years for which the bonds will be outstanding, presumably on a simple, straight-line basis. (By way of contrast, the costs associated with the issuance of stock are usually treated as a reduction of the proceeds received, or perhaps as a direct charge against retained earnings, and hence do not affect net income in any period, although apparently some companies do defer such costs and then amortize them, in a manner akin to the treatment of organization expenses.)

4. PREMATURE TERMINATION OF INDEBTEDNESS

Suppose a bond issue is terminated prior to maturity. Since any discount or issue expense will not have been completely amortized, the question arises as to how to account for those unamortized amounts. For example, assume in connection with the illustration used above that at the end of year 10, when the discount has been reduced to approximately $102,000 (so that the figure on the balance sheet for Bonds Payable less Unamortized Discount would stand at approximately $898,000), and the Deferred Issue Expense asset would have been reduced to $40,000, the company elects to "call" the bonds, that is, pay them off, pursuant to an option contained in the original bond agreement. (Often such an option to terminate a borrowing prior to maturity is conditioned upon the payment of a penalty to the bondholders, generally termed a "call premium".) At first blush it might seem that the company would have little choice but to charge the unamortized discount and issue expense (plus any call premium) to current expense in the year of the termination, since the end of the borrowing means there will not be any future benefit from the borrowed funds with which these items were associated. However, when the source of the funds to pay off the existing bonds is a new issue of bonds (a transaction usually described as a "refunding"), the company is in fact continuing to enjoy the benefit of borrowed funds, giving rise to an argument that in such circumstances these amounts (i. e., the unamortized discount and issue expense associated with the terminated borrowing, together with any call premium) should be amortized over what would have been the remaining duration of the terminated borrowing, or perhaps even treated as a cost associated with the new borrowing and hence amortized over the life of the new debt issue. These arguments were put to rest in 1972 by the Accounting Principles Board:

APB OPINION NO. 26 *

Accounting Principles Board, 1972.

Early Extinguishment of Debt

INTRODUCTION

1. Debt is frequently extinguished in various ways before its scheduled maturity. Generally, the amount paid upon reacquisition

---

* Copyright ⓒ by the American Institute of Certified Public Accountants, Inc.

of debt securities will differ from the net carrying amount of the debt at that time. This Opinion expresses the views of the Accounting Principles Board regarding the appropriate accounting for that difference.

2. *Applicability.* This Opinion applies to the early extinguishment of all kinds of debt . . . [except the conversion of convertible debt].

3. *Definitions.* Several terms are used in this Opinion as follows:

    a. *Early Extinguishment* is the reacquisition of any form of debt security or instrument before its scheduled maturity except through conversion by the holder . . . . All open-market or mandatory reacquisitions of debt securities to meet sinking fund requirements are early extinguishments.

    b. *Net Carrying Amount* of debt is the amount due at maturity, adjusted for unamortized premium, discount, and cost of issuance.

    c. *Reacquisition Price* of debt is the amount paid on early extinguishment, including a call premium and miscellaneous costs of reacquisition. If early extinguishment is achieved by a direct exchange of new securities, the reacquisition price is the total present value of the new securities.

    d. *Difference* as used in this Opinion is the excess of the reacquisition price over the net carrying amount or the excess of the net carrying amount over the reacquisition price.

DISCUSSION

4. *Current Practice.* Early extinguishment of debt is usually achieved in one of three ways: use of existing liquid assets, use of proceeds from issuance of equity securities, and use of proceeds from issuing other debt securities. The replacement of debt with other debt is frequently called refunding.

5. Differences on nonrefunding extinguishments are generally treated currently in income as losses or gains. Three basic methods are generally accepted to account for the differences on refunding transactions:

    a. Amortization over the remaining original life of the extinguished issue.

    b. Amortization over the life of the new issue.

    c. Recognition currently in income as a loss or gain.

Each method has been supported in court decisions, in rulings of regulatory agencies, and in accounting literature.

6. *Amortization Over Life of Old Issue.* Some accountants believe that the difference on refunding should be amortized over the remaining original life of the extinguished issue. In effect, the difference is regarded as an adjustment of the cash cost of borrowing that arises from obtaining another arrangement for the unexpired term of the old agreement. Therefore, the cost of money over the remaining period of the original issue is affected by the difference that results upon extinguishment of the original contract. Early ex-

tinguishment occurs for various reasons, but usually because it is financially advantageous to the issuer, for example, if the periodic cash interest outlay can be reduced for future periods. Accordingly, under this view the difference should be spread over the unexpired term of the original issue to obtain the proper periodic cost of borrowed money. If the maturity date of the new issue precedes the maturity date of the original issue, a portion of the difference is amortized over the life of the new debt and the balance of the difference is recognized currently in income as a loss or gain.

7. *Amortization Over Life of New Issue.* Some accountants believe that the difference on refunding should be amortized over the life of the new issue if refunding occurs because of lower current interest rates or anticipated higher interest rates in the future. Under this view, the principal motivation for refunding is to establish a more favorable interest rate over the term of the new issue. Therefore, the expected benefits to be obtained over the life of the new issue justify amortization of the difference over the life of the new issue.

8. *Recognition Currently in Income.* Some accountants believe a difference on refunding is similar to the difference on other early extinguishments and should be recognized currently in income in the period of the extinguishment. This view holds that the value of the old debt has changed over time and that paying the call price or current market value is the most favorable way to extinguish the debt. The change in the market value of the debt is caused by a change in the market rate of interest, but the change has not been reflected in the accounts. Therefore, the entire difference is recorded when the specific contract is terminated because it relates to the past periods when the contract was in effect. If the accountant had foreseen future events perfectly at the time of issuance, he would have based the accounting on the assumption that the maturity value of the debt would equal the reacquisition price. Thus, no difference upon early extinguishment would occur because previous periods would have borne the proper interest expense. Furthermore, a call premium necessary to eliminate an old contract and an unamortized discount or premium relate to the old contract and cannot be a source of benefits from a new debt issue. For example, a larger (or smaller) coupon rate could have been set on the old issue to avoid an unamortized discount (or premium) at issuance. When such debt originally issued at par is refunded, few accountants maintain that some portion of past interest should be capitalized and written off over the remaining life of the old debt or over the life of the new debt.

9. Another argument in favor of current recognition of the difference as gain or loss is also related to market forces but is expressed differently. If debt is callable, the call privilege is frequently exercised when the market value of the bonds as determined by the current yield rate exceeds the call price. A loss or gain is recognized on extinguishing the debt because an exchange transaction occurs in which the call or current market value of the debt differs from its net carrying amount. For example, the market value of the debt ordinarily rises as the market rate of interest falls. If market values were recorded as the market rate of interest fluctuates, the changes in

the market value of the debt would have been recorded periodically as losses or gains. The bond liability would not exceed the call price.

10.   On the other hand, some accountants holding views opposing current recognition of the difference in income believe that recognizing the difference as gains or losses may induce a company to report income by borrowing money at high rates of interest in order to pay off discounted low-rate debt. Conversely, a large potential charge to income may discourage refunding even though it is economically desirable; the replacement of high cost debt with low cost debt may result in having to recognize a large loss. Thus, a company may show higher current income in the year of extinguishment while increasing its economic cost of debt and lower current income while decreasing its economic cost of debt. For these reasons, these accountants favor deferral.

*   *   *

16.   *Economic Nature of Extinguishment.* In many respects the essential economics of the decision leading to the early extinguishment of outstanding debt are the same, regardless of whether such debt is extinguished via the use of the existing liquid assets, new equity securities, or new debt. That is, the decision favoring early extinguishment usually implies that the net present value of future cash inflows and outflows is maximized by extinguishing the debt now rather than by letting it run to maturity. The savings may be in lower cash interest costs on a new debt issue, in increased earnings per share of common stock if the assets are not earning the interest rate on the outstanding debt, or in some other form. The essential event is early extinguishment. Under this view, the difference is associated with extinguishing the existing debt and is accounted for the same regardless of how extinguishment is accomplished.

17.   To illustrate that view, assume that three firms each have long-term debt outstanding with ten years remaining to maturity. The first firm may have excess cash and no investment opportunities that earn a rate of return higher than the cash savings that would ensue from immediately extinguishing the debt. The second firm may wish to replace the debt with a similar issue bearing a lower coupon rate. The third firm may have excessive debt and may want to replace the debt with a new issue of common stock. The underlying reason for the early extinguishment in all three cases is to obtain a perceived economic advantage. The relevant comparison in the replacement of debt with other debt is with the costs of other debt. The comparison in other cases is with other means of financing. The means by which the debt is extinguished have no bearing on how to account for the loss or gain.

OPINION
*   *   *

19.   *Reduction of Alternatives.* The Board concludes that all extinguishments of debt before scheduled maturities are fundamentally alike. The accounting for such transactions should be the same regardless of the means used to achieve the extinguishment.

20.   *Disposition of Amounts.* A difference between the reacquisition price and the net carrying amount of the extinguished debt

should be recognized currently in income of the period of extinguishment as losses or gains and identified as a separate item. The criteria in APB Opinion No. [30] * should be used to determine whether the losses or gains are ordinary or extraordinary items. Gains and losses should not be amortized to future periods.

21. *Convertible Debt.* The extinguishment of convertible debt before maturity does not change the character of the security as between debt and equity at that time. Therefore, a difference between the cash acquisition price of the debt and its net carrying amount should be recognized currently in income in the period of extinguishment as losses or gains.

* * *

QUESTION

Under Op. No. 26 any call premium incurred in refunding existing debt is in effect treated in the same way as unamortized discount and issue expense, and charged against income in the year of the refunding. Is there a basis for treating call premium differently?

5. "RESTRUCTURING" OF DEBT

In recent years one of the most significant accounting problems relating to debt has been how to handle modifications of debt which result from the debtor's inability to meet its original commitments. For example, suppose a creditor decides that its chances of getting repaid would be improved by agreeing to an adjustment of the terms of the loan, perhaps by reducing the current interest rate (or even the principal) to a more manageable amount from the debtor's point of view. Such transactions were quite common in the middle 1970's, especially in connection with mortgage loans which were jeopardized by high interest rates and a worsening economic climate. If a reduction in the principal amount were viewed as a pro tanto "extinguishment" under APB Op. No. 26, the debtor would have to recognize gain on the transaction (and the creditor would presumably show a loss); and the same might be said of a reduction of the interest rate, since there seems little reason to treat the two cases differently. But there is a certain irony in finding that a company has increased its income as a result of its financial position being so insecure that its creditors are willing to make significant concessions in their own self-interest. On the other side of the coin, the banks and other financial institutions who were the chief holders of such troubled debt (one notable example being New York City municipal obligations, which were candidates for various kinds of restructuring)

---

* [Ed. note]. The original reference here was to APB Op. No. 9, but that has been viewed as amended since Op. No. 9 was superseded by Op. No. 30.

were anxious to avoid showing significant losses, or at least to delay showing such losses as long as possible. In 1975 this was a very hot potato requiring immediate FASB attention, but the Board's initial response (in FASB No. 4, which follows immediately below) was quite limited; it was not until 1977 that a comprehensive resolution of the problem was reached (in FASB No. 15, set out below right after FASB No. 4), a resolution which was greeted with an audible sigh of relief by the financial community.

STATEMENT OF FINANCIAL ACCOUNTING STANDARDS NO. 4 *

Financial Accounting Standard Board, 1975.

Reporting Gains and Losses From Extinguishment of Debt

(An amendment of APB Opinion No. 30)

INTRODUCTION AND BACKGROUND INFORMATION

* * *

2. . . . APB Opinion No. 30 and the related Accounting Interpretation issued by the AICPA staff [see pages 192–194, supra] can be read literally to preclude classifying most if not all gains or losses from early extinguishment of debt as an extraordinary item in the income statement.

3. Since the effective date of APB Opinion No. 30, the Board has had inquiries regarding that Opinion because application of the criteria . . . appears to preclude classifying gains or losses from most transactions or events as extraordinary items in the income statement. Many respondents [also] suggested that the conclusions of APB Opinion No. 26 relating to *early* extinguishment of debt be reconsidered . . . ..

4. The Board concluded that the pervasiveness of [the issues involved in or related to Opinion No. 26] makes broad reconsideration . . . a more comprehensive undertaking than can be accomplished in the near future. The Board also . . . concluded that there is insufficient experience under [Opinion No. 30] to warrant a general reconsideration of the criteria set forth therein at this time.

5. . . . The Board believes that an immediate response is needed to the concern expressed regarding income statement classification of gains and losses from certain extinguishments of debt . . . ..

* * *

STANDARDS OF FINANCIAL ACCOUNTING
AND REPORTING

Income Statement Classification

8. Gains and losses from extinguishment of debt that are included in the determination of net income shall be aggregated and, if material, classified as an extraordinary item, net of related income tax effect. That conclusion shall apply whether an extinguishment is early or at scheduled maturity date or later. The conclusion does not apply, however, to gains or losses from cash purchases of debt made to satisfy current or future sinking-fund requirements. Those gains and losses shall be aggregated and the amount shall be identified as a separate item.

*   *   *

Amendment to Existing Pronouncement

10. This Statement amends APB Opinion No. 30 only to the extent that classification of gains or losses from extinguishment of debt as an extraordinary item pursuant to the first two sentences of paragraph 8 of this Statement shall be made without regard to the criteria in paragraph 20 of that Opinion.

*   *   *

STATEMENT OF FINANCIAL ACCOUNTING
STANDARDS NO. 15 *

Financial Accounting Standard Board, 1977.

Accounting by Debtors and Creditors for Troubled
Debt Restructurings

INTRODUCTION

1. This Statement establishes standards of financial accounting and reporting by the debtor and by the creditor for a troubled debt restructuring. The Statement does not cover accounting for allowances for estimated uncollectible amounts and does not prescribe or proscribe particular methods for estimating amounts of uncollectible receivables.

2. A restructuring of a debt constitutes a *troubled debt restructuring* for purposes of this Statement if the creditor for economic or legal reasons related to the debtor's financial difficulties grants a concession to the debtor that it would not otherwise consider. That concession either stems from an agreement between the creditor and the debtor or is imposed by law or a court. For example, a creditor may restructure the terms of a debt to alleviate the burden of the debtor's near-term cash requirements, and many troubled debt restructurings involve modifying terms to reduce or defer cash

* Copyright © by Financial Accounting
Standards Board, 1977. See acknowledgement, page xviii, supra.

payments required of the debtor in the near future to help the debtor attempt to improve its financial condition and eventually be able to pay the creditor. Or, for example, the creditor may accept cash, other assets, or an equity interest in the debtor in satisfaction of the debt though the value received is less than the amount of the debt because the creditor concludes that step will maximize recovery of its investment.

3. Whatever the form of concession granted by the creditor to the debtor in a troubled debt restructuring, the creditor's objective is to make the best of a difficult situation. That is, the creditor expects to obtain more cash or other value from the debtor, or to increase the probability of receipt by granting the concession than by not granting it.

4. In this Statement, a *receivable* or *payable* (collectively referred to as *debt*) represents a contractual right to receive money or a contractual obligation to pay money on demand or on fixed or determinable dates that is already included as an asset or liability in the creditor's or debtor's balance sheet at the time of the restructuring. Receivables or payables that may be involved in troubled debt restructurings commonly result from lending or borrowing of cash, investing in debt securities that were previously issued, or selling or purchasing goods or services on credit. Examples are accounts receivable or payable, notes, debentures and bonds (whether those receivables or payables are secured or unsecured and whether they are convertible or nonconvertible), and related accrued interest, if any.

. . .

5. A troubled debt restructuring may include, but is not necessarily limited to, one or a combination of the following:

    a. Transfer from the debtor to the creditor of receivables from third parties, real estate, or other assets to satisfy fully or partially a debt (including a transfer resulting from foreclosure or repossession).

    b. Issuance or other granting of an equity interest to the creditor by the debtor to satisfy fully or partially a debt unless the equity interest is granted pursuant to existing terms for converting the debt into an equity interest.

    c. Modification of terms of a debt, such as one or a combination of:

        1. Reduction (absolute or contingent) of the stated interest rate for the remaining original life of the debt.

        2. Extension of the maturity date or dates at a stated interest rate lower than the current market rate for new debt with similar risk.

        3. Reduction (absolute or contingent) of the face amount or maturity amount of the debt as stated in the instrument or other agreement.

        4. Reduction (absolute or contingent) of accrued interest.

6. Troubled debt restructurings may occur before, at, or after the stated maturity of debt, and time may elapse between the agreement, court order, etc. and the transfer of assets or equity interest,

the effective date of new terms, or the occurrence of another event that constitutes consummation of the restructuring. The date of consummation is the *time of the restructuring* in this Statement.

7. A debt restructuring is not necessarily a troubled debt restructuring for purposes of this Statement even if the debtor is experiencing some financial difficulties. For example, a troubled debt restructuring is not involved if (a) the fair value of cash, other assets, or an equity interest accepted by a creditor from a debtor in full satisfaction of its receivable at least equals the creditor's recorded investment in the receivable; (b) the fair value of cash, other assets, or an equity interest transferred by a debtor to a creditor in full settlement of its payable at least equals the debtor's carrying amount of the payable; (c) the creditor reduces the effective interest rate on the debt primarily to reflect a decrease in market interest rates in general or a decrease in the risk so as to maintain a relationship with a debtor that can readily obtain funds from other sources at the current market interest rate; or (d) the debtor issues in exchange for its debt new marketable debt having an effective interest rate based on its market price that is at or near the current market interest rates of debt with similar maturity dates and stated interest rates issued by nontroubled debtors. In general, a debtor that can obtain funds from sources other than the existing creditor at market interest rates at or near those for nontroubled debt is not involved in a troubled debt restructuring. A debtor in a troubled debt restructuring can obtain funds from sources other than the existing creditor in the troubled debt restructuring, if at all, only at effective interest rates (based on market prices) so high that it cannot afford to pay them. Thus, in an attempt to protect as much of its investment as possible, the creditor in a troubled debt restructuring grants a concession to the debtor that it would not otherwise consider.

*   *   *

STANDARDS OF FINANCIAL ACCOUNTING AND REPORTING

Accounting by Debtors

12. A debtor shall account for a troubled debt restructuring according to the type of the restructuring as prescribed in the following paragraphs.

Transfer of Assets in Full Settlement

13. A debtor that transfers its receivables from third parties, real estate, or other assets to a creditor to settle fully a payable shall recognize a gain on restructuring of payables (see paragraph 21). The gain shall be measured by the excess of (i) the carrying amount of the payable settled (the face amount increased or decreased by applicable accrued interest and applicable unamortized premium, discount, finance charges, or issue costs) over (ii) the fair value of the assets transferred to the creditor. The fair value of the assets transferred is the amount that the debtor could reasonably expect to receive for them in a current sale between a willing buyer and a willing seller, that is, other than in a forced or liquidation sale. . . .

14.   A difference between the fair value and the carrying amount of assets transferred to a creditor to settle a payable is a gain or loss on transfer of assets. The debtor shall include that gain or loss in measuring net income for the period of transfer, reported as provided in *APB Opinion No. 30*, "Reporting the Results of Operations."

*   *   *

Modification of Terms

16.   A debtor in a troubled debt restructuring involving only modification of terms of a payable—that is, not involving a transfer of assets or grant of an equity interest—shall account for the effects of the restructuring prospectively from the time of restructuring, and shall not change the carrying amount of the payable at the time of the restructuring unless the carrying amount exceeds the total future cash payments specified by the new terms.[9]   That is, the effects of changes in the amounts or timing (or both) of future cash payments designated as either interest or face amount shall be reflected in future periods.   Interest expense shall be computed in a way that a constant effective interest rate is applied to the carrying amount of the payable at the beginning of each period between restructuring and maturity (in substance the "interest" method prescribed by paragraph 15 of *APB Opinion No. 21*).   The new effective interest rate shall be the discount rate that equates the present value of the future cash payments specified by the new terms (excluding amounts contingently payable) with the carrying amount of the payable.

17.   If, however, the total future cash payments specified by the new terms of a payable, including both payments designated as interest and those designated as face amount, are less than the carrying amount of the payable, the debtor shall reduce the carrying amount to an amount equal to the total future cash payments specified by the new terms and shall recognize a gain on restructuring of payables equal to the amount of the reduction (see paragraph 21).[11]   Thereafter, all cash payments under the terms of the payable shall be accounted for as reductions of the carrying amount of the payable, and no interest expense shall be recognized on the payable for any period between the restructuring and maturity of the payable.[12]

18.   A debtor shall not recognize a gain on a restructured payable involving indeterminate future cash payments as long as the maximum total future cash payments may exceed the carrying amount of the

9.   In this Statement, *total future cash payments* includes related accrued interest, if any, at the time of the restructuring that continues to be payable under the new terms.

11.   If the carrying amount of the payable comprises several accounts (for example, face amount, accrued interest, and unamortized premium, discount finance charges, and issue costs) that are to be continued after the restructuring, some possibly being combined, the reduction in carrying amount may need to be allocated among the remaining accounts in proportion to the previous balances. However, the debtor may choose to carry the amount designated as face amount by the new terms in a separate account and adjust another account accordingly.

12.   The only exception is to recognize interest expense according to paragraph 22.

payable. Amounts designated either as interest or as face amount by the new terms may be payable contingent on a specified event or circumstance (for example, the debtor may be required to pay specified amounts if its financial condition improves to a specified degree within a specified period). To determine whether the debtor shall recognize a gain according to the provisions of paragraphs 16 and 17, those contingent amounts shall be included in the "total future cash payments specified by the new terms" to the extent necessary to prevent recognizing a gain at the time of restructuring that may be offset by future interest expense. Thus, the debtor shall apply paragraph 17 of *FASB Statement No. 5*, "Accounting for Contingencies," in which probability of occurrence of a gain contingency is not a factor, and shall assume that contingent future payments will have to be paid. The same principle applies to amounts of future cash payments that must sometimes be estimated to apply the provisions of paragraphs 16 and 17. For example, if the number of future interest payments is flexible because the face amount and accrued interest is payable on demand or becomes payable on demand, estimates of total future cash payments shall be based on the maximum number of periods possible under the restructured terms.

Combination of Types

19. A troubled debt restructuring may involve partial settlement of a payable by the debtor's transferring assets or granting an equity interest (or both) to the creditor and modification of terms of the remaining payable. A debtor shall account for a troubled debt restructuring involving a partial settlement and a modification of terms as prescribed in paragraphs 16–18 except that, first, assets transferred or an equity interest granted in that partial settlement shall be measured as prescribed in paragraphs 13 and 15, respectively, and the carrying amount of the payable shall be reduced by the total fair value of those assets or equity interest. A difference between the fair value and the carrying amount of assets transferred to the creditor shall be recognized as a gain or loss on transfer of assets. No gain on restructuring of payables shall be recognized unless the remaining carrying amount of the payable exceeds the total future cash payments (including amounts contingently payable) specified by the terms of the debt remaining unsettled after the restructuring. Future interest expense, if any, shall be determined according to the provisions of paragraphs 16–18.

Related Matters

*   *   *

21. Gains on restructuring of payables determined by applying the provisions of paragraphs 13–20 of this Statement shall be aggregated, included in measuring net income for the period of restructuring, and, if material, classified as an extraordinary item, net of related income tax effect, in accordance with paragraph 8 of *FASB Statement No. 4*, "Reporting Gains and Losses from Extinguishment of Debt."

22. If a troubled debt restructuring involves amounts contingently payable, those contingent amounts shall be recognized as a payable and as interest expense in future periods in accordance with paragraph 8 of *FASB Statement No. 5*. Thus, in general, interest

expense for contingent payments shall be recognized in each period in which (a) it is probable that a liability has been incurred and (b) the amount of that liability can be reasonably estimated.   Before recognizing a payable and interest expense for amounts contingently payable, however, accrual or payment of those amounts shall be deducted from the carrying amount of the restructured payable to the extent that contingent payments included in "total future cash payments specified by the new terms" prevented recognition of a gain at the time of restructuring (paragraph 18).

23.   If amounts of future cash payments must be estimated to apply the provisions of paragraphs 16–18 because future interest payments are expected to fluctuate—for example, the restructured terms may specify the stated interest rate to be the prime interest rate increased by a specified amount or proportion—estimates of maximum total future payments shall be based on the interest rate in effect at the time of the restructuring. . . .

24.   Legal fees and other direct costs that a debtor incurs in granting an equity interest to a creditor in a troubled debt restructuring shall reduce the amount otherwise recorded for that equity interest according to paragraphs 15 and 19.   All other direct costs that a debtor incurs to effect a troubled debt restructuring shall be deducted in measuring gain on restructuring of payables or shall be included in expense for the period if no gain on restructuring is recognized.

*   *   *

Accounting by Creditors

27.   A creditor shall account for a troubled debt restructuring according to the type of the restructuring as prescribed in the following paragraphs. . . .

Receipt of Assets in Full Satisfaction

28.   A creditor that receives from a debtor in full satisfaction of a receivable either (i) receivables from third parties, real estate, or other assets or (ii) shares of stock or other evidence of an equity interest in the debtor, or both, shall account for those assets (including an equity interest) at their fair value at the time of the restructuring (see paragraph 13 for how to measure fair value).   The excess of (i) the recorded investment in the receivable [17] satisfied over (ii) the fair value of assets received is a loss to be recognized according to paragraph 35.

29.   After a troubled debt restructuring, a creditor shall account for assets received in satisfaction of a receivable the same as if the assets had been acquired for cash.

17. *Recorded investment in the receivable* is used in paragraphs 28–41 instead of *carrying amount of the receivable* because the latter is net of an allowance for estimated uncollectible amounts or other "valuation" account, if any, while the former is not.

The recorded investment in the receivable is the face amount increased or decreased by applicable accrued interest and unamortized premium, discount, finance charges, or acquisition costs and may also reflect a previous direct write-down of the investment.

Modification of Terms

30. A creditor in a troubled debt restructuring involving only modification of terms of a receivable—that is, not involving receipt of assets (including an equity interest in the debtor)—shall account for the effects of the restructuring prospectively and shall not change the recorded investment in the receivable at the time of the restructuring unless that amount exceeds the total future cash receipts specified by the new terms. That is, the effects of changes in the amounts or timing (or both) of future cash receipts designated either as interest or as face amount shall be reflected in future periods. Interest income shall be computed in a way that a constant effective interest rate is applied to the recorded investment in the receivable at the beginning of each period between restructuring and maturity (in substance the "interest" method prescribed by paragraph 15 of *APB Opinion No. 21*). The new effective interest rate shall be the discount rate that equates the present value of the future cash receipts specified by the new terms (excluding amounts contingently receivable) with the recorded investment in the receivable.

31. If, however, the total future cash receipts specified by the new terms of the receivable, including both receipts designated as interest and those designated as face amount, are less than the recorded investment in the receivable before restructuring, the creditor shall reduce the recorded investment in the receivable to an amount equal to the total future cash receipts specified by the new terms. The amount of the reduction is a loss to be recognized according to paragraph 35. Thereafter, all cash receipts by the creditor under the terms of the restructured receivable, whether designated as interest or as face amount, shall be accounted for as recovery of the recorded investment in the receivable, and no interest income shall be recognized on the receivable for any period between the restructuring and maturity of the receivable.[21]

32. A creditor shall recognize a loss on a restructured receivable involving indeterminate future cash receipts unless the minimum future cash receipts specified by the new terms at least equals the recorded investment in the receivable. Amounts designated either as interest or as face amount that are receivable from the debtor may be contingent on a specified event or circumstance (for example, specified amounts may be receivable from the debtor if the debtor's financial condition improves to a specified degree within a specified period). To determine whether the creditor shall recognize a loss according to the provisions of paragraphs 30 and 31, those contingent amounts shall be included in the "total future cash receipts specified by the new terms" only if at the time of restructuring those amounts meet the conditions that would be applied under the provisions of paragraph 8 of *FASB Statement No. 5* in accruing a loss. That is, a creditor shall recognize a loss unless contingent future cash receipts needed to make total future cash receipts specified by the new terms at least equal to the recorded investment in the receivable both are probable and can be reasonably estimated. The same principle ap-

---

21. The only exception is to recognize interest income according to paragraph 36.

plies to amounts of future cash receipts that must sometimes be estimated to apply the provisions of paragraphs 30 and 31. For example, if the number of interest receipts is flexible because the face amount and accrued interest is collectible on demand or becomes collectible on demand after a specified period, estimates of total future cash receipts should be based on the minimum number of periods possible under the restructured terms.

* * *

Related Matters

* * *

35. Losses determined by applying the provisions of paragraphs 28–34 of this Statement shall, to the extent that they are not offset against allowances for uncollectible amounts or other valuation accounts, be included in measuring net income for the period of restructuring and reported according to *APB Opinion No. 30*. Although this Statement does not address questions concerning estimating uncollectible amounts or accounting for the related valuation allowance (paragraph 1), it recognizes that creditors use allowances for uncollectible amounts. Thus, a loss from reducing the recorded investment in a receivable may have been recognized before the restructuring by deducting an estimate of uncollectible amounts in measuring net income and increasing an appropriate valuation allowance. If so, a reduction in the recorded investment in the receivable in a troubled debt restructuring is a deduction from the valuation allowance rather than a loss in measuring net income for the period of restructuring. A valuation allowance can also be used to recognize a loss determined by applying paragraphs 28–34 that has not been previously recognized in measuring net income. For example, a creditor with an allowance for uncollectible amounts pertaining to a group of receivables that includes the restructured receivable may deduct from the allowance the reduction of recorded investment in the restructured receivable and recognize the loss in measuring net income for the period of restructuring by estimating the appropriate allowance for remaining receivables, including the restructured receivable.

36. If a troubled debt restructuring involves amounts contingently receivable, those contingent amounts shall not be recognized as interest income in future periods before they become receivable —that is, they shall not be recognized as interest income before both the contingency has been removed and the interest has been earned.[24] Before recognizing those amounts as interest income, however, they shall be deducted from the recorded investment in the restructured receivable to the extent that contingent receipts included in "total future cash receipts specified by the new terms" avoided recognition of a loss at the time of restructuring (paragraph 32).

37. If amounts of future cash receipts must be estimated to apply the provisions of paragraphs 30–32 because future interest receipts are expected to fluctuate—for example, the restructured terms

---

24. *FASB Statement No. 5*, paragraph 17 (which continued without reconsideration certain provisions of *ARB No. 50*, "Contingencies"), states, in part: "Contingencies that might result in gains usually are not reflected in the accounts since to do so might be to recognize revenue prior to its realization."

may specify the stated interest rate to be the prime interest rate increased by a specified amount or proportion—estimates of the minimum total future receipts shall be based on the interest rate in effect at the time of restructuring. . . . a creditor shall recognize a loss and reduce the recorded investment in a restructured receivable if the interest rate decreases to an extent that the minimum total future cash receipts determined using that interest rate fall below the recorded investment in the receivable at that time.

38. Legal fees and other direct costs incurred by a creditor to effect a troubled debt restructuring shall be included in expense when incurred.

39. A receivable from the sale of assets previously obtained in a troubled debt restructuring shall be accounted for according to *ABP Opinion No. 21* regardless of whether the assets were obtained in satisfaction (full or partial) of a receivable to which that Opinion was not intended to apply. A difference, if any, between the amount of the new receivable and the carrying amount of the assets sold is a gain or loss on sale of assets.

Disclosure by Creditors

40. A creditor shall disclose, either in the body of the financial statements or in the accompanying notes, the following information about troubled debt restructurings as of the date of each balance sheet presented:

a. For outstanding receivables whose terms have been modified in troubled debt restructurings, by major category: (i) the aggregate recorded investment; (ii) the gross interest income that would have been recorded in the period then ended if those receivables had been current in accordance with their original terms and had been outstanding throughout the period or since origination, if held for part of the period; and (iii) the amount of interest income on those receivables that was included in net income for the period. A receivable whose terms have been modified need not be included in that disclosure if, subsequent to restructuring, its effective interest rate (paragraph 30) has been equal to or greater than the rate that the creditor was willing to accept for a new receivable with comparable risk.

b. The amount of commitments, if any, to lend additional funds to debtors owing receivables whose terms have been modified in troubled debt restructurings.

* * *

*

APPENDIX

ADAMS v. STANDARD KNITTING MILLS *

United States Court of Appeals, Sixth Circuit, 1980.
— F.2d —.

MERRITT, CIRCUIT JUDGE: In this securities fraud case, Peat, Marwick, Mitchell & Co., herein referred to as "Peat," a firm of certified public accountants, appeals from a judgment of the District Court in the amount of $3.4 million, plus pre-judgment interest, plus attorneys' fees of $1.2 million. The suit is a class action based upon causes of action implied under §§ 10(b) and 14(a) of the Securities Exchange Act of 1934 and SEC Rules 10b–5 and 14a–9. It is based on an allegedly false proxy solicitation issued in order to gain shareholder approval of a merger between two corporations, Chadbourn, Inc. and Standard Knitting Mills, Inc., herein referred to as "Chadbourn" and "Standard." The primary issue is whether Peat is liable for a negligent error—the failure to point out in the proxy statement sent to stockholders of the acquired corporation that certain restrictions on the payment of dividends by the acquiring corporation applied to preferred as well as common stock. We hold that in the context of this case Peat is not liable for such conduct and reverse the District Court on the issue of liability.

I. STATEMENT OF FACTS RESPECTING RESTRICTIONS ON PAYMENT OF DIVIDENDS

A. General Terms and Purpose of the Merger

In April 1970, Chadbourn, Inc., a relatively profitable North Carolina hosiery manufacturer listed on the New York Stock Exchange, acquired all of the common stock of Standard Knitting Mills, Inc., a smaller, publicly-held, Knoxville, Tennessee, textile manufacturer, whose stock traded from time to time, although infrequently, in the over-the-counter market. On April 22, 1970, Standard's stockholders at a special meeting agreed to exchange their stock for a package of Chadbourn securities. The meeting occurred after the stockholders received the proxy statement a month earlier from Standard transmitting information about the proposed merger and Chadbourn's financial condition. The proxy statement contained a recom-

---

* Portions of the opinion and many of the
footnotes omitted.

mendation by Standard's management favoring the merger, as well as financial statements of Chadbourn prepared by its accountants, Peat Marwick.

Before the merger, Standard's stock traded at around $12.00 a share, although its book value was carried at approximately $21.00 a share, and Chadbourn's stock fluctuated between $8.00 and $14.00 a share. Standard's stockholders exchanged each share of Standard common for ⅒ of a share of Chadbourn common, plus 1½ shares of Chadbourn convertible, cumulative, preferred stock. The Chadbourn preferred was the main part of the package. According to the terms of the merger agreement, each share of Chadbourn preferred stock given in exchange was supposed to pay annual cash dividends of $.46⅔ a share, and Chadbourn was supposed to redeem 20% of these preferred shares each year at $11.00 a share, beginning in 1975. Each preferred share carried a conversion privilege allowing the preferred stockholder to convert a share of preferred into ⁹⁄₁₀ of a share of Chadbourn common. The general purpose of the package appears to have been to give each Standard shareholder a set of Chadbourn securities with approximately the same market value as their Standard shares but with more liquidity and higher dividends.

Approximately a year after the merger, Chadbourn's sales of hosiery plummeted unexpectedly, and it suffered a loss of $17 million. This loss wiped out its retained earnings and left it with a capital deficit of $7 million. Chadbourn now was unable to redeem or pay dividends on the preferred stock. In October 1972, the former Standard stockholders sued Chadbourn, Standard, their management, their lawyers and the appellant, Peat, which was, as previously stated, the accounting firm that prepared and certified Chadbourn's financial statements in the proxy materials. Plaintiffs entered into a settlement agreement with the defendants other than Peat, under which the former Standard shareholders were awarded control of Chadbourn, renamed "Stanwood Corporation." The District Court did not take into account the value of the settlement received by the plaintiffs in determining damages against Peat. Since we reverse the findings of the District Court on liability, we need not reach questions concerning the measure of damages and the award of attorneys' fees.

B. Restrictions on the Use of Retained Earnings Contained in the Chadbourn Loan Agreements

The first restriction on retained earnings is in a 5-year term loan agreement Chadbourn made with three banks in September, 1969. Chadbourn borrowed $6 million from the banks repayable in installments over the 5-year period. In order to protect the banks, the loan agreement contained a provision which prohibited Chadbourn and its subsidiaries in any year during the term of the loan from redeeming or paying dividends "on its *capital* shares of any class" in an amount in excess of $2 million, less the amount of the repayments on the loan, plus future earnings after the 1968–69 fiscal year.[5] These restrictions would apply to dividend payments on Chadbourn preferred shares issued to Standard shareholders (amounting annually to approximately $450,000) and would apply as well to any distributions to redeem these shares.

The second debt agreement was a little less restrictive. The second contractual restriction on paying out retained earnings is in another debt agreement which Chadbourn also entered into in 1969. Chadbourn borrowed $12.5 million in exchange for an issue of convertible, subordinated debentures. The effect of these restrictions on dividends and distributions was similar, except that under this agreement Chadbourn was free to use its 1968–69 net earnings of $3.1 million, as well as future earnings, for the payment of dividends and stock redemptions.

The net effect of both sets of restrictions on dividends and redemptions, when taken together, was that Chadbourn would either have to continue to make money or refinance its indebtedness in order to meet fully its future dividend and redemption obligations on the preferred stock issued to Standard's shareholders. As is explained above, when the bottom dropped out of its hosiery market and its retained earnings a year after the merger, it could do neither.

C. The Description of the Restrictions on Retained Earnings in the Proxy Statement

Standard's proxy statement dated March 27, 1970, contained a 35-page description of the terms of the transaction and its tax-free nature, comparative earnings and stock prices of Standard and Chadbourn and a description of their history, business, managements and properties. The text was followed by 18 pages of financial statements of both companies, including the opinions of Peat with respect to the Chadbourn financial statements and of Ernst & Ernst with respect to the Standard financial statements.

The plan for the exchange of Standard stock for Chadbourn stock was set out at pages 4–8 of the text under the heading "SUMMARY

---

5. In August, 1967, at the beginning of Chadbourn's 1967–68 fiscal year, Chadbourn had retained earnings of $4.7 million. Its net earnings during the 1967–68 year were $1.6 million so that retained earnings in August, 1968, at the beginning of the fiscal year 1968–69 were approximately $6.3 million. Its net earnings during the 1968–69 fiscal year were $3.1 million so that retained earnings in August, 1969, at the beginning of the 1969–70 fiscal year were approximately $9.3 million. At this time stockholder equity, consisting of total capital of approximately $18.3 million plus these retained earnings, was $27.7 million.

OF PLAN." Pages 6–7 of this portion of the proxy statement accurately describe the two sets of restrictions as follows:

> Under the provisions of a term loan with three banks maturing October 1, 1974, Chadbourn cannot, without the consent of such banks, [1] declare any dividend or [2] make any distribution (other than common stock dividends), or [3] acquire any of its stock if, after such action, the aggregate of all dividends (other than stock dividends), other distributions to stockholders and all amounts paid for the acquisition of its stock plus the amounts of all payments made on the term loan, would exceed $2,000,000 plus Chadbourn's consolidated net earnings since August 2, 1969. The Indenture dated as of March 15, 1969 hereinabove referred to contains certain restrictions on the payment of dividends on capital stock, however, such are less restrictive than those contained in the term loan agreement.

Chadbourn's financial statements as of August 2, 1969, and Peat's opinion, dated October 21, 1969, were published in the back of the March 27, 1970, Standard proxy statement. The liabilities and stockholders' equity side of the balance sheet was shown on page F–5 of the proxy statement. This page sets out amounts for current installments of long-term debt, and the non-current portion of long-term debt, "stockholders' equity," which referred in turn to certain notes, including footnote 7.

Footnote 7, paragraphs (c) and (d) erroneously described the two sets of restrictions as follows:

> (c) As to the note payable to three banks, the Company has agreed to various restrictive provisions including those relating to maintenance of minimum stockholders' equity and working capital, the purchase, sale or encumbering of fixed assets, incurrance [sic] of indebtedness, the leasing of additional assets and the payment of dividends *on common stock* in excess of $2,000,000 plus earnings subsequent to August 2, 1969.

> (d) . . . Further, the indenture has certain restrictive covenants but they are less restrictive than those contained in the note agreement with the three banks. (Emphasis added.)

The word "common" in paragraph (c) referring to the loan agreement was wrong because the relevant provision of the loan agreement restricted the use of retained earnings for the payment of dividends on *"capital* stock of any class," not just "common." Thus the restriction on retained earnings would apply to all distributions to pay dividends or redeem the preferred shares issued to Standard stockholders should they approve the merger.

D. Facts Respecting Peat's Negligence

The facts demonstrate that Peat's omissions were the result of negligence but did not arise from an intent to deceive, or *scienter*, as found by the District Court.

Peat failed to disclose fully in the financial statement the restrictive effect of the loan agreement and indenture on Chadbourn preferred stock. After each entry relating to long-term capitalization, the financial statement directs the attention of the reader to explanatory note 7. Note 7 alone pertains to Chadbourn's long-term debt. Missing from the note is any reference to limitations that the debt agreements placed on Chadbourn preferred stock.

Only in notes 7(c) and 7(d) does Peat mention the restrictive provisions. Note 7(c), which discusses the loan agreement, reports only that "the Company has agreed to various restrictive provisions including . . . the payment of dividends on common stock in excess of $2 million plus earnings subsequent to August 2, 1969." Note 7(d) describes the indenture. It says that "the indenture has certain restrictive covenants, but they are less restrictive than those contained in the [loan] agreement." Thus, there is no indication in either note that the long-term debt restrictions affected the redemption and earnings of preferred stock.

From notes 7(c) and 7(d), a reader easily could derive the following mistaken impression: The loan agreement contains certain restrictions on the payment of dividends by Chadbourn. As note 7(c) explicitly says, the loan agreement restrictions relate to the payment of dividends "on common stock." The indenture contains limitations that are "less restrictive" than those created by the loan agreement. Since the limitations of the loan agreement apply only to common stock, the reader mistakenly could reason that the "less restrictive" indenture constraints appear to have no broader sweep. What note 7 conveys to the reader is the erroneous notion that neither the loan agreement nor the indenture restrictions apply to Chadbourn preferred stock.

The remainder of the proxy solicitation does not entirely correct the misunderstanding created by the financial statement notes. Peat argues that the textual language from the body of the proxy statement, quoted above in subsection C, adequately advised Standard shareholders that long-term debt agreements restricted certain aspects of Chadbourn's preferred stock. We conclude, however, that contrary to Peat's claim, the text is equivocal.

The text states that Chadbourn cannot "declare any dividends" or "make any distributions" under certain conditions specified by the loan agreement. These phrases are placed under the heading "The Chadbourn Common Stock." It would not be irrational to conclude from the location of these statements that the restrictions applied solely to the common stock of Chadbourn. This conclusion would be confirmed by note 7(c), which explicitly states that the loan agreement restricts the payment of dividends on common stock. Moreover, under the section of the text labelled "Provisions Relating to the $.46⅔ Preferred Stock," there is no indication that any debt restrictions exist, much less that they apply to the dividends or redemption of preferred stock.

Nor does the language in the text regarding indenture restrictions correct the misleading impression of note 7(d). The text reports that the indenture contains "certain restrictions on the payment of dividends on capital stock." Like note 7(d), the text fails to mention restrictions on the redemption of Chadbourn preferred stock. The language regarding dividend payment restrictions on capital stock is found in the "Chadbourn Common Stock" section. Its location casts doubt on the argument that "capital stock," the restrictions on which are mentioned in part by the text, was meant in this context to include preferred stock. Adding to the doubt is the absence of any information about the indenture from the "Preferred Stock" section of the text. At best the textual discussion of indenture restrictions is equivocal regarding their reach.

The finding of the District Court that Peat acted with scienter in making the omissions is nevertheless clearly erroneous. We find in the record nothing to indicate that a desire to deceive, defraud or manipulate motivated Peat to omit from the financial statement information regarding the applicability of long-term debt restrictions. Indeed, Stanwood Corporation, the successor to Chadbourn controlled by the former Standard shareholders, hired and retained as vice president and treasurer the Peat associate, Hugh Freeze, who the shareholders' counsel now claim sought to defraud them. If the shareholders and their representatives really believed Freeze intended to defraud them, it seems doubtful that they would have put him in charge of the financial affairs of the corporation.

At most the evidence supports a finding that Peat acted negligently in preparing the financial statements. Peat became aware that note 7 incorrectly described the debt limitation several weeks before the merger vote occurred. The Standard proxy statement was mailed to its stockholders on March 27, 1970. Between March 23, 1970, and April 1, 1970, Chadbourn's outside counsel telephoned Freeze, the Peat manager in charge of the Chadbourn audit, and told him that a description of restrictions relating to Chadbourn's stock had been inserted in the forepart of the Standard proxy statement prior to mailing. The lawyer called to his attention the difference in the description in the proxy statement and the footnote, pointing out that the footnote said "common" rather than "capital stock of any class." In the course of this conversation, Freeze took a copy of the preliminary Standard proxy statement and noted the change by hand in note 7(c). Thereafter, footnote 7(c) was not amended, and no effort was made to call the discrepancy to the attention of Standard stockholders or officials. Freeze did not foresee that the bottom would drop out of Chadbourn's earnings and that what appeared to be a minor error at the time would become a major bone of contention.

The evidence simply suggests a mistake, an oversight, the failure to foresee a problem. We find nothing in the record indicating an intent to deceive or a motive for deception. J. B. Woolsey, Standard's vice president for financial affairs, and presumably other Standard officers, knew of the restrictions and recommended the merger anyway. No stockholder testified that he was deceived. An erroneous statement cannot *ipso facto* prove fraud, and here we find no evidence of anything other than a negligent error.

II. LIABILITY FOR NEGLIGENT MISREPRESENTATION UNDER SEC RULES 10b–5 AND 14a–9

In view of our conclusion that the District Court's findings of scienter are clearly erroneous, we reverse the imposition of liability under Rule 10b–5. In Ernst & Ernst v. Hochfelder, 425 U.S. 185 (1976), the Supreme Court settled the issue. It unequivocally held that liability under Rule 10b–5 requires "intentional misconduct." Id. at 201. The Court said that 10b–5 requires "intentional or willful conduct designed to deceive or defraud investors." Id. at 199.

We turn to the question of the standard of liability under Rule 14a–9 pertaining to statements made in proxy solicitations. There has been relatively little case law on the standard of liability following the Supreme Court decision in J. I. Case Co. v. Borak, 377 U.S. 426 (1964), which established a private right of action under 14(a) and Rule 14a–9. Two circuits have examined the issue. Both have prescribed a negligence standard for the corporation issuing the proxy statement. One held that the negligence standard also applies to outside, nonmanagement directors, Gould v. American-Hawaiian Steamship Co., 535 F.2d 761, 777–78 (3d Cir. 1976); and the other intimated in dicta, without deciding the issue, that a *scienter* standard probably should apply to outside directors and accountants, Gerstle v. Gamble-Skogmo, Inc., 478 F.2d 1281, 1300–1301 (2d Cir. 1973).

In view of the overall structure and collective legislative histories of the securities laws, as well as important policy considerations, we conclude that scienter should be an element of liability in private suits under the proxy provisions as they apply to outside accountants.

* * *

III. COMPUTER DEFECTS

Chadbourn used electronic data processing to record many of its financial records from sales to inventory on hand. The District Court found various deficiencies connected with these computer accounts which, it concluded, Peat should have disclosed in the notes accompanying the proxy statement.

The record contains evidence of poorly documented computer programs, a high level of computer personnel turnover, lack of security in the computer room, erroneously coded data, and poorly designed computer programs that failed to detect improperly coded data. Peat sent several memoranda to Chadbourn's management, documenting the computer weaknesses; and one internal Chadbourn memorandum not written by Peat, stated that the company was "pushed . . . to the brink of bankruptcy" by the unreliability of computer-generated information. The District Court found that Peat's failure to disclose these weaknesses constituted fraud. We disagree.

An outside accountant examines the quality of a company's internal accounting primarily to determine the extent to which he must test a client's records. The more reliable the client's accounting system proves to be, the less testing the accountant must conduct. A by-product of this testing is the discovery of weaknesses in internal accounting. The accountant may bring such weaknesses to the attention of management but he is not always obligated to inform the stockholders. This is not to say that an accountant may keep a blind eye to all wrongdoing while walking through a client's corporate headquarters. He may be held liable to the extent that he intentionally or recklessly disregards the generally accepted, standard body of accounting knowledge. This is not the case here. Although we cannot say the District Court's inference, that faulty computer information materially impaired management's ability to manage, is clearly erroneous, there was no scienter in Peat's failure to disclose. The absence of an intent to deceive is fatal to plaintiff's claim.

According to the Statements on Auditing Procedure,[10] promulgated by the Auditing Standards Executive Committee of the American Institute of Certified Public Accountants (AICPA), the accountant may have a duty to direct management's attention to internal accounting weaknesses he has uncovered. But the Committee imposed

10. See AICPA, Statement on Auditing Procedure, No. 33 at 32 (1963) ; AICPA, Statement on Accounting Standards No. 1 §§ 320, 640 (1973); Carmichael, Opinions on Internal Control, Journal of Accountancy 47 (1970). The AICPA in 1977 promulgated a rule that disclosure to management was required. See AICPA, Statement on Accounting Standards No. 20 (1977).

no requirement that the notes to the certification of financial reports contain a similar disclosure of such weaknesses.

An auditor cannot always make an assessment of the effect of accounting weaknesses on the efficiency of a company. Often such an assessment requires a technical knowledge of a business in which accountants have no expertise. Peat's reliance on the AICPA's committee opinions is sufficient indication of good faith and lack of scienter.

Peat cannot be charged with knowledge of the interplay between poor or inefficient record-keeping procedures and mismanagement. Nor does the record disclose that Peat actually knew of Chadbourn's internal memoranda evaluating the effect of poor computer information upon management. Likewise, the evidence does not support a finding of recklessness.

Finally, undisputed testimony shows that by the time of the proxy solicitations, many of the computer problems had already been solved. The only relevant disclosure would have been that, for the two quarters preceding the merger, Chadbourn's management may not have been sufficiently informed due to temporary computer deficiencies. Accountants are not liable for failing to speculate publicly about this subject.

IV. THE AUDIT

The District Judge also held that Peat failed to conduct its audit according to generally accepted accounting principles (GAAP) and generally accepted auditing standards (GAAS), and therefore fraudulently misrepresented material facts about Chadbourn by certifying the proxy financial statements. The Court found deficiencies in two important areas of the audit, the closing inventory and accounts receivable. We conclude that there is sufficient evidence to support the Court's finding that Peat inadequately tested Chadbourn's financial figures in certain respects, but the evidence falls far short of proving that Peat intended to deceive the stockholders or that its negligence produced financial statements *materially* at odds with the real facts. The question of materiality in this context is whether, given all the financial information, there was a substantial risk that the actual value of assets or profits were significantly less than Peat stated them to be.

The District Judge found errors in five aspects of the inventory valuation: the physical count, the standard cost audit, the conversion from standard to actual costs, the inventory "work forward," and the "lower of cost or market" test. An accurate appraisal of inventory is important in a business such as Chadbourn's because, aside from exaggerating the primary asset listed on the balance sheet, overvaluing the closing inventory lowers the annual cost of sales and thus inflates net earnings.[11] This latter figure is especially sensitive to fluctuation in inventory value when inventory value is disproportionately greater.

1. Physical Count

In conducting a physical inventory, independent accountants do not count every item on their client's premises. The client's employees count inventory items, and usually these counts are documented on accounting forms or "tickets" as to style, quantity, as well as other relevant characteristics. The accountant's responsibility is to conduct statistical tests on a cross-section of these accounting tickets to determine whether the client counts were correct. The client counts need not exactly coincide with the accountant's spot check count, as long as the percentage of discrepancies to total number of goods, is small.

The District Court found that Peat conducted inadequate tests for counts of both finished stockings and greige goods.[12] The finding regarding greige goods is based on testimony by witness Rittenberg that from a total of 1000 to 1500 bins of goods, a Peat employee tested about 100, and that the Peat count on items inside each bin conflicted with Chadbourn's in 40 to 50 of the bins tested. In examining the exhibit from which Rittenberg drew his conclusion, we calculated for the bins tested that the average variance between Peat's and Chadbourn's count, weighted by the total number of goods, was only about four percent. The greige goods inventory, as a whole, was valued at $2 million. This degree of variance in the greige goods account is insufficient to render the inventory figure a material misstatement of fact.

The District Judge's finding regarding the count of finished goods was based on cross examination of testimony of Peat's accountant, William Brasington. After selecting four work papers, Brasington stated that, for one ticket listing representing 199,000 dozen, one style consisting of 1655 dozen was tested and a difference of 28 dozen was found. He "admitted" that this test by itself would have been insufficient but claimed that other testing was done. He also testified that in another instance, a count of 435,000 dozen was not tested at all. It is not a reasonable conclusion, however, that the total amount of testing was insufficient.

11. Costs of sales = value of starting inventory + production costs incurred during fiscal year — value of closing inventory. See W. Conkling & P. Pacter, Attorney's Handbook of Accounting 5–29 (H. Sellin 2d ed. 1971).

Net earnings = Gross sales — cost of sales.

12. Greige goods are unfinished, unshaped stockings.

Brasington vigorously insisted that on the whole testing was adequate. The Record does not indicate the total number of discrepancies found in either Brasington's four work papers or all the work papers combined. Nor does it indicate for what purpose Brasington was asked to select these four work papers. No expert witness claimed that the testing of the physical count was insufficient. Plaintiff's chief witness concerning the audit, Larry Rittenberg, examined Peat's work papers and testified in lengthy detail to the errors and omissions in Peat's work. He did not testify that there were any errors in the physical count.

The District Judge inferred from the counts of the two inventory items that were not fully tested, and from Brasington's failure to produce other work papers, that all the work papers relating to the physical count were deficient. But the record does not show that the four work papers were deficient on the whole.

The four papers were only a part of the testing of the total count. In order to determine whether the testing was deficient there must be evidence from a large enough sample of work papers from which a statistically valid conclusion about the whole may be drawn. The evidence does not support a conclusion that there was a material miscount in these inventory items.

Third, the District Judge found that Peat did not adequately test a computer listing of finished goods that was compiled from the accounting tickets. The testimony cited by the District Court was again taken from the cross examination of Brasington. Basington said that five percent of the listings were tested and that 1 to 2 percent error was found. The District Court evidently interpreted the witness to mean that of the five percent tested, $\frac{1}{5}$ to $\frac{2}{5}$ of the listings were wrong. What the witness clearly meant, however, was that 1 to 2 percent of the sample tested were inaccurate, and interpolating this 5 percent sample to the whole, that 1 to 2 percent of the entire listing might have been inaccurate. This small error is immaterial and supports the validity of Peat's testing.

The District Judge also found that Peat conducted insufficient cut-off tests. A cut-off test is one designed to tag inventory at the plant at which it was first counted so that it is not counted twice if shipped to another plant. The record does not indicate, however, that this affected a material portion of goods.

2. Standard Cost Audit

Next plaintiffs contend that Peat did not test Chadbourn's "build-up" of standard costs. A build-up of standard costs involves an estimate of costs per unit of goods; it starts with production records or engineering studies on the costs of labor and raw materials per good. The costs are totalled and checked style by style for consistency. The "build-up" represents what it should cost to produce goods under realistic day to day manufacturing circumstances barring unusual, unforeseen, and evanescent occurrences. Determining standard cost is a method of allocating total actual costs among different styles, and is an intermediate step in valuing the actual cost of the closing inventory.

The District Court found that Peat's testing of the standard cost build-up was not documented in its work papers, and concluded that Peat never audited the standard cost at all. Plaintiffs have not proved, however, that there was a material risk that a proper audit of the standard cost system would have revealed materially lower costs. Indeed, the evidence tends to support Peat's valuation. Actual costs were extremely close—and slightly higher—than the estimated standard cost, a prima facie indication of a relatively small risk that standard costs were materially lower. Nor does the record indicate unusual circumstances that unduly inflated actual production costs.

In the unlikely event that standard costs for some styles were materially lower, standard costs for other items must have been higher in order for the sum of standard costs to have approached the actual cost so closely.[13] And in order for this mix of under and overvalued standard costs to have effected a material change in the valuation of the closing inventory, plaintiff must show that disproportionately more "overvalued" cost items than "undervalued" cost items were not sold and remained in the closing inventory. Consequently, even assuming Peat did not conduct further testing that the work papers directly indicate, this omission was immaterial. Moreover, there is a total absence of evidence of fraudulent intent.

3. Conversion of Standard to Actual Cost

A third complaint is that Peat knowingly failed to establish standard cost centers for each plant, from which standard costs would be converted to actual costs on a plantwide basis. Instead, Peat computed a weighted average variance between what it perceived to be the actual-to-standard variances for each plant, and then used one company-wide average variance to convert each good's standard cost to its actual cost. The District Judge found on the basis of Rittenberg's testimony that this procedure violated both GAAS and GAAP. Whether or not this finding was clearly erroneous, plaintiff's chief witness specifically refused to conclude that there was a material risk that Peat's calculations thereby inflated the value of the closing inventory.

13. Again this assumes no exceptional production costs. No such exceptions are documented in the record.

A plantwide "standard-to-actual" variance would be computed and utilized in valuing the entire company's inventory, only if there were an overall write-down from actual cost to market value in at least one plant. In order for Peat's method of calculation to result in an inflated valuation, plaintiffs must prove (1) that there had been an overwhelming concentration of goods whose actual cost exceeded market value in plants which had above average actual-to-standard variances, and (2) that there was no overall concentration of such goods in other plants. There is no evidence that such circumstances occurred, and again, the information on which Rittenberg based his opinions could not have provided an adequate foundation for finding a material risk.

4. Inventory Work Forward

Peat observed the inventory approximately four weeks prior to the end of Chadbourn's fiscal year. Peat updated the inventory to its status as of the fiscal year's end, using computer-generated data on the sales transacted (the "gross profit report") subsequent to the taking of the physical inventory. The District Judge found that Peat's reliance on Chadbourn's computer system—with all its weaknesses—constituted a departure from GAAS, and therefore made its certification a material misrepresentation.

Of the long list of deficiencies the most relevant one was that "approximately 25% of customer service source documents [were] incorrectly coded." Testimony by Dalton, the head of Chadbourn's computer operations, indicates that a significant portion of the incorrect coding was of style number. This same style coding was used by the "gross profit report" program to retrieve individual costs for each item sold. This cost information was in turn used by Peat in its inventory work forward. If styles were incorrectly coded, this program which matched up styles with their respective costs would have been unable, by itself, to register the transaction correctly. But we cannot determine whether it would necessarily have provided an erroneous cost.

The District Judge found that Peat did not test the sales data for the work forward; this finding is not clearly erroneous. There is hearsay testimony that Peat conducted such tests in September or October of 1968, several months before the memo documenting the 25% error rate in coding. The District Judge evidently inferred from Peat's failure to document such testing in its work papers, that the testing did not occur. The record also establishes adequate foundation for this inference.

Without examining the computer program documentation and procedures used by Chadbourn's computer operators for erroneously coded data, or conducting a test of the gross profit report data,

Peat did not have any basis to evaluate the risk involved in using the reports. Although witness Rittenberg had no foundation to evaluate and testify on the risks either, we believe it is true that Peat conducted no testing on reports which dealt with $2 million in sales costs. The distinction here is between inadequate testing and no testing at all. The risk that twenty-five percent of styles were incorrectly coded presented the risk that the costs of twenty-five percent of the month's cost transactions totaling $2 million were incorrectly stated. Although the failure here could lead to a material error, there is no evidence that it did and certainly no evidence of scienter.

5. "Lower of Cost or Market" Test

The final step in valuing a physical inventory is the markdown of items whose actual cost exceeds market value. The auditor must test a sampling of sales to determine whether its client has provided adequate markdown—and hence an adequate markdown in inventory value—for goods that are selling below cost. This is done in order to realize losses in inventory value as soon as they occur.

The District Judge found that Peat examined an insufficient number of sales to test Chadbourn's reserves. This is supported by Rittenberg's testimony. However, Brasington, one of Peat's accountants, gave uncontradicted testimony that the valuations proved to be correct from subsequent market studies on individual styles. Subsequent valuations would not have been so close to Peat's original predictions for *so many different styles*, had Peat's testing been materially inadequate. The District Judge's finding here is clearly erroneous.

6. Accounts Receivable

Finally, the District Judge found that Peat failed to "reconcile" confirmations taken at different dates of Chadbourn's accounts receivable. A confirmation of an account receivable is simply a test of whether as of a certain date a customer of Chadbourn actually owes what Chadbourn's records show them to owe. Peat claims that the confirmation tests were adequate because in all, over 80% of accounts were tested. But Peat misunderstands the thrust of the Court's finding. When an accountant does not "reconcile" tests conducted on different dates, this leaves open the possibility that a customer who apparently is acknowledging an old debt, may actually be acknowledging a new one acquired between the two test periods. All confirmations must be confirmations of debts incurred as of a specific date.

The District Judge's finding that these tests were not reconciled is not clearly erroneous. Accounts receivable was listed as approximately $10 million or 15% of total assets of $65 million, and is therefore a material asset. The record, however, is silent on the magnitude of error that could have resulted from conducting confirmation tests on different but relatively close dates. It is improbable—and there is no evidence—that customers' debts increased so radically over a one month period to have materially altered Chadbourn's total accounts receivable. Consequently, plaintiffs have not shown Peat's failure to reconcile dates to have been material.

Accordingly, the judgment of the District Court is reversed.

[Dissenting Opinion]

WEICK, CIRCUIT JUDGE, dissenting . . . ..

* * *

In this appeal, as before stated, it was not our function to conduct a de novo hearing. In an action involving claims of fraud, securities violations, and reckless conduct where the testimony at a bench trial was taken before an experienced District Judge who had the opportunity to and did take testimony of witnesses, observe the demeanor of the witnesses and to make credibility assessments, we are not permitted to set aside his factual findings unless we are satisfied and can demonstrate that they are not supported by substantial evidence and are clearly erroneous. *Fed.R.Civ.P.* 52(a). The majority was unable to demonstrate that the District Judge did not have sufficient evidence to support his findings of intentional fraud or reckless conduct.

In my opinion, the findings of fact adopted by the District Court are supported by substantial evidence and are not clearly erroneous. I would affirm the judgment of the District Court for the reasons herein set forth.

I.

In 1969 Chadbourn, a moderately sized Charlotte, North Carolina manufacturer of hosiery and panty hose, enjoyed substantial sales due to the popularity of panty hose, its major product. Between 1967 and 1969 Chadbourn's earnings had increased many times. For the year ending August 2, 1969, it had sales of $68,074,688 and its 3,800,000 shares were listed on the New York Stock Exchange. During this period the market for panty hose was free of foreign competition and price cutting. In the late 60's Chadbourn embarked upon an aggressive acquisition campaign.

In 1968 and in early 1969 Chadbourn became interested in acquiring Standard Knitting Mills of Knoxville, Tennessee. Standard was a relatively small company whose shares of stock were owned and controlled by Knoxville residents. Its 632,000 shares of common stock were registered with the Securities and Exchange Commission under the Securities Exchange Act of 1934 and were publicly held by 556 persons and were seldom traded. The sales price of the few shares that did change hands was roughly at $11 a share. Twenty-two percent of its stock was held and controlled by Valley Fidelity Bank and Trust Company of Knoxville in a number of fiduciary accounts. Nineteen percent was held or controlled by officers and directors of Standard and their families. The officers and directors of Standard were considered to be substantial people in Knoxville. Although many of its plants were old, it had for many years run a sound business and paid dividends by manufacturing cotton knitwear. In the late 60's three large chain store customers bought approximately 50 percent of its output.

Prior to the merger and during the period of negotiation for the shares of Standard, Chadbourn offered for sale to its shareholders and to the public $12,631,000 of 6½ percent 20 year convertible subordinated debentures due March 15, 1989 pursuant to an Indenture dated March 15, 1969.

On July 28, 1969, Chadbourn and Standard agreed to merge subject to a vote of approval by the Standard shareholders which vote eventually took place at a special meeting of its shareholders held on April 22, 1970. In return for each share of Standard stock Standard shareholders were to receive one and one-half shares of Chadbourn $.46⅔ Cumulative and Convertible Preferred Stock, Jr., Series A, created specifically for the purpose of consummating the Standard merger. In addition, Chadbourn specifically agreed to repurchase the preferred from shareholders of Standard who desired to sell at $11 per share in five yearly installments from 1975 to 1979.

As a result of the merger, Chadbourn acquired a relatively conservative textile manufacturing company that was well entrenched in the Knoxville community. For many years Standard had operated as a sound business enterprise, and indeed, it reported its first operating loss in recent history in the months just prior to the merger with Chadbourn, and also reported earnings weakness for the period immediately after the merger. Three of its customers were large chain stores that were valuable clients. The $.46⅔ dividend, $10 par cumulative convertible preferred financed the acquisition by Chadbourn without any immediate outlay of a large sum of money. Chadbourn thus obtained beneficial control of the company and its earning power. Further, Chadbourn did not need to resort to a bank or to the competitive money markets for financing the merger at a high rate of interest which allowed it to use any bank credit that was available to it for other purposes. Because of the relatively small dividend the most valuable feature of the preferred was its ability to be converted into .6 share of Chadbourn common which fluctuated in value between $8 and $14 per share before the merger. From the point of view of the plaintiff class and subclass, former Standard common shareholders, the merger offered some advantages. In return for their common, plaintiffs were to receive cumulative preferred dividends larger than dividends declared historically on Standard common, each share of preferred was convertible into Chadbourn common, the preferred was readily marketable on the New York Stock Exchange for cash, a small amount of Chadbourn common would be distributed pro rata among holders of the preferred if Standard achieved certain earnings goals, and Chadbourn promised to redeem the preferred at $11 per share in installments from 1975 to 1979 to shareholders desiring redemption.

In September, 1969, approximately two months after the agreement to merge was signed but before it was approved by Standard's shareholders, Chadbourn borrowed six million dollars from North Carolina National Bank, First National Bank of Boston, and the First National Bank of Atlanta. The loan agreement called for twenty consecutive quarterly installment payments of $150,000 and a final lump sum payment of any remaining balance so that the entire loan would be retired on October 1, 1974, if the payments were made several months before Chadbourn agreed to begin redeeming the preferred stock.

An internal Peat memorandum acknowledged on July 24, 1969, the engagement of its services by Chadbourn in preparing a "[p]roxy statement to be filed [with the SEC] for stockholders of Standard Knitting Mills, Inc. in connection with the proposed acquisition of Standard and its subsidiaries by Chadbourn." It was also to be used to solicit votes of Standard shareholders favoring the proposed merger. Peat made the audit during the July 4th 1969 holiday as was customary in the textile industry. It was ultimately dated August 2, 1969.

Peat received $194,424 for its services from Chadbourn in 1969–70. Peat charged $105,000 for the audit and $26,000 for the Standard proxy work. Peat charged a fee that was 125% of its usual fee because "SEC work does require a higher degree of risk," however, Peat admits that it exercised no different degree of care in performing its services for Chadbourn.

The Standard proxy materials in issue were mailed to Standard shareholders on March 27, 1970. The merger was approved by the shareholders at a special meeting for that purpose held on April 22, 1970. At the meeting Mr. Kramer, General Counsel and a Director of Standard, represented that there were no restrictions on the payment of dividends on the $.46⅔ cumulative and convertible preferred. This representation conformed to Footnote 7 of the Chadbourn financial statement contained in Standard proxy materials which was written and certified as correct by Peat. Footnote 7 in pertinent part reads as follows:

(7) Long-Term Debt:

(c) As to the note payable to three banks, the Company has agreed to various restrictive provisions including those relating to maintenance of minimum stockholders' equity and working capital, the purchase, sale or encumbering of fixed assets, incurrence of indebtedness, the leasing of additional assets and the payment of dividends on *common* stock in excess of $2,000,000 plus earnings subsequent to August 2, 1969.

(d) The 6% debentures are . . . .

Further, the indenture has certain restrictive covenants but they are less restrictive than those contained in the note agreement with the three banks. [Emphasis ours]

The footnote incorrectly stated that the restriction upon the payment of dividends contained in the bank loan agreement applied only to Chadbourn common stock. Further, the exact provisions of the restrictive covenants of the Indenture are not set out but are characterized as "less restrictive than those contained in the note agreement with the three banks," implying that only restrictions on payment of dividends on common were contained in the Indenture. There is no mention of restrictions on the payment of dividends on Chadbourn preferred stock contained in the bank loan agreement or the Indenture, and there is no mention whatsoever of any restrictions on redemption of the preferred stock contained in either the bank loan agreement or the Indenture.

Approximately one month after the merger was approved plaintiffs received a proxy from Chadbourn soliciting their votes for approval of a loan and option agreement involving the acquisition of United Hosiery Mills by Chadbourn (the UHM proxy materials). Footnote 7(c) of the financial statement in the UHM proxy materials, which corresponded to footnote 7(c) contained in the Standard proxy materials, supra, had been altered so that the word "common" hereinbefore referred to was changed to the word "capital," thus indicating that restrictions on payment of dividends contained in the bank loan agreement applied to both common and preferred stock. This change was not brought to the attention of the reader in Peat's certification of the Chadbourn financial statement contained in the UHM proxy materials and the change was located on the 55th page of 77 pages of the UHM proxy materials.

Several months after plaintiffs received the UHM proxy materials plaintiffs received the 1970 Chadbourn Annual Report, which contained a financial statement for Chadbourn prepared by Peat. Footnote 6(c) of this financial statement returned to the use of the word "common." A quick reference to the 1969 Chadbourn Annual Report for the purpose of resolving this ambiguity would reveal that the pertinent footnote in the 1969 Chadbourn Annual Report used the word "common" as well. Footnote 7(c) in the UHM materials, therefore, was the only footnote in the certified financial statements in issue received by plaintiffs which indicated that restrictions on the payment of dividends in the bank loan agreement and Indenture applied to both common stock and preferred stock. The 1969 Chadbourn Annual Report, the financial statement in the Standard proxy materials, and the 1970 Chadbourn Annual Report uniformly indicated that the restrictions on the payment of dividends applied to common stock only, and none of the financial statements in issue, including the one in the UHM proxy materials, mentioned any existence of restrictions upon redemption contained in the bank loan agreement and the Indenture.

The loan agreement and the Indenture in fact contained covenants which restricted the payment of dividends upon common and preferred stock and the redemption of common and preferred stock. The bank loan agreement in pertinent part provided that Chadbourn would not:

Section 5.3. Declare or pay any dividend on its capital shares of any class or make any distribution to any shareholders as such (other than dividends or distributions payable solely in common stock of the Company and other than cash paid in lieu of fractional shares in connection with any such dividend payable solely in common stock of the Company), or purchase, redeem or otherwise acquire for value any shares of its stock of any class, if, after giving effect to such action, the aggregate of:

(a) all dividends, other than in common stock of the Company, on its capital shares of all classes, preferred and common, and all other distributions to shareholders as such (other than cash paid in lieu of fractional shares in connection with any dividend payable solely in common stock of the Company) between August 2, 1969 and the time of taking such action; plus

(b) all amounts paid out for any redemptions, purchases or other acquisitions of its stock of any class (other than amounts for redemption of any shares of the Company's 6% Cumulative Preferred Stock, $50 par value) between August 2, 1969 and the time of taking such action; plus

(c) the amount of all payments required to be made, and of all prepayments made, on principal of the Note prior to the time of taking such action;

would exceed the sum of:

(y) $2,000,000; plus

(z) the consolidated net earnings (including special items) of the Company and its subsidiaries accumulated subsequent to August 2, 1969;

provided that any subsidiary may declare and pay dividends.

The pertinent text of the Indenture is less precise. The text in pertinent part reads as follows:

Section 5.05. The Company will not declare or pay any dividends or make any distribution on or with respect to its capital stock, except for dividends payable solely in capital stock of the Company and except for cash paid in lieu of fractional shares in connection with any such dividend payable solely in capital stock of the Company, and will not permit any subsidiary to, directly or indirectly purchase, redeem, or otherwise acquire for a consideration any capital stock of the Company if the aggregate amount of all such payments or distributions after August 3, 1968 would exceed the sum of:

(i) $2,000,000 plus

(ii) the net proceeds (exclusive of any underwriting discounts or commissions or other expenses paid or incurred by the Company in connection therewith) of the sale for cash by the Company of any shares of its capital stock after August 3, 1968 less the amount paid by the Company for the purchase with cash of any shares of its capital stock after August 3, 1968 plus

(iii) Consolidated Net Income realized after August 3, 1968.

Consolidated Net Income from August 3, 1968, to August 2, 1969, was $3.01 million. This language can be read to restrict redemption by Chadbourn subsidiaries only. Peat Marwick argues that the latter interpretation is correct and that Chadbourn itself was never under the terms of the Indenture restricted in its ability to redeem the preferred. There is evidence, however, that the Indenture was drawn with the intent to restrict redemption by Chadbourn. For example, Mr. Johnston, counsel for Chadbourn, disagreed with Peat on precisely this issue. He published a text in a note 8(d) of the financial statement contained in the 1971 Chadbourn Annual Report which indicated that the Indenture restrictions upon redemption also applied to Chadbourn. That footnote in pertinent part reads as follows:

(8) Long-Term Debt:

(d) The 6½% debentures are . . . .

Further, the indenture contains a restrictive provision under which the Company cannot declare any dividends or make any distribution (other than capital stock dividends), or acquire any of its stock if, after such action, the aggregate of all dividends (other than stock dividends), other distributions to stockholders and all amounts paid for the acquisition of its stock would exceed the sum of (i) $2,000,000 plus (ii) the net proceeds of the sale for cash by the Company of any shares of its capital stock after August 3, 1968 plus (iii) consolidated net income realized after August 3, 1968.

This same text was published in the 1972 and 1973 Chadbourn Annual Reports. These restrictions in effect limited the amount available for future dividends and future redemptions by Chadbourn to $2 million plus post-1969 earnings under the bank loan agreement, and $5.1 million plus post-1969 earnings under the Indenture. The promised redemption of the preferred from 1975 to 1979 would cost roughly $10 million if all of the preferred shareholders requested redemption. In the interim Chadbourn was obligated, *inter alia*, to pay the dividends on the preferred, to carry the debt service on the $12,-631,000 Indenture, and to pay off the $6 million bank loan completely.

Chadbourn had to deal with approximately $18.5 million of new indebtedness before it could redeem plaintiffs' preferred as promised. Undisclosed was the fact that Chadbourn had to either earn approximately $16 million before taxes and $8 million after taxes, refinance the $18.5 million of indebtedness, or sell an additional $8 million of new equity securities.

It is clear that Peat had full knowledge of these restrictions when it prepared the Standard proxy financial statements and certified that the financial statements accurately described the financial condition and debt structure of Chadbourn. This certification was false and fraudulent as found by the District Court. Furthermore, between March 23, 1970, and April 1, 1970, prior to the merger, Hugh Freeze, the Peat manager in charge of the Chadbourn audit, received a phone call from Peat's attorney Herbert Browne, Jr., a member of the law firm of Helms, Mullis & Johnston, the firm that prepared parts of the proxy. Brown informed Freeze that the use of the word "common" in footnote 7(c) of the Peat audit was erroneous. Freeze then crossed out the word "common" on his copy of a preliminary draft of the Standard proxy footnote and wrote the word "capital" underneath it. Peat, however, did not alter the proxy, or, if the proxy had already been mailed, Peat took no steps to notify Standard shareholders or the SEC to correct the alleged error before the Standard shareholders voted on the acquisition of Standard by Chadbourn. The District Court could rightly infer that the reason Freeze did not correct the original was because it would have defeated the merger as the Standard shareholders would not have approved it.

There is other direct evidence that Peat had actual knowledge of the alleged error in footnote 7 of the proxy statement before the merger vote was taken. At approximately the same time it was preparing the Standard proxy Peat was also drafting a proxy containing the same financial statement for use in soliciting votes for the acquisition of Continental Strategics Corporation by Chadbourn (the Continental proxy materials). The Continental proxy, like the UHM proxy, contained the correct word "capital" in footnote 7(c). The Continental proxy was mailed on April 8, 1970, approximately two weeks before the vote on the Standard merger. The Continental proxy was not mailed to Standard shareholders because the Standard merger had not yet been consummated.

As indicated, supra, Peat also prepared the UHM proxy which contained the correct word "capital" in footnote 7(c). In a letter to the SEC dated April 20, 1970, two days before the Standard merger vote, counsel for Chadbourn sent to SEC copies of the UHM proxy containing the proper word.

Early drafts of the footnotes from the summer of 1969 when the audit was conducted indicate that Peat originally intended to disclose verbatim the Indenture restrictions on dividend payment. When the existence of the bank loan agreement for $6 million required a revision of the financial statement the following fall, Peat's auditing manager Freeze wrote footnote 7(c) using the word "common." For footnote 7(d) Freeze discarded the verbatim language of the Indenture restricting dividend payment and characterized the Indenture restrictive covenants as "less restrictive than those contained in the note agreement with the three banks." This characterization of the Indenture covenants appeared in all of the certified financial statements in issue until counsel for Chadbourn stated the Indenture dividend restriction in full in the 1971 Chadbourn Annual Report and stated the Indenture restrictions on redemption as well.

Despite all this evidence of deliberate fraud, Peat has the audacity to assert that the false, untrue and misleading statements in footnotes 7(c) and 7(d) of its audit were only "lapsus calami" (Br. at 5), "slip of the pen" (Br. at 29), and a "footnote mistake" (Br. at i). It is unbelievable that the majority of this panel would swallow with hook, line and sinker such an outrageous and ridiculous proposition and to hold that Peat's misrepresentation was only negligent and use it as a basis for reversing a well reasoned opinion of the District Court thereby depriving the many shareholders of Standard of millions of dollars of compensation in which they were justly entitled because of the fraud perpetrated on them by Peat. If it originally was only a slip of the pen, it became a deliberate fraud when Peat's own lawyer called this to the attention of Peat's manager in charge of the audit and the employee corrected the alleged mistake in his copy and did not correct the original because it would have defeated the merger. The characterization of Peat's misrepresentation as a "negligent misrepresentation" adds something new and unheard of in our jurisprudence.

The District Court characterized it differently. It found that Peat's Certificate that it had performed its 1969 Chadbourn audit in accordance with generally accepted accounting standards and auditing practices and false and untrue and that Peat acted "willfully, with intent to 'deceive' and 'manipulate' and 'in reckless disregard of the truth'" in respect to footnotes 7(c) and 7(d) in said audit. In my opinion, the majorities holding should be rejected and the factual findings of the District Court upheld.

In imposing liability the District Court followed the standards of Ernst & Ernst v. Hochfelder, 425 U.S. 185 (1976) with respect to the necessity of proof of scienter as mere negligence is not enough to violate the Act. The District Court in finding scienter stated:

> [n]otwithstanding this stringent element of proof, the court concludes that in all the facts and circumstances of this case, scienter on behalf of defendant has been established by a preponderance of the evidence.

> On two occasions when it counted most, with full knowledge of the correct term, Peat, deliberately, did not correctly describe the stock which was restricted in the payment of dividends by the bank loan which stock also was the particular class plaintiffs would receive by the merger. Furthermore, defendant never fully described either the dividend restrictions on preferred stock contained in the indenture or the redemption restrictions contained in the indenture and loan agreement. Defendant's agents documented Chadbourn's numerous edp defects at the time of the 1969 audit and approximately one year later some corrections had been made but a considerable number of deficiencies still remained—yet defendant did not feel obliged to report this to plaintiffs. Finally with full knowledge of Chadbourn's deficient edp and other internal weaknesses, defendant conducted its 1969 audit as though Chadbourn was as sound as a dollar used to be—clearly deviating from GAAP, GAAS and the provisions of Peat's own audit manual. The court finds and

holds the proof in this case clearly established that, with the knowledge defendant possessed prior to, during and after the 1969 audit compared against the content of the [sic] Peat's 1969 Chadbourn financial statements, defendant acted willfully, with intent to "deceive" and "manipulate" and in "reckless disregard for the truth." App. 389a–90a.

Unlike the present case, in *Ernst & Ernst*, "the respondents specifically disclaimed the existence of fraud or intentional misconduct on the part of Ernst & Ernst." The Supreme Court did not determine whether reckless behavior is sufficient for civil liability under section 10(b) and Rule 10b–5.

In Mansbach v. Prescott, Ball & Turben, 598 F.2d 1017, 1024, No. 77–3226 (6th Cir. May 7, 1979), however, we upheld the sufficiency of recklessness to establish civil liability under the Act and that such claims should be liberally construed in order to effectuate the policies underlying the federal securities laws.[1]

The District Court was correct in finding that the deliberate misstatements and fraudulent omissions in the proxy statement were material. It is clear that no prudent Standard shareholder in his right mind would ever have voted for the merger if he had known of the restrictions on the payment of dividends and on the redemption of the cumulative preferred stock which he was to receive under the terms of the merger. The Standard stockholder had been receiving regular dividends on his Standard common stock. Because of the restrictions on the preferred stock which he was to receive in exchange he would not receive any dividends on the preferred stock for a long time and possibly he would never receive either the dividends or secure the redemption of the preferred shares. Under the law it was not necessary to prove that each shareholder of Standard relied on the representations contained in the proxy statement and financial statement mailed to them and to SEC. Affiliated Ute Citizens of Utah v. United States, 406 U.S. 128, 153–54 (1972); Mills v. Electric Auto-Lite Co., 396 U.S. 375, 384–85 (1970). The majority opinion is inconsistent with the holdings in these cases and with the reasoning of the Supreme Court in Chiarella v. United States, No. 78–1202, 48 L.W., No. 36, pages 42–50.

As before stated 22 percent of the outstanding Standard common shares was held in trust by a Knoxville bank in fiduciary accounts.

1. The majority opinion impliedly overrules our decision in *Mansbach* but this is not an uncommon practice in our court for one panel to overrule the decision of another panel. See article in Harvard Law Review Volume 92:-931, 934, 935 on Appealability of Orders Relating to Ongoing Grand Jury Procedures. General Motors Corp. v. United States. Also as pointed out herein, the applicable decisions of the Supreme Court were not even followed.

Because of the finding of liability by the District Court on the basis of section 10(b) of the Act and Rule 10b–5, I need not address the issues of Peat's liability under section 14(a) and Rule 14a–9, as an aider and abettor.

I also approve of the findings and conclusions of the District Court with respect to causation because materiality was established.

The majority does not discuss issues raised by Peat on the statute of limitations, damages and attorneys' fees. I will therefore not discuss them.

In my opinion, the majority should have treated these matters so that it would not be necessary to remand the case to our court in the event the Supreme Court reversed this court on the issues of liability. This case has already been pending too long in the federal courts.

II.

Although our decision with respect to violations of section 10(b) of the Act and Rule 10b–5 are dispositive of the issue of liability, we also approve the findings and conclusions of the District Court as additional support with respect to Peat's false Certificate of the Chadbourn 1969 audit and the electronic data processing (edp).

The District Court found that Peat violated generally accepted auditing standards and generally accepted accounting principles (GAAS and GAAP) during the audit. Specifically, he found that Peat violated the following standards taken from Statements on Auditing Procedure No. 33 (SAP 33): the second and third general standards:

> 2. In all matters relating to the assignment an independence in mental attitude is to be maintained by the auditor or auditors.

> 3. Due professional care is to be exercised in the performance of the examination and the preparation of the report.

the second standard of field work:

> There is to be proper study and evaluation of the existing internal control as a basis for reliance thereon and for the determination of the resultant extent of the tests to which auditing procedures are to be restricted.

the third standard of field work:

> Sufficient competent evidential matter is to be obtained through inspection, observation, inquiries and confirmations to afford a reasonable basis for an opinion regarding the financial statements under examination.

The Court further found Peat violated Statement on Auditing Procedure No. 41 (SAP 41), which sets forth a procedure for accountants to follow upon discovery of new material information to inform management and others known to be relying on such information. We believe that there is substantial evidence in the record to support such findings, and that they are not clearly erroneous. With respect to the conduct of the audit, no working papers exist to verify that important auditing steps were performed during the audit. Peat's valuation of Chadbourn's inventory was poorly performed. Peat's employee Marston's working papers on the efficacy of Chadbourn's internal controls stated, "[c]ontrols is out of control!" Two letters from Peat to Chadbourn dated September 17, 1969, and December 22, 1970, show that Chadbourn's electronic data processing (edp) problems were widespread and pervasive in all internal accounting systems, yet Peat failed to adequately take these problems into consideration, or to demand a full manual audit at financial year end, only one month later, as required by Peat's own audit manual; indeed, Peat instead relied upon Chadbourn's internal accounting systems to adjust the audit figures so that the financial statement read as of August 2, 1969, instead of July 4, 1969. With respect to the discovery of new material, Peat failed to inform the Standard shareholders of its footnote mistake in the financial statement even though Peat had full knowledge of the alleged mistake well before the merger vote and the accounting profession in SAP 41 specifically set forth a procedure for disseminating such information. Obviously Peat did not correct its mistake because if it had corrected it, Standard would have rejected the merger.

The court further found that Peat's failure to disclose dividend restrictions on payment thereof and redemption of the $.46⅔ preferred stock violated both Regulation S–X (Plf's Ex. 225–A) and Accounting Series Release No. 35. (Plf's Ex. 224).

James Quigley, a full partner of Peats, admitted on cross-examination that it was mandatory that redemption restrictions be disclosed.

In arriving at its factual findings with respect to the audit, the materiality of the omissions and misrepresentations by Peat and in internal control, the District Court was supported by the testimony of Larry E. Rittenberg, an assistant professor, in the department of accounting of the University of Tennessee and George J. Benston, a distinguished professor of accounting and finance at the University of Rochester Graduate School of Management.

Professor Benston testified that Peat's footnote in the financial statement was incorrect because it did not disclose important aspects in the indenture and note agreement and violated Regulation S–X and Accounting Series Release No. 35.

Peat admitted it made a mistake but claimed it was inadvertent. The District Court found no mistake but a fraudulent omission of material facts. It was a fraud not only on Standard's stockholders but also on SEC.

The amicus brief of American Institute of Certified Public Accountants is noteworthy in its failure to discuss the main issue in this appeal, on which our decision is based, namely, the fraudulent footnote 7 of the Chadbourn financial statement contained in the Standard proxy materials written and certified as correct by Peat and mailed to Standard stockholders and filed with SEC. Instead, the Institute treats only one of the many issues in this case, namely, the liability of Peat for failure to disclose in its audit, weaknesses in the internal control of Chadbourn or require Chadbourn to make such disclosure.

If Peat desired to limit its liability it should have never attached to its audit the Certificate which it executed and was found by the District Court to be a false and fraudulent certification.

The District Court made a number of specific findings of fact with supporting record references with respect to Electronic Data Processing (EDP) deficiencies being Nos. 45 to 53 and held that Peat had a duty to disclose them to Standard's stockholders as prudent investors would be entitled to this information. Peat's failure to disclose this material information on its audit constituted a breach of duty of disclosure.

The District Court further made many specific findings of fact with supporting record references with respect to Generally Accepted Auditing Principles and Standards (GAAP and GAAS) being Nos. 54 to 102 from which it can be gleaned that the work performed by Peat was anything but a reliable audit. Finding (102) concludes: "The misrepresentation and omissions of defendant which have been fully documented in the Memorandum Decision and herein, were committed or omitted by Peat willfully, deliberately, with intent to deceive and manipulate and with reckless disregard for the truth."

CONCLUSION

The requirement by law of the proxy statement with its certified audit and financial statement to be sent to the shareholders of an acquired company in a merger and filed with SEC, forms an important function for the protection of investors in the administration of the Securities Act by the Securities and Exchange Commission.

The Act can never be properly administered if deliberate, fraudulent, deceitful and recklessly made proxy statements such as were prepared by Peat for use in a corporate merger and for filing with SEC are ever tolerated. Its characterization by the majority as a "negligent misrepresentation" does not excuse the fraudulent omission by an auditor who owes a duty to disclose the truth. The District Court was correct in pointing out the many glaring deficiencies and fraudulent omissions in Peat's proxy statement and audit for which it was well paid. It should be required to compensate the victims of its frauds as ordered by the District Court.

The judgment of the District Court should be affirmed.

INDEX

References are to Pages

†